"Kärkkäinen's masterful introductio[illegible] is ecumenical, interdisciplinary, and interreligious. But one senses on every page a yearning to be faithful to the church's Scripture and shared tradition. Open this book and feast on the many years of research and reflection from one of the most important theologians of our time."

— FRANK D. MACCHIA, Vanguard University

"Only a theologian of Veli-Matti Kärkkäinen's erudition and pastoral sensitivity can perform this scholarly tour de force. An extremely prolific author, Kärkkäinen distills all the fruits of his immense learning and exact scholarship into this comprehensive volume of systematic theology. Religious pluralism is a theological minefield, and a wise and experienced guide is needed. From this book both beginning theology students and advanced scholars can learn how to reexamine all the *loci theologici* from the perspective of religious pluralism. The fact that the book is written in a highly accessible and clear style makes it a perfect choice as a textbook."

— PETER PHAN, Georgetown University

"With *Christian Theology in the Pluralistic World*, theologian Kärkkäinen delivers the first truly global, comprehensive, contemporary, and evangelical-ecumenical systematic theology. This Christian vision is based on the biblical revelation, is in dialogue with other faith traditions, and takes into account the rest of human knowledge as discovered in the sciences. It is all brought together in a magisterial but eminently readable constructive theological summary."

— ROGER E. OLSON, Baylor University

"The appearance of this thoughtful condensation of Kärkkäinen's audacious five-volume project—framed for classroom use and easy reference to the larger work—makes his exhilarating and challenging bird's-eye view of theology available to students and scholars alike. This is theology that brings into play on every topic the light of relevant scientific perspectives, the comparative insights of religious diversity, and the full breadth of Christianity's ecumenical and global richness."

— S. MARK HEIM, Andover Newton Seminary at Yale

HT501

Fall 2020

Christian Theology in the Pluralistic World

A Global Introduction

Veli-Matti Kärkkäinen

William B. Eerdmans Publishing Company
Grand Rapids, Michigan

Wm. B. Eerdmans Publishing Co.
4035 Park East Court SE, Grand Rapids, Michigan 49546
www.eerdmans.com

Published 2019
Printed in the United States of America

25 24 23 22 21 20 19 1 2 3 4 5 6 7

ISBN 978-0-8028-7465-8

Library of Congress Cataloging-in-Publication Data

A catalog record for this book is available from the Library of Congress.

Contents

Preface

You are holding in your hands a new kind of theology textbook, the first of its kind. It not only introduces you to all basic Christian doctrines in their historical and contemporary perorations, including the current global and "contextual" diversity, but also puts you in a continuous dialogue with four other living faiths and their teachings, namely, Judaism, Islam, Buddhism, and Hinduism. Furthermore, it also delves widely into insights from natural (and behavioral) sciences as far as they have bearing on Christian theology, as, for example, in the doctrine of creation. In sum: this textbook seeks to do everything a first-class theology primer does—and then so much more!

This text is based directly on my five-volume series titled A Constructive Christian Theology for the Pluralistic World (2013–2017): *Christ and Reconciliation* (2013), *Trinity and Revelation* (2014), *Creation and Humanity* (2015), *Spirit and Salvation* (2016), and *Community and Hope* (2017). To communicate and make this highly technical and complex theology available to theology students and other interested readers, the current textbook's aim is clarity, simplicity, and user-friendliness without in any way sacrificing accuracy.

That five-volume series helped conceive the nature and task of Christian systematic (or doctrinal or constructive) theology in a new key. Living as we are in the beginning of the third millennium of the common era in a world shaped by cultural, ethnic, sociopolitical, economic, and religious plurality, it is essential for Christian theology to tackle the issues of plurality and diversity. While robustly Christian in its convictions, building on the deep and wide tradition of biblical, historical, philosophical, and contemporary systematic traditions, its approach is also deeply and widely dialogical, including not only cultural but also religious diversity, as well as the wide influence of sciences and secularism.

By putting the best of doctrinal traditions developed and tested during church history into a dialogue with the current global diversity—as the majority of Christians nowadays can be found in Africa, Asia, and Latin America—this project seeks to challenge the hegemony of aging white European and North American men. It gives equal voice to contributions from female theologians of various agendas such as feminist, womanist, and *mujerista*; women from Africa, Asia, and Latin America; other liberationists, including black theologians of the United States and sociopolitical theologians from South America, South Africa, and Asia; and postcolonialists, as well as others. Rather than considering the insights from these and similar traditions as "contextual" in the sense that they are shaped by the context—whereas "mainstream" views are not—and can therefore be incorporated into the conversation at the author's wish, as "ornaments" or means of enrichment, this project engages these contributions as equal conversation partners with traditional and contemporary systematic views.

Yet another distinctive feature of the five-volume series and this current textbook is that while following the typical systematic outline, theological argumentation in this series also engages a number of topics, perspectives, and issues that are missing by and large in traditional and even most contemporary theologies. These include topics such as violence, race, environment, ethnicity, inclusivity, and colonialism.

I dedicate this volume to the "so great a cloud of" students from five continents, men and women from all Christian traditions: those at Fuller Theological Seminary, a "theological laboratory" to learn from and engage global diversity and plurality in, and also my students, past and present, in Thailand and Finland—and beyond.

As with so many other books, I owe greater gratitude than I am able to express to my Fuller Theological Seminary editor, Susan Carlson Wood. Suffice it to say that her impeccable editorial skills have again helped transform my "Finnish English" into American English! My doctoral student Viktor Toth checked the accuracy of all references and also compiled the indexes.

Since this textbook is based on the five-volume constructive theology series, I also wish to take this opportunity to thank once again all of my research assistants who over many years collaborated in this project, all of them doctoral students at Fuller's Center for Advanced Theological Studies: Getachew Kiros, Leulseged Tesfaye, Naoki Inoue, Amy Chilton Thompson, David Hunsicker, Dan Brockway, Joshua Muthalali, Christopher O'Brian, Jongseock Shin, and Viktor Toth. They helped find sources, finished the meticulous checking of the accuracy of all references, and compiled indexes. Without the help of these doctoral students, representing four continents, the writing process would have taken much longer.

Abbreviations

A&D	*Angels and Demons: Perspectives and Practice in Diverse Religious Traditions.* Edited by Peter G. Riddell and Beverly Smith Riddell. Nottingham, UK: Apollos, 2007
ANF	*The Ante-Nicene Fathers: Translations of the Writings of the Fathers down to A.D. 325.* Edited by Alexander Roberts and James Donaldson et al. 9 vols. Edinburgh, 1885–1897. Public domain; available at www.ccel.org
AOA	*Animals on the Agenda: Questions about Animals for Theology and Ethics.* Edited by Andrew Linzey and Dorothy Yamamoto. Urbana: University of Illinois Press, 1998
Aquinas, *ST*	*The Summa Theologica of St. Thomas Aquinas.* Second and Revised Edition, 1920. Literally translated by Fathers of the English Dominican Province. Online Edition Copyright © 2008 by Kevin Knight. http://www.newadvent.org/summa/
Barth, *CD*	Karl Barth. *Church Dogmatics.* Edited by Geoffrey William Bromiley and Thomas Forsyth Torrance. Translated by G. W. Bromiley. Edinburgh: T&T Clark, 1956–1975. Online edition by Alexander Street Press, 1975
BC	*The Book of Concord: The Confessions of the Evangelical Lutheran Church.* Translated by Theodore G. Tappert. Philadelphia: Fortress, 1959

BEM	*Baptism, Eucharist, and Ministry*. Faith and Order, 1982 *BEM*-B = Baptism section *BEM*-E = Eucharist section *BEM*-M = Ministry section
CA	Confessio Augustana (= Augsburg Confession). In the *Book of Concord*, edited by Theodore G. Tappert. Latin version
Calvin, *Institutes*	John Calvin. *Institutes of the Christian Religion.* Translated by Henry Beveridge. Available at www.ccel.org
CGA	*Creation and the God of Abraham.* Edited by David B. Burrell, Carlo Cogliati, Janet M. Soskice, and William R. Stoeger. Cambridge: Cambridge University Press, 2011
DIRW	*Death and Immortality in the Religions of the World.* Edited by Paul Badham and Linda Badham. New York: Paragon House, 1987
DV	*Dogmatic Constitution on Divine Revelation: Dei Verbum* (Vatican II). Available at http://www.vatican.va
EJ	*Encyclopedia Judaica.* Edited by Michael Berenbaum and Fred Skolnik. 17 vols. 2nd ed. Detroit: Macmillan Reference, USA, 2007. http://www.bjeindy.org/resources/library/encyclopediajudaica/
EMB	*Evolutionary and Molecular Biology: Scientific Perspectives on Divine Action.* Edited by Robert John Russell, William R. Stoeger, SJ, and Francisco J. Ayala. Vatican City and Berkeley, CA: Vatican Observatory and Center for Theological and the Natural Sciences, 1998
EPCW	*Evangelization, Proselytism, and Common Witness: The Report from the Fourth Phase of the International Dialogue between the Roman Catholic Church and Some Classical Pentecostal Churches and Leaders, 1990–1997.* http://www.prounione.urbe.it/dia-int/pe-rc/doc/i_pe-rc_pent04.html
ER	*Encyclopedia of Religion.* Edited by Lindsay Jones. 15 vols. 2nd ed. Detroit: Macmillan Reference USA; Gale, Cengage Learning, 2005
EWEG	*The End of the World and the Ends of God: Science and Theology on Eschatology.* Edited by John Polkinghorne and Michael Welker. Harrisburg, PA: Trinity, 2000
GDT	*Global Dictionary of Theology.* Edited by Veli-Matti Kärkkäinen and William Dyrness. Assistant editors, Simon

	Chan and Juan Martinez. Downers Grove, IL: InterVarsity Press, 2008
HRC	*Handbook of Religious Conversion.* Edited by H. Newton Malony and Samuel Southard. Birmingham, AL: Religious Education Press, 1992
I&E	*Islam and Ecology: A Bestowed Trust.* Edited by Richard C. Foltz, Frederick M. Denny, and Azizan Baharuddin. Cambridge, MA: Harvard University Press, 2003
IRDSW	*Interdisciplinary and Religio-Cultural Discourses on a Spirit-Filled World: Loosing the Spirits.* Edited by Veli-Matti Kärkkäinen, Kirsteen Kim, and Amos Yong. New York: Palgrave Macmillan, 2013
ISHCP	*Islam and Science: Historic and Contemporary Perspectives.* Edited by Muzaffar Iqbal. 3 vols. Surrey, UK: Ashgate, 2012. *ISCHP* 1: *Studies in the Islam and Science Nexus* *ISCHP* 2: *Contemporary Issues in Islam and Science* *ISCHP* 3: *New Perspectives on the History of Islamic Science*
IWWLM	*In Whom We Live and Move and Have Our Being: Panentheistic Reflections on God's Presence in a Scientific World.* Edited by Philip Clayton and Arthur Peacocke. Grand Rapids: Eerdmans, 2004
J&E	*Judaism and Ecology: Created World and Revealed Word.* Edited by Hava Tirosh-Samuelson. Cambridge, MA: Harvard University Press, 2002
JBC	*Jesus beyond Christianity: The Classic Texts.* Edited by Gregory A. Barker and Stephen E. Gregg. Oxford: Oxford University Press, 2010
JWF	*Jesus in the World's Faiths: Leading Thinkers from Five Religions Reflect on His Meaning.* Edited by Gregory A. Barker. Maryknoll, NY: Orbis, 2008
LG	*Lumen Gentium: The Dogmatic Constitution on the Church.* Solemnly Promulgated by His Holiness Pope Paul VI on November 21, 1964 (Vatican II). http://www.vatican.va/archive/hist_councils/ii_vatican_council/documents/vat-ii_const_19641121_lumen-gentium_en.html
LW	*Luther's Works.* American ed. (Libronix Digital Library). Edited by Jaroslav Pelikan and Helmut T. Lehman. 55 vols. Minneapolis: Fortress, 2002.
NP	*Neuroscience and the Person: Scientific Perspectives on Di-*

	vine Action. Edited by Robert John Russell, Nancey Murphy, Theo C. Meyering, and Michael A. Arbib. Vatican City and Berkeley, CA: Vatican Observatory and Center for Theological and the Natural Sciences, 1999
NPNF[1]	*A Select Library of the Nicene and Post-Nicene Fathers of the Christian Church.* 1st ser. 14 vols. Edited by Philip Schaff. Edinburgh, 1886–1880. Public domain; available at www.ccel.org
NPNF[2]	*A Select Library of the Nicene and Post-Nicene Fathers of the Christian Church.* 2nd ser. 14 vols. Edited by Philip Schaff and Henry Wace. Edinburgh, 1886–1880. Public domain; available at www.ccel.org
OHE	*Oxford Handbook of Eschatology.* Edited by Jerry L. Walls. New York: Oxford University Press, 2009. Online edition
OHM	*The Oxford Handbook of Millennialism.* Edited by Catherine Wessinger. New York: Oxford University Press, 2011. Online edition
OHRD	*The Oxford Handbook of Religious Diversity.* Edited by Chad Meister. Oxford: Oxford University Press, 2010
OHRS	*The Oxford Handbook of Religion and Science.* Edited by Philip Clayton. Associate editor, Zachary Simpson. Oxford: Oxford University Press, 2006
Pannenberg, *ST*	Wolfhart Pannenberg. *Systematic Theology.* Translated by Geoffrey W. Bromiley. 3 vols. Grand Rapids: Eerdmans, 1991, 1994, 1998
Pannenberg, *TA*	Wolfhart Pannenberg. *Anthropology in Theological Perspective.* Translated by Matthew J. O'Connell. Philadelphia: Westminster, 1985
PC	*Physics and Cosmology: Scientific Perspectives on the Problem of Natural Evil.* Edited by Nancey Murphy, Robert John Russell, William R. Stoeger, SJ. Vol. 1. Vatican City and Berkeley, CA: Vatican Observatory and Center for Theological and the Natural Sciences, 2007
PE	*The Problem of Evil.* Edited by Marilyn McCord Adams and Robert Merrihew Adams. Oxford: Oxford University Press, 1990
Pelikan, *CT*	Jaroslav Pelikan. *The Christian Tradition: A History of the Development of Doctrine.* Vol. 1, *The Emergence of the Catholic Tradition (100–600).* Vol. 2, *The Spirit of Eastern*

	Christendom (600–1700). Vol. 3, *The Growth of Medieval Theology (600–1300)*. Vol. 4, *Reformation of Church and Dogma (1300–1700)*. Chicago: University of Chicago Press, 1971, 1974, 1978, 1984
QCLN	*Quantum Cosmology and the Laws of Nature: Scientific Perspectives on Divine Action*. Edited by Robert J. Russell, Nancey Murphy, and C. J. Isham. Vatican City and Berkeley, CA: Vatican Observatory and Center for Theology and the Natural Sciences, 1993
RB	*Religion and the Body*. Edited by Sarah Coakley. Cambridge: Cambridge University Press, 1997
RCP	*Repentance: A Comparative Perspective*. Edited by Amitai Etzioni and David E. Carney. Lanham, MD: Rowman & Littlefield, 1997
RTSA	*Resurrection: Theological and Scientific Assessments*. Edited by T. Peters, R. J. Russell, and M. Welker. Grand Rapids: Eerdmans, 2002
SBE	*Sacred Books of the East*. Translated by Max Müller. 50 vols. Oxford: Oxford University Press, 1879–1910. Available at www.sacred-texts.com
SPDA	*Scientific Perspectives on Divine Action: Twenty Years of Challenge and Progress*. Edited by Robert John Russell, Nancey Murphy, and William R. Stoeger, SJ. Vatican City and Berkeley, CA: Vatican Observatory and Center for Theological and the Natural Sciences, 2008
SRPW	*Science and Religion in a Post-colonial World: Interfaith Perspectives*. Edited by Zainal Abidin Bagir. Adelaide: ATF Press, 2005
TCW	"Towards Common Witness: A Call to Adopt Responsible Relationships in Mission and to Renounce Proselytism." WCC and the Vatican, 1997
TRV	*Teaching Religion and Violence*. Edited by Brian K. Pennington. Oxford: Oxford University Press, 2012
TTL	*Together towards Life: Mission and Evangelism in Changing Landscapes*. Commission on World Mission and Evangelism/WCC, 2012
UR	*Unitatis Redintegratio: Decree on Ecumenism* (Vatican II)
WA	Weimarer Ausgabe (Weimar edition of Luther's works)
WCC	World Council of Churches

WHS	*Whatever Happened to the Soul? Scientific and Theological Portraits of Human Nature.* Edited by Warren S. Brown, Nancey C. Murphy, and H. Newton Malony. Theology and the Sciences. Minneapolis: Fortress, 1998

Bible references, unless otherwise indicated, are from the Revised Standard Version of the Bible, copyright 1952 [2nd edition, 1971] by the Division of Christian Education of the National Council of the Churches of Christ in the United States of America. Used by permission. All rights reserved.

Unless otherwise indicated, all citations from patristic writers come from the standard series listed above.

Unless otherwise indicated, contemporary Roman Catholic documents, documents of Vatican II, papal encyclicals, and similar works are quoted from the official Vatican website: www.vatican.va. This includes also dialogue documents with Lutherans, Reformed, Anglicans, Methodists, and Pentecostals.

Contemporary World Council of Churches documents are quoted from their official website: http://www.oikoumene.org/, unless otherwise indicated.

Talmud references are from *The Babylonian Talmud*, translated and edited by I. Epstein, 35 vols. (London: Soncino Press, 1952), available at http://www.come-and-hear.com/tcontents.html.

Mishnah texts are from eMishnah.com (2008) at http://www.emishnah.com/Yoma.html.

The Qur'anic references, unless otherwise indicated, are from *The Holy Qur'ān: A New English translation of Its Meanings* © 2008 Royal Aal al-Bayt Institute for Islamic Thought, Amman, Jordan. This version of the Qur'ān is also available online at http://altafsir.com.

Hadith texts are from the Hadith Collection website: http://www.hadithcollection.com/ (2009-).

Bhagavad-Gita texts are from the translation by Ramanand Prasad, EAWC Anthology, 1988. Available at http://eawc.evansville.edu/anthology/gita.htm.

All other Hindu texts, unless otherwise indicated, are from the Sacred Texts website: http://www.sacred-texts.com/hin/index.htm.

Buddhist texts, unless otherwise indicated, are from "Tipitaka: The Pali Canon," edited by John T. Bullitt. *Access to Insight*, May 10, 2011 (http://www.accesstoinsight.org/tipitaka/index.html).

INTRODUCTION

The Nature and Task of (Systematic) Theology

The Origins and Early Developments

In pre-Christian usage, the term "theology" applied to three different types of study: "mythical" theology of the poets concerning the deities, "political" theology of public life, and "natural" theology as the inquiry into the nature of the deities. Only the last one sought to speak of the deities in a way in keeping with their true nature. Early Christian tradition, while for a long time suspicious of adopting the term "theology," ultimately did so, and it came to refer to Christian doctrines and beliefs derived from the Bible.

In the early centuries, theology was basically the exposition of sacred Scripture. With the rise of universities in medieval times with theology at the center of the academy, a close alliance with pagan philosophies became an important asset, and of course, those non-Christian materials were used critically and cautiously. As a separate theological discipline, systematic theology as we now know it did not appear until the early eighteenth century. That said, systematic theology has a long and distinguished pedigree in the history of the church. This lineage goes back to the very beginnings of Christian tradition, to great doctrinal works by the apologists (defenders of faith against secular philosophical-religious claims) and early theologians such as Irenaeus, Origen, Augustine, and others, all the way to the Middle Ages with grand *Summa theologiae*–type works by Aquinas and others. The nomenclature *sacra doctrina* (sacred doctrine) was common in the medieval era. And then there are the great works of the Reformers, such as Calvin's *Institutes*. These are all precursors to what we call "systematic theologies" today. Alternative current terms for systematic theology include "constructive theology" and "doctrinal theology." In this project, the terms "constructive theology" and "systematic theology" are used synonymously.

When we speak of the birth of systematic theology as a separate discipline in the eighteenth century, we keep in mind that until then what we now call biblical theology (the critical study of the Old and New Testaments), church history, historical theology (the sources and development of postbiblical doctrines), and (Christian) philosophy were all practiced more or less as one enterprise. The diversification of theological disciplines became both useful and necessary because of the width and depth of accumulated tradition and the need to educate clergy. Hence, around this time was also established another separate discipline in the theological curriculum: practical theology—with the focus on preaching, counseling, and church leadership—alongside biblical studies, (Christian) philosophy, historical theology, and church history.

From the establishment of the discipline, the defining feature of systematic theology has been a comprehensive presentation of Christian doctrine, particularly as presented in the Bible and doctrinal tradition.[1] But the systematic task involved not only presentation of the doctrine but also its explanation, proving, and confirmation.

Systematic Theology as a Theological Discipline

For this short orientation to systematic theology, the following description serves as the starting point. Let us set it forth and then parse it in some detail:

> Systematic (or doctrinal or constructive) theology is an integrative discipline that continuously searches for a coherent, balanced understanding of Christian truth and faith in light of Christian tradition (biblical and historical) and in the context of historical and contemporary thought, cultures, and living faiths. It aims at a coherent, inclusive, dialogical, and hospitable vision.

1. In the European context, the term "dogmatics" is often used as the nomenclature. Generally speaking, it is a synonym—as its goal is the study and presentation of Christian "dogmas" (doctrines and beliefs) in historical and contemporary forms.

Systematic theology's nature as an "integrative" discipline points to its most distinctive feature in the current theological curriculum. It means that in order to practice well systematic theology, one has to utilize the results, insights, and materials of all other theological disciplines, that is, biblical studies, church history and historical theology, philosophical theology, as well as ministerial studies. Closely related fields of religious studies, ethics, and missiology also belong to the texture of systematic work. That alone is a tall order. But for this project, the theologian has to engage also nontheological and nonreligious fields such as natural sciences, cultural studies, and the study of living faiths (most importantly, Judaism, Islam, Buddhism, and Hinduism).

The use of materials and insights, at times even methods (such as exegesis or historiography), however, is guided by the principle according to which the systematician must listen carefully to related disciplines but also go beyond their inputs, domains, and questions. While it would be absurd for systematic theologians not to engage deeply and widely relevant Old Testament, New Testament, and historical theological materials, it would also limit severely the constructive task if they were bound to only the questions, issues, contributions, and insights of those fields. The systematic theologian asks many questions—say, in relation to inclusivity, care for environment, or science—that the Bible and much of church history are silent about. At the end of the constructive task, however, the theologian should make sure the proposal is in keeping with biblical revelation and, hopefully, with the best of tradition.

The ultimate goal of constructive theology is not a "system" of doctrine—hence, the nomenclature "systematic" is most unfortunate! Rather, it seeks a coherent and balanced understanding. In terms of the theory of truth, it follows coherence theory. One current way of speaking of coherence is to compare it to a web or a net(work). That metaphor is fitting, as it speaks of the coherence theory's attempt to relate every statement to the other relevant statements and ultimately to the whole.

As the definition above insists, systematic theology's task is not only the presentation and analysis of Christian doctrines and beliefs. It also has a mandate to pursue truthfulness and reliability. This is particularly vital now that, with the waning of the Enlightenment critical principle, no religion can merely assume the authority of its particular scripture or doctrine. Its truthfulness must be demonstrated.

Here we are helped by the groundbreaking work of the late German theologian Wolfhart Pannenberg. Fully confident that there is no return to an idyllic precritical mind-set, he was an adamant supporter of historical-critical study. But unlike many critical scholars, he was also open to events that seem to defy the limits of rationality, including miracles; indeed, Jesus's resurrection from the dead, as a historical fact, became a cornerstone of his critical-rational approach to doing theology. Call it a sort of postcritical stance. Alongside great theologians of the past, including Thomas Aquinas, Pannenberg argued that the "object" of theology is God, but because God is the Creator of all, theologians also study everything in relation to God. Hence, theology's domain is wide and inclusive, not only of the spiritual but also of the secular, not only the church but also the world, including sciences and cultures. All the time, theology's ultimate aim is the pursuit and, if possible, the establishment of the truth of God. But this search will never come to an end on this side of the eschatological consummation; hence, theological statements are always anticipatory in nature.[2]

The definition above noted that systematic theology argues for God's truth also "in the context of historical and contemporary thought, cultures, and living faiths. It aims at a coherent, inclusive, dialogical, and hospitable vision." Here we come to the more distinctive features of this particular textbook and the underlying five-volume series.

Theology for the Pluralistic and Diverse Contemporary World

An Inclusive Vision of Theology

The global Christian church is currently amazingly plural and diverse, not least because of the shift of the majority from the Global North (Europe and North America) to the Global South (Africa, Asia, Latin America). By 2050, only about one-fifth of the world's three billion Christians will be non-Hispanic whites. Therefore, as the Korean Methodist Jung Young Lee reminds us, due to this dramatic demographic shift, "Christianity is no longer exclusively identified as a Western religion. In fact, Christianity is already not only a world religion but also a world Christianity. This means Christianity cannot be understood exclusively from a Western perspective."[3]

Regrettably, theology, the way it has been conducted not only in the past but also by and large even in the beginning of the third millennium, has neither paid attention to diversity nor been inclusive. It has preferred—often to the point of excluding and marginalizing the voices of the other—the voice of the powers-that-be, or the hierarchy, or the scholarly elite.

2. Pannenberg, *ST* 1, chap. 1.

3. Jung Young Lee, *The Trinity in Asian Perspective* (Nashville: Abingdon, 1996), 11.

The "post-" world calls for Christian theology to set inclusivity as a stated goal. Inclusive "theologies are multiperspectival, multidisciplinary, and multicultural."[4] Inclusivity is not blind to the limitations we all bring to the task. Rather, it builds trust and room for each and every one to face one's limitations.[5]

Doing theology in this inclusive and new way does not of course mean that Christian tradition is to be undervalued. That would be not only naive but also counterproductive. Much of contemporary theology in particular locations and contexts draws its energy from a careful, painstaking, and often tension-filled dialogue with and in response to tradition. Therefore, this volume also pays close and sustained attention to historical development of doctrines.

The term "global," often used in these kinds of conversations, has to be handled with great care. Here, "global" means that in the presentation and argumentation of constructive theology, voices, testimonies, and perspectives from around the world and from different agendas will be engaged. It is a communion of local conversations in interrelated dialogue. At the same time, we should be mindful that the term "global" can smack of modernity's preference for "universal" grand projects and concepts.

A Dialogical Vision of Theology

One of the direst liabilities of Christian theology—of the past and currently—is its lack of sustained dialogue with other living faiths, their teachings and claims to truth. Sustained dialogue is necessary not only for practical reasons such as building trust, helping communicate the gospel, and learning from others. Here we speak of the *theological* mandate. Briefly put: if we take theology's "object" as God and everything in relation to God, certainly religious faiths belong to that domain! Studying, comparing, and challenging the truth claims of living faiths should be a most obvious task for any theology worth its salt.

For systematic theology to engage other religions and make their insights part of the systematic argumentation, an interdisciplinary approach is necessary. Three interrelated yet distinct disciplines come into play, namely,

4. Amos Yong, *The Spirit Poured Out on All Flesh: Pentecostalism and the Possibility of Global Theology* (Grand Rapids: Baker Academic, 2005), 240.

5. Jürgen Moltmann, *The Trinity and the Kingdom of God: The Doctrine of God*, trans. Margaret Kohl (San Francisco: Harper & Row; London: SCM, 1981), xii.

religious studies/comparative religions, theology of religions, and particularly comparative theology.

Christian theology of religions seeks to reflect critically and sympathetically on the theological meaning of religions in the economy of God. It seeks to "account theologically for the meaning and value of other religions. Christian theology of religions attempts to think theologically about what it means for Christians to live with people of other faiths and about the relationship of Christianity to other religions."[6] Since theology of religions operates usually at a fairly general level, another discipline is needed, "comparative theology." Gleaning resources not only from Christian theology and theology of religions but also from comparative religion, it investigates "ideas, words, images and acts, historical developments—found in two or more traditions or strands of tradition."[7] Complementing theology of religion's more generic approach, comparative theology makes every effort to consider in detail specific topics in religious traditions. Whereas *comparative religion* seeks to be "neutral" on faith commitments, looks "objectively" at the features of religious traditions, and typically does not allow for the reality of gods/deities of religions, *comparative theology* "marks acts of faith seeking understanding which are rooted in a particular faith tradition but which, from that foundation, venture into learning from one or more other faith traditions."[8] Comparative theology is robustly Christian theology; it is committed to its traditions and contemporary expressions.

To the dialogical vision of theology also belongs the engagement of sciences. Particularly in the doctrine of creation, theological anthropology, and eschatology, contributions from cosmology, physics, quantum theory, evolutionary biology, paleontology, neurosciences and brain study, and philosophy of mind are necessary. This kind of interdisciplinary discourse breaks through the limitations of any specific discipline with standard borders. It seeks mutual learning, interaction, and engagement in its quest for a coherent vision. The term "transversal"—borrowed from mathematics and employed by some leading interdisciplinary theologians—illustrates it well, as it indicates "a sense of extending over, lying across, and intersecting with one another."[9] While this

6. Veli-Matti Kärkkäinen, *An Introduction to the Theology of Religions: Biblical, Historical, and Contemporary Perspectives* (Downers Grove, IL: InterVarsity Press, 2003), 20.

7. Francis X. Clooney, SJ, *Comparative Theology: Deep Learning across Religious Borders* (West Sussex, UK: Wiley-Blackwell, 2010), 9.

8. Clooney, *Comparative Theology*, 10.

9. J. Wentzel Van Huyssteen, *Alone in the World? Human Uniqueness in Science and Theology* (Grand Rapids: Eerdmans, 2006), 20. See further, Calvin O. Schrag, "Transversal

kind of inclusive dialogue may strike one as a completely new way of doing theology, it has important historical precedents. Just think of Thomas Aquinas, who regularly consulted all known sciences, in addition to philosophy (and in some cases, whatever little he knew of other religions), to formulate a Christian view. Many others could be added to the list. While learning even the basics of sciences—similarly to foreign religions—is a painful and tedious task, as systematic theologians writing for the third millennium, study we must!

A Hospitable Vision of Theology

Theology, robustly inclusivistic in its orientation, welcoming testimonies, insights, and interpretations from different traditions and contexts, is an inclusive and dialogical enterprise. It honors the otherness of the other. It also makes space for an honest, genuine, authentic sharing of one's convictions. In pursuing the question of truth as revealed by the triune God, constructive theology also seeks to persuade and convince with the power of dialogical, humble, and respectful argumentation. Theology, then, becomes an act of hospitality, giving and receiving gifts.[10]

Without engaging the rich philosophical debate about the (im)possibility of hospitality and gift giving in a truly altruistic manner, suffice it to state this much. Even though, with the best intentions of showing hospitality and giving a gift, we tend to expect reciprocity, there is no reason to give up the good effort. A wonderful way to describe this effort is to speak of a "gracing relationship." It is a "relationship where both parties are recognized by each other as someone not determined by the conditions of one's own horizon, but rather as an Other, a relationship that is not part of the world and the concrete expectations (or anticipations) of the other. Hence, in such a relationship one is invited into the world of the other by means of an open invitation."[11] Such an open invitation and receiving of the other doesn't have to be perfect; it can still be ideal, a goal.

Rationality," in *The Question of Hermeneutics: Essays in Honor of Joseph J. Kockelmans*, ed. T. J. Stapleton (Dordrecht: Kluwer, 1994).

10. Risto Saarinen, *God and the Gift: An Ecumenical Theology of Giving*, Unitas Books (Collegeville, MN: Liturgical Press, 2005).

11. Jan-Olav Henriksen, *Desire, Gift, and Recognition: Christology and Postmodern Philosophy* (Grand Rapids: Eerdmans, 2009), 44–45.

The Plan and Nature of the Book

This book examines ten central Christian doctrines. For each doctrine, it provides a proper biblical, historical, and contemporary theological discussion. At the same time, where relevant, cultural, sociopolitical, scientific, and other nonreligious fields are also engaged. And throughout, with every doctrine, a detailed explanation of relevant related Jewish, Islamic, Hindu, and Buddhist teachings is conducted and a careful comparison with the Christian doctrine attempted. The book does not assume any previous academic knowledge of either religions or sciences.

Because of a most meticulous and detailed documentation in the five-volume series, this textbook contains only minimal bibliographic references (beyond direct citations). This is to help keep the length of the book manageable and more accessible to a wider audience. The reader seeking details about sources can always turn to the longer series.

1 | Revelation

For Orientation

There hardly is a religion without a belief in and notion of a "divine revelation" of some sort. While this revelation is believed to come in many forms, it also became inscripted, and as a result, sacred books and writings can be found all around the religious world. Christian religion is no exception. As important as is the book—the Bible with the Old and the New Testaments—for the Trinitarian Christian doctrine of revelation, revelation is more than a writing. It is an *embodied*—incarnated, as theological tradition puts it—presence of God among men and women, the "Word made flesh" (John 1:14 KJV).

Due to massive changes in philosophy and religion as a result of the eighteenth-century Enlightenment, our first task will be to consider the possibility and conditions of the divine revelation in the modern/contemporary world. Thereafter, this chapter will seek to outline key insights into the Trinitarian, embodied (incarnated) theology of revelation focused on the Word-made-flesh. Since that revelation is claimed to be accessible in the sacred Jewish-Christian canon, the Bible, its nature and role, will then be carefully considered. That discussion also takes us to the formative debates that culminated at the time of Protestant Reformation of the sixteenth century concerning the role of tradition and the church ("magisterium," the teaching office) in the interpretation and appropriation of Scripture. A number of delicate and complex issues surround that debate.

Thereafter, this chapter will inquire into the relation of this "special" revelation to what men and women know through "natural revelation." Similarly, the role and power of biblical revelation to promote justice, equality, and human flourishing—or facilitate inequality, power struggle, and suffering, as some critics see it—is a topic worthy of careful consideration in the contemporary world. The chapter will end, as will all other chapters of this book, in a quite detailed comparative theological exercise in which Christian Scripture and revelation are compared and contrasted with views of four living faiths.

On the Possibility and Conditions of Revelation in the Modern World

Traditional Doctrine of Revelation

It is curious that whereas a separate *doctrine* of revelation cannot be found among either the biblical or the early theologians—and none of the classic creeds rule on this topic—there is no doubt about a deep "revelational" intuition[1] among Christians prior to the Enlightenment. Only around the time of the Reformation did the *doctrine* of revelation become a theological theme. Deism (the view according to which God, having created the world, has left it to its own devices) in particular called for a defined doctrine of revelation among those who wanted to stick with classical Christian tradition. Whereas in older theology revelation denoted the supernatural communication of "heavenly teachings," in post-Enlightenment theology revelation began to lose this divine quality and came to be equated with human capacity to intuit religious truths and teachings.

In pre-Enlightenment tradition, theology's foundation in the Bible could be assumed. Scripture was taken as divine revelation in both Protestant and Catholic theology.[2] The doctrine of divine inspiration stayed intact until modernity, as exemplified in the verbal inspiration view of Protestant orthodoxy. Guarding verbal inspiration became a critical issue because it was feared that "once one concedes that anything in scripture is of human origin, its divine authority is lost."[3]

Coupled with this principle of "objective certainty" based on verbal inspiration and thus divine authority was the Reformation's, particularly the Reformed tradition's, insistence on the testimony of the Holy Spirit, as ably formulated by Calvin.[4] Spirit and Word are tightly linked in his theology, and it

1. Avery Dulles, *Models of Revelation* (Maryknoll, NY: Orbis, 1992 [1983]), 3–4.

2. E.g., *Dogmatic Constitution on the Catholic Faith*, Vatican I (1780), session 3, chap. 3.

3. Pannenberg, *ST* 1:32.

4. Chap. 7 in book 1 of Calvin, *Institutes*, is titled "The Testimony of the Spirit Necessary to Give Full Authority of Scripture. . . ." See particularly 1.7.4.

is from the Spirit that the Word receives its authentication. But as a result of the gradual weakening of the doctrine of the divine authority of Scripture, the role of the "doctrine of the internal testimony of the Spirit" took on a new meaning: it was now needed to add weight to and strengthen the believer's "subjective experience and certainty," which otherwise would be in danger of being lost.[5]

With the introduction of the Enlightenment critical spirit, all these premises came under critical rejection. Theologically speaking, the Enlightenment brought about the collapse of the "Scripture principle."[6]

Revelation after the Enlightenment

Somewhat ironically, what started initially at the Reformation—the slow consolidation of the right of the individual person to judge in matters of religion linked with his or her access to writings (such as the widely used catechisms), thanks to the invention of the printing press—also helped usher in modernity, a major foe to religion. Not merely rationality per se but the *independent* use of human reason, freed from all authorities, whether ecclesiastical or secular, became the hallmark. Linked with the emerging modern science with its unwarranted belief in the "omnipotence" of rational inquiry, the new application of human reason pushed toward replacing what were taken as ancient superstitions and outdated religious beliefs.

Enlightenment philosophers objected to any notion of "supernatural" intervention of God. Classical liberalism, an offshoot from the Enlightenment (inspired also by humanist and Romantic ideals), gleaned from these influences an immanentist (merely "this-worldly") view of revelation in which inspiration was nothing more than enhancement of natural human capacities for insights into religion.

Instead of "revealed" religion (based on the divinely inspired Scriptures), "natural" or "rational" religion came to the fore. Just consider the title of the British philosopher John Locke, *Reasonableness of Christianity* (1695). Although another Englishman, David Hume, in his *Essay on Miracles* (1748), did not necessarily do away with all notions of the miraculous, his work set such strict rational criteria for deciding the authenticity of miracles that the traditional concept was virtually dismissed.

5. Pannenberg, *ST* 1:34.

6. See the classic work by B. B. Warfield, *Revelation and Inspiration* (New York: Oxford University Press, 1927).

Protestant theology with its turn to individualism was much more vulnerable to the influence of the Enlightenment than the Catholic Church with its tight hierarchy and magisterium (teaching office). The reason is simple: Protestantism was a religion of individual judgment rather than ecclesiastical magisterial teaching. By the opening of the twentieth century, understandably, a number of competing views emerged, to be tackled below.

The Christian tradition's grave difficulties maintaining belief and confidence in divine revelation are ironically in contrast with almost all other major living faiths. Most Hindus, Buddhists, and Muslims, and a number of Jews, still take for granted that kind of belief, as will be discussed at the end of this chapter.

After this historical detour, we can begin developing a distinctively Christian theology of revelation.

The Word-Made-Flesh: Embodied Trinitarian Revelation

The Trinitarian Form of Revelation

The leading twentieth-century theologian, Karl Barth, of Switzerland, intuited clearly the Trinitarian basis of theology of revelation when speaking of "the life of God Himself turned to us, the Word of God coming to us by the Holy Spirit, Jesus Christ."[7] When we hear the word "revelation," we may think of some kind of esoteric and abstract ideas being unveiled, hidden mysteries being uncovered. That is not the biblical and Christian view. Revelation in Christian parlance is about *personal* outreach by the triune God, out of loving desire to establish a lost fellowship. This understanding is beautifully expressed in the Roman Catholic Vatican II (1962–1965) document *Dei Verbum* (*Dogmatic Constitution on Divine Revelation*, #2):

> In His goodness and wisdom God chose to reveal Himself and to make known to us the hidden purpose of His will (see Eph. 1:9) by which through Christ, the Word made flesh, man might in the Holy Spirit have access to the Father and come to share in the divine nature (see Eph. 2:18; 2 Peter 1:4). Through this revelation, therefore, the invisible God (see Col. 1:15; 1 Tim. 1:17) out of the abundance of His love speaks to men as friends (see Ex. 33:11; John 15:14–15) and lives among them (see Bar. 3:38), so that He may invite and take them into fellowship with Himself.

7. Barth, *CD* I/2, 483.

At the heart of revelation is the event in which the loving God seeks to establish a fellowship by assuming human form in the power of the Spirit and thus communes with men and women. This takes us into the most distinctive claim of Christian faith, that is, incarnation, the Word-made-flesh. As the second-century Saint Irenaeus so succinctly puts it, "the Father is the invisible of the Son, but the Son the visible of the Father."[8]

When Christian revelation is placed in the midst of other religions, its distinctive nature comes to the fore: "This is not, as in Islam, the revelation of a set of propositions, as though God were dictating laws or doctrines to be carefully written down. It is not, as in Hinduism, an inner experience of a supreme Self, as though someone had a particularly vivid or intense sense of the Supremely Real. It is not, as in Buddhism, an experience of release from sorrow, desire, and attachment. . . . It is the unlimited Divine Life taking form in a particular human life. It is the realization of the Eternal in a particular historical individual."[9] Because of incarnation, the divine embodiment, the biblical idea of revelation in Judeo-Christian revelation is deeply historically anchored.

Divine Love: The "Why" of Revelation

Why did the triune God choose to reveal himself to humanity? The biblical reply is simple: it is about love. Martin Luther puts it succinctly: "The love of God does not find, but creates, that which is pleasing to it. . . . Rather than seeking its own good, the love of God flows forth and bestows good."[10]

Luther also adds a highly counterintuitive remark according to which this revealing God is at the same time a "hidden" God. As the humiliation, suffering, and crucifixion of the Son of God manifest, God seems to be revealing God's own life and heart through the opposites: rather than in glory, majesty, and power (as the "theologian of the glory" assumes), divine revelation comes in the form of humiliation, submission, and suffering (the domain of the "theologian of the cross").

Hence the Johannine Jesus's saying "He who has seen me has seen the Father" (John 14:9) applies as much to the suffering and humiliated Jesus as to the risen and ascended Lord. As the Korean-born theologian Andrew Sung

8. Irenaeus, *Against Heresies* 4.6.6.

9. Keith Ward, *Religion and Revelation: A Theology of Revelation in the World's Religions* (Oxford: Clarendon, 1994), 193.

10. Martin Luther, *Heidelberg Disputation* #28; *LW* 31:57.

Park, who looks at the meaning of the cross through the lens of the key cultural concept of his first culture, *han*, confesses: "The cross is the symbol of God's han which makes known God's own vulnerability to human sin. . . . God shamefully exposes the vulnerability of God on the cross, demanding the healing of the han of God."[11]

To sum up: Christian theology of revelation is Trinitarian in its form and content. Springing from the Father's love, it is embodied in the Word-made-flesh (see 1 Cor. 2:9–11).

While all theological traditions agree on the main outline of the Trinitarian form and content of revelation as briefly described above, it is understandable that various approaches to and "models" of revelation have been proposed.

Models of Revelation

Revelation as Doctrine

Taking a lead from the late Catholic theologian Avery Dulles's acclaimed *Models of Revelation*,[12] this section seeks to discern and discuss some leading contemporary approaches to theology of revelation. These different models can be seen as complementary.

An intuitive way to conceive revelation is to take it as a deposit of doctrines and teachings. This was common in Protestant orthodoxy, which hammered out a most detailed, systematic presentation of theology. Similar orientations were not uncommon in Catholic theology until Vatican II in the 1960s, which brought about a more personalist approach.

While of course not leaving behind this model, in the twentieth century, theology's turn to history has become a dominant orientation.

Revelation as History

An important way to account for the centrality of history for the Christian view of revelation emerged in the mid-twentieth century, named the "salvation

11. Andrew Sung Park, *The Wounded Heart of God: The Asian Concept of Han and the Christian Doctrine of Sin* (Nashville: Abingdon, 1993), 123.

12. His *Models of Revelation*, chap. 2, gives an overview of various models of revelation.

history" school.[13] Without rejecting the traditional idea of God speaking, the salvation-historical approach conceived of revelation mainly in terms of divine historical acts and events.

Building on this idea but also going dramatically beyond it, Pannenberg suggested in 1961 the idea of "revelation as history."[14] In that model, rather than a particular "salvation history," universal history is the arena of God's revelation. Critical of the salvation-history movement's limiting of revelation merely to salvific events such as the exodus and crucifixion, Pannenberg boldly announced that rather than being understood "in terms of a supernatural disclosure or of a peculiarly religious experience and religious subjectivity," revelation arises out of history-at-large, including also "secular" events. Rejecting the reception of revelation by authority, whether ecclesiastical or divine, Pannenberg called for a critical-historical study of the implications for Christian faith of divine acts everywhere in the world and its history.[15] This claim is diametrically opposed to those who rather wished to divorce revelation from specific historical events, such as F. D. E. Schleiermacher, the leading nineteenth-century classical liberal.

Although Pannenberg's history-driven model did not necessarily do away with all notions of divine speaking ("Word"), it emphasized the indirect nature of God's revelation in the form of historical acts of God. Furthermore, rather than the past, the focus in traditional theology, his main focus looked to the future, the eschatological consummation when the truthfulness of the biblical claims to God would become obvious to everyone. While no certainty of the Christian message was to be had before that, Christ's resurrection, which Pannenberg took as a historical fact, provided a preliminary ("proleptic") confidence.

The most contested claim of Pannenberg's model was that revelation was open to "anyone who has eyes to see," and therefore there is no need for an additional divine illumination or inspiration by the Spirit, as traditionally has been believed. Rather than a "deposit of divine revelation," as in tradition, Scripture becomes a record of historical acts of God to be critically analyzed for their truthfulness and validity. Later, in his monumental three-volume *Systematic Theology* (ET 1991–1998), he softened his position in response to his

13. George E. Wright, *God Who Acts: Biblical Theology as Recital*, Studies in Biblical Theology 8 (London: SCM, 1952).

14. Wolfhart Pannenberg, ed., *Revelation as History: A Proposal for a More Open, Less Authoritarian View of an Important Theological Concept*, trans. David Granskou (London: Collier-Macmillan, 1968 [1961]).

15. Pannenberg, "Preface to the American Edition," in *Revelation as History*, ix.

critics and came to acknowledge that there is revelation both as "word" and as an "event" and that not all revelation is necessarily self-evident due to human sin and other limitations. Yet his basic insight into "revelation as history" still stood and set itself against all notions of "fideism," that is, willingness to believe without any rational argument or evidence.

Critics have noted that Pannenberg's proposal suffers from a one-sided rejection of, or—as in his mature theology of revelation—a marginalizing role of, God's direct communication. In a number of instances in the biblical narrative, Yahweh/Father of Jesus Christ seems to be speaking directly to humanity, and that is to be considered revelation. There are a great many such passages referring to divine speaking (just consider for example Num. 12:5–8).

The way *Dei Verbum* links words and deeds seems to provide the needed balance between tradition's at times too-limited emphasis on the revelatory power of the Word and a Pannenbergian focus on historical events: "This plan of revelation is realized by deeds and words having an inner unity: the deeds wrought by God in the history of salvation manifest and confirm the teaching and realities signified by the words, while the words proclaim the deeds and clarify the mystery contained in them" (#2).

Moltmann also takes his cue from revelation's embeddedness in history in his distinctive proposal.

Revelation as Promise

In his *Theology of Hope* (ET 1964), Moltmann, like Pannenberg, firmly set his gaze toward the future and considered it the center of theology. Linked with rooting theology in history, this center helped him construct an innovative model, namely, revelation as promise.

Moltmann differentiates between two kinds of worldviews, one that is typical of Greek and other pagan philosophies, and the other, of biblical Judeo-Christian religion. Whereas for the former revelation is some kind of "epiphany of the eternal present of being" in light of which truth is seen, in the Bible it is "in the hope-giving word of promise that Israel found God's truth."[16] For those whose hope is set on divine promises, religion is like a journey of nomadic people in search of the promised land. And this is, of course, what the biblical narrative is all about!

16. Jürgen Moltmann, *Theology of Hope: On the Ground and the Implications of a Christian Eschatology*, trans. James W. Leitch (London: SCM, 1967 [1964]), 40–41.

This promise is fully anchored in history and its ebbs and flows, but it is not contained within human history. Promise gives hope for overcoming life's threats and impasses, as the promise of Jesus's resurrection from the dead most dramatically manifests. The promissory nature of revelation puts it in contradiction to how things seem to be working in the world. It makes room for hope.

Moltmann's turn to promise as the framework for the Christian theology of revelation is useful—as long as one does not thereby dismiss the cognitive content of revelation, as Moltmann at times seems to do. A proper content of revelation is required for us to sort out which revelation is from God—and which from another deity! How else can a judgment be made between the claims of religions?

Having discussed theology of revelation regarding its "foundation" in the triune God and various ways to conceptualize its nature, we now ask, What is the nature and role of Scripture?

God's Word in Human Words: The Nature of Scripture as Revelation

Inspiration of Scripture: Divine-Human Dynamic

Until the time of the Enlightenment, the inspiration of Scripture had been understood in terms of more or less direct divine influence on human writers and, as in Islam, as a virtual dictation of finished revelation received by the prophet. Behind this traditional understanding of revelation lies the assumption that revelation is a more or less timeless and changeless "product." Of course, many nuances have been introduced regarding the exact nature and "technics" of how the inspiration process took place. The spectrum ranges from "dictation theory" to inspiration of words to inspiration of thoughts (but not necessarily individual words), and beyond.

The Enlightenment presented a massive rebuttal of key traditional beliefs about Scripture. In response, classical liberalism made inspiration virtually a matter of enhancement of human capacities to gain an insight into matters of religion. The Bible, after all, in this outlook, is basically an important and unique collection of human testimonies to human religious experiences and human interpretations of those experiences, but it is not authority based on divine inspiration.

So, how would a contemporary Christian view of inspiration of Scripture be formulated in the post-Enlightenment world and in light of radical theological changes? The way forward is not a return to a lost, idyllic, pre-Enlightenment mind-set. The value of sober criticism in service of a more reliable knowledge is an undeniable achievement of modernity.

Contemporary theology of inspiration should begin from the importance of incarnation as the guide to a proper understanding. Incarnation, embodiment, means that the triune God, in the project of divine revelation, is fully embedded in human realities. Finite, fallible human minds can only grasp so much—and to only a certain degree—of mysteries beyond the human mind. Rather than God dictating or mechanistically monitoring the choice of exact words in the communication of revelation, it is better to think of inspiration in terms of divine-human synergy. In this outlook, the humanity of the biblical writers is not set aside but is rather affirmed. On the other side, because we are speaking of *divine* intervention, it is a matter of more than just giving eloquence to *human* experiences of religion.

Vatican II's *Dei Verbum* puts this dynamic well. It affirms the *divine* and hence "superhuman" nature of revelation: "Through divine revelation, God chose to show forth and communicate Himself and the eternal decisions of His will regarding the salvation of men" (#6). When it is looked at from the perspective of the Holy Spirit's energizing and guiding activity, there is no need to choose—as has been debated in theology—between the inspiration of the authors and that of the writings themselves. Having first affirmed the divine dynamic in the inspiration of Scripture, *Dei Verbum* then speaks robustly of the *human* side in the process of Scripture's inspiration: "In composing the sacred books, God chose men and while employed by Him they made use of their powers and abilities, so that with Him acting in them and through them, they, as true authors, consigned to writing everything and only those things which He wanted" (#11).

The acknowledgment of the simultaneous divine and human form of Scripture makes it possible also to understand its breathtaking diversity. If God had dropped the revelation from the skies, so to speak, one would expect something like a legal document with precise wording or a step-by-step manual brief enough to be grasped even by the feeble-minded. Not so the Bible—and interestingly enough, neither the Qur'an, which, however, even in current orthodox Muslim theology, is confessed to be directly given to the Prophet and faithfully recorded thereafter; the nature of the Qur'an as a book is difficult to understand.

The authentically mutual divine-human dynamic in inspiration and the preservation of Scripture—as uneven as the mutuality is in the sense that God is the "author" and source—also comes to light in the slow development process of the canon. The human acts of interpretation, memory, comparison between reliable and unreliable sources (as in Luke 1:1–4), weighing of opinions, and so on were an important, God-willed part of the process.

The two classic New Testament texts 2 Timothy 3:16 and 2 Peter 1:21, while often interpreted in a way that supports the more "mechanistic," direct understanding of revelation, seem to be undergirding the kind of dynamic "God's word in human words/human words as God's word" view sketched here. The reference in the former passage to *theopneustos* ("God-breathed"), in the analogy of Yahweh's breathing the breath of life into the first human being (Gen. 2:7), can be understood in terms "of the breathing-out of Scripture in a similar way [to what happened to Adam] as the giving of life and power to the formed words of human writers."[17] As Adam became a "living soul" (*nephesh*), so the human writings, "dead" in themselves, become the living Word of God. The Greek expression *pheromenoi*, in the latter passage, referring to the influence ("moving") of human authors by the Holy Spirit, plays on the metaphor of being driven like a ship by the wind. Rather than the human agency being taken away, as in a contemporary airplane's autopilot mode, the ship sailing under the "wind of the Holy Spirit" reaches its destination gradually in the midst of many struggles.

To affirm the dual nature of Scripture as fully divine and fully human, we must ask what exactly is the relationship between the scriptural text and the divine revelation. Are they to be equated or separated?

Scripture as the Word of God and Human Testimony

According to the "Scripture principle" of pre-Enlightenment theology, particularly in Reformation orthodoxy, the "matter of Scripture" and the scriptural text were more or less identified with each other. When the Bible speaks, God speaks. The fundamentalist movement of the twentieth century materially affirmed the same. On the other side of the hermeneutical spectrum is a "hermeneutics from below," which looks at the Bible as merely *human* testimonies of faith. Just consider this example: "Whereas a text talks about the resurrection of Christ, for example, it is the author's faith in the resurrection expressed in this discourse which is investigated."[18]

Barth's way of negotiating the relationship between the text and revelation offers a third way and contains some real promise even if it also suffers from

17. Ward, *Religion and Revelation*, 216.

18. Jürgen Moltmann, *Experiences in Theology: Ways and Forms of Christian Theology*, trans. Margaret Kohl (Minneapolis: Fortress, 2000), 142 (without necessarily endorsing this view).

some extreme tendencies. The mature Barth is well known as the advocate of the idea of Scripture as testimony or witness to Christ.[19] Thereby Barth was not rejecting the nature of Scripture as the Word of God. He was rather defining its nature as the Word of God in terms of its work as witness. For him, the Bible is God's Word "to the extent that God causes it to be His Word, to the extent that He speaks through it."[20] That is not to deny the human and, in Barth's view, limited and even fallible nature of the biblical witness. The Bible in this witness is thus "a chorus of very different and independent but harmonious voices. An organism which in its many and varied texts is full of vitality in the community."[21]

Where we have to balance and correct Barth is in his one-sided emphasis on the fallibility of the Scripture as witness and his downplaying of the propositional element. To function as a witness, the Scripture has to be reliable, if not free from human errors, and for a divine revelation to be recognized as such it must also have solid propositional content. Yet another liability comes to focus in Barth's view, namely, the claim that the Bible *becomes* God's Word the moment the Spirit so wishes to work. This would make revelation too much a matter of subjective reception by human beings. This concern has nothing to do with the undermining of the importance of Spirit-aided reception of—opening of eyes to—the "spiritual" meaning of the Bible. The concern is about affirming the Bible's "objective," authoritative status regardless of human receptivity or lack thereof.[22]

Even if we concede a divine-human synergy, what about the fact that, as already implied, revelation in the Scripture comes in many forms, from legal codes to poems to teachings to sermons, and so forth?

Metaphors and Revelation

Too often propositions as cognitive statements and metaphors (and symbols) as merely expressive of emotions or values are juxtaposed. Is such juxtaposition valid?

Thomas Aquinas raised the question in the very beginning of his *Summa theologiae*, "Whether Holy Scripture should use metaphors" (1.1.10). After a

19. Barth, *CD* I/1, 88–124.

20. Barth, *CD* I/1, 109; see Frank D. Macchia, "God Says What the Text Says: Another Look at Karl Barth's View of Scripture" (unpublished manuscript, n.d.).

21. Barth, *CD* IV/2, 674.

22. Stanley J. Grenz and John R. Franke, *Beyond Foundationalism: Shaping Theology in a Postmodern Context* (Louisville: Westminster John Knox, 2001), 68.

careful consideration, Thomas concluded that indeed it is proper to use metaphors when interpreting Scripture's meaning and speaking of God. "For God provides for everything according to the capacity of its nature." Indeed, metaphors carry a surplus. Whereas propositional concepts tend to be more limited, the domain of metaphors is wider, more suggestive, and richer. At times, metaphors may say "more," as they seek to express something that transcends the limits of human concepts.

This can be seen everywhere in the Bible. Sometimes God is compared to a compassionate father (Ps. 103:13) or a comforting mother (Isa. 66:13). Behind the metaphorical and symbolic use of language in religion and theology is simply the desire "to make the unexperienceable divine reality comprehensible with the help of metaphors taken from the world which human beings experience."[23] Metaphors are not only useful in that they have a surplus of meaning—they evoke imagination—but they are also necessary.

The reason traditional and contemporary fundamentalist theologies of revelation have not been keen on symbols and metaphors is their alleged dismissal of cognitive content. That symbols evoke imagination and can play with several meanings does not make them meaningless in communicating content; indeed, the polysemy (or multivalence) may help convey dimensions and features that otherwise would be inaccessible.[24] In sum, to affirm the need for the metaphoric and symbolic is not to dismiss the propositional and cognitive. Rather, they are mutually conditioned and together say "more."

Having now established revelation in Scripture, based on the Word-made-flesh as a dynamic divine-human synergy, we reflect more deeply on what constitutes scriptural authority.

How to Determine the Authority and Meaning of Scripture

The Use of the Bible and Its Authority

What makes the Bible the ultimate authority? Is it the way the church uses the Scripture that is determinative, or is it the truthful content Scripture conveys as a function of being revelation? Whereas the latter option has been the normal view in Christian tradition, in contemporary theology the former option has garnered a lot of support.

23. Moltmann, *Experiences in Theology*, 161.
24. Dulles, *Models of Revelation*, 142.

Movements such as postliberalism (G. Lindbeck) make the Bible's authority a matter of its usage by the religious community.[25] Biblical statements, then, receive their authority from their ecclesiastical usage, and the Bible guides and rules the life and faith of the community. The obvious question to the postliberal approach is whether there is any way to negotiate between different traditions and their narratives. Is there any way to negotiate between the Vedas of Hindus, the Qur'an of Muslims, the Book of Mormon, and the Bible? Furthermore, if ecclesiastical usage is the norming norm, what or who is to norm the ecclesiastical usage? There are both good and bad ways of using the Bible. Kevin Vanhoozer's "canonical-linguistic" *Drama of Doctrine* seeks to balance the one-sided emphasis on the community as the source of authority and move to the canon of the Bible. In that sense, Protestantism's *sola Scriptura*, "Scripture alone," can be maintained: biblical canon judges even the ecclesiastical usage.

What is important about postliberalism is that it highlights the role of community in the process of inspiration and authority. If the Bible is the book of the church, then its coming into existence—unlike the Qur'an, which comes without any mediation—has to do with the way the believing community came to discern its unique significance and thus authority. It also helps us balance the one-sided focus of tradition on the inspired nature of the writings themselves. Scripture has been birthed in the bosom of the believing community. In sum:

> Revelation arose not only prior to but also together with the process of canonical scripture. In part, God's revelatory work came in and through the formation of scripture, as under the guiding hand of the Spirit the community of faith sought to understand the ongoing work of God in the world in the light of God's earlier activity as described in the oral and written traditions of the community. The faith community sought as well to determine what God's covenant with their forebears meant for them as they sought to be God's covenant partners in the present. The canonical texts reflect this ongoing conversation within the ancient Hebrew community and the early church.[26]

That it took centuries for the church—under the guidance of the Holy Spirit, as it is believed—to come to a common understanding of what the canon is further accentuates its significance.

25. George A. Lindbeck, *The Nature of Doctrine: Religion and Theology in a Postliberal Age* (Philadelphia: Westminster, 1984).

26. Grenz and Franke, *Beyond Foundationalism*, 72.

Who Decides the Meaning of the Text?

Vanhoozer's canonical-linguistic turn also reminds us of the need to tend to the importance of the "original authorship" of the Bible, although that does not have to mean limiting the meaning only to it. Until the Enlightenment and even some time thereafter, it was taken for granted that what the text means is what the original author meant it to mean. It was believed that there is an "extratextual" reference to realities outside, such as the resurrection of Christ, in the midst of many meanings and many metaphors.[27]

The proper highlighting of the original authorship is a healthy corrective to those postmodern and reader-response approaches that make the contemporary reader the main locus of determining the text's meaning. Take for example the *Postmodern Bible*, which states that our understanding of the text is "inseparable from what we *want* it to mean, from how we *will* it to mean."[28]

The problem is that making the meaning of the text merely a function of the contemporary reader makes it arbitrary. On the contrary, the original canonical meaning is determinative even though it also leaves room for the text's continuous speaking even in new ways to every generation of readers. In the terminology of J. L. Austin's speech-act theory, the biblical texts perform a "perlocutionary" speech-act achieved by the speaker. The surplus of speech-act theory is that it speaks of *speaking*, communication as an act. Hence, it also helps transcend the failing dualism of either words or acts that characterizes many debates in the doctrine of revelation. When applied to the work of the Spirit in and through Scripture, speech-act theory reminds us of the Word of God as creative, enlivening, and transforming "power."[29]

That the message of the Bible, which the Spirit appropriates, is integrally related to the canonical text is not to say that the Spirit is "tied" to the original meaning of the text. Paul Ricoeur has reminded us that once the text is out there, in a real sense of the word, it gains a life of its own. However, this "life" of the text does not have to be so distanced from or unrelated to the original text.

What about the role of tradition?

27. Kevin J. Vanhoozer, *The Drama of Doctrine: A Canonical-Linguistic Approach to Christian Theology* (Louisville: Westminster John Knox, 2005), chap. 9.

28. *Postmodern Bible* (New Haven: Yale University Press, 1995), 14.

29. Grenz and Franke, *Beyond Foundationalism*, 73.

Sola Scriptura, Tradition, and the Authority of the Church

Scripture and Church

For patristic writers, as far as we know, there hardly was an opposition between Scripture and tradition. There was coinherence of Scripture and tradition. This view remained more or less intact until the high Middle Ages—but not all the way up to the Reformation, as is often assumed. It became an important issue a couple of centuries before the Reformation and a topic of fierce debate among theologians. The reason had to do with the new acknowledgment of the significance of exegesis in determining the meaning of biblical statements, before determined by church authority.

Three positions emerged by the time of the Reformation in this fierce debate about the Scripture-tradition relationship:

- the view that every truth necessary for salvation can be found in Scripture, and only therein;
- the standpoint according to which the divine truth is found in both Scripture and the tradition of the church going back to the apostles; and
- the opinion that, since the Holy Spirit abides permanently in the church, the church not only controls the interpretation of Scripture but may also add to revelation.

To this situation spoke the Protestant Reformation's insistence on *sola Scriptura.* That principle, however, was not meant to deny the role of tradition but rather to define the ultimate norm of revelation and faith: written, canonical Scripture.

As a response to the Reformation, the Council of Trent saw it necessary to even further highlight the importance of tradition.[30] As a way of self-correction, Vatican II in the 1960s came to affirm that "there exists a close connection and communication between sacred tradition and Sacred Scripture. For both of them, flowing from the same divine wellspring, in a certain way merge into a unity and tend toward the same end."[31] Hence, in contemporary Roman Catholic understanding, "Sacred tradition and Sa-

30. Council of Trent, Fourth Session, "Decree concerning the Canonical Scriptures," in *The Canons and Decrees of the Sacred and Oecumenical Council of Trent*, trans. J. Waterworth (London: Dolman, 1848), 17.

31. *DV*, #9.

cred Scripture form one sacred deposit of the word of God, committed to the Church."[32]

The "Protestant principle" (Tillich) does not, then, mean neglecting tradition, but rather, as argued above, it means setting the text of Scripture as the highest norm of faith and theology (which currently is the ecumenical consensus). Neither is the Protestant view an attempt to downplay the role of the church in relation to community and tradition. It is a principle of setting the Christian community under the authority and life-giving power of the Word of God. But this has to be done in a nuanced way.

There is a mutual relationship between Scripture and church. The theological critique above of the postliberal insistence on Scripture's authority as the function of its ecclesiastical usage is not to be interpreted as undermining the importance of the Christian community to Bible reading. The role of the community has to be put in proper theological perspective, though. Instead of regarding the ecclesial practice of reading the Scripture as determining the doctrine, it is better to say that the canonical text, as received and affirmed by the church, guides and "regulates" all practices of the church.

Scripture and Living Tradition

In response to the common individualistic misunderstanding of *sola Scriptura*, we have to say, "to locate divine authority in the canon is not to imply that individual readers may presume that they have immediate and unproblematic access to God's word."[33] Fruitful reading always happens in the Christian community and is guided—and if need be, corrected—by living tradition. In other words, "*sola scriptura* does not mean *nulla traditio* ('no tradition')."[34]

Consequently, the Protestant principle of *sola Scriptura* should not be understood as a way of rejecting or undermining the role of tradition; rather, it should be understood as linking the two together. Vatican II's *Dei Verbum* (#2) formulates correctly the principle of mutuality: "Hence there exists a close connection and communication between sacred tradition and Sacred Scripture."

"Tradition" in its theological meaning refers both to the process of communication and to the content. At first it might seem that the very notion of

32. *DV*, #10.

33. Vanhoozer, *The Drama of Doctrine*, 151.

34. Vanhoozer, *The Drama of Doctrine*, 233; citation in the text from Richard A. Muller, "Scripture," in *Oxford Encyclopedia of the Reformation*, ed. Hans J. Hillerbrand (Oxford: Oxford University Press, 1996), 4:37.

tradition suggests something frozen, unchanging, fixed. That, however, is not the case with the Spirit-led tradition among the people of God. In biblical and theological understanding, tradition is not a dead phenomenon. It is, as both Eastern Orthodox[35] and Roman Catholic theology insist, a living, dynamic, and hence, evolving process: "This tradition which comes from the Apostles develop [*sic*] in the Church with the help of the Holy Spirit."[36]

Three more themes await us in the rest of the chapter: the question of natural revelation and natural theology; the relation of revelation to issues of liberation, equality, and inclusivity; and the placement of Christian revelation among living faiths.

Natural Revelation and "Natural Theology"

Why Natural Knowledge of God Is "Natural"

In typical systematic presentations, the question of natural revelation appears in the beginning. Indeed, it has long been tradition to divide the doctrine of revelation into two parts—general and special revelation—and then to speak of the former first. The reason for the reversed order will become clear in the discussion.

Whereas natural revelation and natural theology encountered a massive rebuttal in Barth's neo-orthodox theology, fortunately there are attempts in contemporary theology to take another, more constructive look and consider it as an integral part of a distinctively Christian theology of revelation. This desire is based on the obvious fact that both common sense and Christian tradition have always believed that the "traces" of God are to be found in the world God created. If so, then it must be located under the general framework of the Trinity, and as the British theologian-scientist A. McGrath so wittily puts it, we need to speak of "the dynamics of a *trinitarian* natural theology."[37]

Important here is how one understands the category of "nature." It should not be understood in terms of human nature (i.e., human thinking) being the measure for the authenticity of revelation—that would thwart the biblical warning about God's "folly" being wiser than human wisdom (1 Cor. 1:21)—but rather in terms of God's nature, the source of revelation. True nat-

35. James J. Stamoolis, "Scripture and Tradition in the Orthodox Church," *Evangelical Review of Theology* 19, no. 2 (April 1995): 131–43.

36. *DV*, #8.

37. Title of chap. 6 in Alister E. McGrath, *A Fine-Tuned Universe: The Quest for God in Science and Theology* (Louisville: Westminster John Knox, 2009).

ural revelation is that which corresponds with the true nature of God rather than being based on perverted human imaginations. Also, as God is the creator of everything, this world truly and authentically contains traces of God.

Indeed, until the beginning of the twentieth century, the "natural" knowledge of God by human beings created in the image of God was not widely contested. Biblical passages such as Psalm 19, Romans 1:19–21, and Acts 17:16–34, among others, seemed to affirm it unequivocally. Said Irenaeus: "For by means of the creation itself, the Word reveals God the Creator; and by means of the world [does he declare] the Lord the Maker of the world; and by means of the formation [of man] the Artificer who formed him."[38] In Aquinas's theology, natural knowledge of God was of course an important theme,[39] as it was in Calvin's.[40] English natural theology came to its zenith in William Paley's *Natural Theology; or, Evidences of the Existence and Attributes of the Deity*, in the beginning of the nineteenth century (1802), which utilized the famous metaphor of a clock or watch. In contemporary theology, *Dei Verbum*'s formulation expresses well this confidence in wider Christian tradition: "God, who through the Word creates all things (see John 1:3) and keeps them in existence, gives men an enduring witness to Himself in created realities (see Rom. 1:19–20)" (#3).

The theologian who set himself against all notions of natural theology was Barth, although he did not categorically contest the notion of some kind of natural knowledge of God; he just did not take it for a revelation and, rather than making it an asset, considered it a major obstacle to the saving knowledge of God.[41] So, this vehement opposition to natural theology calls for a careful assessment. But before that, a brief historical look at what natural theology was in early Christian theology is in order to help us understand the critique of Barth and like-minded theologians.

Natural Revelation as Christian Revelation

Fittingly, Moltmann states: "Inasmuch as natural theology has to do with the universality of God, we might also view it as one dimension of revealed theology, for the universality of the one God is also part of God's revelation."[42]

38. Irenaeus, *Against Heresies* 4.6.6.

39. Aquinas, *ST* 1.1.12.

40. Calvin, *Institutes* 1.3.

41. The classic discussion is of course in Barth, *CD* I/2, §17: "The Revelation of God as the Abolition of Religion."

42. Moltmann, *Experiences in Theology*, 73.

This observation is in keeping with the statement above that "natural theology, then, is the talk about God that corresponds to the nature of the divine itself."[43] The important point here is that originally "natural" knowledge of God did not mean knowledge unrelated to God, but rather knowledge derived from God.

Consequently, early Christian theology did not use natural theology (theology based on natural revelation) to develop proofs for the existence of God, and it saw natural theology as an aid in the investigation into the nature of God. It was believed that by looking at nature, God's creation, something important could be learned from God—not of course divorced from but rather hand in hand with the Scripture, the fullest form of revelation.

Not until medieval theology did the understanding of the nature and role of natural theology change drastically; then it came to denote revelation in keeping with human nature. That trend came to its zenith at the time of the Enlightenment. This twist led the modern thinkers to use natural theology as a way to prove the existence of God apart from biblical revelation or even any religious commitments. But that use is diametrically opposed to the original meaning of natural theology.

This was the target of Barth's criticism! Otherwise, he would not have considered natural revelation coming from human nature and hence meaning nothing less than an effort of "domesticating the Gospel."[44] Ironically for him, natural theology thus conceived expresses our "self-preservation and self-affirmation" against God, and hence is essentially a matter of "self-justification."[45] The same kind of misunderstanding seems to lie behind the criticism coming from American Reformed philosophical theology (a.k.a. "Reformed epistemology," as represented by such contemporary luminaries as A. Plantinga, N. Wolterstorff, and W. P. Alston). How else could they claim that "the enterprise of providing support for religious beliefs [starts] from the premises that neither are nor presuppose any religious beliefs."[46] But all theologians at all times have condemned that kind of "natural" theology!

Against this misguided criticism, we have to state that "to show that Christianity is in agreement with natural religion is thus to strengthen the authority of the Christian revelation."[47] Speaking of Reformed theology—and bearing in mind Calvin's support for the natural knowledge of God—it is

43. Pannenberg, *ST* 1:76–77.

44. Barth, *CD* II/1, 142.

45. Barth, *CD* II/1, 136.

46. William P. Alston, *Perceiving God: The Epistemology of Religious Experience* (Ithaca, NY: Cornell University Press, 1991), 289.

47. Pannenberg, *ST* 1:103.

instructive that a faithful disciple of Barth, the late Scot T. F. Torrance, was not only able to overcome his teacher's opposition but also able to advocate a robust Reformed natural theology.[48]

Scripture, Liberation, and Human Flourishing

Christian Theology as Liberation Theology

With full justification, the pioneer black theologian James H. Cone raises this critical question: "Why is it that the idea of *liberation* (inseparable from the biblical view of revelation) is conspicuously absent in theological discussions about the knowledge of God?"[49] Similarly, the Cuban-born Hispanic American Justo L. González laments that so few Christians, particularly those in the majority and in places of power, realize "the political agenda" in the Bible.[50]

As an alternative to an allegedly noncommitted and neutral, objective approach, Cone is "determined to speak a liberating word for and to African American Christians, using the theological resources" at his disposal.[51] This is in keeping with his vision of Christian theology as "a theology of liberation. It is *a rational study of the being of God in the world in light of the existential situation of an oppressed community, relating the forces of liberation to the essence of the gospel, which is Jesus Christ*."[52] A number of liberationists from various global contexts couldn't agree more with this call.[53]

Working for human flourishing is a theological mandate for Judeo-Christian tradition. The Trinitarian revelation that comes to us as divine word and act, as promise that contains hope and knowledge, is not meant only for the life to come, for the "salvation of the soul." It has everything to do with the realities of this earthly life.

48. Thomas F. Torrance, "The Problem of Natural Theology in the Thought of Karl Barth," *Religious Studies* 6 (1970): 121–35.

49. James H. Cone, *A Black Theology of Liberation*, 2nd ed., twentieth anniversary ed. (Maryknoll, NY: Orbis, 1986), 44.

50. Justo L. González, *Mañana: Christian Theology from a Hispanic Perspective* (Nashville: Abingdon, 1990), 83–85.

51. Cone, *Black Theology of Liberation*, xii.

52. Cone, *Black Theology of Liberation*, 1.

53. Gustavo Gutiérrez, *A Theology of Liberation: History, Politics, and Salvation*, trans. and ed. Sister Caridad Inda and John Eagleson (Maryknoll, NY: Orbis, 1986 [1973]; rev. ed. with a new introduction, 1988), 45.

This state of affairs brings to light the difference in ethos between Judeo-Christian faiths and other living faiths. Unlike Islam, Christianity is not merely—or even primarily—a matter of "submission" to the divine, but rather an effort to embody the core values advocated by the Scriptures and profoundly manifested in the Word made flesh. The Jewish Torah, unlike the holy scriptures of Asian religions (particularly of Hinduism), calls for a loving, covenant-based, responsible obedience to God.

Moltmann speaks of "the biblical texts as furthering life" and of a hermeneutics of Scripture that attends to the affirming and strengthening of life and holism. Taking his cue from the biblical promise that the Spirit is the Spirit of life and that this Spirit is behind revelation and Scripture, he lays out this ambitious vision: "What furthers life is whatever ministers to the *integrity of human life* in people and communities . . . whatever ministers to the *integration* of individual life into the life of the community, and the life of the human community into the warp and weft of all living things on earth . . . whatever spreads *reverence for life* and the *affirmation of life* through *love for life* . . . whatever *heals broken relationships* and *liberates life* that has been oppressed."[54] Let us consider various interrelated aspects of that kind of liberating work in relation to Scripture and the doctrine of revelation.

Political Implications of Faith

Should the Christian and the church be politically active? While there are varying opinions as to what extent and by using which means the church should be involved in the work of the society, one thing seems to be indisputable, namely, that—as just mentioned—no faith worth its salt can stay politically neutral. What we believe does influence our choices and behavior. It has political implications.

Isn't it curious that in general conservative and fundamentalist movements tend to be antagonistic to sexual inclusivity, including ministry opportunities for women and other minorities? Such believers hold on to the absolute inerrancy of Scripture yet miss the liberationist impulse. During the years of American slavery, slaves were advised to be obedient to white masters on the basis of biblical statements to that effect.

Liberation has to begin from the house of the Lord! One of the urgent tasks in that regard has to do with inclusion of both women and men.

54. Moltmann, *Experiences in Theology*, 149–50, here 149.

Inclusive Word

Interpretation of texts is not an innocent act. The feminists and other female theologians tirelessly remind us of this. On the basis of a certain kind of Bible reading, oppression, domination, exclusion, and even hatred have arisen. Allegedly scripturally driven arguments have been used in all religions to dominate and subjugate.

Hence, it is urgent to seek to expose the hidden motifs and agendas behind the reading and interpretation. As the Catholic feminist E. Johnson contends, an important part of that task is to unmask ways of speaking of God "that are exclusively, literally, and patriarchally male" and that have led to patriarchalism, exclusivity, and even oppression.[55] Female images, metaphors, and symbols are needed to both challenge and correct the prevailing structures of patriarchalism.

While there might be many reasons for the predominantly male-driven language in the Bible, the sociopolitical and cultural background of biblical times certainly played a major role. That is exactly why, for the sake of liberation and inclusivity, the traditional Christian ways of understanding revelation and doing theology must be subjected to a self-critical assessment in order to establish a more balanced approach. By acknowledging the metaphorical and symbolic nature of revelation without rejecting its proper propositional nature, one is given ample resources for the kind of liberative work this Catholic feminist envisions: "In the midst of emerging emancipatory discourse about the mystery of God from the history of women's experience, biblical language about God in female metaphors becomes a precious discovery."[56]

Revelation and Scripture among Religions

The Challenge and Complexity of Interfaith Engagement of Scriptures

It is now obvious to us even in the American context—and even more obvious in most European settings—that Christian faith can no longer be taken as the religion of the land. Both religious diversity and pervasive secularism have transformed the American and European cultures in dramatic ways. In the

55. Elizabeth Johnson, *She Who Is: The Mystery of God in Feminist Theological Discourse* (New York: Crossroad, 1993), 44.

56. Johnson, *She Who Is*, 77–78.

Global South, religious diversity is taken for granted and is a matter of fact in many areas; secularism is doing much more poorly there.

Unfortunately, interfaith engagement has not occupied the minds of most theologians so far. Sheer lack of knowledge of religions usually nurtures not only misguided remarks about them but also negative attitudes.[57]

How could the comparative work among religions with regard to revelation and Scripture be best done? Or is it a legitimate project at all? Challenges are many and they are great. To begin with, the reservoir of sacred scriptures is amazingly huge among religions—illustrated by Max Müller's classic, *Sacred Books of the East*, in fifty hefty volumes; yet even that "library" misses noteworthy portions of scriptures from various parts of Asia!

Although religious revelation comes in many forms, including nonwritten forms, it is also the case that "in all religions the scriptural word is seen as a means of revealing or realizing the Divine."[58] While most religions have either their canonical or otherwise-determined "primary" scripture, they also have a huge secondary literature that typically is believed to be based on and derive its (relative) authority from the primary revelation.

So far we have spoken of "scriptures" as if the term were self-evident. It is not. Religions vary on what they call scripture. Religions such as Judaism, Islam, and Christianity have a clearly defined and closed canon. In many others, most profoundly in Buddhism, especially in Mahayana traditions, there is hardly any notion of a "closed canon." Hinduism lies somewhere in between, as it has the twofold structure of primary, most-authoritative scriptures, the Vedas (*shruti*), and the secondary *smrti* collections of various types of materials, from epics to songs to folklore and so forth. Even the collection of Vedas, let alone the rest of the Hindu scriptures, is immense.

Scriptures also play different roles in various religions. Whereas Judaism, Christianity, and Islam can be rightly called "religions of the book" because of the necessary and authoritative role played by the written canonical scripture, in Hinduism the spoken word is primary. Furthermore, whereas almost all religions of the world regard their scriptures as inspired and of divine origin, that is not the case with all traditions. Buddhism has no concept of divine inspiration.

57. Timothy C. Tennent, *Theology in the Context of World Christianity: How the Global Church Is Influencing the Way We Think about and Discuss Theology* (Grand Rapids: Zondervan, 2007), 55; see also Michael Amaladoss, SJ, "Other Scriptures and the Christian," *Indian Theological Studies* 22, no. 1 (March 1985): 62–78.

58. Harold Coward, introduction to *Experiencing Scripture in World Religions*, ed. H. Coward (Maryknoll, NY: Orbis, 2000), 1.

Finally, the nature and function of scripture among different traditions vary greatly. For the typical Muslim, the Qur'anic revelation is truly verbatim and relates to all aspects of life. Typical contemporary Jews and Christians consider Scripture the ultimate authority, even though, apart from fundamentalists, they consider its principles and thoughts to be the inspired guide to faith and practice. For most Buddhists, scripture's main role and authority lie in its capacity to convey Buddha's enlightenment and precepts. It is the scripture's "object" rather than the scripture as such that is highly venerated and authoritative. In Hinduism, Brahmins study Vedas as the divinely originated religious (and in many traditions, philosophical) authority, whereas for most Hindus, scriptural content comes in the form of folklore, rituals, artistic forms, and the general cultural environment in India.

With these caveats in mind, let us follow the premier comparative theologian Keith Ward in trying "to articulate a concept of revelation which will be true to the main orthodox Christian tradition, yet which will be open to a fruitful interaction with other traditions, and with the developing corpus of scientific knowledge."[59]

Hindu Scriptures and Authority in a Christian Perspective

The Matrix of Hindu Scriptures

Hindu sacred literature is huge: "No other living tradition can claim scriptures as numerous or as ancient as Hinduism."[60] Hindu scriptures are commonly divided into two categories. First are the Vedas, which are called the *sruti* ("what is heard"), received directly by the *rishis*, "seers." These are the foundational, primary scriptures honored by all Hindu traditions. Second are the secondary scriptures, the *smrti* ("what is remembered"), which are considered to be humanly authored and come in the forms of epics, narratives, and folklore. Basically all forms of Hinduism consider the ancient Vedas as the scripture par excellence. Indeed, it can be said that what keeps Hinduism together and allows it to be discussed as a unified—albeit extremely diversified—tradition is the common belief in the Vedas as foundational, authoritative, divine revelation.

59. Ward, *Religion and Revelation*, 1.

60. Klaus Klostermaier, *A Survey of Hinduism*, 3rd ed. (Albany: State University of New York Press, 2010), 65. Taoism comes close, if not even ranking ahead of Hinduism, in the number and diversity of scriptures.

The Vedic literature is by and large unknown to most Hindus apart from the higher castes (especially Brahmins). Instead, most Hindus get their scriptural teaching from various epics, religious folklore called the Puranas, among which the two most important and widely used are *Ramayana*, a story of Rama, depicted as an incarnation of Vishnu in later tradition, and *Mahabharata* ("Great Epic"), part of which is the Bhagavad Gita, the most important single writing of scripture among all Hindus. Furthermore, unlike in contemporary Christianity, religious and religiously inspired art such as music, dance, and paintings is often taken as revelatory in nature.

To this list one should add an important caveat regarding the most foundational Hindu concept of dharma. Variously translated as "righteousness," "duty," and "ethics/morality," it denotes common human virtues such as generosity, compassion, and abstaining from violence. In addition to this dharma, which is common to all humanity, every human person has a dharma that leads to liberation. Now, where is this dharma to be found? In the Vedas and epics, but also in the practices and behavior of good people and in promptings and insights of one's mind and conscience.

The Vedas originated beginning around 1500 BCE. Each of the four collections (Rig Veda, Sama Veda, Yajur Veda, and Atharva Veda) has four parts: Samhitas, hymns to various deities; Brahmanas, rules for Vedic rituals; Aranyakas, "forest" discussions, symbolic and philosophical reflections on the rituals; and, for the purposes of theological discourse, the most important, the Upanishads, composed around 600 BCE or later.

Theologies based on the Upanishads, called Vedanta, embody much of Hinduism to the West. That said, Vedanta is merely one of the six main schools or traditions of Hinduism,[61] even though it is by far the best known. Second, philosophical in nature, based on the Vedas, it is not necessarily the Hindu religion of common folks. Third, even the Vedanta school has several widely different subtraditions with implications for the doctrine of God, creation, and other topics.

Whereas the Vedas' origin is believed to be divine, the secondary sacred literatures have human authors. But even though their authority is lower than that of the Vedas, their inspired nature is not denied. They play a major role among the masses, particularly the little Bhagavad Gita, the "Bible" of most Hindus. This is the scripture that almost all Hindu households possess. The Hindu devotional literature (*bhakti*) is immense, and it appears in many languages.

61. The six orthodox traditions are Nyaya, Vaisesika, Samkhya, Yoga, Purva Mimamsa, and Vedanta.

Competing Hermeneutics

While all six Hindu traditions consider study and knowledge of scripture the necessary source of theology, two traditions excel in Vedic exegesis: the ritualistic, nontheistic Purva Mimamsa and all Vedanta schools (which, as mentioned, focus on the study of the Upanishads). Profound hermeneutical differences exist between the two main Vedanta traditions devoted to the study of the Vedas, to be briefly visited in the context of the doctrine of God and doctrine of creation. This observation is useful for Christian students who are often bewildered by the internal divisions of their own tradition.

Since Purva Mimamsa is oriented toward ritual and is nontheistic, it regards the Vedas' main purpose as guiding in the right ritual. Hence, the Vedas in this hermeneutic are not looked upon as guides for how to live in the world or, perhaps surprisingly to outsiders, even as information about the deities or immortality. Purva Mimamsa acknowledges gods as legitimate recipients of worship and invocation but eschews inquiry into their nature.

The Vedanta schools, also known as the "Later" (Uttara) Mimamsa, in contrast, engage extensively and painstakingly the task of commenting on the Upanishads, in which they see the revelation of the Ultimate or Absolute, Brahman, as the main theme. Usually Vedanta theologians begin with and concentrate on attentive commentary of Brahma Sutra, including the careful consideration of the nature and works of the deities. But even within this tradition, there are significant divisions between schools (about which more in the next chapter).

Hindu and Christian Views of Scripture: Parallels and Differences

Both Hinduism and Christianity build on scriptural authority. Virtually none of the Hindu schools deviates from scriptural authority.[62] A contemporary Christian may mistakenly assume that with the rise of highly rational, philosophical views of the divine developed among Vedanta traditions, the authority of the (last part of) the Vedas is replaced with a typical post-Enlightenment historical-critical attitude. Nothing could be more off the mark. With all their rational powers, even the philosophically oriented Vedanta scholars build sol-

62. Sarvepalli Radhakrishnan, "The Nature of Hinduism," in *The Ways of Religion*, ed. Roger Eastman (New York: Harper & Row, 1975), 13; Julius J. Lipner, *Hindus: Their Religious Beliefs and Practices* (London: Routledge, 1994), chap. 2.

idly on the divine revelation. The affirmation of Vedic authority is so central to Hinduism as a religious tradition—at least in principle—that those who did not subscribe to it, such as adherents of Buddhism and Jainism, early deviations from Hinduism, were considered heretical. The post-Enlightenment Christian theological rejection of all notions of authority not only in the Christian religion but also, by implication, among other faiths does not exist in Hinduism.

Because of their divine origin and eternal nature, the Vedas are taken to be infallible, free from all error. All orthodox Hindu traditions stick with a strong doctrine of verbal revelation. Materially, they affirm a similar kind of doctrine of the infallibility of sacred scripture as affirmed by classical Christianity and Judaism, as well as Islam. This qualifies the alleged openness of Hinduism to other faiths.[63]

What is the main function of scripture for Hindus? This is a critical comparative theme. The word *veda* derives from the Sanskrit root *vid*, "to know." The knowledge in mind, however, is neither the Western Enlightenment-based "objective" knowledge nor even necessarily the biblical idea of wisdom or knowledge whose goal is the "fear of the Lord." The aim of the knowledge has everything to do with the ultimate goal of the "salvific" vision of liberation (*moksa*). Behind the need for liberation as *moksa* is "ignorance" (*avidya*), lack of true knowledge. This ignorance has to do with the lack of insight into the nature of reality and the Divine (to be explained in the doctrine of salvation below). Even the Upanishads, the most philosophically oriented part of each Veda, do not seek detached abstract knowledge but rather have as their main goal liberation from ignorance. This is markedly different from Christian Scripture's ultimate goal to lead men and women into salvific knowledge of and personal fellowship with the personal triune God who has revealed himself in the Word become flesh.

An essential Christian—as well as Jewish—theme of Scripture focuses on godlike lifestyle and behavior at all levels of human life, whether in the family, society, or the world. At least for the outsider, it looks as if this perspective is not in any way at the heart of Hindu understanding of scripture. Whereas Judeo-Christian faith is deeply anchored in historical events, Hindu religion is not.

Also different are the Christian and Hindu understandings of "inspiration," to use the Christian vocabulary. Whereas in Christian understanding the

63. See Keith Ward, *Images of Eternity: Concepts of God in Five Religious Traditions* (London: Darton, Longman & Todd, 1987), 6; reissued as *Concepts of God: Images of the Divine in Five Religious Traditions* (Oxford: Oneworld, 1998).

divine inspiration of Scripture, even as a genuinely "human" word, is miraculous—that is not the Hindu view of the coming into existence of the Vedas. The reception by the "seers" of the Vedic revelation as oral speech originating in eternity was a matter of "the progressive purifying of consciousness through the disciplines of yoga, [which] had simply removed the mental obstructions to the revelation of the Divine Word." Hence, "in this Vedic idea of revelation there is no suggestion of the miraculous or supernatural."[64] On the other hand, there is nothing like the long struggle of the prophets and other biblical authors with God in real historical events or the notion of progressive revelation, developing and clarifying incrementally over the course of history.

Is There Revelation in Buddhist Traditions?

The Dhamma and Its Proliferation

While it is true that "Buddhism is, in one sense, a religion without revelation . . . [as] there is no active communication from a God in most forms of Buddhism," it is also true that "there is certainly an authoritative teaching in Buddhism, derived from the enlightened insight of Gautama."[65] Ironically, among all religions, Buddhism, with its multiple denominations, has produced the largest mass of sacred texts in various languages.

It makes sense to speak of scripture in Buddhism as long as one keeps in mind some distinctive features that mark it off from other, more "typical" religious traditions. The Buddhist scripture is focused on the founder, the Gautama, who became Buddha as a result of enlightenment. While there is some similarity in this respect with the Christian New Testament with its focus on the founder, Jesus of Nazareth, the founder's role in Buddhism is totally different, as he is a human being rather than a divine Savior. The focus of its scripture is geared toward helping the human in the pursuit of enlightenment.

Following the approximately forty-five-year teaching career of Buddha, each of the early schools developed rich scriptural collections; unfortunately, only the Pali-language Tipitaka ("Three Baskets") was preserved, and that is the "canonical" scripture of the oldest and most traditional Theravada school. After Buddha's death, the First Buddhist Council (486 BCE) was invoked to

64. Harold Coward, *Sacred Word and Sacred Text: Scripture in World Religions* (Maryknoll, NY: Orbis, 1988), 106.

65. Ward, *Religion and Revelation*, 58.

recite the teachings of the Enlightened One. The council established criteria and procedures for the memorization of Buddha's words. Only after about five hundred years was the canonical collection now known as Tipitaka put into writing. As in Hinduism, oral tradition is highly appreciated in Buddhism, even though most schools also highly revere the canonical writings.

According to tradition, Tipitaka was written down in 29 BCE in Sri Lanka under King Vattagamani. Sutta Pitaka contains mainly doctrinal discourses, which appear in shorter poems and longer narratives. Some of those narratives relate to earlier lives of Buddha. A separate, huge collection of former incarnations of Buddha, often numbered around five hundred, is called Jataka, and in English is published in no fewer than six volumes! While noncanonical, this is a highly popular collection, and samples of it circulate widely among Buddhist laypeople. The second "basket" of Tipitaka is the Vinaya Pitaka, which is mainly about (monastic) rules of conduct and discipline. Many of the Buddhist moral principles can be found here, often illustrated with narratives and stories. Abhidhamma Pitaka is the most systematic form of Buddhist thought and beliefs. Alongside the Tipitaka, there are a number of other significant writings such as that of the Buddhist teacher of the fifth century CE Buddhaghosa: Visuddhimagga, "The Path to Purification," a highly significant guide particularly to religious practices among the Theravadans. Most of these writings are not accessible for ordinary Buddhists. Instead, a small portion from the canonical text, called Dhammapada, is close to what we may call the "Buddhist Bible," a slim anthology of verses that for the Jewish-Christian reader brings to mind the Old Testament Proverbs and crystallizes much of the core teaching of the Buddha and Buddhism.

Around the beginning of the common era, the most significant split occurred, giving birth to the Mahayana school. This branch developed a rich and variegated treasure of scriptures as well as a competing hermeneutics alongside the older tradition. Significantly, the Mahayana tradition claimed to build on Buddha's own teaching—thus representing the mentality of some Christian "back to the Bible" restorationist movements—with the alleged "Second Turning of the Wheel of Dhamma." This sermon was believed to be hidden for a while and then rediscovered by this renewal movement—again, a development not unknown in other religious traditions. Mahayana advocates a much more open access to the pursuit of nirvana for all men and women, not only to a few religious.

The development and dissemination of Mahayana tradition throughout various Asian locations are closely connected with the proliferation of sacred literature. As early as the second century CE, the earliest texts were translated into Chinese, and the Tibetan collection of sacred writings was developed a couple of hundred years later. Both the Chinese and Tibetan collections of sutras include a section called "Perfection of Wisdom" (Prajnaparamita), an essential Mahayana teaching about Bodhisattvas (the Enlightened Ones) and the principle of "emptiness" (to be explained later in this text). Once this core text expanded to become huge—over one hundred thousand lines—it was condensed into short texts such as the Diamond Sutra and the Heart Sutra, the best-known parts of the Sanskrit "canon." Quite distinct from the Mahayana tradition, the Tibetan Tantric or Vajranaya school produced large collections of sacred writings as well, including Mahavairochana Tantra, "The Tantra of the Great Vairochana."

While Mahayana and all other Buddhist schools consider Tipitaka to be founding scriptures, Mahayana has produced a number of significant sutras that are rejected by most Theravadans. While the production of rich sacred literature is the hallmark of Mahayana, no canon has been formulated. Hence, there is no fixed pan-Buddhist canon even though Tipitaka is greatly appreciated by all, and only in the Theravada school can the written Tipitaka be said to function as canonical writing.[66]

The Function and Authority of Scripture

Why is there so much sacred literature if it is not salvific in the sense of other religions? Indeed,

> Throughout its history, Buddhist tradition has maintained a paradoxical attitude towards its sacred texts. On the one hand, those texts have themselves been the objects of the utmost veneration: and life, limb, and more have been sacrificed to ensure their unaltered preservation and correct understanding. At the same time, Buddhism avers that the sacred text has, in and of itself, no particular value. Its worth depends entirely on what is done with it, and at best, the sacred text is never more than an aid that must be abandoned by each individual at a certain point on his journey toward the Buddhist goal of enlightenment.[67]

66. Malcolm David Eckel, "Buddhism," in *Eastern Religions: Hinduism, Buddhism, Taoism, Confucianism, Shinto*, ed. Michael D. Coogan (Oxford: Oxford University Press, 2005), 143–52.

67. Reginald A. Ray, "Buddhism: Sacred Text Written and Realized," in *The Holy Book in*

This twofold, dynamic attitude toward the scripture is best illustrated in the famous "Discourse on the Great Decease," which recounts the death of Gautama. On the one hand, it urges the disciple Ananda to be the "lamp" and "refuge" unto himself, and on the other hand, it tells him that the Dhamma is the lamp and refuge![68]

In Buddhist texts one never sees the saying "Thus said Buddha"—as "Thus said the Lord" is customarily seen in the Christian canon. Buddhist texts at times begin with an epithet, "Thus I have heard," and it is most often Gautama himself who is the hearer. And even when the Theravada tradition claims to preserve the "words" of Gautama, always there is the theological assumption that "the *dharma* transcends all words and the capability of language."[69] As Eva K. Neumaier correctly observes: "On the one hand, Buddhists have compiled hundreds of volumes of 'canonical' Buddha words while, on the other hand, maintaining that all words are, at best, only approximations of the truth, and at worst, altogether useless."[70]

So, what do Buddhists believe are the "authority" and defining function of scripture? While there certainly are doctrines in Buddhism, rather than "believing the doctrines" as described in the tightly formulated canons of Semitic religions and Vedic Hinduism, the main function and authority of scripture in all Buddhist schools is to serve as an aid to accessing Buddha's experience of the Awakening.

Often Buddha encouraged his disciples to test every teaching, even his own, in order to attain full conviction. Considering ignorance as the root of evil is of course a shared conviction with Hinduism, even though the role of scripture differs vastly between the two traditions: Vedas are believed to be eternal divine voices whereas Tipitaka is an authoritative access to Buddha's experience and teachings.

Gospel and Dhamma

Surprisingly, a certain parallelism can be discerned between the Christian understanding of Christ as the Word and the Buddhist view of the nature of

Comparative Perspective, ed. Frederick M. Denny and Rodney L. Taylor (Columbia: University of South Carolina Press, 1985), 148.

68. *Mahaparinibbana Sutta* 1.33.

69. Eva K. Neumaier, "The Dilemma of Authoritative Utterance in Buddhism," in *Experiencing Scripture in World Religions*, ed. H. Coward (Maryknoll, NY: Orbis, 2000), 138.

70. Neumaier, "Dilemma of Authoritative Utterance," 138–39.

a revealed word. Samyutta Nikaya says: "He who sees Dhamma . . . sees me; he who sees me sees Dhamma. Truly seeing Dhamma, one sees me; seeing me one sees Dhamma."[71] At the same time, they differ radically, not only because of Buddhism's ambivalence about theistic notions, but also because of its approach to scripture and "revelation" as expounded above. One has to be careful in not overvaluing seeming similarities.

The main differences between Buddhist and Christian notions of revelation have to do with the following: the detachment of revelation from the historical process, the lack of any notion of inspiration of the sacred text, and a very different linking of the sacred words/scripture to the "founders" of the faith—in Christian tradition, Jesus not only speaks authoritatively but *is* the *eternal* Word made *flesh*.

How do Christian and Buddhist notions of authority relate to each other? Two points are in order. First of all, both traditions build on authority. Second, they do this so differently that their views conflict dramatically. The Buddhist conviction about Buddhism's correctness is based on the teachings of the Buddha, in whose life the insight gained led to fulfillment. But since the Buddha is not living physically with us now, the account must be taken by faith. The same goes for Christians, who build on the words of Jesus Christ that are available only through the writings of the early witnesses.

How does Tipitaka take other religious traditions and their scriptures? Estimates vary. The noted Buddhist expert Walpola Rahula—in my understanding—somewhat naively praises the absolute open-mindedness of Buddhist tradition in relation to all other living faiths.[72] As will be detailed in chapter 9, Buddhism's relation to the Other is much more complex. Sympathetically put, it could be labeled "critical tolerance."[73]

The Qur'an and the Bible

Islamic Canon and Sacred Texts

Unlike Hinduism and Buddhism, in which the canon is either vast or hardly defined, but similar to Judeo-Christian traditions, Islam has a clearly defined

71. *Vakkali Sutta* in Samyutta Nikaya, 22.87.

72. Walpola Rahula, *What the Buddha Taught*, rev. ed. (New York: Grove, 1974), 5 particularly.

73. Coward, *Sacred Word*, 157.

canon, the Qur'an. Linked to later exposition and expansion of the Qur'anic materials, there is also a huge and vast Hadith tradition that consists of the sayings of the Prophet and other sages. The sayings and actions of Muhammad narrated in the Hadith are not believed to be revealed, although they are inspired.

By the ninth century, as many as six hundred thousand Hadiths had been recorded, which were then condensed to about twenty-five thousand. By far the most important is the Hadith of Bukkhari; significant also are the Hadiths of Muslim, of Sunan Abu-Dawud, and of Malik's Muwatta. Understandably, Islamic tradition has also produced commentary literature, as have other living faiths. Especially the Sunni exegesis during the first Islamic centuries became famous for its meticulous and tedious work. Along with the mainline Sunni and Shi'ite schools, the mystical Sufi schools have produced an amazingly diverse devotional and mystical literary and poetic treasury.

Although scripture plays an important role in all four living faiths engaged here, in probably no religion is it more central than in Islam. That said, the Qur'an does not do away with earlier revelations, the Jewish First Testament and the Christian Second Testament, but rather considers itself their fulfillment and correction. Similarly to how Hindus view the Vedas, most Muslims consider the Qur'an the eternal speech of God. Again, like Hinduism, oral scripture is the primary mode. It is interesting that the term *Qur'an* in Arabic means both "recitation" and "reading," thus embracing both oral and written aspects.

Unlike in Hinduism, whose *rishis* (seers) merely "hear" the eternal speech in the Vedas, passively, by virtue of having been cultivated spiritually to tap into the divine, the recipient in Islam, the prophet Muhammad, is more than just a passive recipient. Hence, the usual nomenclature of the "messenger" probably says too little of the role of the Prophet.

Unlike the Bible, in which most of the divine speech comes in human form, often embedded in the struggles of human life and in the events of history, and which often contains substantial narratives about key figures such as prophets and apostles, in "the Qur'an, Muhammad receives a direct, fully composed revelation from God, which he then recites to others."[74] While progressive contemporary scholars, mainly based in the West, acknowledge the personal, religious, sociohistorical, and similar contextual factors in the formation of the canon, orthodox Islam regards the Arabic Qur'an as the direct, authoritative speech of God conveyed through the Prophet. In that sense,

74. Coward, *Sacred Word*, 82.

Muhammad's role is critical and unique. An ancient tradition holds that the Qur'an is but a copy of a "Guarded Tablet" in heaven (85:22).

The belief that the revelation of the Qur'an came to Muhammad directly from God does not mean that it all came at one time and in the form of dictation, as it were. According to Q 17:106, "We have revealed it by [successive] revelation." Hadith traditions give vivid accounts of various ways the reception of revelation took place, including through dramatic emotional states,[75] without the struggles having any influence on the revelation.

Although the sacred texts of the living faiths were conveyed originally in particular languages, the Qur'an insists that its original language, Arabic, is also its only "revelatory" language.[76] The Qur'an can only exist in Arabic; all translations fall short of full revelation. The form of Arabic used in the Qur'an is of the tribe of Quraysh, that of Muhammad. Interestingly, stylistically it is identical with none of the known bodies of Arabic. Even the Arabic of the Hadith is different from that of the Qur'an.

The oral form of the Arabic Qur'an is the most foundational and most authentic revelation. Beginning from Muhammad, who was commanded by the angel to commit the revelation to memory and who then recited it to the first disciples, there has been an unbroken line of reciters (*iurra*) of the Qur'an.

Like the New Testament, the Qur'an defines its main and ultimate goal as the salvation of humankind. It also often refers to itself as the guide (14:1; 2:185; among others). The Qur'anic view of scripture is understandably strongly propositional. An extreme view of the infallibility of the Qur'anic revelation and words is affirmed by all orthodox Muslim traditions. According to 2:2, "That Book, in it there is no doubt" (see also 5:15–16; 5:48).

Not surprisingly, the Islamic tradition has paid close attention to careful and authoritative exegesis (*tafsir*) of the Qur'an. Indeed, because the Qur'an lays the foundation for and regulates all aspects of life and society, more is at stake in the hermeneutics of scripture in Islam than with most other traditions. The main difference between the Sunni and Shi'ite schools is that the latter regards the imams as also inspired (and perhaps even infallible), a claim strongly rejected by the Sunni.

75. See *Hadith of Bukhari* 1.1.2 and 3.

76. Q 42:7: "And thus have We revealed to you an Arabic Qur'ān." So also 12:2; 13:37; 16:103; 20:113; 26:195; 39:28.

Qur'an as the Fulfillment of Revelation

What is the relationship of the Qur'an to other scriptures? This is a dynamic and complex question that calls for nuanced reflection. Well known is the statement in Q 42:15 that clearly bespeaks universality: "I believe in whatever Book God has revealed." The Holy Qur'an makes it clear that the divine revelation as guide is available to all nations (Q 35:24). Hence, the current "A Common Word"[77] project between Muslims and Christians took its inspiration from Q 3:64: "Say: 'O People of the Scripture! Come now to a word agreed upon between us and you, that we worship none but God.'"

To balance and complicate this openness and universality, there is an equally important principle of sufficiency and completeness in the Qur'an: "Lo! We have made it an Arabic Qur'ān that perhaps you may understand. And it is indeed in the Mother Book, [which is] with Us [and it is] indeed exalted" (43:3–4). An implication seems to be that all the sacred books of the religions derive from the same divine origin.

On the other hand, Islamic theology of revelation also includes the determined insistence on the supremacy and finality of the Qur'anic revelation, something similar to the Roman Catholic fulfillment theology of religions. Sura 5:44–48 makes this clear by presenting the Jewish Torah and the Christian New Testament as stepping-stones to the final revelation given in the Qur'an. Not only does the Qur'an provide fulfillment; it also provides correction and criteria. It is in light of the Qur'an that the value of other revelations is assessed.

A major challenge to a common reading of Christian and Muslim scriptures is the common Muslim charge of *tahrif*, usually translated as "alteration." At its most basic level, it refers to problems of textual variants and, hence, the lack of the authentic original. It may also denote deliberate altering of the text—the most typical charge being that Ezra altered the Old Testament text. But it can also simply mean a misguided interpretation of the texts. In light of Islamic tradition, this makes sense, as the New Testament contains not only sayings of Jesus but also his activities, not unlike the Hadith of Islam. The current *tahrif* criticism of the Bible uses skillfully—and selectively—the insights of (Christian) historical-critical study in rebutting the truthfulness and reliability of the text.

The dilemma of Muslim-Christian views of revelation does not have to do with the strangeness, but rather with the deep affinity, between these two traditions. As Clinton Bennett aptly puts it:

77. For the project, see A Common Word, http://www.acommonword.com/.

> In many respects, the conservative Christian view of the Bible as infallible and as inspired word for word is closer to how Muslims view the Qur'an than to the liberal Christian view of the Bible as a potentially fallible, human response to experience of the divine. On the Muslim right, the Bible is regarded as so corrupt that it no longer has any value. On the Christian left, an attempt is made to understand how the Qur'an can be accepted as "revelation." One difficulty is that Christians who deconstruct the Bible are likely to transfer this approach to the Qur'an as well, which is unacceptable, even to more liberal Muslims. Yet despite each side's view of the Other's scripture, Christians and Muslims from both the "right" and "left" cite from the Other's scripture to support their views.[78]

Qur'an and Christ as Living Word

It is not the prophet but rather the book that is the closest parallel to Christ. Islam is not based on Muhammad but rather on the Qur'an and Allah. Neither Christ nor Muhammad in Islamic interpretation is divine; only God is. Hence, it is in Christ's role as the living Word of God in relation to the divine revelation of the Qur'an that the deepest commonalities are to be investigated. Rightly it has been noted that whereas Jesus in Christian tradition is the "Word made flesh," the Qur'an in Islam is the divine word "inlibrate."[79]

There are surprisingly deep similarities among the accounts in the Qur'an of the power of its word and Old Testament claims about the word of the Lord and New Testament statements about Christ as the creative word. Consider Q 59:21: "Had We sent down this Qur'ān upon a mountain, you would have surely seen it humbled, rent asunder by the fear of God." The Islamic tradition speaks of the living words of the Qur'an in terms of destruction, healing, tranquillity, and so forth.

78. Clinton Bennett, *Understanding Christian-Muslim Relations: Past and Present* (London: Continuum, 2008), 16.

79. Vincent Cornell, "Listening to God through the Qur'an," in *Scriptures in Dialogue: Christians and Muslims Studying the Bible and the Qur'an Together*, ed. Michael Ipgrave (London: Church House, 2004), 37.

The First and the Second Testaments: Jewish Theology of Revelation

It might strike one as odd to discuss the Jewish view of Scripture last, after the more foreign traditions from Asia and even Islam. That said, unlike some other topics, such as Christology and the Trinity, that are plagued with deep and irreconcilable conflicts, Christian and Jewish traditions hold more in common when it comes to Scripture.

Distinctively, in the Jewish religion the process of reception of revelation is fully embedded in historical events and living tradition. While divine in its origin, the revelation is given and received in the matrix of human life at personal, tribal, national, and international levels.

Importantly, because revelation comes in the unfolding of history, it looks into the future for fulfillment. But being oriented to Yahweh's final intervention, the most significant sign and manifestation of which is the arrival of the Messiah, does not mean that therefore Jewish faith is otherworldly. It is not. Indeed, one of the most significant differences between the Jewish and Christian views of revelation is that the latter is deeply eschatologically oriented and hence its revelational category of promise is also eschatological, as discussed above. Judaism focuses on the implications of revelation for this world.

Furthermore, the focus of Jewish revelation is on ethical and moral obedience. This is not to deny the importance of moral precepts in other living faiths—only consider Buddhism. It is to say that in other living faiths the connection between moral conduct and religious practice, belief in God and righteous walks of life as expressions thereof, is not established in the integral way it is in Judaism—and of course, by implication, in Christianity.

For the Jewish faith, revelation is propositional in nature. Two important considerations help highlight the importance of the propositional nature of revelation. On the one hand, according to ancient tradition—although not supported by recent Jewish historical academic study—Moses basically received the law by divine "dictation." On the other hand, what he received, the detailed lists of commands, exhortations, laws, and practices conveyed by Yahweh, can only be appreciated as cognitive, propositional statements. How different is the content of the Hebrew Bible's law code from the style and content of, say, the Rig Veda of Hinduism!

The center and most sacred part of the Jewish canon, Tanakh,[80] is Torah ("teaching," "instruction"). In written form, it is the "Five Books of Moses."

80. Tanakh is an acronym formed from the first letters of the three sections of Scripture: Torah, Nevi'im, and Ketuvim.

An important counterpart is the Oral Torah, which came to full flourishing with the emergence of rabbinic Judaism beginning around the start of the common era, but which was believed to have been revealed to Moses along with the written Torah.

The two other parts of the canon, albeit not as sacred, are Nevi'im (prophetic books) and Ketuvim ("Writings"). Importantly, what the Christian Bible names "historical books" (Joshua, Judges, 1–2 Samuel, 1–2 Kings) are prophetic here. Since Yahweh is the Lord of history, the post-Enlightenment separation of "secular" and "sacred" history is a foreign idea.

If "prophetic Judaism" (the Judaism until the beginning of the common era) brought about the Hebrew Bible as we have it now, "rabbinic" Judaism produced the huge and varied collections of the so-called Oral Torah; the nomenclature "oral," of course, has to be taken in a qualified sense here. While put into written form in Mishnahs (and commented on in Talmuds), the first transmission of it from Yahweh to Moses is believed to have been oral. While not canonical in the sense of Torah, it is irreplaceable in that it helps make the written Torah living and applicable to ever-new situations. Hence the importance of midrash, the meticulous examination of the written text to find its right and true meaning.

Rabbinic Judaism became the dominant form of the religion following the devastation caused by the destruction of the Second Temple in 70 CE, which of course meant yet another loss of the land and more importantly the temple. While Judaism divided into many groups, all of them held Torah as the canonical Scripture but had varying views concerning the value of extrascriptural tradition.

The Pharisees, the mainstream of rabbinic Judaism after 70 CE, became the custodian of developing tradition. Through painstaking study of the Law (Torah) and the rest of the canon, they uncovered meanings not apparent at a cursory reading. Revelation is thus "progressive," unlike traditional prophetic Judaism, which believes in the reception by Moses of Yahweh's revelation. This huge Oral Torah is classified under the general categories of halakah, ritual and legal practices and traditions, and haggadah, with its focus on homiletics, ethics, exegesis, and theology. The first major such work that also became foundational to the Oral Torah is the Mishnah, compiled in the second century CE. Huge collections of Talmudic tractates—the most important of which are the Babylonian and Palestinian—emerged as commentaries on the Mishnah over several centuries. The Babylonian Talmud, completed in the sixth century CE, is the most important of these works and an indispensable resource for everything Jewish.

In medieval times revisionist movements arose, such as Karaism, which questioned and basically rejected the rabbinic notion of Jewish tradition, and Kabbalism, which, unlike Karaism, did not reject either rabbinic tradition or the Oral Torah, but rather filled it with new meanings, often highly speculative and imaginative.

As important as prophetic and rabbinic Judaism is to that religion, in the contemporary world there are a number of nonorthodox movements, from the Reform movements of the mid-nineteenth century to various liberal schools of our era. While all these movements, in some sense or another, consider Torah the canonical Scripture, they disagree widely about how to deal with the rules (*mitzvoth*) of Torah in the contemporary world.

Scripture between the Two Religions

To locate the Jewish tradition in the multifaith matrix, it is helpful to follow Keith Ward's characterization. He identifies Judaism as seminal and intermediate. It is seminal in its functioning as the basis for two other faiths, Christianity and Islam, and it is intermediate because it is a local or tribal tradition. However—and this is significant for Christian considerations—its view of revelation is universal in that it speaks of Yahweh as the creator and God of all men and women and the whole of creation.

When it comes to the relation of the two peoples of God who share the same Torah as their Scripture, we have to begin with the sad and long track record of Christian anti-Semitism. As early as the second century CE, Marcion wanted the Christian church to reject the Old Testament as canonical Scripture.

When mutual trust is being established, mutual dialogue and common Scripture may begin with issues related to the discussion of current themes such as the implications of the divine Word as incarnate and the Christian "deviation" from the teachings of the First Testament.

The consideration of the theology of revelation takes us naturally to the doctrine of God, the theme of divine revelation.

2 | Triune God

For Orientation

This lengthy chapter falls into two intertwined sections of discussion. As a way of orientation to the first main section of the chapter, we seek to establish the conditions for speaking of God in a contemporary culture plagued with secularism and various kinds of atheistic rebuttals of not only God's existence but also the possibility or meaningfulness of speaking of God. Another "foundational" task concerns the need for clarifying the meaning and value of philosophical and natural theology's "proofs" of God. Thereafter, the material presentation of a contemporary doctrine of God for a pluralistic world is attempted under the novel nomenclature "classical panentheism."

The second main section will first take a careful look at the way the Old Testament–based Jewish monotheism evolved into a Trinitarian monotheism during the first formative centuries of Christian existence and was further clarified and expanded. That discussion naturally leads to the question of the topic known in classical theology as "divine attributes." Thereafter, we continue the discussion on liberative impulses of Christian theology, including an acute subtopic in today's world, namely, violence and God. The chapter ends with a comparative theological look at the triune God among other faith traditions' deities.

On the Conditions and Contours of God-Talk in a Secular World

God in a Secular Age

In ancient cultures, including the biblical ones, the "problem" of God had to do with the simple question, "Which God?," because in polytheistic environments deities were local and there was the rivalry of the gods, well known also in the Bible. Beginning in modernity, the question shifted to "Does God exist?," as atheistic rebuttals emerged. In contemporary postmodern times, the question is, "Does God matter?"[1] In the aftermath of modernity, a secular age has pervaded most of the cultures of the Global North. New atheism has emerged to challenge the belief in God. The huge influence of sciences and scientific worldviews subjects any religion's belief in God to new scrutiny and rebuttal.

Whereas in the past the terms "God" and "gods" were meaningful even among those indifferent to religion, that is no longer the case. For a large number of contemporary people, the word "god" has either become meaningless or has been stripped of any real content. Indeed, since the Enlightenment, it has been assumed and expected that religion would disappear altogether as science and "civilization" march onward. This is known as the "secularization thesis," first forcefully presented by the great intellectuals of the nineteenth century, from Karl Marx to Sigmund Freud and many others. More recently, beginning from the "secular decade" of the 1960s, a number of leading contemporary sociologists of religion and even some theologians have enthusiastically embraced the thesis.

Is the secularization thesis true? The answer is *no*—and *yes*! When it comes to the loss of power of religions over secular institutions such as, say, universities, the thesis appears to be quite accurate. The role of religion in the Global North has significantly diminished. But where the secularization thesis has embarrassingly failed is in its prophecy of the disappearance of religions globally. Contrary to the thesis, the current world is even "more" religious than before, notwithstanding the simultaneous presence of secularism. Furthermore, against all odds, fundamentalist and other traditional forms of religion, within both Christian and other faith traditions, seem to be growing.

So, what is secularism? The Canadian philosopher Charles Taylor contends that there has been a shift away from a culture in which it was virtually impossible not to believe in God to an era in which belief in God is but one

1. See further, Stanley J. Grenz, *Theology for the Community of God* (Grand Rapids: Eerdmans, 1994), 30–33 particularly.

option—and to many a marginal one.[2] Taylor distinguishes three different notions of secularism: the retreat of religion from the public space (type 1), the decline in belief and practice (type 2), and the change in the conditions of belief (type 3). Secularism even in the Global North does not necessarily mean leaving behind all notions of God or transcendence. What has changed in the Global North is that belief in God has become a matter of personal choice. This change of conditions of belief (type 3) is what the original advocates of the secularization theory missed and what really makes the difference. No wonder some talk about "postsecularism."[3]

The most radical attempt in theology to accommodate the entrance of secularism was the short-lived death-of-God movement in the 1960s. Whether it *really* meant to talk about the "death" of God in any literal sense or was a rhetorical device, the ideology could not sustain itself for many years.[4] A much more serious and long-standing challenge to God-talk has been the philosophical attempt to make it simply meaningless, "senseless."

Objections against God-Talk

Part of the so-called Vienna Circle, a number of early-twentieth-century analytic philosophers headed by Ludwig Wittgenstein, argued that only empirically tested statements could be taken as true. Hence, religious and ethical statements were "nonsensical" and meaningless. A growing number of thinkers joined the chorus, among them even some theologians. The problem with this claim is obvious: the demand for empirical verification would of course relate to that sentence as well, and hence make it meaningless!

But even if talk about God is considered meaningful, that does not guarantee its possibility for finite human beings. The reason is simple: God is infinite and beyond human concepts, while human understanding and language are finite and fallible. A theological counterargument is that Christian tradition has always acknowledged the finite, partial, and fallible nature of human knowledge of God—but that with this admission, it has not ruled out the possibility of some kind of real talk about God. Particularly in the Chris-

2. Charles Taylor, *A Secular Age* (Cambridge, MA: Belknap Press of Harvard University Press, 2007).

3. Jürgen Habermas, *Between Naturalism and Religion*, trans. Ciaran Cronin (Cambridge, UK: Polity, 2008).

4. See Veli-Matti Kärkkäinen, *The Doctrine of God: A Global Introduction*, 2nd rev. ed. (Grand Rapids: Baker Academic, 2017), 124–26.

tian East, the limitations of human knowledge of God became a theological theme in the so-called apophatic or "negative" theology for which it suffices to speak of God in indirect, suggestive terms rather than direct, bold statements. That said, apophaticism is not a refusal to talk about God. It is just a humble and modest claim to the knowledge of God.

In the Christian West, the limitation of human talk about God was often framed as an analogical language in which there is some real correspondence between human words and divine reality but not a total equation. Just think of the "Heavenly Father" analogy. There needs to be some correspondence between a heavenly and an earthly father for the analogy to make sense, but there does not have to be a total equation.[5]

In contemporary theology, metaphors acknowledge the partial nature of human knowing, somewhat similarly to tradition's use of analogy. Metaphor "is seeing one thing *as* something else,"[6] and, as discussed in the previous chapter, it also carries a surplus. In sum: God-talk is meaningful and possible when rightly conceived. But what if there is nothing "behind" that talk?

The Atheistic Rebuttals of Faith in God

The Arguments of Modern Atheists

While the phenomenon of atheism predates the Enlightenment, its form and role in ancient societies were vastly different from those of the post-Enlightenment world. Biblical writers simply dismiss as "fools" those who deny God (Ps. 14:1). Those few dissenting thinkers in antiquity such as Socrates, often identified as atheists, were not denying the existence of god(s) after modern atheism, but rather wished to shift the focus from the cult of gods to independent thinking. Indeed, early Christians were charged with "atheism," having left behind the Jewish faith and refusing to worship the gods of the Roman Empire.

On philosophical grounds, severe criticism of the concept of the personal God came from the idealist J. G. Fichte, a pupil of Hegel. Fichte simply could not reconcile the ideas of "personal" and "infinite" with the notion of

5. Whereas "univocal" totally equates the human and divine terms, "equivocal" makes them totally different.

6. Sallie McFague, *Metaphorical Theology: Models of God in Religious Language* (Philadelphia: Fortress, 1982), 15.

God as a being. If a being, then God must be "substance," but that would endanger infinity, as entities in space-time can hardly be infinite. If God were a "person," then God would be an "I" in contrast to other "I's." Again, infinity would be compromised. Counterarguments have been presented against Fichte, whose details we need not to go into here.[7]

A very different atheistic agenda comes from "the last real atheist,"[8] Friedrich Nietzsche. From Charles Darwin he learned that the human mind is hardly anything beyond nature, and hence ethics, arts, and similar human enterprises are nothing more than "natural" rather than being religious in origin. Unlike typical atheists, Nietzsche is not content with merely denying the existence of God. His project is to "kill" God, as he dramatically describes the act of the "madman" in his *Gay Science (The Joyful Wisdom)* and replace him with "Superman."[9]

The most vocal modern advocate of the charge that religion is a matter of human projection is Ludwig Feuerbach. For him, religious talk about God was nothing but a wishful projection into the skies of an idea of a good Father. Not only was that not real, but it was also dangerous, as it diverted people from the pursuit of important personal and societal goals of improving this world. Feuerbach's ideas were picked up by Karl Marx, who wished to offer a new materialist vision to make a difference in this world. Like many of the like-minded, Marx considered religion harmful and dangerous, in his own words, "the opiate of the masses." Hence, "The abolition of religion as the illusory happiness of the people is a demand for their true happiness."[10]

Enter yet another modern atheist, Sigmund Freud, and you face the charge that religion represents the worst kind of sickness of mind. Hence, his project of "curing" our minds from the sickness of religion emerged. In critique, all the forms of modern atheism are based on speculation rather than on serious study of either the history of religions or specific religious texts. Hence, by and large, they are academically worthless. Furthermore, their take on religion is hopelessly one-sided and lacks nuance. Against every misuse of religion can be found numerous historical examples of religious people who lived most noble and selfless lives. At the same time, when critiquing religion

7. For details and sources, see Grenz, *Theology for the Community*, 37–38.

8. Ian S. Markham, *Against Atheism: Why Dawkins, Hitchens, and Harris Are Fundamentally Wrong* (Oxford: Wiley-Blackwell, 2010), title of chap. 2.

9. Friedrich Wilhelm Nietzsche, *Gay Science (The Joyful Wisdom)*, trans. Thomas Common (Lawrence, KS: Digireads, 2009 [1882/1887]), ##125, 79–80.

10. Karl Marx, *Critique of Hegel's Philosophy of Right*, ed. Joseph O'Malley (Cambridge: Cambridge University Press, 1970), 131.

for many of the ills among men and women, these atheists do not bother looking at the meaning of similar kinds of ills produced by secularism.

Contemporary "New Atheism" and Scientific Naturalism

Allegedly basing their atheism on science and "naturalism" (the belief that there is nothing beyond nature), a number of new atheists continue Freud's infamous curing-from-the-sickness-of-religion project, including the two Oxford scholars, ethologist Richard Dawkins and chemist Peter Atkins, as well as the British American popular science writer Christopher Hitchens.[11] These atheists' claims can be summarized as follows.[12] First, the concept of God is incoherent, including notions of divine omnipotence and omniscience as well as the problem of evil. Second, faith means the opposite of reason and belongs to a precritical era. Third, whereas theism is without any rational grounds, atheism can allegedly be shown to be "true." Fourth, because true, atheism is able to provide a healthy worldview whereas theism fails to do that. Part of the contribution of atheism for these three advocates is its tolerance vis-à-vis the intolerance of other faiths. Fifth, atheism helps avoid religious education, which is simply child abuse. Finally, all these writers highlight the integral link between violence and faith in God.

In response, Alister McGrath, himself an Oxford biologist and theologian, notes that, first, "for Dawkins, the natural sciences possess the capacity to explain the world," eliminating the need for collaborating with other academic disciplines, least of all theology and religious studies.[13] This "science explains everything" approach, however, has encountered devastating critique. Not only is there no such thing as "explaining the world," a number of important issues also clearly go beyond the borders of science, such as what was "before" and what "caused" the big bang. Second, the claim that after the advent of Darwinianism no legitimate place is left for God grossly ignores the simple fact that contemporary Christian theology takes for granted Darwinist evolutionist theory. Third, the argument that faith is an attitude without any rational basis clearly conflicts with the universal conviction among theologians that

11. For details, see chap. 1 in Hans Schwarz, *The God Who Is: The Christian God in a Pluralistic World* (Eugene, OR: Cascade, 2011).

12. See Markham, *Against Atheism*, chap. 1.

13. Alister E. McGrath, *The Order of Things: Explorations in Scientific Theology* (Oxford: Wiley-Blackwell, 2006), 24; Alister E. McGrath, *Dawkins' God: Genes, Memes, and the Meaning of Life* (Oxford: Blackwell, 2005).

faith and reason belong together in a dynamic mutual relationship. Fourth, Dawkins's charge of faith in God as a "meme," a "pathological infection,"[14] has absolutely no scientific evidence. Fifth, as argued below, belief in God can hardly be necessarily made a cause of violence. Generally speaking, new atheists routinely confuse "methodological" and "metaphysical" naturalism. Whereas the former is a necessary prerequisite for all scientific work that seeks empirical verification, the latter is an ideological stance with no scientific or empirical court to appeal to.

The "Traces" of God in the Created Reality

Knowledge of God from God's Greatness

As mentioned in the context of natural revelation, common sense and Christian intuition have posited the existence of God on the basis of the created order, including the human person. Indeed, the attempts to "prove" the existence of God/gods go back to antiquity to great philosophers such as Plato and Aristotle. Similarly, other religious traditions know this tradition, including Judaism and Islam, even at times some Asiatic faiths.

Classical theology did not regard the proofs of God as "proofs" in the later apologetic sense, in terms of attempting to show that by the force of logic God's existence must be acknowledged. Rather, the classical proofs were a means of making God-talk reasonable. The proofs were presented by those who already presupposed God's existence.

In Christian philosophical and theological tradition, one of the first formative ways of attempting to prove God's existence was done by the medieval master Anselm of Canterbury. His famous ontological argument is from *Proslogium*: "Even the fool is convinced that there is something, at any rate in the understanding, than which nothing greater can be conceived, for when he hears this, he understands it, and whatever is understood is in the understanding. And certainly that than which a greater cannot be conceived cannot exist in the understanding alone. For if it be in the understanding alone, it is possible to conceive it as existing in reality, which is greater."[15]

14. Richard Dawkins, *The Selfish Gene* (Oxford: Oxford University Press, 1989 [1976]), 192.

15. Anselm of Canterbury, *Proslogium*, chap. 2 in *Anselm of Canterbury: The Major Works*, ed. G. R. Evans and Brian Davies (Oxford: Oxford University Press, 1998), 66.

Although Anselm's main argument was more or less decisively defeated during the Enlightenment times by Immanuel Kant—who raised the obvious question of whether it is really necessary to posit an existence on the basis of an *idea* of an existence[16]—there still is some intuitive value in this highly abstract idea.

Knowledge of God from the World

Along with the ontological, the cosmological argumentation has also occupied the minds of Christian theologians. Thomas Aquinas is best known for the five proofs, presented in the first part of his *Summa theologiae*: the proofs from motion, causality, contingency, grades of perfection, and purpose. Behind the use of cosmological proofs is the intuition that through the experience of the world God has created we can know something of the Creator.

Contemporary theology exercises proper caution when making God the "explanation" of the possibility of the world. While God is in one sense "the first cause," merely looking for the first cause would keep us in the confines of time and space (a fallacy duly critiqued by Kant and others). That said, modestly employed, both cosmological and ontological proofs lend credence to the *idea* and possibility of God the Creator (although they give very little content to the nature of that God).

Yet another set of proofs relates to the nature of the human being as a religious and moral being, classically named anthropological and moral proofs.

The Incurable Religiosity and Morality of Humanity

One important aspect in the anthropological argument can be called "the persistence of the transcendent,"[17] the fact that it seems to belong to human nature to be open to and inquire into the realities beyond the visible world. This is what the sociologist of religion Peter Berger names "a rumor of angels."[18]

16. Immanuel Kant, *The Critique of Pure Reason* [1781], trans. J. M. D. Meiklejohn (A Penn State Electronic Classic Series, 2010), 348, http://www2.hn.psu.edu/faculty/jmanis/kant/Critique-Pure-Reason6x9.pdf.

17. Alister E. McGrath, *The Open Secret: A New Vision for Natural Theology* (Oxford: Blackwell, 2008), chap. 2.

18. Peter L. Berger, *A Rumor of Angels: Modern Society and the Rediscovery of the Supernatural* (Garden City, NY: Doubleday, 1969; Harmondsworth, UK: Penguin, 1970).

Although the anthropological argument seems to make a strong case for the human being's openness and propensity for belief in God, in itself it hardly is able to say anything much of the existence of God. Nor is it meant to; it merely makes talk about religion and God meaningful and rational, perhaps even necessary.

The liability of the anthropological proof is its misuse in support of the atheistic argument. Indeed, that happened with Feuerbach and others, as explained above: belief in God was made a function of human projection. As persistent as that kind of propensity might be, the atheistic argument goes, it is also detrimental and dangerous.

Closely linked with the anthropological is what is traditionally called the "moral argument," which of course was most profoundly developed by Kant in his *Critique of Practical Reason.* He was impressed by "the moral law within" as much as he was by "the starry heavens."[19] This moral law pushes us toward the highest level of morality and judges when we fail. It is difficult to posit a "foundation" for morality apart from God.

Having clarified the conditions for and rebuttals of God-talk and God's existence, we now move to the actual doctrine of God as it has been conceived in Christian tradition and contemporary theology.

The Appeal of Panentheism(s)

"Classical Theism" and Biblical Narrative of God

Much of the energy for a growing number of reinterpretations of the doctrine of God is derived from a desire to revise or, in some cases, even reject the whole project of "classical theism" (see below). If there is any common denominator behind most of these projects, it is a turn to a form of panentheism. What does this all mean? What is at stake in this discussion?

It has become customary to speak of "classical theism" as a generic term designating the approaches of traditional postbiblical developments of early Christian theology that sought to express its faith in the biblical God with the help of Greco-Roman philosophical categories and later found its highest sophistication in medieval scholasticism, post-Reformation Protestant orthodoxy, and

19. Immanuel Kant, *The Critique of Practical Reason*, trans. Thomas Kingsmill Abbott (University Park: Pennsylvania State University Press, 2010), 164, http://www2.hn.psu.edu/faculty/jmanis/kant/Critique-Practical-Reason.pdf.

early modern theology. Classical theism is not limited to Christianity; in many ways, similar kinds of doctrines of God can be found in Judaism and Islam.

The picture of God that emerged out of that philosophical-theological development is considered to be vastly different from the dynamic, narrative, testimonial presentation of Yahweh/the God of Jesus Christ in the biblical canon.[20] Complaints have been many: the God of classical theism, as an "Unmoved Mover," while enjoying his own perfect fullness of being, is distanced from the world, unaffected by the happenings of history, unrelated to Christian life (let alone social and political struggles), and so on. The American process theologian David Ray Griffin's textbook caricature lists the following elements: "pure actuality," "immutability and impassibility," "timelessness," "simplicity," "necessity," "omnipotence and omniscience."[21]

So, how do these developments relate to the biblical narrative and testimonies? As said, the Bible does provide us with a narrative, a story of God that consists of testimonies, parables, metaphors, disputes, and so forth, which are diverse, which sometimes stand in dynamic continuity with us, and which are authentically human. Systematic theologians should be mindful of the warnings of Old Testament theologians not to oversystematize the dynamic biblical narrative.[22]

In some parts of the New Testament, occasional references to the kinds of intuitions classical theism entertains can be found, but even there the Old Testament type of testimonial, narrative presentation is in the fore. The kinds of passages pointing in the direction of classical theism include the apostle Paul's affirmation in 1 Corinthians 8:4–5 that "there is no God but one" and that "so-called gods in heaven or on earth" do not exist. Other examples cited include Acts 14 and 17, where Paul finds parallels with existing philosophical and religious thought forms. A passage from the Pastoral Epistles (1 Tim. 1:17) talks about God in terms that bear obvious similarities to philosophical approaches: "To the King of ages, immortal, invisible, the only God." Terms such as "immortal" and "invisible" clearly ring philosophical tones of the time.

While going beyond the "economic" biblical narrative of God, early theologians had a necessary and useful reason to contextualize it into prevail-

20. For biblical theologies of God, see Kärkkäinen, *The Doctrine of God*, chap. 1; for classical theism, chap. 2.

21. David Ray Griffin, *God, Power, and Evil: A Process Theodicy* (Philadelphia: Westminster, 1976).

22. John Goldingay, *Israel's Gospel*, vol. 1 of *Old Testament Theology* (Downers Grove, IL: InterVarsity Press, 2003), 32; Walter Brueggemann, *Theology of the Old Testament: Testimony, Dispute, Advocacy* (Minneapolis: Augsburg Fortress, 1997), 117.

ing Hellenistic philosophical-religious terminology. Both the development of Christian doctrine and mission to the world needed it.

Take, for example, the classical notion of God as "immaterial substance," that is, God is not physical or material. As abstract as it may sound, it was also useful and necessary at the time when the "only options were that God is either a material or an immaterial substance."[23] Of course, theology had to choose the latter. That our worldview allows us to express the same in different categories is not to put blame on the fathers' efforts.

Panentheism in the Bible and Christian Tradition

Whereas in "classical theism" the God-world relationship is conceived in terms of a clear distinction (though, of course, not separation, as God's presence permeates the whole of creation), "pantheism" makes a total equation between God and the world. No Abrahamic theologian can endorse that. The middle position is known under a somewhat elusive term, "pan*en*theism." Therein, God and world are neither equated (as in pantheism) nor strongly distinguished (as in classical theism). Although a more recent phenomenon, the idea of panentheism (while not so named) is not unknown in tradition either. Consider the bold global statement by Bishop Kallistos of Diokleia: "There are . . . good grounds for asserting that Judaism, Christianity, and Islam are all fundamentally 'panentheist,' if by 'panentheism' is meant the belief that God, while *above* the world, is at the same time *within* the world, everywhere present as the heart of its heart, the core of its core." The long panentheistic orientation—"the delicate equilibrium between transcendence and immanence"—was however impaired as the otherness and distance of God from the world, particularly among the Western theologians, took the upper hand.[24]

The Hebrew Scripture teaches a dynamic panentheistic vision. On the one hand, God is spoken of as the absolutely majestic, transcendent, "incomprehensible," "hidden" Divine (Job 38:4; Isa. 45:15; 55); on the other hand, this same God asks rhetorically, "Am I a God at hand . . . and not a God afar off?" (Jer. 23:23), whose presence men and women cannot avoid wherever they go (Ps. 139:7–8). Similarly, the New Testament speaks of God in dynamic terms. Paul's speech in Acts 17 makes every effort—in one and the same passage!—to

23. F. LeRon Shults, *Reforming the Doctrine of God* (Grand Rapids: Eerdmans, 2005), 11.

24. Kallistos Ware (Bishop of Diokleia), "God Immanent Yet Transcendent: The Divine Energies according to Saint Gregory Palamas," in *IWWLM*, 158–59.

paint the picture of God's transcendence as well as God's immanence as robustly as possible. On the one hand, it goes on to argue that nothing humanly constructed ever is able to contain God, the Creator of the world; on the other hand, the passage reminds us that it is in God that we live and breathe!

Consider approaches to God in Christian history that represent classical panentheism. On the one hand, Eastern Christian tradition makes every effort to ascertain the total "incomprehensibility" and hence transcendence of God, lest the majestic God be made a function of human handling. On the other hand, it elevates spiritual experience, vision, "ascent" to God as the main way of knowing God. That "knowledge" can only be had of God who is "near" us. "In his essence God is infinitely transcendent, utterly beyond all created being, beyond all understanding and all participation from the human side. But in his energies—which are nothing else than God himself in action—God is inexhaustibly immanent, maintaining all things in being, animating them, making each of them a sacrament of his dynamic presence."[25]

Such mystical, experience-based, spirituality-driven conceptions of God appear also in the West in theologians such as the ninth-century John Scotus Eriugena and the fifteenth-century Nicholas of Cusa, as well as in the mystical tradition of the fourteenth and fifteenth centuries.[26] Coming from a different perspective and agenda, the great American preacher Jonathan Edwards of the eighteenth century seems to have affirmed a type of panentheism in this remark: "God is the sum of all being, and there is no being without his being; all things are in him, and he in all."[27]

The Panentheistic Turn in Contemporary Theology

Among twentieth-century theologians, the turn to panentheism has come to full fruition. The most radical form is that of American process theology in which God is not only deeply involved in the affairs of the world but even emerges and evolves with the world; there is, of course, no conception of creation *ex nihilo* ("from nothing") or any certain eschatological outcome.[28] A more classical approach is that of the Roman Catholic priest-paleontologist Teilhard de Chardin, whose cosmic evolutionary spirituality made every effort

25. Ware, "God Immanent Yet Transcendent," 160.

26. See John W. Cooper, *Panentheism: The Other God of the Philosophers—from Plato to the Present* (Grand Rapids: Baker Academic, 2006), chap. 3.

27. As cited in Cooper, *Panentheism*, 74.

28. See Kärkkäinen, *The Doctrine of God*, 126–29.

to harmonize with twentieth-century natural sciences. Mindful of charges of pantheism, he made every effort to affirm the transcendence of God.

Among contemporary theologians, the most widely debated panentheistic *theological* turn is Moltmann's "trinitarian panentheism."[29] A key motif for him is resistance to the classical notion of God's impassibility, that is, God's incapacity to suffer because of perfection. Instead, Moltmann proposes a robust view of "the crucified God" who is deeply involved in the pains and joys of his people and the world.[30] Not surprisingly, the doctrine of creation follows from and supports Moltmann's panentheism. For him creation is the fruit of the loving God's longing for his other and for that other's free response to the divine love. That is why the idea of the world is inherent in the nature of God himself from eternity.[31] Hence, there is a reciprocal relationship between the world and God, which will culminate in the eschaton in the mutual indwelling of God and creation.[32]

Understandably, panentheism "strikes a chord with many feminist thinkers, who regard traditional models that emphasize God's distance and absolute power as being overtly patriarchal. Panentheism, by contrast, emphasizes God's connectedness and responsiveness to the world."[33] The moderate Catholic feminist Elizabeth Johnson's theological vision—based on values of "mutual relations," "radical equality," and "community in diversity"—builds on God as loving communion, as relational, while utterly transcendent, also intimately related to everything that exists. The triune God constantly sustains life and resists destructive powers of nonbeing and violence.[34] Similarly, panentheism has great appeal to eco-feminists[35] and some other ecologically sensitive theologians.[36]

29. So called by Richard Bauckham, *The Theology of Jürgen Moltmann* (Edinburgh: T&T Clark, 1995), 17.

30. Jürgen Moltmann, *The Crucified God: The Cross of Christ as the Foundation and Criticism of Christian Theology*, trans. Margaret Kohl (Minneapolis: Fortress, 1993).

31. Jürgen Moltmann, *The Trinity and the Kingdom of God: The Doctrine of God*, trans. Margaret Kohl (San Francisco: Harper & Row; London: SCM, 1981), 138.

32. Jürgen Moltmann, *The Coming of God: Christian Eschatology*, trans. Margaret Kohl (Minneapolis: Fortress, 1996).

33. Gregory R. Peterson, "Whither Panentheism?" *Zygon: Journal of Religion and Science* 36, no. 3 (2001): 396.

34. Elizabeth Johnson, *She Who Is: The Mystery of God in Feminist Theological Discourse* (New York: Crossroad, 1993), 228–30.

35. Elizabeth Johnson, *Women, Earth, and Creator Spirit* (Mahwah, NJ: Paulist, 1993); Sallie McFague, *The Body of God: An Ecological Theology* (Minneapolis: Fortress, 1993).

36. Among male theologians, an important panentheistic-ecological proposal comes

Moreover, a number of other liberation theologians deeply concerned about suffering, injustice, and inequality in the world have turned to panentheism. The senior American black theologian James Cone reinterprets God's immanence in terms of divine presence in the midst of the struggle for liberation, and transcendence as God's unlimited capacity to bring about changes rather than God's being "'above' or 'beyond.'"[37] Similarly, the Peruvian Catholic Gustavo Gutiérrez builds on a robust panentheistic theology by speaking of the divine presence not only in the world and among human beings in general, but particularly among the poor, marginalized, and exploited ones.[38]

While conservative-evangelical theology by and large has been quite suspicious of the panentheistic turn, "open theism" has introduced God as loving parent, responsive, open to the future, and in constant dialogue with creatures and creation.[39]

Particularly deep interest in panentheism is shown by a growing number of theologians who dialogue with natural sciences. The late British biochemist-priest Arthur Peacocke reminds us of the importance for the doctrine of God of the radically changed worldview in sciences, which bespeaks dynamic interrelationality, complexity, and evolvement, as well as divine immanence.[40]

My *Trinity and Revelation* joined this long line of diverse pantheisms and proposed a new way of negotiating between classical theism and forms of contemporary panentheism; it was somewhat counterintuitively identified as "classical panentheism."[41] The term "classical" means to say that the panentheism advocated is not a new phenomenon in Christian theology, as was also shown above. It is yet to be seen what kind of reception that proposal may encounter.

Having outlined some basic conditions and contours of God-talk and the doctrine of God in Christian theology, we take up the second main section

---

from Matthew Fox, *The Coming of the Cosmic Christ: The Healing of Mother Earth and the Birth of a Global Renaissance* (San Francisco: Harper & Row, 1988).

37. James H. Cone, *A Black Theology of Liberation*, 2nd ed., twentieth anniversary ed. (Maryknoll, NY: Orbis, 1986), 76–78, here 77.

38. Gustavo Gutiérrez, *A Theology of Liberation: History, Politics, and Salvation*, trans. and ed. Sister Caridad Inda and John Eagleson (Maryknoll, NY: Orbis, 1986 [1973]; rev. ed. with a new introduction, 1988), 156–57.

39. Clark H. Pinnock, *Most Moved Mover: A Theology of God's Openness* (Grand Rapids: Baker Academic, 2001).

40. Arthur Peacocke, "Introduction: '*In* Whom We Live and Move and Have Our Being'?" in *IWWLM*, xx.

41. For details, see chap. 10 in Veli-Matti Kärkkäinen, *Trinity and Revelation*, A Constructive Christian Theology for the Pluralistic World, vol. 2 (Grand Rapids: Eerdmans, 2014).

of this chapter, which will first highlight the Trinitarian nature and works of God in the world.

The Role and Importance of the Trinitarian View of God

Whether the Doctrine of the Trinity Is Indispensable

In the words of Orthodox Bishop Kallistos, "The doctrine of the Trinity is not just one possible way of thinking about God. It is the only way. The one God of the Christian church cannot be conceived except as Trinity."[42] That said, for most Christians this doctrine sounds outdated and complex. So, do we "need" the doctrine of the Trinity?

Although we should not join the chorus of those who speak of the eclipse of the Trinity in Christian history, it is also the case that following the patristic era, during which time the basic contours of the doctrine of the Trinity were hammered out, it also began to wane in importance. Routinely, the unity of God preceded the threeness in doctrinal manuals. And while the order of discussion is hardly all-important, it easily leads to the implication that while oneness of God is primary, Trinity is somewhat auxiliary. Certainly, modern theologian Schleiermacher's 800-plus-page *The Christian Faith* serves as an example: fewer than 15 pages are devoted to the Trinity![43]

Recall here Barth's wise word that "doctrine of the Trinity is what basically distinguishes the Christian doctrine of God as Christian."[44] If so, even the theological presentation should reflect it—as it does in Barth, in whose *Church Dogmatics* the Trinity appears in the very beginning.[45]

How to Do Trinitarian Theology

One of the reasons why Christian tradition at times failed to see fully the significance of the Trinity had to do with the way the doctrine came to be

42. Kallistos [Timothy] Ware, "The Holy Trinity: Model for Personhood-in-Relation," in *The Trinity and an Entangled World: Relationality in Physical Science and Theology*, ed. John Polkinghorne (Grand Rapids: Eerdmans, 2010), 107.

43. Friedrich Schleiermacher, *The Christian Faith*, ed. H. R. Mackintosh and J. S. Stewart (Edinburgh: T&T Clark, 1999), 738–51.

44. Barth, *CD* I/1, 301.

45. Barth, *CD* I/1, §§8–12.

formulated. In the course of history, the doctrine was often divorced from the economy of divine works (creation, salvation, sanctification) and came to be based on somewhat abstract speculations. A feeling arose that if the doctrine is so complicated and complex, perhaps it is not for every believer!

Contemporary theology has been attempting to overcome this liability with its turn toward the economic, "from below," approach to God. This turn was brilliantly heralded by the twentieth century's most important Roman Catholic theologian, Karl Rahner: "*The 'economic' Trinity is the 'immanent' Trinity and the 'immanent' Trinity is the 'economic' Trinity*" (Rahner's rule).[46] This simply means that access to any knowledge of God moves up, so to speak, from the observation of God's work in creation, providence, reconciliation, and consummation, to the life of God itself. Whatever can be known of God by the limited, finite human mind is based on the economy of salvation rather than on God's inner life. Yet we can trust that this knowledge of God, however limited and occasional, is reliable because God, as faithful Creator and Savior, is the same in God's own life (immanent Trinity) as in God's works in the world (economic Trinity).

What makes possible the economic approach to the knowledge of the triune God is the gracious embodiment of the divine in the incarnation of the Logos. This indeed makes the Christian belief in the Trinity unique: "unlike the adherents of other faiths, Christians believe that God has entered fully and directly into the created order, and has become *concretely embodied* in the world."[47]

Alongside Barth, Wolfhart Pannenberg also reverses the order. *Systematic Theology* (vol. 1) treats first threeness (chap. 5) and then oneness (chap. 6). There are two interrelated reasons behind this move. First, for him, all systematic theology is but exposition of the doctrine of the triune God and his works. Second, the biblical basis of the Trinitarian doctrine can be found in the coming of Jesus, the obedient Son of the Father, as explicated in the New Testament. Jesus's self-distinction from the Father in becoming fully human, one of us, and his continuing unity with the Father as fully divine are the beginning of the "Trinitarian grammar." Here, again, we see how Rahner's rule is followed.

Moltmann similarly turns to Christology and anchors the doctrine of the Trinity specifically on one event in the history of Jesus, namely, the cruci-

46. Karl Rahner, *The Trinity*, trans. Joseph Donceel (London: Burns & Oates, 1970), 22.

47. David S. Cunningham, "The Trinity," in *The Cambridge Companion to Postmodern Theology*, ed. Kevin J. Vanhoozer (Cambridge: Cambridge University Press, 2003), 186.

fixion: "the cross of the Son stands from eternity in the centre of the Trinity."[48] This is in keeping with Moltmann's focus on divine suffering in defeat of what in tradition came to be named divine impassibility (impossibility for God to suffer in a real sense of the word—and a related conception of immutability, the lack of change in the Deity).

What, then, is the content and way to develop the Christian doctrine of God—from the Old Testament monotheism to the New Testament Trinitarian belief in one God?

One God as Father, Son, and Spirit

The Slow Emergence of the Trinitarian Doctrine

Were we not so familiar with the way God is presented in the New Testament, we would be totally astonished by the difference from the Old Testament. How can it be that there is seamless transition from the Old Testament way of speaking of Yahweh as one God to the talk about God in the New Testament as Father, Son, and Spirit? The answer is simply this: "The initial impetus . . . was spawned by the theological puzzle posed by the early church's confession of the lordship of Jesus and the experience of the indwelling Holy Spirit, both of which developments emerged within the context of the nonnegotiable commitment to the one God of the Old Testament that the early believers inherited from Israel."[49]

The critical stage in moving from a binitarian to a Trinitarian understanding of God had to do with the growing insistence on the Spirit as the "medium of the communion of Jesus with the Father and the mediator of the participation of believers in Christ."[50] The God who raised the Son from the dead by the power of the Spirit (Rom. 1:4) will raise believers from the dead as well (8:11). In the "Spirit Christologies"[51] of the Synoptic Gospels, Jesus is anointed by the Spirit at his baptism and receives a confirmation from the Father, "Thou art my beloved Son" (Mark 1:11 par.).

Pannenberg sums up: "The involvement of the Spirit in God's presence in the work of Jesus and in the fellowship of the Son with the Father is the basis of the fact that the Christian understanding of God found its developed and defini-

48. Moltmann, *Trinity and the Kingdom*, xvi; so also, e.g., 78.

49. Stanley J. Grenz, *Rediscovering the Triune God: The Trinity in Contemporary Theology* (Minneapolis: Fortress, 2004), 7.

50. Pannenberg, *ST* 1:266.

51. See chapters on Christology (chap. 5) and pneumatology (chap. 7) below.

tive form in the doctrine of the Trinity and not in a biunity of the Father and the Son." That said, however, "the NT statements do not clarify the interrelations of the three but they clearly emphasize the fact that they are interrelated."[52]

Not surprisingly, after the New Testament times it took centuries for the church to come up with a defined understanding of how to account for the threeness in the one God. Among the many tactics, a reliable, biblically based way was to establish distinction in the one God by considering the inner relations of the Son, Father, and Spirit. On the basis of the Paraclete (the "Advocate") passages in John 14, Tertullian suggested that the Son distinguished both the Father and the Spirit from himself.[53] This suggests, as Pannenberg puts it a bit technically, that the "self-differentiation of the Son from the Father on the one side and the Spirit on the other forms a basis for the thesis that there is a threefold distinction in the deity."[54] The point made here is clear: the threeness of Father, Son, and Spirit belongs to eternity—eternal loving fellowship ("communion") between them—rather than merely to some "outward" works.

Righting the Heretical Views

The first critical task for the early theology was to establish the full deity of the Son, a process that took quite a bit of time, and somewhat later, that of the Spirit (to be discussed below in chaps. 5 and 7). Ironically, these significant developments came from tackling and defeating heretical views.[55] The key heretical view regarding the Trinity is known as *monarchianism* ("sole sovereignty"). Monarchianism questioned how Christians could maintain absolute monotheism (Deut. 6:4) while believing in "two gods," Jesus Christ and the Spirit, in addition to the Father. For our purposes, there are two subcategories, dynamic and modalistic. Both emerged in the late second and early third century. They stressed the uniqueness and unity of God in light of the Christian confession that Jesus is God.

Dynamic monarchianism[56] preserved the sole sovereignty of the Father by promoting the idea that God was dynamically present in Jesus, making

52. Pannenberg, *ST* 1:268–69.

53. Tertullian, *Against Praxeas*, sec. 9 (in *ANF*, vol. 3), quoting John 14:28 and 14:16.

54. Pannenberg, *ST* 1:272.

55. For a detailed treatment, see Veli-Matti Kärkkäinen, *Christian Understandings of the Trinity: The Historical Trajectory* (Minneapolis: Fortress, 2017).

56. J. N. D. Kelly, *Early Christian Doctrines*, rev. ed. (New York: Harper & Row, 1978 [1960]), 115–19.

Jesus higher than any other human being but God. In other words, God's power (Greek, *dynamis*) made Jesus *almost* God. Thus, the Father's uniqueness was secured. Modalistic monarchianism[57] defended God's sole sovereignty by seeing the three persons of the Trinity not as self-subsistent "persons" but as "modes" or "names" of the same God. Father, Son, and Spirit do not stand for real distinctions but are merely different ways God manifested himself at different times.

In presenting an orthodox response to these views, Tertullian first noted that preservation of the "monarchy" of God, the main concern of monarchianism, did not necessarily require that God be only one person. If the Father thus wishes, the Son may share in the monarchy without thereby destroying it. Therefore, the divine monarchy is no reason to deny the distinction between Father and Son.[58] Tertullian was convinced that the threeness revealed in the divine economy was in no way incompatible with God's essential unity. To combat both modalism and polytheism, he introduced the idea of God as one substance (*substantia*) and three distinct persons (*personae*). Gerald O'Collins defines Tertullian's term "substance" as "the common fundamental reality shared by Father, Son, and Holy Spirit."[59] Tertullian's view was well received and helped to clarify the issue on the Latin-speaking (Western) side, although it represented far from a final settlement.

In Greek-speaking theology, particularly under the leadership of Athanasius and the three Cappadocians (Basil, Gregory of Nazianzus, and Gregory of Nyssa), materially the same Trinitarian formula was expressed in terms of *mia ousia—treis hypostaseis*, "one 'essence'—three 'persons.'" Somewhat technically repeated: sharing the same divine "essence," "the Father possesses the divine substance *without cause* from himself, the Son *by being begotten from the Father* and the Spirit *by proceeding from the Father*."[60] A wonderful example is Basil's description: "For all things that are the Father's are beheld in the Son, and all things that are the Son's are the Father's; because the whole Son is in the Father and has all the Father in Himself."[61] Later he also applied the same principle to the Spirit.

57. Kelly, *Early Christian Doctrines*, 119–23.

58. As paraphrased by Justo L. González, *A History of Christian Thought*, vol. 1, *From the Beginning to the Council of Chalcedon* (Nashville: Abingdon, 1970), 182–83.

59. Gerald O'Collins, *The Tripersonal God: Understanding and Interpreting the Trinity* (Mahwah, NJ: Paulist, 1999), 105.

60. Franz Dünzl, *A Brief History of the Doctrine of the Trinity in the Early Church*, trans. John Bowden (London: T&T Clark, 2007), 107.

61. Basil of Caesarea, *Letters* 38.8 (*NPNF*² 8:141).

In sum: whatever difficulties early theology encountered in trying to establish the understanding of a genuine threeness in the one God, it rightly sought to negotiate between two extremes: tritheism,[62] on the one hand, and modalism, the lack of personal distinctions in the one Godhead, on the other hand. At the same time, what is technically called the subordinationist tendency was strong and deep: it means the subjecting of the Son and Spirit to the Father[63] and in a sense making them somewhat inferior, which was a long-standing challenge to the equality of the three.

God's Life as Communion of Love and Equality

To say that one God exists as Father, Son, and Spirit is to speak of communion, the personal communion of the three. The turn to a relational understanding of personhood—that is, an individual can be "person" in the true sense of the word only if he or she is not seeking to isolate from others but rather is seeking to dwell within a community—has assisted in the rediscovery of communion theology. The Greek Orthodox theologian John Zizioulas's important collection of essays with the telling title *Being as Communion* (1985) has become a clarion call for contemporary theologians. The main thesis of Zizioulas's theology is simple and profound: God is not first "one substance" and only then exists as "trinity"; rather, triune communion is the most essential statement about God, a mutual relationship of love.[64]

Many contemporary theologians, from Moltmann to feminists and other female theologians to other liberationists, see in the communion theology a promise of equality as opposed to hierarchic relations. As the late Catholic feminist C. M. LaCugna puts it: "God, too, lives from and for another: God the Father gives birth to the Son, breathes forth the Spirit, elects the creature from before all time. . . . God's rule is accomplished by saving and healing love."[65] A number of these theologians discern that communion theology may also underwrite cautious panentheism. Behind the appreciation of the communion

62. Consider Gregory of Nyssa, *On "Not Three Gods" to Ablabius.*

63. Justin Martyr's idea of the Son being "second" and the Spirit being "in the third place" in the Godhead is a classic example of a subordinationist view. *First Apology*, sec. 13.

64. John D. Zizioulas, *Being as Communion: Studies in Personhood and the Church* (Crestwood, NY: St. Vladimir's Seminary Press, 1985), 17.

65. Catherine Mowry LaCugna, *God for Us: The Trinity and Christian Life* (San Francisco: HarperSanFrancisco, 1991), 383; see also Karen Baker-Fletcher, *Dancing with God: The Trinity from a Womanist Perspective* (St. Louis: Chalice, 2006).

nature of God is the intuition that, while distinct, God and the world do not represent two totally different realities; they are intertwined.

Some leading theologians from the Global South, particularly Africa and Asia, have sought to envision the communal nature of the one God through the lens of an important cultural asset: ancestorship. This resource is also widely utilized in Christology, as will be discussed below. The Roman Catholic Charles Nyamiti of Tanzania is best known in the African context for such an enterprise.[66] African cultural traditions possess key features conducive to an authentic Trinitarian account such as relatedness, communion, and the central role of intermediaries, both ancestors and spiritual beings. To Nyamiti's credit, while utilizing robustly local cultural-religious ancestral resources, he also builds intentionally on key Christian resources with the intent to remain within creedal tradition. He makes the bold claim that the ancestral way of constructing the classical doctrine is indeed superior to the classical ways, and this for several reasons. For instance, the ancestral way of viewing the Trinity highlights the importance of communion and participation, unlike any other view; the Holy Spirit is seen as integral or internal rather than "external" to the Trinity; the holiness of the Father is an integral part of his being; the ancestors being the models of exemplary conduct illustrates perfectly the Son's role as the perfect image of his Father, in obedience and humility.[67] That said, there are also differences, of which Nyamiti is well aware, between Christian Trinitarian doctrine with Christ as the mediator and ancestral "mediators," and therefore, this comparison also demonstrates contrasts at the same time.

The Unity of the Tripersonal God

What, then, about the unity of the triune God? In recent times the theological pendulum has swung the other way: whereas in tradition the unity of God was the beginning point for the establishment of the threeness, contemporary theology usually begins with threeness (Father, Son, and Spirit) as it appears in the New Testament narrative. That raises the question of how to ensure the unity. Moltmann responds to this question in this way: "What then emerges is a concept of the divine unity as the union of tri-unity" and further clarifies

66. Charles Nyamiti, *African Tradition and Christian God* (Eldoret, Kenya: Gaba, 1972); see also his *Christ as Our Ancestor: Christology from an African Perspective* (Gwero, Zimbabwe: Mambo, 1984).

67. See further, Charles Nyamiti, "The Trinity from an African Ancestral Perspective," *African Christian Studies* 12, no. 4 (1996): 51–52.

that rather than focusing on one divine substance, it focuses on "relationships and communities."[68] On this basis, Moltmann states: "The three divine Persons exist in their particular, unique natures as Father, Son and Spirit in their relationships to one another, and are determined through these relationships. . . . Being a person in this respect means existing-in-relationship."[69]

In the same way, Pannenberg, as mentioned, begins from the threeness and only then goes on to affirm the unity. But Pannenberg, being a more traditional theologian, also works harder in making sure the unity is not compromised in any way. Unlike Moltmann and many other social Trinitarians, but like traditional approaches, he affirms a single divine essence and does not see this affirmation in any way softening the starting point in the three persons. The key is that unlike traditional substance ontology,[70] he bases the unity on a relational ontology and relational understanding of personhood. In other words, he conceives of "the divine essence as the epitome of the personal relations among Father, Son, and Spirit."[71]

The point made by both of these contemporary theologians (albeit somewhat differently) is that, first, threeness rather than unity should be the first Christian statement about God, and the unity—which is of course necessary in order to avoid polytheism—can be affirmed in terms of a relational ontology. That kind of dynamic ontology makes room for a unity that is not antagonistic to diversity within one Godhead.

Having established the threeness of one God—or the oneness of the triune God—we embark upon a big topic in contemporary theology, namely, the triune God's relation to the world and its consummation. This will take us to further details about Rahner's rule, named above, concerning the economic and immanent Trinity, followed by discussion about the divine "attributes." Before that longer discussion, however, we will take up briefly a millennium-long and still-continuing debate known by the technical term *filioque*. It has to do with the derivation of the Spirit in the Godhead and was the "official" theological reason in the first major split of the Christian church in 1054.

68. Moltmann, *Trinity and the Kingdom*, 19.

69. Moltmann, *Trinity and the Kingdom*, 172, among others.

70. "Ontology" is the branch of philosophy that inquires into the nature of "being" or existence. The term "substance ontology" is used to refer to the way classical philosophy until the advent of the modern/contemporary scientific worldview assumed the existence of more or less "solid" substances; the current worldview, after the relativity and quantum theories, on the contrary, envisions the nature of reality in terms of relations, dynamic evolvement, and elusive explanations.

71. Pannenberg, *ST* 1:334.

Filioque *and the East/West Split*

The term *filioque* (Latin: "and from the Son") refers to the addition by Latin Christianity to the Niceno-Constantinopolitan Creed of 381, concerning the dual procession of the Spirit from the Son and the Father, a statement vehemently opposed by the Greek-speaking Orthodox tradition, which always has stuck with the original form of the creed that said the Holy Spirit "proceeds from the Father." This was the major theological reason for the first major breach of the Christian church in 1054.

Why was this word added in the first place? Undoubtedly the New Testament itself is ambiguous about the procession of the Spirit. Whereas (the Johannine) Jesus says that he himself will send the Spirit (John 16:7) or that he will send the Spirit (called *Parakletos* here), who proceeds from the Father (15:26), Jesus prays to the Father in order for him to send the Spirit (14:16) and promises that the Father will send the Spirit in Jesus's name (14:26).

The rebuttals of the Orthodox Church are many and varied—some more solid, others overstatements. What is indisputable is that the Westerners launched this addition unilaterally, without consultation with the East. Similarly, it is true that more often than not the subordination of the Spirit to Jesus has plagued the Christian West with theological corollaries in ecclesiology, the doctrine of salvation, and elsewhere; that is, while Christ has loomed large in these doctrines, the Spirit's role has tended to be marginal.

Even if some of the objections from the East may need qualification, the Eastern critique of the *filioque* is important both ecumenically and theologically. The West acted wrongly in unilaterally changing the ecumenically binding creed. At the same time, it can be argued that *filioque* is not heretical—as the Eastern criticism too often implies—but that it is ecumenically and theologically unacceptable and therefore should be removed. This is the growing consensus of both Protestant and Roman Catholic theologians.[72] An alternative to *filioque* that reads "from the Father through the Son" would be also acceptable to the Christian East. Other such negotiations might be available.

72. For a helpful discussion, see Lukas Vischer, ed., *Spirit of God, Spirit of Christ: Ecumenical Reflections on the Filioque Controversy* (London: SPCK; Geneva: WCC, 1981).

God and World—God's Works in the World

How to Negotiate the Economic and Immanent Trinity

Above it was established, following Rahner's rule, that the knowledge of God proceeds "from below," from the economy of salvation. That knowledge, as incomplete and fallible as it may be due to human limitations, is reliable, as God is faithful. Important theological considerations come to the fore when the rule is being pushed to establish too tight an identity between the economic and immanent Trinity. That could potentially lead to the compromising of the divine freedom, "the total collapse of the immanent Trinity into the economic Trinity [which] result[s] in a finite God who is dependent for divine definition upon the world."[73]

On the other side, insisting on the *distinction* between the immanent and economic Trinity too strongly raises the problem of the idea of God being "immune" to the happenings and needs of the world. In the extreme, it may imply that what happens in the world is a kind of superficial act, as in a play, more or less distinct from the absolutely unmoved deity of eternity. Rahner's rule is of course presented to combat these errors.

The first tendency, toward equating the economic and immanent Trinity, has been a common liability of the newest theology. Some wonder if Moltmann, with all his cautiousness in treating the issue, in some sense ends up collapsing the two. Sayings like the following undoubtedly give rise to that suspicion: "In order to grasp the death of the Son in its significance for God himself, I found myself bound to surrender the traditional distinction between the immanent and the economic Trinity, according to which the cross comes to stand only in the economy of salvation, but not within the immanent Trinity."[74] Similarly, the well-known desire of Moltmann to unite the economic and immanent Trinity in the eschatological consummation points to the same: "The economic Trinity completes and perfects itself to immanent Trinity when the history and experience of salvation are completed and perfected. When everything is 'in God' and 'God is all in all,' then the economic Trinity is raised into and transcended in the immanent Trinity."[75]

Most contemporary theologians seek to walk a thin line, holding tightly to the *distinction* without making it a *separation*. Pannenberg's careful and

73. Ted Peters, *God—the World's Future: Systematic Theology for a Postmodern Era* (Minneapolis: Fortress, 1992), 108.

74. Moltmann, *Trinity and the Kingdom*, 160.

75. Moltmann, *Trinity and the Kingdom*, 161.

nuanced approach serves here as a fine example. As a panentheist, well aware of the need to correct tradition's tendency to make the relationship between history and the divine life more or less independent, Pannenberg is also critical of those contemporary revisions that for him result in the danger of the "absorption of the immanent Trinity in the economic Trinity."[76] While the Creator God is certainly committed to the promised salvation and consummation, God's "future" is not contingent on the events of history.

Having negotiated the economic-immanent distinction, we go on to consider more carefully the way God works in the world. This takes us to the discussion of divine attributes.

How to Speak of the "Divine Attributes"

Following the rule of proceeding from the economic to the immanent Trinity, we will not begin the consideration of God's attributes "from above," as it were—for the simple reason that the human mind can never penetrate infinite divine mystery! Rather, we seek to discern the qualities and characteristics of the triune God in the world by virtue of the divine works, God's relationship with the world and us.

The most reliable account of God's works in the world can of course be found in Scripture. In that light, very appropriate is the complaint by the late Reformed British theologian Colin Gunton that too often theologians used to begin with a "commonsense"—not rarely, quite abstract—listing of attributes and then define what makes God![77] With all its merits, Thomas Aquinas's highly sophisticated description of God may be in danger of that. Having discussed the existence of God in the beginning of his *Summa theologiae* (1.1.2) under the rubric "Essence of God" (1.1.3–11), the Angelic Doctor seeks to describe God in terms of "simplicity," "perfection," "infinity," "immutability," "eternity," and "unity," among other attributes.[78] A number of examples from more recent times could be easily listed.

It is not that these kinds of descriptions of God are wrong; indeed, there is much truth and value in them. Of course, God is "being" above all other beings, without belonging to the same category with other beings! Of course,

76. Pannenberg, *ST* 1:331.

77. Colin E. Gunton, *Act and Being: Towards a Theology of the Divine Attributes* (Grand Rapids: Eerdmans, 2003), 16.

78. That said, the Angelic Doctor also acknowledges in the beginning of the discussion that "we do not know the essence of God" (1.2.1).

God is "simple" in that there are no "parts." And so forth. The liability of these kinds of abstract, "from above," explanations is that they likely claim too much, and even if they don't, their relevance to spirituality, worship, mission, and Christian education is not easily evident. Beginning with the Scripture and economy of salvation, content with humble and modest explanations, would save us from those kinds of dangers. Recall that in the biblical canon, the description of God comes in the form of testimonies, metaphors, symbols, and other familiar ways of speaking.

An important biblical way of speaking of the nature of God has to do with the *name* of God. Unlike in our current culture—but similar to many cultures of the Global South—in the ancient world one's name "gives power over the one who bears it."[79] Indeed, in the biblical narrative, the "name" of Yahweh, like the "word" and "spirit," becomes a semipersonified agent of God, God's representation. Important in this regard is the revealing of the name Yahweh in Exodus 3:14. Notwithstanding wide exegetical disputes[80] about the meaning of the I AM self-designation, the theological lesson is that the naming of God can only be done by God, rather than by other deities or humans, and that God has chosen to leave the meaning open and elusive! Commenting on this passage, the feminist E. Johnson adds a highly interesting caveat. In her search for complementary, corrective, and balanced ways of naming God, she suggests SHE WHO IS. When used not in exclusion to the traditional naming, that feminine description bespeaks inclusivity and belonging.[81]

Ultimately and at its core, the description of God's qualities and capacities—the listing of the divine attributes—is a form of praise and worship. Just consider this one representative biblical testimony in Psalm 136: every "description" of Yahweh and his mighty acts is accompanied by the congregation's response, "his steadfast love endures for ever"! It also reminds us that the God of the Bible is passionate, responsive, and deeply relational.

Before proceeding, a short "methodological" note is in order, regarding a topic dear to and widely debated among classical theologians. Somewhat oversimplified, it can be stated like this: How can we imagine the attributes of God being related to the essence of God, as it were? Are they separable or are they just part of the essence, to put it crudely? As long as substance ontology was the dominant paradigm, theological tradition had to spend a lot of ink

79. Pannenberg, *ST* 1:359–60, here 359.

80. See Stanley J. Grenz, *The Named God and the Question of Being: A Trinitarian Theo-Ontology* (Louisville: Westminster John Knox, 2005), 135–51.

81. See Johnson, *She Who Is*, 241–43.

negotiating this matter. While generally it was agreed that attributes cannot be separate from the essence, opinions varied as to how to establish the necessary connection,[82] the details of which we do not have to engage here. Now that we have moved to a dynamic worldview with relational concepts of the "essence," we have much more leeway. In other words, the attributes tell us of God in relation to the world. At the same time, we can say without much sophisticated speculation that of course they are rooted in the undivided, common essence of God, God who is infinite and uncreated, so beyond our limited concepts and notions.

How should we classify the divine attributes? Tradition built on the important intuition that there is a difference, or at least a distinction, between the "incommunicable" and "communicable" ones; the former are unique to God's nature, whereas the latter, while perfect in God, can, to a lesser degree, also be human attributes. While that distinction is not without merit (particularly with regard to attributes beginning with the prefix "omni-," unique to God), it may also blur the complexity of many attributes such as holiness, which, as an expression of God's infinity, represents both the "*omni*-holiness" (of God) and the partial-developmental holiness of humans.

Here I follow the classification that builds on the notion of divine infinity. As an important philosophical-theological term with much discussion in tradition, the basic cash value of infinity is that it not only distinguishes itself from the finite but also embraces and includes it (it would not be infinite if there were any boundaries to it, namely, the boundary between infinite and finite). Just think of the most well-known and important biblical "definition" of God, God as love: the divine love not only distinguishes itself from all limits, failures, and abuses of human love but also embraces, includes, and overcomes human love. The other important biblical pointer to God, God as eternal, similarly fits the bill, as will be detailed below. Hence, without too tight a categorization or overly technical analysis, we simply speak of God as eternal and as loving.

Eternal God as
- Holy
- Faithful
- All-Wise, -Powerful, and -Present

82. This was the debate between nominalists and realists, that is, between those (the former) to whom descriptions/qualities/etc., such as holiness, were merely "names," and (the latter) to whom they were "really existent."

Loving God as
Compassionate
Good
Merciful
Just and Righteous

Eternal God

The Holy One

The concept of infinity, as defined above—that it both demarcates from and embraces its opposite, the finite—helps in defining the divine holiness. Holiness can be defined as both a characteristic that separates God from everything else and a characteristic that makes it possible to embrace everything. In the Bible, the separation from everything that is not holy stands in the forefront. Theological tradition up until our times has so heavily focused on the first part of the meaning, separation, that the equally essential meaning of the fact that it not only "opposes the profane world . . . [but also] embraces it, bringing it into fellowship with the holy God," has not been duly noted. In other words, the holiness of God "enters the profane world, penetrates it, and makes it holy."[83]

As with any other attribute, we must not be "thinking of God's holiness in isolation from God's identity," or else "a contradiction is inscribed deep into the doctrine of God: the contradiction between God's holiness and his love."[84] They presuppose each other.

Faithful and Everlasting

The commonsense intuition of "eternal" denoting everlasting time that never comes to an end and the Greek conception of "eternal" as the timelessness of God as the one who exists absolutely "outside" or "beyond" time (and its corollary: change) are not so much wrong as they are limited; they miss the deeper meaning of the biblical-theological term. Indeed, "we ought not to conceive of God's eternality as timeless impassibility but as omnipresence with respect to

83. Pannenberg, *ST* 1:399, 400, respectively.

84. John Webster, "The Holiness and Love of God," *Scottish Journal of Theology* 57, no. 3 (2004): 258.

time. God is present in all time, and therefore all time is present to God."[85] The essential point about divine eternality is the reference to the faithfulness and dependability of the biblical God. This is vigorously argued by the American Lutheran R. Jenson, who, after careful biblical scrutiny, concludes that God's "eternity" means "'faithfulness' to the last future"[86] that hence assures us of "the certainty of his [God's] triumph."[87] The Hebrew term *emunah* (faithfulness) is the "reliability of a promise" of Yahweh. Yahweh is not immune to time; rather, Yahweh shows his faithfulness over the course of time.

Highlighting faithfulness and constancy goes hand in hand with the equally important idea of God's everlasting nature in terms of what tradition calls divine "aseity," that God has his existence in himself without anything else, or that God's "incorruptible" nature never comes to an end, as it were. A proper way to affirm those important ideas is to refer to God's livingness, that God has life in himself. "The Spirit of God is opposed to the frailty of all things earthly, of all 'flesh' (Isa. 31:3), for he is the source of all life and thus has unrestricted life in himself."[88] Hence, the right intuition among early theologians affirmed the "incorruptibility" of God based on the biblical affirmations of God's "immortality" (Rom. 1:23). God is not subject to the process of decay that humans and the rest of creation, including the cosmos, are subject to (Ps. 102:26–27).

All-Wise, All-Present, and All-Powerful God

The biblical conviction of God's ever-presence in his creation (Jer. 23:24) as well as his absolute transcending of all that is made, even "heaven and the highest heaven" (1 Kings 8:27), is another way of saying theologically "eternity" and philosophically "infinity." "Whereas God's eternity means that all things are always present to *him*, the stress in his omnipresence is that he is present *to all things at the place of their existence.*"[89]

85. Grenz, *Theology for the Community*, 91.

86. Robert W. Jenson, *The Triune Identity: God according to the Gospel* (Philadelphia: Fortress, 1982), 141; Robert W. Jenson, *Systematic Theology*, 2 vols. (New York: Oxford University Press, 1997, 1999), 1:46–50, 94–101.

87. Jenson, *The Triune Identity*, 141; *Systematic Theology*, 1:157.

88. Pannenberg, *ST* 1:401; for a detailed philosophical discussion, see Wolfhart Pannenberg, *Metaphysics and the Idea of God*, trans. Philip Clayton (Grand Rapids: Eerdmans, 1990), chap. 4 and passim.

89. Pannenberg, *ST* 1:410.

Traditional theology made a distinction between God's "immensity," as one of God's intrinsic or incommunicable attributes, and his "omnipresence," which had to do with God's relation to the world. That distinction, however, must be corrected, as the two are best seen in conjunction. "Precisely as the one who incommensurably transcends his creation, God is still present to even the least of his creatures. As in the case of his eternity, then, there are combined in his omnipresence elements of both immanence and transcendence in keeping with the criterion of the true Infinite."[90]

In theological perspective, the presence of God is explained in terms of the divine Spirit that not only brings about all creatures but also upholds them everywhere. This is deep immanence. At the same time, the Trinitarian doctrine helps explain the transcendence of God since God in his immanent life—as integrally related as that is to the economic life—can never be contained by creation.

God's knowledge (omniscience), widely attested in Scripture, is related to God's presence in creation in that all things are present to God at all times (rather than that God must be "present" everywhere to "know" the things, even though God's omnipresence is not thereby denied either). "When we speak of God's knowledge we mean that nothing in all his creation escapes him. All things are present to him and are kept by him in his presence,"[91] as is classically affirmed in Psalm 139.

Similarly related to God's eternality and infinity is the attribute of omnipotence (Job 42:2; Isa. 45:7; Jer. 32:17; Rom. 1:20; etc.). It manifests itself particularly in the context of creation, to the point that this God "gives life to the dead and calls into existence the things that do not exist" (Rom. 4:17). Omnipotence can of course only be attributed to God, who is both omnipresent and omniscient. "As all things are present to God in his eternity, and he is present to them, so he has power over all things. His omnipresence for its part is full of the dynamic of his Spirit."[92]

Whereas in traditional theology the attribute of omnipotence played a central role, in the beginning of the third millennium any reference to the divine power—or any kind of conception of power, for that matter—raises eyebrows and subjects the speaker to the charge of the abuse of power. It is also integrally related to the suspicion of religion's link with violence. Against those valid suspicions, the Cuban American Justo González rightly notes that

90. Pannenberg, *ST* 1:412.

91. Pannenberg, *ST* 1:379–80.

92. Pannenberg, *ST* 1:415.

the biblical God does not "rule the world with an iron fist, as Pharaoh ruled over Egypt or Pinochet ruled Chile. God does not destroy all opposition with a bolt from heaven, nor is opposition something God has created—like the military dictator who sets up an opposition party in order to claim that his rule is democratic." Does this view compromise the power of God? No, says González. "The Crucified is also the Risen One, who shall come again in glory to judge the quick and the dead. What it denies is an easy jump from creation to resurrection, with no cross."[93]

The God of Love

Infinite Love

The biblical statement "God is love" (1 John 4:8, 16) finds its theological basis in the Trinitarian doctrine: Father, Son, and Spirit love each other eternally, as manifest in the love between Jesus and the Father (John 3:35). Love is the basic essence of God. Hence, we can speak of the divine love as infinite. Utilizing a major cultural concept, deeply relational and communal, the Japanese thinker Nozomu Miyahira calls this inner-Trinitarian love "concord" or "betweenness" among the Father, Son, and Spirit, expressing itself in mutual knowing, entrusting, and glorifying.[94]

The sending of the Son to the world and its salvation manifested the Fatherly love in a profound way (John 3:16), and Jesus opened this shared loving relationship also to those who loved him (John 14:21; 15:9; 17:23), to the extent that the divine love has been poured out into the hearts of his followers through the Holy Spirit (Rom. 5:5). Nothing can separate them from God's love (Rom. 8:31–39).

An essential feature of the divine love is self-giving, gift. God gives himself to the creatures in numerous ways, which we could call the "attributes of the divine love": compassion, goodness, grace, righteousness, and patience.[95]

93. Justo L. González, *Mañana: Christian Theology from a Hispanic Perspective* (Nashville: Abingdon, 1990), 93.

94. Nozomu Miyahira, *Towards a Theology of the Concord of God: A Japanese Perspective on the Trinity* (Carlisle, UK: Paternoster, 2000), 182 and passim.

95. Cf. Pannenberg, *ST* 1:432–42.

The Compassion of the Suffering God

At the heart of contemporary criticism of tradition's way of speaking of God stand two related terms: "immutability" and "impassibility." In the biblical testimonies and in light of the dynamic relational Trinitarian account of God, God can hardly be conceived of as an "Unmoved Mover." Rather, God is a loving, compassionate, "cosuffering" Father.[96]

In the coming of Jesus, God's compassionate heart is opened to us in the most profound way. In light of the suffering Messiah on the cross, theology speaks of the *theopathy* (divine suffering) rather than the *apathy* of God. God's compassionate suffering for us is not passive suffering but rather "active passion," as it defends and advocates for the rights of the weak and marginalized.[97] As Moltmann famously puts it, suffering at the cross is not only salvific to us but also a deeply Trinitarian event. Jesus's cry of dereliction is not only the cry of the innocent victim,[98] but also a cry of the Father who deserts his Son.[99] Therefore, in his pointed style, Moltmann says: "A God who cannot suffer is poorer than any man. For a God who is incapable of suffering is a being who cannot be involved. . . . But the one who cannot suffer cannot love either. So he is also a loveless being."[100]

Korean theologians express the essence of divine love and compassion with the term *han*, "a feeling of acute pain and sorrow in one's guts and bowels."[101] Not only Jesus's death on the cross but also his whole life "bespeaks of the han of God for the children of the poor. . . . Jesus' suffering for three hours on the cross was one thing; his many years' suffering . . . was a profound source of Jesus' han."[102]

96. Elizabeth Johnson, *Quest for the Living God: Mapping Frontiers in the Theology of God* (New York: Continuum, 2007), chap. 3.

97. Moltmann, *Trinity and the Kingdom*, 23.

98. Moltmann, *The Crucified God*, 146–47.

99. Moltmann, *The Crucified God*, 243.

100. Moltmann, *The Crucified God*, 222.

101. Wonhee Anne Joh, *Heart of the Cross: A Postcolonial Christology* (Louisville: Westminster John Knox, 2006), xxi.

102. Andrew Sung Park, *The Wounded Heart of God: The Asian Concept of Han and the Christian Doctrine of Sin* (Nashville: Abingdon, 1993), 125.

Good and Gracious God

Goodness as one of the essential features of the love of the covenant-faithful God is a reason for constant praise and thankfulness in the First Testament:

> Praise the LORD!
> O give thanks to the LORD, for he is good;
> for his steadfast love endures for ever!
> (Ps. 106:1; so also 107:1; 118:1; 1 Chron. 16:34)

Pannenberg reminds us: "In the message of Jesus the God whom he proclaims as Father is characterized supremely, and elevated above all other beings, by his goodness."[103] As the fountain of goodness, the heavenly Father responds to his children not only when they ask him (Matt. 7:11) but also regardless of merit (20:15), whether they are bad or good (5:45).

Tradition maintains that God is good "necessarily"; in other words, God cannot but be good. According to Aquinas, "God is the highest good," unable to "bear any mingling with evil."[104] The goodness of God, of course, has come under questioning because of the existence of evil in the world that God has created good. That most complicated theological question will be discussed in the doctrine of providence.

In biblical teaching, God's goodness and "his saving and forgiving activity as an expression of his mercy (Matt. 18:33; cf. Luke 10:37)" go together. Behind the term "mercy" in its more inclusive sense is the Hebrew concept *hesed*, covenant-based loving-kindness, grace, and favor. "God's merciful turning to the needy, the suffering, and the helpless must thus be seen as a specific expression of his goodness."[105] As an expression of God's goodness that is liberally shown to people without merit (Exod. 33:19; Dan. 9:18; Rom. 9:15–16, 18) and regardless of the quality of their lives, God shows mercy even to those who rebel against him (Dan. 9:9).

God of Righteousness and Patience

In what ways could righteousness be linked with the love of God? Common sense would make a different connection: that righteousness is rather a subcat-

103. Pannenberg, *ST* 1:432.
104. Aquinas, *Summa contra Gentiles* 1.95.3–4.
105. Pannenberg, *ST* 1:432–33.

egory of, or at least linked with, the judgment of God. The integral relation of righteousness to the love of God is established in its biblical link with covenant righteousness. This is exactly what lies behind the Pauline statement: "This was to show God's righteousness, because in his divine forbearance he had passed over former sins; it was to prove at the present time that he himself is righteous and that he justifies him who has faith in Jesus" (Rom. 3:25–26).

Christian theology has been in danger of losing the biblical covenant-based notion of God's righteousness as it has too often conceived of it primarily in penal and judicial terms. Even though Luther's groundbreaking insight was that, rather than penal justice, God's righteousness is salvific righteousness that makes believers righteous, theological tradition still by and large continued to link righteousness with penalty. Only in contemporary theology, thanks to the new perspective on Paul, has the biblical covenant understanding of the righteousness of God been recovered.

At the same time, to fully rediscover the biblical notion of the righteousness of God as part of God's love, its "practical" implications in relation to liberation and justice must be affirmed in a more robust way. According to the black theologian James Cone, "It is important to note . . . that the righteousness of God is not an abstract quality in the being of God, as with Greek philosophy. It is rather God's active involvement in history, making right what human beings have made wrong."[106] The next section, "Divine Hospitality," will develop that theme.

To appreciate the divine patience, we must remind ourselves of the relative freedom and independence granted to creatures by the Creator. Rather than forcing the creatures to live in union with their Creator, he makes space for their independence—and then, notwithstanding their continued rebellion, pursues them for their salvation. Patience is an expression of love that both affirms the independence of the creatures and makes every effort to establish communion. Not for nothing, in several Old Testament passages that list Yahweh's attributes, is patience mentioned along with righteousness, mercy, and grace (Exod. 34:6; Pss. 86:15; 103:8; 145:8). Consider early theologian Tertullian's *Letter on Patience*: "He endures ungrateful peoples who worship the trifles fashioned by their skill and the works of their hands, who persecute His name and His children, and who, in their lewdness, their greed, their godlessness and depravity, grow worse from day to day; by His patience He hopes to draw them to Himself" (chap. 2). A fitting follow-up to the consideration of this and

106. Cone, *Black Theology of Liberation*, 2.

other divine attributes is to delve into their implications and benefits under the heading "Divine Hospitality."

Divine Hospitality

The God of Hospitality and an Unconditional Gift

To speak of God is to speak of giving, gift, and hospitality, in the words of the feminist Letty M. Russell, "reframing the idea of hospitality through identifying characteristics of God's gift of welcome."[107] As Luther puts it, the divinity of the triune God consists in that "God gives" himself in terms of the Word, justice, truth, wisdom, love, goodness, eternal life, and so forth.[108]

In an important study, *Hospitable God*, George Newlands and Allen Smith note: "Though we may not find the word 'hospitable' on every page of the doctrinal tradition about God, we suggest that hospitality provides a summative term which may express eloquently affirmations and concerns which lie at the heart of the Christian gospel."[109] Let us take this insight as a guide.

Hospitality as Inclusion in God-Talk

Oppression and violence can appear in many forms, not least in the way we speak of each other and of God. The traditional way of speaking of the divinity has been dominated and shaped by men. It has taken up issues and perspectives arising out of male experience. Importantly, women theologians have repeatedly reminded us that the way we name the divine shapes not only our theology but also our view of reality at large. So, how should we challenge, correct, and balance religious and theological language and make it inclusive?

We can discern three main tactics. Seeking to replace all traditional talk of God based on predominantly masculine metaphors with something else could be named the "substitution argument." It would randomly exchange

107. Letty M. Russell, *Just Hospitality: God's Welcome in the World of Difference*, ed. J. Shannon Clarkson and Kate M. Ott (Louisville: Westminster John Knox, 2009), 77; for "reframing," see George Lakoff, *Don't Think of the Elephant!* (White River Junction, VT: Chelsea Green, 2004), 15.

108. WA 3:454.4–10, among others.

109. George Newlands and Allen Smith, *Hospitable God: The Transformative Dream* (Surrey, UK: Ashgate, 2010), 22.

something else for "Father" and "Son." Let us name the other extreme, critical of the appeal to the metaphorical nature of God-talk, the "nonsubstitution argument": for those theologians, Trinitarian names are proper names and can never be replaced. In the middle there is the "mediating position," which, while accepting the metaphorical nature of God-language, is not ready to leave behind traditional naming but desires rather to qualify and correct it, as well as find alternative metaphors.

The substitution position considers Trinitarian language not only hopelessly sexist but also supportive of oppressive structures. To heal this problem it turns to the metaphorical nature of God-talk. If God is a mysterious unknown, as even classical theology maintains, it is very hard to point to a specific "name" for God, at least in the sense of a fixed "proper" name. A whole new repertoire of descriptions of God is then available, such as Source, Word, and Spirit; Creator, Liberator, and Comforter; Creator, Redeemer, and Sanctifier; and so forth. The point is that a gender-free way of addressing the triune God would avoid the problems related to traditional discourse.

The nonsubstitutionist position rejects any attempt to replace "Father," "Son," and "Spirit" with other terms. The American Lutheran theologian Robert W. Jenson argues that traditional Trinitarian names form the proper name of God.[110] Proper names are irreplaceable, so the argument goes.

The mediating position wishes to redeem the sexist and patriarchal nature of Christian Trinitarian discourse without replacing "Father," "Son," and "Spirit" with other names, but at the same time argues that other, complementary names should be utilized as well. This view reminds us that "Father" is a relational term rather than a statement of God's gender; Christian tradition has never assigned maleness to the divine.

The mediating position seems to be most promising. On the one hand, it rightly critiques the one-sided, at times oppressive, way of speaking of God only in terms of male images. On the other hand, this making more inclusive of traditional terminology does not mean leaving behind the traditional terminology. Feminist theologians help us seek equivalent images of God as male and female. "The mystery of God is properly understood as neither male nor female but transcends both in an unimaginable way."[111] Despite Christian tradition being male-driven, it has deep resources, including those from Scripture. Elizabeth Johnson suggests these three: Spirit-Sophia, Jesus-Sophia, and Mother-Sophia.[112]

110. Jenson, *The Triune Identity*, xii.

111. Johnson, *She Who Is*, 55.

112. Johnson, *She Who Is*, chaps. 7; 8; and 9.

In other words, we need both the deconstruction of patriarchal language and the reconstruction of complementary, more adequate models for speaking of God.

What about the nomenclature "Father"? The late Catholic feminist LaCugna argues on the basis of the relational note mentioned above that "father" is not a proper name as much as a specific and personal way to identify God. "The total identification of God with Jesus the Son, even unto death on a cross, makes it impossible to think of God as the distant, omnipotent monarch who rules the world just as any patriarch rules over his family and possessions."[113] At the same time, she recommends several analogies appropriate for that purpose such as Mother-Daughter, Father-Daughter, Mother-Son, Lover-Beloved, and Friend-Friend.[114]

God as Communion: A Theological Account of Equality and Justice

One of the main features of divine hospitality as outlined by Russell is "creation of community."[115] The rediscovery of communion theology, as discussed above, has helped contemporary theology envision God as the dynamic, living, engaging community of the three. Indeed, at the heart of Trinitarian communion theology is the insistence that the Trinity is a dynamic, lively symbol. It speaks of relationality, belonging, equalitarianism, and inclusion. As Elizabeth Johnson succinctly puts it, "The symbol of the triune God is the specific Christian shape of monotheism,"[116] which reflects mutual relationality, friendship, radical equality, and nonhierarchical patterns of life. It also embraces diversity.

For many liberationists and others, an integral communion theology is the needed asset to help overcome the rampant individualism of much of modern theology, particularly in the Global North. The Cuban-born Justo González claims that this is one area in which Euro-American theology needs to be mentored and corrected by the theologies of the Global South, in this case by Hispanic tradition, for which "the best theology is a communal enterprise," as opposed to "Western theology . . . [that] has long suffered from an exaggerated individualism."[117]

113. Catherine Mowry LaCugna, "The Baptismal Formula, Feminist Objections, and Trinitarian Theology," *Journal of Ecumenical Studies* 26, no. 2 (Spring 1989): 243.

114. LaCugna, "Baptismal Formula," 244–45.

115. Russell, *Just Hospitality*, 82–83.

116. See further, Johnson, *She Who Is*, 211.

117. González, *Mañana*, 29.

To hospitality based on loving communion belongs resistance to violence. How would that relate to the common assumption that faith in God and religion brings about violence, hatred, and at times bigotry?

Hospitality and Violence

On the Complexity of Linking Violence with Religion

The senior American scholar of public religion Martin Marty argues that "the collisions of faiths, or the collisions of peoples of faith, are among the most threatening conflicts around the world in the new millennium." This is because people of different faiths frequently divide themselves and others into competitive and suspicious groups of "belongers" and strangers.[118] Indeed, violence is part of religion's texture, each and every faith tradition's history[119]—hence, we have provocative book titles such as *Terror in the Mind of God.*[120] That said, violence is also part of the record of atheistic and other secular ideologies; think only of the 70 million purported victims of Communist regimes, among them a large number of believers of various faiths. This means that the alleged relationship between religion and violence must be nuanced, particularly when we face unnuanced claims such as those new atheist Sam Harris makes in *The End of Faith: Religion, Terror, and the Future of Reason.* He argues that since religions necessarily produce violence, the less religion, the better.[121]

It simply is unfounded to believe that with the demise of religion violence would disappear. Indeed, most ironically, some of the most vocal critics of religious violence seem to be content with exercising violence on their own terms. Take as an example Harris. Not only was he an ardent supporter of the Iraq invasion by US forces in 2003, he also finds justifiable the torturing of terrorists[122]—while at the same time condemning mercilessly the torture of

118. Martin E. Marty, *When Faiths Collide* (Malden, MA: Blackwell, 2005), 1–4, here 1.

119. Jack Nelson-Pallmeyer, *Is Religion Killing Us? Violence in the Bible and the Quran* (Harrisburg, PA: Trinity, 2003); Maurice Bloch, *Prey into Hunter: The Politics of Religious Experience* (Cambridge: Cambridge University Press, 1992).

120. Mark Juergensmeyer, *Terror in the Mind of God: The Global Rise of Religious Violence*, 3rd rev. ed. (Berkeley: University of California Press, 2003).

121. For a thoughtful and useful discussion of the blunt linking of violence with Islam by Dawkins, Harris, and Hitchens, see chap. 7 in Markham, *Against Atheism.*

122. Sam Harris, *The End of Faith: Religion, Terror, and the Future of Reason* (New York: Norton, 2004), 192–99.

witches in history![123] A fitting conclusion is that "religion does some harm and some good, but, most people, faced with the evidence, will probably agree that it does a great deal more good than harm."[124]

What about the Alleged Violent Acts of God in the Bible?

What about the scriptural texts that seem to endorse God's violence? Wouldn't those passages alone make any defense of the innocence of the God of the Bible meaningless? On this complex question, the following responses might be useful. First, in every society in the ancient world, violence was rampant and horrible. All living faiths' holy scriptures are ancient texts and share that feature; the Bible is no exception. Second, Christian theology of revelation builds on progressive revelation: God takes people at the level they are at and patiently, over the ages, shapes them. To that progressive revelation also belong nuancing, balancing, and finally forbidding the right to violence. Third, the full revelation in Jesus Christ tells us violence has been superseded and replaced with unconditional love and embrace. Fourth, in our kind of world, violence will not come to an end until the coming of the righteous rule of God.[125]

Finally, in Christian vision, only God has the prerogative to exercise violence. God is all-loving, all-wise, all-patient, all-righteous. We humans are sinful and egoistic. In our hands, violence is always corrupted, evil, and destructive. In the sacrificial death of his Son, God has put violence to an end.[126] Consequently, it is not "less" but "more" religion, civil religion, peaceful religion in society, that may contribute to peace.

Hospitality as Active Advocacy

In Christian vision, following Russell, we can speak of "hospitality as the practice of God's welcome, embodied in our actions as we reach across difference to participate with God in bringing justice and healing to our world

123. Harris, *The End of Faith*, 87–92.

124. Keith Ward, *Is Religion Dangerous?* (Grand Rapids: Eerdmans, 2006), 7.

125. Ward, *Is Religion Dangerous?*; Markham, *Against Atheism*, chap. 5.

126. Miroslav Volf, *Exclusion and Embrace: A Theological Exploration of Identity, Otherness, and Reconciliation* (Nashville: Abingdon, 1996).

in crisis."[127] Hospitable theology not only advocates inclusivity and equality, it also makes every effort to actively promote liberation and freedom. Hospitable advocacy is based on the nature of the God of the Bible as one committed to liberation.

This kind of God, as the senior African American theologian James H. Evans says, is impartial, "no respecter of persons" (see Acts 10:34).[128] At the same time, with this black theologian we can speak of God's "inclusive partisanship," preference for those in need. The need for God's help and intervention arises from particular contexts and situations, and hence, liberative theology is always particular, whether that of female theologians of Hispanic origin working in the context of emerging *mujerista* theologies,[129] theologians from the context of the First Nations of North America,[130] or others.

Rightly, Justo González reminds us that the way God is presented in the Bible implies a "political agenda"; God is not interested only in "spiritual salvation," but also in life here and now.[131] Another senior black theologian, James Cone, debunks the myth that God is "color-blind." Were that true, God would be blind to justice and injustice. Instead, the Yahweh of the Old Testament, the God of Jesus Christ, takes sides with the oppressed against the oppressors. Therefore, for Cone the movement for black liberation is "the very work of God, effecting God's will among men."[132]

Having developed a Christian theology of God, we will discuss its claims among other faiths in two moments. First, focusing on intra-Christian materials, we will present a theological analysis and critique of kinds of religious pluralisms. Thereafter, a careful investigation of the notion of the deity in other faiths as well as their Christian engagement is in order.

127. Russell, *Just Hospitality*, 2; for an extended discussion of "just hospitality," see chap. 5.

128. James H. Evans Jr., *We Have Been Believers: An African-American Systematic Theology* (Minneapolis: Fortress, 1992), 67–76.

129. Ada María Isasi-Díaz, *En la Lucha* [In the Struggle]: *A Hispanic Women's Liberation Theology* (Minneapolis: Fortress, 1993), and Ada María Isasi-Díaz, *Mujerista Theology: A Theology for the Twenty-First Century* (Maryknoll, NY: Orbis, 1996).

130. Robert Allan Warrior, "Canaanites, Cowboys and Indians: Deliverance, Conquest and Liberation Theology Today," *Christianity and Crisis* 49, no. 12 (September 11, 1989): 261–65.

131. González, *Mañana*, 83–85, here 84.

132. Cone, *Black Theology of Liberation*, 6.

Theo-Logical Pluralisms

For Orientation: Typologies of the Theology of Religions

Generally speaking, Christian theology of religions has established three broad categories of Christian approaches to religious diversity:

- "*Exclusivism*" teaches not only that salvation is to be found in the triune God of the Bible, in the salvific work of Christ alone, but also that the person to be saved must hear the gospel preached and give a personal response to it through the Word (and sacraments).
- "*Pluralism*" argues that no religion has the final and ultimate word about God but that all different faiths are more or less equal paths to truth and salvation. There is some kind of "rough parity" between religions.
- "*Inclusivism*" is the most complex response, according to which salvation can be found only in the triune God and the work of Christ (in agreement with exclusivism) but that many people in other faiths who never had a meaningful encounter with the Christian gospel may still be saved because of the universal salvific effects of Christ. This is the official position of the Roman Catholic Church, as stipulated at the Second Vatican Council (1962–1965).[133]

As useful heuristically and pedagogically this now-classic typology may be, it is also being subjected to various kinds of criticisms (the details of which we cannot discuss here), such as that it puts the question of access to salvation at the center and ignores some other themes. Furthermore, terms such as "exclusivism" are far from neutral and may be interpreted ideologically.

We focus in this section on the middle category, pluralism. For the sake of clarity, two groups of pluralisms will be identified. Let us call them first-generation Christian pluralisms and second-generation pluralisms, to be explained below.

A Pluralistic Proposal from the Asian Soil

The somewhat clumsy expression "first-generation pluralisms" refers to the pluralistic Christian theologies of religions that arose in the second half of

133. Veli-Matti Kärkkäinen, *An Introduction to the Theology of Religions: Biblical, Historical, and Contemporary Perspectives* (Downers Grove, IL: InterVarsity Press, 2003).

the last century, building on the modernist epistemology and ethos. These emerged both in the Global North (from the Protestant John Hick, to be discussed below, and Roman Catholic Paul F. Knitter, among others) and in Asia (from the Protestants Stanley Samartha and M. M. Thomas as well as the Roman Catholic Aloysius Pieris). They represent by and large the replacement of Christocentrism with theo-centrism; that is, rather than regarding Christ as the only way to God, a broader and less restrictive access to God from various points of view is advocated. Unlike later versions of pluralism to be discussed in the next subsection, these did not take as their main framework the Trinity, but rather, more generally, the notion of God.

In the context of India and many other Asian countries, with the growing sense of religious tolerance but increased and intensified political and social intolerance, theologians such as Stanley J. Samartha saw clearly the impasse between the traditional exclusivistic Christian confession and the plurality of religious claims. In keeping with the less categorical pan-Asian mindset—whose logic does not so predominantly operate with the Western either/or logic[134]—Samartha took as a clue the category of the divine as "Mystery": "This Mystery, the Truth of the Truth (*Satyasya Satyam*), is the transcendent Center that remains always beyond and greater than apprehensions of it even in the sum total of those apprehensions. It is beyond cognitive knowledge (*tarka*) but it is open to vision (*dristi*) and intuition (*anubhava*)."[135]

The emphasis on Mystery is meant to make room for the mystical and the aesthetic in theology. Samartha believes that Mystery lies beyond the dichotomy of theistic versus nontheistic. He opines that the nature of Mystery makes inadmissible any claim by one religious community to have exclusive or unique knowledge. He seeks to compromise all claims to exclusivity.[136]

Critics of Samartha and the like-minded note that to speak of God as mystery is nothing new in Christian tradition (just think of the long mystical tradition) but that it was not a means of denying the uniqueness of God but was rather a warning to the limited human mind not to claim too much knowledge of God. Likewise, the desire to "soften" the rational claims of the-

134. See Jung Young Lee, "The Yin-Yang Way of Thinking," in *Asian Christian Theology: Emerging Themes*, ed. Douglas J. Elwood (Philadelphia: Westminster, 1980), 87.

135. Stanley J. Samartha, "The Cross and the Rainbow: Christ in a Multireligious Culture," in *Asian Faces of Jesus*, ed. R. S. Sugirtharajah (Maryknoll, NY: Orbis, 1995), 111, emphasis removed.

136. Stanley J. Samartha, *Courage for Dialogue: Ecumenical Issues in Inter-Religious Relationships* (Geneva: WCC, 1981; Maryknoll, NY: Orbis, 1982), 153; see also Samartha's "Unbound Christ: Towards Christology in India Today," in Elwood, *Asian Christian Theology*, 146.

ology and make room for aesthetic and mystical elements is also familiar in Christian tradition. But it has not been used in tradition to compromise the salvific role of the triune God.

God as the "Ultimate Reality"

Having left behind much of the traditional Christian confession, the late John Hick, undoubtedly the most well-known spokesperson of pluralism, compares his turn to pluralistic theo-centrism with the astronomical model of Copernicus that replaced the Ptolemaic view. In that model (analogously to the sun at the center of all religions) stands God, around which all religions, including Christianity, as human interpretations of divine reality, revolve in the analogue of the planets.[137] Rather than divinely revealed truths about God, religions are but human conceptualizations, visions, and experiences. Hence, all religions—which are more or less exclusivistic by nature—are called to soften their own identity and acknowledge the commonality of the religious experience and belief. A related and very critical asset in Hick's turn to pluralism is his understanding of religious and theological language as metaphorical (or mythical): rather than propositional and factual, statements such as "Christ rose from the dead" are to be understood in an elusive and nonliteral manner.

While at first Hick was content to speak of *God*, later, to do justice to his understanding of the nature of religious language and to respond to the justified criticism that his pluralistic conception still favored theistic (and even *mono*theistic) religions, Hick began speaking about the "Ultimate Reality." This term is more flexible than the personal term "God."

In describing religions' access to and knowledge of the Ultimate Reality, Hick utilizes the Kantian distinction between *phaenoumena* (the way we see things) and *noumena* (the thing in itself, which is unknown to us), and maintains that there is a part of the Divine/Reality that is totally unknown to us and a part about which we know at least something. The Hindu concept of *nirguna* Brahma, in contrast to *saguna* Brahma, refers to something that cannot be fathomed at all by human means of knowledge.

What about Hick's view of the Trinity? While not engaging the topic in any detail, it suffices for him to state that there is no way to follow that ancient doctrinal statement. Reluctance to consider Jesus (or the Spirit) as divine alone

137. John Hick, *God and the Universe of Faiths: Essays in the Philosophy of Religion*, 2nd ed. (London: Macmillan, 1977).

would make that belief obsolete. His theology is best described as Unitarian or modalistic. Therein, Father, Son, and Spirit are not meant to be taken "as ontologically three but as three ways in which the one God is humanly thought and experienced."[138]

The critics have been quick to point to a number of problems in Hick's pluralism. First, it could be argued that his proposal is not a neutral "meta-theory" of religions but rather yet another form of a new religion, different from all existing ones. Second, rather than a beacon of tolerance and openness, Hick's demand for the followers of other religions to give up their deepest convictions and adopt a new foreign "religion" smacks of imperialism and of one's own sense of superiority. Third, most contemporary scholars of religions hardly support uncritically Hick's foundational assumption of the common essence of religions; a good case can be made for deep and critical differences. Fourth, the turn to a merely metaphorical notion of language has not been widely adopted. Among other problems, that linguistic turn thwarts the quest for the ultimate truth in any religion. Finally, the abstract and formal concept of the Ultimate Reality is seen by many critics as just that, namely, *abstract and formal.* Its content is empty—or else it begins to favor a certain type of belief system.

Differently from Hick and those like-minded, the second-generation pluralists embrace diversity and take Trinity as a Christian asset.

Trinitarian Ways of Constructing Pluralistic Theologies

Trinity and a Cosmotheandric Vision

The turn to the Trinity as the way to negotiate the relation of the God of the Bible to other faiths has caught the attention of several contemporary theologians.[139] The pioneer in the field is the late American-based half-Indian (from India) and half-Spanish Roman Catholic Raimundo Panikkar. In his small yet highly significant book *The Trinity and the Religious Experience of Man* (1973), Panikkar argued for the viability of a Trinitarian approach based on the groundbreaking idea that not only do all religions reflect a Trinitar-

138. John Hick, *The Metaphor of God Incarnate: Christology in a Pluralistic Age* (London: SCM, 1993), 149.

139. For a discussion and theological assessment, see Veli-Matti Kärkkäinen, *The Trinity and Religious Pluralism: The Doctrine of the Trinity in Christian Theology of Religions* (Aldershot, UK: Ashgate, 2004).

ian substructure, but there is a Trinitarian structure to reality. He coined a neologism, "cosmotheandrism," which simply means the coming together of cosmic, divine, and human. A leading insight for Panikkar is that the Trinity, while a distinctively Christian way of speaking of cosmotheandrism, is also the "junction where the authentic spiritual dimensions of all religions meet."[140]

Following the typical Asian principle of "nonduality" (*advaita*), he resists all dualisms and surmises that the divine and human (as well as cosmic) are not two but rather one in essence (without, however, conflating them, as in pantheism). Following his advaitic logic, Panikkar constructs the Christian doctrine of the Trinity in a most unique way. The Father is "Nothing." This is the apophatic way—but even more than that: the way to approach the Absolute is without name. There is no "Father" in himself; the "being of the Father" is "the Son." Indeed, in incarnation, *kenōsis*, the Father gives himself totally to the Son. What about the Spirit? The Spirit is God's immanence and also the unity between the Father and Son (who, as *advaita* implies, are not two but one).

Panikkar's pluralism is distinctively different from the first-generation pluralism of Hick. On the one hand, there is an openness to find a common core (in this case, through the notion of cosmotheandrism). On the other hand, the uniquely Christian understanding of God and reality is not only not ignored but made programmatic. Not the Hickian kind of dream of an elimination of differences, this is rather a vision of a "convergence," a coming closer together of great faith traditions. "The mystery of the Trinity is the ultimate foundation for pluralism."[141]

Panikkar's Trinitarian theology has also encountered critical questioning. Many wonder if his cosmotheandric Trinity deviates too radically from basic intuitions of the Christian doctrine of God. On the other hand, some pluralist colleagues doubt if other religions really want to accept the claim that cosmotheandrism is a pan-religious idea. Furthermore, problematic to many is Panikkar's advaitic approach to logic and truth.

140. Raimundo Panikkar, *The Trinity and the Religious Experience of Man* (Maryknoll, NY: Orbis; London: Darton, Longman & Todd, 1973), 42.

141. Raimundo Panikkar, "The Jordan, the Tiber, and the Ganges: Three Kairological Moments of Christic Self-Consciousness," in *The Myth of Christian Uniqueness: Toward a Pluralistic Theology of Religions*, ed. John Hick and Paul F. Knitter (Maryknoll, NY: Orbis, 1987), 110.

Trinity and Diverse Religious Ends

The launching pad for American Baptist S. Mark Heim's distinctively Trinitarian pluralism is his 1995 work titled—surprisingly—*Salvations* (plural). Its main argument is that, rather than one common religious end for people of all faiths, there is a diversity of end goals willed by God. The sequel, *The Depth of the Riches: A Trinitarian Theology of Religious Ends* (2001), represents a full-blown vision of the Trinity as the guarantor of more than one goal for the followers of religions, including Christians, to whom communion with God is the highest aim. Diversity in godhead translates into diversity of religious ends for religions.[142]

The obvious critical challenge to Heim is whether this robust emphasis on diversity in the triune God may be in danger of frustrating the equally important conviction of the oneness of God as a result of which classical Christian theology envisions a unity of all people in the eschatological consummation. Be that as it may, it is clear that no Christian theologian ever has jumped from the threeness (diversity) in God to diversity of religious ends; so, this turn is totally unknown in Christian tradition. Furthermore, similarly to Panikkar's Trinitarian pluralism, many wonder if Heim's desire to understand other religions' distinctive religious ends through the framework of Christian faith truly represents pluralism or is rather another form of one religion putting its own interpretation above others.

The Triune God among the Deities of Religions

Any comparative task regarding concepts of the divine among religions is immense and complex. One has to proceed carefully in order not to deny the distinctive features of each tradition. Buddhism in particular poses a significant challenge, as its original Theravada form intentionally seeks to shift the focus in religion away from the deities to the primacy of each person's ethical pursuit of enlightenment.

We will begin with Islam and then proceed to two Asiatic faiths, Hinduism and Buddhism. No separate focused investigation of Jewish tradition is included here, although some of its key ideas will be brought to the dialogue with Islam.

142. S. Mark Heim, *The Depth of the Riches: A Trinitarian Theology of Religious Ends* (Grand Rapids: Eerdmans, 2001), 180.

Allah and the Father of Jesus Christ

Although all Abrahamic faiths are monotheistic, Islam seeks to be most radically so. Affirmed everywhere in Islamic theology, the short sura 112 of the Qur'an puts it succinctly, taking notice also of the fallacy of the Christian confession of the Trinity:

> Say: "He is God, One.
> God, the Self-Sufficient, Besought of all.
> He neither begot, nor was begotten.
> Nor is there anyone equal to Him."

Hence, the basic Muslim confession of *shahada*: "There is no god but God, and Muhammad is the apostle of God." So robust is the belief in the unity of God that for some Muslim philosophers and mystics the principle of unity also applies to reality itself.

An essential aspect of the divine unity is Allah's distinction from all else. The common statement "God is great" (*Allah akbar*) means not only that but also that "God is greater" than anything else. Hence, the biggest sin is *shirk*, associating anything with Allah. Importantly, *shirk* means literally "ingratitude." In other words, "there is only one divine Creator who should be thanked and praised; no other being is to be given the thanks due only to God."[143] In that light it is understandable that, unlike modern forms of Christianity, the Muslim faith encompasses all of life, whether secular or sacred. The five pillars of Islam (profession of faith, prayers, almsgiving, fasting, and pilgrimage) shape all of life.

Muslim theology of God includes the built-in dynamic between the absolute transcendence of God because of his incomparability and uniqueness, on the one hand, and on the other hand, his presence and rulership in the world, which is a call for total obedience. God is sovereign; all reality is totally dependent on Allah.

One of the most well-known ways in Islamic theology to imagine God is the listing of the Ninety-Nine Beautiful Names of God; while not to be found in the Qur'an as such, various kinds of listings of the attributes of Allah can be found in scripture.[144]

143. John B. Carman, *Majesty and Meekness: A Comparative Study of Contrast and Harmony in the Concept of God* (Grand Rapids: Eerdmans, 1994), 323.

144. Samuel M. Zwemer, *The Moslem Doctrine of God: An Essay on the Character and*

As is true for God in the Bible, the Qur'an occasionally uses anthropomorphic metaphors of Allah, such as the "face of God" (Q 2:115; 92:20) or the "hand(s) of God" (48:10; 5:64), although in general Islam is very cautious about picturing Allah. While there is hardly a classified typology of attributes in Islamic traditions, representative is the listing of thirteen attributes mentioned in sura 59:22–24: "He is God, than Whom there is no other god, Knower of the unseen and the visible. He is the Compassionate, the Merciful . . . the King, the Holy, the Peace, the Securer, the Guardian, the Mighty, the Compeller, the Exalted . . . the Creator, the Maker, the Shaper."

As in Christian tradition, early on Islam moved toward "classical theism." Reflecting the features of Christian scholasticism, the rise of Islam *kalam* theology was the culmination of this development. Not unlike what occurred in Christian history, there was a continuing debate between the traditionalists who wished to retain the verbatim biblical account and the Mu'tazilites, a strictly rationalist *kalam* movement drawn to systematic explanations. "A Short Creed by Al-Ashari" reads like a Christian confession, yet it also obviously rebuts Christianity's Trinitarian claims: "We believe . . . that God is One God, Single, One, Eternal; beside Him no God exists; He has taken to Himself no wife (*sahiba*), nor child (*walad*)."[145]

Similarly to Christian scholastics, the Asharites, the mainstream Sunni movement (followers of al-Ashari *kalam* theology), engaged in highly sophisticated disputes about, for example, how to understand the attributes of God in relation to God's essence, and so also entered debates with the Mu'tazilites. Whereas the Mu'tazilites were willing to attach the attributes not to the essence of God but rather to his actions, the Asharites—as well as their most famous scholar, al-Ghazali—linked some attributes to the essence and others to his actions.

Early Muslim theology's relation to pagan philosophy was not much different from that of Christian tradition. There were a great appreciation of and liberal borrowing from the greatest masters of antiquity, including Plato and Aristotle—although never without criticism.[146] It is also noteworthy that

---

Attributes of Allah according to the Koran and Orthodox Tradition (New York: American Tract Society, 1905), chap. 3.

145. In Duncan B. Macdonald, *Development of Muslim Theology, Jurisprudence, and Constitutional Theory* (New York: Charles Scribner, 1903), 294. Available at www.sacred-texts.com.

146. The classic work here is that of al-Ghazali, *The Incoherence of the Philosophers* (Provo, UT: Brigham Young University Press, 1997).

Muslim theologians, particularly the *kalam* scholars, engaged "proofs" for the existence of God, borrowing from Aristotle and others.

Do Muslims and Christians Believe in the Same God?

The term *allah* predates the time of Muhammad. It did not originate in the context of moon worship in Arabia (even though the crescent became Islam's symbol and moon worship was known in that area). The term derives from Aramaic and Syriac words for God. In that light, it is fully understandable that even among Christians in Arabic-speaking areas, the term *Allah* is the designation for God.

So, do Muslims and Christians worship the same God or not? This question is not new to either tradition. As early as the seventh Christian century, John of Damascus, the most celebrated theologian in the Christian East with firsthand knowledge of the Muslim faith, delved deeply into it in the last chapter of his *De haeresibus* (*On Heresies*). Even though he considers Muslims "idol worshipers," John seems to assume that both traditions worship one and the same God. Or consider the Catholic cardinal Nicholas of Cusa of the fifteenth century, who, following the ransacking of the holy city of Constantinople in 1453, in his *De pace fidei* (*On the Harmonious Peace of Religions*) sought a way to achieve a "harmony among religions" and "perpetual peace."[147] At the same time, he also exercised critical judgment on Islam's errors. Even Luther, with his well-known and deep suspicions toward Muslims (and Jews), assumed that "all who are outside this Christian people, whether heathen, Turks, Jews, or false Christians and hypocrites . . . believe in and worship only the one, true God."[148]

The key issue of course has to do with the unity and Trinity. In keeping with the stress on the unity, the Qur'anic teaching categorically rejects any notion of threeness of God, including Jesus's deity (4:171; 5:72–76). A foundational reason for the strict rebuttal of the Christian doctrine of the Trinity is the absolute exaltedness of Allah and the sheer absurdity of the idea of God having a child by a woman. Importantly, often behind the Muslim charge of

147. Nicholas of Cusa, *De Pace Fidei*, ed. and trans. Jasper Hopkins, 2nd ed. (Minneapolis: Arthur J. Banning Press, 1994), #68; available at http://jasper-hopkins.info/DePace12-2000.pdf.

148. Martin Luther, *The Large Catechism*, trans. F. Bente and W. H. T. Dau (St. Louis: Concordia, 1921), art. III, 76.

shirk is an Arian[149] heretical notion according to which Christ is "associated" as closely as possible with God, but is not God. But that view was categorically rejected by Christian creeds as well.

In response to the Islamic charge of *shirk*, Christian theology (in the words of Pannenberg) argues that "the doctrine of the Trinity is in fact concrete monotheism" and in no way compromises authentic monotheism.[150] Some of the earliest Christian theologians already faced the charge of polytheism long before the rise of Islam. Just recall the fourth-century Gregory of Nyssa's *On "Not Three Gods."*

What unites Muslim and Christian theologies is that both traditions speak of God in universal rather than "tribal" terms. Similarly to the Bible, the Qur'anic message "is a message for all people: all people should become Muslims, for God is the sovereign God of all people."[151] Part of the universalizing tendency is the important promise in sura 42:15: "God is our Lord and your Lord. Our deeds concern us and your deeds concern you. There is no argument between us and you. God will bring us together, and to Him is the [final] destination." This same sura also mentions that "had God willed, He would have made them one community; but He admits whomever He will into His mercy" (v. 8), and that "whatever you may differ in, the verdict therein belongs to God" (v. 10). Hence, the reason Muslim theology can unequivocally affirm the identity of the God of Islam and the God of Christianity has to do with the principle of continuity—in terms of fulfillment—between the divine revelations given first to the Jews, then to Christians, and finally, in the completed form, to Islam (2:136; 6:83–89; 29:46).[152] While Christian tradition understands the principle of universality differently, materially it shares the same viewpoint: the God of the Bible, Yahweh, the Father of Jesus Christ, is the God of all nations and the whole of creation. Therefore, both faiths also are deeply missionary by nature.

An important asset to Christian theology for reflecting on the relation of Allah to the God of the Bible is its relation to Judaism. Hardly any Christians would deny that Yahweh and the Father of Jesus Christ are one and the same God. Yet the Jews no less adamantly oppose the Trinitarian confession of faith.

149. Arianism represents an early Christian heresy according to which Jesus Christ was "almost" equal to the Father but not totally; for details, see chapter on Christology.

150. Pannenberg, *ST* 1:335–36.

151. See Hendrik Vroom, *No Other Gods: Christian Belief in Dialogue with Buddhism, Hinduism, and Islam* (Grand Rapids: Eerdmans, 1996), 104.

152. For a current Muslim argument, see Umar F. Abd-Allah, "Do Christians and Muslims Worship the Same God?" *Christian Century* 121, no. 17 (August 24, 2004).

This simply means that Christian tradition is able to confess belief in and worship one God even when significant differences exist in the understanding of the nature of that God. To confess one God does not require an identical understanding of the nature of God.

It is important to clarify the many Islamic misunderstandings about what the Christian Trinitarian confession means. What if it is true that "what the Qur'an denies about God as the Holy Trinity has been denied by every great teacher of the church in the past and ought to be denied by every orthodox Christian today"?[153] These include the typical Muslim misconceptions of the inclusion of Mary with Father and Son, Arianist interpretations, and the blunt charge of tritheism.

Having affirmed that Muslims and Christians believe in the same God, the Dutch Christian philosopher of religion Hendrik Vroom "would like to add that Christians, on the basis of the gospel, are better *able* to know God than Muslims are."[154] This is not an expression of a puffed-up spirit of superiority but rather a confident call to Muslims from a Christian perspective to consider rich values in the Christian Trinitarian conception of faith in one God. Muslim theologians undoubtedly would issue the same challenge to Christians.

Brahman and the Trinitarian God

Comparison in Perspective: Orientational Remarks

A number of well-known challenges and unnuanced assumptions concerning Hindu and Christian views of the Divine complicate any serious comparative theological work, such as the following claims: whereas Christianity has a personal God, Hinduism has an impersonal god; whereas Christianity is monotheistic, Hinduism is polytheistic; whereas in Christianity the Divine can take the form of humanity, in Hinduism the deity remains transcendently distant; and so forth.

Beyond the above-mentioned popular stereotypes, scholarly study must also be mindful of the radical difference regarding the role of doctrine. Whereas for Christianity (and Islam) the doctrinal understanding of God is binding and normative, Hinduism lacks that. As long as one is not going

153. Miroslav Volf, *Allah: A Christian Response* (New York: HarperCollins, 2011), 14.
154. Vroom, *No Other Gods*, 113.

against the authority of the Vedas, the oldest scriptures, one is allowed a lot of leeway. Indeed, while in the final analysis the majority of Hindus would conceive of Brahman (often in the "person" of another god, whether Shiva or Vishnu or any of their associates) as the Ultimate Reality and thus affirm "monotheism," some Hindus can also be more or less nontheistic (although hardly is there any atheistic movement after modern Western atheism) or agnostic about the existence of gods. Furthermore, while by far the majority of Hindu adherents embrace a personal deity (most often in the form of Isvara, typically locally determined), theologically speaking, beyond the personal notion, there is still the "true" impersonal deity. Deep differences in worldview and epistemology also often complicate the task of comparison: Asiatic cultures are by and large cyclical, whereas Abrahamic are linear, and so forth.

Many Gods or One God?

The oldest Vedas, particularly Rig Veda, list a number of deities or *devas* (this term denoting "divine being" rather than god in the current sense of the word). Among them, Indra, the cosmic power, while a fairly late arrival in Vedic religion, plays the central role. Other important figures include Agni, the deity of fire, associated particularly with sacrifices; the lovely Savitri, "Mother Earth"; Aditi; and a host of others.[155]

A critical move toward the embrace of one major notion of the deity amidst the bewildering diversity of *devas* began in classical Hinduism, as represented by the last part of the Vedas, the Upanishads. The well-known answer in Brihadaranyaka Upanishad (3.9.1) in response to the question of how many gods there are altogether, drawn from a Vedic text, is 330,000, which then boils down to one, and this one god is Brahman. The many gods are "only the various powers of them." Ultimately, there is one ultimate divine, Brahman, represented by a number of individual deities.[156]

Here we come to the most important *theo*-logical affirmation in theistic Hinduism: *atman* is Brahman.[157] Whereas Brahman is the ultimate notion of the divine, *atman* is the ultimate reality about us. While everything else in the world, including everything in us, changes, *atman* does not. Though it is

155. Klaus Klostermaier, *A Survey of Hinduism*, 3rd ed. (Albany: State University of New York Press, 2010), chap. 8.

156. Arvind Sharma, *Classical Hindu Thought: An Introduction* (Oxford: Oxford University Press, 2000), 1.

157. Brihadaranyaka Upanishad 4.4.5 and 25; *SBE* 15:175, 181, respectively.

routinely translated as "soul," in no way is that individually driven Western concept a good way to communicate the meaning of the Sanskrit word.

Most typically, three deities are seen as the major manifestation of Brahman: Brahma, the "creator" god; Vishnu, the "preserver" god; and Shiva, the "destroyer," or better, "consummator," god. The distant Brahman comes to be known and worshiped in any of these deities or their associates known as *isa* or *isvara*, the "Lord" or Bhagavan, the Exalted One. Typically the "Lord," be it Vishnu or Shiva—since by and large the worship of Brahma almost completely vanished a long time ago—becomes more or less an exclusive title in popular piety, although, theologically, either one and both of them manifest Brahman. Hence, we have the proliferation of Hindu denominations, among which the most important are Shaivism (followers of Shiva) and Vaishnavism (followers of Vishnu), with an ever-increasing number of subsects. Either related to the main deities or separate from them, local and tribal deities, both male and female, and cults of worship dedicated to them fill India.

While it is of course true that the Hindu conception of Brahman as the ultimate reality leans toward an impersonal notion unlike the personal God of Semitic faiths, it is also true that Hinduism is quite familiar with personal conceptions of deities. Not only does the personal deity come to the fore in the hugely popular and widespread folk piety based on the great epics of *Mahabharata* and *Ramayana*, as well as many Puranas, but even in the later stages of the Upanishads personal notions begin to emerge in various forms.

What is distinctive about Hindu deities is the prominent place of female deities; indeed, "Hinduism possesses a full-blown feminine theology."[158] Usually Shiva and Vishnu are accompanied by their wives, Parvati and Sri (Lakshmi). The prominent female deity is known as Sakti, "power," or Devi, the "Divine Mother." Sometimes Sakti is described as exercising the same powers as Vishnu and Shiva.

Classical Debates about the God-World Relationship

As mentioned above, the relation of Brahman (the Ultimate) to *atman* (the "[World-]Soul") is the most widely debated problem in Vedantic Hindu theology/philosophy (one of the six orthodox schools of Hinduism). In Christian parlance, it is about the relationship between God and world. Among the many Vedanta schools, three are by far the most well known outside India. To

158. Sharma, *Classical Hindu Thought*, 68; see chap. 5 for a useful discussion.

(over)simplify a complex issue, for our purposes here, only two interpretive traditions can be engaged: ninth-century Sankara's *advaita* (nondualism), a radical monism, and eleventh-century Ramanuja's "qualified" nondualism. Whereas the former allows no real distinction between God and the world, Ramanuja's negotiates it delicately without endorsing dualism. (They are both different from the thirteenth-century qualified dualism of Madhva.) These differences come to the fore in the hermeneutics of authoritative commentaries on *Vedanta-Sutras*, a key Upanishadic writing.

Sankara's nondualistic, absolutely monistic *advaita* philosophy's starting point is a strong and uncompromising rejection of any notion of distinction, let alone separation, between Brahman and *atman*. The major fallacy behind separation is what Sankara calls *avidya*, "nescience," which is incapable of distinguishing between relative and absolute being. A familiar illustration is taking a rope for a snake. They only appear similar! As long as one lives under this misguided assumption, one must continue in the cycle of samsara, leading to rebirth and reaping the law of karma, the law of cause and effect. The correct insight into the total and absolute unity of God and world will bring about the ultimate release, leading to "nirvanic" extinction. Sankara is deeply intellectual in orientation, and it appears that knowledge rather than, say, devotion or ethics is the key to the true knowledge of God in this interpretive tradition.

What then is Brahman according to Sankara? The Brahman "is all-knowing and endowed with all powers, whose essential nature is eternal purity, intelligence, and freedom."[159] Clearly, there are again parallels with Abrahamic traditions with their conceptions of God as the omniscient and omnipotent Absolute Being. At the same time, Sankara's God, somewhat differently from that of Ramanuja, to be discussed next, leans strongly toward the impersonal and pantheistic notion, yet in a more complex way. Sankara makes an important distinction between two aspects of the Divine, namely, *nirguna* and *saguna* Brahman. Whereas the former is without any qualities and thus beyond human grasping, the latter has qualities and is thus known. In light of that distinction, in Sankara's impersonal monism, the worship of the *isvara* type of personal deity can be tolerated but of course is known by the "wise" to be a false impression!

It is here that, a few centuries later, Ramanuja comes to challenge his predecessor with this "qualified" monism (known as *visitadvaita*) in which "*brahman*, who is identical with *īśvara* . . . is none other than Visnu. Creation

159. Sankara, *Vedanta-Sutras* 1.1; *SBE* 34, 14.

is the body of *brahman* but not without qualification."[160] His way of speaking of the world as the body of God is paralleled in some contemporary panentheistic Christian conceptions. An important related idea is what Christian and Western philosophical tradition calls "infinity," as "God contains all finite realities, both good and evil, but also transcends them. God is with and without form. . . . [God] is separate from all beings yet united with all beings."[161] Thereby Ramanuja categorically rejects Sankara's *nirguna-saguna* distinction as, in his deeply theistic interpretation of Vedanta tradition, he conceives of *isvara* with an infinite number of supreme and auspicious qualities. That kind of Divine can be worshiped and praised, unlike Sankara's Divine. This affirmation of the supreme Brahman as personal Lord makes it possible to embrace and encourage—much more than just to tolerate as a false belief after Sankara—*bhakti*, devotional tradition, the mainline form of theistic Hinduism among the masses. Ramanuja's thought also considers salvation as a collaboration between divine grace, human effort, and loving surrender to God. All in all, it is easy to see that in many ways Ramanuja's qualified monism reflects theological and devotional aspects closer to the Abrahamic and particularly Christian tradition than those of Sankara.

As mentioned, the negotiation between the unity and Trinity is not a burning issue in Christian-Hindu engagement of God. That said, it is not completely irrelevant either.

Trinitarian God and the One Divine

The obvious starting point for considering any Trinitarian parallels in Hinduism is the above-mentioned "trinity" of classical deities—Brahma, Vishnu, and Siva—named Trimurti. While never widely popular, a strand of Hindu piety developed cultic rites to honor the threeness. Recall that for most all Hindus, different gods (these three or any others) are ultimately the expression of the One—an observation that in principle should be highly compatible with the Christian confession of one God in three persons.

Before getting too excited about this alleged parallel, let us note that a key reason why the threefold conception never played an important role in either the popular or (particularly) the scholarly Hindu world is the virtual disappearance of the cult of Brahma—leaving only two major gods, Vishnu

160. Klostermaier, *Survey of Hinduism*, 377.
161. Carman, *Majesty and Meekness*, 146.

and Siva. Furthermore, even when the three Hindu deities are not conceived of as three gods but rather as manifestations of one, Hindus still routinely consider one of them supreme. Finally, in light of the fact that the deities are related with distinctive primary tasks (like Brahma with creation), it is more appropriate to regard the three as manifestations rather than "persons" of the one god.

Hence, it is understandable that on the Hindu side, the effort to find parallels has been lacking, even if at times it has been quite pronounced for Christian theologians. Ram Moham Roy, the founder of the strictly monotheistic neo-Hindu reform movement Brahma Samaj, states categorically with regard to the Christian Trinity: "After I have long relinquished every idea of a plurality of Gods, or of the persons of the Godhead, taught under different systems of modern Hindooism, I cannot conscientiously and consistently embrace one of a similar nature, though greatly refined by the religious reformations of modern times."[162]

For some, a more promising bridge may be found in the ancient concept of *saccidananda*, of three words meaning "being," "intelligence," and "bliss." Consider this statement by Brahmabandhab Upadhyaya, a famous nineteenth-century Hindu convert to Catholicism: "I adore the *Sat* (Being), *Cit* (Intelligence) and *Ananda* (Bliss), . . . the Father, Begetter, the Highest Lord, unbegotten, the rootless principle of the tree of existence . . . the increate, infinite Logos or Word, supremely great, the Image of the Father . . . [and] the one who proceeds from the union of *Sat* and *Cit*, the blessed Spirit (breath), intense bliss."[163]

Other Hindu converts and reformers have similarly shown more interest in this parallel than in the three deities discussed above. To put these and many other explorations in perspective, the Jesuit Hindu expert F. X. Clooney summarizes in a way worth repeating and affirming: "That the record is mixed should not surprise us. We know that the rich, deep Christian tradition of trinitarian theology, so nuanced and difficult, did not come together easily or suddenly in the earliest Church; rather, it took centuries to put together right insights into the three persons of God. . . . [Similarly] it was very hard indeed to explain in India the fine points of trinitarian thought, and as a re-

162. As cited in Francis X. Clooney, "Trinity and Hinduism," in *Cambridge Companion to the Trinity*, ed. Peter C. Phan (Cambridge: Cambridge University Press, 2011), 316 (I have been unable to secure the original source).

163. Clooney, "Trinity and Hinduism," 317 (I have been unable to secure the original source).

sult many did not see a great difference between Christian ideas of God and Hindu ideas."[164]

Any God(s) in Buddhism?

On the Conditions and Challenges of the Mutual Dialogue

Except for the exchange between Nestorian Christians and Buddhists from the sixth to the eighth century, unlike with Judaism and Islam, Christian and Buddhist traditions did not have much mutual engagement until the first occasional contacts in the nineteenth century. By and large, Christian assessment of Buddhism was plagued by both ignorance and negative judgments leading to typical caricatures such as that Buddhism is atheistic (or idolatrous, as it was mistakenly taken as the adoration of images of the dead Gautama). Christians also routinely considered the Buddhist worldview nihilistic because of the doctrine of *sunyata* (emptiness) and life-denying because of the principle of *dukkha* (suffering), and so forth.

Mutual dialogue faces significant challenges. To begin with, it is routinely asked whether Buddhism is a religion in the same sense as other living faiths. The reason is of course that Buddhism separated itself from the parent religion, Hinduism, because of the latter's overly focused attention on deities and spirits that led to the undermining of one's own effort toward "salvation." Particularly the original Theravada Buddhism still seeks to be faithful to that vision, notwithstanding its acknowledgment of the existence of deities. Even in the currently mainstream movement, Mahayana, notwithstanding strong theistic orientations particularly in folk spirituality, deities and gods are not looked upon as saviors. On the other hand, for all Buddhist denominations, some kind of "ultimate reality" is to be had, even if not god in the traditional sense. As mentioned, Buddha is no savior.

The Buddhist Quest for the Ultimate Reality

Not only is Buddha not a savior, he is also not the "ultimate reality." Furthermore, in contrast to the parent religion, Hinduism, Buddhism strictly rejects the idea of Brahman and *atman* as the ultimate answer. That said, the search

164. Clooney, "Trinity and Hinduism," 320–21.

for the ultimate reality seems to be easier in the mainstream Mahayana tradition. All scholars agree that its foundational idea of *sunyata* is the most likely proposal—but not the only one. Before looking at it, let us briefly consider other suggestions.

The Awakening of Faith,[165] by the second-century Indian dramatist and sage Asvhagosa, suggests one candidate for the ultimate reality. It names it simply "suchness" (and alternatively, "soul" or "mind," depending on the English translation), which "is the soul of all sentient beings," and it "constitutes all things in the world, phenomenal and supra-phenomenal."[166] While impersonal, suchness is active and dynamic, though changeless. Noteworthy is that another key Buddhist concept, foundational to Mahayana, namely, Dharmakaya, the doctrine and wisdom taught by the enlightened Buddha, is at times used as an alternative term for "suchness." These ways of speaking of the ultimate reality seem not too far from a formal concept of deity in philosophical theology (but a far cry from a personal deity).

Yet another classic pan-Buddhist candidate for the ultimate reality could be nirvana (*nibbana*),[167] the ultimate goal of all pursuit for enlightenment. The famous and well-known "Udana Exclamation" (8.1), an ancient authoritative "small saying" among various Buddhist denominations, states it clearly: "There is that dimension where there is neither earth, nor water, nor fire, nor wind; neither dimension of the infinitude of space, nor dimension of the infinitude of consciousness, nor dimension of nothingness, nor dimension of neither perception nor non-perception; neither this world, nor the next world, nor sun, nor moon. And there, I say, there is neither coming, nor going, nor staying; neither passing away nor arising."[168] While this "definition"—of something indefinable!—strikes non-Buddhist sensibilities as negative, it is not, for it points to the final release, hence "salvation" in Judeo-Christian terms.

And now to the concept of *sunyata*. According to the leading academic interpreter of Mahayana Buddhism in the West, Masao Abe of Japan, "The ultimate reality . . . is neither Being nor God, but Sunyata."[169] Notoriously

165. Asvaghosa, *Açvaghosha's Discourse on the Awakening of Faith in the Mahâyâna*, trans. Teitaro Suzuki (1900); available at http://sacred-texts.com/bud/taf/index.htm.

166. Asvaghosa, *Awakening of Faith* II ["General Statement"], 53–54.

167. The former rendering is from Sanskrit and the latter from Pali (the language of the Theravada scriptures).

168. "Nibbana Sutta: Total Unbinding (1)" (*Udana* 8.1), trans. T. Bhikkhu, *Access to Insight (BCBS Edition)*, September 3, 2012, http://www.accesstoinsight.org/tipitaka/kn/ud/ud.8.01.than.html.

169. Masao Abe, "Kenotic God and Dynamic Sunyata," in *Divine Emptiness and His-*

difficult to translate and even harder to understand, *sunyata* literally means "(absolute) nothingness." However, it is not an "empty nothingness." It is only "empty" in terms of being "entirely unobjectifiable, unconceptualizable, and unattainable by reason or will."[170] According to the classic formulation of the "The Heart Sutra," "Form is Emptiness, Emptiness is form. Emptiness does not differ from form, and form does not differ from Emptiness . . . in Emptyness [*sic*] there is no form, no feeling, no recognition, no volitions, no consciousness; no eye, no ear, no nose, no tongue, no body, no mind . . . no ignorance and no extinction of ignorance . . . no aging and death and no extinction of aging and death; likewise there is no Suffering, Origin, Cessation or Path, no wisdom-knowledge, no attainment and non-attainment."[171] Furthermore, importantly, "Sunyata should not be conceived of somewhere *outside* one's self-existence, nor somewhere *inside* one's self-existence."[172] So, what, if anything, can be said of the potential convergences in relation to Christian tradition's doctrine of God?

God and the "Ultimate Reality" in Perspective

Not all Christian interlocutors, after having engaged carefully with the Buddhist concept of *sunyata*, believe that *sunyata* in any real sense could be taken as the Ultimate Reality. Reasons are many, such as that it seems not to be transcendent in the sense that a theistic notion of god or Ultimate Reality is usually envisioned. Related to this, it seems to Christian intuitions that if there is a notion of the divine in Buddhism, it has to be equated with the reality itself, that is, it leads to a sort of pantheism. That assumption seems to be confirmed by Buddhist experts themselves: "God *is* each and everything," and in this "completely kenotic God, personality and impersonality are paradoxically identical."[173] Noteworthy in this regard is the comment by a leading Christian comparative theologian, H. Küng, who concludes that while nirvana, emptiness, and Dharmakaya have "brought about a twilight of the gods or idols" as they have replaced the Hindu gods and Brahman as

---

torical Fullness: A Buddhist-Jewish-Christian Conversation with Masao Abe, ed. Christopher Ives (Valley Forge, PA: Trinity, 1995), 50.

170. Abe, "Kenotic God," 50.

171. Heart Sutra (no translator given, n.p.; available at http://www.sacred-texts.com/bud/tib/hrt.htm.

172. Abe, "Kenotic God," 51.

173. Abe, "Kenotic God," 40, 41.

the ultimate explanation, "they have not put any other gods—not even the Buddha—in their place."[174]

After a careful dialogue with the Buddhist teachings about the ultimate reality, I myself came to this conclusion and recommendation: "First, unlike any *monotheistic* tradition, Buddhism is happy with a plurality of answers to 'one question' without suppressing the diversity; second, unlike any *theistic* tradition, Buddhism, even in its major Mahayana forms, makes every effort to resist the tendency to rely on gods (even if their existence and role in the world thereby need not be denied after modern Western anti-theistic ideology); and third, that therefore, Buddhism and Christianity represent deeply and radically different paths to liberation/salvation. Wouldn't that kind of tentative conclusion serve an authentic, hospitable dialogue better than a forced, I fear, one-sided (!) '*con*-sensus'?"[175]

174. Hans Küng, "God's Self-Renunciation and Buddhist Self-Emptiness: A Christian Response to Masao Abe," in Ives, *Divine Emptiness and Historical Fullness*, 221.

175. Kärkkäinen, *Trinity and Revelation*, 415.

3 | Creation

New Vision for the Christian Theology of Creation

A contemporary theology of creation has the twofold task of critically retrieving the best of theological tradition and tapping into new opportunities and resources in the beginning of the new millennium. Let us highlight briefly the most important ones.

First, the rich biblical and historical tradition of creation theology should be carefully reexamined. Unlike the holistic and embodied biblical (particularly Old Testament) perspectives, theological tradition often holds dualistic explanations that contrast nature and the human, soul and spirit, secular and sacred, and so forth.

Second, Christian theology of creation is a statement not only of creation but, first and foremost, of the Creator. All good theology must be a Trinitarian theology. A Trinitarian doctrine leads to a relational, communal view of creation.

Third, not only because of the impending natural catastrophes due to human exploitation but also for the sake of honoring God's creative act as divine handiwork, creation theology must be an "ecological theology."[1] Such a theology is directed toward the flourishing of creation.

Fourth, the unprecedented influence of natural sciences should be acknowledged in a new way. "The natural sciences today offer to Christian

1. A key theme in Jürgen Moltmann, *God in Creation: A New Theology of Creation and the Spirit of God*, trans. Margaret Kohl (Minneapolis: Fortress, 1993).

theology . . . precisely the role that Platonism offered our patristic, and Aristotelianism our medieval forebears."[2] Rightly the British physicist-priest John Polkinghorne calls the religion-science dialogue a new form of "contextual" theology.[3]

Fifth, the task of constructing a new theology of creation should be conceived of as an ecumenical task—the term "ecumenical" understood in its widest sense, that is, referring to the whole inhabited world, in this case the global Christian family.[4] Along with that, there is a dire need for the theological academy to collaborate across genders, races, and classes, as well as across geographical boundaries.

Sixth, the fact that "all cultures have their myths or theories of creation"[5] both necessitates a most careful consideration of theological implications and, at the same time, offers a platform for mutual conversation. The presence of "creation" myths among other living faiths is an invitation—and an obligation—for Christian theology to engage them in mutual dialogue.

Our first task is to clarify the relationship between religions and sciences with a view toward theological work. Thereafter, a distinctively *Christian* vision of nature, that is, nature as *creation*, is outlined. Building on that conversation, similarly to other doctrines, we apply resources regarding the Trinity to the task. This discussion also helps clarify crucial issues such as the possibility and condition of creation independently from the Creator, the meaning of creation "out of nothing," and the value of creation.

Before continuing the construction of a Trinitarian theology of creation in detailed dialogue with contemporary scientific cosmologies, we take a careful look at the visions of origins and cosmologies in four other living faiths.

Thereafter, two long sections delve into many complicated questions about how to best find consonance with and difference between the most recent knowledge in the natural sciences concerning the origins and evolution of the universe and life on our planet and theological and religious convictions. This includes both the topic of "beginnings," the origins of the cosmos, and its

2. Alister E. McGrath, *A Scientific Theology*, vol. 1, *Nature* (Grand Rapids: Eerdmans, 2001), 7.

3. See John Polkinghorne, *Theology in the Context of Science* (New Haven: Yale University Press, 2009), chap. 1.

4. Peter Lønning, ed., *Creation—an Ecumenical Challenge: Reflections Issuing from a Study by the Institute for Ecumenical Research, Strasbourg, France* (Macon, GA: Mercer University Press, 1989).

5. Colin E. Gunton, *The Triune Creator: A Historical and Systematic Study*, Edinburgh Studies in Constructive Theology (Grand Rapids: Eerdmans, 1998), 1.

continuing sustenance—that is, providence—by the triune God, the Creator. The final main section in this chapter takes up a most urgent and complex issue: suffering, evil, and decay in nature.

Two standard topics are omitted in this context: a full-scale consideration of theodicy, that is, how to defend the goodness of God vis-à-vis rampant evil and suffering in the world (to be discussed in the last chapter of the book, on eschatology). The second theme has to do with (spiritual) "powers," whether good (angels) or evil (demons, evil angels, Satan), to be considered below in chapter 7 on pneumatology.

Theology of Creation in the Matrix of Sciences and Religions

The Significance of Science for Religions and Theology

The simple reason why contemporary theology should be deeply interested in science is that science is a universal phenomenon and, as such, of great interest to people of all religions.[6] There is also the theological reason for dialogue: when "Christians confess God as the Creator of the world, it is inevitably the same world that is the object of scientific descriptions." As a result, theologians have the task of relating their statements to those of scientists.[7]

We begin by relating sciences to Abrahamic faiths and, thereafter, to Asiatic faiths. The bulk of the chapter is then devoted to considering Christian theology's ways of relating to science. The last part of the chapter engages forms of naturalism, including scientism, from the perspective of the religions.

Science and Abrahamic Faiths

The Embrace of Science in Jewish Tradition

No other ethnicity can boast so many leading scientists throughout history and in the contemporary world as the Jewish—from Galileo to Einstein. Of all Nobel Prizes in physics, Jews have gathered almost a third![8] And yet, the

6. Patrick McNamara and Wesley Wildman, eds., *Science and the World's Religions*, 3 vols. (Santa Barbara, CA: Praeger, 2012).

7. Wolfhart Pannenberg, "Contributions from Systematic Theology," in *OHRS*, 359.

8. Noah J. Efron, *Judaism and Science: A Historical Introduction* (Westport, CT: Greenwood, 2007), 1–11.

Jews entered the scientific field relatively late, at the beginning of the twentieth century.

Until modernity, rabbis were sages who were looked upon also as intellectuals in science. In the contemporary world, that role has changed radically, even if there are still conservative rabbis who lean toward a literalist interpretation of Scripture and hence the American Christian Right type of creationism. This separation between the domains of religion and science, however, is a new development. For the defining medieval philosophers such as Moses Maimonides, nothing could have been stranger.

The Old Testament, unlike the Qur'an, does not discuss cosmology as a separate topic; the little it offers is partially borrowed from the environment. Nor is there much attention to nature itself (unlike the Qur'an), although some of the sages, particularly Solomon, are depicted as masters of the knowledge of nature (1 Kings 3:10–14). Rather than being mystical and speculative, for the most part the Old Testament's depiction of nature is that of an orderly cosmos brought about and controlled by Yahweh. This "disenchantment process" helped pave the way for the rise of scientific explorations.

Unlike the Muslims (and some Hindus), the Jews have never entertained the idea of a "Jewish science." Therefore, the sorts of science-religion clashes experienced among Christians (and much later in Muslim contexts) are by and large unknown (except for the more recent Orthodox rabbis' reservations mentioned above). As in mainline Christian tradition, evolutionary theory is currently embraced.

The Islamic Struggle with Modern Science

After the glorious rise of Islamic science, its "golden age" lasted until the eleventh century (CE) and featured such luminaries as Ibn Rushd (Averroes) and Ibn Sina (Avicenna), finally giving way to the "age of decline."[9] That said, however, if one judges the history of Islamic science, current Western scientific and philosophical academia should remember its debt to the Islamic influence on the rise of sciences.

Modern science came to Islamic lands only in the nineteenth century, and currently the Islamic world at large is in the process of catching up; leading Muslim scholars lament the status of scientific education at large

9. Mohamad Abdalla, "Ibn Khaldūn on the Fate of Islamic Science after the 11th Century," in *ISHCP* 3:29–30.

in most Muslim lands. None of the main producers of modern science is a Muslim.

Unlike in the West, in Islamic contexts the link between religion and science is tight, so much so that, according to the Algerian astrophysicist Nidhal Guessoum, even current textbooks are hardly much else than "a branch of Qur'anic exegesis."[10] The Iranian physics professor Mehdi Golshani's book *The Holy Quran and the Sciences of Nature* is a representative example. That said, unlike the Christian tradition (and more recently, Jewish tradition), religion-science dialogue is still a marginal phenomenon among Muslims.

Not unlike scholars and scientists in other religious traditions, Islamic scholars and scientists offer a fairly obvious typology of responses to modern science:

- Rejection of science because of its alleged opposition to revelation.
- An uncritical embrace of the technocratic practical results of Western science in pursuit of power- and competence-equality with (as they are perceived) more developed Western nations.
- An effort to build a distinctively "Islamic science" based on the authority of the Holy Qur'an and Hadith.
- An attempt to negotiate between the legitimacy and necessity of contemporary scientific principles and methods while at the same time critiquing the metaphysical, ethical, and religious implications of the scientific paradigm.[11]

Ironically, the advocates of the first category are rapidly becoming a marginal phenomenon in Islamic lands, not because Muslims by and large would endorse any part of the seeming atheistic ethos advanced by modern scientific culture, but simply because of the uncritical embrace of the instrumental use of science in pursuit of technological, particularly military, competence (category 2). Because of the alleged neutrality and value-free nature of modern science, its practical fruits are being enjoyed unabashedly without much or any concern for the serious philosophical-ethical-religious challenges to core Islamic values. This has raised concerns in the minds of some leading Islamic theologians.[12]

10. Nidhal Guessoum, *Islam's Quantum Question: Reconciling Muslim Tradition and Modern Science* (London: I. B. Tauris, 2011), 180.

11. Adapted from Mehdi Golshani, "Does Science Offer Evidence of a Transcendent Reality and Purpose?" in *ISHCP* 2:96–97.

12. Seyyed Hossein Nasr, "Islam and Science," in *OHRS*, 72.

Deeply critical of and disappointed with the antagonism of the secular scientific paradigm, some Muslim intellectuals have been envisioning the possibility and necessity of an Islamic science.[13] The main complaints against modern science and its "blind" use by Muslims include the lack of critical study of science produced in the West; the assumption of science's value-free, neutral nature; the failure to acknowledge the disastrous effects of modern science on nature; and so forth. What would an Islamic science look like? According to Nasr, it would include "stop[ping] the worship-like attitude towards modern science and technology," returning to an in-depth study of authoritative Islamic sources, studying carefully pure sciences (including at the best institutions in the West) instead of focusing merely on applied fields, and rediscovering and reviving those fields of sciences in which Islam first achieved great competency, namely, medicine, agriculture, architecture, and astronomy.[14]

As an alternative to Islamic science, some leading scientists argue that there should not be in principle a contradiction between whatever science qua science discovers and Islamic faith. They strongly reject the whole idea of Islamic science and argue for the universal nature of the scientific pursuit and therefore its compatibility with Islam.[15]

As in the Christian tradition, a vibrant Muslim creationist movement exercises wide influence among laypeople in various global locations.[16] Another similar kind of science-appealing development has to do with the search for "miraculous scientific facts in the Qur'an,"[17] a highly apologetic enterprise.

Modern Science and Asiatic Faith Traditions

Science in Hindu Outlook

In contrast to the post-Enlightenment Western ideals of total objectivity and objectification of nature, traditionally Hindu vision has integrated scientific pur-

13. Mehdi Golshani, "Islam and the Sciences of Nature: Some Fundamental Questions," in *ISHCP* 1:77–78.

14. Seyyed Hossein Nasr, *The Need for a Sacred Science*, SUNY Series in Religious Studies (Albany: State University of New York Press, 1993).

15. Guessoum, *Islam's Quantum Question*, 129–35.

16. See, e.g., Salman Hameed, "Bracing for Islamic Creationism," *Science* 322, no. 5908 (December 12, 2008), http://science.sciencemag.org/content/322/5908/1637.full.

17. Chap. 5 in Guessoum, *Islam's Quantum Question*.

suit with the religious and ritualistic domain. Religion and science are deeply intertwined. Consider this: "India is the one and only country in the world that simultaneously launches satellites to explore the space *and* teaches astrology as a Vedic science in its colleges and universities." In fact, since 2001, astrology has been taught as a scientific subject in Indian colleges and universities.[18]

Beginning in the mid-nineteenth century, a vast and wide intellectual renaissance started in India that resulted in its current great scientific pursuit; that was also the time a European educational system was introduced (related to the British-led colonialistic project). Understandably, assessments of and attitudes toward modern science have varied. Bhikhu Parekh has famously classified Indian responses to Western (secularizing) influences under three categories: the "critical traditionalists," who believe Indian foundations can be redeemed even if some important aspects of the West are incorporated; the "modernists," who wish to adapt to the European lifestyle; and the "critical modernists," who envision a creative synthesis.[19]

Not unlike some Muslims, a group of Hindu scientists have attempted to develop a credible "Hindu science" (also called "Vedic science") paradigm.[20] Not surprisingly, this project has been subjected under critique both by the scientific community and by some Hindu thinkers.

Buddhist Appraisals of Science

Modern Buddhism's relation to Western science is not totally different from that of Hinduism. Its claims about science emerged in a polemical manner as Buddhists worked hard to convince Westerners, including Christians, that their understanding is not superstition but rather a rational, sound account of reality.[21]

The Buddhologist José Ignacio Cabezón suggests a typology similar to ones devised by Christian theologians. The first model, "Conflict/Ambivalence," represents only a small minority of Buddhists. Generally speaking, a negative

18. Meera Nanda, "Vedic Science and Hindu Nationalism: Arguments against a Premature Synthesis of Religion and Science," in *SRPW*, 30.

19. Bhikhu Parekh, *Colonialism, Tradition, and Reform: An Analysis of Gandhi's Political Discourse* (New Delhi and London: Sage, 1989).

20. See Susmita Chatterjee, "Acharya Jagadish Chandra Bose: Looking beyond the Idiom," in *Science, Spirituality, and the Modernization of India*, ed. Makarand Paranjape, Anthem South Asian Studies (London: Anthem, 2008), chap. 8.

21. Donald S. Lopez, *Buddhism and Science: A Guide for the Perplexed* (Chicago: University of Chicago Press, 2008).

attitude toward science among Buddhists in the contemporary world may have more to do with Western science's general hostility toward religion. By and large, however, rather than conflictual, the Buddhist attitude can be called "Compatibility/Identity." It can manifest itself either in terms of similarity between Buddhism and science or in the idea that "Buddhism is science" and therefore it and science are more or less identical.[22] As in all other faith traditions, there is a growing body of contemporary (mostly popular) literature written by Buddhists around the world concerning the astonishing compatibility between, say, quantum mechanics and compassion or emptiness and relativity theory.[23]

The final category is "Complementarity," which as a middle position seeks to negotiate both similarities (unlike the first option) and differences (unlike the second option). Whereas both Buddhism and science focus on "empirical" investigation of reality, Buddhism complements the reductionist materialism with the inclusion of the mental/spiritual/"inner." Whereas sciences rely only on rational, conceptual, and analytic methods, Buddhism also utilizes intuition, meditation, and "inner" resources. And so forth.[24]

Science and Religion in Mutual Critical Dialogue: A Christian Theological Assessment

The following typology helps us structure Christian approaches to science:[25]

Theology in Continuity with Science
Science in Continuity with Theology
Theology and Science as Separate Realms
Mutual Interaction of Theology and Science

For the first category, classical liberalism is a grand example. With its categorical separation between "nature" (the domain of facts) and "history" (the domain of human values), it made the former the realm of natural sciences and

22. Henry S. Olcott, *The Buddhist Catechism*, 2nd ed. (London and Benares, India: Theosophical Publishing Society, 1903), 95–109. Available at www.sacredtexts.com.

23. Lopez, *Buddhism and Science*, 2–4.

24. José Ignacio Cabezón, "Buddhism and Science: On the Nature of the Dialogue," in *Buddhism and Science: Breaking New Ground*, ed. B. Alan Wallace (New York: Columbia University Press, 2003), 41–56.

25. Anne M. Clifford, "Creation," in *Systematic Theology: Roman Catholic Perspectives*, ed. Francis Schüssler Fiorenza and John P. Galvin (Minneapolis: Fortress, 1991), 1:225–40.

the latter that of "human sciences." Hence, no conflict arises. The critical point about this category is the timidity of its theology to engage natural sciences *critically.* Instead, there is accommodation.

The second category is rooted in the pre-Enlightenment worldview in which theology was seen as the queen of sciences. As long as the Scripture principle stayed intact, the authority of Scripture surpassed that of the sciences and philosophy. On the contemporary scene, the fundamentalist movement known as creationism, with its advocacy of an antievolutionary scientific paradigm as an alternative to mainline natural sciences, represents this category. It is based on literal interpretation of the biblical message, including matters of science, and a search for archaeological/paleontological "evidence" in support of a young earth theory.[26] The obvious problem with this approach is that it lacks scientific credibility and hence even at its best remains a purely religious affair.

The third category is most notoriously represented by Barth and neo-orthodoxy with its fideistic (based on faith alone) elevation of divine revelation as the judge of all matters of knowledge, the rejection of natural theology, and the acceptance of classical liberalism's categorical separation between nature and history. It simply rejects dialogue with sciences, as Barth did in his massive discussion on creation in *Church Dogmatics.*[27] Its main liability, similar to that of the second category, is the failure of theology to have a public voice and also to make its own contribution to the sciences.

The orientation recommended here is "Mutual Interaction of Theology and Science."[28] At Vatican II, the Roman Catholic Church stated that "earthly matters and the concerns of faith derive from the same God" and hence in principle cannot violate each other.[29] Among Protestant theologians, Wolfhart Pannenberg is a leading example. He argues that while theology must be mindful of the differences between its method and that of the natural sciences, it should also remember to make every effort to critically integrate scientific results.[30] Many other leading Protestant theologians agree, including the Reformed theologian Jürgen Moltmann and late T. F. Torrance (as much as he was Barthian in theology). Theology should not merely serve as science's religious interpreter; rather, it should also challenge and contribute to science's quest.

26. Henry M. Morris, *Beginning of the World* (Denver: Accent Books, 1977).

27. Preface to Barth, *CD* III/1.

28. Adapted from Robert J. Russell, *Cosmology: From Alpha to Omega; The Creative Mutual Interaction of Theology and Science* (Minneapolis: Fortress, 2008).

29. *Gaudium et Spes: Pastoral Constitution on the Church in the Modern World* (Vatican II), #36. Available at www.vatican.va.

30. Pannenberg, *ST* 2:70–71.

Alongside sciences, theology's main engagement partner with regard to understanding God's creation is naturalism, a science-related ideological stance.

Naturalism, Sciences, and Theology of Creation

Naturalism refers to "the philosophy that everything that exists is a part of nature and that there is no reality beyond or outside of nature."[31] While some naturalisms are not necessarily religion defeating, all naturalisms seek to explain the world without reference to God, the almighty Creator.[32]

Critics rightly note that naturalism's basic claim cannot be verified within its own logic of reasoning because it is a worldview rather than a science issue. Ultimate questions of the origins of the cosmos are beyond scientific inquiry. To the perennial question of why there is something rather than nothing and who produced it, naturalism cannot give any answer unless it goes beyond its own limits. In contrast to naturalism, Christian theological engagement of science takes up these metaphysical challenges presupposed in any meaningful scientific work and argues boldly for the possibility and necessity of a religious interpretation of nature as creation.

What about other faith traditions with regard to naturalism? By and large, religions categorically oppose scientific naturalism if it means making the world totally void of divine or "supernatural" ("spiritual") Being/Ultimate Reality. Particularly vehemently is it rejected in Islamic tradition.[33] The same can be said of great Asiatic faiths, even Theravada Buddhism.

With the advent of naturalism, the traditional conception of nature and the cosmos as God's handiwork, creation, was replaced by a secular account. This calls for a theological response.

Nature as Creation: A Theological Interpretation

Beginning in the seventeenth century, a radical reinterpretation of nature happened due to the Enlightenment and scientific revolution. Rather than divine

31. Stewart Goetz and Charles Taliaferro, *Naturalism* (Grand Rapids: Eerdmans, 2008), 6.

32. Veli-Matti Kärkkäinen, *Creation and Humanity*, A Constructive Christian Theology for the Pluralistic World, vol. 3 (Grand Rapids: Eerdmans, 2016); chap. 2 constructs a fourfold typology of naturalisms.

33. Hamid Parsania, "Unseen and Visible," in *ISHCP* 1:158.

handiwork, nature was seen as mechanical, measurable, and secular, with no need for metaphysical explanations. The autonomy of nature pushed to the margins the idea of God as the first cause.

As the late Colin Gunton argues, the result was the "tearing apart of belief and knowledge."[34] Ironically, it led to the abuse of nature for human resources, as nature was stripped of any purpose.

Enter postmodern thinkers, particularly of the Continental tradition, and the view of nature in modernity is challenged by massive forces of deconstruction. Whereas modern reason made nature a mechanistic, objectified, and measurable "machine," postmodern deconstruction takes nature as merely a humanly constructed phenomenon.

From a theological point of view, both the modern and the postmodern options are problematic because the theology of creation is based on the assumption that nature is God's creation and human rationality ultimately derives from the Creator's infinite wisdom. Due to the orderliness and rationality of nature, it can be studied and investigated in a proper manner.

Indeed, against common assumptions, even natural sciences are not free from the burden of interpretation: neither scientific observations nor their interpretations are interest-free enterprises. This opens up the possibility and legitimacy of a religious, theological reading of nature as creation.

Christian theology imagines nature as God's creation, a testimony to the Creator's love, goodness, and wisdom. It neither mystifies nor secularizes it. Moreover, a distinctively Christian theology of creation is Trinitarian.

A Trinitarian Theology of Creation

Creation as the united work of Father, Son, and Spirit was beautifully captured by Basil the Great: "And in the creation bethink thee first, I pray thee, of the original cause of all things that are made, the Father; of the creative cause, the Son; of the perfecting cause, the Spirit."[35]

34. Colin E. Gunton, *Enlightenment and Alienation* (Grand Rapids: Eerdmans; Basingstoke: Marshall, Morgan & Scott, 1985), 5.

35. Basil, *On the Holy Spirit* 16.38; for a delightful Trinitarian account of creation in Luther, see *LW* 1:9.

The Love and Goodness of the Father

Why creation? The simple answer is divine love. Theologically put: with the same love that the Father loves the Son in the Spirit, the world is "loved" into being. Luther put it well: "The three persons and one God . . . has given himself to us all wholly and completely, with all that he is and has. The Father gives himself to us, with heaven and earth and all the creatures. . . . The Son himself subsequently gave himself and bestowed all his works, sufferings, wisdom, and righteousness. . . . [And] the Holy Spirit comes and gives himself to us also, wholly and completely."[36] Another way of saying this is to speak of God's goodness, God's essential nature as taught everywhere in Jesus's message about the nature of God as Father (Matt. 5:45; 6:26; 7:11).

Herein is the possibility of creation distinct from God. The Son's self-distinction from the Father "is the origin of all that differs from the Father, and therefore of the creatures' independence vis-à-vis the Father."[37] As the Reformed theologian Gunton puts it, "to create in the Son means to create by the mediation of the one who is the way of God out into that which is not himself."[38] This saves us from pantheism, the equation of God with the world, and from disengagement, the alleged autonomy of creation from the Creator. The Son is the mediator of creation.

The Mediating Role of Christ and Cosmic Christology

Building on the Old Testament teaching on the creative power of the *dabar* (Hebrew term for "word") of Yahweh (Gen. 1:2; Isa. 55:11), the New Testament speaks of *logos* (the Greek term for "word" and "wisdom") as God's agent of creation (John 1:3). With the teaching of Proverbs 8 in mind, Origen maintains that "all the creative power of the coming creation was included in this very existence of Wisdom"[39] that eternally derives from the Father.[40]

36. *LW* 37:366; WA 26:505–6.

37. Pannenberg, *ST* 2:22.

38. Gunton, *The Triune Creator*, 143.

39. Origen, *First Principles* 1.2.2 (in *ANF*, vol. 4); see also Augustine, *The Literal Meaning of Genesis* 2.6, translated and annotated by John Hammond Taylor, SJ, 2 vols., Ancient Christian Writers 41–42, edited by Johannes Quasten, Walter J. Burghardt, and Thomas Comerford Lawler (New York: Paulist, 1982), 54.

40. Origen, *First Principles* 1.2.3.

Significantly, in the Old Testament, this agent, Wisdom, is female, Lady Wisdom (Prov. 1:20–33; Sirach 24; Wisdom of Solomon 1:4–6; 7:22–23; 8:1). The postcolonial Chinese American Kwok Pui-lan notes how the vision of Jesus as Sophia-God may help people conceive of creation as "an organic model" in search of the healing of creation and how well it connects with some wisdom traditions in Asia and beyond.[41]

The New Testament sets the agency of Christ in creation into a cosmic framework (John 1:1–14; Col. 1:15–19; Heb. 1:2–4), a theme found also in patristic theology. In the contemporary worldview with an infinitely large universe, the cosmic creation Christology of early Christianity needs to be rediscovered.

While put in cosmic framework, the New Testament also connects the Word/Christ with incarnation, thus forging an important link between creation and redemption. Indeed, "the same divine rationality or wisdom which the natural sciences discern within the created order is to be identified within the *logos* incarnate, Jesus Christ."[42]

Whereas the self-distinction of the Son from the Father is the condition for the existence and relative independence from God of the created reality, the work of the divine Spirit creates the possibility for its unity with the Creator as well as its coming into life and flourishing.

The Life-Giving Spirit and Cosmic Pneumatology

The Spirit is the uniting link between the Creator and the universe as well as between God and human beings. Corresponding to the cosmic vision of Christology, the biblical witnesses present to us the cosmic Spirit. The *ruach Elohim*, the Spirit of God, "was moving over the face of the waters" (Gen. 1:2). The same Spirit of God that participated in creation over the chaotic primal waters (Gen. 1:2) is the principle of human life (Gen. 2:7). This very same divine energy also sustains all life in the cosmos (Ps. 104:29–30).[43]

Christian tradition, particularly the Protestant tradition, however, has been slow to capture the significance of a cosmic pneumatology. The Spirit's work came to be associated with salvation and the church understood narrowly. Only slowly were the cosmic and creational aspects of the work of

41. Kwok Pui-lan, *Postcolonial Imagination and Feminist Theology* (Louisville: Westminster John Knox, 2005), 164–65.

42. McGrath, *A Scientific Theology*, 1:188.

43. See Sergius Bulgakov, *The Comforter*, trans. Boris Jakim (Grand Rapids: Eerdmans, 2004), 220.

the Holy Spirit rediscovered (as discussed in chap. 7 on pneumatology) in twentieth-century theology. As Pannenberg puts it, "God's Spirit is not only active in human redemption. . . . The Spirit is at work already in creation as God's breath, the origin of all movement and all life."[44]

Moltmann rightly notes that a turn to a robust creational pneumatology pushes theology toward panentheism, as it attempts to "discover God *in* all the beings he has created and to find his life-giving Spirit *in* the community of creation that they share."[45] This has affinity with various indigenous spiritualities from which we can learn much.[46]

Having briefly described the distinctive yet interrelated roles of Father, Son, and Spirit in the work of creation, we now focus on how to establish the independent existence of creation alongside the Creator.

A Sovereign and Loving Creator

The Sovereign Creator

The main theme of the first biblical account of creation—a liturgical text, tightly structured and ordered, as illustrated in its hymnic form—ran counter to the Babylonian creation myths, particularly *Enuma Elish*, which conceive "creation" as a battle between Marduk and Tiamat.[47] Whereas in Babylon the heaven and the earth emerge out of the fatal fight between the gods, in Israel creation is the function of the sovereignty of God resulting in an orderly and good world. By the power of the divine word (and spirit) everything comes into being. God's power also subdues astral entities such as sun and moon or the gigantic living beings of the deep sea. This is nothing less than their demythologization.

The particular term to highlight the Creator's sovereignty is *bara* (Gen. 1:1), "to create." Several other Old Testament texts affirm the sovereignty of God (Pss. 104:14–30; 139:13). The point of the *ex nihilo* ("from nothing") formula is to envision God's work as "absolute" beginning, rather than as fashioning out of existing materials.

44. Pannenberg, *ST* 3:1.

45. Moltmann, *God in Creation*, xi.

46. Diamuid O'Murchu, *In the Beginning Was the Spirit: Science, Religion, and Indigenous Spirituality* (Maryknoll, NY: Orbis, 2012).

47. *Enuma Elish*, in *The Babylonian Genesis: The Story of Creation*, by Alexander Heidel (Chicago: University of Chicago Press, 1942), 1–48.

Interestingly enough, American process theism rejects *ex nihilo* vehemently, viewing "creation" in terms of a reordering of chaos.[48] Its view of God as merely a persuader,[49] working with preexisting materials, can hardly be reconciled with biblical and theological tradition.[50]

Creation as a Free Gift

Is the coming into existence of the cosmos a *necessary* act of God? By and large tradition agreed on the freedom of God in creation although it debated about how to best secure that. Barth vigorously defended the divine freedom and linked it with the equally important idea of God's love as the impetus for creation.[51] Barth followed here the mainstream Christian tradition against those (like Moltmann after him) who in some way or another left the impression that creation is somehow a "necessary" divine act.

Pannenberg rightly notes that God's deity does not require the world; rather the world is "the result and expression of a free act of divine willing and doing."[52] It is only after the free decision to bring about the universe that the Creator, so to speak, is bound to take care of it.

To deepen the discussion from the previous chapter, let us further reflect on the God-world relationship, a key debate in current theology.

The God-World Relationship in a Trinitarian Framework

The Value of Creation

The doctrine of the Trinity allows theology to envision the infinitely loving and resourceful God as the Creator of the world, both transcending it and being deeply embedded in it. This is an authentic personal interaction affirming

48. John B. Cobb Jr. and David Ray Griffin, *Process Theology: An Introductory Exposition* (Philadelphia: Westminster, 1976), 63–79.

49. Lewis S. Ford, *The Lure of God: A Biblical Background for Process Theism* (Philadelphia: Fortress, 1978).

50. Alfred North Whitehead's often-cited statement is this: "It is as true to say that God creates the World, as that the World creates God." *Process and Reality: An Essay in Cosmology*, ed. David R. Griffin and Donald W. Sherburn, corrected ed. (New York: Free Press, 1978 [1929]), 348.

51. Barth, *CD* III/1, 95.

52. Pannenberg, *ST* 2:1.

both intimate connection and real distinction. At the same time, it honors the God-given, limited freedom of creation as distinct but not separate from the Creator.[53]

The depiction of the work of creation as the joint work of the triune God best supports two essential theological values: participation and materiality/physicality. These were concerns of early patristic theology in its vehement attack on Gnosticism, a philosophy centered on dualism between the good spiritual and the evil physical aspects of the world. Because they are created and thus contingent on the Creator, creatures are meant to participate in God. At the same time, we can speak, correctly understood, of "a genuine theological materialism" that affirms both the goodness of all creation and its rootedness beyond itself, in God, the Creator (differently from atheistic materialism and naturalism).[54]

With the focus on physicality as an integral aspect of God's creation, early theology successfully attacked the pagan idea of the eternity of matter. Thereby early theologians helped reaffirm the relative value and goodness of all created reality.

As the work of the triune God, creation has inherent value. It is not instrumental, as in secular modernity. The atheist Ludwig Feuerbach completely missed it: "Nature, the world, has no value, no interest for Christians. The Christian thinks only of himself and the salvation of his soul."[55]

Trinitarian Panentheism and the Search for Intimacy and Distinction

On top of theological problems, the failure to negotiate properly the God-world relationship has sociopolitical implications. Female theologians and postcolonialists have correctly "challenged the image of the separate immaterial God for its collusion with the subordination of women and the devastation of creation."[56]

With good intentions and intuitions, classical theology too often ended up conceiving of God as so transcendent and aloof from the world that the

53. Gunton, *The Triune Creator*, 66.

54. James K. A. Smith, *Introducing Radical Orthodoxy: Mapping a Post-secular Theology* (Grand Rapids: Baker Academic, 2004), 76.

55. Ludwig Feuerbach, *The Essence of Christianity*, trans. George Eliot (New York: Harper & Brothers, 1957), 287, emphasis removed.

56. Mayra Rivera, *The Touch of Transcendence: A Postcolonial Theology of God* (Louisville: Westminster John Knox, 2007), 1.

equally important value of intimacy with creation was left undeveloped. In keeping with the powerful turn to panentheism in contemporary theology, as detailed in the previous chapter, a more balanced view of the intimacy and distinction dynamic can be had. In the words of the contemporary postcolonialist female theologian Rivera, "God is irreducibly Other, always *beyond* our grasp. But not beyond our touch."[57]

Much help for this balanced dynamic between intimacy and distinction can be gleaned from the work of some leading feminist thinkers regarding the importance of metaphors and new "models" of God (S. McFague, J. Soskice, E. Johnson, among others).[58] The literalist, patriarchal, male-dominated language for God easily leads to dualistic, hierarchical, and oppressive accounts of the God-world relationship. Biblically based images such as "God as potter who creates the cosmos by molding it"[59] and "God the creator as mother who gives birth to the universe"[60] are badly needed to critique and enrich theological imagination and liturgical practice.

The Anglican feminist Kathryn Tanner's distinction between "contrastive" and "noncontrastive" accounts of divine transcendence is highly useful. Whereas the former contrasts transcendence and immanence inversely—meaning that the more focus on one, the less on the other—the latter represents intimate involvement with the world. The "noncontrastive" approach saves God from becoming one being among others and rather supports divine transcendence simultaneously with robust presence and activity throughout.[61] The Catholic feminist A. M. Clifford summarizes: "God exists in everything. Paradoxically, God is never really distant from creation, although creatures, since they are unlike God in nature, are necessarily distant from God."[62]

Now we move to origin theologies and myths of other traditions.

57. Rivera, *The Touch of Transcendence*, 2.

58. A useful discussion particularly with regard to creation, including theology-science dialogue, is Sallie McFague, *Models of God: Theology for an Ecological, Nuclear Age* (Minneapolis: Fortress, 1987), 249–71.

59. McFague, *Models of God*, 250.

60. McFague, *Models of God*, 249.

61. Kathryn E. Tanner, *God and Creation in Christian Theology: Tyranny or Empowerment?* (Minneapolis: Fortress, 1988), chap. 2.

62. Clifford, "Creation," 218.

The Nature and Origins of the Cosmos in Religions' Imaginations

The Challenge of Comparing Creation Theologies of Religions

There is only a little truth to the mantra that whereas the Asiatic religions are cosmocentric, the Semitic faiths are anthropocentric; this claim is usually made without a detailed engagement of scriptural and theological traditions. While it is true that in Abrahamic faiths cosmogonies are written mainly from the perspective of humanity, this in no way means that their scriptural traditions lack a cosmic orientation. Indeed, it can also be argued that the Christian vision of eschatological salvation in terms of the renewal of the whole creation particularly supports a robust integrative approach to creation in which both humanity and the cosmos have their own places.

The real differences between Abrahamic and Asiatic traditions have to do with the meaning of history, the intentionality of creation, and the moral dimension. Whereas for Asiatic religions, particularly Hinduism, reality is an "appearance," for Judeo-Christian and Islamic traditions it is the place for "salvation history." Whereas for Buddhism there is no "reason" for the emergence of the cosmos (certainly no divine cause), and for Hinduism creation is a "side effect" (or *lila*, "play"), Jews, Christians, and Muslims hold to an "intentional creation."[63] God creates the world for a purpose.

Creation Theologies in Abrahamic Traditions

All three traditions believe in God, the almighty Creator, who has brought about the cosmos and sustains and guides its life from the beginning to the end. Everything derives from and is dependent on God. The same Creator guides the creation with the help of the laws of creation he has put in place (Q 30:30). There are divine purposes present in creation. While God and world can never be separated, neither can they be equated. God is infinite; cosmos and creatures are finite.

Since Christian theology of creation is based on the Old Testament, there is no need to delve here into a distinctively Jewish theology of creation. Suffice it to note that the major difference has to do with the Trinitarian interpretation of the work of creation by the one God in Christian tradition.

63. Janet M. Soskice, "*Creatio Ex Nihilo*: Its Jewish and Christian Foundations," chap. 2 in *CGA*, 29.

Similarly to the Bible, the Qur'an describes God as the Creator in the absolute sense,[64] that is, God brought into existence that which was not existent "before": "When nothing had yet come into existence, there was the One, the First (*al-Awwal*)," the ineffable one, incomparable (Q 26:11), who never perishes (55:26–27).

Materially close to the Christian view of nature as creation is the Qur'anic interpretation of created order as *muslim*. The term means "submission," from the root "to be whole and integral." The idea behind the term is that one who submits to God avoids disintegration. Creation follows ("submits" to) the laws set up by the Creator. The Qur'an testifies, "to God prostrate whoever is in the heavens and whoever is in the earth, together with the sun and the moon, and the stars and the mountains, and the trees and the animals, as well as many of mankind" (Q 22:18).

No wonder Islam has a long tradition of natural theology not unlike Judaism and Christianity. All created realities are considered "signs" revealing the Creator (Q 30:22). Hence, the study of nature may draw us nearer to God (41:53).

The foundational message signified by creation for Muslim theology is *tawhid*, the unity and oneness of God. Distinguishing itself from the Christian *Trinitarian* theology of creation, the Qur'anic principle of the unity of God (*tawhid*) serves as the theological framework for creation theology.

Markedly different conceptions of the nature and origins of the cosmos come to the fore with the shift to Asiatic faiths.

The Buddhist Vision of the Origins of the Cosmos: "Codependent Origination"

A foundational difference from Abrahamic faiths is that none of the Buddhist traditions consider the Divine as the "Creator." This applies even to Mahayana traditions, which show much more pronounced interest in deities than Theravada traditions. In that sense, Buddhism is a "naturalist" philosophy closer to contemporary scientific materialism but with the crucial difference that even in its nontheistic orientation it is the spiritual/mental that is primary. Buddhism is not atheistic.

Buddha himself had no interest in speculations about the origins, and as is well known, he often warned his followers about not getting into such

64. Muzaffar Iqbal, *Islam and Science* (Aldershot, UK: Ashgate, 2002), chap. 2.

speculations, as they are useless for the ultimate pursuit.[65] That said, it is ironic that Buddhist cosmology is rich, variegated, and highly sophisticated.[66]

There is no absolute "origin" or "creation" in Buddhism. According to Lotus Sutra, the "catechism" of the Mahayana tradition, the cosmos was "not derived from an intelligent cause," nor has it any purpose.[67] Rather, the cosmos is everlasting and without beginning.[68]

Instead, all Buddhist schools agree with "dependent origination." The famous scriptural passage reads thus:

> "When this is, that is."
> "From the arising of this comes the arising of that."
> "When this isn't, that isn't."
> "From the cessation of this comes the cessation of that."[69]

In other words, according to the principle of effect, everything emerges in an interrelated manner through various sequences, finally consummating into ultimate liberation.[70] Everything is in a continuous process of change. The world passes through cycles of evolution and dissolution, *ad infinitum*, similarly to Hinduism. "Behind" this continuous process of the dependent origination is the process of the arising and cessation of *dukkha* (the first "Noble Truth").

As mentioned, rather than using "suffering" (or "pain" or "stress") for *dukkha*, it is best to leave the term without English translation to avoid misunderstanding. It is intentionally an ambiguous word. With all their differences, all Buddhist schools consider *dukkha* to be the main challenge in life and, consequently, extinction of *dukkha* to be the main goal.

65. Majjhima Nikaya Sutta 63, in *The Middle Length Discourses of the Buddha*, trans. Bhikkhu Ñānamoli and Bhikku Bodhi (Kandy, Sri Lanka: Buddhist Publication Society, 1995).

66. W. Randolph Kloetzli, *Buddhist Cosmology: Science and Theology in the Images of Motion and Light* (Delhi: Motilal Banarsidass, 1989), and Akira Sadakata, *Buddhist Cosmology: Philosophy and Origins*, trans. Gaynor Sekimori (Tokyo: Kōsei Publishing, 1997).

67. Lotus Sutra 5.80; *SBE* 21.

68. Lotus Sutra 13.19; *SBE* 21.

69. Samyutta Nikaya 12.61.

70. Samyutta Nikaya 12.2; P. A. Payutto, *Dependent Origination: The Buddhist Law of Conditionality*, trans. Bruce Evans (Bangkok: Buddhadhamma Foundation, 1995), chap. 1.

Hindu Cosmologies of Origins

While, like Buddhism, Hinduism does not know the doctrine of *creation*, it is unusually rich in religious cosmologies and sacred cosmogonies. At the same time, Hinduism speaks of origins in diverse voices characteristic of its enormous plurality.

Notwithstanding the lack of a doctrine of "creation" strictly speaking, Gita freely speaks of the Deity as the creator and sustainer of the world.[71] He is also *Om*, the eternal "echo," the sound originating from the mythic past. But even then, there is no teaching about a onetime creation "from nothing."

A distinctive Hindu teaching in various scriptural traditions affirms that God and nature are the same.[72] The description of "creation" in Brihadaranyaka Upanishad (1.4) is a case in point: Brahman first made himself split into two, bringing about male and female; out of female came cow and bull, out of them mare and ass, and so forth. Out of his body parts, further things were created.[73] No wonder the cosmos is sometimes compared to a cosmic being, a living organism.

What is more similar to the Semitic faiths is that "Hindu scriptures attest to the belief that the creation, maintenance, and annihilation of the cosmos is completely up to the Supreme Will."[74] Gita puts it in a way that closely resembles the New Testament statement about Christ (Rev. 1:8): "I am the beginning and the middle and the end also of all beings."[75] What is radically different from the Abrahamic traditions is that all Hindu scriptural traditions also affirm rebirth and a cyclical worldview: hence, "creation" does not mean the absolute beginning, as in the Semitic traditions.

As mentioned repeatedly, the most well-known scriptural tradition of Hinduism in the West is that of the Upanishads, the last (latest) part of the Vedas and the main Vedanta schools. It is here that the sophisticated philosophical discussions of origins and of the relation of the cosmos to Brahman occur. Notwithstanding important internal differences, all Vedanta schools agree with the rest of the Vedic literature, "That Self [*atman*] is indeed Brahman."[76] How

71. Gita 7; *SBE* 8:74, 76; 13:106.

72. Keith Ward, *Religion and Creation* (Oxford: Clarendon, 1996), 79–80.

73. Brihadaranyaka Upanishad 1.4.5; *SBE* 15:86.

74. O. P. Dwivedi, "Dharmic Ecology," in *Hinduism and Ecology: The Intersection of Earth, Sky, and Water*, ed. Christopher Key Chapple and Mary Evelyn Tucker, Religions of the World and Ecology (Cambridge, MA: Harvard University Press, 2000), 6.

75. Gita 10; *SBE* 8:88.

76. Brihadaranyaka Upanishad 4.4.5; *SBE* 15:176.

the details of this foundational statement are worked out calls for a short explanation, corresponding to the God-world issue in Christianity.

The main comparative point is this: Hindu cosmology is based on a pantheistic equation between "God" and the world, called technically *advaita*, nondualism (lit. "not-two"). As to the nuances of this nonduality principle, the Vedanta schools of absolute dualism (Sankara) and qualified dualism (Ramanuja) have carried on hundreds of years of highly sophisticated debates. When compared to Abrahamic faiths, those nuances are just that, *nuances*, and they all fail to make a distinction. Even in the most pan(en)theistically oriented versions of Christian theology, the world is not conceived to be a nondifferentiated extension of the Lord, as it is in Hinduism. There is an "unbridgeable gulf" between those theistic faiths that see the Creator as infinitely greater than the creatures and those that equate the two.[77]

Creation in Evolution: An Evolving Cosmos

A Changed Worldview

Before looking at the scientific explanations of the origins of the cosmos, a brief look at the dramatic worldview changes is in order. Probably none surpasses the importance of the shift from substance ontology, aligned with dualisms of various sorts, to relationality and holistic explanations. Related to it, instead of a static universe, we now conceive of a highly dynamic, evolving cosmos.

In the physical sciences, the most dramatic change since Newton, along with relativity theories (on which more below), is the shift from classical to quantum physics.[78] Quantum theory has helped overcome once and for all the naive mechanism and full determinism that were often assumed in the older paradigm. What quantum theory reveals is that not only at the smallest, subatomic level (where quantum theory primarily functions), but also at the macrolevel, nature reveals surprises, irregularities, and unpredictability—notwithstanding amazing regularity of processes. Still, the laws of nature are in place and natural phenomena are (relatively speaking) deterministic—other-

77. R. C. Zaehner, *Mysticism, Sacred and Profane: An Inquiry into Some Varieties of Praeternatural Experience* (Oxford: Clarendon, 1957), 204.

78. John Polkinghorne, *The Quantum World*, Princeton Science Library (Princeton: Princeton University Press, 1985).

wise no scientific observations would be possible. What the unpredictability means is that determinism is not ironclad and that—at least according to the major (Copenhagian) interpretation of quantum theory—natural processes and events are probabilistic in nature.

Indications of indeterminacy are well known, such as the wave/particle duality (that is, light appears both as wave and as particle) and the incapacity to measure both the momentum and position of the particle.[79] Or consider the highly counterintuitive quantum "entanglement" (Bell's theorem), according to which, without any "real" reason, the measurement of two chance events—imagine the measurement of the spin of two electrons when they travel as a result of the decay of an atom—shows definite nonlocal correlation; that is, while it cannot be said that these two chance events really influence each other, they are to a certain extent inseparable.

Add to these the whole new field of chaos theory, which shows that, while causality (rightly understood) is of course not to be put aside, the more developed the processes, the less *mechanistically* causal they are—even if they are basically deterministic! Consider the famous "butterfly effect": the slightest change affecting climate in one part of the world, when amplified, may cause a huge storm on the other side of the globe!

In this kind of "open universe," the process of emergence is constantly at work. The basic definition of "emergence" is "that new and unpredictable phenomena are naturally produced by interactions in nature; that these new structures, organisms, and ideas are not reducible to the subsystems on which they depend; and that the newly evolved realities in turn exercise a causal influence on the parts out of which they arose."[80] Emergence theories seek to defeat explanatory reduction—also known as "physical closure"—which seeks to explain everything in the world in terms of physical processes and entities.[81]

79. The famous "superposition" principle, roughly speaking, says that a particle can be said to be both "here" and "there," not of course simultaneously but probabilistically, that is, we can never know for sure. Consider also other celebrated quantum examples of indeterminism and counterintuitiveness, namely, the "double-split experiment"; that is, imagine a beam of electrons shot through a metal plate with two narrow slits; the results clearly imply that these particles have behaved more like waves as they appear to have entered both slits!

80. Philip C. Clayton, *Mind and Emergence: From Quantum to Consciousness* (Oxford: Oxford University Press, 2004), vi; for the history, see chap. 1.

81. Nancey Murphy, "Reductionism: How Did We Fall into It and Can We Emerge from It?" in *Evolution and Emergence: Systems, Organisms, Persons*, ed. Nancey Murphy and William R. Stoeger (Oxford: Oxford University Press, 2007), 19–39.

The Origins of the Universe in Light of Contemporary Cosmology

The Standard Big Bang Cosmology

As an academic discipline, contemporary cosmology faces a number of challenges and opportunities.[82] Not only does it utilize a variety of disciplines in its study of origins, evolution, and the ultimate fate of the entire universe, it also relates to questions for which obviously there are no empirical answers, such as why there is something rather than nothing.

Notwithstanding a number of continuing debates, the global natural scientific community considers the big bang theory the standard, established position with huge experimental support.[83] Briefly put, the standard model argues that the cosmos came into being about 13.8 billion years ago from a singularity of zero size and infinite density (usually marked as $t = 0$ in which t denotes time), and has since expanded to its current form. Since the Hubble discovery in the 1920s, we know that the galaxies are receding from us, and therefore that the cosmos is "expanding." Important evidence for this expansion and the big bang came from the discovery in the 1960s of the microwave background radiation that is believed to be an echo from the original big bang.

The big bang model is based on relativity theories (and later quantum theories). Whereas Albert Einstein's 1905 special relativity theory linked space and time together in a space-time continuum and thereby made all points of observation relative rather than absolute, the 1916 general relativity theory included gravity. Radically revising the Newtonian theory in which space and time were understood to be some kind of separate backgrounds or "containers" in which matter moved, Einstein established space-time as a four-dimensional manifold (three space and one time dimension) that "can stretch, warp, and vibrate."[84] Furthermore, whereas Newton's 1680s theory of gravity applied only to bodies at rest or moving slowly ("slow" in relation to the speed of light!), Einstein's theory applied to bodies in all conditions. That is because gravitation was thought of no longer in terms of a "field" but rather as a distortion of space and time. As the physicist John Wheeler's famous dictum puts it: "Matter

82. NASA/WMAP [Wilkinson Microwave Anisotropy Probe] Science Team, "Cosmology: The Study of the Universe," last modified June 3, 2011, http://map.gsfc.nasa.gov/universe/WMAP_Universe.pdf.

83. Consult Kate Grayson Boisvert, *Religion and the Physical Sciences* (Westport, CT: Greenwood, 2008).

84. Robert J. Spitzer, SJ, *New Proofs for the Existence of God: Contributions of Contemporary Physics and Philosophy* (Grand Rapids: Eerdmans, 2010), 15.

tells space how to curve" and "space tells matter how to move."[85] Think of the surface of a balloon with colored spots while it is being blown up: it is not that the spots are moving (even though they are) but that the surface of the balloon is expanding!

Now, on this basis, the big bang theory builds naturally: observing the galaxies flying apart as indications of constant expansion, it simply looks back in time to the point when the expansion started; finally you come to the "beginning point." For that to work, the so-called cosmological principle is assumed, that is, the distribution of matter in the universe is homogeneous and isotropic when averaged over very large scales. An important support to this assumption, besides extensive observational evidence related to the even distribution of galaxies, among others, came from the 1960s discovery of cosmic microwave background radiation, the remnant heat from the big bang: it seems to have a highly uniform temperature over the large scale. Further support for the big bang model has come from the defeat of its onetime challenger, the so-called steady state theory of Hoyle, Bondi, and Gold, of the late 1940s. This theory supposes that although the universe is constantly expanding, new matter is also being created to keep a constant density over time.

Important refinements to the classical big bang theory, originally proposed in the 1920s by the Roman Catholic priest-physicist Georges Lemaître, have been made since. Currently we know that immediately after the big bang, during the extremely short period of time (so-called Planck time, 10^{-43} seconds, the shortest measure of time) named the "inflation period," dramatic developments occurred.[86] What is strange and counterintuitive is that contemporary science is not able to explain what happened during that immensely short period immediately following the bang, since no known laws of nature apply to it. The current relativistic laws of nature can explain how the cosmos has evolved since, that is, after 10^{-43} seconds till today. What happened "before" that, hence, must be a matter of quantum laws; oddly enough, it is the kind of happening our known laws—and hence also terminology—cannot grasp at all!

Here also is the culmination of undoubtedly the biggest unresolved riddle in contemporary natural sciences: how to reconcile with quantum theory, which studies the tiniest, smallest particles within the atom, the theory of relativity, which is able to explain the functioning of everything big.[87] Separately,

85. C. W. Misner, K. S. Thorne, and J. A. Wheeler, *Gravitation* (New York: Freeman, 1973), 5.

86. "What Is the Inflation Theory?" NASA/WMAP Science Team, April 16, 2010, http://map.gsfc.nasa.gov/universe/WMAP_Universe.pdf.

87. The problem is often presented briefly as that of unification: How can we give a

these two theories have been proven true beyond much doubt. However, all mathematical attempts to make them collaborate embarrassingly fail—hence, the continuing search for a "theory of everything"[88] that would be able to explain both the smallest and the biggest.[89]

All life in the universe is basically made of three components: protons, neutrons, and electrons. But what is astonishing is that—totally opposite of what was believed—the universe overall is not made mainly of this "baryonic matter," as it came to be called. On the contrary, most of the universe is something "dark," namely, "dark matter" (23 percent) and "dark energy"[90] (72 percent), which leaves only a few percent for the "stuff" life is made of.[91] While much is still unknown about both dark matter (a form of matter so dense that it neither emits nor absorbs any light and therefore cannot be detected) and particularly dark energy, the latter is important in helping explain the 1998 discovery that the expansion of the universe is speeding up.[92]

Revised Scientific Cosmologies

Although this standard big bang theory is still the foundation of all scientific cosmologies, revisions and challenges are under way. They can be elusively named quantum cosmologies. The most well known is the one presented by the British thinker Stephen Hawking and his American colleague James Hartle. Indeed, Hawking famously came to radically revise his earlier view of the big bang, shifting from an initial singularity to a boundary-less scenario that still presupposes the "beginning" (and thus, finite nature of the universe with regard to the beginning), although no beginning in time (no

---

unified explanation of the four fundamental forces: gravity, electromagnetism, and the strong and weak nuclear forces?

88. John D. Barrow, *New Theories of Everything* (Oxford: Oxford University Press, 2007).

89. Brian Greene, *The Elegant Universe: Superstrings, Hidden Dimensions, and the Quest for the Ultimate Theory*, 2nd ed. (New York: Vintage Books, 2000).

90. "Dark Matter," Berkeley Cosmology Group, http://astro.berkeley.edu/~mwhite/darkmatter/dm.html.

91. We also know now that to use the term "atom" (as a convenient reference to the three above-mentioned components) is technically wrong, as the term means "uncut." Each atom in itself is an extremely—perhaps infinitely—complex "microcosm." It is only the limitations of measurement devices that hinder our going beyond "quarks" and similar "smallest" things we can infer currently.

92. "Cosmology: The Study of the Universe," Wilkinson Microwave Anisotropy Probe, last updated June 3, 2011, http://map.gsfc.nasa.gov/universe/WMAP_Universe.pdf.

singularity). Why this move? The main reason goes back to the fundamental riddle of contemporary natural sciences, mentioned above—the impossibility of reconciling classical and quantum physics. Hence, what if the assumption of singularity—which is entailed by classical physics—is not needed in the quantum world? Hartle-Hawking's "no-boundary" model builds on that premise. Its difference from the standard model can be easily depicted with the following illustration: imagine a piece of wood in the shape of a cone. In the standard model there is a sharp edge, in other words, a singularity, $t = 0$. In the no-boundary model the edge is rounded off, smooth; hence, there is no singularity, no beginning in time. Hawking also draws from there an unwarranted metaphysical conclusion: "'The boundary condition of the universe is that it has no boundary.' The universe would be completely self-contained and not affected by anything outside itself. It would neither be created nor destroyed. It would just BE."[93]

The Hartle-Hawking proposal is merely one of many elusively known quantum cosmologies, the details of which cannot be engaged here.

How would all this relate to the theological doctrine of creation?

The Theological Meaning of the "Beginning" of the Universe Ex Nihilo *among Abrahamic Faiths*

A common assumption among pagan philosophies was that if God is eternal, then creation is as well. Some Christian theologians, particularly Origen, came to believe that on Platonic presuppositions the immutability and eternity of God led to the eternity of the world.[94] By and large, however, early theology rejected the eternity of the world. Rather than creation taking place in time, time itself comes into being in creation, as Augustine argued.[95] Over the centuries this became the "canonical" view in Christianity. Similarly, on the Jewish side, Maimonides set forth robust objections to the Aristotelian claim for the eternity of the world because of its incompatibility with scriptural teaching.[96] Interestingly, some medieval Islamic scholars (Ibn Rushd, Ibn Sina, and others) were open to the eternity of the cosmos.

93. Stephen Hawking, *A Brief History of Time*, updated and expanded tenth anniversary ed. (New York: Bantam Books, 1998 [1988]), 141.

94. Origen, *First Principles* 1.2.10.

95. Augustine, *City of God* 11.6.

96. Moses Maimonides, *The Guide for the Perplexed*, trans. M. Friedländer (sacred-texts .com [1903]), 2.13–29.

If the universe is not eternal, there has to be some kind of beginning; but what does that mean? Terminologically and materially, it may mean many different things—as already the discussion of current scientific cosmologies indicates: beginning *of* time; beginning *in* time; beginning as in "origin," the ultimate "source" or "cause" of everything.

The main theological thesis for the theistic doctrines of creation in Abrahamic faiths is clear and unambiguous: it is about the contingency of the universe on the Creator. In other words, however the question about the relation of time to the big bang or similar scientific view of the "beginning" may be negotiated, theology's claim for the ultimate contingency of creation upon the Creator stays intact (e.g., Qur'an 7:54). This is a major difference from Asiatic faiths.

But how to best describe the "beginning" in theology? A shorthand response is *ex nihilo* ("out of nothing"). It took about a millennium for Judaism to adopt the *doctrine* of *ex nihilo*, even when the *idea* at large was there.[97] The reason is that Genesis 1:1–2 can be interpreted in terms of God working with "materials" already in existence and not necessarily as *ex nihilo*. The rest of the biblical teaching, however, eventually won the day in favor of "out of nothing."[98]

While the Christian fathers rightly acknowledged that *ex nihilo* was not directly taught in the Bible, as early as the second century the doctrine was established. It helped reject the Platonic notion of the eternity of matter and the idea of the divine architect fashioning the cosmos out of materials already available.[99] With *creatio ex nihilo*, early tradition also ruled out pantheism, which equates God and matter, and the necessity of creation.

While the doctrine of *ex nihilo* rules out views according to which the Creator worked with "preexisting" materials, it does not rule out the emergence of novelty, surprises—evolution! On the contrary—and in contrast with Deism—Christian tradition teaches that the same Creator who brought about reality from nothing, in *creatio continua* not only maintains but also helps bring about new forms and new phenomena.

97. Ernan McMullin, "Creation *Ex Nihilo*: Early History," in *CGA*, 11–23.

98. Menachem M. Kellner, *Dogma in Medieval Judaism from Maimonides to Abravanel* (Oxford: Oxford University Press, for the Littmann Library of Jewish Civilization, 1986), 213–17.

99. Paul Copan and William Lane Craig, *Creation out of Nothing: A Biblical, Philosophical, and Scientific Exploration* (Grand Rapids: Baker Academic, 2004).

The Coherence between the Big Bang Cosmologies and "In the Beginning" Doctrines of Creation

There are several reasons why scientists reject the idea of the eternity of the universe and consider it finite at least with regard to the beginnings. The most obvious reason has to do with the second law of thermodynamics, which states that all cosmic (and smaller) processes happen only in one direction. Without energy from outside, equilibrium comes with decay and disorder.

No wonder that theologians—many of whom at first might have been startled by the big bang theory—soon came to welcome it as an idea compatible with the biblical teaching on "in the beginning." Often cited is Pope Pius XII's embrace of the big bang, which is all the more astonishing in light of his resistance to evolutionary theory![100] At the same time, theologians have also been wise not to uncritically push the parallelism for the obvious reason that scientific results are prone to change, as has already happened with the introduction of quantum cosmologies. That said, the theologian should not underestimate the analogical importance of the big bang cosmology as one of the ways to correlate theological claims with scientific ones in a mindful manner. "What one *could* readily say, however, is that if the universe began in time through the act of a Creator, from our vantage point it would look something like the Big Bang that cosmologists are now talking about. What one cannot say is, first, that the Christian doctrine of creation 'supports' the Big Bang model, or second, that the Big Bang model 'supports' the Christian doctrine of creation."[101]

What about the Hawking-Hartle proposal of the denial of the beginning in time? Would it cause problems for theology? Hawking himself believes this is the case, drawing the unwarranted conclusion that in the absence of beginning *in time*, no Creator is needed. Happily, his conclusion is faulty (and falls outside strict science). The doctrine of creation in no way restricts divine activity to the bringing about (in the beginning) of the universe. The doctrine of creation is also about continuing creation, providence, and divine action. The relation of the "beginning" to time matters little or nothing. In the words of the British theologian Simon Oliver, "Whether one accepts the Big Bang understood as a temporal boundary to the universe, as in the inflationary

100. Pius XII, "The Proofs for the Existence of God in the Light of Modern Natural Science" (address to the Pontifical Academy of Sciences, November 22, 1951).

101. Ernan McMullin, "How Should Cosmology Relate to Theology?" in *The Sciences and Theology in the Twentieth Century*, ed. A. R. Peacocke (Notre Dame: University of Notre Dame Press, 1981), 39.

theory, or the Hawking model of a beginningless universe which is nevertheless finite, neither approximates to the doctrine of creation *ex nihilo*. Natural science cannot truly think the *nihil*."[102]

One set of questions that current cosmology raises has to do with time and space as created entities.

Creation's Space-Time in Theological Perspective

Theologically Problematic Notions of Time

The awkward expression "space-time" reminds the reader of the obvious fact that in the post-Einsteinian worldview neither time nor space has the kind of "absolute" existence it had in classical physics.[103] Rather, we speak of a space-time continuum.

Augustine correctly made time a created entity.[104] This correct insight, however, was coupled with another, highly suspicious supposition that if time has its origin in God, then God somehow must exist "outside" time. This idea of placing God outside time led to a highly problematic juxtaposing of eternity and time that in turn led to two mistaken notions, that either one thinks of God's eternity as something "timeless" or one thinks of it as an unending time.

Einstein's relativity theories brought to the surface the biggest challenge to theology, namely, the negotiation between what are called flowing time (or A-time) and block time (or B-time). The former is the commonsense notion in which the present is real and so is also the flow of time from past to present to future, whereas the latter is the majority view among physicists. For natural scientists, the current understanding of space-time implies that time and space have an equal ontological status, and thus it is unnecessary to distinguish between past, present, and future. Analogically, think of space laid out there completely.[105]

That said, it is not totally correct to say that all notions of "absolute" time are canceled by relativity. It is rather that the more or less fixed notions of "present," "past," and "future" become elusive and somewhat confused. Nor

102. Simon Oliver, "Trinity, Motion and Creation *Ex Nihilo*," in *CGA*, 134.

103. Gideon Goosen, *Spacetime and Theology in Dialogue* (Milwaukee: Marquette University Press, 2008), chap. 3.

104. Augustine, *City of God* 11.6.

105. William Lane Craig, *Time and Eternity: Exploring God's Relationship to Time* (Wheaton, IL: Crossway, 2001), 32–66 and chaps. 4; 5.

is it correct to say that the theories of relativity and of block time deny change (because of tenselessness). Indeed, most ironically, it is exactly the relativity theory that made it possible for cosmology to move away from the static to a dynamic, evolving universe!

Theological Contours of Our Conceptions of Space-Time

So, what is at stake for theology in the debate? This question may be(come) one of the defining and most critical issues in the theology-science conversation. One of the problems with B-time involves the question of authentic human freedom if the future does not mean potentialities. Furthermore, divine freedom in light of the insistence on the openness of the future to God also seems to be at stake. Also, it would be extremely difficult to envision an authentic form of Christian eschatology apart from some kind of reality of unfolding of history and time (an issue to be taken up in that context). With these considerations in mind, let us look at several reasons that support the flowing-time template.

Among the scientific reasons to oppose or at least radically qualify the block-time conception, the first is obvious, namely, the second law of thermodynamics (entropy), which seems to require unidirectionality and irreversibility of time. Similarly, the majority interpretation of quantum physics with its indeterminacy principle makes much less sense (if any) if the future is not potentially true and open for processes to evolve in an indeterminate way.

These and related reasons lie behind the fact that notwithstanding the majority of physicists supporting the block theory, the issue is far from resolved among scientists. Hence, some leading religion-science experts such as the American physicist-theologian R. J. Russell have proposed credible alternatives to block time in the changed postrelativity (and post–quantum theory) era of ours.[106] Without going into details, suffice it to state this: here are credible scientific, philosophical, and particularly theological reasons for theologians to continue defending the real "historicity" of the universe and hence the dynamic nature of time.

In this light, back to mistaken notions of time mentioned above. Rather than imagining God "outside" time, it is appropriate to claim that in his omnipresence and deep engagement with the world, God transcends (space-)

106. Robert J. Russell, *Time in Eternity: Pannenberg, Physics, and Eschatology in Creative Mutual Interaction* (Notre Dame: University of Notre Dame Press, 2012).

time. Incarnation alone tells us that God exists in space-time—but as the almighty Creator, God can certainly not be contained within. God is both "in" and "outside" simultaneously! Also, rather than marking the "end" of time (timelessness) or merely unendingly long time, eternity is the source of earthly time and will bring it to fulfillment, as explained in chapter 10 on eschatology.

What about *space*-(time)? Let it suffice to say this much: whereas in the past space has been conceived either as a "receptacle" or as a "container" of all objects, leading to Newton's "absolute space" idea, or as "relational," a positional quality of material objects being related to each other, relativity theories stripped off the separate existence of space. There is a space-time continuum, integrated with matter and energy.[107] Theologically speaking, similarly to time, we should imagine God both "in" (his own space) and "outside," to ensure immanence and transcendence.[108]

Having examined the issues of the "beginnings" of the universe and its space-time, we now focus on the "beginnings" of life-forms. The much-discussed notion of the "anthropic principle" builds that bridge.

Emerging Life

The Conditions of Life: The Biopic (Anthropic) Principle

The universe is extremely "fine-tuned" to bring about creative processes, particularly life. The values of the universal constants controlling the interrelationships among space, time, and energy in the universe seem to be extremely fine-tuned to allow any kind of life condition. Indeed, it would appear to be much more likely that life conditions were not in place.[109] A critical part of these constants has to do with initial conditions "between the opposing tendencies of the contractive pull of gravity (drawing matter together) and the sum of expansive effects." Unless these tendencies are extremely fine-tuned, not only would life not be possible but nothing else could be possible either.[110]

This fine-tuning is also the condition for the emergence of humanity, the highest known life-form. Recall the physicist Freeman Dyson's oft-cited note

107. Ian G. Barbour, *Religion in the Age of Science* (New York: Harper & Row, 1990), 107–8.

108. Thomas F. Torrance, *Space, Time, and Incarnation* (Edinburgh: T&T Clark, 1968), 11.

109. Alister E. McGrath, *A Fine-Tuned Universe: The Quest for God in Science and Theology*, Gifford Lectures, 2009 (Louisville: Westminster John Knox, 2009), 119–21.

110. John Polkinghorne, "The Anthropic Principle and the Science and Religion Debate," *Faraday Paper* 4 (2007): 1–4.

that "the more I examine the universe and study the details of its architecture, the more evidence I find that the universe in some sense must have known that we were coming."[111] This is the famous "anthropic principle,"[112] which, in fairness to the complexity and novelty of all life in the universe, should be named the "biopic principle."

The theological appropriation of the biopic principle and design argument, understandably, is not only the commodity of Christian tradition. Currently, one can find it strongly presented in Islamic tradition as well.[113] The Qur'anic passage from 21:16 is often invoked: "Not for (idle) sport did We create the heavens and the earth and all that is between!"[114] The fine-tuning argument can also be found in Jewish theology.[115] In contrast, it seems that Buddhist cosmology is prone to dismiss the whole argument because of the rejection of both creation and Creator.[116] Most likely the same applies to Hindu cosmology.

So far we have talked about religious responses to fine-tuning. Naturalists and atheists disagree. Whereas for theists, it speaks of the Creator, for atheists and naturalists fine-tuning is either accidental or, thanks to "multiverse" theory (the existence of infinitely many parallel universes), inevitable as one of the possibilities. Be that as it may, science alone cannot resolve the issue; it is ultimately a theological and metaphysical one.

Whatever the religious interpretation, the fine-tuning principle points to the emergence of life on our planet.

The Continuing Mystery and Diversity of the Emergence of Life

Creation is striking not only because of its unbelievably rich diversity—more than two million existing species of plants and animals known, many more

111. Freeman J. Dyson, *Disturbing the Universe* (New York: Harper & Row, 1979), 250.

112. John D. Barrow and Frank J. Tipler, *The Anthropic Cosmological Principle* (Oxford: Oxford University Press, 1986).

113. For an up-to-date discussion, see Guessoum, *Islam's Quantum Question*, chap. 7 (on design) and chap. 8 (on the anthropic principle).

114. Trans. Abdullah Yusuf Ali, at www.altafsir.com.

115. Nathan Aviezer, "The Anthropic Principle: What Is It and Why Is It Meaningful to the Believing Jew?" *Jewish Action*, Spring 1999, n.p., http://www.ou.org/publications/ja/5759spring/anthropic.pdf.

116. Matthieu Ricard and Trinh Xuan Thuan, *The Quantum and the Lotus: A Journey to the Frontiers Where Science and Buddhism Meet*, trans. Ian Monk (New York: Three Rivers, 2001).

to be discovered—but also because of the sheer fact of its multiplicity; yet all organisms are related by common ancestry. Not only to the religious imagination but even to science, the emergence and nature of life is a mystery without explanation—heightened by the fact that "the universe is *essentially* lifeless."[117] As a scientific field, "origin-of-life" studies, which look at the emergence of life on Earth in the wider context of cosmic evolution, is a fairly recent enterprise.

Organic life has emerged extremely slowly on our planet. After the advent of the most elementary forms of bacterial life, it would take over 2 billion years to have higher forms. What is the theological response? Theology's task is neither to compete with the scientific account, which relies on principles of randomness (and regularity of nature), nor to seek an alternative explanation as to *how* the logistics of the emergence and diversification of life-forms took place. Theology's task, rather, is to inquire into the metaphysical implications and conditions.

The Creator who in the first place established the natural laws that govern the evolvement and sustenance of the vast cosmos seems to be utterly patient with letting those regularities—combined with accidents—produce ever-more sophisticated life reaching up to the highest that we know, namely, consciousness. Even though we quite accurately know what kind of biological and chemical processes, in addition to metabolism and the capacity to reproduce, are the essential conditions for living beings in contrast to physical objects, we are far from providing the ultimate answer.[118]

A significant step that may take us closer to the mystery of life is the highlighting of the capacity to carry information (just think of DNA).[119] Information, truly, stands at the heart of contemporary inquiry into what life is and whence it comes.[120] Theologically we can state that if God is not only the original creator but also the one who continuously creates and acts in the world, it means that "the stuff of the world has a continuous, inbuilt creativity."[121]

117. John F. Haught, *Is Nature Enough? Meaning and Truth in the Age of Science* (Cambridge: Cambridge University Press, 2006), 57.

118. McGrath, *Fine-Tuned Universe*, chap. 10.

119. Bernd-Olaf Küppers, *Information and the Origin of Life* (Cambridge, MA: MIT Press, 1990).

120. John Polkinghorne, "Theological Notions of Creation and Divine Causality," in *Science and Theology: Questions at the Interface*, ed. M. Rae, H. Regan, and J. Stenhouse (Grand Rapids: Eerdmans, 1994), 236.

121. Arthur Peacocke, "Chance and Law in Irreversible Thermodynamics, Theoretical Biology, and Theology," in *Chaos and Complexity: Scientific Perspectives on Divine Action*, ed. Robert John Russell, Nancey Murphy, and Arthur R. Peacocke (Vatican City and Berkeley,

So far scientific evolutionary theory has been taken for granted. Let us close this section by providing theological reflections on it.

Evolutionary Theory in Religious and Theological Assessments

Darwinism in a Christian Theological Viewpoint

The relation of Christians to the evolutionary theory of Darwin has traveled a long and winding road: from cautious acceptance in the beginning years, to vehement opposition subsequently by many, and finally to its embrace by mainline Christianity in its theistic form—notwithstanding continuing opposition among the conservative churches (particularly in the United States but also elsewhere). Particularly challenging has been the application of the evolutionary scheme to the evolvement of humanity.

Against popular misconceptions, the idea of evolvement and evolution of the created reality is neither a new and novel idea stemming from modern science nor something that is either religious or antireligious in its core. Just consider the first creation story in Genesis chapter 1: it presents creation in terms of a sequence of events and forms, even when its presentation understandably differs in details from contemporary science.

Although Charles Darwin was not the original modern inventor of what we now call evolutionary theory, he became its most eloquent public disseminator. The key ideas of his 1859 *Origin of Species by Means of Natural Selection* are well known: random variations among species; the struggle for life due to the increase of populations at a geometrical rate; the best chance of survival for those with the most useful variations; and the passing on of the most useful traits to the next generation by the possessors of those traits.[122]

As is well known, Darwin himself was not an atheist; neither did he see his theory denying the idea of the Creator God. While his remarks in the second edition of *The Origin of Species* on the "grandeur in this view of life, with its several powers, having been originally breathed by the Creator into a few forms or into one"[123] might have been inspired by desire to avoid conflict with religious authorities, they also point to the possibility of a theistic interpreta-

CA: Vatican Observatory and Center for Theological and the Natural Sciences, 1995), 139–42, here 139.

122. Hans Schwarz, *Creation* (Grand Rapids: Eerdmans, 2002), 3–20.

123. Charles Darwin, *Origin of Species*, in vol. 49 of *Great Books of the Western World*, ed. Robert Maynard Hutchins (Chicago: Encyclopaedia Britannica, 1952), 243.

tion of evolutionary ideas. No wonder, particularly in the American context, that evolutionism was cast in a theistic framework from the beginning and was not at first greatly resisted by the churches. It was rather the atheistic, cosmically oriented interpretation by Darwin's interpreters that helped emerging evolutionary theory take a decidedly antireligious turn.

Darwin's subsequent main work, *The Descent of Man in Relation to Sex* (1871), was likely to rouse more resistance from religious circles. In hindsight, it is somewhat ironic that while the resistance to Darwinism soon intensified in the United States, after a fairly smooth embrace of evolutionism, the opposite was the case on the Continent and the British Isles.

While it would be a fatal mistake for Christian theology to oppose evolutionary theory in principle, we should also be mindful of the abuses of the theory. Indeed, evolutionism has emerged as "a secular religion."[124] Social Darwinism has been used as a means of shaping economic and sociopolitical programs deeply antagonistic to the values of human dignity and the equality of all. Most drastically, in the hands of Nazis, some communists, and other tyrants, traces of evolutionism have funded cruelty and violence. That said, theologically it can be concluded that contemporary evolutionary theory, rather than being an enemy of a theistic view of creation, "has given theology an opportunity to see God's ongoing creative activity not merely in the preservation of a fixed order but in the constant bringing forth of things that are new."[125]

Evolutionary Theory among Religions

Among Jews, a basically similar kind of development has taken place as happened among Christian communities. The leading rabbis of the nineteenth century, along with most traditional communities in the United States, vehemently opposed evolutionism, while some others saw it as compatible with Jewish faith.[126] Mainline Jewish theology nowadays sees no conflict with the theistic interpretation of evolution, including human evolution. Indeed, proportionally more Jews in the United States accept evolution than do Christians.

124. Brendan Purcell, *From Big Bang to Big Mystery: Human Origins in the Light of Creation and Evolution* (Hyde Park, NY: New City Press, 2012), 115.

125. Pannenberg, *ST* 2:119.

126. Geoffrey Cantor and Marc Swetlitz, eds., *Jewish Tradition and the Challenge of Darwinism* (Chicago: University of Chicago Press, 2006).

Islam has the greatest difficulty in finding a constructive way to deal with evolutionism.[127] So fierce is the opposition that it is not uncommon to find fatwas (more-or-less binding legal-religious rulings) on it.[128] What is striking in Muslim countries is that not only a large majority of the general public but also university students and professors strongly and consistently oppose evolution, particularly human evolution. Even among American Muslims, fewer than half accept evolution.[129] The most important reason for opposition is the question of Adam.

Among the main Asiatic faith traditions, evolutionary theory has caused hardly any concern. Regarding Buddhism, there are a number of reasons for this. First, Gautama considered questions of origins to be secondary and marginal. Second, at least in some key Buddhist scriptural accounts, as discussed above, an evolutionary view (though not in its modern form) can be discerned. Third, the idea of no-self and impermanence leans toward evolvement and evolution.

Similarly, the Hindu traditions consider the origins and development of the whole reality in terms of evolvement and a common ancestry. Moreover, for Hindus, even the gods may assume animal features.[130]

The last big topic to discuss is the conditions of the Creator acting in the world, a highly disputed theme for contemporary theology and philosophy, traditionally named the doctrine of providence.

Providence and Divine Action

Providence in Theological Tradition

A theist—at least in Abrahamic traditions—is bound to speak of God's intentional, loving care, maintenance, and guiding of the cosmos and its processes.

127. Mahmoud Ayoub, "Creation or Evolution? The Reception of Darwinism in Modern Arab Thought," chap. 11 in *SRPW*.

128. See the Fatwa Center of America's ruling against human evolution in 2010 at www.askmufti.com.

129. A Pew Research Center poll reports that only 45 percent of American Muslims embrace evolutionary theory. See "Appendix A: U.S. Muslims—Views on Religion and Society in a Global Context," Pew Research Center, April 30, 2013, http://www.pewforum.org/2013/04/30/the-worlds-muslims-religion-politics-society-app-a/.

130. David L. Gosling, "Darwin and the Hindu Tradition: 'Does What Goes Around Come Around?'" *Zygon: Journal of Religion and Science* 46, no. 2 (June 2011): 348.

The theme is so prevalent in the Bible that it is useless to even begin to compile lists: providence is comprehensive and inclusive of all creation. Similarly to creation, providence speaks of contingency, as Augustine put it, "But the universe will pass away in the twinkling of an eye if God withdraws His ruling hand."[131]

Tradition has made the commonsense distinction between "general" providence, the all-embracing maintenance of the world's order and life, and "special" providence, which encompasses redemptive and saving acts of God as well as particular divine "interventions" related to prayers and miracles.

In "general providence" we can distinguish several types of interrelated forms of contingency and dependability:[132]

- Preservation within *nature* is expressed in the regularity of seasons and the cycles of sun and moon, in the predictability and lawfulness of complex processes (such as chemical reactions), and in the evolutionary process of the cosmos and life at large.
- Preservation through *moral conduct* takes place with the help of conscience, natural law, and a general sense of morality.
- Preservation through the *historical* process is the most contested form of providence because history's unfolding is ambiguous and open to many interpretations.

In another, related way of accounting for the complex unity and pervasiveness of divine providence, theological tradition established three interrelated categories: preservation (proper), concursus, and governance. Whereas providence proper relates to the general "maintenance," the doctrine of concursus affirms the invitation for creatures to collaborate with the Creator, so affirming their freedom and independence, to the point that they may also deviate from God. Along with providence and concursus, tradition also speaks of world governance, loving guidance toward the desired end goal by the Creator. It speaks of God's faithfulness to his creation.

That said, the modern person faces a number of challenges to trusting divine providence, particularly righteous governance. Just think of the two world wars, the Jewish Holocaust, and innumerable other worldwide crises, from poverty and hunger to natural catastrophes. They all question God's goodness.

131. Augustine, *The Literal Meaning of Genesis* 4.12.22 (trans. Taylor, 1:117).
132. Following the typology of Schwarz, *Creation*, 189–212.

What is the final goal of providential world governance? For the Protestant scholastics, it was the glory of God. We can follow tradition in that from the perspective of the creatures, giving glory to God is indeed the highest calling. From God's perspective, however, we have to say that "God does not need this, for he is already God in himself from all eternity." This notion combats the common atheistic and even religious suspicion that God is ultimately guided by a form of self-seeking and self-love. Rather, we have to say that God's love and faithfulness to his creation will become evident in cooperation and governance, the goal of which is the redemption and fulfillment of creation.[133]

This is all good and important, but now, as already implied, serious challenges have risen as a result of changing worldviews.

Divine Acts in History and Nature

What Is at Stake, and What Are the Challenges for Theology?

With the emergence of modern science, it seemed there was no need for God to intervene in the world process after having created the world and caused it to follow its laws and regularities. The establishment of the principle of inertia[134] further helped consolidate a purely naturalistic, mechanistic explanation of the world. When combined with atheism, naturalism made God as provider obsolete. Evolutionary theory with its focus on chance further helped make divine acts obsolete. P. Clayton formulates it succinctly: "Physical science, it appears, leaves no place for divine action. Modern science presupposes that the universe is a closed physical system, that interactions are regular and law-like, that all causal histories can be traced, and that anomalies will ultimately have physical explanations. But traditional assertions of God acting in the world conflict with all four of these conditions: they presuppose that the universe is open, that God acts from time to time according to his purposes, that the ultimate source and explanation of these actions is the divine will, and that no earthly account would ever suffice to explain God's intentions."[135]

133. Pannenberg, *ST* 2:56–57, here 56.

134. Inertia refers to an object's tendency to stay in the existing state or motion until an outside force causes a change.

135. Philip C. Clayton, "The Impossible Possibility: Divine Causes in the World of Nature," in *God, Life, and the Cosmos: Christian and Islamic Perspectives*, edited by Ted Peters, Muzaffar Iqbal, and Syed Nomanul Haq (Surrey, UK: Ashgate, 2002), 249.

Not surprisingly, theologians reacted in more than one way. Conservatives continued the affirmation of divine acts without concern for science, and liberals virtually left behind any factual notion of divine acts as they were conceived to be merely subjective responses to religious influence.[136] Neo-orthodox theologians, with all their resistance to classical liberalism, subscribed to the "nature-history" dualism, thus removing God and his acts from the realm of the sciences.

Dissatisfied with these options, a growing group of contemporary theologians are aiming at an alternative that, while sensitive to the necessity (for biblical-theological reasons) to affirm divine acts, wishes to do so in a way that would not contradict physical sciences. The most promising is the model named noninterventionist objective divine action (NIODA).[137]

An All-Embracing Trinitarian Theology of Divine Action

Advocates of NIODA have developed a comprehensive and robust theology of real ("objective") divine action, but in a way that avoids intervention. At the same time, it seeks to avoid the "God-of-the-gaps" fallacy approach in which the only room left for God is that which cannot (yet) be explained by human reason. Its account of divine action is multifaceted and allows for divine action to happen directly (without God having to perform any prior act) or indirectly (by setting into motion a sequence of events) as well as in either a mediated way (God acting in, with, and through the existing processes) or an immediate way (*ex nihilo*). It affirms both the bottom-up approach, which refers to the effects of the lower level on upper levels, and top-down causality, that is, the "higher" level influences the "lower," as when the mind guides human decisions and behavior. Also important is the whole-part causality in which a system or process acts causally beyond what its individual parts (as aggregates, technically put) would do separately. This happens particularly in complex systems such as human societies. That said, God acts as "personal" agent in the world who has a living relationship with the world.[138]

Recall that according to quantum theory, the world process, while regular, is not absolutely deterministic, leaving "natural" openings for God's all-

136. See Nancey Murphy, *Beyond Liberalism and Fundamentalism: How Modern and Postmodern Philosophy Set the Theological Agenda* (Valley Forge, PA: Trinity, 1996).

137. Robert J. Russell, "Challenges and Progress in 'Theology and Science': An Overview of the VO/CTNS Series," in *SPDA*, 3–56.

138. Arthur Peacocke, "The Sound of Sheer Silence: How Does God Communicate with Humanity?" in *NP*, 237.

present, all-wise, and all-powerful influence (without turning into a God-of-the-gaps liability). No wonder, among the NIODA and other science-theology scholars, both quantum theory and chaos theory have been widely investigated concerning indeterminism, that is, their capacity to provide a meaningful opening for divine action.

As with any other doctrine, providence and divine action is also Trinitarian in its shape. With the same love that the Father loves the Son, he loves the universe, his creation, by continuously providing for its life, meaning, and hope for the future. The Son as Logos and mediator of all creaturely work of God is the one in whom everything is held together. Through his Spirit the triune God is present in, under, above, and below, so to speak, all natural processes.

A key to a ubiquitous and comprehensive theology of divine action is the Trinitarian doctrine of divine omnipresence—which also entails divine omniscience: "All things are present to him and are kept by him in his presence,"[139] as classically affirmed in Psalm 139. In this sense, the establishment of divine action with the help of quantum theory (in its ubiquitous form) points in the right direction, "reemphasizing God's operational presence in the most basic processes of nature known to us,"[140] that is, even the subatomic. This is of course not to compromise but rather to establish transcendence as well. Even in his deepest immanence, God as the almighty sovereign Creator also transcends God's creation.

This divine action also encompasses special providence and divine action.

Special Providence and Miraculous Acts of God

What Is a Miracle?

After the Enlightenment, it has been difficult for the modern person to affirm the possibility of the miraculous. As divine "interventions," they would be but violations of the laws of nature.

Obviously, the term "miracle" is linked with the "supernatural." That term (in distinction from "natural"), however, is to be used with great care. For

139. Pannenberg, *ST* 1:380.

140. Niels Henrik Gregersen, "Special Divine Action and the Quilt of Laws: Why the Distinction between Special and General Divine Action Cannot Be Maintained," in *SPDA*, 194.

early theology, the supernatural-natural distinction did not exist if it meant, as in modernity, the distinction between two realms, that of God and that of the sciences, respectively. All of reality was governed by God. What they called miracle was an event for which they did not know the explanation, but it was not contrary to nature.

The term "supernatural" did not establish its theological usage until medieval times, when it came to mean something "going beyond" (*super*) nature, "above the wonted order and course of nature, as to raise the dead,"[141] but even then, not something against nature. What makes miracle miraculous is not that it is against nature, but that "it surpasses the faculty of nature,"[142] and hence is God's work, hidden to human understanding.

Things changed dramatically in modernity. As soon as nature was considered to be running on its own powers, miracles came to be perceived as violations of nature's laws. God's miraculous interventions were not only not needed but soon became obsolete and even impossible to conceive. And if granted, they could easily become an asset to the God-of-the-gaps logic. The most serious challenge to miracles comes from contemporary science's claim for physical closure and determinism. So, what might be a constructive way for contemporary theology to go in this matter?

The Miraculous in a Theological Perspective

How credible is the charge that the miraculous is a violation of the laws of nature? Two responses help defeat it. First, happily, that claim is tied to the now-outdated, mistaken view of strict determinism that quantum theory has dispelled; it has lost its power. Second, and most importantly, against those who reject special divine action, Keith Ward rightly wonders that while believing that "God, a supernatural being, has caused, and continues to cause, the whole universe to exist . . . how plausible it is, then, to say that such a God will refuse to operate in the world in particular ways."[143]

Theologically speaking, Christ's resurrection as the most profound divine action known to us reveals the ultimate meaning of the miracle. Rather than going against nature, it transcends and lifts up the natural. It points to

141. Aquinas, *ST* 3a.13.2.

142. Aquinas, *ST* 1.105.7.

143. Keith Ward, "Personhood, Spirit, and the Supernatural," in *All That Is: A Naturalistic Faith for the Twenty-First Century*, by Arthur Peacocke, ed. Philip Clayton (Minneapolis: Fortress, 2007), 155.

the eschatological consummation when, according to the biblical promises, creation "will be set free from its bondage to decay" (Rom. 8:21). In resurrection, even death will be defeated (1 Cor. 15:55).

Part of the doctrine of creation and providence has to do with nature's suffering and potential for flourishing.

The Suffering and Flourishing of Nature

For Orientation

Although the mystery of evil is likely to remain that—a *mystery*—any theistic faith, even those outside the Abrahamic traditions, has to account for the presence of evil in light of God's goodness. The problem is particularly pressing for Abrahamic faiths that insist on God's fairness, love, and goodness. Rampant suffering and acts of evil in the world, in relation both to humanity (moral evil) and to nature (natural evil), not only constitute a major atheistic challenge concerning the existence of God. Even more importantly, suffering poses the question of what kind of God there is, if there is one.

Traditionally, the topic of suffering and evil has been discussed under the rubric of theodicy (that is, how to justify the goodness and power of God vis-à-vis rampant evil and suffering in God's creation), and its focus has been almost exclusively on pain and suffering in human life. Nature's suffering has been ignored. This project seeks to correct this lacuna and focus here on the suffering in nature and nature's prospects for well-being. The next chapter on humanity will then pick up human flourishing, and the last chapter, on eschatology, will tackle the theodicy question.

In Search of an "Evolutionary Theodicy"

Nonhuman Suffering in Theological Tradition

What about animals' and nonhuman living organisms' suffering? While Christian tradition has not totally ignored nonhuman suffering, it has been routinely linked with what has happened to humanity. Briefly put: suffering and death in the world were introduced following the perfect paradise state as a result of the fall of the first human couple. That explanation, however, is not credible anymore scientifically, nor is it mandated biblically, as will be discussed in the next chapter. Also, in Christian tradition a main reason for overlooking animal pain is the nonrational and therefore subordinate and utilitarian view of animals,[144] a stance hardly in keeping with the whole of biblical theology. Hence, there is a need for theological reflection on suffering in nature apart from humanity (but not unrelated to it).

What about plants (and other nonsentient entities)? Do they feel pain? Science does not speak with one voice at the time of this writing. What we know is that plants seem to have some kind of biochemical injury mechanisms and, for example, may release hormones that could indicate a sensation.[145] Perhaps we should find another term, because "pain" entails a nervous system—or use the term strictly analogically.

Entropy and Suffering in Nature in a Theological Perspective

The wider framework for a theological consideration of suffering and pain in nature is the kind of world God has decided to create in which all created life is finite and necessarily subject to death and decay. To be born is to face death. The physicist Richard Carlson reminds us: "Starting with the products of the Big Bang, time, and the development of more and more complex entities, previously developed material in concert with the laws of the universe eventually resulted in the highest level of evolution. On Earth, given its finite size and resources and the need for millions of years to achieve this level, creaturely death is required as part of the process. In fact, it can be said that new life has always depended on the death of the now living."[146] In this light, the traditional idea of death being the direct result of human sin is untenable.

Entropy and suffering also seem to be instrumental to evolution and development. Or to put it another way: the emergence of complexity and intelligence requires a long process of wastefulness. This insight seems to apply to both the biological world and to physics.[147]

Among several "evolutionary theodicy" proposals concerning how to relate the goodness of God to the presence of entropy, evil, and suffering in

144. Dorothy Yamamoto, "Aquinas and Animals: Patrolling the Boundary?" chap. 7 in *AOA*; Scott Ickert, "Luther and Animals: Subject of Adam's Fall?" chap. 8 in *AOA*.

145. Frank Kühnemann, "When Plants Say 'Ouch,'" Deutsche Welle, February 5, 2002, http://www.dw.de/when-plants-say-ouch/a-510552.

146. Private e-mail communication, September 7, 2013.

147. William R. Stoeger, SJ, "Entropy, Emergence, and the Physical Roots of Natural Evil," in *PC*, 93.

nature, a promising one is called a "consequentialist natural theodicy" (CNT). It argues that natural evils are an unintended by-product or consequence of God's free choice to create the kind of world in which we live, an evolving world. Correctly understood, CNT contends that God had no choice but to permit physical and biological natural evil in our kind of world, having in his freedom and love decided to bring about the world.[148] This reasoning leaves a number of important questions without an answer. Perhaps the most pressing is this: granted that natural evil is necessary for this kind of world, one wonders if *this much* natural evil is necessary.

Be that as it may, only with the turn to eschatological consummation can any long-standing hope be gained. Indeed, although it seems like entropy, and its ultimate effect, death, is ruling in this cosmos, the biblical vision has in view the final cosmic redemption with the overcoming of the second law of thermodynamics (Rom. 8:21–22). Hence, eschatology is a proper place to engage the topic again.

Part of nature's suffering is due to human action.

The Pollution of Creation: Ecological Resources and Challenges among Religions

The Role of Sacred Traditions in Relation to Nature

The pollution of creation is a well-documented, major crisis threatening not only the well-being but even the *being* itself of our planet, so much so that "if current trends continue, we will not."[149] This raises the question of the role of religions in helping overcome the impending eco-catastrophe. Happily, unlike in the past, most religions nowadays make claims to being "green."

Although there is no denying religions' guilt for the environment's pollution—just think of some fundamentalist Christians' intentional neglect in hopes of an imminent eschatological consummation—the persistent criticism against a necessary link between natural disaster and religion[150] is untenable.

148. Nancey Murphy, "Science and the Problem of Evil: Suffering as a By-Product of a Finely Tuned Cosmos," in *PC*, 131–51.

149. Daniel Maguire, *The Moral Core of Judaism and Christianity: Reclaiming the Revolution* (Philadelphia: Fortress, 1993), 13.

150. Lynn White Jr., "The Historical Roots of Our Ecological Crisis," *Science*, n.s., 155, no. 3767 (March 10, 1967): 1203–7, http://www.drexel.edu/~/media/Files/greatworks/pdf_fall09/HistoricalRoots_of_EcologicalCrisis.ashx. For rebuttals, see Richard C. Foltz, "Islamic En-

A related misconception is that whereas Abrahamic faiths are detrimental to the environment, Asiatic faiths by nature are "green." Is that so?

On another front, critics routinely ignore the enormously devastating effects on nature by atheists, from the former Soviet Union to China and beyond. Religion seems not to explain much here.

How "Green" Is the Buddhist View of Nature?

In support of Buddhism's green attitude, a number of features are routinely mentioned, from its alleged nonanthropocentrism, to its focus on this-worldly ethical pursuit rather than centering on transcendental salvation, to Buddha's compassion toward all beings, to its nondualistic approach to the world (in contrast to Judeo-Christian dualism).[151]

On the contrary, reports from Buddhist experts are far more cautionary and in many cases negative altogether.[152]

Why this negative self-assessment? The most obvious reason has to do with the very "foundations" of Buddhism. Rather than the Christian vision of a new creation that encompasses the renewal of the whole of creation and all creatures, the Buddhist vision of seeking liberation from *dukkha* is deeply anthropocentric, individualistic, and oblivious to nonhuman beings. Unlike in Abrahamic traditions in which nature has intrinsic value as the handiwork of a personal Deity, in Buddhism and its cyclical view of time/history, nature is doomed to a repeated cycle of emergence and destruction *ad infinitum*. This hardly leaves much energy or vision for the protection of this vanishing world. All in all, these kinds of theological reasons that seem to obliterate or frustrate environmental pursuits and ethics among Buddhists are almost never mentioned in the popular promotional literature hailing "green" Buddhism.

---

vironmentalism: A Matter of Interpretation," in *I&E*, 249–79; Norman Lamm, "Ecology in Jewish Law and Theology," in Lamm, *Faith and Doubt: Studies in Traditional Jewish Thought* (New York: Ktav, 1972).

151. Martine Batchelor and Kerry Brown, eds., *Buddhism and Ecology* (London: Cassell, 1992).

152. Ruben L. F. Habito, "Environment or Earth Sangha: Buddhist Perspectives on Our Global Ecological Well-Being," *Contemporary Buddhism* 8, no. 2 (2007): 131–47.

Hinduism's Ecological Resources and Dilemmas

The significance of ecological attitudes among Hindus is immense in light of the huge environmental problems in India and surrounding areas.[153] There is no doubt that, as in Buddhism, the cyclical worldview of Hinduism potentially leans toward being oblivious to the conservation of the earth. Furthermore, Hinduism's concept of the appearance nature of reality or the cosmos as *līlā* ("play," that is, an unintended "by-product") similarly may cause the faithful to consider this earth a secondary, temporary dwelling place, on the way to the "real world."

A number of other critical questions await response before the issue of Hinduism's relation to ecological concerns can be even tentatively defined: Can the strongly ascetic[154] Hindu outlook (in pursuit of one's own deliverance) contribute to the communal and cosmic good? What is the role of karma, the bondage to the world because of deeds in the past and present, with regard to environmental care? What about the deeply *theologically* based and (originally) divinely sanctioned hierarchic nature of society (the caste system) when it comes to ecological concern?

On the other side, there are some beautiful, inspiring scriptural resources extolling the beauty of nature. Just consider the long "Hymn to Goddess Earth" in Atharva Veda.[155] Many other such beautiful nature hymns can be found particularly in Rig Veda (1.115; 7.99; 10.125; and so forth), somewhat similar to the nature psalms in the Hebrew Bible.

The Emergence of Ecological Awareness among the Jews

There are important resources to facilitate the flourishing of nature in Abrahamic faith: the task of vice-regency given by God both in Hebrew-Christian and Islamic scriptures (see the theological anthropology discussion below); the importance of history and time (because of a linear rather than cyclical worldview); the covenant spirituality of the Hebrews that binds human beings to God, other humans, and nature; and so forth.

153. Dwivedi, "Dharmic Ecology."

154. Christopher Chapple, "Asceticism and the Environment: Jainism, Buddhism, and Yoga," *Cross Currents* 57, no. 4 (2008): 514–25.

155. Atharva Veda, section 10: Cosmogonic and Theosophic Hymns, 12.1, *Hymns of the Atharva-Veda* together with extracts from the ritual books and the commentaries; *SBE* 42, n.p.

Similarly to others, the Jewish religion has acknowledged only recently the value of work for the environment.[156] Reasons are many and understandable: the survival of the small dispersed nation, particularly in the Holocaust world, including continuing threats from the surrounding nations, has not facilitated concern for the natural environment. Although secular Jewish eco-minded individuals have excelled in green activities beginning from the 1960s,[157] it was mainly among some Jews in the United States that the religiously driven pursuit started.[158]

It is not true that nature was absent from Jewish life in the past; just consider the many nature-related blessings and prayers in liturgy, many of them based on Old Testament texts.[159] The annual feast of Sukkot, also known as the Feast of Tabernacles, during which people live in small huts for a week commemorating not only the forty years of survival in the desert but also nature and agriculture, is a great nature event. It is called nowadays the "Jewish Environment Holiday." Jewish scriptural tradition also testifies to the faithfulness of the Creator for the sustenance and well-being of nature (Gen. 8:22, among others).

Similarly to the Muslim tradition, Jews are cautious not to make nature an idol. Related to this concern is the debate among some leading eco-theologians whether to consider the earth sacred or not. According to Hava Tirosh-Samuelson, the following three bases for care of nature are routinely mentioned: "protection of vegetation . . . ; awareness of the distress of animals; and predicating social justice on the well-being of the earth itself." They all belong to and derive from the covenantal theology foundational to all Jewish tradition.[160]

The Islamic View of Nature as "Sign" and Its Implications for the Environment

The US-based Muslim intellectual S. H. Nasr has harshly critiqued the technocratic use of nature in the modern West, and on the other hand, has high-

156. See Arthur Waskow, "Is the Earth a Jewish Issue?" *Tikkun* 7, no. 5 (1992): 35–37.

157. See Mark X. Jacobs, "Jewish Environmentalism: Past Accomplishments and Future Challenges," in *J&E*, 449–80.

158. For the Shomrei Adamah ("Keepers of the Earth") organization founded in 1988 by Rabbi Ellen Bernstein, see http://ellenbernstein.org/.

159. Neil Gillman, "Creation in the Bible and in the Liturgy," in *J&E*, 133–54.

160. Hava Tirosh-Samuelson, "Introduction: Judaism and the Natural World," in *J&E*, xxxviii.

lighted the spiritual and moral dimension of the ecological crisis.[161] This is fully in keeping with mainline Islamic tradition, which attributes even the environmental crisis ultimately to "the loss of a relationship between humans, the natural realm, and Allah."[162]

Islamic creation theology's foundational idea of creation as "sign" may have immense ecological impetus, as it links all creatures to the Divine. A related ancient Islamic resource is the concept of balance. Similarly to the heavens, which are sustained "by mathematical balance," human beings should be balanced, straight, and honest in relation to each other and to natural resources.[163]

What role and place does creation (nature) have vis-à-vis humanity? According to Muslim teachers, the resources of the creation, unlike in modern science, are not meant for consumption by humanity but rather ultimately are meant for God's service. This is of course not to deny the great benefits of natural resources to men and women but rather to put the matter in perspective.

Eco-Theological Resources in Christian Tradition

The standard criticisms against Judeo-Christian tradition's incapacity to deliver eco-friendly attitudes were responded to above. At the same time, many theologians believe that Christian theology should be able to hold in a dynamic tension an attitude of reverent admiration for the beauty of creation in its endless diversity and creativity, and a deepening concern for nature's vulnerability and suffering from the current global economic-industrial rape. This reverence does not have to make nature either divine or a "sacrament," even though there are sacramental elements in nature. The de-divinizing of nature affirms creation as *creation*, finite and vulnerable, as well as valuable because of its goodness.

What is very important for contemporary theology is to consider carefully the meaning of the mandate in Genesis 1:26–27 to act as God's faithful vice-regents. It does not justify abuse but rather is a call to responsible service on behalf of the good creation. Regretfully, the command to "subdue the earth"

161. Seyyed Hossein Nasr, *Man and Nature: The Spiritual Crisis in Modern Man*, rev. ed. (Chicago: Kazi Publishers, 1997 [1967]).

162. Saadia Khawar Khan Chishti, "*Fiṭra*: An Islamic Model for Humans and the Environment," in *I&E*, 69–71.

163. Comments in the Holy Qur'an, trans. Yusuf Ali, 5177–78, cited in İbrahim Özdemir, "Towards an Understanding of Environmental Ethics from a Qu'ranic Perspective," in *I&E*, 13.

was too often taken in its literal sense in Christian tradition. Although there is the minor alternative "green" tradition in Christianity that includes mystics and saints to whom nature had intrinsic value and human dominion represented stewardship and care for creatures, in the main, Christian tradition conceived of nature as having been made for humans and their benefit, and as a result, it was seen through a utilitarian lens.

The task of an ecological Christian theology is twofold: it has to clarify and help avoid ways of thinking and speaking of nature as creation that are detrimental to her survival and well-being, and it has to search for resources—theological insights, metaphors, approaches—that may help foster the flourishing and continuing shalom of God's creation. Particularly helpful in this enterprise has been highlighting the Spirit's work for continuous healing of creation, a topic to be picked up below in the chapter on pneumatology. Similarly, a careful negotiation of the dynamic between the value of creation in this era and the eschatological hope for final redemption and consummation (attempted in the last chapter) has the potential of yielding fruitful results.

4 | Humanity

Humanity in a Radically Changed Context

Theological Anthropology in Transition

Traditionally Christian theology has emphasized the difference of humanity from the rest of creation rather than its continuity with it. A radical change in contemporary theology has to do with the emphasis on continuity. Surprisingly, the first two creation narratives in the Old Testament point to a dynamic mutuality among creatures. The emergence of a sequence of forms—or "generations of the heavens and the earth when they were created" (Gen. 2:4a)—culminating in the creation of humanity, makes the creation an interrelated web, a network. This is not to undermine the uniqueness of humanity in relation to God but rather to remind us of our indebtedness to all that God has created.

Dramatic changes in the sciences and philosophy have caused enormous shifts: from a naive cosmology with our planet at the center of reality, astronomy and physics moved it out to the margins of a vast galaxy among billions of galaxies; evolutionary theory and biology definitively linked humans with the rest of creation; and neurosciences have revealed astonishing bases of human decisions, emotions, and will in brain functions. Particularly challenging has been the application of the evolutionary scheme to humanity. The explosive increase in knowledge about humanity in recent years, rather than making religious and theological reflection obsolete, on the contrary intensifies the need.

The goal and task of theological anthropology "is to set forth the Christian understanding of what it means to be human. Christian anthropology views the human person and humankind as a whole 'in relationship to God.'"[1] Traditionally and conveniently, it falls into two interrelated major parts, namely, humanity as the image of God, and the image of God in relation to (original) sin and the Fall.

Jewish faith's response to evolutionary theory with regard to humanity has been by and large comparable to that of Christianity. After initial opposition by some leading rabbis and traditional communities, particularly in the United States, mainline Jewish theology has come to see no conflict with the theistic interpretation of Darwinism. Among Abrahamic faiths, Islam continues to have the greatest difficulty in relating to evolution particularly in relation to humanity, as was chronicled in the previous chapter. Among the main Asiatic traditions, evolutionary theory has not caused much concern.

The Plan of the Chapter

The first section engages the evolvement of modern humans in the long line of hominids, focusing on how to define uniqueness and dignity in light of contemporary knowledge of the evolutionary process. That discussion will lead to the distinctively theological investigation of humanity under the classical rubric of the *imago Dei.*

Thereafter, the discussion engages major philosophical-theological proposals concerning the nature of human nature particularly with regard to current neuroscientific study and its interpretations of the nature of human nature. This discussion is intimately connected with the question of determinism and free will. In keeping with the interfaith orientation of this primer, the following section continues the comparative task with a focused look at how humanity and human nature are conceived in four living faiths.

The traditional topics of original sin and fall, the second part of theological anthropology, will be taken up thereafter. The last section will continue the discussion of the conditions of flourishing, with the focus on human flourishing.

1. Stanley J. Grenz, *The Social God and Relational Self: A Trinitarian Theology of the* Imago Dei (Louisville: Westminster John Knox, 2001), 23.

An Evolving Humanity: Uniqueness and Dignity in Scientific Perspective

The Evolvement of Human Uniqueness

The Long Hominid Lineage

The closest predecessors of modern *Homo sapiens* are the hominids.[2] The genetic evidence indicates that the oldest group of hominids goes back 5 to 7 million years in history. The australopithecines are routinely mentioned as the first known hominid species; their origin spans a period of 4–5 million to 1.5 million years ago. They all walked on two feet and showed evidence of an important growth of brain size.

The development of the hominids peaked about 2 million years ago. It may be significant that all hominid fossils older than 1 million years are limited to Africa. Bipedalism is routinely taken as the first defining mark of the hominid. The expansion of the brain beginning from *Homo habilis* 2 million years ago, followed by *Homo erectus*, and the use of tools and a dietary shift to include meat are other definitive early developments.

About a million years ago, out of several species of hominids, only *Homo erectus* remained and started to expand to Europe and parts of Asia. About a half-million years ago, an even more developed form of *Homo erectus* appeared, called "archaic *sapiens*." While definitely not yet *Homo sapiens*, this species is a bridge to the *sapiens*. It is debated whether this evolvement of the hominid that led to the rise of *Homo sapiens* was gradual or punctual.[3]

Although the species originated in Africa (according to the mainstream scholarly opinion), the final decisive stage of development on the way to the emergence of the modern human being happened in (western) Europe. The history of modern humans is fairly short when compared to that of the hominid, and in that shift the presence of *Homo neanderthalensis* plays a role; that species is dated to the Middle Paleolithic era (400,000/200,000–45,000 years ago). Notwithstanding scholarly debates, it is agreed that they lacked artistic capacities and that their intellectual skills were far from those of modern humans. Despite their long existence, they made virtually no progress in the use of tools.

2. Matt Cartmill and Fred H. Smith, *The Human Lineage* (Hoboken, NJ: Wiley-Blackwell, 1989).

3. Roger Lewin, *The Origin of Modern Humans* (New York: Scientific American Library, 1993), 15–32.

According to a widely held scholarly interpretation, the most dramatic development, called the "creative explosion" or "cultural big bang," took place with the shift from the Middle to the Upper Paleolithic era 45,000–35,000 years ago: "it is during this time that human consciousness and intelligence emerged, and with it creative, artistic, and religious imagination."[4] Ian Tattersall and Jeffrey H. Schwartz, two leading paleoanthropologists, summarize it well: "*Homo sapiens* is not simply an extrapolation or improvement of what went before it . . . our species is an entirely unprecedented entity in the world, however mundanely we may have come by our unusual attributes."[5] This emerging scholarly consensus helps critique the earlier, linear view of development, on which, ironically, much of the theologically based critique of human evolution is often based.

Human Uniqueness in Scientific and Philosophical Understanding

The standard paleoanthropological definition of human uniqueness lists features such as development in tool production, increased technological changes, use of ornaments, significant changes in economic and social organization, and so forth. This is important but still wanting. Neuroscientists and psychologists wish to add to the list:

1. *Language*: the capacity to communicate complex, abstract ideas, rather than merely repeat
2. *A theory of mind*: an ability to consider the thoughts and feelings of another person
3. *Episodic memory*: a conscious historical memory of events, persons, times, and places
4. *Conscious top-down agency*: conscious mental control of behavior and influence
5. *Future orientation*: ability to run mental scenarios of the future implications of behaviors and events
6. *Emotional modulation*: a complex social and contextual cognition that serves to guide ongoing behavior and decision making[6]

4. J. Wentzel Van Huyssteen, *Alone in the World? Human Uniqueness in Science and Theology* (Grand Rapids: Eerdmans, 2006), 64.

5. Ian Tattersall and Jeffrey H. Schwartz, *Extinct Humans* (New York: Westview, 2000), 9.

6. Warren S. Brown, "Cognitive Contributions to Soul," in *WHS*, 103–4.

Even this fairly sophisticated list requires amplification with features such as the capacity to discern beauty and other aesthetic experiences; the importance of feelings such as falling in love or deep disappointment; the gift of imagination that "travels faster" than the speed of light; and, say, the sense of humor.

As much as some rudimentary forms of "consciousness" may be found in some animals, these are a far cry from human consciousness and lack the human mind's capacity for self-transcendence, that is, humans knowing that they know! Similarly, as much as higher animals may be able to "learn" to use—or imitate—words taught by humans, that skill has little to do with human symbolic behavior, including syntax and semantics.

Human Genetics and Culture in Relation to Uniqueness

Since the discovery in the 1950s of the structure of DNA[7] and subsequent discoveries, genetics has become a massive enterprise in our society. Even in popular knowledge, phenomena such as the mitochondrial DNA (mtDNA) are quite well known. Transmitted only by the mother, mtDNA tells us that the human race shares a common origin in terms of maternal origins, although not a single human person. (In contemporary estimation, it takes at minimum a group of about ten thousand people to give rise to a lasting population.) Astonishingly, the variation in the mtDNA among humans is almost zero, while among other mammals it may be significant—and that despite the much wider geographical diversity of humans.

But what about the genetic commonality of humankind—the fact that 98–99 percent of our genetic heritage is shared with chimpanzees? Does it demonstrate that humans are only more advanced mammals? No, genetic similarity in itself explains only so much. Consider this: humans and dandelions share about 25 percent of their DNA, and humans and daffodils no less than 33 percent.[8] Hence, the genetic similarity between humans and chimpanzees is not what matters, but rather, "just how strange we are compared to all other living species on this earth."[9]

7. Of course, DNA itself was known much earlier, beginning from the end of the nineteenth century.

8. Jonathan Marks, *What It Means to Be 98% Chimpanzee: Apes, People, and Their Genes* (Berkeley: University of California Press, 2002), 29–31.

9. Brendan Purcell, *From Big Bang to Big Mystery: Human Origins in the Light of Creation and Evolution* (Hyde Park, NY: New City Press, 2012), 191.

At the threshold of the appearance of modern human beings (about 50,000–75,000 years ago), anatomy and behavior, so to speak, parted ways. Whereas until then they progressed in tandem, thereafter behavioral and cultural change began to accelerate in a dramatic way.[10] The all-important role of culture to human evolvement is too often dismissed in neo-Darwinism (and sociobiology), which emphasizes nature's determinism at the expanse of novelty such as self-consciousness.[11]

Because human behavior is guided by rationality, not merely by instincts and drives (as is the case with infants), its evolution is not determined by genes or even the environment. It is a complex and complicated process of dynamic factors. Cultural activities and capacities, including learning, reflection, emotional attentiveness, and many others, significantly shape us. The genetic and cultural information comes together in an absolutely unique way in *Homo sapiens.* "Since the genetic and cultural have coevolved and coadapted together, they are one reality, not two."[12]

The Evolvement of Mental and Cultural Capacities

Linguistic and symbolic capacities[13] are essential elements of our cultural adaptation. While all higher animals communicate in some way or another, only humans use language. This is made possible by the extraordinary development of human brain capacity and aided greatly by the specifics of the vocal tract. Not only the size of the brain matters (although its significance in human, including hominid, evolution should be duly noted), but also specifics about the brain. At a weight of only three to four pounds in adults (with a man's brain slightly heavier), the brain contains 10 billion neurons communicating with each other through synapses that number about 10^{12}.[14] What is amazing

10. Richard Milner and Ian Tattersall, "Faces of the Human Past: Science and Art Combine to Create a New Portrait Gallery of Our Hominid Heritage," *Natural History*, February 2007, n.p., http://www.naturalhistorymag.com/htmlsite/master.html?http://www.naturalhistorymag.com/htmlsite/0207/0207_feature.html.

11. Simon Conway Morris, *The Crucible of Creation: The Burgess Shale and the Rise of Animals* (New York: Oxford University Press, 1998).

12. Philip Hefner, "Biocultural Evolution: A Clue to the Meaning of Nature," in *EMB*, 330.

13. See Terrence Deacon, "The Symbolic Threshold," in *The Symbolic Species: The Co-Evolution of Language and the Brain* (New York: Norton, 1997), 79–92.

14. Sean A. Spence, *The Actor's Brain: Exploring the Cognitive Neuroscience of Free Will* (Oxford: Oxford University Press, 2009), 17; this section is indebted to that book.

about brains is simply that although obviously physical (material), they give rise (or at least are necessary) to mental acts!

The crossing over the symbolic threshold is, roughly speaking, dated around 75,000 years ago. The capacity for language requires also proper development of the vocal tract. In humans those capacities are without parallel when compared even to the highest animals. We are truly "the symbolic species."[15] The move from proto-language to human language is so tremendous that many biolinguists and cognitive archaeologists relate it to the "human revolution."[16] Human language makes possible the openness of humanity to the future and progress beyond physical (and other) limitations. Openness may also help explain the unbelievable drive for continuing innovation, improvement, and inventions in human culture—a feature unknown even among the hominids, let alone other animals. No wonder the difference between humans and other species is "not just a difference of degree. It is a difference in kind."[17]

Enter biblical-theological resources into the conversation.

Humanity as the Image of God: A Theological Account

The Image of God as a Dynamic Goal

Christian theology's most significant anthropological concept, *imago Dei*, claims to provide a foundational account of the human person and humanity in relation to the Creator, other creatures, and the cosmos as a whole. Notwithstanding the scarcity of direct references to the concept in the biblical canon—after three occurrences in the beginning (Gen. 1:26–27; 5:1; 9:6), the concept disappears until it is picked up in a couple of New Testament passages (1 Cor. 11:7; James 3:9)—from early on theological tradition made it an umbrella term. That said, there is no one fixed meaning of *imago Dei*. The main reason for the diversity of interpretations is that the biblical materials themselves do not explicitly elaborate on its meaning.

15. Deacon, "Symbolic Threshold."

16. See Derek Bickerton, "Did Syntax Trigger the Human Revolution?" in *Rethinking the Human Revolution: New Behavioural and Biological Perspectives on the Origin and Dispersal of Modern Humans*, ed. Paul Mellars et al. (Cambridge: Short Run Press, 2007), 99–105.

17. Ian Tattersall, *The World from Beginnings to 4000 BCE* (New York: Oxford University Press, 2008), 101.

Whereas in early theology the "structural" view—the idea that there is something within the structure of human beings that makes us the image of God, whether reason or will or something similar—was in the foreground, by the time of the Reformation, the "relational" view came to be preferred. In relational interpretations, what is crucial about the image of God is humanity's placement in reference to God (and derivatively, other human beings). Without necessarily leaving behind either one of these approaches, in modernity, influenced also by the emerging evolutionary theory, the "dynamic" view came to dominate. In that outlook, human beings are considered to be on the way, so to speak, to their final destination. The image of God is the divinely set destiny as much as a present reality.[18]

Among the patristic interpreters, reason came to dominate the structural view,[19] often coupled with will.[20] While these do not exhaust the biblical meaning of the term, undoubtedly reason and will are necessary for the establishment of freedom, including moral freedom. An important related implication of human freedom is the equality of all human beings, including both sexes. Indeed, freedom also relates to slaves and even lepers.

As important as these capacities are, contemporary theology reminds us that none of them alone, not even "soul," can be named as the meaning of the image. When the Bible refers to the image of God (Gen. 1:26–27), it refers to the whole human person. The image also includes the body, as the eschatological hope is directed toward the resurrection of the body.

The dynamic view has established itself in modern and contemporary thought without necessarily leaving behind older models. It is only in eschatological fulfillment that the fullness of the image of God can be achieved.[21] In other words, the image of God is a goal to be reached. The American Lutheran theologian Ted Peters fittingly calls this the "proleptic" framework, in which "the image of God in humans [is viewed] as the call forward, as the divine draw toward future reality. We are becoming."[22]

18. Grenz, *Social God*, particularly chap. 4.

19. Augustine, *Confessions* 13.32.

20. E.g., Justin Martyr, *First Apology* 28.

21. Grenz, *Social God*, 146.

22. Ted Peters, *God—the World's Future: Systematic Theology for a Postmodern Era* (Minneapolis: Fortress, 1992), 147.

A Trinitarian Theology of the Image of God

The Triune God and Humanity in Relation

Whatever else the image of God means, it means that humanity is referred to God, or as the New Testament specifies it, to Christ, the "original" and ultimate image of God (2 Cor. 3:18). If the Son is God's self-expression, that means that in some real sense humanity also expresses God and divine qualities.

Understanding the *imago* as based in our relatedness to God is the only way to ensure that all human beings, regardless of their capacities—whether rational, emotional, relational, or other—exist in the state of the image of God. Otherwise, for example, the intellectually disabled could not be. Even when it comes to relationality, the basis has to be God relating to the human being, rather than the measure of the human person's capacity to relate. Namely, there are people who do not have the capacity to reciprocate relationality.

Having been placed before God means that the ultimate goal of humanity is to seek and honor God as the Creator and live in communion with other people God has created in his image as well. Indeed, an essential feature of the Jewish-Christian understanding of the image is its universal nature: not only each human person but also humanity as a whole exists in the image of God. If the human destiny is referred to the Creator, that means it cannot be achieved alone.

Honor and dignity are granted to all men and women, as one of the meanings of the "image" in ancient cultures is linked to the king. In the Bible, however, this royal implication is not limited to the king alone but is extended to all of humanity, and in that way may also fund the idea of democratization. The royal language, so to speak, is here applied to common folks as well. Universality is also further consolidated by the conviction that however one negotiates the relation of the *imago* to sin, there is wide agreement that likeness-to-God was not lost as a result of the Fall; the most sin can do here is to blur and weaken the meaning of the status of humanity as the image of God.

An important implication of the relatedness to the Creator is the mandate and responsibility to serve as God's vice-regents. The God-given task to name the creatures points to this role (Gen. 2:19–20). In the ancient world—as in some cultures in our day—naming means exercising power and authority. In evolutionary history, the development of language is of course needed for naming.

What about nonhuman creatures in relation to the image of God? As appealing as the suggestion that all creatures are equally in the image might be, theologically it is not valid. Only humanity is directly addressed and placed in a unique position of vice-regency and responsibility by the Creator. Related to uniqueness, the human being comes into existence by a special divine resolve rather than a general creative word, as does the rest of creation.

The Dignity of Human Life

Christian tradition routinely used to locate the uniqueness and dignity of human life in the immortal soul. While understandable, that move is hardly supported by the biblical data; what is, however, affirmed in the biblical teaching is the link between the image of God and the inviolability of human life (Gen. 9:6). In keeping with the discussion above, the locus of the dignity is the whole human being (and humanity at large) set in relation to God.

While not uniquely a biblical or Christian idea,[23] only the status of the image of God and "destiny of fellowship with God [confer] inviolability on human life in the person of each individual."[24] From this Pannenberg draws an important conclusion: "A feature of the dignity that accrues to us by virtue of our being destined for fellowship with God is that no actual humiliation that might befall us can extinguish it."[25] Not surprisingly, by the time of the Enlightenment, some leading thinkers sought to establish human dignity apart from God. Among the atheists, the project of severing it from God came to its zenith. Contemporary "scientific" atheists such as Richard Dawkins have made this a major project.

But what does the concept "dignity" exactly mean in this context? "Each and every human being has been set apart for designation as a being of elevated status and dignity. Each human being must therefore be viewed with reverence and treated with due respect and care, with special attention to preventing any desecration or violation of a human being."[26] The reference to the Creator does not of course mean that only those who acknowledge the Creator can be granted full dignity. The universal nature of humanity as the image of God relates the dignity to all. This is also the theological basis for the equality of all.

23. See the *Charter of the United Nations* (June 26, 1945), preamble, http://www.un.org/en/sections/un-charter/introductory-note/index.html.

24. Pannenberg, *ST* 2:176.

25. Pannenberg, *ST* 2:177.

26. David P. Gushee, *The Sacredness of Human Life: Why an Ancient Biblical Vision Is Key to the World's Future* (Grand Rapids: Eerdmans, 2013), 16–36, here 24, emphasis removed.

Although the conviction that humans represent the most highly developed creatures and have a unique dignity has been used in Christian tradition to dissociate humans from the rest of creation, that claim does not necessarily have to imply separation. It can be reasoned, rather, that exactly as the most highly developed creatures, men and women have the biggest responsibility to be mindful of their deep links with the rest of the life of the cosmos and the well-being of the planet in which they find their dwelling place.

Having now established the meaning of the image of God, including dignity, in a Trinitarian theological perspective, we discuss what behavioral and natural sciences are saying of humanity.

Sociality, Emotions, and Embodiment: A Holistic Account of Humanity

A Communal and Relational Account of Personhood

Both biblical scholars and neuroscientists are telling theologians that critical values shaping human personhood include sociality, embodiment, and emotionality, along with rationality, of course. These values go back to the fundamentals of a biblical view of humanity and the implications of a Trinitarian, relational theology of the human being as the image of God.

In theological anthropology, commensurately, we view the human being as a relational being, in relation to God, to fellow human beings and creation, as well as to oneself. Rather than being isolated, personhood is relational, communal, networked. Relationality and communion theology are the way to defeat modernist individualism. Herein theology also has much to learn from scholars in the Global South. For example, in African settings, authentic humanity is defined in terms not of individuality but rather of commonality and belonging.[27]

Indeed, sociality and relationality are deeply embedded in human development and its evolutionary history. Mental life is shaped and formed by social context, including socialization and language.[28] Particularly important in this regard is the uniquely human capacity to discern other people as persons with their own subjectivity as well as intentions and activities (facilitated by "mirror

27. Joe M. Kapolyo, *The Human Condition: Christian Perspectives through African Eyes* (Downers Grove, IL: InterVarsity Press, 2005), 39.

28. Leslie A. Brothers, *Friday's Footprints: How Society Shapes the Human Mind* (New York: Oxford University Press, 1997).

neurons"); this makes it possible to impute mental states to others and predict their behavior (the "theory of mind").

Alongside sociality, embodiment is an essential value in a contemporary scientific account of the human person. How would Christian and other faith traditions relate to that claim?

Embodied and Emotional Human Personhood

The attitude toward the body among religions is confused and complex.[29] The Jewish appreciation of the body is distinctive among religions due to the this-worldly focus on salvation and eschatology. That said, it is not correct to say that whereas Judaism is interested in the body, Christianity is interested in the soul; the doctrine of the resurrection of the body (let alone the incarnation) makes that merely a generalization.

The Islamic scriptures share the idea of human beings created out of dust and returning to dust, and that the dead will be resurrected on the judgment day. Somewhat like (Orthodox) Judaism but unlike Christianity, Islam does not distinguish between the religious and the secular; hence, the body is always looked at from a religious perspective, as is everything else. The Islamic law then regulates in much detail the right and wrong use of the body.

In various Hindu scriptures, as can be expected from such a wide array of traditions, many diverse attitudes to the body can be discerned: from honoring and embrace to contempt and shame. The highly influential *Laws of Manu* exhibit a diversity of attitudes toward the body, from contempt for its uncleanliness and uneasiness with its nature, including harsh misogyny (6.76–77), to acknowledgment of its "natural" nature and value (with regard to conception and birth, 9.31–42), to affirmation of the body of both men and women (10.70–72).[30] In the midst of such diversity of views, it is fair to say that fundamentally the Hindu tradition can hardly be taken as body-affirmative.

In keeping with Hinduism, Buddhism in the main not only is dualistic in a general sense (body-soul) but also believes the body will come to an end at death. Like other ascetic teachings, Theravada Buddhism's canonical texts that deal with monastic life and spiritual exercises not only reject all bodily sexuality but also depreciate it. Mahayana traditions' appraisal of the body is more

29. Sarah Coakley, "Introduction: Religion and the Body," in *RB*, 1–12.

30. *The Laws of Manu*, trans. George Buhler, *SBE* 25, http://www.sacred-texts.com/hin/manu.htm; Wendy Doniger, "The Body in Hindu Texts," in *RB*, 169–73.

complex and would require a study beyond this primer. Suffice it to say that in all the main Buddhist traditions, clinging to the body is a hindrance to enlightenment and should be renounced; the body is impermanent, disposable, while the soul is "eternal," or at least qualitatively radically different from the body.

The Christian philosopher-theologian P. Clayton reminds us of the necessity of a holistic, multidimensional account of human personhood of embodiment: "We have thoughts, wishes, and desires that together constitute our character. We express these mental states through our bodies, which are simultaneously our organs of perception and our means of affecting other things and persons in the world. . . . [The massive literature on theories of personhood] clearly points to the indispensability of embodiedness as the precondition for perception and action, moral agency, community, and freedom—all aspects that philosophers take as indispensable to human personhood and that theologians have viewed as part of the *imago dei.*"[31]

Indeed, a number of key Christian convictions fund embodiment, including the pronouncement of all creation "good" in the creation story, the incarnation, the resurrection of the body, and the belief that, according to the "sacramental principle," God's presence and grace are conveyed in "flesh," as is evident particularly in the Eucharist. Rather than flight from the body, a Christian view of creation funds intimacy, closeness, and mutuality. Moltmann aptly summarizes the reason for the importance of embodiment: "*God as Creator is no closer to spirit than God is to physical matter.*"[32]

To the bodily life belong cognition, emotions, passions, and desires. One of the most far-reaching discoveries of the famed neuroscientist Antonio Damasio is that of the embodied nature of both emotions and cognition.[33] What has recently been named "Descartes's error" was his failure to highlight the role of emotions at the expense of reason (ironically, in that his last book was titled *The Passions of the Soul*, 1649!) and making emotion the servant of reason. For Descartes, reason and emotion operated in different provinces of the brain, and the former took the lead. In light of current neuroscientific research, the opposite is the case.

Recently we have also discovered that emotional (and moral) states such as empathy, shame, trust, regret, and detecting the emotional states of others

31. Philip C. Clayton, "The Case for Christian Panentheism," *Dialog* 37, no. 3 (Summer 1988): 205.

32. David H. Kelsey, *Eccentric Existence: A Theological Anthropology*, 2 vols. (Louisville: Westminster John Knox, 2009), 1:56.

33. Antonio R. Damasio, *Descartes' Error: Emotion, Reason, and the Human Brain* (New York: Grosset/Putnam, 1994).

not only are tightly linked with certain neural activities but are also embodied and socially shaped. Finally, not only are emotions and intelligence tightly linked with each other, also linked with them is embodiment, as illustrated in the subtitle of a widely acclaimed book by Damasio: *Body and Emotion in the Making of Consciousness* (1999). Indeed, add to the equation sociality, and we can envision the human being in her wholeness and complexity.

Consider also the critical implications of embodiment to a holistic account of gendered human existence: "Because we are embodied, we are gendered, sexual beings,"[34] a topic worthy of closer theological reflection.

"Male and Female He Created Them"

Not only embodiment but also the male-female relationship has been a problem among most religious traditions. For example, Islam's depreciation of women, coupled with deep body-soul dualism, is well known.[35] Similar examples can of course be found in other faith traditions—and secular ideologies.

What is unique about the (second) biblical creation narrative is the account of the creation of the woman, not only of humanity in general or of man, as in other creation myths of the time. The theological implication is that sexual distinction belongs to the essential and formative nature of human creation. Sexuality, then, is deeply social in nature.[36] Sexuality is also integrally linked with embodiment: only embodied beings can be either sex. It is generally agreed that the designation of woman as "helper" (Gen. 2:18) is not a way of making the female subordinate or the servant of man; the use of the Hebrew term (*'ezer*) in the biblical narrative does not warrant that.

Christian theology has traveled a long road to establish the full equality of women and men. The denigrating sayings about women by leading theologians from Augustine to Aquinas all the way to modernity are well known.[37] Regretfully, the same applies not only to other Abrahamic faith traditions but also to other religions.[38] What is highly curious is that even

34. James K. A. Smith, *Introducing Radical Orthodoxy: Mapping a Post-secular Theology* (Grand Rapids: Baker Academic, 2004), 77.

35. Q 2:223, 228. The allowance of polygamy, notwithstanding rules concerning fair treatment of wives, also points to subordination (see Q 4:3).

36. Grenz, *Social God*, chap. 7.

37. Elizabeth Johnson, *She Who Is: The Mystery of God in Feminist Theological Discourse* (New York: Crossroad, 1993), 104–20 particularly.

38. Diana Y. Paul, *Women in Buddhism: Images of the Feminine in the Mahāynana*

the Enlightenment philosophy did not have resources to rehabilitate the equality of women. Rather than equality, Kant advocated the idea of complementarity, assigning "soft" and modest features to women and the opposite to men.

What, then, is the theological significance of the sexual distinction? Genesis 1:26–27 is no more "gender-free" than it is complementarian. Although the theologian does not have to be "essentialist" about womanhood (or manhood), common sense says that maleness and femaleness are something "real."[39] Complementarianism's liability is that it makes one-half of humanity receiver, the other half giver. The radical middle position between essentialism and constructivism that appeals to many current theologians can be called "critical essentialism." *Critical* essentialism does not deny the commonsense intuition of real differences between male and female. Rather, it argues that "such differences—whatever they may be—will not be accepted as warrants for social systems which grant men in general authority and power over women in general."[40] In keeping with that is Moltmann's comment that the lasting theological meaning of having been created as male and female is that "to be human means being sexually differentiated *and* sharing a common humanity; both are equally primary."[41]

Before continuing the discussion of the nature of human nature, let us attempt another comparative exercise, this time focusing on the meaning of the image of God in two sister faith traditions.

The Image of God among Abrahamic Traditions

In all Abrahamic faiths the discussion of humanity is placed in relation to God and in the context of finite, moral life. Deeply embedded in the Jewish tradition is of course the belief shared with Christians of humanity having been created in the image of God. Jewish tradition, however, speaks with res-

---

Tradition, 2nd ed. (Berkeley: University of California Press, 1985); A. S. Altekar, *The Position of Women in Hindu Traditions: From Prehistoric Times to the Present Day*, 2nd ed. (Delhi: Motilal Banarsidass, 2005).

39. Serene Jones, *Feminist Theory and Christian Theology: Cartographies of Grace* (Minneapolis: Fortress, 2000), chap. 2.

40. Lisa Sowle Cahill, *Sex, Gender, and Christian Ethics* (Cambridge: Cambridge University Press, 1996), 1–2.

41. Jürgen Moltmann, *God in Creation: A New Theology of Creation and the Spirit of God*, trans. Margaret Kohl (Minneapolis: Fortress, 1993), 222.

ervations about the *tselem*, "image of God," in order to avoid speaking of God too anthropomorphically.[42]

Although in the Qur'an there is no direct statement about humanity being created in the image of God (as there is in the Hadith), the corresponding idea is there. The well-known passage of 30:30 comes close to it: "So set your purpose for religion, as a *hanīf*[43]—a nature given by God, upon which He originated mankind. There is no changing God's creation." Here the term *fitrah* (nature) is used, which clearly has resemblance to the image in Christian-Jewish vocabulary. Somewhat similarly to the biblical testimonies, the human being is made of clay in the Qur'an (Q 23:12–14). Not only that, but the one made of clay is also breathed into by the Spirit of God, and therefore even the angels prostrate themselves before him (15:26–30). In the Hadith, the idea of the image of God appears: "Allah, the Exalted and Glorious, created Adam in His own image."[44]

The technical term *fitrah*, used of human nature—"an inborn natural predisposition which cannot change, and which exists at birth in all human beings"[45]—has a number of interrelated meanings, including moral intuitions and religious instinct. According to a well-known Hadith statement, "Everyone is born according to his true nature and the command pertaining to the demise of the children of the infidels and of the children of the Muslims. There is none born but is created to his true nature (Islam). It is his parents who make him a Jew or a Christian or a Magian quite as beasts produce their young with their limbs perfect. Do you see anything deficient in them? . . . The nature made by Allah in which He has created men there is no altering of Allah's creation; that is the right religion."[46] On the basis of this teaching, in Muslim tradition *fitrah* is universal, not limited to Muslims alone, and is an immutable feature of humanity. Very closely resembling the Christian idea of the innate knowledge of God, it "is the faculty, which He has created in man-

42. See Jonathan Schofer, "The Image of God: A Study of an Ancient Sensibility," *Journal of the Society for Textual Reasoning* 4, no. 3 (May 2006), http://jtr.shanti.virginia.edu/volume-4-number-3/the-image-of-god-a-study-of-an-ancient-sensibility/.

43. The exact meaning of the term is somewhat unclear (hence left without English rendering here). A number of times it refers to "faith" (of Abraham) and also has the connotation of a nonpolytheistic faith. See Arthur Jeffery, *The Foreign Vocabulary of the Qur'ān* (Leiden: Brill, 2007), 112.

44. Sahih Muslim, 40, #6809.

45. Yasien Mohamed, *Fitrah: The Islamic Concept of Human Nature* (London: Ta-Ha, 1996), 13.

46. Sahih Muslim, 33, #6423 (the last sentence is a citation from Q 30:30); similarly Sahih Bukhari, 60, #298.

kind, of knowing Allah." As a result, belief in Allah (the confession of *tawhid*) is "natural" to human beings.[47] Therefore, Islam is at times called *din al-fitrah*, the religion of human nature, that is, religion that is in keeping with natural human instincts and inclinations (believed to be confirmed by Q 3:17)—a claim shared by Christian theologians regarding their own tradition.

All three Abrahamic traditions affirm the dignity of humanity in relation to God, the Creator. Just compare these two statements from Islamic and Judeo-Christian writings, respectively: "When any one of you fights with his brother, he should avoid his face for Allah created Adam in His own image."[48] "Whoever sheds the blood of man, by man shall his blood be shed; for God made man in his own image" (Gen. 9:6).

A common theme for all three traditions is the idea of humanity as God's viceroy on earth. This idea is deeply embedded in Jewish tradition based on the biblical teaching. In Islam, the idea of vice-regency is typically described in terms of caliph. According to Qur'an 2:30, when God announced to the angels, "Lo! I am about to place a viceroy [*khalīfah*] in the earth," they demurred and wondered if God knew the risks involved because of the frailty of human nature! In response the Lord taught them how to name the creatures, and that was a cause of marvel among the angelic beings. By extension, key figures such as Noah are appointed as a caliph as God's prophet and servant (10:71–73). A highly significant implication of the comprehensiveness of the vice-regency is the curious saying of 33:72: "Indeed We offered the Trust to the heavens and the earth and the mountains, but they refused to bear it and were apprehensive of it; but man undertook it." Importantly, the saying continues that the vice-regent is "wrongdoer and ignorant" and that God is on the lookout for those who act wrongly (v. 73).[49]

Taking careful notice of this wide consensus among the three Abrahamic faiths concerning the uniqueness of humanity because of the relation to God, we will register in the following other key themes concerning humanity and also engage the other two Asiatic faiths. Before that, the next section will take up the complex question of the nature of human nature, building on the evo-

47. Mohamed, *Fitrah*, 16. See also *Ibn Taymiyyah Expounds on Islam: Selected Writings of Shaykh al-Islam Taqi ad-Din Ibn Taymiyyah on Islamic Faith, Life, and Society*, compiled and translated by Muhammad 'Abdul-Haqq Ansari (Virginia: Institute of Islamic and Arabic Sciences in America, 2007), 3–4, http://ahlehadith.files.wordpress.com/2010/07/expounds-on-islam.pdf.

48. Sahih Muslim, 32, #6325.

49. For details, see Kenneth Cragg, *The Privilege of Man: A Theme in Judaism, Islam, and Christianity* (London: Athlone Press, 1968), chap. 2.

lutionary and theological results reached so far and engaging in some detail the results and approaches of neuroscience.

The Nature of Human Nature

The Confused State of Thinking about Human Nature

Despite deep differences in visions of human nature, virtually all religions agree that humanity is more than merely material; they affirm a spiritual (philosophically: idealist) view. At one end of religions, there is the view that only the spiritual dimension of humanity matters, not the bodily dimension, nor individuality in any sense (*advaita* Vedanta of Sankara). Thus, the whole point of the spiritual quest is to overcome the illusion of dualism. While the other major Vedanta school allows for some form of duality (the qualified nonduality of Ramanuja), the basic view of humanity is not much different. While radically different in many ways, the main schools of Buddhism, with their denial of the persistence of "self," envision "salvation" in terms of transcending embodiment and thus also individuality. Despite internal differences, all three Abrahamic faiths envision human nature as embodied soul or spirited body. They also make human existence finite and thus not immortal. Particularly in Jewish-Christian traditions, embodiment/materiality is an essential part of human nature, either because of a "this-worldly" eschatology (Judaism) or because of life in the resurrected body in the new creation (Christianity).

In contrast to religious views, among scientists who study human nature and among nonreligious philosophers, by far the most common notion of human nature is physicalist (materialist) monism. Apart from a minority of scientists as well as (conservative) theologians and philosophers, in academia monistic (physicalist) explanations rule (notwithstanding the many internal debates regarding details). While in Christian and some other religious traditions the focus of human uniqueness used to be the soul, in contemporary science and culture it is the brain! Historically and globally speaking, however, this state of affairs is astonishingly strange: most common people, regardless of religious, geographical, and racial features, have intuitively stuck with some sort of dualist way of thinking of human nature.[50] Not surprisingly, both his-

50. Jesse M. Bering, "The Folk Psychology of Souls," *Behavioral and Brain Sciences* 29 (2006): 453–98.

torical and current Christianity throughout the global church take dualism as the received tradition.

Unlike in the past when all Christian theologies were dualist, affirming the body-soul dualism as a default position, contemporary theology faces more than one option. In light of the current scientific knowledge, theology has come to a new appreciation of the fact that even mental capacities are tightly and integrally linked with the physical base. That is one reason why traditional dualism has become a minority position. Interestingly, Pannenberg surmises that this shift away from dualism is "in line with the intentions of the earliest Christian anthropology." While still making a clear distinction between body and soul, important early patristic thinkers defended the psychosomatic unity against Platonism's deep dualism. However, that attempt to hold on to the idea of body-soul unity soon gave way to dualism for the simple reason that, in keeping with the times, even those theologians who championed the psychosomatic unity did not thereby reject the idea of the soul as an independent entity.

Human Nature in Theological and Biblical Traditions

The Rise to Dominance of Dualisms

The roots of body-soul dualism can be traced back to Hellenistic philosophy (which in itself was not a unified tradition but rather a constellation of many traditions). Typically in that tradition, *soma* (body) denoted something alien. For Plato and others, death marked the separation of the soul from the body. Soul is eternal and remains, while the body is decaying and fleeting. Soul is the higher aspect of humanity while the body is lower. Platonism influenced significantly the earliest Christian anthropologies, although not uniformly and not without growing criticism.

Plato's pupil Aristotle's conception of the soul is markedly different from his teacher's. For him, the soul is the "form" (or actuality) of the body.[51] Rather than an entity, soul is more like a life principle, "that aspect of the person which provides the powers or attributes characteristic of the human being," but not only the human being but also all other living entities, such as animals and plants.[52]

51. Aristotle, *On the Soul* 2.1–3, trans. J. A. Smith, Internet Classics Archive, http://classics.mit.edu//Aristotle/soul.html.

52. Nancey Murphy, *Bodies and Souls, or Spirited Bodies?* (Cambridge: Cambridge University Press, 2006), 13.

Later Christian theology under the leadership of Thomas Aquinas adopted this "hylomorphic" view.

By the time of Augustine, the shift toward a more robust dualism along with the stronger hierarchic view of soul and body (the former higher than the latter) had taken the upper hand. It was natural to make soul the seat of the image of God. The key aspect of the soul is rationality (and will). Although Aquinas followed Augustine in locating likeness to God in rationality,[53] with the help of Aristotelianism, he also took important steps toward rediscovering key aspects of the original biblical unity of human nature. His baptizing of Aristotle's idea of the soul as the "form" of the body[54] became church dogma in the Catholic Church. Its basic intuition points away from dualism that makes soul and body separate substances.

The third major turning point in Christian—and secular—thinking on human nature had to do with the rise of modernity and modern science. The prime architect of the modern account of human nature is the modernist René Descartes, whose thought marks the zenith of body-soul dualism. At the same time, he also goes further into dualism by making body a "nonthinking thing," comparable to a machine.[55] The soul's main and only task is rational. Jumping to the twentieth century, we discern that Karl Barth, among others, came to affirm dualism.[56]

Dualisms under Theological Assessment

Contemporary theology has a twofold task. First, it is essential to discern and continue affirming the legitimate intuitions that lie behind the dominant dualisms of tradition. Second, their liabilities and failings should be affirmed and corrected in critical dialogue with sciences and other religions.

On the problematic side, dualisms (of various sorts) locate the image of God and human uniqueness in the soul rather than in the human person as a whole, a move not present in the Bible. Second, dualisms tend to elevate reason above other features of human nature. Third, dualisms suffer from the downplaying of the body, emotions, and passions. The critical question then

53. Aquinas, *ST* 1.93.4, 6.

54. Aquinas, *ST* 1.76.1.

55. René Descartes, *Meditations on the First Philosophy* [1641], sixth meditation, 17, in *The Method, Meditations, and Philosophy of Descartes*, trans. John Veitch (Washington, DC: M. Walter Dunne, 1901), http://oll.libertyfund.org/titles/1698.

56. Barth, *CD* III/2, 325.

is, "If the body does not belong to the *imago Dei*, how can the body become 'a temple of the Holy Spirit'?"[57] Finally, dualisms seem to run against much of current neuroscientific knowledge (on which more below).

The important intuitions behind dualisms of Christian tradition are well worth preserving and cultivating, namely, that there is "more" to human life and dignity than just the material;[58] that affirming morality and an ethical base calls for "more" than material explanation; and that there is hope for life eternal, and therefore, even at the moment of my personal death, I am not forgotten by God.

Contemporary theology must hold on to these intuitions when revising anthropological conceptions. Two important tasks are being tackled to meet this need: a reconsideration of the biblical teaching on human nature and a careful theological assessment of the ways human nature is understood in current sciences and philosophy (of mind). Let us first look at the biblical materials and thereafter at scientific and philosophical perspectives.

Biblical Insights into Human Nature

Not surprisingly, until the beginning of the twentieth century, theology took it for granted that dualism of body and soul is the canonical opinion based on the Scripture. This consensus began to be challenged and later overturned by twentieth-century critical scholarship. Particularly significant was the recovery of the holistic, unified, and nonanalytic view of humanity in the Hebrew Bible. A further shift was the rediscovery of the importance of the physical to the biblical account of human nature. It was also found out that what is called "soul" in the Old Testament (*nephesh*) rather means "life" or "living [being]."[59] R. Bultmann's influential interpretation of *soma* as denoting the whole person in the New Testament also played a role here.[60]

What about the New Testament, which at least on its face seems rampantly dualistic? Indeed, it was a commonplace to claim that whereas the Old Testament is holistic, the New Testament is dualist. Against that, critical

57. Moltmann, *God in Creation*, 239.

58. See Keith Ward, *More Than Matter: Is Matter All We Really Are?* (Grand Rapids: Eerdmans, 2011).

59. "Soul," in *A Dictionary of the Bible*, ed. James Hastings (Edinburgh: T&T Clark, 1902).

60. Joel B. Green, *Body, Soul, and Human Life: The Nature of Humanity in the Bible*, Studies in Theological Interpretation (Grand Rapids: Baker Academic, 2008), 14–16, 54–61.

scholarship replied that there hardly is a uniform New Testament presentation of human nature, and that even if dualistic language is common, the New Testament may not intentionally teach dualism.[61] In sum: "A survey of the literature of theology and biblical studies throughout the twentieth century, then, shows a gradual displacement of a dualistic account of the person, with its correlative emphasis on the afterlife conceived in terms of the immortality of the soul. First there was the recognition of the holistic character of biblical conceptions of the person, often while still presupposing temporarily separable 'parts.' Later there developed a holistic *but also physicalist* account of the person, combined with an emphasis on bodily resurrection."[62]

While the "liberal" theological traditions have by and large owned this shift, the "conservative" ones for the most part have resisted it and continued to stick with dualism.[63] Notwithstanding opposition by the traditionalists, there was no stopping the rise of the monistic interpretation with an emphasis on physicality.

Human Mind and Nature in Current Scientific and Philosophical Perspectives

How to Interpret the Integral Connection between Brain Events and the Mental

As recently as the late eighteenth century, no causal link between, say, the capacity of speaking and brain activity was discerned! Later, in the nineteenth century, it took dramatic events such as the oft-referred-to Phineas Gage instance to wake up society to the tight link between the brain and human behavior. In 1848, an explosion caused a tamping iron to pierce the skull, exiting from the top of the head, of this twenty-five-year-old New England railroad worker. This led to a serious change in his personality, making this once-stable person emotionally and socially bankrupt—yet without any visible effects at all! The obvious lesson from this poor rail worker's incident is simply that

61. Joel B. Green, "'Bodies—That Is, Human Lives': A Re-examination of Human Nature in the Bible," in *WHS*, 159–63.

62. Murphy, *Bodies and Souls*, 10.

63. An influential advocate of dualism is philosopher John W. Cooper, *Body, Soul, and Life Everlasting: Biblical Anthropology and the Monism-Dualism Debate*, 2nd ed. (Grand Rapids: Eerdmans, 2000).

brains and neurons have much to do with emotions, sociality, and thoughts.[64] There is no lack of more recent such reports.

Rapid developments in psychology and neurosciences have yielded an amazing array of information about the deep and wide connections between the brain and human behavior. It has been shown that certain brain systems are linked with particular mental and physical activities, such as language capacities, types of memory functions, and error detection and compensation. Highly interesting is blind sight. People blind due to brain damage can still detect objects without being able to "see" them. Not only are behavioral, cognitive, and emotional functioning and activities linked with the brain, there is also an integral connection between neuronal processes and decision making in ethical and moral domains. And even more: a tight link has been detected between religious activities such as prayer, meditation, speaking in tongues, and others, and neuronal processes.[65]

What are the implications for theology of this close linking of neural/brain events and human behavior/mind? A particularly important issue is whether the mental is not only a "real" property but can also exercise causal influence downward. The challenge simply is how the mental—our beliefs, desires, intentions, plans—can have real influence in a world that, according to the sciences, operates along the regularities of natural laws, including brain activities and processes. Theologians face mounting opposition from advocates of the "brain/mind identity theory" (that mental events are but neuronal events, and vice versa), those who hold to "psychosocial parallelism," in which physical events are caused by physical causes and mental events by mental causes, to "epiphenomenalism," in which mental life is nothing but a by-product of brain processes, and even to "eliminativism," which bluntly rejects that mental events are real in the first place. All these theories of the mind-body relationship not only challenge theologians but also—if shown to be true—fatally defeat anyone holding the commonsense (and necessary) intuition of the reality of mental life and its effects. In particular, the existence of consciousness poses an urgent question. This is the famous zombie question regarding a being without a consciousness (even if behaving like the rest of us).

Although neuroscientists are naturally drawn to the identity theory, a competing view particularly among philosophers known as "nonreductive physicalism/materialism" is gaining much attention. Nonreductive physical-

64. Damasio, *Descartes' Error*, chaps. 1; 2.

65. Patrick McNamara, *Where God and Science Meet: How Brain and Evolutionary Studies Alter Our Understanding of Religion*, 3 vols. (Westport, CT: Praeger, 2006).

ism, put simply, considers the mental an emergent novel property (or capacity or event) that "supervenes," that is, is dependent on the subvenient base, the physical, but that it cannot be reduced to its base. To give an example: even if human imagination emerges from (and supervenes on) the physical base (the brain), having emerged, it is "more" than that and nonreducible to its base.

What about "Nonreductive Physicalism"?

Identity theory and its siblings are based on "reductive physicalism" and believe that human behavior and choices have their causal base in the physical processes, a view known as "bottom-up" causation. Hence, higher-level capacities such as mental abilities are nothing but the sum of their lower-level physical processes. Nonreductive *physicalism* agrees with part of this agenda by claiming that all higher capacities have a physical base. But it vehemently disagrees with a reduction of the higher to its physical base. In other words, having emerged (from the physical base), mental capacities cannot be reduced back to their base: they have become something "more." Hence, some theologians and Christian philosophers are ardent defenders of nonreductive physicalism while strongly rejecting reductive physicalism. For them, even religiosity has an ultimately physical base but cannot be reduced to it.[66] Not surprisingly, most advocates refuse to use the term "soul" any longer for the simple reason that there is no use left for it.[67]

Nonreductive physicalism insists robustly on the possibility of free will. To do so, it needs to affirm not only bottom-up but also top-down causation and whole-part causation (that is, the "system" as a whole is more than its parts). It emphasizes the possibility of mental causation. Nonreductive physicalists also remind us that human behavior and mental life are shaped significantly by the context, including culture, human relationships, learning and training, and similar domains. Human behavior is intentional and purposeful and is able to assess the results and conditions.

With all its advancement, it is easy to see the basic philosophical dilemma of nonreductive physicalism particularly with its claim for *physicality* as the ultimate base and explanation: "say yes, and you seem to end up with

66. Nancey Murphy and Warren S. Brown, *Did My Neurons Make Me Do It? Philosophical and Neurobiological Perspectives on Moral Responsibility and Free Will* (Oxford: Oxford University Press, 2007).

67. Murphy, *Bodies and Souls*, ix.

a reductive physicalism; say no, and you aren't really a physicalist after all."[68] It also shares the underlying problem common to all physicalisms, namely, that of the higher mental capacities, consciousness. How can matter *mean* (if mental life has its basis in the brain, which obviously is materialist)? Notwithstanding a number of responses, few believe that consciousness—let alone self-consciousness—has been satisfactorily explained so far. In light of relativity and quantum theories, there is also a growing doubt as to what "materialism" ("physicalism") really means. The "matter" the current natural sciences speak about seems to be quite different from what we thought matter is!

Theological Accounts of Human Nature beyond Dualism

Theologians at large oppose reductive materialism—and with good reasons. So, what about those to whom even the nonreductive option is a nonstarter for reasons mentioned. Generally speaking, not many theologians have been willing to jump on to the physicalist bandwagon. The reasons for that resistance are obvious. It simply is not intuitive for a religionist to think of ontology merely in terms of a staunch physicalist claim. Behind that attitude is the deeper claim that even for nonreductive physicalists who are not atheists, physicalism is only the penultimate option. All theistic traditions consider the Ultimate to be spiritual; certainly that is the case for all Abrahamic faiths.

Even if a smaller and smaller number of contemporary theologians see promise in traditional dualistic accounts of the human being, a widely held view is an integral and holistic account of human nature as spirited body or embodied spirit—or something like that. Moltmann's vision of "a *perichoretic* relationship of mutual interpenetration and differentiated unity"[69] between body and soul and Pannenberg's "personal unity of body and soul"[70] speak the same language.

What about those to whom even that kind of chastised dualism may not go far enough, particularly in terms of accounting for what the neurosciences are revealing about the integral physical link between the mental and the physical? If they are not excited by the turn to physicalism (even in its nonreductive form), then another kind of monism is the way to go. In this perspec-

68. Philip C. Clayton, *Mind and Emergence: From Quantum to Consciousness* (Oxford: Oxford University Press, 2004), 130.

69. Moltmann, *God in Creation*, 259.

70. Main heading in Pannenberg, *ST* 2:181.

tive, important is the philosopher-theologian Philip Clayton's reminder that a promising proposal is a "monism" that is not physicalist in itself, although it takes physicality most seriously.[71]

What would be the benefits of replacing monistic physicalism with a revised notion without going back to dualism? It would allow for a more holistic and diversified ontology of things in creation characterized, or qualified, by the various modal aspects. Thereby it would not try to say the last word on a topic that in light of current scientific knowledge is still open-ended (and might remain so for a long time!). It would help theologians stick to the foundational metaphysical assumption of the primacy of the spirit(ual) while holding fast to the embodied nature of humanity and an integral link between the mental and the physical.

A new constructive proposal by the author is named "multidimensional monism,"[72] which doesn't take the physical as the ultimate but rather argues that some kind of ideal (spiritual) is primary, but in a complex and mutually dynamic way. This model agrees with Clayton, who rightly notes that if all mental phenomena are claimed to derive from the physical, it "then becomes extremely unclear (to put it gently) why, *from the perspective of one's own theory of the human person*, a God would have to be introduced at all (except perhaps as a useful fiction)."[73] Now, that does not of course mean that a Christian physicalist couldn't introduce God. But the point is that it is very difficult.

This proposal takes as a necessary and minimum premise that human beings are "psychosomatic unities rather than dual beings composed of a spiritual soul housed within a material body,"[74] what the New Testament scholar N. T. Wright calls "differentiated unity."[75] A multidimensional monism model borrows from and builds on Polkinghorne's "dual-aspect" monism that seeks to go beyond the classical options of materialism, idealism, and dualism in light of the current multilayered, complex, and dynamic understanding of reality, including human nature. Dual-aspect monism means to say that neither the mental nor

71. Clayton, *Mind and Emergence*, 4.

72. Veli-Matti Kärkkäinen, *Creation and Humanity*, A Constructive Christian Theology for the Pluralistic World, vol. 3 (Grand Rapids: Eerdmans, 2016), chap. 12.

73. Philip C. Clayton, "Neuroscience, the Person, and God: An Emergentist Account," in *NP*, 204.

74. John Polkinghorne, "Anthropology in an Evolutionary Context," in *God and Human Dignity*, ed. R. K. Soulen and L. Woodhead (Grand Rapids: Eerdmans, 2006), 93.

75. N. T. Wright, "Mind, Spirit, Soul and Body: All for One and One for All; Reflections on Paul's Anthropology in His Complex Contexts" (paper presented at Society of Christian Philosophers Eastern Meeting, March 18, 2011).

the physical is primary or, when left alone, determinative. In analogy with quantum theory's superposition principle—that an entity can be said to be in two different states at the same time—both presuppose and influence each other.[76]

What about continuing the use of the term "soul"? While nonreductive physicalists' refusal to use it is understandable, it seems warranted to keep the term in the Christian thesaurus. First, the theologian's task is to help the faithful grasp its redefinition, as they have for many other terms whose meanings have changed, such as "creation." Second, the term "soul" is so widely and frequently used in the biblical canon—and consequently, everywhere in Christian tradition—that its dismissal seems unfounded and counterproductive. Third, there is also the interfaith consideration: although different religious traditions may mean different things when using the term, the cancellation in Christian tradition would not only look awkward and confusing to others but would also seriously hinder dialogue.

Freedom and Determinism—Divine and Human

This section continues the theological discussion of human nature by focusing on freedom in two interrelated contexts: in relation to current rebuttals of freedom in neurosciences, and in relation to the long-standing theological investigation of freedom in relation to God's foreknowledge and omniscience. When it comes to the divine and human relationship, the "compatibilist" option allows determinism along with free will, whereas the "incompatibilist" view (which includes the subgroup "libertarians" and is sometimes synonymous with it) demands that the person should have been able to choose otherwise (hence, the view can also be called "counterfactual free will").

A (Theological) Defeat of Neuroscientific Determinism

The word is out there that neuroscience has resolved an issue so far only reflected on philosophically and theologically. Some enthusiastic popularizers go so far as to say that current science has made all talk about free will obsolete and wrong: "Free will is an illusion."[77]

76. John Polkinghorne, *Faith, Science, and Understanding* (New Haven: Yale University Press, 2000), 95–97 particularly.

77. Sam Harris, *Free Will* (New York: Free Press, 2012), 5, emphasis removed.

So, what exactly is neuroscience saying about volition, freedom, and free will? In the early 1980s, the neuroscientist Benjamin Libet with his colleagues conducted the now classic experiment using EEG (electroencephalography) to measure the brain's electrical activity to study the antecedents of voluntary action, that is, what happens in a brain just before one "chooses" to act voluntarily. Subjects were asked to flex spontaneously their finger or wrist at their choosing. The result was that some milliseconds before flexing, signals could be discerned in the vertex (midline of the skull).[78] This basic observation with repeated patterns and refinements led to this highly counterintuitive sequence: brain event > intention to act > action. In other words, it seems that it is not mind > free will but brain (the physical "mindless" base) that ultimately influences human behavior. The situation is, however, much more complicated, and this and similar study settings have been subjected to devastating critique (the details of which do not concern us here). Hence, its conclusions are hardly freedom defeating.

Contrary to Libet-type approaches, philosophers and theologians consider human action and choices in a wider network of influences and factors. Real "action" is part of a large network of factors, including language, social relationships, beliefs and convictions, as well as education and training, including the person's own shaping of one's life as a result of the pursuit of good. Human freedom also entails decision not to act if there are reasons to do so. In sum: rather than paying attention to fleeting, millisecond-long mental events, in real voluntary action we should speak of a mental *state* that consists of awareness, knowledge, reflection, emotions, imagination, and other mental events—by a fully embodied person, in the network of one's community/communities, life experiences, and so forth. Practicing human life is a lifelong project and is essentially just that, a *practice.* Human behavior, morality, and the good life are a matter of patient character formation, practicing of virtues, and formation of habits in constant interaction with other people and communities.

Let us now introduce God's omnipotence and omnipresence into the discussion of freedom.

78. B. Libet et al., "Time of Conscious Intention to Act in Relation to Onset of Cerebral Activity (Readiness-Potential)," *Brain* 106, no. 3 (1983): 623–42.

Divine Foreknowledge and Human Freedom

Traditional Approaches

The problem of the possibility and conditions of human freedom arises as soon as one sets forth the theological claim that all that happens is not only foreknown by God but also divinely determined. Classically Augustine's interlocutor Evodius wondered "how God can have foreknowledge of everything in the future, and yet we do not sin by necessity." Evodius is stuck between a rock and a hard place because "[it] would be an irreligious and completely insane attack on God's foreknowledge to say that something could happen otherwise than as God foreknew."[79]

In many ways the simplest and most commonsensical solution to our problem is what can be called the "simple foreknowledge view." Although it has some contemporary advocates, it is the Thomistic view assuming that because God is a simple being (that is, there is no "composition" such as that between essence and existence), God's "act of understanding must be His essence."[80] Since God's knowledge of everything is simple, there is no room for contingency (at least ultimately): God's knowledge never changes, and therefore, more or less divine determinism must be assumed. The Augustinian-Calvinistic view based on a very robust account of divine sovereignty and a thin account of human freedom materially represents this ancient tradition. Should one wish to speak of human freedom, compatibilism seems to be the only option. As to *how* compatibilism is possible, this view does not usually offer any sophisticated explanations.

One who sought to provide at least some kind of explanation of how the simple foreknowledge view might work is Boethius, with his "eternity solution": because God is timeless ("eternal" in this specific understanding), the question of who/what decided certain events in a particular human being's life does not arise; there is no interval between, say, t_1 and t_2 (t = moment of time). Apart from the difficulty with that concept of time (and eternity), as discussed in the previous chapter, there are other theological and logical reasons to reject the eternity view it espouses.

An innovative proposal trying to hold on to both divine sovereignty and human freedom came from the sixteenth-century Spanish Jesuit Luis de

79. Augustine, *On the Free Choice of Will* 3.2, trans. Thomas Williams (Indianapolis: Hackett, 1993).

80. Aquinas, *ST* 1.14.4.

Molina. He sought to reconcile two claims long thought to be incompatible, namely, that God is the all-knowing governor of the universe and that individual freedom can prevail only in a universe free of absolute determinism.[81] The Molinist concept of middle knowledge holds that God knows, though he has no control over, truths about how any individual would freely choose to act in any situation. Given such knowledge and then creating such a world, God can be truly providential while leaving his creatures genuinely free.[82] Molinism goes further than compatibilism (without leaving behind compatibilist intuitions), which merely holds together divine determinism and human freedom without explanation. Molinism seeks to explain *how* God knows the contingent future. Whereas "natural knowledge" is the knowledge of necessary truths (and all logical possibilities), and "free knowledge" encompasses the actual world as it is, "middle knowledge" is the knowledge of the "counterfactuals" of all feasible worlds, that is, what humans might do in any given context. It is best to understand the "moments" in God's knowledge as *logical* rather than temporal moments. The promise of the proposal is that it makes it possible to be "an incompatibilist about causal determinism and human freedom (in the relevant sense), but a compatibilist about God's omniscience (foreknowledge) and such freedom."[83]

Contemporary Theology on Freedom and Sovereignty

In contemporary theology, yet another way to negotiate the issue is proposed by "open theists" and their "free will" theory, which seeks to reconcile divine foreknowledge and human freedom by seriously redefining foreknowledge: while "omniscient," God can only know those future events that are possible to be known, but not those that are so much contingent on human choices (or nature's events) that it does not make sense to speak of their knowledge yet.[84]

81. William Lane Craig, *The Only Wise God* (Eugene, OR: Wipf & Stock, 1999).

82. See Kenneth Perszyk, "Introduction to Molinism," in *Molinism: The Contemporary Debate*, ed. Kenneth Perszyk (New York: Oxford University Press, 2011), 4–5. An accurate, nontechnical introduction to Molinism is William Lane Craig, "The Middle Knowledge View," in *Divine Foreknowledge, Four Views*, ed. James K. Beilby and Paul R. Eddy (Downers Grove, IL: InterVarsity Press, 2001), 119–43.

83. John Martin Fischer, "Putting Molinism in Its Place," in Perszyk, *Molinism*, 209 (not Fischer's own opinion).

84. William Hasker, *Providence, Evil, and the Openness of God* (New York: Routledge, 2004), among other publications.

The price paid, namely, compromising—or at least significantly redefining—divine omnipresence, causes concern to many theologians. It seems to many that foreknowledge is necessary for God's proper governance (providence) of the world, including foreseeing the future even though not necessarily after Augustinian-Calvinist determinism in which God's foreknowledge secures the future by knowing and *determining* his decrees. In that sense, Molinism is still an appealing option to many theologians. Its "twin pillars" are then a belief in the traditional notion of providence (the idea that everything that happens is "specifically" intended or else permitted by God) and libertarianism, the existence of freedom of the will. That said, not only open theism and other options but also Molinism has faced critique, particularly with regard to the concept of counterfactuals (the complicated philosophical questions that go beyond the level of this primer).

Recently, a proposal named the "Trinitarian-Pneumatological-Molinist" account of freedom has been proposed by the author.[85] According to this proposal, the Spirit's universal presence makes possible, permeates, sustains, and guides the life of creation to which a relative independence has been given by the grace of God. In this approach, the possibility of divine action is nothing external but rather an essential part of God's continuing presence in the world. If all creative life, including human life, is a function of and is being constantly energized, sustained, and "lured" by the ever-present Spirit, then also human freedom happens within the framework created by the Creator. In such a pneumatological context, the omniscience of the triune God is understood as the divine omnipresence in creation, and thus no event or process evades it. Rather than curtailing the freedom of creatures, the Creator freely grants it. Rather than fully determining the choices and life of humans, the omnipresent-omnipotent-omniscient triune Creator prepares and determines the creaturely environment for such conditions that make possible certain types of free choices but do not determine them, although they are known to God. Even if the human person does not freely choose the ideal option(s), the Creator's will is not thereby frustrated, or else only strict determinism follows. The triune God honors the choices of the creatures, although those choices never come close to frustrating the eternal divine economy of salvation ("salvation" most inclusively understood, encompassing all of creation, the cosmos).

What about other Abrahamic traditions? Whereas Judaism at large takes for granted an authentic human freedom, Islam's stance is more complicated. Although Islam by and large affirms human freedom, not surprisingly there

85. Kärkkäinen, *Creation and Humanity*, chap. 13.

are different schools of thought.[86] The oldest view tended to be predestinarian in orientation. They applied the cause-and-effect relation evident in creation to human actions as well and attributed both right and wrong to Allah. In many ways, this currently marginal Islamic view resonates with the stricter deterministic interpretations of Christian tradition. The "neutral" view came to the fore after the mid-eighth century (CE), and was supported by the libertarian criticism of the "classical" view. Rather than divine determinism, God's justice and fairness came to the forefront. This school interpreted the ambiguous Qur'anic passage, "And God brought you forth from the bellies of your mothers while you did not know anything" (16:78), to mean that the newly born infant is like a blank slate, devoid of either good or evil. Only in the course of growth does either inclination take over. The neutral hermeneutics thus put an emphasis on free will and its implications. This view, then, shifts toward what in later tradition became a highly influential Muslim interpretation, the "positive" view, which basically takes *fitrah* as a state of intrinsic goodness. For that mainline Islamic tradition, two foundational affirmations must be held in balance: belief in the sovereignty of God, and his power behind everything that happens in the world.

Humanity and Human Nature in Religions' Teachings

The Embodied Ensouled Human Being: The Jewish Vision

As counterintuitive as it may sound at first, during the early periods of Old Testament history "the Jews were materialists," that is, they hardly had a developed eschatology and, therefore, even the blessings of God were mainly regarded in terms of earthly goods.[87] A number of older Jewish traditions were influenced deeply by other Platonic traditions, as exemplified in Wisdom of Solomon, including the evil nature of the body (1:3) and the preexistence of the soul (provided it comes from God, 8:13). In Philo, the most famous Hellenistic Jew, the Platonic influence came to its zenith.

Later in tradition, the eleventh-century Spaniard Solomon Ibn Gabirol (a.k.a. Avicebron) creatively engaged the Hellenistic (and also to some extent Islamic) tradition and contributed significantly to issues of self, soul, and per-

86. For a detailed discussion, see Mohamed, *Fitrah*, chap. 2.

87. Raymond Martin and John Barresi, *The Rise and Fall of Soul and Self: An Intellectual History of Personal Identity* (New York: Columbia University Press, 2006), 42.

sonal identity. His *Fountain of Life*[88] suggests a novel form of "materialism" in which, except for God, all substances, whether spiritual or physical, are composed of matter and form. The human soul (like that of the angels) is a kind of "spiritual matter." Avicebron's hylomorphism, thus, is a creative combination of Aristotelianism and Platonism; as in Plato, the soul acts something like the captain of the ship.[89]

The leading medieval Jewish philosopher, Moses Maimonides, set the tradition firmly in the Aristotelian camp and influenced greatly Christian scholarship. On the one hand, Maimonides built on the Hebrew Scriptures' emphasis on the integral relationship between body and soul, and on the other hand, he continued the religious/philosophical tradition of allowing some kind of independence to the soul, particularly after death.[90] Postmedieval rabbinic theology in particular came to rediscover not only the anthropomorphic orientation of early tradition but also the importance of the bodily nature of the human being to the image of God.

According to the twentieth-century Russian-born American rabbi Samuel S. Cohon, "the Jewish conception of human nature reaches its fullest expression in the belief that man is endowed with a divine soul." The immortal soul (immortality given by God) in the rabbinic teaching is "the life-principle and innermost self of man, [which] reveals and praises God, the abiding principle, the life and mind of the world."[91] Judaism thus operates dualistically, making a distinction between the material and immaterial (spirit, soul) without in any way implying moral dualism of good and evil, as in Platonism. This is in keeping with the normative rabbinic view of human nature regarding the human person as body and soul, the former linking with the earth, the latter with heaven. While closely related to the body, the soul is also independent and continues after death.[92] That said, Jewish dualism is thoroughly holistic and integral.

The Christian commentator may note several things about Jewish anthropology. First, as discussed, the Old Testament anthropology, while employing a number of nonanalytic terms, majors in a holistic, embodied view of human nature with due acknowledgment of community and the link with

88. http://www.sacredtexts.com/jud/fons/index.htm.

89. Martin and Barresi, *Rise and Fall*, 85.

90. Moses Maimonides, *The Eight Chapters of Maimonides on Ethics (Shemonah Perakim)*, trans. and ed. Joseph I. Gorfinkle (New York: Columbia University Press, 1912), 37–46.

91. Samuel S. Cohon, *Jewish Theology: A Historical and Systematic Interpretation of Judaism and Its Foundations* (Assen: van Gorcum, 1971), 346.

92. Cohon, *Jewish Theology*, 389–90.

earlier generations. Second, this is in keeping with not only the Old Testament but also Jewish emphasis on "salvation" in this life, with much less stress on future eschatology than Christian tradition. Third, like its Christian counterpart, Jewish anthropology was heavily shaped throughout history by influences from philosophical and religious traditions. In sum: it seems to me that a highly integrated hylomorphist account of humanity with the acknowledgment of soul and belief in the resurrection of the body is an important current Jewish view.

The Human Being as Body and Soul: The Islamic Vision

Although the Islamic view of humanity is realistic, acknowledging many limitations and failures of human nature, the principle of *fitrah*, as discussed above, elevates the human person to a unique place among the creatures.[93] Notwithstanding some exegetical disputes, a number of sayings point to this divinely given status, for example, "Verily We created man in the best of forms" (Q 95:4; also 40:64). Humanity's status also appears in her inviolable dignity and invitation to serve as Allah's viceroy, discussed above. The Qur'anic creation accounts contain several references to humans having been presented before angels before they were created and having been assigned the lofty status of God's coregents (20:21). God's blessings and providence have been lavished upon humanity (7:10; 31:20; 17:70). The reason why the Qur'an (unlike Hadith) dares not to use the Jewish-Christian expression of the image of God is to safeguard the utter transcendence of Allah (42:11). That said, the Qur'an teaches that the Creator is "nearer to him than his jugular vein" (50:16). After all, the human being made of clay is also breathed into by the Spirit of God (15:26–29).[94]

Islamic anthropology is deeply dualistic. The Qur'an and subsequent Islamic theology speak of the soul everywhere. In keeping with Abrahamic faiths, the normative Islamic tradition rejects the eternity and preexistence of the soul.

Aristotle became the guiding philosophical influence in Muslim anthropology. Avicenna (Ibn Sina) and Averroes, the leading scholars, were dualist;

93. Q 4:28; 10:12; 14:34; 16:4; 17:11; 33:72; 70:19; etc.

94. Mona Siddiqui, "Being Human in Islam," in *Humanity: Texts and Context; Christian and Muslim Perspectives*, ed. Michael Ipgrave and David Marshall (Washington, DC: Georgetown University Press, 2011), 16–17.

body and soul are separate substances, and personality is located in the soul and has total independence from the body. Gleaning from Platonic sources, Avicenna viewed soul as "an immaterial substance, independent of the body," spiritual in its essential nature.[95] As in earlier influential medieval philosophers in his tradition, reason and intellect are for him the key aspects of the soul's capacities.[96]

The twelfth century—when a number of Islamic, Jewish, and Greek (Plato, Aristotle) works were translated and disseminated—was a fertile time for interfaith debates about the soul-body problem.[97] Thomas Aquinas and Mulla Sadra, another Muslim authority, were united in criticizing the Neoplatonically based body-soul dualisms in which the body is a mere instrument in the employ of the soul. They put forth a hylomorphic account. Unlike Avicenna, Sadra worked toward a highly integrated body-soul connection.[98]

Generally speaking, current Muslim theology continues affirming traditional body-soul dualism, and only a few individual revisionist scholars have dared to tackle issues such as whether there is a soul in light of scientific knowledge.[99] As evident from this brief discussion, basic theological intuitions about humanity are very similar to the Christian tradition; the only major exception has to do with the doctrine of sin and the Fall, to be discussed below.

The Many Hindu Visions of Humanity

Hinduism at large envisions *jiva*, "the living being" (sometimes also translated as "soul"), in terms of three bodies, namely, a physical ("gross"), a subtle, and a causal body. The causal body is a kind of "blueprint" that causes the human being to be what it is. The "subtle" body is the "mental" part of human nature with mind, intellect, activity of sense organs, vital energy, and so forth. As long

95. *Avicenna's Psychology* [*De Anima*; *The Treatise on the Soul*], trans. and ed. Fazlur Rahman (Oxford: Oxford University Press, 1952), 3.

96. Martin and Barresi, *Rise and Fall*, 82–84.

97. Reza Rezazadeh, "Thomas Aquinas and Mulla Sadrá on the Soul-Body Problem: A Comparative Investigation," *Journal of Shi'a Islamic Studies* 4, no. 4 (Autumn 2011): 415–28.

98. Daftari Abdulaziz, "Mulla Sadra and the Mind-Body Problem: A Critical Assessment of Sadra's Approach to the Dichotomy of Soul and Spirit" (PhD diss., Durham University, 2010), http://etheses.dur.ac.uk/506/.

99. For such an example, see Mahmoud Khatami, "On the Transcendental Element of Life: A Recapitulation of Human Spirituality in Islamic Philosophical Psychology," *Journal of Shi'a Islamic Studies* 2, no. 2 (2009): 121–40.

as the human being falsely assumes separate individuality because of *avidya*, "ignorance," and has not yet grasped the insight of the identity of *atman* with Brahman, the subtle body represents the continuity in the process of transmigration (at death, the physical body is left behind and decays).[100] Consider also the importance of the appearance nature of reality in Hindu cosmology and imagination. Understanding the visible world as merely an appearance of the "real" world of the spirit (ultimately everything is *atman*, that is, Brahman) is of course not to say that therefore the world does not exist; the world exists but as appearance, and can easily mislead men and women to cling to what is *maya*, transitory and impermanent. Although one has to be careful in maintaining that the Semitic faiths are historical and Hinduism is not, it is also the case that history or embodiment certainly is not at the center of Indian vision.

In light of the appearance nature of reality, it is understandable that foundational to a Hindu understanding of humanity and human nature is the sharp distinction between the *real* self and the *empirical* self that lives in the phenomenal world. Whereas the latter is made of "stuff" such as earth, water, and light, and includes the "subtle body" of vitality (breath, mind, intelligence), it is not the "real" me, contrary to common intuitions. The real self is the *atman*, the eternal and formless, indeed the Brahman ("Spirit," "God," the Divine). This does not of course mean that "I" would not exist at all; even appearances, or dreams, or illusions exist in some sense. What the mainline Hindu philosophy is saying is that I do not exist "ultimately" or "really." To realize this truth is the key to release.

Here we also come to internal divisions among the Vedanta theologies, already discussed in several contexts. Sankara's *advaita* school argues for an absolute, uncompromising nondualism and, hence, identity of Brahman (god, divine, "spirit") and *atman* (self or soul). In contrast with this view, Ramanuja's *visistadvaita* allows for a qualified nondualism that refutes absolute identity between Brahman and *atman*, although it insists on their inseparability. Related to it, Vaishnava traditions, based on the teachings of the Bhagavad Gita, teach the eternity of each individual self.[101] This is taken to mean the existence of an infinite number of selves with no beginning and no end. This interpretation differs from that of *advaita*, according to which only the Absolute Self exists and all other "selves" are but appearances thereof.

100. Arvind Sharma, *Classical Hindu Thought: An Introduction* (Oxford: Oxford University Press, 2000), chap. 10.

101. Bhagavad Gita, chap. 2 (*SBE* 8:44): "Never did I not exist, nor you . . . ; nor will any one of us ever hereafter cease to be."

The Vaishnavites also believe that the souls are created by God, the Absolute Soul, and are to serve the Lord (Krishna or similar).[102] In this sense, there is some commonality between how the souls are related to Krishna and the relation of individuals to Christ in Christian tradition. Somewhat similarly, Krishna is both unchanging and changing in nature and considers devotees dear to him.[103] While devotion to Krishna seems to require a continued personal life and some form of embodiment, even the Vaishnava view rejects the idea that the self is to be identified with the material body.

Notwithstanding a wide variety of views among Hindus, it seems to me that Hindu anthropology is deeply dualistic. Consider this summative statement by the late Swami Adiswarananda: "According to Hinduism, man is essentially a soul that uses its body and mind as instruments to gain experience."[104] Part of this teaching is the separation between the apparent and real self as well as the eternity of the "soul." Clearly, these tenets are in deep conflict with all current notions of the natural sciences. Furthermore, the *advaita* view seems irreconcilable to Abrahamic theistic belief due to its ultimate conflating of the divine and the human (pantheism in Abrahamic traditions). Finally, Christian anthropology that resists body-soul dualism and lifts up the importance of embodiment and sociality definitely looks in the opposite direction from any attempt to divide human nature between the apparent and the real, and to consider the bodily only as the temporary "tool" of the eternal spirit.

Interdependence, No-Soul, and Dukkha*: The Buddhist Vision*

Three foundational and wide-reaching Buddhist principles govern talk about human nature: the principle of *dukkha*, interdependent origination, and the no-self teaching. The first two have been explained in the previous chapter, on creation. Interdependent orgination (or causal interdependence), we recall, relates not only to the physical but also to other dimensions of reality, including the human.

102. Keith Ward, *Religion and Human Nature* (Oxford: Clarendon, 1998), 37–38.

103. The classic passage of devotion is in Gita, chap. 18 (*SBE* 8:128): "Dedicating in thought all actions to me, be constantly given up to me, (placing) your thoughts on me"; for mutual devotion, see also chaps. 12 (*SBE* 8:99–102) and 18 (see Ward, *Religion and Human Nature*, 39, 43).

104. Swami Adiswarananda, "Hinduism," part 2 (Ramakrishna-Vivekananda Center of New York, 1996), http://www.ramakrishna.org/activities/message/message15.htm.

Not only humans but everything else is impersonal or selfless (*anatta*, "no-self"). "What we call a 'being,' or an 'individual,' or 'I,' according to Buddhist philosophy, is only a combination of ever-changing physical and mental forces or energies."[105] There is no "self" or "soul" that is permanent. Calling the person a "self" is just an elusive, conventional way of referring to that fleeting combination of elements. To be liberated from the illusion of being permanent and hence clinging to something requires the "salvific" insight into the true nature of reality (release from samsara, the cycle of rebirths).

How would a Christian respond to the Buddhist teaching of no-soul? Keith Ward rightly notes that "from a theistic viewpoint, it will seem to be false that there is no enduring Self and that there is no permanent and noncontingent reality—for God is precisely such a reality." In that sense, "the whole Buddhist world-view and discipline leads away from theism."[106] Indeed, in the absence of self, it is impossible—at least for the Western mind—to imagine "who" is the one who clings to life due to desire, suffers from the effects of karma, and particularly comes to the enlightening realization (if it ever happens) that the samsaric cycle is now overcome. This also has to do with what seems to me a deep and wide difference of orientation between Semitic faiths and Theravada Buddhism, namely, the notion of individuality and the individual's relation to others. Furthermore, it seems to be impossible to think of ways to affirm the dignity of human personhood if there is nothing "permanent."

It is often assumed that the Buddhist notion of humanity is pessimistic and gloomy. But it is not. It is rather realistic. As is well known, Gautama gave a long litany of things in life that are enjoyable and should be enjoyed, from economic security to wealth to happiness on account of living a good life.[107] Indeed, says Rahula, "a true Buddhist is the happiest of beings" because he or she has no fears or anxieties.[108]

What about the Buddhist notion of the nature of human nature in terms of body-soul/physical-spiritual distinctions? On the one hand, the Buddhist view of humanity is deeply holistic and resists dualisms. In keeping with the interrelatedness principles of Buddhist cosmology, all "five constituents" that she is made of interrelate and collaborate. On the other hand, ultimately the spiritual quest moves away from embodiment, and in that sense a perennial dualism is present. What about the soul? Although it is not difficult to establish

105. Walpola Rahula, *What the Buddha Taught*, rev. ed. (New York: Grove, 1974), 20.

106. Keith Ward, *Religion and Revelation: A Theology of Revelation in the World's Religions* (Oxford: Clarendon, 1994), 166.

107. See, e.g., *Anana Sutta: Debtless* (Anguttara Nikaya 4.62).

108. Rahula, *What the Buddha Taught*, 27.

the usage of the term "soul" in the Buddhist thesaurus, it is difficult to determine its meaning in relation to the typical terminology in Abrahamic faiths and Western philosophical traditions. For example: What is the meaning of "the soul of all sentient beings . . . that constitutes all things in the world"?[109] Hard to tell.

At this juncture we move from the first to the second part of theological anthropology, to sin and fall.

The Misery of Humanity: Sin and "Fall"

Challenges to the Doctrine of Original Sin in Current Theology

Although the sinfulness of humanity, as Reinhold Niebuhr succinctly put it, is "one of the best attested and empirically verified facts of human existence,"[110] it is customary nowadays to begin theological talk about sin with either an apology or a humorous saying. Undoubtedly, one reason for the obscurity and marginality of the doctrine is the dissolution of many of the traditionally held beliefs related to the doctrine of original sin and the Fall, partially due to changes in cosmology and the introduction of evolutionary theory.

Notwithstanding many disagreements among the Christian traditions concerning the hermeneutics of "fall" and "original sin," there is no denying the simple fact that while "no religious vision has ever esteemed humankind more highly than the Christian vision," no other tradition has also "judged it more severely."[111] That said, the *interpretations* of the doctrine of original sin in Christian tradition are far from unanimous.

An Appraisal of the Growth of Tradition

The Old Testament virtually refuses to offer any reason for the presence of sin in human life, and even the New Testament, apart from some well-known

109. See, e.g., Asvaghosa, *Awakening of Faith* II, 53–54, in *Açvaghosha's Discourse on the Awakening of Faith in the Mahâyâna*, trans. Teitaro Suzuki (1900), www.sacred-texts.com/bud/taf/index.htm.

110. Reinhold Niebuhr, "Sin," in *A Handbook of Christian Theology*, ed. Marvin Halverson and Arthur A. Cohen (New York: World, 1958), 349.

111. Paul King Jewett, with Marguerite Shuster, *Who We Are: Our Dignity as Human; A Neo-Evangelical Theology* (Grand Rapids: Eerdmans, 1996), 57.

Pauline references, is silent about its ultimate origins. Even if in Pauline theology (recall that Adam and the Genesis narrative do not appear at all in the Gospels) the universality of sin is traced back to Adam (Rom. 5:12), there is not yet an idea of sin "as a fated universal legacy that proliferates generation after generation like a congenital disease."[112] And although Paul teaches the universal occurrence of death (Rom. 5:12, an idea familiar also to Jewish tradition), he does not speak of inheritance of sin in any technical sense. Rather, individuals suffer as a result of their sins. Orthodox theology followed that tradition in understanding the example and sin of Adam as representing the whole race instead of linking this notion to the idea of inheritance of sin. Pannenberg rightly comments that "the thesis of the universality and radicalness of sin would not have required for its proof the acceptance of a *transmission* of the *individual* sin of the first parents of the human race."[113]

Importantly, patristic theology for centuries did not have a developed doctrine of sin other than a deep intuition of the fallen and sinful nature of humanity. Freedom and responsibility were high values to early theologians in a culture plagued with fatalism and Gnostic determinism (that assumed the evil nature of all things physical). Rather than sin and guilt, the redemptive and reconciliatory work of Christ were in the forefront.

While in the Latin West the Augustinian doctrine was consolidated particularly in opposition to Pelagianism, whose understanding of sin was very thin alongside the confidence in human capacity to live pleasing to God even on its own, the Christian East took a decidedly different standpoint: the human person was regarded as mortal even before the Fall, and hence death per se could not be punishment for the Fall; human nature was good by virtue of existing as the image of God, and free will was not destroyed by the Fall, only impeded. Hence, sin was rooted in human freedom. The East followed the Hebrew mind-set with no idea of original sin. According to Eastern theology, we do not inherit sin but rather its consequences when we sin, its corruption rather than guilt alone. While the universality of sin was affirmed, it was often described in terms of woundedness or sickness. As did early tradition, they denied that infants were born in sin.[114] Because of freedom of will, a "return" to the state of grace is open at all times, although after the Fall moral and other weaknesses in us abound. Rather than being

112. Pannenberg, *TA*, 121.

113. Pannenberg, *TA*, 123.

114. See further, Tatha Wiley, *Original Sin: Origins, Developments, Contemporary Meanings* (New York: Paulist, 2002), 50–51.

annihilated, the likeness (to God) is obscured or tainted. Irenaeus had already established the powerful vision of Adam and Eve as yet immature "children" undergoing growth and development toward perfection.[115] The Christian East looks into the future, the ultimate goal of perfection (deification, that is, union with God). Furthermore, although the Greek fathers trace sinfulness back to Adam, they do not teach that "we participate in Adam's actual guilt, i.e., his moral culpability, nor [do they] exclude the possibility of men living entirely without sin."[116]

The definite *doctrinal* formulation of original sin was established in the Latin West no earlier than the fourth and fifth centuries under the leadership of Augustine. In the West, the blessedness of life in the original paradise was further idealized, making Adam virtually a perfect being. Pride was the reason for the Fall, which resulted in concupiscence (a strong desire and inclination to sin) and death. Western writers also deemed it necessary to establish in a more rigid way the theory of the transmission of sin, which eventually led to the Augustinian notion of hereditary transmission. In sum: the Fall "from grace" was complete and disastrous—but God is not to be blamed, only the human being.[117]

According to the Augustinian-Western logic, when Adam sinned, we participated in it. This interpretation was supported by the faulty Vulgate translation of Romans 5:12, which translated the Greek *eph ho* as "in whom."[118] That means we all participate in Adam's guilt.[119] Sinfulness is propagated by virtue of sexual union, even in the case of baptized parents—an interpretation consistently rejected by the Eastern Church.

An asset in the hereditary interpretation of sin came from the traducianist view of the origin of soul (that the origin of the human soul comes from both parents concomitantly, and hence there is a "physical" connection between the infant and the parents). Only redemption in Christ can save the human being from this *condition* of sinfulness derived from Adam. The Pelagian opposition to the Augustinian doctrine was rejected, and Augustinianism

115. Irenaeus, *Against Heresies* 3.22.4; 3.23.5; 4.38.1–2.

116. J. N. D. Kelly, *Early Christian Doctrines*, rev. ed. (New York: Harper & Row, 1978 [1960]), 347–48.

117. William E. Mann, "Augustine on Original Sin and Evil," in *Cambridge Companion to Augustine*, ed. Eleonore Stump and Norman Kretzmann (Cambridge: Cambridge University Press, 2001), 40–48.

118. Kelly, *Early Christian Doctrines*, 353–54.

119. Augustine, *Treatise on the Merits and Forgiveness of Sins, and on the Baptism of Infants* 3.14 (in *NPNF*[1]).

was ratified by ecclesiastical decrees and became the mainstream Western tradition.[120]

With some modifications (particularly by Thomas Aquinas), this Augustinian-driven account of the origin and influence of sin became dominant in the Christian West in Catholic, Anglican, and Protestant traditions (with further modifications in each of these theologies). The important Thomistic tweaking, still programmatic in the Catholic Church, notes the difference between "natural" capacities such as reason and will and "supernatural" gifts, namely, faith, hope, and love. Whereas the former were merely tainted by the Fall, the latter can be had only by virtue of divine grace. The Fall hence entails privation of original righteousness. This is a less radical account of the effects of the Fall in Catholicism than the account in Lutheran and Calvinist traditions, although both depend on Augustine. If possible, Calvin even intensified the Augustinian interpretation, speaking of "natural depravity which we bring, from our mother's womb, though it brings not forth immediately its own fruits, is yet sin before God, and deserves his vengeance."[121]

Notwithstanding internal differences and nuances, Christian tradition's (particularly in the Christian West) account of the nature and consequences of the Fall and sin includes, in some form, the following:

- The literal reading of Genesis 2–3 with its corollaries: the origins of humanity in one couple and their perfect state of innocence and immortality
- The hereditary view of the transmission of sin
- The concept of original sin as entailing guilt and condemnation in relation to human responsibility and self-determination
- The overly individualistic account of sinfulness

The Problem of Sin and Fall in Modern Theology

In the aftermath of the Enlightenment, modern theology rejected, for scientific and cultural reasons, a number of traditional beliefs about sin. Echoing the modern mind-set, Schleiermacher's highly revisionist theological account of original sin in terms of arresting the God consciousness serves as an example;

120. Wiley, *Original Sin*, 66–75.

121. John Calvin, *Commentary on the Epistle of Paul the Apostle to the Romans*, on 5:12 (n.p.), http://www.ccel.org/ccel/calvin/institutes.html.

it can hardly be reconciled with the traditional belief in universal sinfulness in any sense.[122] While much closer to normative Christian tradition, neither does the Danish melancholic Kierkegaard's identification of the main problem of humanity with despair[123] satisfy most theologians. Therein, sin can easily be interpreted as nothing more than a matter of existential feeling and sadness.

If these thin accounts of sin are judged to say too little of the nature and influences of sin, what might be some guiding principles for theologians in search for a thicker interpretation—yet with the needed corrective to traditional corollaries? How would theology after the advent of evolutionary theory and a radically changed account of the origins of the cosmos formulate the problem of what is wrong with us?

Sin and "Fall" in Contemporary Theology

In Search of "Thick" Accounts of Sin

Only in light of the dignity of humanity by virtue of the *imago Dei* can we meaningfully speak of the Fall and sin. That, however, does not mean a return to the idyllic idea of a perfect original state, not only because the biblical narrative does not mandate it but also because it is scientifically untenable. Also, several feminists have wondered, for example, if making pride the main source of the Fall is too male-driven an interpretation and may hide human liabilities more familiar to the other gender such as dependence, negation of self, and undermining one's own capacity.[124]

While sensitive to these kinds of cultural and scientific changes, theologians should not make sin merely a human issue. Sin, as deeply as it relates to human persons at personal and collective levels, is also a God-ward phenomenon. It is violation against the commands of holy God.[125]

122. See Friedrich Schleiermacher, *The Christian Faith*, ed. H. R. Mackintosh and J. S. Stewart (Edinburgh: T&T Clark, 1999), §62.

123. Søren Kierkegaard, *Sickness unto Death: A Christian Psychological Exposition for Upbuilding and Awakening*, ed. and trans. Edna H. Hong and Howard V. Hong (Princeton: Princeton University Press, 1983), 17.

124. Valerie Saiving, "The Human Situation: A Feminine View," in *Womanspirit Rising: A Feminist Reader in Religion*, ed. Carol P. Christ and Judith Plaskow (San Francisco: Harper & Row, 1979), 37.

125. Cornelius Plantinga, *Not the Way It's Supposed to Be: A Breviary of Sin* (Grand Rapids: Eerdmans, 1995), chap. 1.

At the same time, theology of sin should hold on to the goodness of human nature as God's creation and so avoid making sin in some sense (a necessary) part of human nature. It does not really take sin to make an authentic human being! Sin does not belong to human nature; sin is an intrusion. Nor should theology link sin with the natural, beautiful, and good enjoyments of earthly life.

Original Sin and the Fall in Light of Current Evolutionary Theory

Current knowledge of human development clearly conflicts with the traditional view that all humans descended from a single pair. What about the idea of the perfect estate, the cornerstone of the traditional idea of original sin? As mentioned, happily for theologians, a plain reading of Genesis 3 hardly leads to the idea of the perfect state. Nor does the biblical narrative teach that as a result of disobedience, human nature was changed; it merely states that the first humans were banished from the garden.

Long before the emergence of the questions posed by modern science, beginning with the fathers, biblical expositors have been aware of many problems with the literal understanding of Genesis 2–4, including the fact that while Genesis 2–3 speaks of a couple (Adam and Eve), Genesis 4 refers to a larger population of humans. While traditional exegesis took Genesis 3 as actual history (etiology), most contemporary scholars consider it in some way a description of the state of humanity, perhaps as a universal symbol of the whole of humanity and/or history of every person.[126] All these interpretations are in keeping with the name "Adam," which means humanity or human person in general.

One promising way to consider the biblical Fall narrative is to take Adam and Eve as representatives of a collective of "last" hominids in their transition to modern *sapiens* in terms of the capacity to exercise free will and self-consciousness, as well as deeper self-awareness, including a new awareness of God.[127] Perhaps these "first" humans, while having becoming aware of God and God's requirements, more often than not rejected them. One could even imagine that this awareness was "particularly clear, uncluttered by the spiritual darkness that eventually clouded the minds of the human race because of its turning away from God."[128] But this does not have to mean any kind of perfect

126. See Schleiermacher, *Christian Faith*, §§70–72, 282–304.

127. John Polkinghorne and Nicholas Beale, *Questions of Truth: Fifty-One Responses to Questions about God, Science, and Belief* (Louisville: Westminster John Knox, 2009), 68.

128. Robin Collins, "Evolution and Original Sin," in *Perspectives on Evolving Creation*, ed. K. B. Miller (Grand Rapids: Eerdmans, 2003), 470.

knowledge after tradition nor perfect innocence, let alone immortality. On the contrary, they were subject to temptations, the desire to turn away from the "voice" of the Lord, inclinations they had inherited from their evolutionary past, including also vulnerability to all kinds of perversions, violence, abuse, self-centeredness, and the like. Analogous to the way humanity inherits all other traits and capacities in an integral genetic-cultural matrix, the spiritual darkness and bondage, including associated violence, can be said to be spread throughout generations.

This proposal seems to be in keeping with Paul's teaching in Romans 1, which, unlike chapter 5, has been curiously absent in the discussion. It looks as if 1:18–32 is meant to present Paul's "Fall" narrative. Without any theory of how or when, Paul simply states that human persons, who knew God through the divine presence and traces in nature, turned away from following God and thus were given to darkness and perversion of behavior.

What about Romans 5:15–19, which seems to assume a literal interpretation of Adam as "one man" (repeated several times)? First, it is clear that Paul (and even Jesus) shared the (then) commonly held beliefs about the biblical narrative, including Adam's historicity. But upholding this common, time-bound notion is not necessarily to affirmatively teach this idea as necessary to the doctrine.[129] Just think of the doctrine of creation in the Bible; that it assumes ancient cosmology and six days is not its message to us. Second, when this passage is placed in the wider context of the Epistle to the Romans, it is clear that "Paul does not *begin* with Adam and move *to* Christ"[130] and his salvific work. Hence, the wider context in Romans highlights the sinfulness and plight of humanity in need of salvation rather than being fixated on historical-etiological concerns about Adam. Third, even if Paul assumes the individuality of Adam, he contrasts Adam with the Last Adam and thus treats both as corporate representatives.

Sinfulness and Misery as Universal but Not Hereditary

If sin and its judgment are being transmitted somehow "naturally" (even biologically), humans can hardly be held responsible for their sinful actions.

129. Richard Swinburne, *Revelation: From Analogy to Metaphor* (Oxford: Clarendon, 1992), 28–33.

130. Peter Enns, *The Evolution of Adam: What the Bible Does and Doesn't Say about Human Origins* (Grand Rapids: Brazos, 2012), 82.

Hence, sin cannot be regarded as a fate that comes upon human beings as an alien power against which they are helpless.

Having seen this clearly, Pannenberg sought to locate the origin and spreading of sin in the tension between "centrality" and "exocentrism."[131] While the former is shared with other creatures, the latter is uniquely human. Exocentrism, the unique human feature, can easily be perverted by, rather than treating others respectfully, manipulating and taking advantage of them. In relation to nature, it becomes exploitive and oppressive. In other words, rather than turning to and honoring God, the Creator, the human being focuses on himself or herself. Thereby the human person also misses one's destiny in fellowship with God. Each new member to the human family comes to the world with a weakened will and propensity to turn away from God and serve only selfish needs. Ultimately, only to humans can it be attributed as guilt, on the basis of divine revelation and our special direct relation to God.

Whatever tactic is chosen in trying to explain the effects of the Fall, it is essential for theology to continue affirming key intuitions of original sin in tradition while correcting its time-bound problematic notions in tradition: human beings are sinful before they commit a sinful act (notwithstanding the fact, mentioned above, that guilt will be imputed only in light of personal responsibility); sin, therefore, is located at a deeper level than any individual act; and the universality of sin is the presupposition for the universality of redemption in Christ. Sinfulness is a bigger thing than just each human person because humanity forms one family.[132]

Sin as Personal and Structural

One of the formative shifts in the theology of sin during the second half of the twentieth century has to do with the balancing of highly individualistic interpretations with communal, structural, social, and relational interpretations—in other words, extending the meaning of sin beyond the personal. Women theologians, postcolonialists, and other liberationists from various global contexts are on the forefront in pushing theology to consider sociopolitical sins, in many cases even environmental sins, as an integral part of the Christian doctrine of sin.[133]

131. See Pannenberg, *TA*, 84.

132. Denis Edwards, "Original Sin and Saving Grace in Evolutionary Context," in *EMB*, 377.

133. Derek R. Nelson, *What's Wrong with Sin: Sin in Individual and Social Perspective from Schleiermacher to Theologies of Liberation* (London: T&T Clark, 2009).

The senior Peruvian liberationist Gustavo Gutiérrez reminds us that "sin, the breach with God, is not something that occurs only within some intimate sanctuary of the heart. It *always* translates into interpersonal relationships, and hence . . . is the ultimate root of all injustice and oppression—as well as of the social confrontations and conflicts of concrete history."[134] For the African American theologian Garth Kasimu Baker-Fletcher, sin "means becoming aware of the ways in which Afrikans [*sic*] (male and female, rich and poor) are engulfed in a demonic system of whiteness/Euro-domination/oppression that has colonized both their bodies and their innermost thoughts, desires, and feelings."[135]

The integral connection between the personal and the social is needed to do justice to the all-pervasiveness of sinfulness and redemption. At the same time, contemporary theology should not make individual persons helpless victims of circumstances and so thwart personal responsibility before God and fellow human persons.

Now it is time to engage other traditions' views of what's wrong with us.

Human Misery in the Vision of Religions

Sin and Fall in Abrahamic Traditions

Among the Semitic faiths, there is no unified conception of human misery. Jewish and Muslim theologies insist on human freedom to choose and responsibility for the choice. That said, all sister faiths place the discussion of sin in relation to God and, derivatively, in the human domain. All of them, though somewhat differently, consider the "origin" of sinfulness in the deviation of humanity from the Creator. Not surprisingly, all three scriptural traditions therefore share the common narrative of the Fall and its consequences even when their interpretations differ from each other quite dramatically. In many ways, Jewish and Muslim interpretations share more in common with each other than Christian interpretations do with them.

Good and evil inclinations in Jewish tradition. Jewish theologians rightly acknowledge that in the Genesis 3 story there is "no doctrine of the fall of

134. Gustavo Gutiérrez, *The Power of the Poor in History: Selected Writings* (Maryknoll, NY: Orbis, 1983), 147.

135. Garth Kasimu Baker-Fletcher, *Xodus: An African American Male Journey* (Minneapolis: Fortress, 1996), 86.

the race through Adam, of the moral corruption of human nature, or of the hereditary transmission of the sinful bias."[136] Adam plays no role in the rest of the Old Testament story. Jewish tradition also rejects his immortality before the Fall.

Instead of original sin, the Jewish (rabbinic) tradition speaks of two tendencies or urges in every human being, namely, *yetzer ha tov* and *yetzer ha ra'*, for good and for evil, respectively. Even though the "inclination" to evil in itself is not evil, it is a matter of which of the two is the guiding force in life. Hence, the main term for repentance from evil is *teshuvav*, literally "turning."[137] Every human being is engaged in the constant fight between the two urges.

This is not to undermine the seriousness of the sinful tendency. Just think of how radically the Yahwist account in Genesis speaks of the wide diffusion of moral evil (4; 6:5–12; 8:21; 9:20–27; 11:1–9). According to the biblical testimonies, human wickedness is great, and even the imaginations of the heart are evil (6:5; 8:21). In other words, the evil urge is present at birth. But each person is responsible for sinful behavior; such responsibility is not inherited. Although the evil inclination plagues the human person, it does not rob the person of all moral integrity, nor cause lostness as in Christian tradition. It is of utmost importance for Judaism to affirm the freedom from depravity and innate evil of human nature despite the serious inclination toward evil. Second Baruch (19:3; 48:42–43; 54:15, 19; 59:2) teaches that even after Adam's sin that brought about death, each new generation has to choose its own path.

That much can be said in general about traditional interpretation in Judaism. There are also differences of orientation. At the beginning of Christianity, at least three somewhat different conceptions of sin fought for recognition in rabbinic theology: first, corruption of humanity as hereditary; second, a vague connection between Adam's sin and subsequent generations' liability to punishment; and third, all sin as the fruit of the human person's own actions. Whereas the rabbinic tradition operated mainly, though not exclusively, with the third paradigm, Pauline and subsequent Christian tradition went with the first two (with the exception of Eastern Christianity, which also wanted to include key elements of the third).[138]

Both Jewish and Christian traditional ways of reading the Genesis narrative have undergone radical revisions as a result of the scientific advances

136. Samuel S. Cohon, *Essays in Jewish Theology* (Cincinnati: Hebrew Union College Press, 1987), 220.

137. Louis Jacobs, *A Jewish Theology* (London: Darton, Longman & Todd, 1973), 243.

138. Cohon, *Essays in Jewish Theology*, 240–70.

concerning human evolution. At the same time, for the continuing dialogue to be meaningful, the differences between *theological* interpretations of the effects and the "source" of human sinfulness should be acknowledged.

Free will and human disobedience in Islam. The Islamic tradition never envisioned Adam and Eve in terms of perfect paradise imagery as in Christian tradition. Its account of humanity is realistic, as illustrated in Qur'an 95:4–6: "Verily We created man in the best of forms. Then, We reduced him to the lowest of the low, except those who believe and perform righteous deeds, for they shall have an unfailing reward." In a number of places the Qur'an speaks of weaknesses, frailties, and liabilities of humanity.[139] That said, according to mainline Muslim teaching, human nature is, generally speaking, good—or, at least, it is not sinful and corrupted as in Christian teaching.

Although Islamic tradition, similarly to others, has had internal negotiations particularly with regard to the presence (or lack) of evil inclinations, the normal Islamic theology assumes a more or less neutral view that takes the beginning of human life as a blank slate, thus emphasizing the role of free will—not unlike Christian Pelagianism. The mainline teaching in tradition and contemporary Islamic theology is by and large the "positive view"[140] of human nature.

That the Qur'an does not know the doctrine of original sin or the idea of moral depravity[141] does not mean that the concept of "fall" is not part of the Muslim tradition. The fall narrative can of course be found in the Qur'an—indeed, in three related narratives.[142] But its implications (like Judaism's) are different from those of Christian theology. In the (chronologically) earliest narrative (20:115–27), after becoming forgetful of the covenant, all angels were invited by God to prostrate themselves before Adam, and they did, but Satan (named Iblis), who then promised to take Adam and Eve to the tree of immortality and knowledge, declined. They ate the fruit, became ashamed, and tried covering themselves with leaves. "And Adam disobeyed his Lord and so he erred" (v. 121). God called Adam again and advised him to leave the garden that had now become an "enemy" (ob-

139. Q 4:28; 10:12; 14:34; 16:4; 17:11; 33:72; 70:19; 96:6; 103:2.

140. See chap. 2 of Mohamed, *Fitrah*.

141. Muhammad Iqbal, *The Reconstruction of Religious Thought in Islam* (Lahore, Pakistan: Ashraf Press, 1960), 85.

142. For a detailed discussion, see Torsten Löfstedt, "The Creation and Fall of Adam: A Comparison of the Qur'anic and Biblical Accounts," *Swedish Missiological Themes* 93, no. 4 (2005): 453–77. He notes (453) that there are striking similarities between Qur'anic and later Christian pseudepigraphal narratives (as in the Gospel of Bartholomew).

viously because Satan was said to be there, v. 117). God promised to guide the human or else blindness would follow for the one who previously was able to see. The punishment of blindness would be revealed on the day of resurrection, and even more severe forms of punishment might follow. The later account in 2:30–38 repeats very closely the Genesis 3 story with only a few significant deviations. The third major passage, 7:10–25, speaks of the disobedient nature of Adam in starker terms and also mentions the going out of the garden in more certain terms (v. 27). Furthermore, all the accounts speak of enmity and distress as a result of the disobedience for which Adam himself (rather than Satan or Eve) is mainly responsible (albeit tempted and lured by Satan).

What is totally missing in Islamic theology of sin is the idea of transmission of "original sin" from one generation to another and its punitive effect on the progeny. Adam (along with Eve and Satan) himself is to be blamed for disobedience, not later generations. Importantly, the Qur'anic narrative does not link the Fall with lostness, as does Christian tradition.

The Human Condition in the Vision of Asiatic Faiths

Craving and dukkha*: The Buddhist analysis.* Gautama once used the simile of cloth to illustrate the difference between the pure mind and the defiled mind. The impure cloth absorbs all bad into its fabric, the end result of which is "an unhappy destination [in a future existence]," whereas a happy future awaits the pure minded. Particularly dangerous, so Buddha teaches, is the appeal of sensuality in its many forms.[143] With right knowledge and true effort, the purification from all defilement can be attained. Even when the devotee looks upon the example of the Buddha, finds teaching in Dhamma, and has the community of *sangha*, the person is one's own savior.

Following the *dukkha* principle, there is the persistent force of craving (*tanha*), which not only clings to life in general but is also accompanied with greed, hatred, and delusion. Although the craving and passion may be most intense, behind the human misery, *dukkha*, is the yearning to cling to what is merely fleeting, decaying, impermanent. That is the main problem for humans.

Whence this (evil) craving? As with all other topics, Buddha declined from speculating and rather focused on defeating it with the help of moral

143. *Maha-dukkhakkhandha Sutta: The Great Mass of Stress of Majjhima Nikaya* 13.

pursuit and right insight. (That there are in the Pali Canon mythical stories of the origins of craving does not change theologically the main orientation.) From the Christian perspective, the only thing these two traditions have in common is the universal human condition as something requiring liberation, insight, or salvation.

Ignorance and "superimposition": The Hindu diagnosis. The beginning point for the generic consideration of "sin"—human misery—in Hinduism at large is the notion of dharma that represents the positive standard against which all deviations must be compared. It is the "duty," the correct way of life, including all activities and spheres of life. Its opposite is *adharma.* Somewhat similarly to Buddhism, Hindu traditions have developed detailed lists of vices to avoid, including delusion, greed, and anger, the roots of all vices.[144] Not unlike most religious traditions, Hinduism makes a distinction between great and lesser sins. The most grievous offense is the killing of Brahmin, which is unforgivable and occasion for the death penalty. Other examples of a great sin include drinking intoxicating beverages and stealing. In principle all great sins are unpardonable, with no possibility for atonement. For lesser sins penance and atonement may be available. In keeping with the caste system, killing a person of a lower caste might be a less severe crime than slaughtering a cow![145] Although there is some commonality with the Abrahamic faiths' conception of sin, the difference is also deep. Whereas sin is ultimately transgression against God, *adharma* is basically a deviation from the "impersonal" law of the cosmos, reality.

Adharma is to be put in the wider context of Hindu philosophy of human "bondage" to *avidya*, "ignorance." Ignorance makes one cling to *maya*, "fiction," and thus subject to effects of karma, leading to rebirths over and over again. Only with the removal of this "ignorance" can the soul's essential nature as pure spirit be restored.[146]

Living faith traditions not only envision human misery and liberation from it but also imagine what would make a good life. Let's call it human flourishing and pick up the conversation started in chapter 3 on the flourishing of nature.

144. Bhagavad Gita 16.21.

145. Klaus Klostermaier, *A Survey of Hinduism*, 3rd ed. (Albany: State University of New York Press, 2010), 168–72.

146. See further, Klostermaier, *A Survey of Hinduism*, chap. 13.

Human Flourishing—and Suffering—in Theological Perspective

The Beauty and Ugliness of a Good Human Life: The Context for Flourishing

The context of human flourishing is the quotidian, the proximate context of humanity, as finite and hence ambiguous. It belongs to the nature of finite existence that there are hurdles, riddles, and unresolved problems.[147] To creaturely, finite life belong physical limitations, the most dramatic of which is the ultimate disintegration of our bodies over the years. Likewise, to human life and nature's ordinary life belong sickness and disability, none of which takes away from human dignity and value. This is because humanity's status as the image of God in terms of being related to God saves theology from anchoring human dignity in the possession of a quality or commodity. One's relation to the Creator is not affected in the least by one's disabilities, not even intellectual ones. Even if the disabled person due to intellectual or emotional deficits is not able to relate to God, God is able to relate to him or her.

In our contemporary fast-paced society, health easily becomes an idol, or at least idealized; just consider the World Health Organization's definition of health as "a state of complete physical, mental and social well-being and not merely the absence of disease or infirmity."[148] Secular definitions consider health and human flourishing in terms of functionality—meaning that opposite to healthy is "dysfunctional." To this theology counters: "Only what can stand up to both health *and* sickness, and ultimately to living *and* dying, can count as a valid definition of what it means to be human."[149] This is of course not to deny that healthy life is preferred over sickness, nor is it a superficial way to glorify suffering. It is but a *theo*-logically driven way to save life from standards external to created life in the kind of finite world God has placed us in. (Nor is this to thwart the promise of healing that was part of Jesus's ministry and mandate to his followers, an important theological topic to be studied in detail in chapter 8, on salvation.)

147. Kelsey, *Eccentric Existence*, 1:201.

148. From the preamble to the Constitution of the World Health Organization as adopted by the International Health Conference, New York, June 19–22, 1946 (Official Records of the World Health Organization, no. 2, 100), entered into force on April 7, 1948, http://www.who.int/about/definition/en/print.html.

149. Moltmann, *God in Creation*, 273.

A theology of human flourishing entails a proper theology of disability, a topic notoriously difficult to all religious traditions and cultures.[150] Notwithstanding some exceptions, into the twentieth century, prejudices, omissions, and negative attitudes prevailed. Hence, an essential task for contemporary theology is to correct and redirect these attitudes on the way toward a "redemptive theology of disability."[151] A related new challenge to Christian churches, as well as to other faith traditions, is to stand for and unwaveringly affirm the full humanity and dignity of HIV/AIDS patients, a problem easily forgotten now that some modest medical advances are in use and development.[152]

Human flourishing at the personal and communal level can only fully happen in tandem with efforts toward equality, justice, and liberation of all. Let us begin from resources in other faiths.

Resources for the Pursuit of Human Flourishing and Liberation among Religions

Liberative Impulses and Obstacles among Religions

The three Abrahamic traditions share not only the idea of the inviolable dignity of human nature because of the relation to God, but also the equality of both sexes and all races. That these traditions have not always upheld these ideals—and more often than not, have acted outright contrary to these beliefs—will not make null this foundational belief.

While the Qur'an does not know the later concept of "race," it affirms the equality of all using different terminology: "And of His signs is the creation of the heavens and the earth and the differences of your tongues and your colours. Surely in that there are signs for all peoples" (30:22; similarly also 49:13). "Sign" is of course a technical term speaking of creation as pointer to God, as discussed above. No wonder all humanity shares the same divine destiny (4:124). Even gender does not count as a criterion of superiority. In Islam, women are as human as men. They are not evaluated on the basis of their gender, but on the basis of their faith and character. That said, authorita-

150. Amos Yong, *Theology and Down Syndrome: Reimagining Disability in Late Modernity* (Waco, TX: Baylor University Press, 2007), chaps. 2; 5.

151. Yong, *Theology and Down Syndrome*, 42.

152. WCC, *Churches' Compassionate Response to HIV and AIDS*, September 6, 2006, http://www.oikoumene.org/en/resources/documents/wcc-commissions/international-affairs/human-rights-and-impunity/churches-compassionate-response-to-hiv-and-aids.

tive Islamic tradition also includes well-known teachings that contradict these Qur'anic teachings[153] and are used as bases for the submission of women. It is the task of prophetic Muslim theology to negotiate this tension for the sake of liberation.

In the structure of the Buddhist faith is deeply built an intriguing irony with regard to its liberative potential. On the one hand, comparable to the Judeo-Christian Ten Commandments and Jesus's Sermon on the Mount, Buddhism lists its key ethical principles and actions—the Eight-Fold Path—at the center of its faith. On the other hand, particularly Theravada's non-theistic human-centered soteriology and the principle of kamma (according to which one reaps what one has sown and others should not be quick to interfere) clearly point toward isolationism rather than social activism. A related ambiguity about the tradition is that although Gautama by and large was a pacifist, the Buddhist category of soldiers emerged claiming that true detachment (the main aim of all Buddhist practices) had freed them to fight without any anxiety about either their own lives or the lives of others.[154] As in other faith traditions, in modern times attempts to rediscover and creatively reinterpret tradition to fund work for liberation have emerged among some Buddhists.[155]

In India, the divinely sanctioned caste system (notwithstanding its official abolition in the twentieth century) forms a major challenge to that tradition's liberative potential for Christian theologians, particularly because of its violent and unjust exclusion of masses of people like the Dalit. The caste system goes back to the hierarchical division of society into four classes (*varna*)[156] based on Eternal Dharma as taught in the Scriptures.[157] Under the four classes (with innumerable subclasses) is the bottom caste, the "Untouchables," known under the self-designation of the Dalit, which means "oppressed, ground down." In sum: deeply ingrained in the caste system is the ontological difference of people, some privileged, others less so. Being divinely sanctioned, it is essentially a *theological problem.* Notwithstanding some important reform

153. See, e.g., Q 2:223, 228.

154. For twentieth-century warriors, see Brian Daizen Victoria, *Zen War Stories* (London: Routledge, 2003).

155. Ken Jones, *The New Social Face of Buddhism: A Call to Action* (Somerville, MA: Wisdom, 2003).

156. The four classes are Brahmans, Kshatriyas, Vaishyas, and Shudras. Etymologically referring to "color," *varna* was related to different skin colors.

157. Rig Veda 10.90. The foundational scriptural basis is found in *Laws of Manu*. Bhagavad Gita 18.41–48 outlines briefly the basic tasks of each caste.

efforts beginning from the nineteenth century,[158] the structures of inequality totally shape the life of Hindus living in India and some related areas.

What is the capacity of Christian theology to resist dehumanization and related attacks against the value of human life?

Against Dehumanization and Desecration

Human history is full of examples of desecration of human life, too many to begin to list—and the most horrific ones in the modern world are in atheistic societies from China to the former Soviet Union and beyond, except for the Nazi crimes against the Jews.[159] Dehumanization, however, is not only about genocide and such horrific crimes; it may be related to ethnicity, race, and immigration. Dehumanization takes many forms; it often likens people to animals in pejorative ways. It may present women (or children or even men) as mere sexual objects in pornography and commercials.

Judeo-Christian theological tradition stands firmly against all dehumanization and makes every effort to reclaim the immense value of each human being created in the image of God. Unbeknownst to many, leading patristic teachers built on the scriptural traditions to find a theological basis for affirming the equality of all human beings, created in the image of God. They established the freedom of religion on the same basis. Particularly prior to Christendom, the church stood against war, abortion and infanticide, judicial torment and killing, and the bloody mayhem of the arenas.[160] Although this biblically based vision was seriously frustrated by Christendom, faithful witnesses even during the darkest times were never missing. In that light, modern critics of Christianity who have expressed deep doubts about its capacity to uphold human dignity are mistaken.

At the same time, Judeo-Christian tradition insists that no amount of humiliation, torture, blaming, degradation, or other inhumane treatment can remove the humanity of a human being. Joining forces against dehumanization is a task not only for the whole global ecumenical church but also for joint interfaith work. This is also the right way to repent from innumerable acts of dehumanization perpetrated—and still under way—in the name of religion.

158. Mohandas K. Gandhi, *Non-Violent Resistance (Satyagraha)* (New York: Schocken, 1951).

159. Gushee, *Sacredness of Human Life*, chap. 9.

160. Gushee, *Sacredness of Human Life*, chap. 4, with a number of examples from early writers.

Identity, Race, and Belonging in a Postcolonial World

The *context* of the quotidian has dramatically changed in the international and globalized world. The term "hybrid" has been launched by postcolonial thinkers to speak of the bewildering diversity of societies and communities in terms of cultures, nationalities, races, identities, and other markers. The Korean American theologian Sang Hyun Lee speaks of marginality in terms of "liminality," which refers to "the situation of being in between two or more worlds, and includes the meaning of being located at the periphery or edge of a society."[161]

In this complex world, theology reminds us that human dignity on the basis of the image of God allows no separation due to race or skin color.[162] All human races share a common origin. Racial differences are minute and form no basis for ranking people groups. The theological grounding of human dignity also critiques and resists ethnocentrism—the belief in the supremacy and unique value of one's own group. Racism builds on ethnocentrism and is often coupled with violence and harassment. When coupled with colonialism and slavery, as has happened with blacks and the First Nations[163] of America, it means making human beings a commodity, as horribly illustrated in the apartheid system of South Africa. In South Korea the *minjung* were treated not only as nameless and faceless but also as persons without rights and dignity.[164] In India, the Dalit similarly have been the objects of harsh racist and dehumanizing actions.[165] And so forth.

Theology's response to all forms of racism, whether explicit or subtle, is an unwavering *no*. For the human being, having been created in the image of God, racist attitudes toward another person or group is a twofold sin: the perpetrator commits a sin against another human being, and the perpetrator arrogantly denies the permanent value of the Creator's work of humanity.

161. Sang Hyun Lee, *From a Liminal Place: An Asian American Theology* (Minneapolis: Fortress, 2010), x.

162. J. Kameron Carter, *Race: A Theological Account* (Oxford: Oxford University Press, 2008).

163. Dee Brown, *Bury My Heart at Wounded Knee* (New York: Holt, Rinehart & Winston, 1971).

164. Byung Mu Ahn, "Minjung: Suffering in Korea," in *The Lord of Life: Theological Explorations of the Theme "Jesus Christ—the Life of the World,"* ed. William H. Lazareth (Geneva: WCC, 1983).

165. Sathianathan Clarke, Deenabandhu Manchala, and Philip Vinod Peacock, eds., *Dalit Theology in the Twenty First Century: Discordant Voices, Discerning Pathways* (New Delhi: Oxford University Press, 2010).

Furthermore, the perpetrator is dividing one united humanity into two classes, those fully human, and others only partially human.

Violence and War

Religions and Violence

Even a cursory look at the statistics is sorrowful reading concerning the pervasiveness of violence against and abuse of people, including children, youth, women, and others of the most vulnerable.[166] Although faith in God per se is not a cause of violence (see chap. 2), there is no denying that violent acts are often occasioned by religious motifs.

The greatest challenge to all Abrahamic faiths in this regard is the concept of holy war. In Judaism,[167] holy war has important limits: war must be carried on as ordered by and meant for the glory of Yahweh, and it is not by human force of arms but rather by the power of Yahweh that victory is won. Very problematic is the concept of *herem*, total annihilation of enemies and their goods (the Amalekites being the prime example). Whereas current liberal Jews consider *herem* merely a theological principle (of total devotion to God), religious Zionists apply the principle to Palestinians and other nearby Arabs. Similarly to Christian hermeneutics, mainstream Jewish scholarship considers this a matter of development of revelation in Scripture. In marked contrast from the Old Testament, the Talmud by and large supports peace and active peacemaking, without advocating pacifism.[168]

For Islam, the key violence-related challenges are not only holy war but also the way jihad is interpreted, whether as "the greater jihad," a personal struggle over spiritual obstacles and temptations, or as "lesser jihad," a call to a holy war. Like the Old Testament, the Qur'an sets out fairly unambiguous rules for just war, including holy war: after seeking spiritual guidance from Allah, war should be resorted to only as the last means; jihad should be led by an imam or at least a Muslim leader; the enemies should be given an oppor-

166. "World Report on Violence and Health," ed. Etienne G. Krug et al., World Health Organization (Geneva, 2002), http://whqlibdoc.who.int/publications/2002/9241545615_eng.pdf.

167. Michael Dobkowski, "'A Time for War and Time for Peace': Teaching Religion and Violence in the Jewish Tradition," chap. 2 in *TRV*.

168. Haim Gordon and Leonard Grob, *Education for Peace: Testimonies from World Religions* (Maryknoll, NY: Orbis, 1987), chap. 3.

tunity to accept Islam first—or if followers of another Abrahamic faith, merely Islamic political rule with a special tax and *zakat*, "almsgiving."[169] A number of contemporary reformists from various Muslim locations have spoken for the nonviolent way. Similarly, some revisionist scholars and clergymen have advocated for a pluralistic, tolerant, and democratic Islamic theory of society.[170]

To an outsider, Hinduism offers a highly complicated case with regard to violence. Well known is the term *ahimsa* ("noninjury," "nonviolence"). As in other traditions, the scriptural texts exhibit a confused approach to violence, both condoning and restricting it.[171] What seems to be clear is that war is embedded in the Hindu system, as one of the four main castes of people consists of soldiers. It is the dharma of the Kshatriya to carry on with that profession. Indeed, in the most famous scriptural Hindu epic (Bhagavad Gita), Arjuna consults Krishna, one of the many avatars of Vishnu, about whether he should refrain from fighting in a battle against the group that includes his relatives. Arjuna is told he should fight because he is a soldier, and failing to do so would mean failing the dharma. From a Christian perspective, all arguments in favor of violence are deeply problematic, notwithstanding the presence of the "just war" concept (widely debated).

Not only is the popular picture of Buddhism as a peaceful and pacifist religion unnuanced, but Buddhist history knows the use of violence. Even more, some of its key concepts such as karma and rebirth have been used to legitimate violence; the former in terms of justifying all kinds of diseases and ills as "judgment," and the latter as a way of helping ease an evil person's karmic effects by ending life.[172] The main historical figure, Asoka (third century BCE), who was instrumental in the early spread of the religion, helped convert masses as part of his military conquests. In the contemporary world, Buddhist nationalisms and fundamentalisms (similarly to Hindu and Muslim movements) are well known among scholars. In other words, regretfully, even the followers of the Lotus flower have resorted to violence, including even His Holiness the Dalai Lama, who earlier in his career approved the use of violence against the true enemies of the people.[173]

What about a Christian take on violence?

169. C. W. Troll, H. Reifeld, and C. T. R. Hewer, eds., *We Have Justice in Common: Christian and Muslim Voices from Asia and Africa* (Berlin: Konrad-Adenauer-Stiftung, 2010).

170. Abdulaziz Abdulhussein Sachedina, *The Islamic Roots of Democratic Pluralism* (New York: Oxford University Press, 2001).

171. *Laws of Manu* 7.

172. Brian Daizen Victoria, "Teaching Buddhism and Violence," in *TRV*, 77–87.

173. Victoria, "Teaching Buddhism and Violence," 82–83.

A Theological Defeat of Violence

This important question is discussed in relation to a number of Christian doctrines: God (chap. 2), the cross and atonement (chap. 6), eschatological judgment (chap.10), and the church's peace-building efforts (chap. 9). In the Christian worldview, neither the world nor faith in God is based on violence but rather on love and hospitality. This can be seen even in the Judeo-Christian creation stories in which the Creator God is not fighting other deities or powers but, rather, brings about the world out of sheer love. Theology of creation based on the divine pronouncement of the goodness of creation (Gen. 1:31) refuses to ontologize violence, war, and conflict.

Acting on the basis of hospitality rather than violence, Christians should therefore be guided by the spirit of openness, inclusion, and welcoming the other. They can either "embrace"—receive the other with outstretched arms—or "exclude," go with these evil dispositions and acts, and be unwilling to make space for the other.[174] The will to embrace is based on and derives from the self-donation of the triune God that comes to its zenith on the cross.

Yet another arena of human flourishing has to do with work, economics, and finances—particularly in the globalized world.

Work, Economy, and Land

Toward a Theology of Work

While theologians have devoted numerous books and studies to matters such as the sacraments, which take place during a short session on Sunday, only a handful of studies have been devoted to work, which occupies men and women throughout the week.[175] Related issues such as the effects of globalization and global markets, the growing gulf between the haves and the have-nots, increasing migration, and new forms of slavery call for theological reflection.

Why do we work? Is it merely an effect of the Fall (Gen. 3:17b–19)? Or is it a main way to achieve human happiness, as classical economic theory surmised (Adam Smith)? Or, perhaps, as the Reformers taught us, work is

174. Miroslav Volf, *Exclusion and Embrace: A Theological Exploration of Identity, Otherness, and Reconciliation* (Nashville: Abingdon, 1996), 30.

175. John Paul II, *Laborem Exercens*, "On Human Work" (1981); Herbert Schlossberg, Vinay Samuel, and Ronald J. Sider, eds., *Christianity and Economics in the Post–Cold War Era: The Oxford Declaration and Beyond* (Grand Rapids: Eerdmans, 1994).

a Christian vocation. Be that as it may, Christian theology is both realistic (Gen. 3) and appreciative, unlike the depreciating attitude prevalent in the ancient world. Early theology made work respectable (often referring to Adam's example in paradise; Gen. 2:15). On the basis of biblical injunctions (1 Thess. 4:11; 2 Thess. 3:10), the necessity of working was affirmed. Often it was connected with the doctrine of sanctification and a belief that new life in Christ would manifest its fruit in everyday labor and lifestyle.[176]

Miroslav Volf's important study *Work in the Spirit* reminds us that if work is related to the divine purpose of creation that points to new creation, then work gains its ultimate meaning from the anticipation of God's new future. While judged, creation will not be fully annihilated with the coming of God's new creation but rather will be preserved and brought to perfection. That affirms the goodness and intrinsic value of human work as part of the divine "cultural" mandate. Human work thus is a form of cooperation with the Creator (Gen. 1:26–27).[177]

At the same time, we should not idealize work. It is rather to include this essential human theme under the theological lens. Theologians must also be reminded of the harsh, complicated, and tiring circumstances and conditions under which work is often done—along with the rest of our lives in its daily ordinariness.

The "Economy of Grace": A Theological Consideration of Global Economics

Apart from liberationists, theologians have by and large been silent about the evil economic and political structures that plague and oppress men and women, especially the poor and marginalized. An essential part of "hypermodern" globalization has to do with "culture industries" that promote consumption, backed by massive advertising and marketing. Unlike the agrarian societies of the past, currently we live in a global "risk society."[178]

What could theology say to global economics? From a minimum set of conditions for an economic system that is fair, the following three conditions probably gain wide acceptance: freedom and dignity of individuals; satisfac-

176. Miroslav Volf, *Work in the Spirit: Toward a Theology of Work* (Eugene, OR: Wipf & Stock, 2001), 69–74.

177. Volf, *Work in the Spirit*, 76–102.

178. Ulrich Beck, *Risk Society: Towards a New Modernity*, trans. Mark Ritter (London: Sage, 1992).

tion of the basic needs of all people, with special reference to the weak; and protection and flourishing of nature.[179] These conditions are based on creation theology's stewardship principle, the inviolability of each human person as the image of God, and the communion of human persons with the rest of creation, as well as the greatest commandment. They do not dictate details of economic systems or planning, but they guide the thinking and work of Christians in charge.

Rather than the hegemony of desires in the consumption society, theology recommends "Sabbath economics: the theology of enough."[180] This is a contingent, dependent security, creaturely existence in the quotidian. Rather than glorifying abundance, Jesus's "downward economic mobility" is the guide: "Apparently unemployed, he seems to have been sustained by the generosity of others (Luke 8:3), homeless, having 'nowhere to lay his head' (Matt. 8:20; par. Luke 9:58)."[181]

A Christian response to economic matters can be named an "economy of grace."[182] Despite the many similarities between the market system and Christian ethics such as the value of work and industry, personal and communal responsibility, as well as demand for fairness, there are a number of differences, such as competition, greed, and maximization of foreign profit. While both view the human being as a creature of desire, "Christian anthropology imagines the end of the human being as praise of God; the market system views the end of the human being as maximized utility." The market calls for unending pursuit of the satisfaction of needs. In the Christian vision, true "enjoyment" can only be had in God and "in participation in the abundance of God's communion through God's grace."[183] Whereas the market system constantly creates new desires, theology knows that only in relationship with God and the neighbor can fulfillment be found.

179. Volf, *Work in the Spirit*, 15–17.

180. George Browning, "Sabbath Reflections 5: Capitalism and Inequity versus a Gospel Mandate," Anglican Communion Environmental Network, 2012, http://acen.anglicancommunion.org/media/61249/Sabbath-Study-5.pdf; Ched Myers, *The Biblical Vision of Sabbath Economics* (Massachusetts: Bartimaeus Cooperative Ministries, 2007); Walter Brueggemann, "The Liturgy of Abundance, the Myth of Scarcity," *Christian Century*, March 24–31, 1999, https://www.religion-online.org/article/the-liturgy-of-abundance-the-myth-of-scarcity/.

181. Kelsey, *Eccentric Existence*, 1:629.

182. I am following here M. Douglas Meeks, "The Economy of Grace: Human Dignity in Market System," in *God and Human Dignity*, ed. R. K. Soulen and L. Woodhead (Grand Rapids: Eerdmans, 2006), 196–214. For a more detailed discussion, see his *God the Economist: The Doctrine of God and Political Economy* (Minneapolis: Fortress, 1989).

183. Meeks, "The Economy of Grace," 205.

Faithfully acknowledging their debt to the Creator, the church is supposed to stand on the side of those who are oppressed and marginalized—not only to feed the hungry and offer a cup of water to the thirsty, but also to stand up against injustice. The discussion of ecclesiology (chap. 9) will deepen this topic.

Migration, Displacement, and Slavery

One phenomenon in the contemporary postmodern milieu is the return of the nomadic lifestyle, known throughout history, including in biblical times. The sociologist Zygmunt Bauman has famously made a distinction between "tourists" and "vagabonds." Whereas the former travel because they can, the latter are on the move because they don't have a choice. Vagabonds are useless to global markets, as they don't make good consumers; they are the outcasts, the marginalized, but they form the majority of the world and are growing rapidly.[184] In this "new world" where whole masses are "disposable people,"[185] slavery has not been eradicated. Part of the wider slavery problem is the increase in labor and sex trafficking, which includes also children and the underaged and a high number of female victims.[186]

The victims of (economically and politically) forced migration and all forms of slavery and trafficking not only lack human value but also lack even minimal living conditions—and almost all of them are landless. For the contemporary Global North mind-set, landlessness may not sound like a problem because even land is made a commodity. However, land is a deeply personal, communal, cultural, and religious issue. It has to do with identity, belonging, self-worth—and God![187]

One-half of the over 200 million migrants in the world are Christians,[188] and a number of them suffer from other forms of dehumanization. Of course, that is not the only reason to act, but that alone should suffice. Christian the-

184. Zygmunt Bauman, *Globalization: The Human Consequences* (New York: Columbia University Press, 1998), chap. 4.

185. Kevin Bales, *Disposable People: New Slavery in the Global Economy*, 2nd ed. (Berkeley: University of California Press, 2004).

186. See the US Committee for Refugees and Immigrants website: http://refugees.org/explore-the-issues/our-work-with-survivors-of-human-trafficking/human-trafficking-basics/.

187. Walter Brueggemann, *The Land: Place as Gift, Promise, and Challenge in Biblical Faith*, Overtures to Biblical Theology 1 (Philadelphia: Fortress, 1977).

188. *Christian Century*, April 4, 2012, 15–16.

ology's continuing upholding of the dignity and equality of all human beings created in the image of God loses credibility if the most vulnerable and marginalized are not on its radar screen. There is also an opportunity for interfaith collaboration. Much promise can be found in the emerging ecumenical field of migrant theologies and initiatives.[189]

189. Gioacchino Campese, CS, "The Irruption of Migrants: Theology of Migration in the 21st Century," *Theological Studies* 73 (2012): 3–32; "Practising Hospitality in an Era of New Forms of Migration," World Council of Churches, February 22, 2005, http://www.oikoumene.org/en/resources/documents/wcc-commissions/international-affairs/human-rights-and-impunity/practising-hospitality-in-an-era-of-new-forms-of-migration.html.

5 | Christology

Introduction: The Doctrine of Christ in Transition

A Revised Plan of Doing Christology

Although Christology stands at the very heart of Christian theology,[1] particularly the last two hundred years have also testified to ever-diversifying and intense debates about what Christology is in the aftermath of modernity and in our increasingly globalized world. The positive side effect of this debate has been an unprecedented interest and productivity in key christological topics, particularly in Protestant theology and, from the mid-twentieth century on, also in Roman Catholic theology.

One reason for the proliferation of interpretations has to do with the chosen "method," that is, how to approach the task. Hence, the discussion here begins with some remarks on the method. Thereafter, differently from tradition, a careful look at the theological significance of Jesus's earthly life and ministry is attempted. An integral part of that discussion is the investigation of the theological meaning of Jesus's earthly ministry in various global contexts and in varying life situations and agendas. Closely related is also the consideration of the theological meaning of Jesus's ministry and emerging confession of faith in his person within the wider Jewish messi-

1. John Onaiyekan, "Christological Trends in Contemporary African Theology," in *Constructive Christian Theology in the Worldwide Church*, ed. William R. Barr (Grand Rapids: Eerdmans, 1997), 356.

anic context. Regretfully, Christologies of the past and current times have routinely dismissed the earthly life of Jesus and almost exclusively focused on fairly narrowly framed doctrinal issues of "two natures" and related dogmatic issues.

Thereafter, as an important preface to standard doctrinal topics, a theological reflection on the meaning of Chalcedon's creed is in order. While the ancient creeds still serve as the ecumenically binding and guiding criterion for christological doctrines, they also have to be put in proper perspective for the sake of the diverse global world.

The Christian confession of the deity and humanity of Jesus Christ, based on the historical and theological claim of his resurrection, will occupy the first main section of the doctrinal clarifications. That discussion both affirms the material content of the classical creeds and seeks to revise it in light of contemporary systematic, historical, and biblical research. The interrelated topics of incarnation and *kenōsis*, preexistence, virgin birth, and sinlessness will be studied following presentation of that framework.

The rest of this chapter will again focus on topics by and large missing in standard christological presentations: first, the relationship between Christ and the Spirit, called "Spirit Christology"; second, a theological response to religious pluralisms; and third, a careful engagement of four living faiths' claims regarding Jesus and their own savior figures, if any.

On the Christological "Method" and Approaches

The traditional methodological problem of Christology is negotiating between Christology "From Above" and Christology "From Below." While the former begins from the lofty biblical titles such as Christ and Lord and the deity and uniqueness of Jesus Christ as formulated in the ancient creeds, the latter delves into the historical-critical questions concerning the human person Jesus of Nazareth and the credibility of his claims. The From Below method is understandably the product of Enlightenment criticism.[2] A particularly crucial question here is to what extent the Council of Chalcedon (451) and preceding councils faithfully and appropriately developed the testimonies, narratives, titles, and incipient creedal traditions of the New Testament; if otherwise, we are forced to conclude with the nineteenth-century historian Adolf von

2. Colin Brown, *Jesus in European Protestant Thought (1778–1860)* (Durham, NC: Labyrinth, 1985).

Harnack's *History of Dogma* that the development of tradition is nothing but the "deterioration of dogma."

From Above advocates typically represent the more traditional and conservative segment of the theological guild—and the mainstream of all theologians prior to the Enlightenment. While doing critical biblical work, they also presuppose that by and large what the creeds are saying is true. But a few From Above advocates either totally ignore the value of a historical basis for christological claims and only concentrate on Jesus's existential meaning "to me" (R. Bultmann) or choose to believe what the creeds are saying without requiring (or at times even resisting the need for) historical-critical evidence (K. Barth).

Some From Below advocates end up virtually abandoning most of the creedal pronouncements, from preexistence to atoning death on the cross to resurrection. They fail to see evidence for the validity of these claims in light of Jesus's history. Other From Below scholars, like the systematician Pannenberg and New Testament scholar N. T. Wright, follow strictly the methods of historical-critical study but end up being convinced that biblical-creedal claims to the divinity and humanity of Jesus Christ and the corollary doctrines faithfully reflect the theological meaning of the Jesus event.

This post-Enlightenment juxtaposition, while still heuristically useful, is no longer considered a crucial methodological issue. Common sense tells us that the distinction between the two approaches is not either-or but rather both-and; they are clearly complementary. The obvious danger of the From Above view, divorced from the history of Jesus, is the violation of the biblical insistence on Jesus, the human person, as the way to the knowledge of God (John 14:6). The danger of one-sided From Below is that it can at its best discover an interesting religious teacher without any theological significance. The Quest of the Historical Jesus project that started in the early nineteenth century represents the culmination of this development.[3] This method easily dissolves into mere "Jesuology" that dismisses the preexistent and exalted Christ altogether. The mutual conditioning of From Below and From Above means that the historical investigation is in the service of the theological one. The mutual conditioning means to correct the long-standing bias in scholarship to "keep history and theology, or history and faith, at arm's length from one another."[4]

Another traditional juxtaposition, the divide between the person and work of Christ, also should be qualified. While the distinction should be

3. Veli-Matti Kärkkäinen, *Christology: A Global Introduction*, 2nd rev. ed. (Grand Rapids: Baker Academic, 2016), chap. 4.

4. N. T. Wright, *The Resurrection of the Son of God* (Minneapolis: Fortress, 2003), 5.

maintained, it has to be maintained carefully and in a way that does not posit separation. Who one is (ontology) and what one does (functionality) cannot be distinguished in such a categorical way as older theology did—neither is it useful to do so. Who Jesus Christ is determines what he does; what he does reflects and grows out of who he is. The biblical testimonies contain very little abstract speculation of who Jesus is. The healing of the man at the pool of Bethesda is a telling example (John 5:2–15). The paralyzed man came to "know" Jesus only through his salvific works, healing and forgiveness ("Sin no more"; v. 14); whatever little he knew of Jesus, he went out to proclaim good news about him (v. 15).

Rather than speaking of "method" in a technical sense and an abstract manner, the current systematic/constructive theology discusses various issues related to the most viable "approach" to or perspectives on doing Christology.

Toward a More Dynamic and "Practical" Christology

The radically changed worldview and context in which faith and theology happen in the beginning of the third millennium call for a new and fresh account of Christology. An aspect in the evolving project is the rediscovery of Jesus's own historical and religious background, that is, Jewish faith and Jewish culture, a theme sorely missed in tradition. It is embarrassing how often traditional and contemporary systematic theologies have not been too attentive to the relation of the New Testament Christology to its Old Testament roots. This has divested theology of the integrally Jewish messianic dimension. Fortunately, contemporary Jesus research as conducted by biblical scholars has shown remarkable interest in the Jewishness of Jesus.

Among the systematicians, Moltmann is an exception to the rule by beginning his major monograph on Christology with a careful investigation of "Jewish messianology";[5] importantly, the subtitle of his christological monograph is *Christology in Messianic Dimensions.* Moltmann rightly takes the Old Testament messianic hopes and metaphors as the presupposition of Christian theology of Christ, Israel's Messiah. To understand and embrace those is essential for both Christian self-understanding and a proper relation to her parent faith.

5. Jürgen Moltmann, *The Way of Jesus Christ: Christology in Messianic Dimensions*, trans. Margaret Kohl (Minneapolis: Fortress, 1993 [1989]), xv.

Alongside the interest in the Jewishness of Jesus, Moltmann's *The Way of Jesus Christ* has also replaced the older static and abstract approach with a more dynamic one in which Jesus Christ is grasped "in the forward movement of God's history with the world."[6] Consequently, the outline of the discussion is not structured according to the typical dogmatic topics—divinity, humanity, and natures—but rather according to various "moves" or stages on the way of Jesus Christ from his birth to earthly ministry to cross to resurrection to current cosmic role to parousia. This kind of Christology "on the way" is by its nature biblical Christology, based as it is on the gospel story. Moltmann also reminds us that unless Jesus's earthly life is rediscovered in theology, what he calls "christopraxis" will be lost, that is, Christology's implications for life in community, discipleship, social concern, and healing.[7]

Understandably, liberation Christologies and Christologies from the Global South opt for a biblical approach and From Below method in the service of liberation, inclusivity, and equality. Womanists have focused on the "deeds of the historical Jesus and not the idealized Christ, in keeping with the liberative traditions of the religious community."[8] The black male theologian James H. Cone critiques the classical Christology of the creeds for neglecting the grounding of the "christological arguments in the concrete history of Jesus of Nazareth," as a result of which too "little is said about the significance of his ministry to the poor as a definition of his person."[9] Because the Nicene fathers were not slaves themselves, their Christology was removed from history and the realities of the world. Instead, they saw salvation in spiritual terms alone, this black theologian contends.[10]

For the liberation Christologies to achieve their goal, not only the material presentation but also the method has to be reconsidered. Cone suggests six sources: black experience, history, culture, divine revelation and Scripture, as well as tradition.[11] Although this suggestion is hardly radical or highly innovative when compared to, say, the so-called Wesleyan Quadrilateral (Scripture, tradition, reason, experience), it reminds us of the need for Christology to be sensitive to a particular context.

6. Moltmann, *Way of Jesus Christ*, xiii.

7. Moltmann, *Way of Jesus Christ*, 43.

8. JoAnne Marie Terrell, *Power in the Blood? The Cross in the African American Experience* (Maryknoll, NY: Orbis, 1998), 108.

9. James H. Cone, *God of the Oppressed*, rev. ed. (Maryknoll, NY: Orbis, 1997; originally New York: Seabury, 1975), 107.

10. Cone, *God of the Oppressed*, 181.

11. James H. Cone, *A Black Theology of Liberation*, 2nd ed., twentieth anniversary ed. (Maryknoll, NY: Orbis, 1986), 23–34.

These new "turns" and emphases do not of course make contemporary Christology any less interested in continuing retrieval of the significance and implications of classical topics of the "two-nature" Christology of Chalcedon. It does, though, put them in a wider perspective of the whole history of Jesus Christ, including Jesus's earthly life and ministry.

The Theological Meaning of Jesus's Earthly Life and Ministry

His Earthly Ministry in Theological Perspective

As said, regretfully, the theological significance of Jesus's earthly life and ministry has been marginal in Christologies. Even if there are remarks on, say, miracles, the goal has been apologetic rather than theological. The lion's share of discussions goes to the events around the cross and resurrection. This all happens in the wider context of discussions of Jesus's divinity, humanity, and unity with God. As Moltmann aptly puts it in reference to ancient creeds, between "born of the Virgin Mary" and "suffered under Pontius Pilate" there is but a comma![12] This is markedly different from the Gospels, in which the teachings, healings, exorcisms, pronouncements of forgiveness, table fellowship, and prophetic acts receive most of the space.

Classical liberal Christology with its radical From Below method helped rediscover many aspects of Jesus's earthly ministry. However, at the same time, it missed almost totally the "Christ of faith," that is, the confession of faith in Jesus Christ as God-man, the Savior and Lord. Ironically, even its account of the earthly ministry was deeply skewed, as everything "supernatural" such as healings and exorcisms was barred. The Sermon on the Mount became nothing more than a fine piece of ethical teaching, as its radically eschatological nature focused on the dawning coming of God's kingdom was eliminated.

In correction, over against the creeds' lack of focus on the earthly life and liberalism's reductionist account thereof, Moltmann suggests an amendment, an addition to the creed:

> Baptized by John the Baptist,
> filled with the Holy Spirit:
> to preach the kingdom of God to the poor,
> to heal the sick,

12. Moltmann, *Way of Jesus Christ*, 150.

to receive those who have been cast out,
to revive Israel for the salvation of the nations, and
to have mercy upon all people.[13]

New Testament scholars agree that Jesus initiated his public ministry in the context of the baptism of John the Baptist.[14] By submitting himself to baptism, Jesus identified himself with the covenant people, who were in need of the baptism of repentance. At the same time, Jesus's baptism can be seen as an anticipation of the "baptism" of suffering and death (Mark 10:38), thus also pointing to the cross and resurrection. Jesus himself, the Baptizer in the Spirit, was baptized by the Spirit as the Father audibly voiced approval. The One on whom the Spirit descended in the form of the dove had a vision of open heavens, a profound sign of salvation and eschatological hope. The return of the Spirit after hundreds of years of absence meant nothing less than the return of Yahweh to visit his people, "the beginning of the end-time deliverance of men and women, the new creation and the manifestation of God's glory."[15]

Thereafter, as an itinerant preacher and healer, Jesus was on the way most of the time; his route took him to towns and countryside, homes and synagogues. Occasionally he also visited pagan areas. Jesus broke national, religious, cultural, and sexual barriers by associating with people not usually involved with a Jewish rabbi. He assumed authority over the precepts of Torah, Sabbath, and the temple, foundations of the exclusive nature of salvation confined to only the covenant people. Particularly his involvement with the "sinners," including table fellowship (Matt. 9:10–13 and par.), became a radical challenge to the religious establishment. The poor (Matt. 11:5; Luke 4:18) and the children (Mark 10:13–16 and par.) were especially dear to Jesus.

Feminists are rightly calling theology to return to the Jesus of the Gospels because in his ministry and behavior "the femaleness of the social and religiously outcast who respond to him has social symbolic significance as a witness against . . . patriarchal privilege."[16] According to the Womanist theologian Jacquelyn Grant, reading the Bible narrative about Christ, who was

13. Moltmann, *Way of Jesus Christ*, 150.

14. Robert L. Webb, *John the Baptizer and Prophet: A Socio-Historical Study* (Sheffield: Sheffield Academic, 1991).

15. Moltmann, *Way of Jesus Christ*, 92.

16. Rosemary Radford Ruether, *Sexism and God-Talk: Toward a Feminist Theology* (Boston: Beacon, 1983), 137.

inclusive in his love toward women and other marginalized people in the society, black women found a Jesus they could claim, and whose claim for them affirms their dignity and self-respect.[17]

Jesus's Role as Teacher among Religions

Totally different from the later liberal interpretations in which Jesus appears to be a kind, ethical teacher cultivating the inner life of individuals and communities, the Jesus of the Synoptic Gospels announced both a personal and a public message. The announcement was about the kingdom of God that "was a warning of imminent catastrophe, a summons to an immediate change of heart and direction of life, an invitation to a new way of being Israel."[18] Although public and "naked," his teaching came mostly in the form of the parables, which of course are open to more than one interpretation. While based on well-known Old Testament and Jewish metaphors, they spoke of the in-breaking in his own person of the righteous rule of God.

Not surprisingly, Jesus's ethical teaching and nonviolence have elicited positive responses among religions.[19] In the words of Jewish historian Joseph Klausner, "there is not one ethical concept in the Gospels which cannot be traced back to Moses and the prophets."[20]

Although the Qur'an (19:32) readily acknowledges Jesus's compassionate nature—and considers him one of the "prophets"—his role as teacher is marginal in the Qur'an. Occasionally, it corrects his teaching (3:50). Indeed, what the Qur'an emphasizes is that God teaches Jesus "the Scripture, and wisdom, and the Torah, and the Gospel" (5:110).

Alongside compassion, Buddhists value Jesus's teaching, particularly the Beatitudes, love of the enemy, the admonition to repay evil with kindness, and the stress on charity and equanimity. That said, what is repulsive to all

17. Jacquelyn Grant, "Womanist Theology: Black Women's Experience as a Source for Doing Theology, with Special Reference to Christology," in Barr, *Constructive Christian Theology in the Worldwide Church*, 346–47.

18. N. T. Wright, *Jesus and the Victory of God*, vol. 2 of *Christian Origins and the Question of God* (Minneapolis: Fortress, 1996), 172.

19. For Muslim, Hindu, and Buddhist testimonies, see *JBC*, 127–30, 185–88, 196–99.

20. Pinchas Lapide, *Israelis, Jews, and Jesus*, trans. Peter Heinegg (Garden City, NY: Doubleday, 1979), 6, quoting from Joseph Klausner, *Jesus of Nazareth: His Life, Times, and Teaching*, trans. Herbert Danby (New York: Macmillan, 1925), without page reference.

Buddhist views is Jesus's emphasis on the kingdom and eschatological rule of God. This rejection also applies to the other three religions engaged here.

Miracle-Worker

The Theological Meaning of Healing and Deliverance

Jesus was also an itinerant "miracle-worker," healer, and exorcist. Whereas premodern theology took the miraculous acts as proof of the divinity of Jesus of Nazareth, the Enlightenment epistemology bluntly rejected their factual and historical nature. At its best, classical liberalism took the miracles as "myths" elicited by the powerful encounter with Jesus; even if they never happened, they still were of great value in pointing to the influence of Jesus on his followers. Both of these paradigms are problematic theologically. Unlike the precritical interpretation, the key New Testament passages that speak of incarnation and divinity do not resort to miracles as their support. And unlike the reductionistic modernist rejection of the miraculous, contemporary epistemologies and worldviews allow us to accept the possibility of the miraculous, as was discussed in the context of divine action (chap. 3).

Fortunately, with the spread of Christianity to the Global South, the modernist refusal to grant the possibility of the miraculous has faced a major challenge. Among the several titles appropriate for Jesus Christ in African cultures, one is the Healer.[21] Health means not only lack of sickness but also well-being in a holistic sense. Sickness is a result not only of physical symptoms but also of spiritual causes. Unlike their counterparts in the West, African Christians reject both the secularist worldview and missionaries' Western conceptions of reality and the spiritual. "Orthodoxy" has left Christians helpless in real life, and so an alternative theology has been needed that relates to the whole range of needs that includes the spiritual but is not limited to abstract, otherworldly spiritual needs. Indeed, for many African Christologists, healing is the central feature of the life and ministry of Jesus Christ. A parallel can be found between the figure of Jesus of the Gospels as the itinerant healer and the traditional African medicine man. Both practice

21. For an important recent discussion, see Timothy C. Tennent, *Theology in the Context of World Christianity: How the Global Church Is Influencing the Way We Think about and Discuss Theology* (Grand Rapids: Zondervan, 2007), 109–22.

a holistic form of healing on the physical, mental, and social levels, even on the environmental level. Of all Christian traditions, Pentecostalism and later charismatic movements have focused on the role of Jesus Christ as the healer.

What is the theological meaning of the mighty deeds of Jesus? They indicate God's approval of the ministry of Jesus. Rather than done by Beelzebub, the mighty deeds are the function of the Spirit of God (Mark 3:20–30). Similarly to the parables, the mighty deeds, including exorcisms, point to the coming of the kingdom of God: "But if it is by the Spirit of God that I cast out demons, then the kingdom of God has come upon you" (Matt. 12:28).

At the same time, the mighty works also link with the Old Testament and its prophetic fulfillment in their restoring to membership and community those who, through sickness or possession of evil spirits, had been excluded. Jesus's healing bodily contact with people considered "untouchable," such as the woman with bleeding (Mark 5:24–34), meant that "Jesus challenged the ideology that women's bodies were polluted by refusing to consider that he became unclean by touching her."[22]

The healing ministry of Jesus is a robust statement about the all-inclusiveness of God's salvation; it includes the physical and emotional as well as the spiritual. Healings also were signs of profound sympathy, of cosuffering (Matt. 14:14). Finally, healings and other mighty deeds anticipate eschatological fullness (for theology of healing, see chap. 8).

Healings and Miracles among Religions

Miracles are of course known among religions. What makes Islam unique is that, on the one hand, the Qur'an does not chronicle any specific miracle performed by Muhammad, since the miracle of the Qur'an itself—as the Word of God—is by far the biggest and most important miracle. On the other hand, the Qur'an recounts several miracles of Jesus, such as healing the leper and raising people from the dead. The Qur'an also knows miracles such as shaping a living bird out of clay based on the apocryphal gospels (5:110). A remarkable miracle is the table sent down from heaven spread with good as the divine proof of Jesus's truthfulness as the spokesperson for God and the divine providence (5:112–15). That said, Jesus's miracles do not make him

22. John R. Levison and P. Pope-Levison, "Christology: 4. The New Contextual Christologies: Liberation and Inculturation," in *GDT*, 178.

divine; indeed, miracles belong to the repertoire of prophets, and they attest to their authenticity.

Understandably, most Hindus, similarly, have no quandaries with miracles reported as by Jesus. When it comes to Buddhism, Mahayana traditions are particularly familiar with miraculous stories of Gautama Buddha and other enlightened ones. However, similarly to Islam, what is radically different among Buddhist thinkers is the interpretation of the meaning of miracles. The capacity to perform miracles points to the fact that Jesus was an extraordinary individual, but it does not point to deity or link with the kingdom of God, as outlined above.

Separately from numerous miracles recounted in the Old Testament, Jewish appraisal of the New Testament claims to Jesus's miracles is more complicated. They are routinely considered to be "magic," often with the Old Testament–based suspicion about an effort to establish one's credentials on the basis of miracles since, as Deuteronomy 13 reminds us, a (messianic) pretender may excel in miraculous acts and yet lead astray the people of God.

Jesus in the Matrix of Diverse Global Contexts and Challenges

The Emergence of "Global" Testimonies to Christ

For countless Christians in the Global South, faith in Christ used to mean a necessary and uncritical renouncing of their previous culture and beliefs. Yet, speaking of the biggest Christian continent currently, "Jesus was in Africa even before the rise of Christianity," in that his family found a hiding place in Egypt and one of the first converts was Ethiopian, among other early allusions.[23] Recall also that a number of early theologians such as Tertullian, Cyprian, and Augustine were North Africans.

One area to test the fruitfulness of a global approach to Christology involves something that played a significant role in traditional Christology but has become marginal in contemporary theology, namely, the various "titles" assigned to Christ. African theologians have discerned parallels between the New Testament teaching concerning Jesus Christ and the traditional African worldview and beliefs. The ancient idea of *Christus Victor*, the powerful

23. Anton Wessels, *Images of Jesus: How Jesus Is Perceived and Portrayed in Non-European Cultures* (Grand Rapids: Eerdmans, 1990), 98–99, here 98.

Christ who rose from the dead and defeated the opposing powers, speaks of overcoming the spell and threat of spirits, magic, disease, and death. Similarly, the "Redeemer" rescues people from enslavement to the evil forces that surround them.[24]

A distinctive approach to appropriating Jesus Christ's local and contextual meaning is attempted in Asian[25] and African[26] contexts by employing the culturally relevant ancestry terminology and imagery. The Roman Catholic C. Nyamiti's widely acclaimed *Christ as Our Ancestor* (1984) is one of the trailblazers. Ancestors mediate between humans and the divine, and they occupy a sacred status. They remind us of the close link between the living and the dead. It does not take too much imagination to see here some thematic parallels with Jesus Christ.

Critical Western scholarship should not dismiss these contextual interpretations as precritical inventions but rather take them as legitimate interpretations of the churches of the continent that is now the "most Christianized" of all. At the same time, similarly to all other constructions, they merit sympathetic critique, including whether they succeed in affirming an orthodox account of the full humanity and divinity of Jesus Christ and his place in the Trinity.

Jesus and Liberation

Christology as a Form of Liberation Theology

One of the complaints of liberation theologians and theologians from the Global South is that traditional theology is too quick to move to abstract speculations of Chalcedonian "metaphysical" Christology. Jesus's role as social critic, challenger of prejudices and conventional ways of society, as well

24. Charles Nyamiti, "African Christologies Today," in *Faces of Jesus in Africa*, ed. R. J. Schreiter (Maryknoll, NY: Orbis, 1991).

25. Jung Young Lee, "Ancestor Worship: From a Theological Perspective," in *Ancestor Worship and Christianity in Korea*, ed. Jung Young Lee (Lewiston, NY: Edwin Mellen, 1988), 83–91; Peter C. Phan, *Christianity with an Asian Face: Asian American Theology in the Making* (Maryknoll, NY: Orbis, 2003), 135–45.

26. Kwame Bediako, *Jesus in African Culture: A Ghanaian Perspective* (Accra: Asampa, 1990); Mika Vähäkangas, "Trinitarian Processions as Ancestral Relationships in Charles Nyamiti's Theology: A European Lutheran Critique," *Revue Africaine de Théologie* 21 (1997): 61–75.

as his table fellowship with the marginalized do not loom large in that kind of Christology. The Roman Catholic Peruvian Gustavo Gutiérrez rightly insists that the turn to liberation, rather than being an optional move, is "a question *about the very meaning of Christianity and about the mission of the Church.*"[27]

The most recent Jesus research has highlighted the social, political, and ideological importance of Jesus's radical egalitarianism. According to John Dominic Crossan, that is "something infinitely more terrifying than (contemporary democracy)."[28] There is an important link with Buddhist tradition here. It, too, began as a reformist movement, albeit of a different kind. Whereas Jesus aimed his criticism mainly at social structures and religious practices that marginalized and oppressed the weaker classes of the society, Gautama's desire was to renew Indian religious beliefs and practices in search of a new ethical approach. Buddha was not uninterested in social issues, but neither were they at the forefront of his thought.[29]

A growing number of Christian theologians from various contexts and agendas—female theologians in search of sexual equality, other liberationists looking for sociopolitical and economic equality, and postcolonialists with the desire to unmask the injustices of colonialism—are asking whether the principles of inclusivity, openness, justice, equality, and reconciliation could be highlighted in traditional Christologies.

"Can a Male Savior Save Women?"

The feminist Rosemary Radford Ruether's now classic question, "Can a male savior save women?"[30] has become a clarion call for a liberationist questioning of traditional Christologies by women of various agendas, (white) feminists, (African American) womanists, (Latina) *mujeristas*, and women from Asia, Africa, and Latin America. Female images are needed to both challenge and correct overly literalist and patriarchal ways of speaking of the Divine and so introduce alternative symbols and metaphors of the divine, "discourses of

27. Gustavo Gutiérrez, *A Theology of Liberation: History, Politics, and Salvation*, trans. and ed. Sister Caridad Inda and John Eagleson (Maryknoll, NY: Orbis, 1986 [1973]; rev. ed. with a new introduction, 1988), xi.

28. Cited in José Ignacio Cabezón, "Buddhist Views of Jesus," in *JWF*, 17.

29. Christopher S. Queen and Sally B. King, eds., *Engaged Buddhism: Buddhist Liberation Movements in Asia* (Albany: State University of New York Press, 1996).

30. Rosemary Radford Ruether, *To Change the World: Christology and Cultural Criticism* (New York: Crossroad, 1981), 45–56.

emancipatory transformation."[31] It is not without significance that whereas in the New Testament Logos is linked with Jesus of Nazareth, the Jewish male, its Old Testament background also stems from the concept of Wisdom (Hebrew *hokmah*, Greek *sophia*) that is widely taken as a female symbol and certainly functions so in Proverbs ("Lady Wisdom"). Furthermore, many actions attributed to "Jesus-Sophia" involve activities, characteristics, and gestures that are as much female as male. At the same time, the biblical Sophia also bespeaks justice and peace, having incarnated and thus identified with suffering humanity.[32]

What about the fact that biblically the Word-made-flesh is male? From the historical and cultural point of view, that choice is fully understandable. That cultural milieu affirmed the predominance of the masculine sex; all religions' "founders" and holy persons were men. Yet despite divine incarnation in a Jewish male, Logos as the universal principle of reality is of course beyond gender. Had the incarnation occurred in the form of the female sex, the corresponding problem would be how to include the male sex. Hence, replacing male-dominated talk about the divinity with female-dominated talk is counterproductive. It would sharpen rather than help resolve the issue of lack of inclusivity. A true human being can only exist as either male or female.

Black Christ?

James Cone points out that since the Christ of the dominant forms of Christianity is presented as a white Christ tailored to the values of modern white society, there is a need for a black Christ: "If Jesus Christ is to have any meaning for us, he must leave the security of the suburbs by joining blacks in their condition. What need have we for a white Jesus when we are not white but black? If Jesus Christ is white and not black, he is an oppressor, and we must kill him."[33] Later on, Cone softened his rhetoric against the "white Christ," granting that his early theology was too much a reaction. But even then, he continued to hold the opinion that the "*norm of all God-talk which seeks to be black-talk is the manifestation of Jesus as the black Christ who provides the necessary soul for black liberation.*"[34]

31. Elizabeth Johnson, *She Who Is: The Mystery of God in Feminist Theological Discourse* (New York: Crossroad, 1993), 5.

32. Johnson, *She Who Is*, 165–67.

33. Cone, *Black Theology of Liberation*, 117.

34. Cone, *Black Theology of Liberation*, 38.

Cone's standpoint joins the long conversation among African American religious thinkers and theologians concerning the necessity and meaning of a black Christ/Messiah: from Alexander Young's "Ethiopian Manifesto" (1829) to Howard Thurman's *Jesus and the Disinherited* (1949) to Albert Cleage's *Black Messiah* (1968). Cleage's most controversial claim is that Jesus of Nazareth, as a member of his people, was literally black. As a corrective, J. Deotis Roberts's *Black Theology in Dialogue* (1987) conceives of the "black Messiah" symbolically. This nuanced and insightful christological interpretation makes it possible both for blacks and for whites to affirm the idea of the black Christ/Messiah as a contextual interpretation, similar to, say, the African title of the Ancestor.

The Face of Jesus in the Poor

The Latin American Catholic term "integral liberation" denotes Jesus's liberating ministry that takes into consideration different dimensions of life, whether social, political, economic, or cultural. The idea of integral liberation insists that "spiritual" and "earthly" belong integrally together. Those that Jesus delivered—the sick, the demon possessed, those outside the covenant community—became signs of the coming kingdom and its power of liberation and reconciliation.

Alongside this "sacramental approach" to Christology, Leonardo Boff advocates a "socioanalytical presentation of Christology." It attempts sociopolitical structural change by drawing from theology and sociopolitical analysis.[35]

Liberationists have rightly argued that Christ's presence is to be found among the poor, not in an exclusive sense (maintaining that Christ is present *only* in the poor) but in an inclusive way, stating that Christ is present *at least* among the poor and the outcasts. Recall that Jesus himself was poor. A significant majority of the "common people" of the world are poor and marginalized, such as the Dalits (caste-less) of India and *minjung* ("masses of people") in Korea. Alongside the doctrinal and proclaimed "Christology of the *kerygma*," a liberationist Christology is also called for.[36]

35. Leonardo Boff, *Jesus Christ Liberator: A Critical Christology for Our Time*, trans. Patrick Hughes (Maryknoll, NY: Orbis, 1978), 269–78.

36. Sathianathan Clarke, Deenabandhu Manchala, and Philip Vinod Peacock, eds., *Dalit Theology in the Twenty First Century: Discordant Voices, Discerning Pathways* (New Delhi: Oxford University Press, 2010); Byung Mu Ahn, "Jesus and the People (Minjung)," in *Asian Faces of Jesus*, ed. R. S. Sugirtharajah (Maryknoll, NY: Orbis, 1993), 163–72.

Christ, Power, and the Empire

Why should Christology be mindful of power issues? Simply because the figure of Christ has been used both by Christian and by secular authorities in a way that has supported and facilitated colonialist enterprises. At the end of the fifteenth century, when South America was discovered under the leadership of Christopher ("The Christ-Bearer") Columbus and taken over by the conquistadors (Spanish soldiers), the figure of Christ was introduced to the first nations of the continent. The Christ presented to the Indios represented the side of the powerful and the ruler. This was followed by enormous suffering among the masses due to colonialism, linked with Christ's legacy.[37]

Not only in Latin America but also in many parts of Asia "it was largely colonization and evangelization in tandem that brought and propagated the western understanding of Jesus," foreign to the culture and hostile to its customs and beliefs.[38] The shadow of the "European Jesus" superimposed by the colonialists of the past centuries is a continuous challenge to Asian theologians as they are in the process of rediscovering the "Asian faces of Jesus"[39]—and this in the midst of religious plurality and rampant poverty.

These examples from various global contexts suffice to remind contemporary theology to be mindful not only of dogmatic-doctrinal issues around Jesus the Christ but also of cultural-religious and sociopolitical issues. Moving now to doctrinal issues is not to leave these issues behind.

The Chalcedonian Tradition: A Horizon for Understanding Christ

Christological Creedal Affirmations and Their Rebuttals[40]

How to Explain the Presence of God in Jesus

Classical christological traditions are based on creedal traditions, the so-called two-nature Christology, culminating in the "definition" (creed) of Chalcedon

37. Wessels, *Images of Jesus*, 58–61.

38. José M. de Mesa, "Making Salvation Concrete and Jesus Real: Trends in Asian Christology," January 1, 1999, 2, available by permission of *SEDOS* on the Network for Strategic Missions: http://www.strategicnetwork.org/index.php?loc=kb&view=v&id=07429&mode=v&pagenum=1&lang=.

39. Sugirtharajah, *Asian Faces of Jesus*.

40. Based directly on Kärkkäinen, *Christology*, chap. 3.

in 451, following the Nicene-Constantinopolitan (381) and other creeds. What possibly could be their significance and authority for the third millennium's secular and religiously pluralistic culture? Before responding to that significant theological question, we will look briefly at the main affirmations of classical creedal Christology. This also requires a mapping out and clarification of the key heretical challenges to "orthodoxy."

Somewhat counterintuitively, a main debate present in the New Testament was not so much about whether Christ was divine but rather if Christians could affirm fully Christ's humanity—so much so that in the Johannine community, belief in Christ's humanity became the criterion for true orthodoxy (1 John 4:2–3). But in the postbiblical incipient Christian theology, founded in the strict monotheism of Judaism, the problem soon became how to deal with the claim that Jesus of Nazareth had been raised from the dead and made equal to the Father.[41]

In the second century, the christological debate centered on the question of the divinity of Christ; most early church fathers took it for granted that Christ was human. This is not to ignore some heretical groups that either denied or contested his true humanity—the most important of which are Ebionites (from a Hebrew term meaning "the poor ones"), primarily a Jewish sect that regarded Jesus as an ordinary human being, the son of Mary and Joseph, and docetists (from the Greek word *dokeō*, "to seem" or "to appear"), according to which Christ was completely divine but his humanity was merely an appearance—but rather to say that these were fairly easily defeated.[42] Docetism had a divine Savior who had no real connection with humanity. Ebionitism had only a human, moral example but no divine Savior.

The first major attempt to express in precise language the New Testament's dual emphasis on Christ as both a human being and a divine figure came to be known as Logos Christology, with the help of the second-century apologists (Justin Martyr and others) who sought to establish a correlation with Greek philosophy and Judaism. The idea of logos, referring to wisdom, learning, philosophy, and divine insight, was known among the Greeks and had a solid Old

41. J. N. D. Kelly, *Early Christian Doctrines*, rev. ed. (New York: Harper & Row, 1978 [1960]), 87.

42. Docetism was related to a cluster of other philosophical and religious ideas that are often lumped together under the umbrella term "gnosticism" (from the Greek term *gnōsis*, "knowledge"). This term is elusive and may denote several things. The most important contribution gnosticism made with regard to docetism was the idea of dualism between matter and spirit. It regarded spirit as the higher and purer part of creation, whereas matter represented frailty and even sinfulness. William C. Placher, *A History of Christian Theology* (Philadelphia: Westminster, 1983), 45–49, 68–70.

Testament background (the Hebrew term *dabar*). Taking John 1:14 as his key text, Justin Martyr argued that the same logos that was known by pagan philosophers had now appeared in the person of Jesus of Nazareth; indeed, philosophers had taught that the reason in every human being participates in the universal logos. The Gospel of John teaches that in Jesus Christ the logos became flesh.[43]

Origen, the leading second/third-century church father from the Eastern Christian church, taught that in the incarnation the human soul of Christ was united with the Logos with this analogy: "If a lump of iron is constantly kept in a fire, it will absorb its heat through all its pores and veins."[44] As a consequence of this union between the Logos and Jesus of Nazareth, Jesus is the true God. One of Origen's most profound contributions was the establishment and clarification of Christ's preexistence, a conviction that was already present among earlier theologians but only as an incipient, elusive idea. Origen taught that the Father had begotten the Son by an eternal act; therefore, Christ existed from eternity.

The Unique Status of the Father in Relation to the Son

As soon as the divine status of the Son of the Father came to be established, the relation to the uniqueness of the Father called for clarification. This task led to a group of views soon to be deemed heretical known by the term "monarchianism," which means "sole sovereignty." For our purposes, there are two subcategories of this view: dynamic and modalistic monarchianism from the late second and early third centuries. They stressed the uniqueness and unity of God to the measure that either made the status of the Son lower than that of the Father or subsumed what the later Trinitarian doctrine calls three "persons" (Father, Son, Spirit) under each other.

The way dynamic monarchianism sought to preserve the "sole sovereignty" of the Father was founded on the idea that God was dynamically present in Jesus, thus making him higher than any other human being but not yet God. Whether at baptism or resurrection (or perhaps at the moment of virgin birth), God's power (Greek *dynamis*) made Jesus *almost* God but not equal to the Father, by which the Father's uniqueness was secured.[45] This view was condemned by the Synod of Antioch in 268.

43. Justin Martyr, *First Apology* 45.

44. Origen, *First Principles* 2.6.6 (in *ANF*, vol. 4).

45. The most well-known proponents were Theodotus, a Byzantine leather merchant, and Paul of Samosata. Kelly, *Early Christian Doctrines*, 115–19.

In modalistic monarchianism, the three persons of the Trinity are not self-subsistent "persons" but are "modes" or "names" of the same God (in one version, successive revelations of the same God). They are like three "faces" of God, with a different one presented depending on the occasion. Whereas dynamic monarchianism seemed to deny the Trinity, indicating that Jesus is less than God, modalistic monarchianism appeared to affirm the Trinity. Both, however, tried to preserve the oneness of God the Father, though in different ways. Modalistic monarchianism was considered heretical by the church, as was its dynamic counterpart. The account of Jesus's baptism, during which the Father spoke to his Son and the Spirit descended on the Son, alone seemed to contradict the idea of modalism.

But even the orthodox position had to struggle with the question, If Christ is divine but is not the Father, are there not two Gods? Tertullian, one of the ablest early Christian theologians, coined much of the Trinitarian vocabulary. He sought to clarify this problem with a series of metaphors: "For the root and the tree are distinctly two things, but correlatively joined; the fountain and the river are also two forms, but indivisible; so likewise the sun and the ray are two forms, but coherent ones. Everything which proceeds from something else must needs be second to that from which it proceeds, without being on that account separated."[46] By analogies such as these, Tertullian and others believed they had clarified the New Testament distinction between Father and Son without leading to belief in two gods. But one may seriously ask whether this is the case. Metaphors such as the one depicting the Father as the sun and the Son as a ray imply subordinationism, that Christ is inferior to the Father. In fact, these ideas and related problems associated with defining Christ's relation to the Father led to the emergence of a new set of questions.

How to Define Christ's Deity in Relation to the Father: Arianism

As soon as Christian theology had combated monarchianism, it faced an even more challenging problem named Arianism, after Arius, a priest of Alexandria (even though historically it is unclear whether Arius himself ever expressed the ideas associated with his name). According to his opponents (on whose reports we have to depend here), Arianism taught that God the Father is absolutely unique and transcendent, and God's essence (the Greek term *ousia*

46. Tertullian, *Against Praxeas* 8 (in *ANF*, vol. 3); see Kelly, *Early Christian Doctrines*, 110–15, 149–53.

means both "essence" and "substance") cannot be shared by another, not even the Son. Consequently, the distinction between Father and Son was one of substance (*ousia*); if they were of the same (divine) substance, there would be two gods. Rather than sharing the same "essence" with the Father, the Son is the first and unique creation of God. A saying attributed to Arius emphasizes his main thesis about the origin of Christ: "There was [a time] when he was not." That would of course make the Son a creature rather than preexistent god.[47]

Behind Arianism is either the monarchianist kind of concern to preserve the uniqueness of the Father, stemming from Jewish monotheistic intuitions, or, as a segment of more recent scholarship surmises, perhaps a Greco-Roman cultural resistance to associating the deity with suffering and death. Although for the Greco-Roman world the idea of a human becoming divine is not a problem (as it was to Jewish intuitions), the attempt to link the divine with earthly sufferings is totally impossible. Hence, compromising the full deity of the Son would help preserve this assumption.

Be that as it may, mainstream Christian theology had to respond to this challenge because it seemed to compromise the basic confession of Christ's deity. The ablest defender of the full deity of Christ, the Eastern father Athanasius of Alexandria argued in response that the view that the Son was a creature, albeit at a higher level, would have a decisive consequence for salvation. Only God can save, whereas a creature is in need of being saved. Thus, if Jesus were not God incarnate, he would not be able to save us. Furthermore, both the New Testament and church liturgy call Jesus "Savior," indicating that he is God. Worship of and prayer to a Jesus who is less than God would also make Christians guilty of blasphemy.[48]

In the spirit of Athanasius's and other mainline theologians' responses to Arius, the Council of Nicea (as formulated in the 381 Constantinopolitan Creed)[49] defined Christ's deity in a way that made Christ equal to God the Father. The text says:

> We believe . . . in one Lord Jesus Christ, the Son of God, begotten of the Father [the only begotten, that is, of the essence of the Father, God of God], Light of Light, very God of very God, begotten, not made, being of one substance [*homoousios*] with the Father; by whom all things were

47. Kelly, *Early Christian Doctrines*, 226–31.

48. Kelly, *Early Christian Doctrines*, 240–47, 284–89.

49. The creedal text referred to as the Nicene Creed is from the 381 Constantinople Council, which gave it final formulation. Hence, often it is named the Nicene-Constantinopolitan Creed.

> made [both in heaven and on earth]; who for us men, and for our salvation, came down and was incarnate and was made man; he suffered, and the third day he rose again, ascended into heaven; from thence he shall come to judge the quick and the dead.

An appendix at the end listed Arian tenets to be rejected:

> But for those who say: "There was a time when he was not"; and "He was not before he was made"; and "He was made out of nothing," or "He is of another substance" or "essence," or "The Son of God is created," or "changeable," or "alterable"—they are condemned by the holy catholic and apostolic Church.[50]

According to the creed, Christ was not created but was "begotten of the substance of the Father." The key word was the Greek *homoousios*, which created great debate. It means literally "of the same substance" or "of the same essence," indicating that Christ was equal in divinity to the Father. Not all theologians were happy with that definition (notwithstanding universal affirmation of Christ's deity by the orthodox party). Especially theologians from the Eastern wing of the church, the Greek Church, would have preferred the Greek term *homoiousios*. The difference is one *i*, which makes a difference in meaning: *homoi* means "similar to," whereas *homo* means "the same." In other words, this formulation would not make Christ identical with the Father but similar to the Father. Greek theologians were concerned that the stricter formulation could lead to modalism, whereas for Latin-speaking theologians the "similar to" clause could be taken to imply support for subordinationism (leading up even to endorsing Arian heresy).

This difference of opinion between the Greek- and Latin-speaking churches did not lead to a division or a permanent labeling of either side as heretical, but it did highlight a growing gulf between the Christian East and (what became later) the Christian West. They began to develop their own distinctive approaches to Christ, namely, the Antiochian and Alexandrian schools. Each school produced a distinctive Christology, which in turn gave rise to distinctive christological heresies. This is a critical stage on the way to the Chalcedonian "solution" in 451.

50. Philip Schaff, ed., *The Creeds of Christendom*, 3 vols. (New York: Harper & Row, 1877; 6th ed. reprint, Grand Rapids: Baker, 1990), 1:28–29.

The Divinity and Humanity of Christ: "One-Nature" and "Two-Nature" Heresies Combated

In the aftermath of Nicea, a complex issue came under consideration: Granted that Christ is divine, how are Christ's two natures—divine and human—related to each other? Among the leading centers of Christian learning and authority (along with Constantinople, another leading Eastern center, and Rome in the West, among others), Alexandria and Antioch came to define the issue of "two natures" from different perspectives.[51]

Alexandrian Christology emphasized soteriological questions and expressed its doctrine of salvation in terms of deification or divinization (Greek *theōsis*), that is, union between the divine and human. In doing so, Alexandrians' main focus was naturally on the divinity of Christ—to the point that (while not, of course, denying the human nature) theirs was a much more "one-nature" Christology (technically called monophysitism, from Greek terms meaning "one" and "nature") in comparison with the "two-nature" view of Antioch.

In contrast, the Antiochean school sought to hold together the divine and human natures, paying more attention to the theological significance of the latter than their Alexandrian counterparts. For Antioch, Christ's earthly life and obedience played a more important role. One can easily imagine that out of these two Eastern church orientations distinctive kinds of heretical views could emerge when taking either focus to the extreme: on the Alexandrian side, a strong leaning toward *monophysitism* led some to the virtual denial of Jesus's human nature, and on the Antiochean side, the distinction between the two natures was claimed by opponents to result in separation of the natures altogether.

The explanation of Cyril of Alexandria, a leading Alexandrian theologian, emphasized the reality of the union of the two natures in the incarnation to the point that after that union, one nature existed, for the Logos had united human nature to itself. This raised the question of what kind of human nature was assumed. Did Christ's nature encompass all of human nature? A heretical view called Apollinarianism tried to answer these questions in a less than satisfactory way.[52] Apollinarius of Laodicea worried about the increasingly

51. Although geographically both cities belong to the Christian East (and were thus Greek speaking), during the centuries they also gave impetus to the division between Greek and Latin Christianities (or the Christian East and Christian West, respectively, which formalized itself only after the formal split in 1054).

52. There are other forms of one-nature heretical views, including the obscure Eu-

widespread belief that the Logos assumed human nature in its entirety because, in his estimation, it would lead to the belief that the Logos was contaminated by the weaknesses of human nature. If so, the sinlessness of Christ would be compromised. To avoid this unacceptable view, Apollinarius suggested that if a real human mind in Jesus were replaced by a purely divine mind, obviously immune to any sinful tendencies, that would solve the issue. But the problem, which his opponents rightly noted, was that this move renders the human nature of Christ incomplete. One of the Cappadocians, Gregory Nazianzen, concluded that it would effectually lead to the compromising of Jesus's role as Savior because only part of the humanity would be assumed by the saving incarnation; that kind of Christ could not fully identify with humans.[53]

Another kind of heretical challenge emerged in Antioch's Christology with a more fully "two-nature" approach. Particularly in response to Apollinarianism, there was a need for "a thoroughly realistic acknowledgment of the human life and experiences of the Incarnate and of the theological significance of His human soul." In that sense Antioch "deserves credit for bringing back the historical Jesus."[54] It taught that redemption calls for obedience on the part of humanity. But of course humans are unable to, so God's initiative is needed: the Redeemer unites humanity and divinity and thus establishes an obedient people of God. This view defends the two natures of Christ: he was at one and the same time both God and a human being. Not surprisingly, the Alexandrians criticized Antioch for denying the unity of Christ.

Against this criticism, the Antiochians' response spoke of the "perfect conjunction" between the human and the divine natures of Christ. In keeping with this, Antioch's leading theologian, Theodore of Mopsuestia, strongly opposed the apparent neglect of Christ's human nature by the Alexandrians, emphasizing that Christ assumed both genuine human body and "soul" (will and rationality). On the basis of biblical teaching, Theodore believed that in Jesus's case the taking on of humanity did not include a sinful nature. Theodore also strongly argued that the two natures of Christ do not compromise his unity. That said, one strand of the Antiochian school did in fact emphasize the two natures so much that it affirmed a view that seemed to separate the humanity and the divinity from each other, making them more or less separate entities. This view is known as Nestorianism.

---

tychianism, after Eutyches, an elderly monk and archimandrite, rejected in more than one council, including Chalcedon. Kelly, *Early Christian Doctrines*, 33–34.

53. Gregory Nazianzen, *Letter to Cledonius the Priest against Apollinarius*, epistle 101, in *NPNF*[2] 7:440. For Orthodox responses to Apollinarianism (with the focus on the two Cappadocians Gregory of Nyssa and Gregory of Nazianzus), see Kelly, *Early Christian Doctrines*, 295–301.

54. Kelly, *Early Christian Doctrines*, 302; for the basic teachings of Antioch, see 301–9.

Similarly to Arianism, the label "Nestorianism" is questionable because we do not know for sure whether Nestorius, patriarch of Constantinople in the first part of the fifth century, actually taught this doctrine. The controversy surrounding Nestorianism arose over the use of the term *theotokos* (God-bearing) in regard to Mary. Was Mary, the mother of Jesus, the mother of God? Nestorius, as a spokesman for a larger group, stated that *theotokos* is appropriate insofar as it is complemented by the term *anthropotokos* (human-bearing). However, Nestorius's own preference was *Christotokos* (Christ-bearing). What was at stake in these technical terminological distinctions? Nestorius maintained that it is impossible to believe that God would have a mother; no woman can give birth to God. Instead, what Mary bore was not God but humanity, a sort of instrument of divinity. Nestorius feared that if the term *theotokos* were applied to Mary without qualifications, it would lead to either Arianism, according to which Jesus was not equal to God, or Apollinarianism, which taught that Jesus's human nature was not real. In the East, however, the term *theotokos* was widely used by Alexandrians. It was often coupled with another ancient concept, *communicatio idiomatum* ("communication of attributes"), which played a significant role in various doctrinal contexts throughout history. With regard to Jesus's two natures, the expression means that what pertains to one nature also pertains to the other. In other words, because we can say that Mary bore the human baby Jesus, we can also at the same time say that Mary bore the divine person Christ. What, then, made Nestorius's doctrine unorthodox? Historical and conceptual problems aside, his Alexandrian opponents simply charged him with believing that Jesus had two natures joined in a purely moral union but not in a real way (as *communicatio idiomatum* suggests). Although Nestorius repudiated this interpretation of his view, this interpretation continued until it was rejected at the Council of Ephesus in 431.

The Chalcedonian "Solution": Its Main Affirmations

With the Nicean faith in its preamble, the creed from the Council of Chalcedon (451) attempted to solve the christological debates in a way that could be embraced by both Alexandrians and Antiochians. The controlling principle of Chalcedon holds that provided Jesus Christ was both truly divine and truly human, the precise manner in which this is articulated or explored is not of fundamental importance. Although the council was unable to state definitely how the union of the two natures occurred, it was able to say how this union *cannot* be expressed. One could perhaps say that, on the one hand, Chalcedon functioned as a signpost pointing in the right direction, and on the other hand, it was a fence separating orthodoxy and heresy.[55]

> We, then, following the holy Fathers, all with one consent, teach men to confess one and the same Son, our Lord Jesus Christ, the same perfect in Godhood and also perfect in manhood; truly God and truly man, of a reasonable [rational] soul and body; consubstantial [coessential] with the Father according to the Godhood, and consubstantial with us according to the Manhood; in all things like unto us, without sin; begotten before all ages of the Father according to the Godhood, and in these latter days, for us and for our salvation, born of the Virgin Mary, the Mother of God, according to the Manhood; one and the same Christ, Son, Lord, Only-begotten, to be acknowledged in two natures, inconfusedly, unchangeably, indivisibly, inseparably; the distinction of natures being by no means taken away by the union, but rather the property of each nature being preserved, and concurring in one Person and one Subsistence, not parted or divided into two persons, but one and the same Son, and only begotten, God the Word, the Lord Jesus Christ, as the prophets from the beginning [have declared] concerning him, and the Lord Jesus Christ himself has taught us, and the Creed of the holy Fathers has handed down to us.[56]

Chalcedon takes great pains in affirming, on the one hand, the true humanity and deity of Jesus Christ and, on the other hand, both the unity and duality of this God-man. These affirmations could only be defined negatively with the help of four terms: "unconfusedly," "unchangeably," "indivisibly," and "inseparably." Even though distinguished, the two "natures" in one person are not to be separated or conflated; in other words, divinity and humanity cannot be a mixture that would lead to a "third nature."[57]

Tradition presupposed that in the New Testament both divine and human attributes are predicated of one subject, Christ (the divine Word, Logos), as seems to be the case in passages such as Acts 3:15 and John 17:5, among others. Logos, the divine Word, is the "subject" of the Incarnate One, expressed in tradition with the help of the term "hypostatic union." The divinity and

55. For these expressions, I am indebted to my Fuller colleague Professor Emeritus Colin Brown.

56. Schaff, *The Creeds of Christendom*, 2:62–63. For a short, important discussion of Chalcedon's theology, see Kelly, *Early Christian Doctrines*, 338–43.

57. See the influential "Leo's Tome": Leo I, "Letter [XXVIII] to Flavian Commonly Called Tome," 3; also 4; *NPNF*² 12:40–41.

humanity of Jesus Christ inhere, mutually indwell each other, without separation, without mingling of natures.

The Liabilities and Problems of Chalcedonian Tradition

Chalcedon is, as the late premier historian of dogma J. Pelikan memorably put it, "an agreement to disagree."[58] How do we assess its merits and liabilities in our contemporary setting? Do we have to stick with its formulations to be "orthodox"? A number of complaints and criticisms have been leveled against the two-nature, "incarnational" Christology of Chalcedon. The criticisms can be grouped under the following categories.

The Chalcedonian Christology has also been blamed for political bias, namely, for deriving its ethos from the church's alliance with the powers that be of the Constantinian empire. According to the feminist theologian Rosemary Radford Ruether, the "orthodox Christology" helped the marginal religious sect evolve "into the new imperial religion of a Christian Roman Empire."[59] That charge, however, has been successfully combated by the historical observation that it was rather the non-Chalcedonian Arian party that was more prone to look for earthly power sympathies.[60] No more convincing is the charge that Chalcedonian Christology led to the "patriarchalization of Christology" and a hierarchic view of the cosmos and the governing of the world. This claim grossly exaggerates the role of doctrine in the ascendancy of Christian religion into the place of power. Second, it ignores the fact that the development of Christian doctrine was in itself a long and complex process; hence, attempting to discern one leading motif, such as desire to enforce power structures, can hardly be supported by historical evidence.

Many wonder if the two-nature Christology by default tends to shift focus from the "lowliness" of Jesus, his suffering and anguish, to his divinity, exaltation, and triumph. Also, as long as the human nature assumed by the eternal Logos is conceived as a nonpersonal human nature, it is difficult to think of a particular human person. Doesn't it look more like "the human garment of the eternal Son"?[61] It is challenging to see any kind of identity between that kind of generic human nature and ours.

58. Pelikan, *CT* 1:266.

59. Ruether, *Sexism and God-Talk*, 122.

60. George Huntson Williams, "Christology and Church-State Relations in the Fourth Century," *Church History* 20, no. 3 (1951): 3–33; and 20, no. 4 (1951): 3–26.

61. Moltmann, *Way of Jesus Christ*, 51.

Several of these problems go back to difficulties in finding a satisfactory way to link the "two natures" with each other. Too often, traditional Christology has attempted to differentiate between the two natures on the basis of general—even static—metaphysics rather than the particular history of Jesus Christ himself. This tendency leads to nonpersonal models of explanation and tends to neglect the notions of true, vulnerable human nature.[62] The doctrinal discussion below seeks to respond to this very important issue.

A significant weakness of Chalcedonian Christology is the lack of focus on the whole history of Jesus the Christ; in other words, its horizon is hopelessly narrow. A glaring omission is the silence in the creeds of everything that has to do with the earthly life of Jesus, including his compassion, teaching, healings, exorcisms, and pronouncements of forgiveness. This is a real concern and has been responded to in this text.

Liberation theologians of various sorts have harshly critiqued the christological formulations of Nicea and Chalcedon, along with classical atonement theories, for their failure to relate to the issues of liberation and to instead concentrate exclusively on theological issues.[63] Liberationists claim they have little interest in Chalcedonian issues and wish to focus on Jesus's earthly ministry and life.[64] A brief theological response is simply this: rather than juxtaposing or leaving behind doctrinal considerations that would end up with a merely human teacher and advocate without any divine authority and eschatological consummation to usher in, let us make the liberationist impulse (similarly to the interfaith dimension) an integral part of christological discourse, as this text does.

Many critics of Chalcedon wonder if it can be saved from being equated with mythological parallels in gnosticism and religions. Myths about gods ascending and descending abound in religions. Notwithstanding some thematic parallels, the New Testament narrative of Logos does not present a gnostic redeemer myth in which a deity visits the earth for a while and then returns to the heavenly realm. Contrary to these temporary visits of gods in the myths, in Christian understanding God became human rather than changed into a human. And even after the ascension, the glorified Lord bears the marks of the incarnation.

In sum: these objections to the creedal tradition, even if some of them are less credible, are important to bear in mind and, if need be, incorporate in the continuing doctrinal work in Christology. This correction, however, does not warrant leaving behind the Chalcedonian model of explanation.

62. See Moltmann, *Way of Jesus Christ*, 53.

63. Cone, *God of the Oppressed*, 104.

64. Kelly Brown Douglas, *The Black Christ* (Maryknoll, NY: Orbis, 1994), 111–13.

The Continuing Relative Value of the Christology of the Creeds

The task of contemporary theology is to correct, expand, and reorient Christology, building critically on the basis of tradition and also using the Chalcedonian formula as the minimum criterion. Many of the problems mentioned above go back to the use of the terms "person" and "nature" in an abstract sense. However, they are to be defined and regulated ecclesiastically and theologically. They are not intended to mean that this is everything the Christian church says of Christ. Nor is it the case that everyone means—or even, originally, meant—the same thing with these terms. The martyred pastor Dietrich Bonhoeffer put it well: "The Chalcedonian Definition is an objective, but living, statement which bursts through all thought-forms."[65]

Of old, this creed has been called the Chalcedonian "definition." However, as the British theologian Sarah Coakley brilliantly notes, it is less a definition in the modern sense of the word and more—building on the etymology of the Greek term for definition, *horos*—a "horizon."[66] The many meanings of *horos*, "horizon," "boundary," "limit," "standard," "pattern," and "rule," remind us of the way early Christianity understood and employed a creedal statement: it was a "rule of faith" (*regula fidei*). The term "rule" here means guidance, limits, standards, and boundaries that help the community of faith to rule out heretical views and point to the shared consensus even when everything—or often, many things—in the rule is not exactly defined.[67] With Chalcedon we speak of something believed to have really happened in a way that can only be expressed as a rule of faith, rather than as a highly accurate "scientific" analysis. The late Jesuit K. Rahner reminds us that every theological formula, including Chalcedon, is "beginning and emergence, not conclusion and end . . . which opens the way to the-ever-greater-Truth."[68]

The genre of the definition is not a detached, "objective," systematic explanation of the details of how to understand "nature" or "union" or similar key terms. Rather, as a rule of faith, it is a "grid" through which reflections on

65. Dietrich Bonhoeffer, *Christ the Center*, trans. John Bowden (New York: Harper & Row, 1960), 92.

66. Sarah Coakley, "What Does Chalcedon Solve and What Does It Not? Some Reflections on the Status and Meaning of the Chalcedonian 'Definition,'" in *The Incarnation: An Interdisciplinary Symposium on the Incarnation of the Son of God*, ed. Stephen T. Davis et al. (Oxford: Oxford University Press, 2004), 160.

67. The term "symbol" for early creeds served the same function (and cannot be read in the "thin" sense of contemporary usage).

68. Karl Rahner, "Current Problems in Christology," in *Theological Investigations* 1, trans. Cornelius Ernst (London: Darton, Longman & Todd, 1965), 149; see also 150.

Christ's person must pass. As such, it only says so much, and even of those things it sees important to delineate, it does not say everything. Indeed, it leaves open a host of issues. Behind Chalcedon, similar to all rules of faith in early Christianity, is the soteriological (salvific) intent. Having confessed belief in the God-man, Jesus the Savior, Christians naturally wanted to say as much as they could about the person and "nature" of the Savior.

Creeds and Global Christianity

An important afterword to the discussion of the criteriological role of Chalcedon—especially in light of global Christianity—is the continuing legacy of the so-called non-Chalcedonian Christologies. It is impossible to understand the history of Christianity in the largest continent of the world, Asia, without acknowledging the crucial role played by two christological "schools" that deviate from the Chalcedonian tradition: Nestorianism and monophysitism. Nestorianism was *the* theological cause for the first major division in the church, between the Christian East and the Christian West, Europe and Asia, after the patristic era.

The gospel was introduced to China and surrounding areas by Nestorians during various times in history beginning in the seventh century. Its "two-nature" Christology was greatly interested in the human nature of Christ, allegedly because "it had long been known for its care for the poor and hungry," and therefore saw it fitting to "emphasize Christ's humanity, for only a completely human Christ could be an ethical and moral example."[69] The Nestorian interpretation has been immensely influential in the history of the largest continent of the world. The other "heresy" in the eyes of the advocates of the Chalcedonian creed, monophysite Christology, has similarly exercised a significant role in many parts of Asia, including India, and North Africa. It is understandable that a Hindu milieu with a wide embrace of the category of the divine would be particularly fertile soil for one-nature (divinity-driven) conception. The challenge and mandate to the global theological and ecclesiastical community are to find ways of affirming Chalcedon's "horizon" while affirming diverging orientations, which undoubtedly have borne good fruit.

Having examined established creedal orthodoxy and its meaning for us, we are ready to tackle a number of key christological doctrines before beginning the interfaith work.

69. Samuel Hugh Moffett, *A History of Christianity in Asia*, vol. 1, *Beginnings to 1500* (San Francisco: HarperSanFrancisco, 1992), 171.

Resurrection and the Identity of Jesus Christ

Resurrection as the Confirmation of Jesus's Deity

According to Paul, Jesus was "designated Son of God in power according to the Spirit of holiness by his resurrection from the dead" (Rom. 1:4). The significance of the resurrection for Christology lies in the fact that not only the title Son of God but basically all titles used in the early church stem from the Easter event, including the title Lord (*kyrios*). Paul also argues that the resurrection was the event of justification of Jesus's work of salvation (Rom. 4:25).

In Christian tradition, several proposals have been set forth as likely candidates for establishing the deity of Jesus, such as sinlessness, teaching "with authority" (Mark 1:22, 27), death on the cross, and Jesus's own claims to messiahship.[70] While important in themselves, none of these proposals has the capacity to constitute his deity. Even though human history knows no persons without sin, finding one wouldn't necessarily make that person a god, any more than would the most insightful and wonderful teaching per se. Jewish history knows a number of self-made messiahs who issued all kinds of claims without any basis in history or personality. Death on the cross is not any kind of unique event in human history; at its best, crucifixion could make Jesus a (failed) self-made messiah, after a host of other such figures in the Jewish milieu, or an innocent martyr.

We are thus left with resurrection as the most appropriate candidate for establishing Jesus's deity. When combined with his own claims of having been sent by his Father and the Father's promise of raising him up on the third day, resurrection can be seen as the divine vindication. That came on the day of Easter, and it was thus interpreted by the early church (Acts 13:30, among other passages). "The resurrection of Jesus Christ is the great verdict of God, the fulfilment and proclamation of God's decision concerning the event of the cross."[71]

At the same time, we should avoid the implication that resurrection "made" Jesus divine. That would be of course nothing but a version of adoptionism. Hence, the Pauline expression "designated Son of God" (Rom. 1:4) has to be read in a way that avoids this error.

For resurrection to function as vindication, its historical facticity has to be confirmed; that is the reasoning of Paul in 1 Corinthians 15.

70. Stanley J. Grenz, *Theology for the Community of God* (Grand Rapids: Eerdmans, 1994), 251–56.

71. Barth, *CD* IV/1, 309.

The Debate about the Historicity of the Resurrection

The biblical idea of resurrection is without parallels in religions. Even though religions know myths of gods rising and dying, those represent different genres and motifs. No wonder the gentile audience found the claim to resurrection incredible (Acts 17:32). Even in the Old Testament and Judaism, the resurrection of one single person, including the Messiah, before the resurrection of all at the end is totally unknown. Radically revising Jewish hopes, early Christianity saw in the resurrection of Jesus the beginning of the end times, culminating in the resurrection of all (1 Cor. 15:12–21).

Since the Enlightenment, the affirmation of resurrection as a historical event in terms of bodily resurrection has been hotly contested. Contemporary scholarship appeals to the following objections: there is no access to such historical knowledge; there is no analogy for such a resurrection; and there is no evidence.[72]

The first argues that instead of the history of resurrection, we have access only to the beliefs in resurrection of the disciples, a subjective experience in hearts of the disciples rather than a real event.[73] The obvious counterargument is that this view represents a typical positivistic[74] objection, according to which things such as raising people from the dead do not happen.

Second, the charge that there is no analogy to resurrection goes back to the old "rule" of Ernst Troeltsch, according to which an analogical corresponding happening is required to qualify an event as historical.[75] That cannot, of course, be provided with reference to Jesus's resurrection, which is a onetime event. The counterargument reminds us that being a onetime event, however, does not in itself disqualify it from being a historical event.

Third, the objection to the lack of evidence for the resurrection ignores many factors that, while hardly sufficient in themselves, may be taken as supporting the possibility of the event. Not among the least is the unexplainable rise of the new religion, Christianity, after the crucifixion of its leader. What caused the change in the attitude and faith of the followers? Furthermore,

72. N. T. Wright, *Resurrection of the Son of God*, 16–20.

73. Rudolf Bultmann, "New Testament and Mythology," in *Kerygma and Myth: A Theological Debate*, ed. Hans Werner Bartsch (New York: Harper & Row, 1961), 39–42.

74. According to logical positivism, a philosophical movement from the beginning of the twentieth century, only empirically tested claims can be taken as true and only those kinds of events can be expected to happen.

75. Ernst Troeltsch, "On the Historical and Dogmatic Methods in Theology [1898]," trans. Jack Forstman, in *Gesammelte Schriften*, 2:728–53 (Tübingen: J. C. B. Mohr, 1913).

the two main pillars of evidence for the historicity of the resurrection are the appearances of Jesus to a great number of eyewitnesses and the empty tomb tradition.[76] The empty tomb tradition was not contested by contemporaries—even though its validity as a historical claim was widely doubted by many twentieth-century biblical scholars. Had the claim to the empty tomb been a fabrication, how could the preaching about the resurrected Christ have taken place in Jerusalem, the place of execution and burial?

In sum: the belief in the physical resurrection of Jesus from the dead is not necessarily a matter of faith totally apart from historical investigation and rational reasoning. That said, the limits of historical inquiry alone should be acknowledged. No amount of historical evidence or logical reasoning is meant to establish indubitable certainty beyond questioning.

Resurrection and the Unity of Jesus Christ with Humanity

Whereas older Christology had the question of Jesus's deity at the center, in recent times the focus has shifted to the question of his humanity. Whereas in older theology the starting point of affirming Jesus's humanity was the union of the Logos with the human Jesus at the incarnation, in contemporary theology it is customary to begin with the affirmation of the humanness of Jesus of Nazareth and inquire into how this "low" Christology came to be developed into a "high" one.

A mediating approach is based on two kinds of sources and perspectives. The first one follows the narrative of the New Testament authors and observes how they were able to speak of the full humanity of Jesus Christ while at the same time affirming his divine status. The second, similarly to the question of the deity, builds on the confirmatory role of the resurrection from the dead. The foundational question about the humanity of Jesus investigates this: "in what sense, if any, can we meaningfully use the word 'god' to talk about the human Jesus, Jesus as he lived, walked, taught, healed, and died in first century Palestine?"[77] In affirming the true humanity of Jesus Christ, we are claiming that "in this historical life we find not only the true deity, but also essential humanity."[78]

76. Raymond E. Brown, *The Virginal Conception and Bodily Resurrection of Jesus* (New York: Paulist, 1992), 92–124.

77. N. T. Wright, "Jesus and the Identity of God," *Ex Auditu* 14 (1998): 42.

78. Grenz, *Theology for the Community*, 272.

Rather than beginning from abstract speculations as to how the divine and human can come together in one person, the "economic" approach of the Gospel writers and other New Testament writers seems to give a naive (in a good sense of the term) and innocent description of the human person who lived under normal human conditions. The dangers to Logos Christology, as if the deity lurked behind the guise of humanity, must be countered with the robust narratives of the New Testament, which include development and growth (Luke 2:40). Even the more "theological" account of John's Gospel speaks of Jesus as weary and thirsty (John 4:6–7). Jesus showed human emotions such as sorrow (11:35) and anguish (12:27). Jesus struggled in trying to accept God's will (Matt. 26:39), including in his prayer life (Heb. 5:8–9). Remarkable is the statement in Hebrews (4:15)—a clause that also found its way into the creed—that Jesus was tempted in every way as we are except that he never committed a sin. The same anonymous author also speaks of the one who "had to be made like his brethren in every respect," including suffering and temptations (2:17–18). Astonishingly, he had to learn "obedience through what he suffered" (5:8).[79]

Whereas the oneness of Jesus with humanity can be gleaned from the historical records in the New Testament, the uniqueness of the humanity of Jesus the Christ can only be established on the basis of the resurrection. Resurrection vindicated not only his divine status as the Son who was sent by his Father but also his claim to humanity and his earthly ministry. Only in light of the resurrection can we also establish Jesus's humanity as the paradigm for all human existence.[80]

The affirmation of the humanity of the One who was also fully divine takes us to the most distinctive Christian claim: incarnation.

"The Word Became Flesh": A Theology of Incarnation

Whether It Was Fitting and Necessary for God to Assume Human Flesh

The doctrine of the incarnation and the corollary doctrines of preexistence and virgin birth are all different ways of speaking about the unique relation between Jesus's divine origin and his human existence. Incarnation is widely testified to in the New Testament (John 1:14; 14:7; 1 John 4:2; Rom. 8:3; 1 Cor. 8:6; Col. 1:15–17; Phil. 2:6–8; Gal. 4:4–6). Incarnation and preexistence are

79. Hans Schwarz, *Christology* (Grand Rapids: Eerdmans, 1998), 234–35.
80. Grenz, *Theology for the Community*, 281.

mutually related teachings. If the former is affirmed without the latter, adoptionism follows. Similarly, any talk about the *Christian* view of incarnation without the presupposition of the deity of Christ—which would lead, as in the Gnostic Gospel of Philip, to the affirmation of every human person's divinity—results in an impasse.

Before delving into the details of incarnation, Thomas Aquinas asks whether it was fitting for the divine to become a human being (*Summa theologiae* 3.1.1). He lists a number of potential objections, such as that the divine has been without flesh from eternity, that the infinite difference between the divine and human makes it impossible for the divine to be "contained" in a human life, and so forth. Yet, at the end Aquinas finds it fitting for the perfect goodness to communicate itself for the sake of others. Building on these and related insights, the philosopher Richard Swinburne argues the same: since human nature is good, it is fitting for God to assume it; by doing so, God shows great appreciation of human nature and bestows great dignity on it, and so forth.[81]

Not only that, but early theology had already established a link between incarnation and creation at large, as is profoundly evident, for example, in Athanasius's *On the Incarnation of the Word*: "For this purpose, then, the incorporeal and incorruptible and immaterial Word of God comes to our realm, howbeit he was not far from us before. For no part of Creation is left void of Him: He has filled all things everywhere, remaining present with His own Father" (2.8).[82]

"Why" Incarnation?

Tradition has given two answers. The first, obvious answer is that the incarnation of the Son was necessitated by human sin and disobedience; this question was profoundly addressed by Anselm's *Cur Deus Homo?* (Why did God become human?) and the whole history of "atonement theories" (to be studied in the next chapter). The second answer is that "God intended the incarnation of the Son of God from eternity. His intention was formed together with the idea of the world" in terms of preparation for the coming of the Son to humanity.[83] According to Moltmann, in the first answer creation only has a functional

81. Richard Swinburne, *The Christian God* (Oxford: Clarendon; New York: Oxford University Press, 1994), 218–20.

82. See also Irenaeus, *Against Heresies* 3.18.1.

83. Jürgen Moltmann, *The Trinity and the Kingdom of God: The Doctrine of God*, trans. Margaret Kohl (San Francisco: Harper & Row; London: SCM, 1981), 114.

value rather than its own remaining value. In the second outlook, the incarnation of the Son completes creation. In the first, human sin and obedience are the "reason" for the coming of the Son; in the latter they are its "occasion."[84]

The distinction between "reason" and "occasion" helps us consider these responses as complementary rather than either/or: whereas the Fall does not have to be the ultimate reason, it certainly was its occasion. Athanasius is a great example here. Whereas he underscores the importance of linking incarnation with creation, he also speaks everywhere of the human lostness and need for the Savior to come and die and be raised from death for our salvation.

The incarnation is not a passing moment in the divine life. If it were, the event would be closer to ancient mythologies in which deities change into human beings (and may again "go back" to the divine mode of being). As the Athanasian Creed says, the incarnation happened "not by conversion of the Godhead into flesh, but by taking of that manhood into God."[85] In that sense we can speak of "permanent incarnation."

The way Christian tradition has spoken of the divine embodiment within the structures of this created reality in the person of Jesus of Nazareth has to do with the idea of two "natures" in one "person."

Two "Natures" in One "Person"

The difficult question that has haunted the Christian theology of incarnation since the beginning is the most obvious: how to even begin to speak of the coming together of the infinite (divinity) and finite (humanity) in one and the same person.[86]

In the patristic theology leading up to Chalcedon, the problem was often tackled in relation to questions such as how to explain the miracles or suffering and death of the one person. Theodore of Mopsuestia, with his Nestorian leanings, tried to explain the logic in terms of attributing miracles to the divine nature and suffering and death to the human nature.[87] This view endangers the unity of the one person and can be interpreted in a way that supports Nestorian heresy.

84. Moltmann, *Trinity and the Kingdom*, 114–15.

85. In *Historic Creeds and Confessions*, ed. Rick Brannan, 6, available on Christian Classics Ethereal Library website: http://www.ccel.org/ccel/brannan/hstcrcon.html.

86. See Friedrich Schleiermacher, *The Christian Faith*, ed. H. R. Mackintosh and J. S. Stewart (Edinburgh: T&T Clark, 1999), 393.

87. Consult Kelly, *Early Christian Doctrines*, chaps. 11 and 12.

A useful beginning point is to note that we should always avoid abstract and formal speculations when speaking of the unique coming together of two natures in one person in Jesus Christ and focus on this particular, unrepeatable event. The New Testament narrative can then be taken as the main guide. The two key passages in the New Testament on which the Chalcedonian incarnational Christology is anchored—Philippians 2:5–11 and John 1:14—hardly contain any abstract description of the divine Logos suddenly descending on a man, Jesus of Nazareth. Paul does not even mention Logos! His point is that the historical person Jesus refused to clutch his divine prerogatives and instead chose the path of the obedient servant, all the way to death on the cross. His exaltation by the Father was the result of his obedient life as a whole. What about John? Doesn't he speak of the preexistent Logos who became flesh? Yes, he does, but not exactly in the way classical tradition has framed the issue. Rather than highlighting any specific moment in Jesus's life, even the virgin birth, which in tradition soon became the locus of incarnation, John "appeals to eyewitnesses who observed our Lord's earthly life. On the basis of personal observations of Jesus' life (not his birth), these persons bear testimony to the incarnation" (John 1:14). In that sense, the confession "the Word became flesh," rather than a presupposition, is the conclusion on Jesus's person on the basis of his whole history.[88]

Let us continue deepening the meaning of the incarnation of Jesus Christ by zooming in on his "self-emptying."

He "Emptied Himself"

Incarnation and Self-Emptying Relate to the Whole Life of Jesus Christ

Quite early, patristic thought made a shift to equating the incarnation of the Logos with the birth of Jesus. That, however, is a problematic turn, for in the New Testament teaching, the "reference is to the totality of his life and work." Also, the Johannine sayings about the sending of the Son (John 3:16) speak of passion and death rather than birth.[89]

The reason we cannot equate incarnation with the birth of Jesus is that then the whole life and history of Jesus would not matter. Not only would that seriously hinder the full establishment of Jesus's humanity, but it would also make the incarnation of the Logos an "external" affair. In the eyes of the New

88. Grenz, *Theology for the Community*, 309–11, here 310.
89. Pannenberg, *ST* 2:301–2, here 301.

Testament writers, Jesus's human life mattered. In the many New Testament references mentioned above that establish the full humanity of Jesus, the New Testament writers speak daringly of the humanity and self-emptying of Jesus Christ. The mention in Hebrews of the shaping of Jesus's character in order for him to be "a merciful and faithful high priest" (Heb. 2:17b) sounds dangerously semiheretical to those for whom the incarnation was "fixed" at conception/birth. Or think of the statement that, having been made "perfect through suffering" (2:10), he "became the source of eternal salvation to all who obey him" (5:9)!

This narrative, testimonial approach of the New Testament, relating to the whole life of Jesus, is really the key to a proper understanding of the incarnation and related topics.

Toward a Theology of Kenōsis

Christ's "self-emptying," *kenōsis* (Phil. 2:7), is neither a renouncing nor even a temporarily turning off of the use of divine powers—which, when taken to its logical end, would lead to the heretical denial of the full divinity of the incarnated Son—but rather the voluntary submission of the earthly Jesus to his Father's will, as a number of Johannine sayings (John 5:19, 30, 36, among others) and the sayings from Hebrews quoted above affirm. Unlike the first Adam, the will of the new Adam totally corresponded to the will of God as "an expression of his free agreement with the Father."[90]

Recall here an early debate from the Third Council of Constantinople (680–681) concerning the question of Jesus's human will in relation to the divine will. The rejection of the heretical monothelitism ("one-will") and endorsement of the "two-will" doctrine[91] meant to affirm a genuine human volition, which in Jesus's case was totally voluntarily subjected to the Father. This also helped defeat monophysite ("one-nature") errors. As a human person, Jesus set himself below his God and thus assumed the place that belongs to the human being. The self-surrender to the death on the cross, with the cry "Father, into thy hands I commit my spirit!" (Luke 23:46), was the ultimate point of his self-distinction and self-emptying.

This self-emptying, therefore, is not best expressed with the idea of a renunciation of divinity (divine essence) but rather with the idea of a renunciation "of any equating of himself with the Father."[92] Rather than being something con-

90. Pannenberg, *ST* 2:315–16, here 316.
91. Pelikan, *CT* 1:340–41; 2:68–75.
92. Pannenberg, *ST* 2:377.

trary to the divine nature of the Son, this act is rather the "activation" of his deity. Barth saw this in a profound way: "in this condescension, He is the eternal Son of the eternal Father."[93] In other words, Jesus's self-emptying, his making himself dependent on the will and love of his Father, is in keeping both with the true divinity of the Son as revealed to us and with the true humanity as created by God. Dependency, contingency, and reference to the other characterize human nature; that is presented to us most purely and innocently in Jesus's humanity.

This voluntary subordination to his Father's will often comes to the fore in the New Testament narrative with regard to the Spirit. Jesus attributed his power to the Spirit given him by his Father (Matt. 12:28; Luke 4:18; 11:20). In that outlook, the earthly Jesus was dependent on the Spirit for his ministry, teaching, and miracles, as well as for overcoming temptations.[94]

"Yet Was without Sin": Sinlessness

Traditional and Revisionist Accounts of Sinlessness

In Christian tradition prior to the time of the Enlightenment, by and large, the sinlessness of Jesus was unequivocally affirmed. This belief was based on New Testament statements such as Hebrews 4:15, which says that Jesus "in every respect has been tempted as we are, yet without sin" (so also 7:26; 9:14; 1 Pet. 2:22; 1 John 3:5; 2 Cor. 5:21). At Chalcedon, the view was reaffirmed. The thick account of Jesus's sinlessness came to be expressed technically as *non posse peccare* (not able to sin), which says more than the thinner expression *posse non peccare* (able not to sin).

Early theologians were well aware that with the affirmation of the sinlessness also came the affirmation of the different nature of Jesus's humanity from our empirical nature—yet that was not seen as threatening but rather as facilitating the redemptive work of Jesus Christ.[95] The basis for the affirmation of sinlessness, apart from biblical references, was seen in Jesus's total obedience and moral perfection, as well as his union with God.[96]

Because of a looser understanding of the union of the two "natures" of Christ, Nestorius came to compromise or at least reformulate the classic view

93. Barth, *CD* IV/1, 129.

94. Clark H. Pinnock, *Flame of Love: A Theology of the Holy Spirit* (Downers Grove, IL: InterVarsity Press, 1996), 88.

95. Irenaeus, *Against Heresies* 5.14.3; Tertullian, *On the Flesh of Christ* 16.

96. Origen, *First Principles* 2.6.3–4.

of sinlessness. Having affirmed that Jesus took human likeness "in order to abolish the guilt of the first man and in order to give to his nature the former image which he had lost through his guilt," Nestorius underscored the assumption of sinful nature to the point that the classic view was rejected.[97] Not surprisingly, the Fifth Ecumenical Council of Constantinople (553) rejected similar ideas related to Theodore of Mopsuestia as heresy.[98]

In the aftermath of the Enlightenment, a number of ways of either rejecting or revising the doctrine emerged. Concerning the liberal Schleiermacher, it is even hard to tell what he truly thought of the issue.[99] What is clear is that for many twentieth-century "liberals," the idea was impossible to affirm. Coming from a different perspective, but also influenced by liberalism, religious pluralists such as John Hick bluntly reject the whole idea of the sinlessness of Jesus. Hick finds him guilty, for example, of racial prejudice (Mark 7:27) and use of violence in the temple (Matt. 21:12).[100]

Unrelated to the Enlightenment, a few influential traditional theologians have ended up affirming Jesus's human nature as sinful because of their uncompromising stress on his identity with sinful humanity. Because Jesus "became involved in the predicament of the whole flesh" of ours, "He was not the perfectly good man,"[101] Dietrich Bonhoeffer surmised. Similarly for Barth, the "flesh" assumed by the Logos "is the concrete form of human nature marked by Adam's fall."[102]

How to Establish Sinlessness

When considering the historical basis for the affirmation of sinlessness, we should bear in mind that Jesus's opponents leveled a number of charges against him concerning not only lifestyle-related issues such as gluttony but also the most serious of all in the Jewish context—blasphemy. Yet any of these can be negotiated, and one can infer from the New Testament testimonies of his followers that he committed no sin. That said, ultimately the affirmation of sin-

97. Nestorius, *The Bazaar of Heracleides*, translated from Syriac and edited by G. R. Driver and Leonard Hodgson (London: Oxford University Press, 1925), bk. 1, part 1, 68.

98. "The Decretal Letter of Pope Vigilius," *NPNF*² 14:322.

99. Schleiermacher, *The Christian Faith*, 385.

100. John Hick, ed., *The Metaphor of God Incarnate: Christology in a Pluralistic Age* (London: SCM, 1993), 77, 110.

101. Dietrich Bonhoeffer, *Christology*, trans. John Bowden (London: Collins, 1966), 112.

102. Barth, *CD* I/2, 151.

lessness has to be—again—an inference from the resurrection that confirmed his claims to deity. Mere sinlessness doesn't of course make the human person divine; but God, by definition, cannot sin.

Theologically, at stake is our salvation. If Jesus were a sinner, he could not save us, the fathers correctly argued. On the other hand, only that which was "assumed" in the incarnation can be saved. This means that if Jesus's humanity is so different from ours that in his incarnation and innocent suffering our fallen human nature was not assumed and healed, our salvation is in jeopardy. Early theology clearly gave soteriological considerations the upper hand.

The theological consideration of the possibility of reconciling the doctrine of sinlessness and the full humanity of Jesus has to keep in mind the nature of the original human nature. True humanity as the image of God does not of course entail sinfulness. Our fallen humanity rather represents corruption. Indeed, rather than asking first how a pure, sinless humanity of Jesus Christ can represent humanity, we have to wonder how our fallen humanity can still be said to represent humanity!

To say that Jesus was fully engaged in the human predicament, yet sinless, is to acknowledge that as human he was deeply affected by the effects of the fallen world, without himself participating in sinful acts. He shared our lot in the fallen and sinful world, full of pain, suffering, and injustice.

What about temptations? Whereas Christian tradition has struggled to understand the authenticity of temptations alongside affirmation of his sinless nature, the Gospels make the temptations a matter of Jesus's relation to the Father. All three temptations raise the question of "If you are the Son of God . . ." So temptations are about obedience. Beyond that, the difference between Jesus and us is that temptations in humans originate from within the fallen nature (James 1:14), whereas in Jesus's case, they originate from outside. Yet that did not weaken their appeal, particularly when, as in the desert, he faced hunger after forty days.

If these considerations make the argumentation lean toward *non posse peccare*, necessary sinlessness, is thereby the true freedom of Jesus Christ being compromised? In other words, can one be authentically free and "not able to sin"? Recall the rejection of the "one-will" view in favor of "two wills" (Constantinople in 681), meaning that Jesus had a true human will. On top of that, we have to realize that authentic freedom does not require the possibility of sin—or else, God would not be free! As Augustine argued, "the will that cannot sin at all is more free than the will that can either sin or not sin."[103] The

103. Paraphrased in Pannenberg, *ST* 2:258n287.

freedom of Jesus Christ was not predetermined, semiautomatic submission but rather true freedom *in God*. Freedom essentially is a relational concept; misuse of freedom, sinning, means breaking the relationship.[104]

Finally, following Chalcedon, in the one person of Jesus Christ, in a hypostatic ("personal") union, two natures (divine and human) coexist perichoretically. The human nature assumed by the Logos is manifested in Jesus of Nazareth in its purest and most original form, in loving and willing obedience of the Son to the Father. Along with a full affirmation of the identification of the human Jesus with our humanity, that identification avoids sinfulness, as sin does not belong to the essence of human nature.

"He Came Down from Heaven": Preexistence

In Christian tradition, affirmed in the Nicene-Constantinopolitan Creed, the doctrine of preexistence means that the second person of the Trinity, the Son of God, became human in Jesus of Nazareth. Tradition doesn't of course teach that the man Jesus existed in any real sense before the incarnation, but that God the Son existed prior to the incarnation. Preexistence and incarnation thus belong together and mutually presuppose each other.

It took early Christian theology some time to formulate its view of the nature of preexistence due to the vacillation between a purely ideal preexistence, as existing in the mind of God, and "real" ("personal") preexistence. Tertullian's view of the eternal generation of the Word[105] made a significant contribution to the solidification of the doctrine.

Contemporary scholarship has cast serious doubts on the doctrine's biblical support.[106] The standard opinion is that preexistence can only be found developed in John, whereas Pauline and other New Testament traditions contain at the most only ambiguous references. J. D. G. Dunn claims that what Paul and the author of Hebrews affirm can at the most be named an "ideal" preexistence.[107] In rebuttal, a strong case is made for the wider attestation of

104. This section is indebted to Demetrios Bathrellos, "The Sinlessness of Jesus: A Theological Exploration in the Light of Trinitarian Theology," chap. 9 in *Trinitarian Soundings in Systematic Theology*, ed. P. L. Metzger (New York: T&T Clark, 2005), 113–26.

105. Tertullian, *Against Praxeas* 7.

106. Consult Douglas McCready, *He Came Down from Heaven: The Preexistence of Christ and the Christian Faith* (Downers Grove, IL: InterVarsity Press, 2005).

107. James D. G. Dunn, *Christology in the Making: A New Testament Inquiry into the Origins of the Doctrine of the Incarnation*, 2nd ed. (London: SCM, 1989 [1980]).

the idea in the canon (1 Cor. 8:6; Phil. 2:6–8; Col. 1:15–17: Gal. 4:4; Heb. 1:2; among others).[108]

For classical liberals, preexistence was either a myth or something ideal, in keeping with a thin doctrine of incarnation such as Schleiermacher's idea of "inspiration," God-filled man, not the God-man.[109] The revisionist view of twentieth-century British bishop J. A. T. Robinson continues that line of thinking, in that Christ "completely embodied what was from the beginning the meaning and purpose of God's self-expression."[110] Religious pluralists such as Hick adopt the liberal view and make it an asset in attempting to relate to religions and religious plurality.[111] The problem with liberal and pluralistic interpretations is the random and artificial reinterpretation of tradition, both biblical and historical, which then also leads to the denial of Christ's divinity and, as a result, the doctrine of the Trinity.

In sum: the traditional idea of the incarnation is impossible without preexistence, and vice versa. The doctrine's lasting meaning is "that Christ *personally* belongs to an order of being other than the created, temporal one. His personal, divine existence transcends temporal (and spatial) categories. . . . Eternity transcends time but without being apart from it."[112]

"Born of the Virgin Mary"

Although direct references to virgin birth in the New Testament are scarce (Matt. 1:18–22; Luke 1:26–36), belief in the supernatural virginal conception of Jesus soon became a universally held view in early Christian theology, including creedal traditions. Tradition is saying that there was a supernatural conception of Jesus by the Holy Spirit in the Virgin Mary apart from normal sexual intercourse (Matt. 1:18–22).

Not until the rise of the quest of the historical Jesus in modernity was there a widespread rejection or radical reinterpretation of the traditional belief in the virgin birth.[113] Not surprisingly, conservative segments of the church

108. N. T. Wright, *The Climax of the Covenant: Christ and the Law in Pauline Theology* (Minneapolis: Fortress, 1993), 56–98; Pannenberg, *ST* 2:369.

109. Schleiermacher, *The Christian Faith*, §97.

110. John A. T. Robinson, *The Human Face of God* (London: SCM, 1972), 179.

111. Hick, *Metaphor of God Incarnate*, 12.

112. Gerald O'Collins, SJ, *Christology: A Biblical, Historical, and Systematic Study of Jesus* (New York: Oxford University Press, 1995), 249–50.

113. See David F. Strauss, *The Life of Jesus Critically Examined*, translated from the 4th

reacted vehemently.[114] The later fundamentalist movement listed belief in the virgin birth (understood in the traditional sense) among the "five fundamentals" to be affirmed and believed. No other contemporary theologian has stressed the theological importance of the virgin birth as much as Barth: "The mystery of the revelation of God in Jesus Christ consists in the fact that the eternal Word of God chose, sanctified and assumed human nature and existence into oneness with Himself, in order thus, as very God and very man, to become the Word of reconciliation spoken by God to man."[115]

Contemporary mainline New Testament scholarship does not regard the virgin birth as a historical event but rather as a "theological" or symbolic one, for example, in terms of total human surrender to God of the human being as embodied in Mary's attitude.

Even though the New Testament does not make a direct link between virgin birth and preexistence, early in Christian theology that link came to be established. Early theology taught that it was Logos, the preexistent Word of God, that was conceived in the Virgin Mary. This is a legitimate development of incipient New Testament ideas. The further development in early theology toward the affirmation of Jesus's sinlessness in terms of virgin birth, on the contrary, is both unnecessary and problematic. This explanation is totally foreign to the New Testament. That position betrays two mistaken anthropological views, namely, that in human conception the role of the (earthly) father could be excluded, and that, even if it could be, that would help safeguard the infant from the influence of the Fall (as that influence was supposed to come mainly from the father). Nor has the virgin birth anything to do with marginalizing, let alone blaming, sexuality and normal human birth as sinful.

In Christian theology and piety, Mary is rightly honored as the "mother of God" (*theotokos*). Mary plays a unique role in the salvation history and thus should be honored appropriately. The creedal statements about Mary have little to do with the role of Mary per se and everything to do with Christology. In light of the fact that there is no theological teaching about Mary in the New Testament in terms of her as "mother of Christ," Christian theology has to appraise critically and sympathetically the traditions about Mary that emerged early in Christian theology; that discussion will be taken up in the chapter on ecclesiology (chap. 9).

German ed. by George Eliot, 2nd ed. in 1 vol. (London: Schwann Sonnenschein; New York: Macmillan, 1892), §26 (particularly 130–31).

114. For a survey, see Thomas Boslooper, *The Virgin Birth* (London: SCM, 1962).

115. Barth, *CD* I/2, 122.

Put in the wider context of religions, Islam strongly affirms the importance of Jesus's virgin birth.[116] But of course, Islam rejects Jesus's deity.

So far, while delving briefly into interfaith engagements, we have engaged mainly Christian (and Jewish) traditions. The last two, lengthier sections of this chapter open windows into other religions and theological responses to religious diversity and religious pluralism(s).

Christological Challenges of Theological Pluralism(s)

Revisionist Interpretations of the Incarnation

Whereas until the Enlightenment incarnation was taken as a onetime, unique event, thereafter both some leading philosophers (G. W. F. Hegel) and theologians (D. E. F. Strauss, Hegel's pupil) began to envision it in terms of a collective divine presence, perhaps even reaching to the whole of humanity.[117] Later, Bishop J. A. T. Robinson's view of incarnation as "a breakthrough of cosmic consciousness" in his *Human Face of God*[118] continued the same line. The use of the concept of myth helped establish the case that, when speaking of incarnation, we are not talking of a historical-factual event but of an elusive idea.[119]

The leading religious pluralist of our times, the late John Hick, not only builds on this legacy but also sharpens and revamps it with a view to rapidly growing religious, cultural, and worldview plurality.[120] Having left behind the Trinity (see chap. 2 above), he unabashedly represents "low Christology," in which incarnation means that all human beings, who only differ from each other in degree, are "Spirit-filled, or Christ-like, or truly saintly."[121] This is the key claim in *The Metaphor of God Incarnate: Chris-*

116. Qur'an 19:16–36; 3:42–59; Neil Robinson, *Christ in Islam and Christianity* (New York: State University of New York Press, 1991), chap. 15.

117. Strauss, *Life of Jesus*, 779–81.

118. J. A. T. Robinson, *Human Face of God*, 204.

119. Donald G. Bloesch, *Jesus Christ: Savior and Lord* (Downers Grove, IL: InterVarsity Press, 1997), 120–31.

120. John Hick, ed., *The Myth of God Incarnate* (London: SCM, 1977).

121. Cited in Gerald O'Collins, SJ, "The Incarnation: The Critical Issues," in *The Incarnation: An Interdisciplinary Symposium on the Incarnation of the Son of God*, ed. Stephen T. Davis et al. (Oxford: Oxford University Press, 2004), 2 (and wrongly attributed to J. Hick, "Incarnation," 205; I have been unable to find the original reference).

tology in a Pluralistic Age. What incarnation is all about is making real the presence of the divine to all men and women rather than a historical-factual statement about the God-man, Jesus Christ. It is to be taken seriously but not literally.

From this base emerges a number of revisionist christological notions that crystallize his version of religious pluralism:

1. Jesus did not teach that he himself was God incarnate.
2. The Chalcedonian two-natures doctrine of the person of Christ cannot be expressed in a religiously adequate fashion.
3. The historical and traditional two-natures doctrine has been used to justify great evils, such as wars, persecution, repression, and genocide.
4. The life and teaching of Jesus challenge us to live a life pleasing to God.
5. This metaphorical understanding of the incarnation fits with a doctrine of religious pluralism, whereby Christ's life and teaching are seen as one example of the religious life that can also be found, in different ways and forms, in other major world religions.[122]

Not surprisingly, critics have challenged him severely (not repeating criticisms presented in chap. 2). First, his universal rather than particular historical notion of incarnation is against biblical and creedal traditions. Second, Hick's system makes all talk about Trinity nonsensical, as Christ is not divine in the first place. Third, his "turn" to metaphorical and mythical language blocks the way to a solid historical-critical study of Jesus traditions. Fourth, only few are ready to acknowledge that Hick's radically revisionist account of Jesus the Christ is any more "neutral" or objective than is the interpretation of those who are timewise and culturally much closer to Jesus, particularly his earliest followers.[123]

In sum, any denial of Jesus Christ's incarnation as a particular, unique, nonrepeatable event severely undercuts Christian orthodoxy.[124] The question has everything to do with the way Logos, the divinity, and Jesus, the man, are being linked with each other. "Because *Logos* is a title for Jesus, there is no other *Logos* or Son except Jesus of Nazareth. When we speculate about the

122. As summarized succinctly in Oliver D. Crisp, *Divinity and Humanity: The Incarnation Reconsidered* (Cambridge: Cambridge University Press, 2007), 155–56.

123. Alister E. McGrath, conclusion to chapter 3, "A Particularist View: A Post-Enlightenment Approach," in *Four Views on Salvation in a Pluralistic World*, ed. Dennis L. Okholm and Timothy R. Phillips (Grand Rapids: Zondervan, 1996), 206.

124. O'Collins, "The Incarnation," 1.

Logos apart from Jesus' historical life, we lose the significance of the term as a christological title."[125] This is but to follow the New Testament, which links the Logos (of John 1) to one man, Jesus of Nazareth.

The Uniqueness of Christ Revisited

The leading Roman Catholic pluralist, Paul F. Knitter, who later in his career turned robustly to a liberationist theology of religions, started by echoing the views of Hick and similar pluralists in turning to a theo-centric Christology as the key to "a more authentic dialogue."[126] Rather than approaching the question of religions from the standpoint of Jesus Christ as the normative norm, Knitter came to focus on the theo-centric consciousness of Jesus Christ and his preaching of the coming of the kingdom of God. For him, Jesus Christ is "unique" in that he is an authoritative revelation of God, but there may be other savior figures among other religions. This, for Knitter, does not undermine the Christian's commitment to Christ but rather makes him or her more capable and willing for dialogue and practical work.

A critic notices instantly that Knitter's proposal suffers from many of the same problems that Hick's does. The turn to theo-centric Christology contradicts the biblical insistence on Jesus as the only way to God. It also opposes the classical Trinitarian canons, as it is not possible to confess belief in the Trinity if Jesus Christ is not the divine Son. Its value for a robust dialogue is also limited, as it does not allow the representatives on the Christian side to present their own views in an authentic and open way.

An important step in some current pluralistic theologies of religions is the turn to liberation as the focal point, represented by Knitter's "eco-liberationist" pluralism, "a globally responsible, correlational dialogue among religions."[127] Rather than doctrinal and theological understanding, religion's main contribution is facilitating and inspiring work for social and ecological improvement. In this template, Knitter now locates the uniqueness of Jesus in his capacity to elicit a proper incentive to liberative work. In contrast with what he calls his own church's "constitutive Christology," Knitter's "representational"

125. Grenz, *Theology for the Community*, 309.

126. The title for part 3 of Paul F. Knitter, *No Other Name? A Critical Survey of Christian Attitudes toward the World Religions* (Maryknoll, NY: Orbis, 1985), 169.

127. Section title in Paul F. Knitter, *One Earth, Many Religions: Multifaith Dialogue and Global Responsibility* (Maryknoll, NY: Orbis, 1995), 15.

Christology speaks of Jesus as "a *decisive/definite* and as *universally meaningful* embodiment or manifestation of God."[128]

Calling religions to work together for the betterment of this planet and life therein is something all (theistic) religions echo. This is not contested. What the critics of the eco-liberationist approach contest has to do with the neglect of the doctrine. Furthermore, is it legitimate to expect all religions to share a common vision of the good life?

Whereas this current section represents Christian theology of religions, the following takes up comparative theology on Christ.

Jesus Christ among Religions

The Jewish Messiah—the Christian Messiah

The Jew—between the Jews and Christians

"When one asks the basic question of what separates Jews and Christians from each other, the unavoidable answer is: a Jew," says the Jewish New Testament scholar Pinchas Lapide.[129] One of the ironies of history is that for eighteen hundred years or more, Jewish theologians by and large ignored Christian claims that Jesus is the Messiah, and their perceptions of Jesus were very negative.[130] The most important early Jewish source on Christ, *Toldot Yeshu* (fifth or sixth century?),[131] radically alters the Gospel narratives and in general advances a highly polemical and mocking presentation. For example, Jesus's miracles are attributed to sorcery or other similarly forbidden sources.[132]

The rabbinical writings contain a definite and direct rebuttal of the claim to the divine Sonship of Jesus, "a blasphemy against the Jewish understanding of God." The Christian doctrines of the incarnation, atonement through the cross, and of course the Trinity, among others, "remained alien to normative

128. Paul F. Knitter, *Jesus and the Other Names: Christian Mission and Global Responsibility* (Maryknoll, NY: Orbis, 1996), 53.

129. Pinchas Lapide, *The Resurrection of Jesus: A Jewish Perspective* (Minneapolis: Augsburg, 1983), 30.

130. Michael J. Cook, "Jewish Perspectives on Jesus," in *The Blackwell Companion to Jesus*, ed. Delbert Burkett (Oxford: Wiley-Blackwell, 2011).

131. Ernst Bammel, "Christian Origins in Jewish Tradition," *New Testament Studies* 13, no. 4 (1967): 317–35.

132. Susannah Heschel, "Jewish Views of Jesus," in *JWF*, 149–50.

Judaism and taboo to the rabbis."[133] That said, the resistance was less targeted against the historical figure of Jesus of Nazareth and more against what was considered Pauline Christology and the subsequent patristic and creedal tradition.

In the aftermath of the Enlightenment, and with the newly opening opportunities for Jews to participate in wider European society, interest in Jesus emerged, partly to help justify Judaism as a religion. Another famous Moses, namely, Mendelssohn, painted a picture of Jesus as a thoroughly Jewish religious figure, so much so that, "closely examined, everything is in complete agreement not only with Scripture, but also with the [Jewish] tradition."[134]

Encouraged by the quest of the historical Jesus and classical liberalism's subsequent interest in the "real" Jesus, divorced from the layers of dogmatic and creedal traditions, the Jewish quest for Jesus as a Jew was energized. At the same time, the Jewish search for the Jewish Jesus also wanted to develop "a counterhistory of the prevailing Christian theological version of Christianity's origins and influence."[135] Among the Christian students of Jesus Christ, recent decades have brought about an unprecedented interest in the Jewishness of Jesus, beginning with the first generation of the "New Perspective (on Paul)" in the 1970s.

Is Christology Inherently Anti-Semitic?

The destruction of Jerusalem by the gentiles in 70 CE alone should have led Christians to reach out to their suffering Jewish brothers and sisters in sympathy and love—yet it did not! Anti-Semitism has a sad and long track record in Christian tradition.[136]

There is a suspicion among many current Christian theologians that something in Christian faith, particularly in Christology, makes it inherently anti-Semitic. The feminist Rosemary Radford Ruether has famously argued that "theologically, anti-Judaism developed as the left hand of christology."[137] Ruether wonders if it is possible to confess Jesus as Messiah without at the

133. Lapide, *Israelis, Jews, and Jesus*, 76–77.

134. In Heschel, "Jewish Views of Jesus," 151.

135. Heschel, "Jewish Views of Jesus," 152.

136. C. Klein, *Anti-Judaism in Christian Theology*, trans. Edward Quinn (Philadelphia: Fortress, 1978).

137. Ruether, *To Change the World*, 31.

same time saying, "the Jews be damned."[138] Both Christian and Jewish scholars have found Ruether's presuppositions to a large extent mistaken for the simple reason that "the appearance of anti-Judaic thought in certain documents in the New Testament does not lead to the conclusion that anti-Judaism is necessarily the left hand of Christology." For example, the parable of the vineyard in Mark 12, which Ruether considers a showcase for inherent anti-Jewishness, is not necessarily so.[139]

This is not to contest or ignore the critique, at times harsh critique, of Jewish faith and people in the New Testament. Whereas before the destruction of Jerusalem in 70 CE we find very little attributing the death of Jesus to Jews, in the later Christian writings the tone gets harsher, and crucifixion is attributed to the Jews alone. A particularly harsh critique of the Jews comes to the fore in Matthew 23, but that is not necessarily different from or untypical of the harsh criticism of one Jewish group by another Jewish group at the time.[140] Even when the whole people is addressed, usually the target of the criticism is the religious or political leadership that is deviating from the will of God.

Has the Messiah Come?

Understandably, the question of the Messiah both joins and deeply divides these two faiths. Although too often not acknowledged, the Christian Messiah is a Jewish Messiah. Why then the Jewish rejection? The main reason a typical Jew cannot acknowledge the arrival of the Messiah is simply that nothing has changed in the world; indeed, everything in the conditions of this world seems to speak against the arrival of the Messiah.[141]

Without downplaying and certainly not dismissing this profound difference in understanding of what the coming of Messiah and the ensuing redemption mean, Moltmann poses the "gentile" question to the Jews: "*Even before* the world has been redeemed so as to become the direct and universal

138. Rosemary Radford Ruether, *Faith and Fratricide: The Theological Roots of Anti-Semitism* (New York: Seabury, 1974), 246.

139. Thomas A. Idinopulos and Roy Bowen Ward, "Is Christology Inherently Anti-Semitic? A Critical Review of Rosemary Ruether's *Faith and Fratricide*," *Journal of the American Academy of Religions* 45, no. 2 (1977): 196.

140. Raymond E. Brown, *An Introduction to the New Testament* (New York: Doubleday, 1997), 222.

141. Michael S. Kogan, *Opening the Covenant: A Jewish Theology of Christianity* (Oxford: Oxford University Press, 2008), 90–95.

rule of God, can God already have a chosen people, chosen moreover *for the purpose of this redemption*?" Furthermore: "Does Israel's election not destroy Israel's solidarity with the unredeemed humanity, even if the election is meant in a representative sense?"[142]

Be that as it may, Christian Christology must resist any notion of imperialism, whatever form it may take. The Messiah confessed in Christian theology is the crucified one "who heals through his wounds and is victorious through his sufferings . . . the Lamb of God, not yet the Lion of Judah."[143] This kind of "theology of the cross" makes it possible for Christian theology to tolerate and appreciate the Jewish "no" rather than assuming that God has abandoned the people of Israel because of their reluctance to acknowledge the Messiah (Rom. 9).

A dialogue about Messiah and other corollary christological issues between Christians and Jews is meaningful only if there is mutual trust to allow both parties to represent their positions faithfully. The challenge to the Jewish faith is to stop "constructing Jewish conceptions of Jesus . . . and try to confront Christian claims about him as we [Jews] actually hear them from Christians." That said, it is also important for Christian theologians to acknowledge that the Jews have the right and prerogative to conceive Jesus within their own faith before they wish to look through a Christian lens.[144] Jews also have a right to comment on Christian doctrine of Christ. That also provides an opportunity for Christians to learn more about their own faith.

Jesus in Light of Islamic Interpretations

The Muslim-Christian Engagement

Vatican II's *Nostra Aetate* sums up the general Muslim perception of Jesus: "Though they do not acknowledge Jesus as God, they revere Him as a prophet. They also honor Mary, His virgin Mother; at times they even call on her with devotion."[145] That said, Christian-Muslim relations are plagued—and hopefully enriched—by a number of ironies. "It is a curious fact of history that whilst Muhammad has been frequently criticized in western and Christian

142. Moltmann, *Way of Jesus Christ*, 30.

143. Moltmann, *Way of Jesus Christ*, 32.

144. Kogan, *Opening the Covenant*, 112.

145. *Nostra Aetate: Declaration on the Relation of the Church to Non-Christian Religions* (Vatican II), #3.

writings, Muslims hold the central figure of Christianity in high esteem." Not only that, but "Islam is the only religion other than Christianity that *requires* its adherents to commit to a position on the identity of Jesus"![146] Indeed, Islamic tradition considers Jesus to be "Muslim."[147]

There are roughly one hundred references or allusions to Jesus (and his mother Mary) in the Qur'an alone.[148] Jesus stands in the long line of prophets, from Noah, Abraham, and Moses, second only to the Prophet himself. His virgin birth is affirmed, similarly his miracles, as discussed above. His teaching is appreciated, though with some reservations, as also discussed. That said, Jesus appears to be also a very divisive figure because of deep theological differences.

Indeed, ambiguity about Jesus has characterized Muslim-Christian exchange from the beginning. There were problems on both sides. On the Christian polemical side, from the beginning of the encounter a handful of arguments have persisted, often used in an uncritical and unnuanced manner against any Muslim interpretation of Jesus: (1) What the Qur'an says of Jesus is hopelessly distorted. (2) There are clear mistakes in the Qur'anic presentation of Jesus. (3) Muhammad received much of his information from heretical or otherwise suspect sources.[149] For a long time a typical Muslim engagement would add to the existing references in the Qur'an and Hadith mainly on the basis of Christian legends and Gospel materials, including gospels not ratified by Christians, especially the Gospel of Barnabas, whose influence even today is immense in anti-Christian polemics.[150]

On the Conditions of a Dialogue

In many ways it is neither fair nor useful to compare Jesus Christ to Muhammad. First of all, even though Christ is named a "prophet" in the Qur'an, it is Muhammad who is the "seal of the prophets" and thus occupies a unique role. Second, unlike Christian faith, which is determined by belief in Christ, Islam is

146. Gregory A. Barker and Stephen E. Gregg, "Muslim Perceptions of Jesus: Key Issues," in *JBC*, 83.

147. Tarif Khalidi, ed. and trans., *The Muslim Jesus: Sayings and Stories in Islamic Literature* (Cambridge, MA: Harvard University Press, 2001).

148. Kenneth Cragg, *Jesus and the Muslim: An Exploration* (London: George Allen & Unwin, 1985; Oxford: Oneworld, 1999), chap. 2; Oddbjørn Leirvik, *Images of Jesus Christ in Islam*, 2nd ed. (London: Continuum, 2010), 20–24.

149. N. Robinson, *Christ in Islam*, chap. 2.

150. Leirvik, *Images of Jesus Christ*, 132–44.

not based on Muhammad but rather on the Qur'an and Allah. Neither Christ nor Muhammad in Islamic interpretation is divine; only God is.

The closest parallel to Christ in Islamic faith could be found in Christ's role as the living Word of God, in relation to the divine revelation of the Qur'an—even though in the Hadith collections a number of sayings seek to clarify the relation between Muhammad and Jesus. Among them is the important, oft-quoted, and highly respectful statement by Muhammad of Jesus: "Prophets are brothers in faith, having different mothers. Their religion is, however, one and there is no Apostle between us (between me and Jesus Christ)."[151] Muhammad's own relation to Christianity and Christian tradition in general, especially in the early phases of his career, was fairly positive and constructive.

Because neither the person nor the work of Christ is in any way as central to Islam as it is to Christianity, the portrayal of Jesus in the Qur'an is set in a different context. Jesus is put in the line of a number of Old Testament prophets beginning with Moses and Abraham. Furthermore, Mary's role is much more prominent in the Qur'anic presentation. Both of the two suras that contain the most references to Jesus, 3 and 19, are named after Mary.

Even the fact that Jesus is a miracle-worker in the Qur'an, unlike Muhammad, does not imply that he should be lifted up higher than the Prophet of Islam; the miracles wrought by Jesus are similar to those performed by Moses and other such forerunners of Muhammad. In other words, the most the miracles can do for Jesus is to confirm his prophetic status; they cannot confirm his divinity. Even the fact that Jesus is described as sinless in Hadith and legendary tradition—whereas it is not quite certain if Muhammad is—does not make Jesus superior.

The only title that is uniquely reserved for Jesus in the Muslim tradition is Messiah (e.g., 4:171). It is, however, difficult to determine the distinctively Islamic interpretation of that term. It is significant that the same sura also names him as "a spirit from Him" (God). In Christian tradition, of course, Messiah, the Anointed One, is integrally connected with the Spirit of God. But its meaning in Islamic tradition remains an unresolved question.

A tempting way to try to ease the tension between two vastly different portraits of Jesus in these two religions would be to "water down" the New Testament account of Jesus—for the sake of the dialogue. The classic work in Christian-Muslim relations by Kenneth Cragg, *The Call of the Minaret*, warns of that orientation. It recommends that for the sake of a genuine dialogue,

151. Sahih Muslim, *Kitāb al-Fadā'il*, 30, #5835, quoted in Leirvik, *Images of Jesus Christ*, 38.

Christians should present Jesus to Muslims in the fullness of his personality as it is revealed in the Gospels.[152] Thus, to be content with only Jesus the prophet-teacher would not do justice to the Muslim's need.

On the other hand, Hans Küng advises Muslims to evaluate Jesus on the basis of the historical sources of the Gospels: "If we on the Christian side make an effort to reevaluate Muhammad on the basis of Islamic sources, especially the Qur'an, we also hope that for their part the Muslims will eventually be prepared to move toward *a reevaluation of Jesus of Nazareth on the basis of historical sources* (namely, the Gospels) as many Jews have already been doing."[153]

The Divinity of Jesus in Islamic Estimation

Islam categorically rejects the claim to Jesus's divinity. It would constitute the greatest sin, that of "association" (with Allah), the *shirk*. Recall that even Muhammad is merely a human person. Even the affirmation of the virgin birth (Q 21:91) has no divine implications. Consider one of the most significant passages about Jesus in the Qur'an, where he is named both Allah's "word" and "spirit" (4:171). Even that does not imply deity!

The Qur'an contains only a handful of direct references to the Christian claim of Jesus as the Son of God and his divinity, and it bluntly denies the claim (4:171; 9:30; 19:35). Similarly denied is the idea of Allah having a son (2:116; 4:171; 17:111; 39:4; 72:3). In the first place, the all-sufficient One has no need for anything (10:68). The idea of sonship is also denied in the Qur'an because it is seen as linked with Allah having a consort (6:101).

The Islamic View of Incarnation

The Muslim rebuttals of the Christian doctrine of the incarnation of Jesus Christ, as presented in the anti-Christian Muslim literature during its first centuries, can be classified under two broad sets of arguments.[154] First, incarna-

152. Kenneth Cragg, *The Call of the Minaret*, rev. ed. (Maryknoll, NY: Orbis, 1985 [1956]), 258–60.

153. Hans Küng, "A Christian Response [to Josef van Ess, 'The Image of God and Islamic Mysticism, the Image of Man and Society: Islamic Perspectives']," in *Christianity and World Religions: Paths of Dialogue with Islam, Hinduism, and Buddhism*, ed. Hans Küng, with Josef van Ess, Heinrich von Stietencron, and Heinz Bechert (New York: Doubleday, 1986), 111.

154. Reda Samuel, "The Incarnation in Arabic Christian Theology from the Beginnings

tion is inconsistent with both Muslim and Christian Scripture. Muslim scholars quoted Qur'anic passages that refute Jesus's divinity (e.g., 5:72, 73) while employing Qur'anic passages that speak of the mere humanity of Jesus (e.g., 5:75). As for the Bible, Muslim scholars devoted considerable attention to the sayings that speak of Jesus's humanity, such as his being the son of David and Abraham (Matt. 1:1), and that indicate that he ate, drank, slept, traveled, rode a donkey, suffered, and died; similarly, his need to pray, his temptations, and so forth. On the other hand, Muslim commentators downplayed the importance of Christian interpretation of a few passages in which they saw direct claims to Jesus's divinity. Second, these early Muslim commentators argued that the Christian doctrine of incarnation is inconsistent with Muslim and Christian teachings at large. On top of this argumentation was the central Muslim idea of *tawḥid*, the oneness of God, which by default rejects all notions of not only incarnation but also the corollary Christian doctrine of the Trinity. *Tawḥid* was seen as taught not only by the Qur'an but also by the Bible, especially the Old Testament (Deut. 6:4).

A related concern among Muslim commentators is the incompatibility of incarnation with God's transcendence, affirmed firmly in both faiths. The idea of God becoming flesh violates, in Muslim sensibilities, the principles of God's glory and greatness. Furthermore, Jesus's physical conception and birth as part of the doctrine of incarnation were seen as incompatible with both Christian and Muslim teachings. A logical problem here is the exact moment the two natures were united, whether in conception or birth or afterward. A final Muslim concern about the incarnation is that it involves *shirk*, the greatest sin of all, associating with God what should not be associated with him.

Although the impasse continues, deepening mutual dialogue is not useless. It would be particularly important for the sake of mutual learning. As mentioned regarding the Trinity, a number of Islamic beliefs about Christ (and the Christian God) are gleaned from heretical sources.

---

to the Mid-Eleventh Centuries" (PhD tutorial, Fuller Theological Seminary, School of Intercultural Studies, Spring 2010).

Jesus and Buddha

The Slow Emergence of Buddhist-Christian Engagement

Unlike the relationship with Islam, the interaction between Jesus traditions and Buddhist traditions has not been wide and deep until the twentieth century. Particularly in Theravada tradition, given the fact that Buddha taught no fewer than forty-five years, the teaching ministry of Jesus, comprising only three years at most, does not easily gain respect. That said, in terms of life history there are obvious similarities between Shakyamuni (Gautama) Buddha and Jesus of Nazareth, even if the historical details of Gautama's life are very scarce, including the lack of precise dating of his birth.[155] Miraculous elements attach to the birth of both founders, including cosmic signs and phenomena, as well as ominous threat; both faced temptations, one in the forest, the other in the desert; both became itinerant preachers and teachers who also were considered miracle-workers; both were men of prayer and meditation; and so forth.[156]

Although Buddhists have been kind in their assessment of the figure of Jesus Christ, occasionally criticisms such as the illicit status of Mary and the coming of Jesus at such a late moment of history are presented. Potentially the Mahayana tradition's stress on the transcendent and "salvific" presence of Buddha might find bridges with Christian faith more easily. The major difference, however, is its vision of multiple Boddhisattvas (Enlightened Ones) vis-à-vis the Christian faith's focus on one single savior.

With all their appreciation of Jesus's ethical life, ministry, and teaching, the biggest obstacle is the claim to Jesus's divinity and corollary creedal beliefs. Leading Tibetan Buddhist scholar and practitioner José Ignacio Cabezón specifies the problem in this way: "The problem lies not in the claim that Jesus is the incarnation or manifestation of a deity. What I find objectionable is (a) the Christian characterization of the deity whose incarnation Jesus is said to be, and (b) the claim that Jesus is unique in being an incarnation."[157] That the idea of incarnation in itself is not a problem for Buddhists is based on the belief prevalent among all Mahayana Buddhists that the universe is populated by

155. Gajin Nagao, "The Life of the Buddha: An Interpretation," *Eastern Buddhist*, n.s., 20, no. 2 (1987): 1–31.

156. Leo D. Lefebure, *The Buddha and the Christ: Explorations in Buddhist and Christian Dialogue* (Maryknoll, NY: Orbis, 1993), chap. 2.

157. Cabezón, "Buddhist Views of Jesus," 21.

enlightened beings who, having attained the buddhahood, have the capacity to incarnate for the welfare of others.

To consider Jesus as incarnate on the basis of his extraordinary teaching, miracles, and ethical life is not to say that therefore he "possessed the quality of maximal greatness (enlightenment), that is, that he was a Buddha."[158] In many respects, Jesus might be better compared with a Boddhisattva, a Buddha-in-the-making, who for the sake of others is willing to suffer and postpone one's own enlightenment (as happens in Mahayana traditions). In the (Japanese and Chinese) Pure Land tradition, similarly, Jesus can be respected as a Boddhisattva, a compassionate being who helps others, a manifestation of Amitabha.[159] Even then there is no ultimacy to the role of Jesus after the Christian tradition. Even wider differences separate the Theravada tradition and Christian interpretation of Jesus, as Theravada does not emphasize the idea of enlightened manifestations of the divine incarnating for the benefit of others.[160]

Behind the Buddhist refusal to grant a salvific role to Jesus lie a number of doctrinal presuppositions. In Buddhist thought, every sentient person is responsible for his or her destiny. The idea that salvation of men and women would be dependent on any historical event such as the cross is totally unknown to Buddhism. After all, mere belief or doctrine cannot save the human person; only effort toward enlightenment can lead to the end goal.

The Buddhist Rita M. Gross makes the insightful observation that Christian tradition tends to "locate truth in the messenger, whereas Buddhism tends to focus on the message." This is linked with the fact that Christian tradition has a tendency "to personify the ultimate while Buddhists tend toward nonpersonal metaphors about ultimate reality."[161]

Incarnation in Buddhist Perspective

What about the doctrine of incarnation? Are there any similar motifs or parallels between the two religions and the founding figures? Anyone who knows Buddhism in its everyday manifestation—even in the Theravada form—knows

158. Cabezón, "Buddhist Views of Jesus," 21–22, here 22.

159. Amitabha is the original Sanskrit name for the central Buddha in Pure Land; it means literally "Infinite Light." In Japanese, the title is Amida. See further, Alfred Bloom, "Jesus in the Pure Land," chap. 3 in *JWF*, 31.

160. Sister Ajahn Candasiri, "Jesus: A Theravadan Perspective," in *JWF*, 25.

161. Rita M. Gross, "Meditating on Jesus," in *Buddhists Talk about Jesus, Christians Talk about the Buddha*, ed. Rita M. Gross and Terry C. Muck (New York: Continuum, 2000), 44.

how highly Buddha is venerated. The story of Brahman Dona in the Pali Canon is illustrative. Having found Buddha's footprints, Dona, in amazement and awe, went to ask Buddha of their origin. Buddha explained that they belong to neither a *deva* (celestial being) nor a spirit nor a human being since all those forms of existence still are stuck within the bounds of samsara leading to rebirths. Instead, Buddha has transcended all that—and that's what makes him *Buddha*![162]

The state of buddhahood is also the key to the Buddhist notion of incarnation. Buddha makes an identification with Dhamma (the doctrine, teaching): "He who sees Dhamma . . . sees me; he who sees me sees Dhamma."[163] Undoubtedly, there is some important resemblance with the Johannine Jesus's words about the unity between him and the Father (John 10:30). Indeed, Buddhist tradition speaks of the kind of "visible Dhamma" in terms of the life of the person who has freed himself or herself totally from hatred, delusion, and greed.

The final form of the (Mahayana) Buddhist doctrine of incarnation is the idea of *trikaya*, three bodies: first, "Transformation Body," the earthly Buddha, a transient and illusionary form of existence; second, "Enjoyment Body," the form of existence for the sake of others; and third, "Dhamma Body," the ultimate form of existence that indeed is no longer a "form" of existence but is formless. In other words, the last "body" transcends the form and laws of existence. It is inconceivable and ineffable.[164] Although there are some interesting similar motifs between the Buddhist and Christian doctrines of incarnation, including the ascent-descent/descent-ascent dynamic, "salvific orientation," and the dialectic between the "historical" and "suprahistorical" forms of existence, even a cursory look reveals profound differences, many of which have been alluded to above.

Sunyata and Self-Emptying

The most promising connecting point between (Mahayana) Buddhism and Christology can be found in the correlation of the main concepts of *sunyata* and the self-emptying of Christ. As discussed (chap. 2), notoriously difficult to translate and even more complicated to understand, *sunyata* literally means

162. Anguttara Nikaya 4, 36 ("Tipitaka: The Pali Canon," ed. John T. Bullitt, *Access to Insight*, May 29, 2010, http://www.accesstoinsight.org/tipitaka/index.html).

163. Samyutta Nikaya 22.87.

164. Perry Schmidt-Leukel, "Buddha and Christ as Mediators of the Transcendent: A Christian Perspective," in *Buddhism and Christianity in Dialogue*, ed. Perry Schmidt-Leukel, Gerald Weisfeld Lectures, 2004 (London: SCM, 2005), 157–59.

"(absolute) nothingness." However, it is not "empty nothingness," since it is what in Western terms should be called the ultimate, absolute reality.[165]

In a comparative commenting on Philippians 2:5–8, Masao Abe notes, first, the "abnegation of Christ as the Son of God," and second, that this self-emptying "indicates the self-sacrificial love of Christ for humankind," as a manifestation of the "unfathomable depth of God's love." This Japanese Buddhist opines that the abnegation was full and thoroughgoing. By that he means that a radical transformation took place as "the Son of God abandoned his divine substance and took on human substance," all the way to the cross. Indeed, he concludes that "Christ as the Son of God is *essentially* and *fundamentally* self-emptying or self-negating." This (and some other related moves, particularly a revision of the doctrine of preexistence) allows him to provide a seemingly self-contradictory account of incarnation based on the logic of *sunyata*: "The Son of God is not the Son of God (for he is essentially and fundamentally self-emptying); precisely because he *is not* the Son of God he *is* truly the Son of God (for he originally and always works as Christ, the Messiah, in his salvational function of self-emptying)."[166] For Christian intuitions—and Western logic—this is a difficult passage to accept and understand.

The Christian commentator Pannenberg wonders what really is the meaning of Abe's talk about the seemingly contradictory (at least to Western logic) notion of emptiness not only emptying everything else but also itself. In Christian theology this did not mean that Jesus ceased to be the Son of God. Christian theology also takes preexistence as a necessary dogmatic assertion.[167]

Christ and Avatars in Hindu-Christian Engagement

The Hindu Appreciation of Jesus's Ethics and Teaching

Although it is probable that as early as the first century there was a Christian presence in India, no evidence of Hindu perceptions of Jesus survives; we

165. Masao Abe, "Kenotic God and Dynamic Sunyata," in *Divine Emptiness and Historical Fullness: A Buddhist-Jewish-Christian Conversation with Masao* Abe, ed. Christopher Ives (Valley Forge, PA: Trinity, 1995), 50; Heinrich Ott, "The Convergence: Sunyata as a Dynamic Event," in Ives, *Divine Emptiness and Historical Fullness*, 127–34.

166. Abe, "Kenotic God," 32–33.

167. Wolfhart Pannenberg, "God's Love and the Kenosis of the Son: A Response to Masao Abe," in Ives, *Divine Emptiness and Historical Fullness*, 247–48.

have to wait until the seventeenth century for that. The earliest modern Hindu interpretation of Jesus was offered in the early nineteenth century by Raja Ram Mohun Roy, who focused on Jesus's ethical meaning and denied divine incarnation.[168]

Beginning from the end of the nineteenth century, a new wave of interpretations of Christ emerged that was deeply rooted in the religious (Hindu) soil of Asia, the so-called Indian Renaissance or neo-Hindu reform. Consider these book titles: Raimundo Panikkar's *Unknown Christ of Hinduism* and M. M. Thomas's *Acknowledged Christ of the Indian Renaissance.* The contemporary Indian theologian Stanley J. Samartha's *Hindu Response to the Unbound Christ* reminds us that while many Indians attached themselves to the person of Jesus Christ—who reflects the features of Hindu avatars (incarnations of Hindu gods such as the famous Krishna or Vishnu)—they also detached that person from the institutional church.

Several Hindu writers were excited by the social teachings of Christ but did not make a personal commitment to him, for example, Swami Vivekananda of the Ramakrishna order, who elevated Jesus among the highly revered figures of Buddha and Krishna, generally believed to be the incarnation of Vishnu. Well known is Mahatma Gandhi's Jesus as an ethical teacher, reflecting the same principles that guided his own pacifistic fight for the liberation of the Indian people, namely, *satyagraha* (the search for truth) and *ahimsa* (nonviolence).[169]

Finally, there are Hindus who have become Christians but insist they have remained Hindus, the best known of whom is Brahmabandhab Upadhyaya. His spirituality is based on a deep personal experience of the person of Jesus the Son of God, who becomes at once his guru and his friend. Whether or not Jesus was divine is not the point.[170]

By and large, Hindu perceptions of Jesus are positive. This is similar to Buddhist views and different from a number of Jewish and Islamic views. With sweeping generalizations, the Hindu perceptions, including the twentieth-century ones, can be described in this way: "(1) Jesus is a rational teacher of universal values; (2) Jesus is an incarnation of God among other incarnations;

168. R. Neufeldt, "Hindu Views of Christ," in *Hindu-Christian Dialogue: Perspectives and Encounters*, ed. Harold Coward (Maryknoll, NY: Orbis, 1990), 162–75.

169. Mohandas K. Gandhi, *The Message of Jesus Christ* (Bombay: Bharatiya Vidya Bhavan, 1963 [1940]).

170. See Jacob Kavunkal, "The Mystery of God in and through Hinduism," in *Christian Theology in Asia*, ed. Sebastian C. H. Kim (Cambridge: Cambridge University Press, 2008), 28–30.

and (3) Jesus is a spiritual teacher. These positions are not, of course, mutually exclusive."[171]

What makes the mutual dialogue between Hindus and Christians both promising and challenging is that there are few, if any, doctrinal boundaries that are exclusively Hindu or required of followers to belong. Add to that a bewildering variety of beliefs, rites, rituals, favorite local gods and goddesses—and you get a feel of a "religion" very different from most other living faiths.

The Divinity of Jesus in Hindu Estimation

Among the Hindu commentators are those who consider Jesus of Nazareth a mere human teacher, albeit a highly respected and honored one. These interpreters of Christ also reject the belief of Jesus as the incarnation of God. Materially these interpretations echo many of the views of classical liberalism. There are also those such as Keshub Chunder Sen who, replacing the doctrine of the Trinity with the Biunity of Father and Spirit, fall short of regarding Jesus as the divine incarnation, his "Divine Humanity."[172]

Many contemporary Hindu interpreters of Jesus, perhaps a majority of them, are willing to grant divine status to Jesus Christ, something parallel to Krishna, the avatar of Vishnu. That said, important qualifications and clarifications are in order. It is a commonplace in Hindu thought to believe that some dimension of the human being is divine. The possibility of realization of the divine lies within the reach of any human being; however, in most cases that does not happen. Jesus is one among those in whom the realization of the divine took place.[173] Hence, Jesus's importance lies in his role as the symbol of the potential of the realization of the divine in the human person. In that outlook, even the cross may be appropriated as the form of an ultimate self-sacrifice.[174]

Some strands of Hinduism such as the Hare Krishna movement consider Jesus as Guru. It focuses on love and devotion rather than on doctrine, particularly toward Krishna, the avatar of Vishnu. The ultimate goal of this pursuit is active love and desire for God. Avatars, divine embodiments, empowered

171. Gavin D. Flood, "Jesus in Hinduism: Closing Reflection," in *JBC*, 202.

172. Editors' explanation as an introduction to Chunder Sen's Lectures, 25–27, reproduced in *JBC*, 165–66, here 165.

173. Chakravarthi Ram-Prasad, "Hindu Views of Jesus," in *JWF*, 85.

174. Ram-Prasad, "Hindu Views of Jesus," 85.

with divine *shakti* (power), help revive the devotion to God. Jesus is one of those divinely empowered incarnations.

If possible, even higher status is granted to Jesus in *The Gospel of Sri Ramakrishna*, written by the great nineteenth-century Bengalese guru Ramakrishna Paramahansa. He even claimed to have a number of mystical encounters with Jesus.[175] His most famous disciple, Swami Vivekananda—best known for his influential speech at the first World's Parliament of Religions in Chicago (1893) and as the founder of Vedanta Societies—wrote the highly honoring preface to the (unfinished) Bengali translation of Thomas à Kempis's *Imitation of Christ.*[176]

Incarnation and Avatars

With all the differences and diversities in Hindu traditions, it is safe to say that in classical Hinduism, the one Brahman in its "manifested" form is known as the Hindu Trimurti, namely, Brahma (the "Creator God"), Vishnu (the "Preserver God"), and Shiva (the "Destroyer God" [or "Completer God"]). As it is the task of Vishnu to make sure the universe and its order will not be destroyed in an undue manner, through various forms of avatars, Vishnu intervenes in the affairs of the world. This "descent," as the word literally means, can be expressed in terms of the word "incarnation," as the often-cited passage in Bhagavad Gita (4.7–8) renders it:

7. Whenever, O descendant of Bharata, there is decline of Dharma, and rise of Adharma, then I body Myself forth
8. For the protection of the good, for the destruction of the wicked, and for the establishment of Dharma, I come into being in every age.[177]

The purpose, hence, of the "coming down" of God is the establishment of dhamma, the right order, "righteousness." It has little to do with the Christian notion of atonement.

Hindu mythology includes numerous accounts of incarnations. Among those, an established doctrine widely shared by various Hindu strands is ten

175. Sri Ramakrishna, *The Gospel of Sri Ramakrishna: Translated into English with an Introduction by Swami Nikhilananda* (New York: Ramakrishna-Vivekananda Center, 1984 [1942]), 34; reproduced in *JBC*, 173.

176. *The Complete Works of Vivekananda*, 8:159–60, reproduced in *JBC*, 177–79.

177. Trans. Swami Swarupananda, http://www.sacred-texts.com/hin/.

incarnations of Vishnu beginning from a fish and tortoise and continuing all the way to Rama and Krishna, the two most cherished avatars of all, and finally to the Buddha.[178] Furthermore, unlike Christian tradition, it is customary for Hindu thought to conceive of avatars in degrees, from a partial to a fuller to a fullest measure of incarnation. This is in direct contrast to the traditional Christian view of incarnation. So is also the idea of multiple "descents" of the divine.

Like the Christian Raimundo Panikkar, Hindus customarily make a distinction between Jesus and Christ. "There is a difference of meaning between *Jesus* and *Christ*. Jesus is the name of a little human body in which the vast Christ Consciousness was born. Although the Christ Consciousness manifested in the body of Jesus, it cannot be limited to one human form."[179] In this framework, "Christ" does not mean a particular individual but rather "the state of realization of Truth." Hence, each and every one of us can become Christ.[180]

178. Arvind Sharma, *Classical Hindu Thought: An Introduction* (Oxford: Oxford University Press, 2000), 6–7, 82–86.

179. Paramahansa Yogananda, *Man's Eternal Quest* (Los Angeles: Self-Realization Fellowship, 1975), 297.

180. Swami Abhedananda, *Vedanta Philosophy* (Calcutta: Ramakrishna Vedanta Math, 1959), 40.

6 | Reconciliation

How to Do the Doctrine of "Atonement" in Contemporary Theology

The introductory discussion of the "method" in Christology in the previous chapter noted that while the traditional distinction between the work ("atonement") and person (identity) of Christ should be handled with great care, for pedagogical and heuristic purposes it continues to be utilized. Although the previous chapter focused on topics usually categorized under the person of Christ, even a cursory look back at the discussion reveals that some key themes investigated, such as incarnation and resurrection, are certainly deeply soteriological as well.

While no single word in the biblical canon refers to the Trinitarian work of the salvation of humankind and the whole creation, Christian tradition has used "atonement" most frequently: hence the term "atonement theories." Older discussions of atonement usually focused on the suffering and death of Christ on the cross; in Eastern Christianity the resurrection also loomed large. Tradition also dealt with incarnation when incarnation was seen as an integral part of the salvific act. The life, ministry, miracles, and preaching of Jesus were not typically highlighted. It was also typical for investigations to focus, at times almost exclusively, on the christological dimensions, whereas the role of the Father was brought to the picture either in terms of the "object" of atonement or as counterpart to the Son. The Spirit's role was not crucial at all.

In contemporary treatments of atonement, a number of orientations both challenge and complement earlier approaches. This discussion will look at the work of salvation through the Trinitarian framework as a salvific event and process, initiated and completed by the joint work of Father, Son, and Spirit. While based on biblical-theological materials, contemporary discussion also takes stock of the globalization of the world with cultural diversity and hybridity, and the interaction with other living faiths. In keeping with this, themes such as violence, power, and inclusivity, as well as sociopolitical dimensions, will also be brought to bear on the discussion.

As a corrective to earlier juridical, often individualistic, and at times "static" ways of interpreting the work of salvation, Adam Kotsko recommends a "social-relational" perspective in which relationality and communal aspects are appropriately acknowledged.[1] Along the same lines, Moltmann warns us of the danger of an individualistic reading of atonement tradition and its "spiritualization," which divorces it from earthly realities and relegates it only to the eschaton.[2] Over against any reductionist account of salvation, we need to speak of reconciliation in holistic terms: "In the theological sense, salvation is whole salvation and the salvation of the whole, or it is not God's salvation; for God is 'the all-determining reality.'"[3]

To embrace and highlight these current turns in the theology of atonement, the term "reconciliation" has been adopted as the main concept. It includes everything traditional atonement-language captured and, as will be explained below, a more comprehensive and inclusive account of the work of salvation wrought by the triune God.

The first section to follow seeks to look carefully at the growth of Christian "atonement theories," both biblical and historical, appreciating the diversity of viewpoints. The growth of traditions will be assessed as to their liabilities and problems, as well as their continuing value for contemporary theology. Thereafter, an issue too often ignored in theology, namely, violence and the cross, will be taken up. In addition, the contemporary theological construction of reconciliation seeks to develop a fully Trinitarian account of reconciliation, to be followed by a careful reflection on the implications and contribution to the church's mission in the world. It will focus on how the Christian church as reconciled community can live out and work toward the reconciliation of men and women with God as well as among themselves, and will include both spiritual-theological and sociopolitical issues. That reflection will naturally lead into the last section of the chapter, which picks up the

1. Adam Kotsko, *The Politics of Redemption: The Social Logic of Salvation* (London: T&T Clark, 2010), chap. 1 particularly.

2. Jürgen Moltmann, *The Way of Jesus Christ: Christology in Messianic Dimensions*, trans. Margaret Kohl (Minneapolis: Fortress, 1993 [1989]), 45.

3. Moltmann, *Way of Jesus Christ*, 45.

interfaith engagement from the end of the last chapter, now centering on the question of "salvation."

A Sympathetic-Critical Assessment of Classical Atonement Traditions

The Diversity of Biblical Metaphors and Symbols[4]

In the theology of the four evangelists, to the work of reconciliation belong Jesus's life, ministry, and teaching and—as the summit—his suffering, cross, resurrection, and ascension. The rest of the New Testament expands the salvific meaning of the salvific Christ event. It employs a number of metaphors, symbols, and images to highlight its many dimensions and benefits. The metaphors are drawn from the Old Testament and various cultural and religious sources familiar to the contemporary culture. They include the court of law (e.g., justification), world of commerce (e.g., redemption), personal and communal relationships (e.g., reconciliation), cult and worship (e.g., sacrifice), as well as the battleground (e.g., triumph over evil). While later Christian tradition, particularly in the Christian West, has looked at Jesus's execution primarily through the lens of punishment and pain, for the writers' contemporary culture, the passion narrative is also about utmost public humiliation and rejection by God and community. All the metaphors are interwoven, not only in the passion narrative and execution but also in the whole history of Jesus Christ, including the pouring out of the Spirit at Pentecost.

The impending violent death loomed on the horizon for the Jesus of the New Testament Gospels; no wonder he had a hard time trying to convince his followers of its necessity (Mark 8:31–38 par.). Behind the impending death, the Gospel authors discern the divine plan—as evidenced in the frequent use of the Greek *dei* ("must," "have to"; Matt. 16:21; Mark 8:31; Luke 9:22; etc.). It was a death "for many," which becomes virtually a technical term. That said, precious few passages on the lips of Jesus seek to describe in any detail the theological meaning of his death. The Markan Jesus's sayings of giving "his life as a ransom for many" (Mark 10:45) and pouring out his "blood of the covenant . . . for

4. Throughout this section, discussion is indebted to Mark D. Baker and Joel B. Green, *Recovering the Scandal of the Cross: Atonement in New Testament and Contemporary Contexts* (Downers Grove, IL: InterVarsity Press, 2000), chaps. 2 and 3; highly useful are also Stephen Finlan, *Problems with Atonement: The Origins of, and Controversy about, the Atonement Doctrine* (Collegeville, MN: Liturgical Press, 2005); Stephen Finlan, *Options on Atonement in Christian Thought* (Collegeville, MN: Glazier, 2007).

many" (14:24) are among such sayings. "Ransom" is connected with the ideas of deliverance and release drawn from the Roman slave trade and the hopes of the Old Testament people of God under foreign tyrannies. The metaphor of covenant blood is connected with Yahweh's faithful acts in saving, freeing, and protecting his people on the basis of covenants often sealed with blood (as in Gen. 15).

It was left to Pauline traditions to offer a rich and variegated depiction of the many dimensions of the saving significance of Jesus's work for us. Often Paul mixes a number of metaphors in one passage. Romans 8:3 contains no fewer than three in one sentence: sacrificial (sent in the flesh), judicial (condemning sin), and scapegoat (condemnation "in the flesh"). Second Corinthians 5:14–6:2 is a grand example of the conflation of metaphors. While "reconciliation"—bringing together two distanced parties (as also in Rom. 5:10–11; Col. 1:20; and Eph. 2:16)—towers here as the main metaphor, others in the passage include "substitution," "representation," "forgiveness," "sin offering," "(cosmic) renewal," "righteousness," and divine "favor." Similarly, Galatians 3:10–14 offers a whole spectrum of metaphors having their background in the Old Testament and Greco-Roman culture. Or think of the reference to the Passover Lamb in 1 Corinthians 5:7 that comes from the same cultic word recalling the formative event in Exodus. Furthermore, in some parts of his corpus Paul uses images drawn from the battlefield, cosmic or earthly, which speak of the defeat of powers (Col. 2:15), and the closely related metaphors of new creation and cosmic renewal pointing to the final victory of Christ over all powers (2 Cor. 5:16–17; Eph. 2:14–15).

The Lukan way of appropriating salvific metaphors is highly distinctive. Particularly the materials in the book of Acts are critical in that they claim to represent authentic samples of the missionary preaching of the early church encompassing both Petrine and Pauline ministries. Alongside the cross, there is a strong focus on the resurrection and ascension, as well as on the pouring out and power of the Holy Spirit. The Pentecostal pouring out of the Spirit on all flesh (Acts 2) marks the beginning of the last days. The crucified Messiah has now been made the risen and ascended Lord (2:36) who brings about forgiveness and restoration to the people of God (5:30–31). Healings as a foretaste of a holistic salvation and promises of the coming eschatological fulfillment are an integral part of the early church's preaching (Acts 3; 4).

An even more distinctive approach to atonement is depicted in the extensive Johannine traditions with their great rhetorical devices such as speaking of the cross in terms of "lifting up" (John 3:14–15; 8:28) and glorification of the Son of Man (13:32)! Familiar Old Testament metaphors of the sacrificial lamb (1:29) are joined with metaphors of water and cleansing (13:10–11; 15:3), which also relate to pneumatological aspects of salvation (4:13–15; 7:37–39). John's epistles are fond of images of "light" and "purification" (1 John 1:5–7; 2:9; 3:3), forgiveness (1:8–9), and sacrifice for sins (2:2; 3:5). The book of Revelation uses several Old Testament images in the cosmic context, including the victorious Lamb (Rev. 5:5, 9).

The book of Hebrews is fully embedded in Old Testament imagery of the temple, priesthood, sacrifices, and covenant. First Peter, while conversant with images of salvation such as the hope for the eschatological inheritance (1 Pet. 1:3–5, 13, 23), lays emphasis on what later theology calls the "moral example" view—the invitation to imitate the suffering and cross of Christ (2:12, 19, 21–25; 3:14–17).

In sum: no single metaphor can capture the fullness of salvation; many metaphors are needed. Furthermore, the domain of atonement is integrally related to the whole history of Jesus. To put it another way: it is the Trinitarian history of Jesus Christ. Finally, the salvation offered is inclusive and holistic: enlightenment, forgiveness of sins, renewal, healing, empowerment, and release from the powers. Similarly, its scope encompasses personal, communal, and cosmic levels.

Historical Interpretations of Atonement

The Classic View

It took a long time for a theology of atonement to develop. Importantly, at no time were there any fixed statements about atonement in ancient creeds. While the apostolic fathers' writings contain a number of references to Christ's work, the fathers exhibit no desire to come up with fixed formulae for doctrines such as they did for the Trinity and the person of Christ. Also, as discussed in chapter 4, there was no theologically developed doctrine of sin yet. Hence, for the apologists the issues of correcting ignorance and bringing enlightenment were central.[5]

This state of affairs and the cosmic orientation of much of early theology gave rise to what Gustaf Aulén, in his classic work *Christus Victor*, calls the "classic view" of atonement. For the first millennium or so, Christian theology understood atonement mainly in terms of Christ's victory over evil powers and

5. J. N. D. Kelly, *Early Christian Doctrines*, rev. ed. (New York: Harper & Row, 1978 [1960]), 165–70.

a total redemption and liberation. Two key terms used are "recapitulation" and "ransom." The second-century bishop of Lyons, Irenaeus, is the leading advocate of the recapitulation view. Cosmic in its orientation, and closely linked to incarnation, this approach saw mortality rather than sinfulness as the ultimate "power" to be defeated. Behind this interpretation is an understanding of the Fall as an unfortunate "accident," natural to humanity-in-childhood, rather than a tragic "fall from grace" as later formulated by the Western Church. The incarnation then means that Christ "recapitulates" in himself all the stages of human life, including those that belong to our state as sinners—not only individual human lives, but even the whole "history of humankind" and indeed of the creation. By his incarnation and human life, Christ reverses the course on which Adam by his sin started to lead humanity. Christ communicates immortality to those who are united to him by faith and effects a transformation in their lives (*Against Heresies* 3.17.4). In a single sentence, Christ "has therefore, in His work of recapitulation, summed up all things" (5.21.1).[6] While this is not everything Irenaeus said of atonement—he also knew, for example, redemption through the blood (3.5.3; 5.16.9)—recapitulation is the key.

The other version of the *Christus Victor* model employed the imagery of ransom, as is evident in Gregory of Nyssa and Origen, and has its secular background in the act of releasing slaves by payment. Gregory used the famous—or rather, infamous—image of God paying the ransom through deceiving the devil with the trickery of a fishhook. Hidden under human nature was Christ's deity, which the devil devoured as bait and thus helped destroy his own power.[7] Immediately following the hook allegory, Gregory also interpreted Christ's work in terms of "healing touch," a metaphor similar in many ways to recapitulation; like other fathers, he freely used other images as well. This is in keeping with the emerging, open-ended, and multifaceted conception of the salvific work of Christ among the fathers.

Later Atonement Theories

By and large this classic view, particularly the recapitulation version, became the dominant explanatory model of the Eastern Church, the Greek-speaking church. On the Latin side (notwithstanding some occasional support for Irenaeus's view), the formulation of atonement theories developed even more

6. Behind the idea of recapitulation is Eph. 1:10.

7. Gregory of Nyssa, *The Great Catechism* 26.

slowly, despite the evolvement of the stark Augustinian concept of original sin. Anselm of Canterbury's *Cur Deus Homo?*, from the eleventh century, offers a logical and theological reasoning for the necessity of the incarnation. In the context of medieval feudal society, with its hierarchy and desire for harmony, sin was seen as a disturbing factor. Rather than being a debt to the devil, sin is the failure to render to God his due, a blockage to divinely intended happiness to humanity. The just God is not able to forgive sin without payment for the lost honor; hence, satisfaction is needed, proportional to the seriousness of the violation. Satisfaction can be paid only by God through the God-man through his voluntary death, which was not occasioned by his own need but was rather a voluntary self-offering as our payment.

Anselm's contemporary Peter Abelard provides a radical revisioning of the interpretation of atonement that also asks the same question of "why" the incarnation in his "Exposition of the Epistle to the Romans." Abelard insists that God indeed has the right of ownership to humans and that it is perfectly appropriate for God to forgive without any "satisfaction" if God so wishes. Jesus's death provides a compelling example to follow. Jesus embodies God's sacrificial love. Thus, we have the nomenclature "moral example view." This was made possible by Abelard's quite thin theology of sin and the Fall.

This view of atonement was embraced by various later movements and thinkers critical of vicarious satisfaction. Understandably, the Enlightenment thinkers found much to commend in the moral example view. It fit well with Immanuel Kant's idea of Jesus as the moral ideal rather than the crucified one. Liberal Protestants, similarly, considered this interpretation appealing, as is evident in Schleiermacher's theology. One of the most influential defenders of the moral example view in the early twentieth century was Hastings Rashdall, who spoke of the "moral ideal which Christ taught by His words, and illustrated by His life and death of love," the only "ideal given among men by which we may be saved."[8]

Instead of Abelard's view, though, the Anselmian interpretation became the dominant view during the Middle Ages, and the classic view remained less well known in the Christian West even though in the East the Irenaean understanding became the main tradition. Thomas Aquinas helped consolidate the satisfaction view in the context of the Western Church's emphasis on sacrifice and the debt of sin.[9]

8. Hastings Rashdall, *The Idea of Atonement in Christian Theology* (New York: Macmillan, 1919), 463.

9. Aquinas, *ST* 3.48.2–4.

The Protestant Reformers, particularly the Reformed side, continued in the line of the Anselmian view.[10] Similarly, Martin Luther built on the Anselmian tradition even though he also helped rediscover in a fresh way the classic view of the fathers. The Reformers' view is often labeled the "penal substitution" view, which implies its Anselmian basis coupled with the need for a sacrificial-expiatory death on the cross as a way to deal with condemned humanity's lot because of sin. In Calvin's Reformed theology and particularly among his followers, both in Reformed orthodoxy following the Reformation and in the ensuing conservative/fundamentalistic Princeton orthodoxy at the turn of the twentieth century, the consolidation of the penal substitution hermeneutics often became the test of orthodoxy. A leading, highly influential Reformed theologian was Charles Hodge. He argues that it is axiomatic that forgiveness requires "satisfaction," and that can be had only through "punishment" in terms of Christ's "sacrifice."[11] Karl Barth, while in many ways diverging from his Reformed tradition, in his massive discussion of the topic of atonement under the telling heading "The Judge Judged in Our Place," defends unabashedly the substitutionary nature of atonement as Christ becomes the sin-bearer and the condemned.[12]

A Theological Appraisal of Atonement Traditions[13]

The recapitulation view helps theology make an integral connection between incarnation, life, death, resurrection, and ascension—in other words, the whole history of Jesus. It reminds theology of the obvious insight that as dramatic a problem as sin is, mortality is the ultimate problem. The recapitulation view empowers development of a more holistic, inclusive view of salvation linking "spiritual" and "physical," personal and communal, as well as the human and cosmic dimensions of reality. Its obvious weakness is a thin theology of the cross, which hardly is in keeping with the Gospel writers' focus on the passion and the cross.

10. D. F. Wright, "The Atonement in Reformation Theology," *European Journal of Theology* 8, no. 1 (1999): 37–48.

11. Charles Hodge, *Systematic Theology*, vol. 3 (Grand Rapids: Eerdmans, 1973 [1872]), 480–544.

12. Barth, *CD* IV/1, 211–82.

13. G. R. Driver, *Understanding the Atonement for the Mission of the Church* (Scottdale, PA: Herald Press, 1986), chap. 2; Robert H. Culpepper, *Interpreting the Atonement* (Grand Rapids: Eerdmans, 1966), chap. 3; Baker and Green, *Recovering the Scandal*, chap. 5.

When it comes to the other version of the classic view, one shouldn't necessarily be put off by the infamous "tricking the devil" rhetorical device. The more substantial challenge is the mistaken view of the rights of the devil. While the New Testament puts the fallen "world" (*kosmos*) under the power of Satan (1 John 5:19), that does not imply the "possession" of the world by Satan. Even talk about "debt" in relation to the devil is not helpful; if sin accrues a debt, it is rather a debt the creature owes to the Creator. The ransom theory rightly highlights the need for personal, communal, and cosmic release from the powers that both resist the will of God and claim—illegal!—authority over the creatures and creation. By implication, the hope for freedom from all sorts of powers, including sociopolitical or sexist as in liberation theologies, is grounded in the history of salvation rather than a utopia.

While not often highlighted, the Anselmian way of explaining the atonement agrees in important ways with the classic view, particularly the recapitulation version, in its integral linking of atonement to incarnation. Even if the Anselmian theory may shift the focus from incarnation to the "satisfaction payment," its instincts lean into a more comprehensive view of the history of Jesus. The main contribution of the Anselmian model turns out to be its greatest liability as well: the attempt to interpret atonement in light of and against the medieval hierarchic and honor-keeping culture and society. On the one hand, this is a legitimate contextualization strategy. On the other hand, as long as that contextualization exercise is not perceived as such—as a *contextualization*—it is in danger of not only subsuming the theological theme under cultural constraints, but also of making that revised understanding *the* interpretation. Later history of theology, culminating in the penal substitution version, is a testament to that potential problem.

Highlighting (God's) honor rather than (human) guilt in itself is a contextual asset since in many parts of the world, ancient and contemporary, honor is a central cultural category. However, the liability of Anselm's way of conceiving of the divine honor is that it seems to operate with a formal, abstract principle. The biblical theology operates with covenant-based, relational, and personalistic notions of the divine honor. This helps distinguish between the abstract, judicial notion of justice in the medieval society, which lays the background for the Anselmian model, and the notion of justice in terms of living rightly and in keeping with the committed, grace-based covenant relationships of the Bible. The Anselmian viewpoint, thus, has to be reminded of the need to see the work of salvation as not stemming so much from God's offended honor, making God the main object of the atonement, requiring satisfaction, as from the unbounded love of the Creator for the creatures gone astray and leaving the covenant relationship. According to the biblical witness, God is the subject of reconciliation (2 Cor. 5:18–20).

If the original satisfaction model considers the need for atonement through the lens of the divine honor violated, the penal substitutionary version, and its development, highlights the theme of guilt, which leads to punishment and thus the need for a sacrifice. Much critique has been leveled against the penal substitution approach in recent years: the view of justice focusing on penalty and satisfaction as well as God's wrath in terms of anger; the guilt- and penitence-oriented ethos as the function of the later medieval/Reformation culture; the Trinitarian implications that seem to set the Son and Father over against one another, and at the same time leave no role for the Spirit; overindividualism and ignorance of communal, sociopolitical, and cosmic dimensions of salvation; dissociation from the whole history of Jesus, in terms of both his life and ministry and his resurrection and ascension; lack of ethical incentive; and the model's claim for sole orthodoxy. Furthermore, a number of contemporary critics point to the problematic of violence and scapegoating—a topic weighty enough to be taken up in the following section. Let us take up these criticisms.

While there is no denying the presence of punishment and even retaliation in the New Testament (Rom. 2:6–11; Matt. 13:42, 50; Revelation), the emphasis in salvation is not on retaliation but rather on rescue and repair. Critics are right about the need to make sure Trinitarian canons will be honored. Rather than Jesus—in his humanity, as it is often depicted—offering his life in the sense of appeasing an angry Father, a biblically and theologically more appropriate way to speak of substitution is to name it "representation."[14] "God was in Christ reconciling the world to Himself" (2 Cor. 5:19 NASB). Christ's humanity is not so much a "substitute" as it is the divinely appointed means of total identification and representation of humanity. The penal substitution view—like the other main models—needs to be put in proper perspective, which includes an effort to relate it to other models as well as to wider theological considerations. While guilt is part of the human problem, it is not all that plagues humanity. Furthermore, guilt is not only about personal life, it also relates to communal and other structural sins. Mortality and decay as well as bondage and slavery to powers, as the classic view contends, are problems too. Forgiveness and renewal of life, rather than merely an abstract satisfaction or another kind of divine transaction, should be the focus when speaking of guilt, repentance, and forgiveness. The

14. Christopher Marshall, *Beyond Retribution: A New Testament Vision of Justice, Crime, and Punishment* (Grand Rapids: Eerdmans, 2001), 61; Dorothee Sölle, *Christ Our Representative* (Philadelphia: Fortress, 1967).

integral ethical result of atonement should be rediscovered when resorting to the metaphors of the penal substitution model. Finally, one's theology of atonement should not be made a test of orthodoxy as at times happens among the more traditional communities. The penal substitution hermeneutics is only one among many perspectives on the work of salvation.

What about the moral example view and its historical successors? It is routinely—and rightly—noted that while the older interpretations of atonement are "objective" in terms of locating the main effect of atonement in God (however, that is being negotiated), the Abelardian view is "subjective." As any half-truth, it is just that, a *half*-truth. In both cases, it is still God—in Christ—who is acting. The objective versus subjective distinction can only be determined from the perspective of humanity's side. It has biblical support both in some sayings of Jesus and in 1 Peter, among others, as explained above in the biblical section. It reminds us of the integral connection between Jesus's suffering and our following in the footsteps of the Suffering Servant. However, taken in isolation from other New Testament perspectives, it fails to account for many critical aspects of atonement such as dealing with human sin in terms of transgression against God and cosmic implications of salvation. Similar to other theories, it has to be seen as one of many.

Violence, Cross, and Atonement

Criticism against the Violent Notions of Atonement

Accusations against the violent nature of traditional theories of atonement, particularly in relation to satisfaction and penal substitution models, abound.[15] The main critiques against the alleged violent nature of the Christian account of the atonement usually argue from some of the following points of view.

First, for many it is unacceptable to assume a God in need of or as an agent of violence. The satisfaction (and by inference, penal-satisfaction) model is said to pervert the picture of a loving, merciful God in producing a "sadomasochistic theology and practice based on the idea of an 'offended' God who can only be mollified through the payment of innocent blood."[16]

15. Hent de Vries, *Religion and Violence: Philosophical Perspectives from Kant to Derrida* (Baltimore: Johns Hopkins University Press, 2002); Leo D. Lefebure, *Revelation, the Religions, and Violence* (Maryknoll, NY: Orbis, 2000).

16. Rosemary Radford Ruether, *Introducing Redemption in Christian Feminism*, Introductions in Feminist Theology 1 (Sheffield: Sheffield Academic, 1998), 100.

Second, it is a commonplace to note that violence fosters violence and should thus be abandoned. It has been argued that the notion of "retributive justice" behind the criminal justice system of the Western nations, according to which the level of punishment is rationed to the severity of the evil deed, has its roots in the satisfaction view of atonement.[17]

Third, a number of female theologians have encountered satisfaction-based models as means of legitimizing female suffering and patriarchy as well as child abuse. They argue that Christian theology of the cross has encouraged women, who already are usually the (falsely) legitimized victims of violence, to continue suffering, modeling the suffering Jesus.[18]

Fourth, a number of scholars have tried to negotiate the allegedly violent nature of many biblical texts by arguing that either the Bible does not teach (divine) violence or, even though it does, we should not use such violence. An example of the first tactic is the claim that rather than God punishing his Son for the sins of humankind, men and women brought punishment over their own lives by rejecting the divine reign of God.[19] Regarding the latter tactics, few theologians—apart from, say, religious pluralists, or those having otherwise left behind Christian identity—have offered viable arguments.

Finally, the most penetrating critique of violence in relation to the cross comes from the French Catholic convert René Girard, an anthropologist, philosopher, and religious scholar.[20] In his theory, human beings are imitators who end up desiring the same things as their rivals; this "mimetic desire" often leads to violence between groups. To control this chaotic violence, collective violence is redirected at one victim, the scapegoat. Once this scapegoat has absorbed the blame and violent emotions of the community, violence is released and peace and reconciliation follow. Religion becomes the means to control and direct the scapegoat mechanism. Myths of cultures and religions, rather than revealing violence as violence, make it a sacred act for the benefit (salvation) of the culture; the victim as the bearer of collective blame has been rightly removed.

The implications for the biblical narrative in general and the passion story of Jesus are of course evident (although the theory itself was first devel-

17. Timothy Gorringe, *God's Just Vengeance: Crime, Violence, and the Rhetoric of Salvation*, Cambridge Studies in Ideology and Religion 9 (Cambridge: Cambridge University Press, 1966), chap. 1.

18. Ruether, *Introducing Redemption*, 95, 98–99; chap. 7.

19. Raymund Schwager, *Jesus in the Drama of Salvation* (New York: Crossroad, 1999).

20. René Girard, *Things Hidden Since the Foundation of the World*, trans. Stephen Bann and Michael Metteer (Stanford, CA: Stanford University Press, 1987), particularly chap. 1; *The Girard Reader*, ed. James G. Williams (New York: Crossroad, 1996), chaps. 1, 3, 4.

oped apart from the biblical story). Girard's basic thesis is that there is nothing sacrificial about the death of Jesus on the cross.[21] On the contrary, unlike the mythical concealing of violence, the biblical narrative exposes violence as violence and helps make an end of the cycle. Indeed, Jesus "dies, not as a sacrifice, but in order that there may be no more sacrifices."[22] A major way in which the death on the cross is exposed as violence is the resurrection. In religious myths, the sacrificed one does not rise from the tomb.[23]

A Theological Assessment of Violence Critiques

Girard should be credited with helping Christian theology—as well as any other religious traditions willing to hear his message—to expose hidden violence in religions. His attempt to eliminate violence from religion is to be congratulated for its aim. Yet there are severe problems as well. His theory is of course thoroughly modernist in suggesting a grand universal narrative. Furthermore, it is based on the ontology of violence rather than on an ontology of hospitality.[24] Theologically, the main problem is that he claims "there is nothing in the Gospels to suggest that the death of Jesus is a sacrifice, whatever definition (expiation, substitution, etc.) we may give for that sacrifice."[25] On the contrary, the point of the biblical story of Jesus's obedient self-sacrifice is that his is the ultimate and last sacrifice. Christ's sacrifice is once and for all (Heb. 7:27). No more sacrifices or shedding of blood is needed—that has ceased to be a means of atonement (10:14; 9:14). Not only Jesus's death on the cross but also his life and ministry speak for the cessation and overcoming of the cycle of violence. According to Miroslav Volf, "the Crucified Messiah" absorbs aggression, challenges violence by unearthing scapegoating and struggling actively against it. Ultimately, according to Volf, Christ's cross is an act of embrace of his opponents. The death of Christ means atonement for sins. It also makes it possible for human beings to embrace enemies.[26]

21. Chap. 11, "Nonsacrificial Death of Christ," in *The Girard Reader*.

22. Girard, *Things Hidden*, 210; see S. Mark Heim, *Saved from Sacrifice: A Theology of the Cross* (Grand Rapids: Eerdmans, 2006); Anthony W. Bartlett, *Cross Purposes: The Violent Grammar of Christian Atonement* (Harrisburg, PA: Trinity, 2000).

23. Heim, *Saved from Sacrifice*, 126.

24. Hans Boersma, *Violence, Hospitality, and the Cross: Reappropriating the Atonement Tradition* (Grand Rapids: Baker Academic, 2006), 134.

25. Girard, *Things Hidden*, 180.

26. Miroslav Volf, *Exclusion and Embrace: A Theological Exploration of Identity, Otherness, and Reconciliation* (Nashville: Abingdon, 1996), 291–95.

Regarding other criticisms presented above: as much weight as they may carry—and they are worth careful reflection—not all contemporary theologians are convinced that violence should be removed from the Christian account of the atonement. While the charge against the "sadomasochistic" God hardly deserves a serious theological response, behind the rhetoric there is the serious theological question of how to conceive of the work of salvation as the joint work of the triune God. Too easily traditional models of atonement yield a picture of the suffering Son in the hands of the just and demanding Father. The corrective can be found in a solid Trinitarian communion theology based on mutual love, respect, and joint work rather than domination and abuse. Subjugation, abuse, or similar perverted motives have nothing to do with this kind of God-in-communion.

Breaking the cycle of violence must begin with honest and scandalous acknowledgment that the crucifixion was a profound event of violence.[27] Contrary to popular conceptions, all three main traditions connect atonement with violence, including the one that often is not supposed to do so, the moral example view. It is not only Jesus's life and teaching but particularly his death that inspires loving response in us. So it seems as though the only way to avoid all notions of violence is to ignore both biblical and historical traditions.

While Christian tradition has reached nothing like a consensus on this matter—as the debates about, say, "just war" illustrate—theology by and large has been open to the idea of the justification of limited violence under certain circumstances with a view to a higher good. Thus, a medical doctor's amputation of a patient's leg to save his or her life is not violence. Killing, hitting, abusing, or speaking badly of my neighbor or a stranger is always and without limitations violence.[28] Furthermore, while humans have no right to violence (perhaps, apart from civil disobedience and "just war"), God does. This is Volf's argument. Taking his cue from the vision of Revelation 19, he concludes: "The end of the world is not violence, but a nonviolent embrace without end. . . . The world to come is ruled by the one who on the cross took violence upon himself in order to conquer the enmity and embrace the enemy. The Lamb's rule is legitimized not by the 'sword' but by its 'wounds.'"[29]

A more detailed and deeper scrutiny of key theological issues related to a Trinitarian theology of atonement in Christian tradition, including suffering,

27. Martin Hengel, *Crucifixion in the Ancient World and the Folly of the Message of the Cross* (Philadelphia: Fortress, 1977).

28. See further Boersma, *Violence, Hospitality, and the Cross*, 43–52.

29. Volf, *Exclusion and Embrace*, 300–301.

sacrifice, and execution of the innocent Messiah, is needed to fully capture this essential topic. This will be the focus of the next section.

Toward a Trinitarian Theology of Reconciliation

Suffering God and Crucified Messiah

Human Agency and Divine Plan behind Sufferings

So, is there a place in contemporary theology to speak of the suffering and violent death of the Messiah? At stake in this question is the foundational question of the nature of God. No other contemporary theologian has underscored this more than Jürgen Moltmann, who boldly considers "the cross of Christ as the foundation and criticism of Christian theology."[30] In the preface to *The Crucified God*, he claims that "whatever can stand before the face of the crucified Christ is true Christian theology. What cannot stand there must disappear."[31]

Jesus's willingness to suffer "for us" is depicted in the New Testament in the context of his obedience to his Father's will (Heb. 5:8–9); that passage speaks of the learning of obedience through suffering, a statement that "should not be seen as contrasting filial closeness to the Father" but rather as an expression of the "tension between learning obedience in time and pretemporal sonship." Jesus's obedience to the Father, then, "is not alien obedience of the slave . . . [but rather] an expression of his free agreement with the Father."[32]

Jesus was put to death as a messianic pretender and blasphemer who was believed to have violated the law and tradition, as well as to have usurped the status of God. There was also a collision with religious authorities, as he was regarded as a rebel. Even though he first came into conflict with his own people, it is clear from the Gospel narratives that the gentile (Roman) authorities executed Jesus.[33] In the words of the postcolonialist theologian Mark Taylor, "Jesus' death on the cross is best viewed as what that event concretely was, an imperial execution."[34] This has significant theological implications: "Roman

30. Subtitle to his *The Crucified God: The Cross of Christ as the Foundation and Criticism of Christian Theology*, trans. Margaret Kohl (Minneapolis: Fortress, 1993).

31. Moltmann, *The Crucified God*, x.

32. Pannenberg, *ST* 2:316.

33. Moltmann, *Way of Jesus Christ*, 160–64.

34. Mark Lewis Taylor, *The Executed God: The Way of the Cross in Lockdown America* (Minneapolis: Fortress, 2001), xiv.

participation in the events leading to the execution of Jesus perhaps was the occasion for extending the understanding of the death of Jesus as expiation to the Gentile world represented by Rome."[35] The Christology of the Roman Catholic Aloysius Pieris of Sri Lanka links Asia's poverty and spirituality to Jesus's "double baptism" in "the Jordan of Asian religions and the Calvary of Asian poverty." This is Jesus's immersion in the Asian context and life that led him finally to the cross; he was executed by the power elite. The powerful crucified him on "a cross that the money-polluted religiosity of his day planted on Calvary with the aid of a colonial power (Luke 23:1–23)."[36] Whatever "reasons" were behind the murder of Jesus, political factors, including religious-political as well as socioeconomic factors, were part of it, even though it was also part of the divine plan.[37]

How to Speak of Suffering without Glorifying It

Jesus's physical sufferings were real. Yet even more painful was the rejection, first by his own people and then ultimately by his Father. "To suffer and to be rejected are not identical. Suffering can be celebrated and admired. It can arouse compassion. But to be rejected takes away the dignity from suffering and makes it dishonourable suffering. To suffer and be rejected signify the cross."[38]

Several critical qualifiers are in order to put the emphasis on suffering and the cross in a proper perspective. First, theologically it is not appropriate to consider only the last days of Jesus through the lens of his suffering, as has often happened in tradition. As Andrew Sung Park pointedly puts it: "It is not right to limit the crucifixion of Jesus Christ to the three hours of suffering on the cross. The crucifixion of Jesus must be understood as extending to his whole life. Jesus lived the life of taking up his cross everyday."[39] Second, the highlighting of the critical role of the cross in Christian faith and theology has nothing whatsoever to do with glorification of suffering in general or of Christ's suffering in particular.

Third, contemporary theology has to be mindful of potentially ideological and suspicious tones in speaking of suffering because of its link with

35. Pannenberg, *ST* 2:426.

36. Aloysius Pieris, SJ, *An Asian Theology of Liberation* (Maryknoll, NY: Orbis, 1988), 49.

37. Contested by Taylor, *The Executed God*, 108.

38. Moltmann, *The Crucified God*, 55.

39. Andrew Sung Park, *The Wounded Heart of God: The Asian Concept of Han and the Christian Doctrine of Sin* (Nashville: Abingdon, 1993), 124.

violence and its alleged effect of sanctifying the passive suffering of many who already suffer at the hands of others. Women, particularly in the Third World, may be such victims, and religion can be used as a pretext. Rightly, many female theologians have critiqued the (ab)use of Jesus's suffering as a pretext for condoning forced, passive suffering of women and other victims,[40] or even worse, enforcing the silence of women and children about their abuse.[41] Those unchristian acts and attitudes have nothing to do with the Christian gospel of reconciliation and must be rejected categorically. Nothing in the gospel story about the voluntary obedience of the Son of God, even to the point of surrendering his life as sacrifice for the salvation of the world, suggests that for women to claim their value they should sacrifice themselves and refrain from pursuing their own needs. The gospel's call to sacrifice one's own needs for the sake of one's neighbors in the service of the love of God is a voluntary, intentional personal decision to "imitate Christ" and may lead to personal fulfillment and contentment.

Christ's sufferings had both an active and a passive side. On the one hand, the sufferings of Christ were voluntary, not imposed by others as in domestic violence or brutal wartime rape. On the other hand, Christ represents the victim rather than the perpetrator. Christ, the Suffering Servant, also resisted power structures, abuse of the weak, and any instrumental treatment of the other. Suffering and pain are reprehensible and objectionable not only to women or other minorities. We all abhor them. They are not to be glorified.

Suffering and Divine Sympathy

As explained above, in the Trinitarian account of the sufferings of Christ, in the anguish and death of the Son of God, there are the presence and sympathy of the Father. God's presence is most concrete and deepest in the midst of our suffering. Hence, for many "the suffering of Jesus gave . . . a sense of comfort, for God in Jesus understood their pain and grief and shared their heavy load."[42] The Korean-born theologian Andrew Sung Park looks at the meaning

40. Rita Nakashima Brock, *Journeys by Heart: A Christology of Erotic Power* (New York: Crossroad, 1988), 56.

41. Joanne Carlson Brown and Rebecca Parker, "For God So Loved the World," in *Christianity, Patriarchy, and Abuse: A Feminist Critique*, ed. J. Carlson Brown and C. R. Bohn (New York: Pilgrim, 1989), 2.

42. Julie M. Hopkins, *Towards a Feminist Christology: Jesus of Nazareth, European Women, and the Christological Crisis* (Grand Rapids: Eerdmans, 2005), 53; see also 56.

of the cross through the lens of a key cultural concept of his first culture: *han.* That multifaceted concept denotes suffering and pain, "a sense of unresolved resentment against injustices suffered, a sense of helplessness, . . . a feeling of acute pain and sorrow in one's guts and bowels."[43] Incarnation and crucifixion speak to the theme of *han*: "The all-powerful God was crucified. The cross is the symbol of God's han which makes known God's own vulnerability to human sin. . . . The cry of the wounded heart of God reverberates throughout the whole of history."[44]

Fully mindful of the feminist critique of violence and suffering in traditional atonement theories, another Korean American theologian, the postcolonialist Wonhee Anne Joh, is convinced that "the power of the cross also points simultaneously to the possibility of a radical form of love that can be linked with the Korean concept of *jeong.*" That crucial cultural concept "encompasses but is not limited to notions of compassion, affection, solidarity, relationality, vulnerability, and forgiveness."[45]

Christ as Sacrifice

Notwithstanding its strangeness to most (but not all!) contemporary cultures, it is important to consider carefully the continuing relevance of the metaphor of sacrifice.[46] For the first Christians, many of whom were Jewish, the temple cult with its sacrifices as a means of atonement was very familiar, and it is no surprise that they applied that framework to the salvific work of Jesus on the cross. In the New Testament, the whole life and self-offering of Christ are depicted as sacrifice; consequently, his followers are exhorted to offer their lives as a "living sacrifice" (Rom. 12:1).

In the context of Christ's salvific self-sacrifice, humanity is not offering to God something to "appease" an angry God, but rather, God who was in Christ (2 Cor. 5:19) is both the giver and receiver of the final, ultimate,

43. Wonhee Anne Joh, *Heart of the Cross: A Postcolonial Christology* (Louisville: Westminster John Knox, 2006), xxi. (Joh attributes this definition to Han Wan Sang but gives a mistaken reference to another author; I was unable to trace the original source.) A careful discussion of the many meanings of *han* can be found in Park, *Wounded Heart of God*, chap. 1 particularly.

44. Park, *Wounded Heart of God*, 123.

45. Joh, *Heart of the Cross*, xiii.

46. Henri A. Blocher, "The Sacrifice of Jesus Christ: The Current Theological Situation," *European Journal of Theology* 8, no. 1 (1999): 23–36.

onetime (Heb. 10:10) gift of sacrifice. "The death of Christ as a sacrifice must therefore be an act in which Christ becomes, theologically speaking, handed over [*paradidōmi*] to God."[47]

S. Mark Heim observes the obvious in that the rejection of the penal substitution theory by many is strongly supported by their aversion to any notion of Jesus's death as a sacrifice.[48] Take black theologians Karen Baker-Fletcher and Garth Kasimu Baker-Fletcher as examples: They wonder if all notions of sacrifice in this context merely enforce the surrogacy role assigned to black women. They suspect any sacrificial notion as a "particularly 'male' construction within our community that one must be willing to 'die' for something in order for it to be valuable."[49] Heim rightly critiques the leaving behind of all notions of sacrifice because those ideas "are rooted in scripture and tradition for good reasons. We cannot understand Jesus' death without understanding that it was a sacrifice, since this is the basis for knowing what it was doing to end sacrifice."[50] The "scandal of the cross" must remain, not as a way of affirming the legitimacy of violence, let alone abuse, but rather as a way to embrace the "promise of the cross": redemption, liberation, salvation, and finally the end of violence.[51]

A total *no* to traditional accounts of atonement faces the danger of virtually being silent about the divine salvific initiative in Christ. Consider the interpretations of the womanist theologian Delores Williams: "redemption had to do with God, through Jesus, giving humankind new vision to see the resources for positive, abundant relational life."[52] God giving us a new vision hardly speaks of the divine initiative in any way similar to classical tradition!

One of the meanings of sacrifice in most cultures involves doing away with pollution and uncleanness. Christ's sacrifice is a metaphor of dealing with that "dirt" that separates us from the all-holy God. The importance of sacrificial rites in African traditional religions has prompted some theologians to speak for the importance of the sacrifice motif in the communication of

47. Risto Saarinen, *God and the Gift: An Ecumenical Theology of Giving*, Unitas Books (Collegeville, MN: Liturgical Press, 2005), 84.

48. Heim, *Saved from Sacrifice*, 294.

49. Karen Baker-Fletcher and Garth Kasimu Baker-Fletcher, *My Sister, My Brother: Womanist and Xodus God-Talk* (Maryknoll, NY: Orbis, 1997; reprint, Eugene, OR: Wipf & Stock, 2002), 103.

50. Heim, *Saved from Sacrifice*, 294.

51. See also Volf, *Exclusion and Embrace*, 25–27.

52. Delores S. Williams, *Sisters in the Wilderness: The Challenge of Womanist God-Talk* (Maryknoll, NY: Orbis, 1993), 165.

the gospel related to this theme.[53] There is also a fellowship theme in African religion related to sacrifice. People gathered together around the sacrifice believe in the presence of the deity; thus, "sacrifice usually brings Deity/deity and worshippers together in an intimate fashion."[54]

Vicarious suffering is related to Jesus's role as our representative. Jesus suffered and died for us not as an "individual" but as a representative of the community. He died for the whole world. In the words of C. S. Song, Jesus is "the crucified people."[55] In this light, the feminist critique of the lack of relatedness of Jesus in his death on the cross sounds odd.[56]

How to Correct "Penal Substitution" and "Satisfaction" Theologies

A proper way to rehabilitate the positive and necessary aspects of the substitutionary and penal substitutionary traditions is to expose their occupation with juridical, individualizing, and de-historicizing tendencies.[57] The presence of legal notions in the explanation of the sacrificial death on the cross is not the problem; the problem is how law and legality are understood. This juridizing tendency of atonement tended to trump the Trinitarian unity of the work of salvation and cast it in a semimechanistic economy of exchange, which has promoted the typical Protestant notion of forensic justification.

An overindividualistic account of atonement both strengthens and is the result of the juridizing effect, rampant in modern Western culture. Individualism fosters the conception of sin and the Fall that has thin social and cosmic implications. God's dealings with his people in the Old Testament, the life of Jesus, implications for Trinitarian life, as well as the relational, communal, and cosmic elements become sidelined. A scholarly consensus in contemporary biblical studies holds that the biblical understanding of law, founded as it is on the covenant, is based on Yahweh's faithfulness and call to a mutual relational faithfulness.

The need to frame reconciliation in a thoroughly Trinitarian context has been repeated over and over again. The following section will delve deeper into that critical theme.

53. J. O. Ubruhe, "Traditional Sacrifice: A Key to the Heart of the Christian Message," *Journal of Theology for Southern Africa* 95 (1996): 16.

54. Ubruhe, "Traditional Sacrifice," 17.

55. Choan-Seng Song, *Jesus, the Crucified People* (New York: Crossroad, 1990).

56. Brock, *Journeys by Heart*, 60.

57. See also Boersma, *Violence, Hospitality, and the Cross*, chap. 7.

The Trinitarian Work of Salvation

While there is wide agreement about the need to construct a Trinitarian theology of reconciliation, not every reference to Trinity suffices. Failing is the medieval Richard of St. Victor's view that "The Father punishes, the Son expiates, the Spirit forgives."[58] This not only challenges the classic rule of the unity of the work of the triune God in the world, but it also proposes violence within the life of the Trinity. The "rule" of the Cappadocian Basil sets theology on a proper road. The Father is the "original cause," the Son the "creative cause," and the Spirit the "perfecting cause."[59]

While not uniform, the works of the persons of the Trinity are united. God who was in Christ (2 Cor. 5:19) took the initiative and reconciled the world to himself; through the life-giving Spirit the crucified Son was raised to new life; and through the mediation of the Spirit the salvific benefits are communicated to humanity and to the creation.

As Moltmann puts it, when it comes to the cross, the Trinitarian account begins from the cry of dereliction: "Basically, every Christian theology is consciously or unconsciously answering the question, 'Why hast thou forsaken me.' . . . In the face of Jesus' death-cry to God, theology either becomes impossible or becomes possible only as specifically Christian theology."[60] The ultimate "reason" for the death of Israel's Messiah for the world was godforsakenness. This differentiates Jesus from Socrates, the Stoics, the Zealot martyrs and other "noble martyrs" of Israel, and even Christian martyrs. Jesus died in anguish and with crying (Mark 14:33; 15:37 par.; Heb. 5:7), not only because of physical pain, as real as that was, but also because of rejection (Mark 15:34).

As much as this cry is the expression of deepest human anguish, on the lips of the dying Jesus of Nazareth, the Son of God, it is also the "climax of his self-distinction from the Father."[61] As obedient Son, rather than "count[ing] equality with God a thing to be grasped" (Phil. 2:6), he accepted the fate of humanity and thus let death expose his finitude. At the same time, the "divine absence from the world reached its peak of intensity in the dereliction of the Son on the cross."[62] Jesus's death on the cross means suffering in our stead; he

58. Richard of St. Victor, *De verbo incarnato* 11, cited in Finlan, *Problems with Atonement*, 85.

59. Basil the Great, *On the Holy Spirit* 16.38.

60. Moltmann, *The Crucified God*, 153.

61. Pannenberg, *ST* 2:375.

62. Pannenberg, *ST* 2:392.

takes the fate of the God-fleeing sinners. Thus, the "judgment in the cross of the Son became for the world its access to salvation."[63]

This tells us that the God of the dying Son Jesus Christ does not shy away from the suffering of either his Son or of the world but rather makes the suffering his own and so overcomes it in hope. All suffering becomes God's so that God may overcome it.[64] At the cross, the Father suffers in deserting his Son. The Son suffers the pain of being cut off from the life of the Father, and the Father suffers the pain of giving up his Son. By doing so, God "also accepts and adopts it [suffering] himself, making it part of his own eternal life."[65] Therefore, following Moltmann, the cross is not only an event between God and humanity. What "happened on the cross was an event between God and God. It was a deep division in God himself, in so far as God abandoned God and contradicted himself, and at the same time a unity in God, insofar as God was at one with God and corresponded to himself."[66] Thus, the cross belongs to the inner life of God, not only occurring between God and estranged humanity.[67] "God's being is in suffering and suffering in God's being itself, because God is love."[68] Rather than a neutral observer of world events, the God of love "suffers from the love which is the superabundance and overflowing of his being."[69] Perhaps the best parallel in human life is the self-sacrificial, persistent, and caring love of a parent.

When we see atonement as the unified work of the triune God, it becomes evident that "God does not love us because Christ died for us, but that Christ died for us because God loves us, and his sacrifice is an expression of this love. The cross of Christ was not given by man to change God, but given by God to change man."[70] The principle of inner-Trinitarian mutuality characterizes the cross.

The Spirit's role comes to the fore particularly in the raising up from the dead of Jesus. The Father raised his Son from the dead through the power of the life-giving work of the Spirit (Rom. 1:4; 8:11). In terms of its salvific effects, the work of the Spirit, whose ultimate aim is the glorification of the Father

63. Pannenberg, *ST* 2:392.

64. Moltmann, *The Crucified God*, 246.

65. Jürgen Moltmann, *The Trinity and the Kingdom of God: The Doctrine of God*, trans. Margaret Kohl (San Francisco: Harper & Row; London: SCM, 1981), 119.

66. Moltmann, *The Crucified God*, 244.

67. Moltmann, *The Crucified God*, 249.

68. Moltmann, *The Crucified God*, 227.

69. Moltmann, *Trinity and the Kingdom*, 23.

70. Culpepper, *Interpreting the Atonement*, 131.

through the Son, serves the consummation of redemption and atonement since it brings about the "overcoming of mortality and consummation by participation in the eternal life" of the infinite God.[71] Rightly it can be said, "An exposition of atonement which leaves out Pentecost, leaves the atonement unintelligible—in relation to us."[72] This brings us to the next topic in the Trinitarian theology of reconciliation, namely, the importance of the resurrection, a topic introduced in the previous chapter.

The Salvific Significance of Christ's Resurrection and Ascension

Resurrection as Our Justification and Hope for the Whole Cosmos

Resurrection is an integral part of the salvific work of the triune God; it is a Trinitarian moment. The Father raised his Son from death through the power of the Spirit (Rom. 1:3–4). As the eternal bond of love, the life-giving Spirit represents divine unity in the midst of deepest separation.

In the preaching and theology of the early church, the linking of the cross with the resurrection and ascension became a key theme: Acts 2:23–24; 3:14–15; 4:10; 5:30; 10:39–40; Romans 6:3–11; 8:34; 1 Peter 1:19–21; 3:18, 21–22. Resurrection is the seal of our salvation, as Christ "was put to death for our trespasses and raised for our justification" (Rom. 4:25). It is evidence of God's vindication of the condemned and executed Jesus.

It is also highly significant that Acts also links the cross and forgiveness and physical healing. The apostles proclaimed the gospel of healing on the basis of the resurrection and ascension of Christ and the pouring out of the Holy Spirit (Acts 3:12–16; 4:8–12).

Importantly, in New Testament theology Christ's resurrection is an eschatological event. It points not only to the future of our own hope for resurrection but even beyond, to the future of this world and creation. Hence, we can say with Moltmann that in this event Christian theology sees "not the eternity of heaven, but the future of the very earth on which his cross stands." Even more: "It sees in him the future of the very humanity for which he died."[73]

While eschatological, referring to the future hope, resurrection is also a powerful sign and energy of hope for today's struggle for equality and justice.

71. Pannenberg, *ST* 2:396.

72. R. C. Moberly, *Atonement and Personality* (London: John Murray, 1924 [1901]), 151.

73. Jürgen Moltmann, *Theology of Hope* (London: SCM, 1967 [1964]), 21; so also 194.

The African American theologian Garth Kasimu Baker-Fletcher rightly notes that resurrection represents the liberation of the "self from the shackles of Euro-dominated death" and the "release of our inner captive so that we might rise to new life as self-affirming Afrikans [*sic*]."[74]

Ascension, the Cosmic Rule, and Consummation of Salvation

By and large contemporary theology, with the exception of the Eastern Orthodox tradition, has ignored the topic of the ascension. In the Eastern Church this feast was known as *analepsis*, "taking up," and also as the *episozomene*, "salvation," denoting that by ascending into his glory Christ completed the work of our redemption.[75]

For the early church, atonement, resurrection, and ascension played a critical role in preaching and teaching. Alongside Luke-Acts (Luke 24:50–53; Acts 1:9–11; 2:32–36; 5:30–32), ascension is mentioned quite frequently in various contexts (Eph. 4:8–10; Phil. 2:6–9; 3:20; 1 Tim. 3:16; 1 Pet. 3:22; Heb. 2:9; 12:2). The cosmic Christology of many church fathers built on this tradition in its highlighting the importance of the ascension. Similarly, building on the New Testament witness (John 15:26; 16:7; Acts 1:4–11; 2:1–4; Eph. 4:10), patristic theology made the relation between ascension and Pentecost an integral topic.[76]

To consider reconciliation as the joint process of the triune God expands the horizon of interpretation beyond the resurrection of the crucified Messiah. It highlights the significance of Christ's being lifted up to the right hand of the Father—"to receive the crown for the work of Redemption"[77]—and vestment with cosmic rule in the anticipation of the consummation of salvific purposes toward humanity and creation. It inspires a powerful anticipation of the final consummation. The state of humanity amidst wars, violence, injustice, and godlessness reminds us of the obvious fact that the reconciliation of the world still awaits its culmination. The theology of Hebrews makes a profound statement, first reminding us of the finality of Christ's sacrifice (9:26), by speaking

74. As paraphrased by J. Denny Weaver, *The Nonviolent Atonement* (Grand Rapids: Eerdmans, 2001), 117.

75. Georges Florovsky, "And Ascended into Heaven," *St. Vladimir's Seminary Quarterly* 2, no. 3 (1954): 23–28.

76. Veselin Kesich, "Resurrection, Ascension and the Giving of the Spirit," *Greek Orthodox Theological Review* 25, no. 3 (Fall 1980): 249–60.

77. Cyril of Jerusalem, *Catechetical Lectures* 14.23.

of the continuing intercessory ministry of the ascended Christ (9:24), as well as the hope of his return (9:28).

According to the medieval master Thomas Aquinas, by virtue of the ascension, our "souls are uplifted to Him" as it fosters faith, hope, and love. The Angelic Doctor lists the following "effects": preparing the place for us (John 14:2–3); interceding for his own (Heb. 7:25); and giving gifts (Eph. 4:10).[78] Thomas also discusses extensively the ascended Lord's "judiciary power," universal rule over all humankind and angels.[79] In Protestant theology, the Heidelberg Catechism lists materially similar kinds of benefits of the ascension, including the pouring out of the Spirit.[80] No Protestant theologian made as much of ascension as Barth.[81] A real event of history rather than myth, it is the "proleptic sign of the parousia" of the One who now "lives on the God-ward side of the universe, sharing His throne, existing and acting in the mode of God."[82]

Some leading liberationists have seen much promise in this doctrine. In Boff's vision, the risen and ascended Christ has penetrated the world in a profound manner—now ever-present according to his own promise (Matt. 28:20). The resurrection has revealed the cosmic dimension of Christ, for in him all creation has come into existence and he is the goal of all.[83] Indeed, the rediscovery of ascension as an integral part of the salvific work of the triune God may help the church's proclamation in various cultural and religious settings and contexts. In many African and Asian contexts, the question is about power over evil forces. The missiologist Herbert Hoefer rightly notes that what "is striking is that each answer to such issues of present living draws upon the fact of Jesus as ascended Lord." Resurrection and ascension help theology and missiology to offer a response that goes beyond guilt and touches on important issues such as honor, shame, immortality, and meaning.[84] The ensuing discussion of soteriology will further develop these insights.

78. Aquinas, *ST* 3.57.6.

79. Aquinas, *ST* 3.59.

80. Heidelberg Catechism, q. 49, in *Historic Creeds and Confessions*, ed. Rick Brannan, 22, available on Christian Classics Ethereal Library website: http://www.ccel.org/ccel/brannan/hstcrcon.html.

81. Barth, *CD* IV/2, §64 is titled "The Exaltation of the Son of Man."

82. Barth, *CD* III/2, 454.

83. As explained by William J. La Due, *Jesus among the Theologians: Contemporary Interpretations of Christ* (Harrisburg, PA: Trinity, 2001), 175.

84. Herbert Hoefer, "Gospel Proclamation of the Ascended Lord," *Missiology* 33, no. 4 (2005): 43–48.

Reconciliation as the Church's Mission in the World

Reconciliation as Holistic Salvation and "Re-Creation"

Casting the doctrine of atonement in a proper Trinitarian framework and in the context of God's faithfulness to his creation helps us widen and make more inclusive the work of atonement by focusing on the multifaceted meaning of the term "reconciliation"—healing and bringing together broken relationships. Of all the metaphors of salvation, reconciliation has the potential of being the most inclusive and comprehensive, encompassing ideas such as "cosmic reconciliation, the Hebrew notion of *shalom*, the meaning of the cross, the psychological effects of conversion, the work of the Holy Spirit, the overcoming of barriers between Christians, the work of the church in the world, peacemaking, movements towards ethnic reconciliation and the renewal of ecological balances between humanity and its natural environment."[85] Originally, the term derived from the secular Hellenistic language of diplomacy. The goal of reconciliation is "the restoration of the sin-broken fellowship of humanity with its Creator, the source of its life."[86]

Reconciliation is more than sacrifice, redemption, and substitution—even though for its validity it assumes those aspects. Alongside the cross, reconciliation includes resurrection, Christ's cosmic rule, and the founding of Christian community for the sake of proclaiming and embodying the gospel of reconciliation. The language of reconciliation "refers both to an event in the past and to an enduring relationship in the present, which is claimed to be eschatologically ultimate."[87]

Reconciliation also forges an important link between creation, atonement, and consummation. "If the God of redemption who is revealed in Jesus Christ is the same as the Creator of the world and the human race, then we must view his saving work as an expression of his faithfulness to his creative work."[88]

In Paul, the main passages about reconciliation are about communal and racial reconciliation, as well as the cosmic restoration of relations (Rom.

85. Ross Langmead, "Transformed Relationships: Reconciliation as the Central Model for Mission," *Mission Studies* 25, no. 1 (2008): 6.

86. Pannenberg, *ST* 2:449.

87. Christoph Schwöbel, "Reconciliation: From Biblical Observations to Dogmatic Reconstruction," in *The Theology of Reconciliation*, ed. Colin E. Gunton (London: T&T Clark, 2003), 19.

88. Pannenberg, *ST* 2:297.

5:9–10; 2 Cor. 5:18–20; Eph. 2:16; Col. 1:19–22). In the first chapter of Colossians (vv. 16–22), having lifted up Christ as the principal and agent of creation, Paul speaks of his role as the head of the church and then bursts into a glorious hymn: "For in him all the fulness of God was pleased to dwell, and through him to reconcile to himself all things, whether on earth or in heaven, making peace by the blood of his cross. And you, who once were estranged and hostile in mind, doing evil deeds, he has now reconciled in his body of flesh by his death" (vv. 19–22a). This is a remarkable vision of reconciliation encompassing creation, atonement, God's communal intentions, and new creation—viewpoints not too often highlighted in Christian atonement tradition. The second chapter of Ephesians, similarly, puts the vision of reconciliation into the widest possible horizon. Galatians 3:28, which speaks of the racial (Jews and gentiles), societal (free and slaves), and sexual (female and male) "one[ness] in Christ," is another remarkable statement about the power of reconciliation.[89]

Recent conflicts in South Africa, the former Yugoslavia, Syria, Afghanistan, and elsewhere have brought the need for reconciliation into a new focus. Reconciliation between persons, people groups, and nations requires both truth telling and love, remembering and forgetting, giving and receiving. The church's role, based on the gospel of reconciliation, will be discussed below in chapter 9, on the church.

One of the ways of responding to the work of reconciliation is to continue working for liberation of the oppressed and marginalized.

Reconciliation and Holistic Liberation

Liberationists of various stripes have rightly critiqued traditional atonement theories for their "abstractness" with little or no attention to inequality, oppression, exploitation, sexism, abuse, and similar sociopolitical problems. They have contended that violent accounts of atonement, on the one hand, lack needed ethical incentive and, on the other hand, have helped marginalize certain segments of humanity, particularly women, the poor, and other minorities. Behind these rightful criticisms is the question of whether Christian theology of reconciliation is supposed to deal merely with the "spiritual" or also with the "mundane" spheres of life. The unambiguous answer to this question is that in the Christian vision of the world, history embraces both

89. Douglas A. Campbell, "Reconciliation in Paul: The Gospel of Negation and Transcendence in Galatians 3:28," in Gunton, *The Theology of Reconciliation*, 39–65.

the "secular" and the "sacred." In this sense, history is one, created and made possible by God. Hence, Christ's "redemptive work embraces all the dimensions of existence and brings them to their fullness. The history of salvation is the very heart of human history."[90]

Liberationists rightly remind Christian theologians of an often-too-narrow outlook on salvation and insist that sociopolitical aspects not be overlooked. In Gutiérrez's terminology, traditional theology errs in viewing salvation as exclusively "quantitative," that is, as "guaranteeing heaven" for the greatest number. According to him, in the Latin American context, there is an urgent need to reinterpret salvation in "qualitative terms," as a way of social, political, and economic transformation.[91] Christian reconciliation includes personal, social, and institutional dimensions, as well as this-worldly and eschatological hopes.[92]

This holistic, all-embracing vision is funded by the conviction that Christ's cross and resurrection are not innocent politically; on the contrary, they imply political claims. Even though crucifixion was a fairly common means of execution, in Jesus's time it was reserved particularly for revolutionaries and self-made messiahs. "The cross already said, with all its violent symbolic power, that Caesar ruled the world, and that those who stood in his way would be both shamed and obliterated."[93] Resurrection and ascension claim that if Jesus is the Lord, then Caesar is not![94]

In his salvific work, Christ not only conquers principalities and powers but also issues a judgment on unjustified human violence, cruelty, oppression, and tyranny. Christ, the Suffering Messiah, is on the side of the sufferers. He both opposes violence and empowers those in need of power and persistence for the work of liberation. Speaking from the South African context, liberationist G. O. Abe expresses this vision in a powerful way: "The true gospel message of Jesus Christ should inspire theologians, especially Africans to rescue the afflicted and liberate the oppressed, the victims of injustice. All forms of dominant inhuman and unchristian attitudes and structures which cause

90. Gustavo Gutiérrez, *A Theology of Liberation: History, Politics, and Salvation*, trans. and ed. Sister Caridad Inda and John Eagleson (Maryknoll, NY: Orbis, 1986 [1973]; rev. ed. with a new introduction, 1988), 86.

91. Gutiérrez, *A Theology of Liberation*, 83–85.

92. Gutiérrez, *A Theology of Liberation*, chap. 9 particularly.

93. N. T. Wright, "Redemption from the New Perspective?" in *The Redemption: An Interdisciplinary Symposium on Christ as Redeemer*, ed. Stephen T. Davis, Daniel Kendall, SJ, and Gerald O'Collins, SJ (Oxford: Oxford University Press, 2004), 79.

94. N. T. Wright, *The Resurrection of the Son of God* (Minneapolis: Fortress, 2003), 225.

human suffering and agony should be analysed and vigorously combated for effective salvation of all."[95]

An important part of the missionary task of the church as it lives out and proclaims the gospel of reconciliation involves relations with other living faiths. The last section of this chapter will take up that discussion.

Christian Theology of Reconciliation among Religions

Jewish and Christian Visions of Reconciliation

With his announcement of the imminence of God's righteous rule dawning in his own ministry, "Jesus came to move the covenant people to conversion to its God."[96] That his own people were not willing to receive him as the Messiah did not thwart divine saving purposes. Ironically and counterintuitively, it was only after the rejection of his own people that Jesus's death on the cross made him the "Savior of the nations."[97]

The influential Jewish philosopher of religion Franz Rosenzweig, in his mature work *The Star of Redemption*, came to affirm the role of the Christian church in the preaching of the gospel to the gentiles. The contemporary Jewish ecumenist Lapide continues that reasoning.[98] Where the Christian theological standpoint focused on the universal and unique salvific role of Jesus Christ has to challenge this Jewish reasoning involves the idea of Judaism and Christianity as two roads to the Father. "I am the way, and the truth, and the life; no one comes to the Father, but by me" (John 14:6). This is not to deny but rather to confirm the biblical notion that "salvation is from the Jews" (John 4:22).

Before delving into comparison of potential similarities in the understandings of atonement between the two religions, a wider context of salvation and reconciliation should be kept in mind. Rather than through a vicarious sacrifice, the normal way for a Jew to be saved is simply by following the Torah, the divinely given law. As discussed in chapter 4 on theological anthropology, Jewish theology does not hold to the Christian tradition's view of the Fall that necessitates divine initiative, such as the death on the cross. Furthermore,

95. Gabriel Oyedele Abe, "Redemption, Reconciliation, Propitiation: Salvation Terms in an African Milieu," *Journal of Theology for Southern Africa* 95 (1996): 3–12.

96. Pannenberg, *ST* 2:311.

97. Pannenberg, *ST* 2:312.

98. Franz Lapide, *Jewish Monotheism and Christian Trinitarian Doctrine: A Dialogue by Pinchas Lapide and Jürgen Moltmann*, trans. Leonard Swidler (Philadelphia: Fortress, 1981).

as also discussed, the otherworldly goal of salvation in the afterlife is not as central either in the Old Testament or in later forms of Judaism as it is in Christian tradition.

In that light, it is remarkable that it was on the basis of Hebrew Scriptures such as Isaiah 53:4–6 that Christian theology came to interpret the vicarious suffering of the Messiah.[99] Particularly the early Christian views and early rabbinic views evolved in close connection with the Old Testament atonement traditions. It is of utmost importance to acknowledge that "the sacrificial concept of Jesus' death was not developed in response to gentile ideas but, rather, as a Jewish conception of the righteous one who reconciles us to God by his sacrifice of suffering and death."[100] In both religions, sacrifice is an atoning act that also calls for human response.[101]

How then would Jewish tradition interpret such key New Testament statements as "Behold, the Lamb of God, who takes away the sin of the world!" (John 1:29)? According to Steven Kepnes, Jews may gain insight into its meaning through the lens of the biblical notions of purity and impurity, sacrificial offices and systems, including the rituals of the sanctuary, as well as the temple. Reference to the Lamb who takes away sin, of course, is based on the slaughtering of lambs for the expiation of sins. Christ's self-sacrifice also connects with Jewish liturgical days such as Yom Kippur.[102] Differences, however, are noteworthy. Even though Jesus may be called metaphorically the High Priest, in Jewish faith the high priest conducts the sacrificial act whereas in Christian faith Jesus is the sacrifice, the sacrificial Lamb. This is not to say that Jewish faith doesn't know substitutionary suffering for others; of course it does, in terms of both the "Suffering Servant" of Second Isaiah and righteous martyrs, as during the Maccabean era. Still, the onetime finished self-sacrifice of Jesus after the Christian interpretation is markedly different from the continuing sacrificial cult administered by the priesthood in Judaism. Not only the finality of the sacrifice of Jesus but also its universality marks it as different from the understanding of the Jewish tradition. Jesus's sacrifice, even as the work of the triune God, is contingent on the relation to his person, a claim without

99. Michael S. Kogan, *Opening the Covenant: A Jewish Theology of Christianity* (Oxford: Oxford University Press, 2008), 116.

100. John C. Lyden, "Atonement in Judaism and Christianity: Towards a Rapprochement," *Journal of Ecumenical Studies* 29, no. 1 (Winter 1992): 51.

101. Lyden, "Atonement in Judaism and Christianity," 47–48, 50.

102. Steven Kepnes, "'Turn Us to You and We Shall Return': Original Sin, Atonement, and Redemption in Jewish Terms," in *Christianity in Jewish Terms*, ed. Tikva Frymer-Kensky et al. (Boulder, CO: Westview, 2000), 297–301.

parallel in Judaism and a stumbling block to its monotheism. The role of the Messiah in Judaism is to serve as the agent of reconciliation, but not as the one who reconciles—only Yahweh can do that. Finally, a foundational difference has to do with the offer and object of the sacrifice. Whereas in Judaism people offer the sacrifice to Yahweh, in Christian theology (2 Cor. 5:18) it is God who reconciles the world to himself.[103]

From the Christian side, if God was in Christ and reconciled the world to himself, then the "ambassadors" are sent out to make the plea that all people, whether Jews or gentiles, "be reconciled to God" (2 Cor. 5:19–20). The Jewish theologian Michael S. Kogan puts succinctly the dynamic tension facing Christian theology with its belief in Christ as the Messiah: "to be faithful to the New Testament command to witness for Christ to all peoples and to convert all nations, while, at the same time, affirming the ongoing validity of the covenant between God and Israel via Abraham and Moses."[104] At the center of this tension lies the obvious but important fact that "historically Christianity has been theologically exclusive and humanistically universal, while Judaism has been theologically universal and humanistically exclusive." Christian theological exclusivism, however, is qualified by the equally important conviction that Christ died for all and that therefore all people from all nations can be beneficiaries of this salvific work.[105]

Progress on this foundational issue poses a challenge to both parties. Kogan formulates it well: if the Jews desire for Christians to affirm the continuing validity of the covenant after the coming of Jesus Christ, then the Jews are confronted with this challenge: "Are Jews really ready and willing to affirm that God, the God of Israel and of all humanity, was involved in the life of Jesus, in the founding of the Christian faith, in its growth and spread across much of the world, and in its central place in the hearts of hundreds of millions of their fellow beings?" Kogan answers *yes* to this question, and he is of the opinion that those of his fellow Jews who do not are no more "enlightened than those Christians who still refuse to affirm the Jews' ongoing spiritual validity as a religious people."[106] The implications of this complicated issue have to be worked out in detail in the chapter on ecclesiology.

103. Lyden, "Atonement in Judaism and Christianity," 50–53.

104. Kogan, *Opening the Covenant*, xii.

105. Kogan, *Opening the Covenant*, xii–xiii.

106. Kogan, *Opening the Covenant*, xiii; see also 13.

The Christian Theology of the Cross in Light of the Islamic Interpretation

Not only with regard to the source of salvation but also, consequently, with regard to the means of salvation, there is a sharp difference between Christianity and Islam: "The cross stands between Islam and Christianity. Dialogue cannot remove its scandal, and in due course a Muslim who might come to believe in Jesus has to face it."[107] One of the reasons the suffering Messiah does not appeal to Muslims is that "paragons of success and vindication" such as Abraham, Noah, Moses, and David are much more congenial to the vision of God's manifest victory on earth. The image of the suffering and crucified Messiah is reprehensible to Islam, virtually implying that God failed.

The single most important dividing issue between Islam and Christian faith is the crucifixion. The Qur'anic explanation for the crucifixion (and incidentally the only explicit reference) in 4:157–59 reads as follows:

> (157) And because of their saying: We slew the Messiah, Jesus son of Mary, Allah's messenger—they slew him not nor crucified him, but it appeared so unto them [or: "but a semblance was made to them"];[108] and lo! those who disagree concerning it are in doubt thereof; they have no knowledge thereof save pursuit of a conjecture; they slew him not for certain.
>
> (158) But Allah took him up unto Himself. Allah was ever Mighty, Wise.
>
> (159) There is not one of the People of the Scripture but will believe in him before his death, and on the Day of Resurrection he will be a witness against them.

Although Muslim tradition does not speak with one voice, the almost universal Muslim conviction is that Jesus of Nazareth did not die on the cross but rather a substitute was put in his stead. As to the identity of the substitute, a number of candidates are listed, usually headed by Simon of Cyrene or Judas Iscariot.[109] Instead of dying on the cross, Jesus was taken up to heaven by Allah[110]

107. George H. Bebawi, "Atonement and Mercy: Islam between Athanasius and Anselm," in *Atonement Today*, ed. John Goldingay (London: SPCK, 1995), 185.

108. Translation of Neil Robinson, *Christ in Islam and Christianity* (New York: State University of New York Press, 1991), 106.

109. See Oddbjørn Leirvik, *Images of Jesus Christ in Islam*, 2nd ed. (London: Continuum, 2010), 67–69.

110. See Clinton Bennett, *Understanding Christian-Muslim Relations: Past and Present* (London: Continuum, 2008), 51–52.

to wait for the return to earth at the eschaton (to be discussed in the chapter on eschatology).

Among a number of interrelated issues, two major exegetical questions surround the interpretation of Q 4:157–58, namely, the meaning of "Allah took him up unto Himself" (v. 158) and "a semblance was made" (v. 157, following Robinson's rendering). The former has to do with what really happened to Jesus if he was not put to death on the cross. The latter relates to the question of who, instead of Jesus, was crucified. Muslim commentary literature on these passages is endless, and Christian apologetics has also engaged them widely from the beginning. Christian apologetics has advanced two different positions as a response to the standard Muslim denial of Jesus's death on the cross.[111] The first one is that the Qur'an is inconsistent in, on the one hand, affirming the death of Jesus (19:33; 3:55) and, on the other hand, denying it (4:157). The second apologetic manner of argument has advanced the thesis that, indeed, the Qur'an is not denying the crucifixion (based on a careful negotiation of several passages, whose complex details we cannot go into here). It goes without saying that Muslim counterapologetics has hardly been impressed. It is not unfair to state that the discussion—after more than a millennium—is still in a stalemate.

In sum: the whole of Muslim theology unanimously "denies the expiatory sacrifice of Christ on the Cross as a ransom for sinful humanity."[112] Nor would such a sacrificial, atoning death be needed, similarly to Judaism, because of the lack of the doctrine of the Fall and sinfulness after Christian tradition. No wonder attacks against the Christian teaching of the crucifixion have played a significant role in Muslim anti-Christian polemics and continue to do so, as illustrated in the widely influential pamphlet by the Indian–South African Ahmed Deedat, *Crucifixion or Cruci-fiction?*

Reconciliation and "Savior" in Buddhist Perspectives

A foundational difference between the Buddhist and Christian visions is that "Savior has no place in the Buddhist worldview. An individual must control and be responsible for his or her own destiny."[113] One is one's own refuge, and

111. Robinson, *Christ in Islam and Christianity*, 108–9.

112. Mahmoud Ayoub, "Towards an Islamic Christology, II: The Death of Jesus, Reality or Delusion (a Study in the Death of Jesus in Tafsīr Literature)," *Muslim World* 70, no. 2 (1980): 94.

113. Satanun Boonyakiat, "A Christian Theology of Suffering in the Context of Ther-

no one else—not even Buddha—can save one from the law of kamma.[114] Buddhists simply "balk at the idea that any deity is capable of granting salvation to others simply through an act of will."[115]

The death on the cross of the Savior for the sins and salvation of others is an idea totally unknown in all traditions of Buddhism. That said, the generic idea of redemptive or "vicarious" suffering on behalf of others is not unknown in Buddhism—think, for example, of the commonly known story in Thai (Theravada) Buddhism of the sixteenth-century Queen Srisuriyothai's self-sacrifice to save her people under the threat from the king of Burma.[116] Apart from this kind of noble human self-sacrifice, resorting to any kind of vicarious act done by another person, even a divinity, would mean shrinking from one's own responsibility to deal with one's kamma. In Mahayana Buddhism, the Boddhisattva—unlike the *Arahat* of Theravada, who has stepped into nirvana—is willing to postpone his own entrance into the *nibbana* to help others reach the goal. Even that, however, is the function not of a "savior" but rather of a "good neighbor."

What about Pure Land Buddhism? Is the path outlined by this Buddhist tradition compatible with the Christian view of salvation? No, it is not, although there are remarkable common themes, unlike in any other major form of Buddhism. The main savior figure is Boddhisattva Dharmakara, who, through the rigorous and pure practice of forty-eight vows, reached enlightenment and became Amitabha Buddha. He opened the path of salvation in primordial times by establishing the Western Pure Land and made it possible for all sentient beings reborn in that land to reach enlightenment, "salvation."[117] "The Buddha embodied his virtue in his Name for all beings, enabling them to enter the Pure Land at death. Through their faith in, and meritorious recitation of the Name, they are saved by its power."[118] With all his great reservations of all human religiosity, Barth felt deep sympathies for the Pure Land tradition,

---

avada Buddhism in Thailand" (PhD diss., Fuller Theological Seminary, School of Theology, 2009).

114. John R. Davis, *Poles Apart: Contextualizing the Gospel in Asia* (Bangalore, India: Theological Book Trust, 1998), 98–104.

115. José Ignacio Cabezón, "Buddhist Views of Jesus," in *JWF*, 23.

116. "Phra Chedi Sri Suriyothai," on Bangkoksite.com, http://www.bangkoksite.com/AyutthayaPage/ChediSriSuriyothai.htm.

117. Boddhisattva is a Buddha-in-the-making aiming at enlightenment. Indeed, there is more than one Pure Land in those traditions. Wherever there is an enlightened Buddha, there is Pure Land. The Western Pure Land created by Boddhisattva Dharmakara is the main Pure Land and combines teachings and features of others.

118. Alfred Bloom, "Jesus in the Pure Land," chap. 3 in *JWF*, 33.

the existence of which was "a providential disposition" parallel to Reformed Christianity based on the logic of grace. He considered carefully the form of Pure Land developed by Shinran with an appeal to faith.[119]

Reconciliation and the Cross in Hindu Assessment

Similarly to Buddhism, Hinduism does not know reconciliation through a vicarious death by another person—not even the main theistic traditions. Raja Ram Mohun Roy, who had a high regard for Jesus as an ethical teacher, expresses the Hindu opposition to the Christian idea of atonement in his correspondence with an anonymous Christian priest. Against the Christian minister's reasoning that Jesus can be called a "Saviour of men" only if "he died in their stead to atone for their sins" rather than just helping them live an ethical life, Roy contends that the title "Saviour" is "applied frequently in the divine writings to those persons who had been endued with the power of saving people." In support, Roy refers to Old Testament Scriptures such as Obadiah 21, Nehemiah 9:27, and 2 Kings 13:5, which use the term translated in many renderings as "savior." Furthermore, Roy notes that Jesus himself at times refers to his salvific work on the basis of "the inculcation of the word of God," as in John 14:3, 5:24, and 6:63. For Roy, the conclusion follows that, on the one hand, there is no way to attribute any "atoning" power to Jesus's influence and that, on the other hand, it wouldn't diminish Jesus's significance for him to be revered as a "Divine Teacher."[120] Apart from exegetical inaccuracies, Roy accurately expresses the radical difference between the two faiths regarding the topic of "salvation."

In other words, the biblical idea of Jesus as the Lamb of God (John 1:29) sacrificed for the sins of the world is foreign to all Hindu strands. That said, as mentioned earlier, the idea of self-sacrifice for the sake of others and their well-being is very much part of Hindu thought. The sacrificial lamb imagery can only make sense if it is understood in its "cosmological"—we could probably also say metaphorical—sense and linked with the basic Vedic principle of *rita* (right order). This multifaceted term denotes cosmic order as well as moral order, and in relation to sacrifices, also the right order of sacrifices. Sacrifices

119. Barth, *CD* I/2, 340–42, here 342.

120. *The English Works of Raja Ram Mohun Roy*, vol. 3, *The Precepts of Jesus—a Guide to Peace and Happiness; Extracted from the Books of the New Testament Ascribed to the Four Evangelists with Translations into Sungscit and Bengalee* (Calcutta: Baptist Mission Press, 1820), part I, 172–75; reproduced in *JBC*, 162–64.

offered to gods were the basic means of securing order in ancient Hinduism. Indeed, "sacrifice" is named in Rig Veda the "center of the universe."[121] The New Testament and early Christian atonement theories include perspectives that are related to these kinds of cosmic ramifications of the cross. However, in Christian tradition they are integrally related to the biblical narrative of the triune God breaking the power of evil and resistance to divine purposes in Christ, reconciling everything in heaven and earth with God.

One aspect of salvation in Christian theology has to do with forgiveness. That is not a totally foreign idea to Hinduism, even though it is not a central one. Bhagavad Gita (18.66) says, "Relinquishing all Dharmas take refuge in Me alone; I will liberate thee from all sins; grieve not." To properly understand this statement, one has to stick with the Hindu view of what "sin" is, namely, "that which keeps the mind attached to sense perception and objects of the senses. Such attachment produces restlessness, which clouds perception of the soul."[122]

That said, the idea of grace properly understood is not unknown in Hinduism, particularly in Vaishnavism (Vishnu-god-based theistic religion) and as taught particularly in the Bhagavad Gita. That topic will be carefully studied in chapter 8, on salvation.

Whereas Christian tradition emphasizes "the God who is offering salvation," Hinduism, even Shaivism, let alone Saivism (Siva-god based) and other traditions, emphasizes "the effort of the individual seeking salvation."[123] Put otherwise: "In the Christian doctrine of Grace, therefore, we confront an act of God," whereas in the Hindu view, liberation is a matter of human initiative and accomplishment.[124] Ultimately, the Christian view of salvation is linked with the salvific work of the triune God in the context of the cross.[125]

121. Rig Veda 1.164.35.

122. Cited in Sandy Bharat, "Hindu Perspectives on Jesus," in *The Blackwell Companion to Jesus*, ed. Delbert Burkett (Oxford: Wiley-Blackwell, 2011), 256.

123. Sabapathy Kulandran, *Grace in Christianity and Hinduism* (Cambridge: James Clarke, 2000 [1964]), 245.

124. Kulandran, *Grace in Christianity and Hinduism*, 242.

125. Chap. 2 in John Brockington, *Hinduism and Christianity* (New York: St. Martin's, 1992).

7 | Holy Spirit

In Search of a Plural, Holistic Pneumatology

Could the Doctrine of the Spirit Be Empowered in Our Secular World?

A profound cultural and religious change has taken place in the post-Enlightenment Global North. Whereas before the Enlightenment era, among all cultures and religions, talk about spirituality, spirits, and the Spirit (of God) was taken as "natural," now the contemporary European-American secular mind-set—as well as, most ironically, much of university-based academic theology—considers spirit talk "supernatural" and fanciful.

What can be called "cosmology of personal agency" has a long and lasting legacy in human history. In such a cosmology, beyond the physical causes are spirits, even divine spirits. In contrast to this spirit sensitivity, most people in the post-Enlightenment West live under "natural cosmologies" that are essentially monist (materialist).[1]

The practical implication of this foundational difference is that whereas for many people the Spirit experience is the most intimate and familiar part of life, for others it is virtually unknown and abstract. Under the category of "many people" to whom spirit talk is still real and vibrant belong by far the majority of the people of the world—and the large majority of Christians now

1. Amos Yong, "On Binding, and Loosing, the Spirits: Navigating and Engaging a Spirit-Filled World," in *IRDSW*, 4–5.

living in the Global South make up about two-thirds of all the faithful. This is too often neglected in academic theology.

Although Christian faith, let alone academic theology, should never resist critical inquiry and new (scientific) perspectives stemming from modernity—as if there might be a return to precritical religion of old—neither should contemporary pneumatology, the doctrine of the Holy Spirit, simply capitulate under the power of secular influence. A new kind of constructive pneumatology, building on rich biblical and historical Spirit traditions, and in active dialogue with the scientific, secular, and religiously pluralistic culture, should be the goal. Such a new approach can be named the "plural paradigm."

From a "Unitive" to a "Plural" Paradigm of Pneumatology

In the introduction to his acclaimed pneumatological volume *The Spirit of Life* (ET 1992), Jürgen Moltmann laments that "a new paradigm in pneumatology has not yet emerged."[2] To remedy this, he proposes a "holistic pneumatology."[3] "On the one hand, it must comprehend human beings in their total being, soul and body, consciousness and the unconscious, person and sociality, society and social institutions. On the other hand it must also embrace the wholeness of the community of creation, which is shared by human beings, the earth, and all other created beings and things."[4] Moltmann's program is pointing in the direction of a "plural paradigm."

In "unitive" pneumatology, only one Spirit (of God) is considered, while the rest of the spiritual realities are dismissed; this means that Spirit(s)/spirits in other religions are not engaged, and neither are spiritual powers and energies. In that paradigm the Spirit's work is mainly considered in relation to "spiritual" realms such as revelation, "order of salvation" (the topic of the next chapter), church and sacraments, and so forth. As an alternative, in a "plural" paradigm the Spirit's work is discerned also in history, politics, arts, and other "secular" realms. Furthermore, the Spirit of God is accounted for within a highly pluralistic cosmology with many spirits, powers, and spiritual realities.[5] Briefly put, the Spirit's domain is wide and inclusive.

2. Jürgen Moltmann, *The Spirit of Life: A Universal Affirmation*, trans. Margaret Kohl (Minneapolis: Fortress, 2001), 1.

3. In the German original, the subtitle (*Eine ganzheitliche Pneumatologie*) means "holistic" or "comprehensive" pneumatology (the ET, *A Universal Affirmation*, fails to capture this).

4. Moltmann, *The Spirit of Life*, 37.

5. Kirsteen Kim speaks of the same distinction using the terms "one-spirit" and "many-

Why is this shift needed? This shift is needed because of the diversity of biblical testimonies to the Spirit; the emergence of Pentecostal/charismatic testimonies; the growth of dynamic Christianity in the Global South, linked with cultural and religious plurality; the rise of postmodern philosophies with celebration of diversity; as well as transformations in scientific paradigms. And very importantly, the encounter with other faiths and their spirited cosmologies presents another reason.

Indeed, many promising signs of a search for a new paradigm are on the horizon. There is a desire to widen and make more inclusive the theological understanding of the ministry of the Spirit. In that wider and more inclusive outlook—while not leaving behind traditional topics such as the Trinity, Scripture, and salvation—the Spirit is also connected with topics such as creation, humanity, and eschatology, as well as political, social, environmental, and other "public" issues. This is a great corrective to tradition.

That said, by and large Christian pneumatologies, even with these necessary and important improvements, are still imprisoned in the paradigm of "unitive" pneumatology. Other spirits, powers, and energies are not seen as worthy of academic discussion and inclusion in respectable pneumatological presentations. Particularly striking is the lack of relating the *Christian* understanding of the Spirit(s) to the understandings of other living faith traditions.

As said, there is no returning to the outdated premodern worldview in hopes of revitalizing the Christian doctrine of the Spirit. Rather, we need a robust and courageous return to a more complex, plural, and multilayered account of reality in the midst of which the Spirit of the almighty God is at work in innumerable ways.

The Plan of the Chapter

The structure of this chapter follows the underlying insight in which the work of the Spirit is being envisioned in mutually related concentric circles, as it were, beginning from the most comprehensive and "universal" sphere:

---

spirit" pneumatologies and cosmologies. "The Potential of Pneumatology for Mission in Contemporary Europe," *International Review of Mission* 95, nos. 378–79 (2006): 338. Similarly, Yong's distinction between "natural" and "cosmology of personal agency" reflects the same foundational intuitions.

The Spirit in the Trinity
The Spirit in Creation
The Spirit in the Cosmos
The Spirit among Religions

The order of discussion is intentionally from the largest context to the private, from the Spirit's work as the principle of life, bringing forth and sustaining all creaturely existence; to the Spirit's relation to other cosmic spirits and powers, including those of other religions; to the "public ministry" of the Spirit in culture, history, politics, economy, and the arts. Before anything else, the immediately following section will establish the deity of the Spirit along with the Father and Son. For a plural pneumatology that seeks to relate the Spirit of the Jewish-Christian Bible to other spirits in the created reality, including those of other religions, it is of utmost importance to clarify and defend the Christian confession of her deity. Christian confession of the deity of the Spirit belongs of course to the domain of the doctrine of the Trinity and hence continues from chapter 2 above. In classical theology, this chapter could also be named "pneumatology proper," in distinction from the "order of salvation" (*ordo salutis*), which delves into diverse salvific works of the Spirit of God at personal and communal levels, the topic for the following chapter.

The Spirit of the Triune God: The Doctrine of the Holy Spirit

The Slow Progress of the Doctrine of the Spirit

After the introductory section's argument for a shift from a unitive to a plural paradigm of pneumatology, one should not conclude that therefore a thinner doctrinal formulation of the deity of the Spirit and Spirit's place in the Trinity would follow.[6] On the contrary, those who seek to relate the Spirit of God to the spirit(s) of other religions and spirits/powers/forces in the cosmos and society recognize the need to think clearly and accurately about the distinctive nature of a Christian Trinitarian confession of the Spirit.

6. Consult Stanley M. Burgess, *The Holy Spirit: Ancient Christian Traditions*; *The Holy Spirit: Eastern Christian Traditions*; *The Holy Spirit: Medieval Roman Catholic and Reformation Traditions* (Peabody, MA: Hendrickson, 1984, 1989, 1997); Veli-Matti Kärkkäinen, ed., *Holy Spirit and Salvation: The Sources of Christian Theology* (Louisville: Westminster John Knox, 2010).

The development of pneumatological doctrine progressed even more slowly and painstakingly than did the doctrinal understanding of Christ and the Trinity. Indeed, "Long before the Spirit was a theme of doctrine, He was a fact in the experience of the community."[7] The Indian ecumenist Stanley J. Samartha captures well this point: "To most Christians the Holy Spirit is associated not so much with doctrine as with life. It is in the unwrapping of the gift of God in Jesus Christ that the Spirit becomes alive in the hearts and minds of Christians. The Spirit inwardly nourishes the new life in Christ and guides the community of believers in their acts of witness and service in the world."[8]

It is understandable then that in the early centuries it was not uncommon to see confusion between the "Spirit" and "Word" (Son),[9] as evident, for example, in the famous apologist Justin Martyr's claim that "it is wrong, therefore, to understand the Spirit and the power of God as anything else than the Word, who is also the first-born of God."[10] No less a giant than Origen advocated the strange idea of the derivation of the Spirit from the Logos and the Spirit's created nature.[11] Understandings of the origins and "derivation" of the Spirit similarly remained somewhat vague, often conceived in emanationist terms.[12] Or consider this: some early fathers spoke of threeness in terms of God, Word, and Wisdom.[13] Because of the lack of a confession of the full deity of the Spirit, at times the Spirit was ranked as the "third" member in the Divine Society.[14]

Why the slow tempo of the doctrinal development? Reasons are many. Both in biblical traditions and in people's general mind-set, the Spirit is more subtle and less concrete a phenomenon than Son and Father. It is far easier to find metaphors and symbols for Father and Son that have an everyday counterpart. Related to the elusive nature and "shyness" of the Spirit is also the biblical perception that the Holy Spirit never draws atten-

7. Eduard Schweizer, "Pneuma," in *Theological Dictionary of the New Testament*, ed. Gerhard Friedrich, trans. and ed. Geoffrey W. Bromiley, 10 vols. (Grand Rapids: Eerdmans, 1964–1976), 6:396.

8. Stanley J. Samartha, "The Holy Spirit and People of Other Faiths," *Ecumenical Review* 42, nos. 3–4 (July 1990): 250.

9. 2 Clement 14; Shepherd of Hermas, Similitude 9.1.

10. Justin Martyr, *First Apology* 33; also Tertullian, *Against Praxeas* 7, 8 (in *ANF*, vol. 3).

11. Origen, *Commentary on John* 2.6.

12. Athenagoras of Athens, *A Plea for the Christians* 10.

13. Theophilus of Antioch, *Theophilus to Autolycus* 2.15; Irenaeus, *Against Heresies* 4.20.3.

14. Justin Martyr, *First Apology* 13.

tion to herself but rather turns our attention to the Son and through the Son to the Father. Furthermore, the naming of the Spirit as the "bond" of love between the Father and the Son might have contributed to the lack of articulating the personal nature of the Spirit. While certainly this idea has both a biblical basis and theological validity, it may also turn into a nonpersonal conception of the Spirit. "Love" or "bond" doesn't have to be as "personal" as Father and Son.

The Eastern Orthodox Church persistently reminds us of still another reason for the slow progress in doctrinal understanding of the Spirit. It has to do with the *filioque* clause, which may have subordinated the Spirit under the Son and thus made theological reflection on the Spirit less urgent. Since that topic was quite extensively treated in the chapter on the Trinity, it will not be taken up here.

Toward the Consolidation of the Deity of the Spirit

Against modalistic teachers, Tertullian established the distinction among Father, Son, and Spirit on the inner relations of the Trinitarian members. On the basis of the Paraclete passages in John 14, Tertullian suggested that the Son distinguished both the Father and the Spirit from himself.[15] While distinguished from each other, the Trinitarian persons also share unity, which later creedal tradition referred to as *homoousios* (consubstantial). Tertullian surmised that the Johannine Jesus's saying "I and the Father are one" means that Father and Son are of "one substance" (2), and this denotes an identity of substance rather than numerical unity (25). By extension, the Son and Spirit are of the same substance with the Father (3). Thus, we can speak of God's one "substance" and three distinct yet undivided "persons" (2).

Technically this is what the Western Church's semicanonized way of expressing its faith in the Trinity says (*una substantia, tres personae*). Materially, this formulation leads to the full establishment of the deity of the Spirit. Among the Greek fathers, Origen finally came to this idea—after much vacillation—when he affirmed that "nothing in the Trinity can be called greater or less, since the fountain of divinity alone contains all things by His word and reason, and by the Spirit of His mouth sanctifies all things."[16]

15. Tertullian, *Against Praxeas* 9, quoting John 14:28 and 14:16. Hereafter, references from this work will be given in parentheses in the text.

16. Origen, *First Principles* 1.3.7 (in *ANF*, vol. 4).

In Defense of Full Deity of the Spirit against Heresies

As in the formulation of christological and Trinitarian doctrines, much of the energy behind the development of pneumatological doctrine came from the threat and challenge of heretical views. The fourth-century Greek-speaking Alexandrian theologians were fighting against heretical views of the Spirit on several fronts, including against the *Tropicii* (Tropici), a group that was not willing to give the same divine status to the Spirit as to the Son. Like the Arian heresy in Christology, the Tropici's view rejected the full equality of the Spirit vis-à-vis other Trinitarian members.[17] Athanasius's *Letters to Serapion on the Holy Spirit* insisted on the indivisibility of the Trinity as a proof of the equal status of the Spirit.[18]

Gregory of Nazianzus's *On the Holy Spirit* vehemently rejected all heretical notions of the created nature of the Spirit: if there ever was a time when the Father was not—meaning he was not eternal because there was a beginning—then the Son would not be eternal either, nor by derivation the Spirit.[19]

Basil the Great's *On the Holy Spirit* was the main tool in rejecting another major pneumatological heresy: that perpetrated by the Pneumatomachoi, the "fighters of the Spirit" who undermined the Nicean orthodoxy and thus echoed Arian misgivings about the Son's equality with the Father. The reference to the Spirit's preexistence was one of the tactics to oppose this "pneumatological Arianism."[20]

Basil's brother Gregory of Nyssa penned *On the Holy Trinity of the Godhead of the Holy Spirit to Eustathius* and *On the Holy Spirit against the Followers of Macedonius*, in which he defended the Cappadocian conviction of the equality of the Spirit. With Arian and Eunomian tendencies, Macedonius compromised the Spirit's divinity and full equality with the Father. Against those heresies, Gregory argued that the Holy Spirit is "essentially holy," as are the Father and the Son. As are the other two members of the Trinity, the Spirit is characterized by divine attributes similar to those of Father and Son.[21] Indeed, everywhere the Greek fathers affirmed boldly the equality of the Spirit with the Son.[22]

In the Latin-speaking church, Saint Augustine's clarification of Trinitar-

17. Athanasius, *Letters to Serapion* 1.21, in Khaled Anatolios, *Athanasius*, Early Church Fathers (London: Routledge, 2004), 220–21.

18. Athanasius, *Letters to Serapion* 1.20, in Anatolios, *Athanasius*, 219.

19. Gregory of Nazianzus, *On the Holy Spirit* 4.

20. See Basil, *On the Holy Spirit* 19.49.

21. Gregory of Nyssa, *On the Holy Spirit against the Followers of Macedonius*, in *NPNF*² 5:323.

22. J. N. D. Kelly, *Early Christian Doctrines*, rev. ed. (New York: Harper & Row, 1978 [1960]), 258–63.

ian and pneumatological contours helped further consolidate the deity of the Spirit. Although all Trinitarian members are holy, what makes the third person unique is that the "Holy Spirit is a certain unutterable communion of the Father and the Son."[23] In other words, "He is the Spirit of the Father and Son, as the substantial and consubstantial love of both."[24] While acknowledging that any of the members of the Trinity could be called love on the basis of biblical passages such as 1 John 4:7–19 and Romans 5:5, Augustine came to the conclusion that the Spirit particularly can be called Love, the bond of love uniting Father and Son, and derivatively, uniting the triune God and human beings.[25]

The New Testament statements such as "God is spirit" (John 4:24) and "The Lord is the Spirit, and where the Spirit of the Lord is, there is freedom" (2 Cor. 3:17) helped the bishop to clarify the twofold reference of the term "Spirit": on the one hand, it speaks of God's nature as "invisible and incomprehensible," and on the other hand, as the Gift of God given to the believer, in other words, as the name of the third person of the Trinity.[26] More daring than the Cappadocians, Augustine felt comfortable in calling the Holy Spirit "Very God, Equal with the Father and the Son."[27]

The Creedal Establishment of the Spirit's Status and Role in the Trinity

The authoritative formulation of the Spirit was finally ratified in the ecumenical creeds. Whereas the fathers at Nicea were irreducibly brief in their confession—"And [we believe] in the Holy Ghost"[28]—in the Creed of Constantinople I (381) the consubstantiality of the Spirit was officially confirmed: "And [we believe] in the Holy Ghost, the Lord and Giver-of-Life, who proceedeth from the Father, who with the Father and the Son together is worshipped and glorified, who spake by the prophets."

Although far from any kind of systematic statement, the Constantinopolitan elaboration of aspects of pneumatological doctrine and the Spirit's tasks is worth noting.[29] First, the equal status of the Spirit was officially con-

23. Augustine, *On the Trinity* 5.11.12.

24. Augustine, *Tractates on John* 105.

25. Augustine, *On the Trinity* 15.17.31.

26. Hilary of Poitiers, *On the Trinity* 2.31–32.

27. Augustine, *On the Trinity*, the preamble to chap. 6 in book 1, 22 (1.6.13).

28. *NPNF*² 14:3.

29. I was inspired by Donald Thorsen, *Explorations in Christian Theology* (Grand Rapids: Baker Academic, 2010), chap. 19.

firmed in that the Holy Spirit is to be "worshipped and glorified" together with the Father and the Son. Related to this is the mention of the proceeding of the Spirit from the Father, reminding us of the Trinitarian structure of the creed and confession of faith in the Spirit. Second, naming the Spirit the "Giver-of-Life" makes an integral connection with the doctrine of salvation. (Unlike twentieth-century theologians, the drafters of the creed most probably did not intentionally link the life-giving Spirit with creation.)

Third, the soteriological connection is brought home also in the nomenclature "Holy" Ghost, in other words, the Spirit's sanctifying work in the life of the believers. Fourth, in keeping with later theological developments, the connection between the inspiration of prophetic Scripture and the Holy Spirit was established at Chalcedon (echoing New Testament statements such as 2 Tim. 3:16 and 2 Pet. 1:20–21).

Fifth, considering more broadly the wider context of the third article of the creed, we note that the Spirit is linked closely with the church and liturgy. The ecclesiological connection is further enhanced by the statement about belief in the one, holy, apostolic, and catholic church and the communion of saints immediately following belief in the Spirit. It might also be significant that this same article, after the Spirit and the church, also mentions belief in the forgiveness of sins. Soteriological and ecclesiological themes are interrelated in that, according to the earliest faith of Christians, salvation and forgiveness can only be had in the church. Furthermore, there is not only the ecclesiological but also the eschatological context for the confession of the Spirit. The article ends with a statement about the resurrection of the body and eternal life. While later theology by and large missed the integral connection between eschatology and pneumatology, in the biblical testimonies the link is established with the expectation and fulfillment of the pouring out of the Spirit as the launching of the final days (Joel 2 and Acts 2).

The Communion of the Spirit, Son, and Father

The Fellowship of the Holy Spirit

The distinctively *Christian* understanding of the divine Spirit is Trinitarian in its experience and form. Trinitarian understanding of God allows both for the reciprocal, mutually dependent understanding of relations between Father, Son, and Spirit and also for an account of the God-world relationship based on mutuality rather than distance.

As discussed in chapter 2 on the Trinity, the turn to a relational understanding of personhood has helped the rediscovery of communion theology, whose roots go back to the New Testament witness, according to which the Spirit is the principle of *koinōnia.*

The late Canadian Baptist Clark Pinnock grasped deeply and put in perspective the profound theological implications of a robust relational communion theology of the divine Spirit with the focus on the "liveliness of the Trinity and the identity of the Spirit within a loving relationality":

> Let us consider the Spirit as One who bonds the loving fellowship that God is and creates access to the Father through the Son (Eph 2:18). The Spirit reaches out to creatures, catches them up and brings them home to the love of God. . . . Spirit is the ecstasy that implements God's abundance and triggers the overflow of divine self-giving. . . . The universe in its entirety is the field of its operations . . . and the Spirit is present everywhere, directing the universe toward its goal, bringing to completion first the creational and then the redemptive purposes of God.[30]

The Spirit's role in the Trinity is integrally related not only to the Father from whom she derives but also to the Son. This brings us to "Spirit Christology"—a dominant theme in the New Testament, particularly in the Synoptic Gospels—or "pneumatological christology."[31] No Son without the Spirit. No Spirit without the Son.

"Spirit Christology"—Christological Pneumatology

The integral, mutually conditioned relationality between the two is evident everywhere in the Gospels and is also assumed in the rest of the New Testament. Jesus's birth (Matt. 1:18–25; Luke 1:35) and its announcement (Luke 1:35, 67); his baptism (Matt. 3:16; Mark 1:10; Luke 3:22; John 1:33); his testing in the wilderness (Matt. 4:1; Mark 1:12; Luke 4:1); his anointing (Luke 4:18–21); his ministry with healings, exorcisms, and other miracles (Matt. 12:28; Luke 4:18; 11:20); the eschatological ministry of Jesus as the Baptizer in the Spirit (Matt.

30. Clark H. Pinnock, *Flame of Love: A Theology of the Holy Spirit* (Downers Grove, IL: InterVarsity Press, 1996), 21, 50; see also 60.

31. Jürgen Moltmann, *The Way of Jesus Christ: Christology in Messianic Dimensions*, trans. Margaret Kohl (Minneapolis: Fortress, 1993 [1989]), 73–74.

3:11)—these are all attributed to the Spirit. Importantly, Jesus was also raised to new life by the power of the Spirit (Rom. 1:4), so much so that he "became a life-giving spirit" (1 Cor. 15:45).

The roots of Spirit Christology go deep into the Old Testament; recall that *Messiah* means literally "the Anointed One." Particularly in the prophetic literature, the messianic figure appears as anointed and empowered by the Spirit of God (Isa. 11:1–8; 42:1–4). Rightly then, Moltmann reminds us that "Jesus' history as the Christ does not begin with Jesus himself. It begins with the *ruach*/the Holy Spirit."[32] In that sense it can also be said that the workings of the Spirit precede those of the Son.[33] As the Son of God, Jesus Christ is "a Spirit-creation."[34]

In the development of the christological doctrine, as investigated in chapter 5, the deity of Christ came to be explained by and large with the concept of the Logos, the Word. As legitimate as that development may be, it is also useful to be reminded of the deep Spirit-orientation in the New Testament. That said, in no way should these two models (Spirit Christology and Logos Christology) be taken as opposites or alternatives. They are complementary. A wonderful example here is Tertullian, a great architect of Logos and two-nature Christology (or "two-substance" Christology, as he preferred to call it) who also advocated a robust Spirit Christology.[35]

Having now established the deity of the Holy Spirit in the context of the Christian doctrine of the Trinity, we begin the work of relating the Spirit to the works of the triune God in the world, as well as to claims about the Spirit(s) in the cosmos and among other faith traditions. The first task is to look at the work of the divine Spirit in the world God has created, the role of the Spirit in creation.

The Spirit in Creation

A Trinitarian Account of Creation

Recall that the chapter on the doctrine of creation sought a robustly Trinitarian account of creation. Let us now further highlight the Spirit's role therein. In his exposition of the creation narrative in Genesis (1:2), Luther paints this

32. Moltmann, *Way of Jesus Christ*, 73.

33. Moltmann, *The Spirit of Life*, xi, 60.

34. Walter Kasper, *Jesus the Christ*, trans. V. Green (London: Burns & Oates; New York: Paulist, 1976), 251.

35. See Tertullian, *Against Praxeas* 5 and 6.

most delightful and poetic Trinitarian picture of the Spirit at work in creation: "The Father creates heaven and earth out of nothing through the Son . . . the Word. Over these the Holy Spirit broods. As a hen broods her eggs, keeping them warm in order to hatch her chicks, and, as it were, to bring them to life through heat, so Scripture says that the Holy Spirit brooded, as it were, on the waters to bring to life those substances which were to be quickened and adorned. For it is the office of the Holy Spirit to make alive."[36]

Promisingly, beginning from the mid-twentieth century, the Spirit's role in the work of creation has been rediscovered in theology. The following section will investigate the implications of that profound development in order to prepare us for a deeper, constructive reflection on the pneumatological-Trinitarian theology of creation.

The Theological Rediscovery of Cosmic Pneumatologies

The Spirit's role as the omnipresent agency bringing and sustaining all life (Gen. 1:2; Ps. 104:29–30) is one of the many treasures of the contemporary pneumatological "renaissance." As the eco-feminist Elizabeth Johnson reminds us, "Of all the activities that theology attributes to the Spirit, the most significant is this: the Spirit is the creative origin of all life. In the words of the Nicene Creed, the Spirit is *vivificantem*, vivifier or life-giver. . . . The Spirit is the unceasing, dynamic flow of divine power that sustains the universe, bringing forth life."[37]

This kind of profound statement importantly places the ministry, role, and work of the Spirit in a robust cosmic, evolutionary, and scientific context.[38] Lutheran theologian Wolfhart Pannenberg has spoken robustly of the need to overcome the reductionist tendencies in the Christian conception of the Spirit and forge an integral link with the whole of creation.[39] He underlines the continuity among the many works of the Spirit from creation to providence to personal faith to the life of the church to resurrection.[40] As noted, his Re-

36. Luther, *Lectures on Genesis 1–5*, in *LW* 1:9; for comments, see Regin Prenter, *Spiritus Creator: Luther's Concept of the Holy Spirit* (Philadelphia: Muhlenberg, 1953), 192.

37. Elizabeth Johnson, *Women, Earth, and Creator Spirit* (Mahwah, NJ: Paulist, 1993), 42.

38. Denis Edwards, *Ecology at the Heart of Faith: The Change of Heart That Leads to a New Way of Living on Earth* (Maryknoll, NY: Orbis, 2007), chap. 3.

39. Wolfhart Pannenberg, "The Doctrine of the Spirit and the Task of a Theology of Nature," *Theology* 75 (January 1972): 11–12.

40. Pannenberg, *ST* 3:1.

formed colleague Jürgen Moltmann's *Spirit of Life* has similarly stressed the integral relationship between the Holy Spirit's role in salvation and creation.[41]

Moltmann further notes that a turn to a vigorous creational pneumatology pushes theology toward panentheism, as it attempts to "discover God *in* all the beings he has created and to find his life-giving Spirit *in* the community of creation that they share."[42] In light of the fact that, as Moltmann's *Spirit of Life* powerfully argues, the Spirit of God is present as a life force immanent in all the living, in body, in sexuality, in ecology, in political life, and so forth, we can therefore speak of "immanent transcendence."[43] This orientation coheres with "classical panentheism" as recommended in chapter 2.

All these and many related current developments toward a cosmic and creational pneumatology, coupled with a panentheistic way of conceiving the God-world relationship, also build important bridges for science-theology engagement in the doctrine of creation and divine action.

The Life-Giving Spirit of Creation

Only with a return to a holistic and comprehensive biblical account of the *ruach Yahweh* as the life principle, energizing and supporting all life of the cosmos, including the physical/material, could theology correct the pneumatological deficit.[44] That turn also helps rediscover the ancient conviction that "there is a cosmic range to the operations of the Spirit, the Lord and giver of life." Indeed, nothing less than that the "universe in its entirety is the field of its operations."[45]

According to the biblical testimony, *ruach Elohim* "was moving over the face of the waters" (Gen. 1:2), "breathing" life (2:7) into creatures.

> By the word of the Lord the heavens were made,
> and all their host by the breath [*ruach*] of his mouth. (Ps. 33:6)

This very same divine energy also sustains all life in the cosmos. All creation is "enspirited by God"[46] and needs the divine breath for its continuance and activity:

41. Moltmann, *The Spirit of Life*, 8–9.

42. Moltmann, *God in Creation*, trans. Margaret Kohl (Minneapolis: Fortress, 1993), xi; similarly, Johnson, *Women, Earth, and Creator Spirit*, 42.

43. Moltmann, *The Spirit of Life*, 36.

44. Moltmann, *The Spirit of Life*, 40.

45. Pinnock, *Flame of Love*, 49–50.

46. Jay Byrd McDaniel, "Where Is the Holy Spirit Anyway? Response to a Skeptic Environmentalist," *Ecumenical Review* 42, no. 2 (1990): 171.

> When you [Yahweh] send forth your spirit [*ruach*], they are created;
> and you renew the face of the ground. (Ps. 104:30 NRSV)

Similarly, when Yahweh "take[s] away their breath [*ruach*], they die / and return to the dust" (v. 29).[47]

To do justice to the infinite nature of the cosmic breath of life, contemporary theology is aided by metaphors and symbols drawn from Christian testimonies in various global contexts. The Korean-born theologian J. Y. Lee speaks of "cloth as a metaphor of the Spirit [that] protects and sustains all things on earth. Unlike the shield, a masculine metaphor of protection, it is closely associated with a feminine image in Asia. Women weave cloth and use it for the protection and decoration of the body."[48]

The "Earthly" and Embodied Nature of the Creator Spirit

Christian tradition has been keen on not compromising the sovereign transcendence of God and the divine Spirit—and rightly so; even when speaking of the Spirit's role in creation, one must resist domesticating the universal creative Spirit of God, within the framework of creation. That said, there is much theological potential in boldly envisioning the Spirit in "earthly" and embodied terms. In the witty expression of the American religious scholar Eugene F. Rogers Jr., "The Spirit, who in classical Christian discourse 'pours out on all flesh,' had, in modern discourse, floated free of bodies altogether."[49] As a result, "the Spirit has grown dull because [it is] unembodied."[50]

The removal of the spirit from the "earthly," however, is misguided. The most profound theological statement against divorcing the divine Spirit from creation and the physical is the incarnation, an event of embodiment. Consider the statement by Moltmann: "If we wish to understand the Old Testament word *ruah*, we must forget the word 'spirit,' which belongs to Western culture."[51] Unlike in Greek, Latin, and contemporary Western languages in which

47. See John Calvin, *Commentary on Psalms 93–119*, in *Commentary on the Psalms*, trans. James Anderson, vol. 4 (Grand Rapids: Christian Classics Ethereal Library, n.d.), on 104:29, https://www.ccel.org/ccel/calvin/calcom11.html.

48. Jung Young Lee, *The Trinity in Asian Perspective* (Nashville: Abingdon, 1996), 104.

49. Eugene F. Rogers Jr., *After the Spirit: A Constructive Pneumatology from Resources Outside the Modern West* (Grand Rapids: Eerdmans, 2005), 1.

50. Rogers, *After the Spirit*, 3.

51. Moltmann, *The Spirit of Life*, 40.

spirit is taken as an antithesis to the bodily and material, in the Old Testament, the basic term (Yahweh's) *ruach* means strong wind or tempest. Its theological meaning is the principle of life.

The emerging ecological pneumatology has made this a leading theme. One of its ablest trailblazers, M. I. Wallace, confesses: "I believe that hope for a renewed earth is best founded on belief in God as Earth Spirit, the compassionate, all-encompassing divine force within the biosphere who inhabits earth community and continually works to maintain the integrity of all forms of life."[52] Consider what Athanasius said: "For no part of Creation is left void of Him: He has filled all things everywhere, remaining present with His own Father."[53]

In light of a number of nature-based biblical metaphors of the Spirit such as the "animating breath," "the healing wind," "the living water," and "cleansing fire," it is totally legitimate to link the Spirit with nature.[54] This is not to undermine the divine uniqueness of the Spirit but rather to speak of the divine infinity in which finite and infinite are both transcended and embraced simultaneously. In the words of the postcolonialist M. Rivera: "God is irreducibly Other, always beyond our grasp. But not beyond our touch."[55]

An important benefit from affirming the panentheistic immanence of the transcendent Creator Spirit in the world relates to one of the most urgent tasks for contemporary theology: the preservation of the earth (discussed already in chap. 3, to be taken up again in the last chapter). In green pneumatological imaginations, the Holy Spirit has been depicted as the "Wounded Spirit,"[56] due to our devastation of God's creation. The task of a properly conceived green pneumatology is to help us imagine metaphors of flourishing, thriving, blossoming, and greening. A counterpart to that task is to cultivate our sensibilities toward the endangerment of nature and its diverse species. Both aspects help cultivate pneumatological sensibilities in the service of nature care.

Having briefly developed some key themes in the cosmic-creational pneumatology, we will finish this section by returning to the science-theology

52. Mark I. Wallace, *Fragments of the Spirit: Nature, Violence, and the Renewal of Creation* (New York: Continuum, 1996), 6.

53. Athanasius, *On the Incarnation of the Word* 2.8.

54. Wallace, *Fragments of the Spirit*, 8.

55. Mayra Rivera, *The Touch of Transcendence: A Postcolonial Theology of God* (Louisville: Westminster John Knox, 2007), 2.

56. Mark I. Wallace, "The Green Face of God: Recovering the Spirit in an Ecocidal Era," in *Advents of the Spirit: An Introduction to the Current Study of Pneumatology*, ed. Bradford E. Hinze and D. Lyle Dabney (Milwaukee: Marquette University Press, 2001), 450–53.

dialogue in the doctrine of creation with a view toward pneumatological resources.

The Divine Spirit and the Natural Sciences: In Search of Correlates

Since the main principles of the most current scientific account of the origins and workings of the cosmos were treated in some detail in chapter 3 on creation, there is no need to repeat them here. Let us rather reflect on pneumatological implications of statements such as these: "Suppose for a moment that, as theists believe, an eternal divine Spirit really did create this cosmos. Suppose that it was God's intent to produce beings capable of knowing God and working in harmony with the Spirit."[57] These statements elicit the question of whether there are any bridges between the claims of Christian Trinitarian-pneumatological belief in creation as God's handiwork and those of the current evolutionary scientific paradigm.

Indeed, the twentieth century saw many radical shifts in the scientific paradigm itself that, while challenging to theology, also offer new ways to consider the role of the Spirit in the cosmos. Wolfgang Vondey observes: "Post-Newtonian physics speaks of the physical universe in terms of such concepts as energy, radiation, magnetism, waves, and field theories. Recent theological investigations speak of the Holy Spirit in surprisingly similar terms, among them the notions of energy, radiation, space, force, field, and light."[58]

Pannenberg, among theologians, has tried his hand at this effort to link pneumatology and scientific explanations: "The presence of God's Spirit in his creation can be described as a field of creative presence, a comprehensive field of force that releases event after event into finite existence."[59] He is not doing this comparison naively; the theologian is well aware of profound differences as well. But the point to our discussion is this: even in the domain where sciences function in the contemporary world, the Spirit of God, the Creator, is not absent. Much work awaits us in this emerging correlation of Christian pneumatology and scientific accounts of the universe and life therein.

57. Philip C. Clayton, "The Spirit in Evolution and in Nature," chap. 13 in *IRDSW*, 187.

58. Wolfgang Vondey, "The Holy Spirit and the Physical Universe: The Impact of Scientific Paradigm Shifts on Contemporary Pneumatology," *Theological Studies* 70 (2009): 4.

59. Wolfhart Pannenberg, *An Introduction to Systematic Theology* (Grand Rapids: Eerdmans, 1991), 49.

The Cosmic Spirit and (Spiritual) Powers

Radical Shifts in the Interpretation of Spirits and Powers in Theology

Angels and Powers in Christian History

In the Bible and early theology, the spiritual realities and beings were taken fully seriously, even if their nature and functions were yet to be theologically developed. Perhaps wisely, "regarding the devil and his angels, and the opposing influences, the teaching of the Church has laid down that these beings exist indeed; but what they are, or how they exist, it has not been explained with sufficient clearness."[60] The fathers' reservation may also have stemmed from the prevalence of belief in angels and spirits among surrounding cultures.

As is well known, the worldview of the ancients not only was open to notions of supernatural forces, but it took them as something thoroughly "natural." The world was filled with spirits, spiritual powers, "spiritual warfare," and similar experiences and intuitions. Just consider the cosmology of the New Testament, whether Jesus's own ministry or the worldview of the Apocalypse, and you get the picture.[61] The cosmos was "spirited."

Building on the rich biblical reservoir, Christian tradition, beginning from the fathers, developed a rich and creative angelology, which culminated in the highly speculative presentations in medieval theology, the most well known of which is the nine-layer cosmic vision in *The Celestial Hierarchy* of Pseudo-Dionysius the Areopagite.[62] Although less speculative, even medieval masters such as Aquinas devoted huge intellectual efforts to a detailed scrutiny of angelology.[63] That said, by and large Christian tradition has followed Calvin's "rule of modesty and sobriety"[64] when speaking of angels.

In contrast with tradition, modern thinkers rejected or seriously marginalized belief in spiritual beings; they virtually rejected everything that did

60. Origen, *First Principles*, preface, 6.

61. Peter G. Bolt, "Jesus, the Daimons and the Dead," chap. 5 in *The Unseen World: Christian Reflections on Angels, Demons, and the Heavenly Realm*, ed. Anthony N. S. Lane (Carlisle, UK: Paternoster, 1996).

62. *The Celestial Hierarchy*, in Dionysius the Areopagite, *Works*, trans. John Parker (1899), 2:1–66; available at http://www.tertullian.org/fathers/index.htm#Dionysius_the_Areopagite.

63. Aquinas, *ST* 1.50–64 and 106–14. An accessible discussion of angels in Augustine, Pseudo-Dionysius, Aquinas, the Reformers, and Milton can be found in Stephen F. Noll, "Thinking about Angels," in Lane, *The Unseen World*, 2–13.

64. Calvin, *Institutes* 1.14.4.

not cohere with "natural religion." At the end of Schleiermacher's doctrine of creation, his discussion of angels—in keeping with his methodology—argues that while there is no principled reason why such beings could not exist, they are irrelevant to "religious feelings" and thus there is no need to try to settle the issue.[65]

Not surprisingly, for the majority of scholars of the twentieth century, "an ontology of angels, fallen or unfallen, is hardly credible."[66] Ironically—and often against their will—Protestant missionaries who went out to the mission lands also tended to proliferate "secular" impulses that included a thin view of angels, at times even virtual rejection of them.[67] However, folk psychology still resists the overly critical scholarly opinion: according to a 2008 Pew survey, a large majority of American adults (79 percent) believe in miracles, and almost as many (68 percent) believe that angels and demons are active in the world.[68] In postmodern times, we also know well that a resurgence of interest in angels and spiritual experiences in the general population, including its literature and entertainment,[69] as well as in some quarters of the secular academy,[70] has taken place.[71]

The Resurgence of Interest in Powers in Twentieth-Century Theology

To the great surprise of many, beginning in the middle of the twentieth century, an interest in angels, demonic forces, and spiritual beings resurfaced in theology. The biggest contribution came from Karl Barth.

Barth's overly long methodological preface to angelology[72] rightly calls for a middle way between the "far too interesting mythology of the ancients"

65. Friedrich Schleiermacher, *The Christian Faith*, ed. H. R. Mackintosh and J. S. Stewart (Edinburgh: T&T Clark, 1999), §42 epithet, 156.

66. David O'Connor, *God and Inscrutable Evil: In Defense of Theism and Atheism* (Lanham, MD: Rowman & Littlefield, 1998), 114.

67. Paul G. Hiebert, "The Flaw of the Excluded Middle," *Missiology: An International Review* 10, no. 1 (1982): 35–47.

68. Pew Research Center, "Summary of Key Findings," *Pew Forum on Religion & Public Life / U.S. Religious Landscape Survey* (2008), 11–12.

69. Amy Summers-Minette, "Not Just Halos and Horns: Angels and Demons in Western Pop Culture," chap. 13 in *A&D*.

70. Cathy Gutierrez, ed., *Handbook of Spiritualism and Channeling* (Leiden: Brill, 2015).

71. HBO TV miniseries *Angels in America*; see http://www.hbo.com/movies/angels-in-america.

72. Barth, *CD* III/3. Hereafter, page references from this work will be given in parentheses in the text.

and the demythologization of the modern (369), and advises sticking with biblical teaching alone (372). Angels are God's ambassadors. But the Bible does not speak of their nature (410), only of their work in the service of God (451–52), as "ministering spirits" (Heb. 1:14; *CD* III/3, 452). They are representatives of heaven and witnesses to the divine activity. In contrast to earlier theology, Barth emphatically rejects the theological tradition's view of demons as fallen angels (251). Instead, he relates the demonic to the semimagical elusive concept of "Nothing" (*das Nichtige*), a domain of utmost "opposition and resistance," against which "God asserts Himself and exerts His positive will" (327, 351).

In the aftermath of Barth, a different type of reenvisioning of powers started on both sides of the Atlantic focusing on their influence on sociopolitical structures and ideologies. This could happen in more than one way. While traditionally the powers have been conceived as more or less spiritual realities,[73] in this new approach they could also be imagined as spiritual and, at the same time, created social realities.[74] This was the approach of the little but significant book by the Dutch Reformed theologian Hendrikus Berkhof, *Christ and the Powers*. Speaking of powers as structures undergirding all human and societal life, he envisions them as providing cohesion and preserving from disintegration: these structures can be social units such as family or tribe, religious or other ideological beliefs.[75] The American Mennonite theologian John H. Yoder, who translated Berkhof's book, developed the idea in his *Politics of Jesus* by further analyzing the structures into religious, intellectual, moral, and political categories.[76] The late Canadian Baptist theologian Stanley J. Grenz's "structures of existence" concept continues this interpretation; he envisions them as "those larger, suprahuman aspects or dimensions of reality which form the inescapable context for human life and which therefore condition individual and corporate human existence."[77]

Following this both-and hermeneutics of powers, Grenz underlines that although the structures have no independent reality apart from humankind,

73. Clinton E. Arnold, *Ephesians: Power and Magic—the Concept of Power in Ephesians in Light of Its Historical Setting* (Cambridge: Cambridge University Press, 1989).

74. G. B. Caird, *Principalities and Powers: A Study in Pauline Theology* (Oxford: Clarendon, 1956).

75. Hendrikus Berkhof, *Christ and Powers*, trans. John H. Yoder (Scottdale, PA: Herald Press, 1962), 30–35.

76. John Howard Yoder, *The Politics of Jesus* (Grand Rapids: Eerdmans, 1972), 145.

77. Stanley J. Grenz, *Theology for the Community of God* (Grand Rapids: Eerdmans, 1994), 228.

they also transcend humanity and lie beyond human control. As such they are "quasi-independent" and "quasi-personal."[78] Here comes the link to the biblical, particularly the Pauline, way of speaking of principalities and powers: This means that between the structures of existence and the biblical talk about angels and spirits, there is no total identification.[79] Because originally the structures were meant to facilitate human life, they were created good by God. However, they can be abused and manipulated for evil—and they often are. As structures of cohesion, "by holding the world together, they hold it away from God, not close to Him."[80] Now, as a result, "[through] the diabolical misuse of structures, evil realities bring humans into structural bondage," including slavery to powers and demand for uncompromising loyalty. The structures become a channel for evil, though still under the Lordship of Christ.[81] Ultimately part of God's creation and Christ's reconciliation, "the structures will one day conform to the reign of God." Because of this eschatological vision, Christians can anticipate that Christ's continuing cosmic rule breaks into the realm of the structures of existence.[82]

A related, alternative interpretation of powers merely as immanent structures, though genuinely influencing affairs of society and human life, comes from the late American New Testament scholar Walter J. Wink, whose trilogy on the powers has become a contemporary classic.[83] For Wink, the powers are "the spiritualities of institutions, the 'within' of corporate structures and the inner essence of outer organizations of power." The outer aspect consists of "political systems, appointed officials, the 'chair' of an organization, laws," whereas the "invisible pole, an inner spirit or driving force . . . animates, legitimates, and regulates its physical manifestation in the world."[84] Although dismissing as outdated the concepts of "angels," "principalities and powers," as well as "Satan" after the worldview of the ancients—which is also "accidentally" that of the biblical writers—Wink takes the powers as "real" (albeit not in the traditional sense). They are social, cultural, political, financial, global powers. What do we do with the powers according to Wink? They must be "redeemed"

78. Grenz, *Theology for the Community*, 230.

79. Grenz, *Theology for the Community*, 231.

80. Berkhof, *Christ and the Powers*, 30.

81. Grenz, *Theology for the Community*, 233–35, here 233.

82. Grenz, *Theology for the Community*, 235.

83. For a summary, see Walter Wink, *The Powers That Be: Theology for a New Millennium* (New York: Doubleday, 1998).

84. Walter Wink, *Naming the Powers: The Language of Power in the New Testament* (Philadelphia: Fortress, 1984), 5.

because they were good originally, then became evil.[85] The key to redeeming powers is in the Jesus kind of lifestyle: nonviolent, peaceful, and free. That life is set against the "domination system of the powers" of the world.[86] With traditional theology, Wink believes in the final reconciliation of the powers, but in contrast with tradition, he envisions reconciliation pantheistically in terms of the "sublimation of evil into the godhead."[87] In sum: Wink's unique contribution is that, on the one hand, with the modernists (and liberal theology) he rejects the time-bound metaphysical conception of powers by making them by and large immanent. But in contrast to the modernists, he considers those powers not only real but also robustly influential beyond the physical and visible.

Leading Pentecostal theologian Amos Yong has taken up the earlier powers proposals and reconstructed them in a highly creative and insightful manner in the wider context of plural pneumatology, "spirit-filled cosmos"[88] (on which more below). Before engaging critically these contemporary Christian interpretations of powers and attempting a constructive proposal, let us inquire into the experiences and theological meaning of the powers in other faith traditions.

Spirits and Powers among Living Faith Traditions

Angels and Demons in Abrahamic Traditions

Although belief in angels, demons, and spiritual beings among secular Jews (a majority of whom reside in the United States) is mixed, over half of them no longer affirm the traditional belief;[89] among religious Jews, that belief is still high, and spiritual powers have a definite place in the scriptural tradition.[90] As

85. Walter Wink, *Engaging the Powers: Discernment and Resistance in a World of Domination* (Minneapolis: Fortress, 1992), 65–85.

86. See Wink, *Engaging the Powers*, 44.

87. Walter Wink, *Unmasking the Powers: The Invisible Forces That Determine Human Existence* (Philadelphia: Fortress, 1986), 39.

88. Amos Yong, *The Spirit of Creation: Modern Science and Divine Action in the Pentecostal-Charismatic Imagination* (Grand Rapids: Eerdmans, 2011), 173–225; see also his *In the Days of Caesar: Pentecostalism and Political Theology* (Grand Rapids: Eerdmans, 2010), 121–65.

89. Pew Research Center, "Summary of Key Findings," 11–12.

90. Among the main Jewish movements in the New Testament era, only the Sadducees refused to believe in spirits (Mark 12:18; Acts 23:8).

is well known, the Old Testament term *malak* (messenger) can be used of both divine and human agents; only the context determines the meaning. A special category is the "angel of Yahweh" (Gen. 19; Exod. 14:19; among others), at times identifiable with God himself. Somewhat like Christian tradition in which medieval theology brought about the most sophisticated angelology, in the mystical Jewish Kabbalah the most creative reflection on spiritual beings emerged.

The appearance of demons, evil spiritual beings, in the Old Testament is infrequent, particularly in the postexilic period—although throughout the canon there are less pronounced and more elusive themes of cosmic conflict and chaos (Job 3:8; 38:8–11; Pss. 29:3–4; 89:9–10; Isa. 51:9–11).[91] Unlike Asiatic and other pagan traditions, biblical tradition always subordinates the role of both good and evil angels to Yahweh, and thus avoids dualism. Even the role of Satan, which gradually evolved through history, is that of a subordinate—in some cases, even Yahweh's servant (as in Job). This clear and uncompromising distinction between God and other spiritual beings carried over to Christian tradition beginning from the fathers.

Of the three Abrahamic faiths, it is in Islam that angels and spiritual beings play the most significant role, whether in scriptural tradition or in (folk) piety.[92] Belief in angels is one of the key tenets of Islam, and their denial is regarded as a rejection of the Word of God. Their importance is also highlighted in that, unlike Jewish-Christian tradition, there is a well-known scriptural teaching about angels' creation prior to that of humans and about Allah's consultation with them before creating humans (Q 38:71–72). Somewhat similarly to the Old Testament, the Qur'an provides various kinds of artistic portraits of angels (such as having hands and two, three, or four wings; Q 35:1; 6:93) and speaks of their ministering in various kinds of tasks of service and messaging, including intercession (Q 53:25). A further similarity is an allusion to the hierarchy of angels, Gabriel being the most prominent, and Michael second. The most important angelic task is that of Gabriel as the messenger from whom Muhammad receives the divine revelation. No wonder highly sophisticated angelologies were constructed by leading Islamic philosophers and theologians.

A special class of heavenly beings, the jinn—hugely important in folk Islam—are mentioned often in the Qur'an. They are made of fire (as opposed to humans, who are made of clay). They are endowed with freedom of the

91. Gregory A. Boyd, *God at War: The Bible and Spiritual Conflict* (Downers Grove, IL: InterVarsity Press, 1997), 73–113.

92. Peter G. Riddell, "How Allah Communicates: Islamic Angels, Devils and the 2004 Tsunami," chap. 8 in *A&D*; Bill A. Musk, "Angels and Demons in Folk Islam," chap. 10 in *A&D*.

will, and there is ambiguity about whether they are evil or good; mostly they are taken as evil. Jinn are believed to interact in various ways with humanity. In folk religion, they are frequently invoked for magical and miraculous purposes. Spiritual healers often address the jinn as part of their rituals.[93]

Spiritual Beings and Powers in Asiatic Faiths

The role and nature of angelic beings and powers in Asiatic faith traditions are more complex than in monotheistic traditions. In Hinduism, the contours and definitions are quite elusive. It is often particularly difficult to make a clear distinction between deities and nondivine spiritual beings.[94] In contrast to Abrahamic traditions, even the main deities (such as Vishnu) get entangled in numerous ways in the lives and workings of what Western terminology would name less-than-divine beings. Furthermore, not all demons are evil, as in Abrahamic traditions.[95] The belief in reincarnation blurs any absolute distinction between human and "superhuman" (angelic, demonic) beings. To make the issue more complicated, even *devas* (the godlike or divine beings) are subject to reincarnation; also, it is not impossible for humans in some cases to be reincarnated as *devas*. Because of the complex, multimillennial history of religious and cultural beliefs, it is no wonder that there is a rich diversity of beliefs and traditions and rituals related to either invoking good spirits or trying to cast away evil spirits.

Buddhist traditions have wide and rich demonological traditions with many local colors.[96] Somewhat similar to the temptations of Jesus on the eve of his public ministry, in early Buddhist tradition Mara, the arch-devil, along with his three daughters, Rati (Desire), Raga (Pleasure), and Tanha (Restlessness), sought to dissuade Gautama from achieving enlightenment.[97] Al-

93. Gordon D. Newby, "Angels" and "Jinn," in *The Oxford Encyclopedia of the Modern Islamic World*, ed. John L. Esposito, *Oxford Islamic Studies Online*, http://www.oxfordislamicstudies.com/article/opr/t236MIW/e0061.

94. Chris Gnanakan, "The Manthiravadi: A South Indian Wounded Warrior-Healer," chap. 7 in *A&D*, 141.

95. Walter Stephens, "Demons: An Overview," in *ER* 4:2275; Michael Witzel, "Vedas and Upanisads," in *The Blackwell Companion to Hinduism*, ed. Gavin Flood (Oxford: Blackwell, 2003), 71–73.

96. See Amos Yong, *Pneumatology and the Christian-Buddhist Dialogue: Does the Spirit Blow through the Middle Way?* (Leiden: Brill Academic, 2012), chap. 9.

97. Ananda W. P. Guruge, "The Buddha's Encounters with Mara the Tempter: Their

though the Theravada tradition soon (against its initial intentions, one may argue) began to develop quite sophisticated visions of spiritual beings, that development was even more massive in the various Mahayana traditions and their extremely rich folk piety. Mahayana was also deeply influenced by local cultures, particularly in China, Japan, Tibet, and beyond.

This brief discussion of "other spirits" in four living faiths reveals that there is a remarkable consistency concerning the place of spiritual beings across different traditions, both monotheistic, polytheistic, and "non"-theistic (Theravada). Similarly, belief in spiritual beings seems not to be limited to any cultural or geographical location or to any specific racial group. It is also clear that the basic structure and orientation of the religion, whether strictly monotheistic or not, determines the place of the powers vis-à-vis the Ultimate Reality. In Abrahamic faiths, they are strictly put under the lordship of God. Furthermore, it seems that a division into evil and good forces is a basic human religious intuition even when the boundary line may be variously (or at times ambiguously) drawn. Finally, it is clear that all major faith traditions assume the belief in the influence of the spirits on the affairs of humans and the world. It is curious that what is now considered the normative opinion in post-Enlightenment academia in the West—that spirits are but an archaic, outdated, and mistaken imaginary fantasy—is historically a new and novel view.

Angels and Powers in a Contemporary Theological Account

Does It Make Sense to Speak of Spiritual Powers in Our Scientific Culture?

There is no denying the radical difference between the general worldview of post-Enlightenment Christian theology and the biblical-patristic ethos (stretching all the way to the advent of modernity) regarding the discernment and acknowledgment of spirits and spiritual realities. Even among those moderns who continue affirming belief in the "Great Spirit" (God), belief in lesser spirits has been in steady decline. However, while this trend is strong among Christian theologians, it is much less so among scholars of other faith traditions.

Representation in Literature and Art," *Access to Insight (BCBS Edition)*, November 30, 2013, http://www.accesstoinsight.org/lib/authors/guruge/wheel419.html.

The difficulty with and refusal to acknowledge other spirits have everything to do with the rise to prominence—first among the scientists and philosophers and soon thereafter among theologians and scholars of religions—of various forms of naturalism, the idea that all that there is, is nature; there is no transcendent or spiritual reality—as *reality*. Since the topic was discussed in the doctrine of creation, let it suffice to merely repeat here that naturalism is *an ideological* view of the world and reality. It is not mandated, nor can it be verified by science or philosophical argumentation. (The same of course applies to theism, belief in God and/or divine beings.)

Related is the difficulty for the scientific mind—used to thinking of world processes as following (more or less) deterministic laws of nature—to envision something as counterintuitive as divine action and divine (or divinely created) spiritual beings. In the same chapter on creation, the possibility and conditions of divine action were discussed and defended. Suffice it to say here that once "real" divine action is assumed, no compelling reason would rule out belief in angels, demons, and other spiritual powers. It is particularly critical that academic theology face this inconsistency: How can one believe in the "Great(est) Spirit," God, and fail to be open to the workings of "smaller spirits" created by the same God?

Contemporary theology should also mind much more actively the virtual universality of belief in spirits and spiritual powers throughout global Christianity, as well as among followers of other religious traditions. Those testimonies and experiences must be incorporated into our theological reasoning. Among Pentecostal and charismatic Christians, belief in spiritual beings is taken for granted and engagement with them is a daily experience. The belief in spiritual beings includes the existence of angels and demons, and their influence on the world and human affairs. In this light, it seems both methodologically and materially obscure and unwarranted for theologians to categorically deny the possibility of such spiritual workings.

Having now clarified some of these pertinent orientation issues, we engage key theological questions about this topic.

Assessing the Biblical Teaching on Powers

Biblical testimonies to angels and spiritual powers abound—with the curious exception that there is nothing about angels or other spiritual beings in the creation narratives of Genesis 1–2. That observation, however, does not diminish the importance of considering spiritual beings as created beings in light of later biblical testimonies (particularly those of the New Testament). The importance of affirming their created nature is to place them under the Creator.

In the New Testament, spiritual realities are often treated in a manner that suggests a nonpersonal nature. Just think of expressions such as seven spirits or lampstands, torches, stars, and so forth (Rev. 1:4–20). The mention of four winds (Rev. 7:1; cf. Heb. 1:7) is a reference to cosmic forces, including heavenly "hosts," stars (Isa. 40:26). Importantly, the New Testament also uses nomenclature such as "principalities," "powers," and "thrones" (Rom. 8:38–39; 1 Cor. 15:24; Eph. 1:21; 1 Pet. 3:22).[98] From a pneumatological point of view, what is really significant is the naming of heavenly, angelic forces as "spirits" (*pneumata*) (Heb. 1:14; 12:9; Rev. 1:4; etc.), including "ministering" spirits (Heb. 1:14). What is clear is that all these powers are both created in Christ (Col. 1:16) and subjected under his Lordship (2:15). Barth was thus mistaken in denying that the Scripture says something about the nature of angels, particularly that they are created, are subjected under Christ's Lordship, are ministering spirits, and so on. His opinion is also mistaken for the obvious fact that any description of function assumes some knowledge of the agent.

On the Nature and Origin of Angels and Demons

Departing from Christian tradition, Barth also failed to affirm the fallen nature of some angels and total lack of connection between demonic and good angels. On the contrary, according to the biblical testimonies, the powers are fallen (1 Pet. 3:22; cf. Gen. 6:1–4), an idea that led to the belief in the fall of angels in Jewish apocalyptic (echoed in 1 Pet. 3:19). Although one may not wish to affirm the whole mythical-speculative tradition of the angelic fall after Jewish-Christian tradition, there are no grounds for categorically excluding the demonic spirits from the rest of the spiritual beings, that is, angels. At the same time, the biblical account gives precious few details, if any, of how the powers fell. That said, although fallen, the powers will be redeemed, as Berkhof, Yoder, Grenz, Wink, Yong, and others have rightly argued (Col. 1:15–20; Eph. 1:20–21).

The relation of the "spirits" to the Absolute Spirit is a complicated matter in light of biblical testimonies. Unlike with any other creatures, there is at times a virtual identification of God with angels (Gen. 18:2; 21:17–21; 31:11–13; Exod. 3; Judg. 13:21–23; and so forth). This identification was the reason for Barth's

98. Clinton E. Arnold, *Powers of Darkness: Principalities and Powers in Paul's Letters* (Downers Grove, IL: InterVarsity Press, 1992).

mistaken notion that therefore angels do not have independent being;[99] but that cannot be, because creaturely existence by definition means independence from the Creator.

What about the origin of angelic beings? As said, even the creation narratives do not discuss that topic. In keeping with evolutionary theory, it can be argued that spiritual beings can be envisioned as emergent realities that evolve gradually as part of God's long-term creative process. That said, we have to leave open several questions: on the basis of biblical revelation, we do not know "when" (timewise) angelic beings emerged; tradition's assumption that they are "older" than humans seems to be well taken. How their emergence relates to the evolvement of the physical/material is similarly an unresolved issue in theology. For disembodied beings, as angels are conceived in Christian tradition, to speak of emergence out of the physical does not seem warranted,[100] particularly because even the physical in theistic belief derives ultimately from the spirit(ual). Nor do we know if the evolutionary process of spiritual beings continues or not.

What about the personal nature of angels?[101] In contrast to the current theological majority view but in concurrence with Christian tradition, there are compelling reasons to affirm their personal nature in some real sense. There are two grounds for this. First is the uncontested biblical teaching. Christian tradition had good biblical reasons for conceiving of angels and demons as spiritual agents with intelligence and will (1 Kings 22:19–21; Dan. 10:5–21; Matt. 4:3–11; Mark 5:6–13). Even Pannenberg, who contests their personhood, has to admit that "the forces that are in the service of God's lordship over creation may obviously become autonomous centers of powers."[102] The other reason for affirming some type of personality for angels is related to the emergence argument: as in humans, who have gradually emerged into self-conscious beings with personality, there is no reason in principle to deny that possibility for other beings in the cosmos. That said, in keeping with a plural pneumatology, contemporary theology can easily imagine various types of angelic beings from "personal" to ecclesial (Rev. 2–3), to institutional/corporeal (such as the principalities and powers), to terrestrial (as in Judg. 13:20; Heb. 1:7; Rev. 7:1–2; 16:5), all the way to celestial spirits and forces (Job 38:7; Isa. 40:26; Luke 2:13; Heb. 12:22; Rev. 5:11).[103]

99. Barth, *CD* III/3, 480.

100. Contra Yong, *The Spirit of Creation*, 213.

101. Pannenberg (*ST* 2:106) calls this the "greatest difficulty besetting the traditional doctrine of angels."

102. Pannenberg, *ST* 2:105.

103. For details, see Yong, *The Spirit of Creation*, 214–16.

What about the demonic powers? If evil at large is but the privation of good and thus not an ontological reality (but rather its destruction and perversion, as Augustine and much of Christian tradition have taught), it seems reasonable to think that notions of demons' personal nature must be much more reserved than with regard to angels. This is not to deny their objective nature as an emergent reality but rather to argue that even then they are parasitic.[104] Like good angels, evil, demonic beings can be envisioned under many categories, from the archetypal primeval chaos, to destructive powers, to "domination systems" (social, historical, political, economic, religious, and so on), to regional and geographic entities, and even "anticelestially as fallen angels."[105]

A Theological Assessment of Wink's Immanentist Proposal

What about the debate concerning the powers' immanentist nature? Wink has of course done a great service in exposing the modernist reductionism in its denial of powers. His desire to tackle the biblical text in light of Christian tradition and the post-Enlightenment world is to be acknowledged. What bothers theologians is Wink's totally nonmetaphysical, immanentist interpretation of powers. The theologian may also wonder why one should juxtapose the traditional (and contemporary) "literal" understanding—despite its many problematic applications and experiences—with the current understanding related to powers. Couldn't a plural cosmology have them both? The dual interpretation may best do justice to the diversity of the New Testament materials and also to the theological intuitions of the church. Not only in Paul but also in the Lukan corpus we see the dual reference to the nature of the powers. In the Lukan interpretation the angels/powers are both spiritual (Luke 9:1; Acts 1:8; 8:19; 26:18) and sociopolitical (Luke 12:11; 20:20; 22:25; Acts 9:14; 26:10, 12).[106]

Wink's proposal leads us to the last theme in this section, namely, the question of "spiritual warfare" and tackling the demonic, topics routinely missing in systematic theology works but pertinent to a large number of Christians among all churches in the Global South and Pentecostals/charismatics everywhere.

104. Yong, *In the Days of Caesar*, 162–63.
105. Yong, *The Spirit of Creation*, 218–19.
106. Yong, *In the Days of Caesar*, 149.

Encountering Evil Powers and the Demonic: A Theological Assessment

Resistance among the Theologians

One of the topics that the allegedly *critical* (Western) theological scholarship does not dare touch is the demonic. One wonders how that intentional omission aligns with a truly critical mind-set. Recall William James's warning to his psychology colleagues: "The refusal of modern 'enlightenment' to treat 'possession' as a hypothesis to be spoken of as even a possibility, in spite of the massive human tradition based on concrete experience in its favor, has always seemed to me a curious example of the power of fashion in things scientific."[107]

Barth saw the topic of the demonic and powers so inconsequential to theology that he offered only a "quick, sharp glance" at it.[108] It is ironic that even the most current theologians are simply silent about the whole topic, including Moltmann with his "world-embracing" pneumatological program! (To Moltmann's credit, however, he includes a section on exorcism in the New Testament testimonies to Christ.) With all their criticism of injustice, suffering, and evil in the world, neither feminist and other female pneumatologists nor postcolonialists or other liberationists dare to engage this topic.

The situation is totally different in the Gospels, which describe vividly the acts of demons or evil spirits as they afflict humans. Pauline traditions similarly are no strangers to the demonic (1 Cor. 10:20–21; 1 Tim. 4:1).[109]

A Theological Appraisal of a "Warfare Theodicy"

While appreciative of Wink's achievements, the American open theist G. Boyd attempts to correct his nontranscendent orientation and offer in-

107. William James, "Report on Mrs. Piper's Hodgson-Control," *Proceedings of the English Society for Psychical Research* 23 (1909): 118, cited in Paul Rhodes Eddy and James K. Beilby, "Introduction: Introducing Spiritual Warfare; A Survey of Key Issues and Debates," in *Understanding Spiritual Warfare: Four Views*, ed. James K. Beilby and Paul Rhodes Eddy (Downers Grove, IL: InterVarsity Press, 2012), 18.

108. Barth, *CD* III/3, 519.

109. Consult works of Jeffrey Burton Russell: *The Devil: Perceptions of Evil from Antiquity to Primitive Christianity* (Ithaca, NY: Cornell University Press, 1977); *Satan: The Early Christian Tradition* (Ithaca, NY: Cornell University Press, 1981); *Lucifer: The Devil in the Middle Ages* (Ithaca, NY: Cornell University Press, 1984); and *Mephistopheles: The Devil in the Modern World* (Ithaca, NY: Cornell University Press, 1986).

stead a robust "warfare theodicy" that would allow for the dual interpretation of evil powers. Boyd's basic contention is that not only in the biblical world but also in ancient cultures at large, as well as in the global cultures outside the hegemony of the (European-originated) Enlightenment, the dominant worldview acknowledges evil and good spiritual powers as real.[110] There is a battle between God and Satan, who is allied with his spiritual powers. Yet not all evil in the world can be attributed to Satan; some evils are due to bad human choices and yet others to "natural" evil. No wonder Boyd not only prefers the ancient *Christus Victor* model as the main model of salvation but even considers it the "biblical" model.[111] At the heart of *Christus Victor* is the cosmic battle between God and resisting powers, conquered by Christ, alongside the Father and Spirit. Encouraging Christians to participate in the "good fight" against the evil forces, he is confident that prayer can make a real difference as it participates on God's side in the continuing battle.

Boyd's warfare theodicy's theological benefit is twofold. First, it succeeds in highlighting a more comprehensive account of the demonic when compared to that of Wink. Second, Boyd's model also urges Christians to do something about the demonic and its powers. That said, it is also beset with problems, two of which merit comment in this context. First, notwithstanding the wide attestation in the Bible of "warfare" (power-laden) images, by no stretch of imagination can it be said that this set of images is *the* dominant one. Therefore, second, it is far from certain that one specific metaphor of salvation, in this case *Christus Victor*, should be made the dominant one, much less the only one.

What about exorcism and "spiritual warfare," that is, casting out evil spirits and dealing with demonic influences through prayers and spiritual rites, activities widely present not only in the biblical canon but also in Christian history and currently among many quarters of global Christianity and among Pentecostals/charismatics?

110. G. Boyd, *God at War*; for a summary, see chap. 1 in Gregory A. Boyd, *Satan and the Problem of Evil: Constructing a Trinitarian Warfare Theodicy* (Downers Grove, IL: InterVarsity Press, 2001).

111. G. Boyd, *God at War*, chap. 9.

How to Think Theologically about Exorcism and "Spiritual Warfare"

Its Prevalence in the Bible, among Religions, and in Global Christianity

Not only demons and evil spirits but also the rituals and techniques of exorcism were widely common in the ancient world, and are common also throughout contemporary living traditions, whether in Buddhism,[112] Hinduism,[113] Islam,[114] or elsewhere. Furthermore, no one contests that the New Testament narrative presents a portrait of Jesus as an itinerant healer and exorcist.[115]

The theological meaning of exorcisms and healings can be discerned in the wider context of Jesus's ministry and person. They indicate the power and approval of God at work in his life. In the early church, the practice of exorcism and casting out devils continued, along with healings and other miraculous acts, as an integral part of the church's regular activity of prayer, liturgy, sacraments, and missionary outreach (Acts 5:16; 8:7; 13:6–12; 16:18). Even a few mass exorcisms are recounted, such as the one in Ephesus (Acts 19:11–12).

Arbitrarily determining these narratives to be historically false fables while taking the teaching and pronouncing of forgiveness by Jesus and the early church as authentic is hardly a "neutral" scholarly judgment. Behind it is a deeply skewed modernist epistemology that has a hard time exercising self-criticism against its own unspoken presuppositions.

Theological-Pastoral Guidelines

According to the Pentecostal theologian Amos Yong, who is deeply engaged in the religion-science and interfaith dialogues, resistance to demonic forces may take many forms, including "prayer, fasting, the charisms, spiritual warfare in its various guises, as well as through the methods of

112. Yong, *Pneumatology*, 208–17.

113. Morris E. Opler, "Spirit Possession in a Rural Area of Northern India," in *Reader in Comparative Religion: An Anthropological Approach*, ed. William A. Lessa and Evon Z. Vogt (Evanston, IL, and White Plains, NY: Row, Peterson, 1958), 553–66.

114. "Simple Guide on Islamic Exorcism," https://islamicexorcism.wordpress.com/.

115. Graham H. Twelftree, *Jesus the Exorcist: A Contribution to the Study of the Historical Jesus* (Tübingen: Mohr-Siebeck, 1993).

exorcism deployed by Jesus himself." Then he elaborates in an important manner:

> If the traditional rite of exorcism was designed to expel evil and destructive spiritual realities from the lives of people, then contemporary rites expose and unmask the privative and perverted nothingness of demonic realities. Exorcisms thus can function at various levels:
>
> - Personally, resulting in healing of fractured self-identities (e.g., in terms of Jungian theory);
> - Socially, resulting in reconciliation between people (i.e., in terms of the enactment of spiritual warfare against greed);
> - Politically, resulting in shalom that includes justice (namely, in terms of undermining territorial spirits).[116]

At the same time, theology's task is to subject the habits of exorcisms and spiritual warfare to critical analysis. This critical task relates particularly to a fairly new phenomenon under nomenclatures such as "power encounter," "territorial spirits," "spiritual strongholds," "spiritual mapping," and the like. In some independent Pentecostal/charismatic circles and Global South communities, these kinds of applications of the ancient deliverance motif have received increasing attention.[117] In (semi)popular literature advocating this hermeneutic, it is common to identify spiritual warfare at various levels: "ground level," dealing with influences of the evil in individuals; "occult level," defeating false ideologies such as Satanism, New Age, or Masonry; and "strategic level," fighting "high ranking principalities and powers as . . . demonic entities [which] are assigned to geographical territories and social networks . . . also referred to as territorial spirits."[118] Among these advocates, the theme of spiritual warfare is made central in preaching, teaching, missionary strategizing, and the general ethos of Christian life.

Unfortunately, solid critical scholarly literature produced by the advocates of this kind of "spiritual warfare" is missing, and therefore it is very difficult to offer a fair and comprehensive theological assessment. The foundational

116. Yong, *The Spirit of Creation*, 223; for more details, see Yong, *In the Days of Caesar*, chap. 8.

117. C. Peter Wagner [and Rebecca Greenwood], "The Strategic-Level Deliverance Model," in Beilby and Eddy, *Understanding Spiritual Warfare*, 173–98; for a scholarly presentation and assessment, see Nigel Scotland, "The Charismatic Devil: Demonology in Charismatic Christianity," chap. 4 in *A&D*.

118. Wagner [and Greenwood], "The Strategic-Level Deliverance Model," 179.

challenge to advocates is this: Why would they wish to apply contemporary critical methods of investigation in medicine, law, sociology, and, say, agriculture, but not in religion and theology? Because of lack of critical scholarship, there tends to be a deep black-and-white mentality in the rhetoric and defense of this kind of spiritual warfare. Just consider the uncritical and alarmingly mistaken listing of "enemies," including "Eastern religions" (named as Satanism!). Related is the spiritualizing tendency that sees "spirits" behind abortion, homosexuality, and certain spiritual practices. Apart from the lack of support from biblical sources and tradition, this spiritualizing also begins to cut the legs out from under a careful and thoughtful ethical-moral consideration and search for proper help. The fact that this paradigm has to be rejected theologically and pastorally should not lead critical scholarship to throw out the baby with the bathwater. The need for this dynamic balance also relates to the topic of the next section: the discernment of the Spirit of God among the spirits and truth claims of other religious traditions.

Discerning the Holy Spirit among Religions

As the Indian theologian Joseph Pathrapankal states, the Spirit is "the foundational reality which makes possible for the humans to exercise their religious sense and elevate their self to the realm of the divine."[119] No wonder, then, that part of the cosmic orientation of all traditional and most contemporary cultures in the Global South involves the deep and wide sense of spirits and spiritualities in religions.

Hence, the importance of the theme of the discernment of the Spirit and spirits in the religiously plural world. But, as another Indian theologian, Stanley J. Samartha, notes in recent years, the question of the discernment of the spirits has "somewhat aggressively thrust itself on the theological consciousness of the church"[120] without the needed readiness. Not surprisingly, discussions of the topics in theological textbooks are lacking.[121]

First, the two cousin Abrahamic faiths will be engaged, to be followed by the Asiatic traditions. The final section seeks to develop theological guidelines and criteria.

119. Joseph Pathrapankal, "Editorial," *Journal of Dharma* 33, no. 3 (1998): 299.

120. Stanley J. Samartha, *Between Two Cultures: Ecumenical Ministry in a Pluralist World* (Geneva: WCC, 1996), 187.

121. Stanley J. Samartha, *Courage for Dialogue: Ecumenical Issues in Inter-Religious Relationships* (Geneva: WCC, 1981; Maryknoll, NY: Orbis, 1982), 76.

Ruach *in Jewish Traditions*

Rabbinic and Mystical Interpretations

Because Christians share with Jews the major part of the sacred Scriptures, no separate study of the Old Testament pneumatologies is needed here. In the vast rabbinic literature, interest in the Shekinah, the divine immanence of Yahweh, overshadows discussion of the *ruach*.[122] An obvious reason for focusing less on the "Holy Spirit" in postbiblical Jewish theology seems to be apologetic, that is, the avoidance of too close a connection with the New Testament and emerging Christian theology of the Spirit. Be that as it may, we have to take into consideration also the well-known (but also widely debated) fact that according to the rabbinic sources, God's Spirit has left Israel. That, however, never meant that interest in the Spirit was therefore lost. Based on the scriptural teachings, the rabbinic literature considers *Ruah ha-Kodesh*, "holy spirit" or "spirit of holiness," to be the divinely given power of prophecy and leadership.[123]

Pneumatology in Judaism has undergone significant revisions and transformations, including diverse medieval movements. The Zoharic literature, compiled in the late thirteenth century, represents a culmination of the mystical Kabbalistic traditions and a response to Christian teachings of the Holy Spirit. The focus is on mystical spiritual experience and the union with God. As in rabbinic literature, the Holy Spirit is identified with the Shekinah. It accompanies the people of God and represents the powerful divine immanence in the world, including guidance of the people of God.[124]

Something curious about the pneumatology of *Zohar* is not the existence of evil spirits or "nonholy spirit," but that it "posits secondary 'holy spirits,' that derive from the *Shekinah* and other emanation-related holy spirits."[125] Even angels can be called holy spirits.

122. Joshua Abelson, *The Immanence of God in Rabbinical Literature* (London: Macmillan, 1912).

123. Julie Hilton Danan, "The Divine Voice in Scripture: *Ruah ha-Kodesh* in Rabbinic Literature" (PhD diss., University of Texas at Austin, 2009), http://repositories.lib.utexas.edu/bitstream/handle/2152/17297/dananj31973.pdf?sequence=2.

124. Elliot B. Gertel, "The Holy Spirit in the Zohar," *CCAR Journal: A Reform Jewish Quarterly* 56, no. 4 (2009): 80–102.

125. Gertel, "Holy Spirit in the Zohar," 88.

Contemporary Jewish Pneumatologies

From a Christian perspective, it is interesting to note the influence of Greek-Hellenistic and later modernist philosophies on the conception of the Spirit in Judaism as well. The chapter entitled "The Holy Spirit" in Hermann Cohen's (d. 1918) *Religion of Reason out of the Sources of Judaism* built on the Enlightenment. It follows strictly an ethical-moral (Kantian) model, beginning with the question: "What is human morality?"[126] The only "religious" meaning of the Holy Spirit relates to holiness. The presentation of the theme of the spirit in Samuel S. Cohon's *Jewish Theology: A Historical and Systematic Interpretation of Judaism and Its Foundations* (1971) follows the same kind of immanentist and humanity-focused line.

A markedly different approach is the pneumatology of the contemporary American rabbi Rachel Timoner's 2011 *Breath of Life*, which bears much resemblance to current Christian pneumatologies. Unlike her predecessors, Timoner links *ruach* with "life-giving breath, a simple wind, and the spirit that animates creation."[127] She also forges a link with redemption in a most holistic manner, a move missing in tradition. In keeping with Christian pneumatologists, Rabbi Timoner also discusses topics such as "embodied spirit"[128] and deep interconnection and relationality between the physical and mental/spiritual, personal and communal, human and the rest of creation, and so forth.

The Spirit of Yahweh and the Holy Spirit

Between the Jewish and Christian theologies, talk about the Spirit has to do with how to conceive of the Spirit of the one God in relation to the divine persons (Father, Son, Spirit). Even when that discussion is not likely to lead to unanimity, the conversation partners speak of one and the same God, the Spirit.

Despite deep differences, Christians and Jews should appreciate the great cross-fertilization between the two traditions when it comes to pneumatology. Christian pneumatology owes everything to the Jewish scriptural traditions of

126. Hermann Cohen, *Religion of Reason out of the Sources of Judaism*, translation and introduction by Simon Kaplan, 2nd rev. ed. (New York: Frederick Ungar, 1972 [1919]), 100.

127. Rachel Timoner, *Breath of Life: God as Spirit in Judaism* (Brewster, MA: Paraclete Press, 2011), xviii.

128. Timoner, *Breath of Life*, 17–19.

the Spirit of God.[129] The far-reaching reorientations in contemporary Christian pneumatologies that have dramatically widened the sphere and ministry of the Holy Spirit are but rediscoveries of the Old Testament teaching on *ruach Yahweh*.

The other Abrahamic faith's conception of the Spirit bears significantly less similarity to Christian pneumatology.

Ruh *in the Qur'an and Islamic Spiritualities*

The Spirit in the Qur'an

The Muslim teaching about the Spirit is deeply indebted to older Abrahamic traditions. The basic term *ruh* is, of course, a Semitic cognate with shared meanings of breath, wind, and air. The twenty Qur'anic references to *ruh* can be divided into four "sense-groups."[130] The first group relates to the sayings about the angels and the spirit (97:4). Here the Spirit is (semi) personified.

The second sense-group concerns the sharing of Allah's spirit with humans. Herein the Qur'an makes a definite shift from a (semi)personal agent to an impersonal breath, as in Genesis 2:7. Interestingly, this breathing relates only to Adam (Q 15:29; 32:8; 38:72) and Jesus (4:171), including the passages in which Mary's virginal conception is mentioned (4:171; 19:17; 21:91; 66:12). What is the meaning of the Qur'anic saying that Jesus is a spirit from Allah? Neither divinity, nor trinity as the same sura hastens to add: "So believe in God and His messengers, and do not say, 'Three'" (4:171).

The third sense-group of *ruh* sayings in the Qur'an is the least understood: "Say: 'The Spirit is of the command [*amr*] of my Lord'" (17:85; also 16:2; 40:15; 42:52). The exact meaning of *amr* is disputed: "command" or "affair" or something else?

The final sense-group relates to the important theme of "Holy Spirit," the "Spirit of Holiness." These occurrences emerge at the end of the Prophet's ministry, as he also becomes better informed on Christian faith and the role of Jesus. Three times it is linked with Jesus in terms of Allah "strengthening" or

129. Michel René Barnes, "The Beginning and End of Early Christian Pneumatology," *Augustinian Studies* 39, no. 2 (2008): 169–86.

130. Thomas J. O'Shaughnessy, *The Development of the Meaning of Spirit in the Koran* (Rome: Pont. Institutum Orientalium Studiorum, 1953).

"confirming" him (2:87, 253; 5:110); some other faithful ones are also strengthened with a spirit from Allah (58:22).

Mystical and Charismatic Experiences of the Spirit in Sufism

Grassroots-level enthusiasm over spiritual experience, similar to that of other faiths, appears in Islamic mystical Sufism and related movements. The rapid and steady growth of Sufism and such spiritualist movements is explained at least partly by the full embrace of the spiritual experience and manifestations.[131] No wonder that throughout the years "power encounter" and miraculous acts have been enthusiastically acknowledged and claimed to lie behind many conversions.[132] Particularly important is Sufism's virtual identification of the Spirit of Holiness/Holy Spirit with God himself.

While doctrinally suspect, Sufi mysticism focuses on love and spiritual unity as well as on spiritual experiences. It is said of Husayn ibn Mansur al-Hallajah, a famous ninth-century Sufi mystic, that he "was so full of the Holy Spirit that he could no longer distinguish himself from God," an abomination to the establishment, leading to his crucifixion in 922.[133]

Discerning Differences and Searching for Commonalities

The many common points include the close relationship of *ruh* to Jesus, including the virginal conception, its relationship to the Word of God, the ministry of strengthening the faithful, and so forth. At the same time, one must be careful not to interpret common theological terms such as "spirit" and "word" without taking into consideration the underlying deep theological differences.

An interesting interfaith debate has to do with how to translate and interpret the identity of the Johannine metaphor of the Holy Spirit, Paraclete. There is a long and wide tradition, particularly in folk Islam, of identifying the Paraclete with Muhammad. The dispute goes back to the interpretation of Qur'an

131. Duncan B. Macdonald, "The Development of the Idea of Spirit in Islam: II," *Moslem World* 22, no. 2 (1932): 166.

132. Sobhi Malek, "Islam Encountering Spiritual Power," in *Called and Empowered: Global Mission in Pentecostal Perspective*, ed. Murray W. Dempster, Byron D. Klaus, and Douglas Petersen (Peabody, MA: Hendrickson, 1991), 180–97.

133. James Kritzeck, "Holy Spirit in Islam," in *Perspectives on Charismatic Renewal*, ed. Edward D. O'Connor (Notre Dame: University of Notre Dame Press, 1975), 110.

61:6: "And when Jesus son of Mary said, 'O Children of Israel I am indeed God's messenger to you, confirming what is before me of the Torah and bringing good tidings of a messenger who will come after me, whose name is Ahmad.' Yet when he brought them, they said, 'This is manifest sorcery!'" The *parakletos* ("Counselor") of John 16:7 is equated with *Ahmad* of Qur'an 61:6 (in many English renderings, the "Praised One"). In Islamic tradition a version of Muhammad's name is Ahmad.[134] There are, however, a number of problems with this identification, the most obvious one being that there is absolutely no textual evidence for it in Greek manuscripts of the New Testament. Furthermore, it is doubtful if Muhammad himself would have endorsed this interpretation.

One related theme that may find commonality between Islamic and Christian spiritualities has to do with "remembering." The main task of the Johannine Paraclete is to "bring to your remembrance all that I [Jesus] have said to you" (John 14:26). The theme of remembering is crucial to Islamic tradition; indeed, the Qur'an itself is named *Al-Dhikr*, the "Reminder." Hence, the central exhortation and promise: "So remember Me, I will remember you; and be thankful to Me, and be not ungrateful towards Me" (Q 2:152).[135]

Atman *and the Holy Spirit: Pneumatology in Hindu-Christian Perspective*

Atman Is Brahman

Hindu traditions are united in their belief in the Spirit(ual) as the ultimate reality.[136] What is much more challenging is defining more precisely how to best express in Hindu terms what Christian faith means by "God is spirit" (John 4:24). Reasons for difficulty are many, including that the demarcation lines in Hinduism between "personal" god/deity, spiritual powers, and energies, including those in nature, are fluid and open-ended. Note also that Hindu philosophy knows a number of words that could be translated (something like) "spirit": *atman*, *antaryamin*, and *shakti*, to name the most obvious ones.

Be that as it may, any inquiry into the "pneumatology" of Hinduism must begin with the most foundational statement in Vedic Upanishadic texts:

134. William Montgomery Watt, "His Name Is Ahmad," *Muslim World* 43, no. 2 (1953): 110–17.

135. Kenneth Cragg, *Jesus and the Muslim: An Exploration* (London: George Allen & Unwin, 1985; Oxford: Oneworld, 1999), 260–62, 269, 272–74.

136. M. M. Thomas, "The Holy Spirit and the Spirituality for Political Struggles," *Ecumenical Review* 42, nos. 3–4 (1990): 216.

"that Self [*Atman*] is indeed Brahman,"[137] a topic already dealt with in various chapters above. As the ultimate reality, Brahman is beyond all qualities, definitions, limits; to use Western philosophical terminology, it is absolutely infinite.

Still the question persists: How exactly is this related to pneumatology within this framework? Are there any parallels with Abrahamic faiths?

In Search of Parallels between Hindu and Christian Concepts of the Divine Spirit(s)

In light of the deep spirituality of Indian cultures and religions, it comes as no surprise that Indian Christian theologians have shown remarkable interest in the Holy Spirit through the lens of Indian spiritualities.[138] This search for potential correlations between the two "pneumatologies" has employed two kinds of tactics. One focuses on the concept of "spirit" per se; the other places the Spirit in the Trinitarian context and looks for any links.[139]

As a representative of the first category, we may look at the alleged connecting point between the concept of *shakti* and God's Spirit. *Shakti* is extraordinary power and energy, not limited to the workings of humans but also related to some deities, particularly Durga and Kali, the prominent female deities. Even more important with regard to parallels with the Holy Spirit is the belief in *shakti* as the energy of creation; at times it is called the "Universal Creator."[140] For Panikkar, this was a key: from the Hindu perspective, the Spirit can be described as the "Divine *Sakti* penetrating everything and manifesting God, disclosing him in his immanence and being present in all his manifestations."[141]

More work has been done with the second category, spirit in relation to Trinity. Having investigated Trinitarian parallels in chapter 2, we now highlight

137. Brihadaranyaka Upanishad 2.5.2; *SBE* 15:113.

138. See Robin H. S. Boyd, *An Introduction to Indian Christian Theology* (Madras: Christian Literature Society, 1969), 241–43.

139. P. V. Joseph, *Indian Interpretation of the Holy Spirit* (Delhi: ISPCK, 2007); Kirsteen Kim, "The Holy Spirit in Mission in India: Indian Contribution to Contemporary Mission Pneumatology" (presentation at Overseas Christian Missionary Society, April 6, 2004), http://www.ocms.ac.uk/docs/TUESDAY%20LECTURES_Kirsteen.pdf.

140. B. J. Christie Kumar, "An Indian Appreciation of the Doctrine of the Holy Spirit: A Search into the Religious Heritage of the Indian Christian," *Indian Journal of Theology* 30 (1981): 29.

141. Raimundo Panikkar, *The Unknown Christ of Hinduism: Towards an Ecumenical Christophany*, rev. ed. (Maryknoll, NY: Orbis, 1981), 57.

the Spirit's role therein. In reference to the ancient concept of *saccidananda* ("being," "wisdom," "bliss"), discussed in the chapter on Trinity, some Indian theologians have seen parallels between *Ananda* (bliss) and the Holy Spirit, the bringer of joy and blessedness.[142] While this Hindu interpretation cannot be reconciled with Christianity for obvious reasons such as its lack of "personhood," as a *Hindu* interpretation it deserves attention. But as said before, the general cash value of the attempts to find a parallel between Christian Trinity and Hindu Trimurti is meager at least in light of investigation done so far. Nevertheless, continuing these dialogical exercises is necessary and useful.

Pneumatology in Buddhist-Christian Perspective: The Quest for the Ultimate Reality

If possible, the search for correlates between the Christian Holy Spirit and conceptions of the Spirit in Buddhist traditions is even more complicated a task, beginning with (Theravada's) intentional flight away from the deities. That said, Buddhist "theology" and cosmology are still foundationally idealist, that is, based on the primacy of the spirit(ual) rather than natural (materialist). Having discussed the issue of an ultimate reality (chap. 2), we need merely mention here that the only viable candidate for comparison would be *sunyata* (emptiness).

Indicative of the scarcity of comparative precedents and lack of specification in rare cases where *sunyata* and *pneuma* have been set in parallel is the leading Christian comparative pneumatologist Amos Yong's stance. He obviously assumes at the general level some commonality but fails to specify it in any exact manner. Indeed, Yong rightly mentions at the outset that "in the Buddhist case *shunyata* functions in a non-theistic context," and therefore he finds it useful to relate it to pneumatological anthropology and the discussion of creation at large rather than to the Holy Spirit strictly speaking.[143]

Another potential comparative parallel could be found between Christian Spirit and the "three bodies" (*trikaya*) doctrine of the Mahayana, discussed in the chapter on Christology, particularly its middle category, the "blissful body" (*sambhogakaya*). But even that stays at such a general level that

142. Peter May, "The Trinity and Saccidananda," *Indian Journal of Theology* 7, no. 3 (1958): 92.

143. Yong, *Pneumatology*, 59; a similar tactic is followed in his *The Cosmic Breath: Spirit and Nature in the Christianity-Buddhism-Science Trialogue* (Leiden: Brill, 2012).

at the moment, for the sake of this primer, we can simply register the effort.[144] That said, the parallels also are severely limited by the Christian confession of the Spirit as God.

Trinitarian Guidelines for the Discernment of the Spirit(s) among Religions

We have noted the turn to the Spirit as a potential tactic to ease an interfaith impasse.[145] Although assessments vary, a consensus agrees on the need to develop theological guidelines for the discernment of the Spirit(s) among religions.[146]

The discernment of spirits in the biblical canon is set in a different context from the multifaith world of ours, as it usually connects discernment with the encounters with false prophets. Interestingly, the postbiblical church linked discernment with issues of spirituality and morality.[147] The New Testament's contribution is that the "discernment of spirits" is named as one of the gifts of the Holy Spirit (1 Cor. 12:10).[148]

Alongside these tasks, an urgent domain of investigation relates to the discernment among religions, a topic the Bible addresses only very marginally. Theologically speaking, the task of spiritual discernment encompasses the domains of both the church and the world. An emerging ecumenical consensus considers the main question to be not merely about "*whether* or not the Spirit is at work among people of other faiths" but rather about "how to *discern* the presence and work of the Spirit."[149]

144. J. C. Cleary, "Trikaya and Trinity: The Mediation of the Absolute," *Buddhist-Christian Studies* 6 (1986): 65.

145. Amos Yong, *Beyond the Impasse: Towards a Pneumatological Theology of Religions* (Grand Rapids: Baker Academic, 2013); Gavin D'Costa, "The Holy Spirit and the World Religions," *Louvain Studies* 34, no. 4 (2010): 279–311.

146. Veli-Matti Kärkkäinen, "'How to Speak of the Spirit among Religions': Trinitarian 'Rules' for a Pneumatological Theology of Religions," *International Bulletin of Missionary Research* 30, no. 3 (July 2006): 121–27; Yong, *Pneumatology*, 8–21.

147. Joseph T. Lienhard, "On 'Discernments of Spirits' in the Early Church," *Theological Studies* 4 (1980): 505–29; Amos Yong, "Discernment; Discerning the Spirits," in *GDT*, 232–35.

148. Eduard Schweizer, "On Distinguishing between Spirits," *Ecumenical Review* 41 (July 1989): 406–15; F. Martin, "Discernment of Spirits, Gift of," in *The New International Dictionary of Pentecostal and Charismatic Movements*, ed. Stanley M. Burgess and Eduard M. van der Maas, rev. and expanded ed. (Grand Rapids: Zondervan, 2002), 582–84.

149. Samartha, "Holy Spirit and People," 259.

There are "no simple phenomenological criteria by which we can test the presence of the Holy Spirit."[150] Ultimately, it is a theological and spiritual process of judgment and assessment. Christology is the most important criterion: "Every spirit which does not confess Jesus is not of God" (1 John 4:3). As Newbigin used to say, "the Holy Spirit does not lead past, or beyond, or away from Jesus."[151] The appeal to ethical and liberative praxis, along with Christ, is also important.[152]

We have to keep in mind at all times that our task is discernment, not controlling the Spirit of God. "To ask whether or how the Holy Spirit is at work in the world is to remind the church that the Spirit is not under our control and that it may even challenge us to repent and reform."[153] A work in progress, discernment is not only provisional but also communal and deeply ecumenical in nature; ultimately, it calls for engagement beyond faith traditions.

So far we have discussed the Spirit's role in the Trinity, the cosmos, creation, and among religions. In the following chapter, his work in salvation will be discussed—as most widely understood, including the personal, communal, and sociopolitical (even peace-building) realms. Finally, the Spirit's role in the church is the theme for chapter 9.

150. Paul G. Hiebert, "Discerning the Work of God," in *Charismatic Experiences in History*, ed. Cecil M. Robeck (Peabody, MA: Hendrickson, 1985), 151.

151. Lesslie Newbigin, *The Light Has Come: An Exposition of the Fourth Gospel* (Edinburgh: Handsel, 1982), 216–17.

152. Amos Yong, "The Holy Spirit and the World Religions: On the Christian Discernment of Spirit(s) 'after' Buddhism," *Buddhist-Christian Studies* 24 (2004): 199.

153. Jeremy M. Bergen, "The Holy Spirit in the World," *Vision: A Journal for Church and Theology* 13, no. 1 (Spring 2012): 84.

8 | Salvation

From the "Order of Salvation" to "Salutary Communion"

Ordo Salutis *in the Past and in Contemporary Theology*

Prior to the Reformation, there was very little interest in outlining the temporal or logical sequence of the process of salvation. Thereafter, Protestant orthodoxy in particular developed highly sophisticated presentations of "steps" in the reception and experience of salvation wrought by the Holy Spirit.[1] Some biblical passages, especially Romans 8:29–30, were often invoked as establishing a precedent. A typical definition is this: "The ordo salutis describes the process by which the work of salvation, wrought in Christ, is subjectively realized in the hearts and lives of sinners. It aims at describing in their logical order, and also in their interrelations, the various movements of the Holy Spirit in the application of the work of redemption."[2]

Understandably the order of topics varies among traditions. Whereas for Lutherans, justification through faith comes first, for the Reformed the starting point is election. Hence, following Christ's work finished at the cross, the *ordo* is discussed under rubrics such as "the application of salvation by the grace of the Holy Spirit," and includes topics of election, calling, faith, justification,

1. See Richard A. Muller, *Christ and the Decree: Christology and Predestination in Reformed Theology from Calvin to Perkins* (Durham, NC: Labyrinth, 1986), 79–96.

2. Louis Berkhof, *Systematic Theology* (Grand Rapids: Eerdmans, 1996), 415–16, emphasis removed.

regeneration, union, sanctification/renewal, and glorification. Understandably for the Arminians, because of their unique understanding of election and predestination, the order is somewhat different: outward call, faith/election, repentance, regeneration, justification, perseverance, and glorification. In response to the Reformation, the Catholic Church's Council of Trent began from water baptism and divine-human cooperation in the preparation of the sinner for justification.[3] Generally speaking, "Protestants have tended to think through the categories of justification and sanctification. The Roman Catholic tradition has often seen salvation through the lens of transformation and renewal. Eastern Orthodox traditions have emphasized participation and deification."[4] While embracing the Protestant type of understanding of salvation, Anabaptists also focus on discipleship and "practical Christianity," and Pentecostals on empowerment and healing.

Contemporary international and ecumenical theology, particularly in the Global South—except for the conservative Reformed theologies and traditions under their influence[5]—shows little interest in this kind of analytic exercise. The Lutheran Wolfhart Pannenberg's soteriological discussion, while detailed and long, hardly mentions the term and refuses to follow any certain order.

Jürgen Moltmann's creative revision of soteriological discussion in his pneumatology points out correctly that the analytic steps refer to "different aspects of the one single gift of the Holy Spirit."[6] Moltmann begins with the consideration of "the Spirit of life" and highlights the importance of the Spirit to all of life, including bodily life (chap. 4). The next stage is the "liberation of life," where he speaks of social and political freedom (chap. 5). The "justification of life" speaks not only of the individual's justification but also of justice for the oppressed and other victims, including the structures of societies (chap. 6). The "rebirth to life" relates to "new creation" both at the individual and cosmic levels and hence radically expands the notion of "regeneration" (chap. 7). Similarly, the "sanctification of life" calls for holiness in personal life as well as the need to honor the sanctity of all life (chap. 8). In contrast to usual

3. For details, see Veli-Matti Kärkkäinen, "*Ordo Salutis*," in *GDT*, 622–23.

4. Richard Lints, "Soteriology," in *Mapping Modern Theology: A Thematic and Historical Introduction*, ed. Kelly M. Kapic and Bruce L. McCormack (Grand Rapids: Baker Academic, 2012), 260.

5. See the conservative Calvinist Baptist Millard J. Erickson, *Christian Theology*, 3 vols. in 1 (Grand Rapids: Baker, 1984), 907–84.

6. Jürgen Moltmann, *The Spirit of Life: A Universal Affirmation*, trans. Margaret Kohl (Minneapolis: Fortress, 2001), 82; references in parenthesis are to this work.

discussions, Moltmann also includes the "charismatic powers of life," including speaking in tongues and healing, in his *ordo salutis* (chap. 9). He finishes by developing a theology of mystical union that would achieve a balance between action and meditation (chap. 10).

In keeping with the plural paradigm of pneumatology, contemporary theology aims at a less analytical and abstract "order" and a more comprehensive and inclusive "sketch" of many dimensions of God's gift of salvation. It also corresponds to the plurality of metaphors and images of atonement and reconciliation. Furthermore, unlike the primarily Reformation-driven guilt-, judgment-, and penitence-oriented accounts of justification that dominated the soteriologies of the Christian West, current international theology seeks to do justice to many needs and dimensions of salvation.

To do justice to these many related moves, we have renamed *ordo salutis* "salutary communion."[7] This vision includes the whole salvation history, the importance of community, the sociopolitical and "secular" domains, as well as ultimately the whole cosmos.

The Plan of the Chapter

Building on the plural paradigm of pneumatology constructed in the previous chapter, we will describe the visions of salvation in four living faiths first in the order to be engaged throughout the chapter. The topics named election and calling in the traditional *ordo salutis* will be investigated and reconceived thereafter under "The Divine Favor and Invitation for Eternal Fellowship." Next, conversion, repentance, and forgiveness of sins, similarly, will be surveyed and reconstructed under the heading "(Re-)Turning to God—and to the Neighbor," including a robust interdisciplinary and interfaith aspect. This will be followed by the longest section, "One with God: Justification, Deification, and Sanctification," which includes the classical themes, following the same template.

To correct the astonishing lacuna in all presentations of *ordo salutis*, the ensuing section is titled "Healing, Restoration, and Empowerment." It focuses on theology of healing, restoration, and human flourishing, as well as an ecumenical theology of "Spirit baptism" with a view to empowerment, energizing,

7. F. LeRon Shults and Steven J. Sandage speak of the "*salutary ordering* of persons in community," in *Faces of Forgiveness: Searching for Wholeness and Salvation* (Grand Rapids: Baker Academic, 2003), 156.

and gifting for ministry. Because healing is a common theme among religions, this discussion will engage insights and challenges from other faith traditions as well.

Thereafter, as an integral part of the Christian vision of salvation, we will return to sociopolitical issues, including reconciliation and peacebuilding among peoples. The chapter will end with a short epilogue: "The Faithfulness of God and the End of Human Yearning," which also anticipates eschatological fulfillment of the salvific work of the triune God (chap. 10).

Visions of "Salvation" and Liberation among Religions

Salvation as Redemption and Submission in Abrahamic Faiths

Notwithstanding marked differences among the Semitic faiths concerning human misery (as discussed in theological anthropology), all three faiths place humanity before God. Though somewhat differently, they all consider the "origin" of sinfulness in humanity's deviation from the Creator.

Redemption in Jewish Theology

Because in the normative Jewish (rabbinic) tradition the human person is tasked to choose and follow good inclinations rather than evil, the main term for repentance from evil is *teshuvav*, literally "turning" (to God).[8] Rather than "salvation," Jewish theology speaks typically of "redemption," which appears well over a hundred times in the Old Testament; its key idea has to do with deliverance. While not limited to national deliverance, the idea is present in most Jewish traditions even beyond Zionism.[9]

What about faith and belief? According to Israel Abrahams, in the Jewish "Bible there are no articles of faith or dogmas in the Christian or Islamic sense of the terms." Rather than invitation to believe (in an intellectual sense), the biblical call is for faithfulness. The reason for the absence of catechism (in the Christian sense) is the emphasis on conduct and ethics. That is not to deny

8. Steven Kepnes, "'Turn Us to You and We Shall Return': Original Sin, Atonement, and Redemption in Jewish Terms," in *Christianity in Jewish Terms*, ed. Tikva Frymer-Kensky et al. (Boulder, CO: Westview, 2000), 293–319.

9. Donald Daniel Leslie et al., "Redemption," in *EJ* 17:151–55.

the presence of theological reflection and doctrines in later Judaism. Those came, however, largely because of apologetic need and external pressure. The Shema (Deut. 6:4) is of course the basis and foundation of Jewish faith. Yet monotheism is more than a belief; it is the central thrust of Jewish (and Islamic) faith tradition.[10]

Rightly or wrongly, Jewish theology considers the Christian version of redemption as focusing on the spiritual. This has to do also with the radically different messianic theology, as discussed in Christology. For the Jews, the arrival of the Messiah means the reconciliation and radical reversal of affairs in the world. Recall also that the Jewish concept has nothing to do with a vicarious atonement after Christian tradition. Following the Torah is the way of salvation. The central teaching of Torah is about covenant, and that calls for faithfulness and obedience.

What about contemporary Jewish theology? Notwithstanding great diversity, this much can be said: "In modern Jewish thought redemption has been viewed as referring to the eventual triumph of good over evil, to the striving of individuals to self-fulfillment, to the achievement of social reforms, and also in terms of the reestablishment of a sovereign Jewish state."[11] This is in keeping with the this-worldly orientation of Jewish theology beginning from the Old Testament.

Submission in Islam

Knowledge of the right path and willingness to submit to Allah are the main salvific needs in Islam. Redemption is not a divine gift but rather a result of right choice. Wrong choices cannot be atoned along the lines of Christian theology.

This is not to deny the presence of grace and mercy in Islam, as is evident in the Qur'an's repeated idea of Allah as merciful (24:21).[12] That mercy, however, does not translate into an idea of "justification by faith." Everything is about submitting to the will of Allah, particularly by observing the five pillars (confession of faith, alms, prayers, fasting, and pilgrimage). Access to Paradise will be granted as a "reward for what they used to do" (56:24).

10. Israel Abrahams, Jacob Haberman, and Charles Manekin, "Belief," in *EJ* 3:290–91.

11. Leslie at al., "Redemption," 17:154–55, here 154.

12. Kenneth Cragg, "God and Salvation (an Islamic Study)," *Studia Missionalia* 29 (1980): 154–66.

In sum: "salvation" in Islam means simply submission to Allah. But the fact that salvation ultimately depends on whether or not one wishes to submit does not mean that believing is marginalized. One cannot submit if one persists in ignorance of the revealed will of God. Belief goes hand in hand with repentance (3:16–17; 19:60) and "the works of righteousness," that is, good deeds (4:57).

While deliverance from sin does not have to be excluded from the Islamic vision of salvation, deliverance from eternal punishment, often depicted as the "fire"[13] of hell, seems to be at the forefront.[14] What about "assurance of salvation"? Although Qur'anic promises to those who believe and do good deeds seem assuring, there are also warnings throughout not to fall away (6:82; 4:13). Although one may lose salvation, every believer can also trust Allah's "guidance" (an almost technical term in the Qur'an referring to the divine help for believers, as in 4:51; 6:157; 17:84; 28:49; 67:22; and so forth).

Like other faith traditions' mystical movements, Sufism focuses on personal devotion and repentance. Union with God—theologically a most scandalous idea in light of normal Muslim teaching—comes to the forefront.

The Human Condition and Release in Asiatic Traditions

Moksa, Release, in Hindu Vision(s)

Outlining "salvation" in Hinduism is utterly difficult, not only because there are hardly any binding doctrinal tenets, but also because of its amazing diversity with endless local variations. What is safe to say is that the standard for what is right and true among all Hindu movements is dharma, the "duty," the correct way of life. Its opposite is *adharma.* It is not only or primarily about deeds and behavior but belongs to the wider context in Hindu philosophy of human "bondage" to *avidya*, "ignorance." Ignorance makes one cling to *maya*, "fiction," and thus subject to the effects of karma, leading to rebirths over and over again. Only with the removal of this "ignorance" can the soul's essential nature as pure spirit be restored. To summarize, in most Hindu traditions, release from ignorance is the key, and that leads to ultimate "liberation," *moksa.*

13. See, e.g., surah 2 in the Qur'an.

14. James Robson, "Aspects of the Qur'anic Doctrine of Salvation," in *Man and His Salvation: Studies in Memory of S. G. F. Barndon*, ed. Eric F. Sharpe and John R. Hinnels (Manchester: Manchester University Press, 1973), 205–6.

What about grace in Hindu doctrine? It can be found in theistic Hinduism and, indeed, is a steady part of the *bhakti* (devotional) tradition, particularly in the Bhagavad Gita. Consider this oft-quoted verse (18.58): "When your mind becomes fixed on Me, you shall overcome all difficulties by My grace."[15] Regarding the pursuit of salvation, theistic forms of Hinduism such as Vaishnavism emphasize *bhakti*, devotion to a personal god.[16]

Beyond this broad picture, three major orientations are routinely mentioned: one focused on devotion (*bhakti*), a second one on knowledge (*jnana*), and the third on effort (or work, karma).[17] They are complementary (Gita 2.47–48). For the masses, the devotional theistic Vaishnavism is the way of salvation, following Gita: "But, to those who worship Me as the personal God, renouncing all actions to Me; setting Me as their supreme goal, and meditating on Me with single minded devotion; I swiftly become their savior." A hugely popular figure of devotion is Krishna, the most important *avatara* of Vishnu (discussed in Christology). Only the strict *advaita* of Sankara rejects or, at its best, tolerates *bhakti*; most all other traditions are open to it.

Among the philosophically minded elite, particularly within the strict *advaita* of Sankara, the knowledge-based way is to pursue release from ignorance. The third path, work driven, holds a most fundamental position and is not necessarily an alternative to the other two. It is connected with liberation because liberation consists in the complete freedom from karma and from all its consequences. Each person, possessing divine nature, can attain liberation by the person's own moral choices and good deeds. In the twentieth century, the most well-known advocate of this path has been Mahatma Gandhi, who also, typical of a general trend, combined it with *bhakti*; for him, the Gita was a "spiritual dictionary."[18]

Enlightenment: Buddhist Visions of Liberation

The chain of kamma due to ignorance can only be broken through enlightenment, a result of right insight. Even Buddha is not a savior but rather an

15. Similarly 18.62.

16. John B. Carman, *Majesty and Meekness: A Comparative Study of Contrast and Harmony in the Concept of God* (Grand Rapids: Eerdmans, 1994), 94–96.

17. Klaus Klostermaier, *A Survey of Hinduism*, 3rd ed. (Albany: State University of New York Press, 2010), chap. 9 (karma), chap. 12 (*jnana*), and chap. 15 (*bhakti*).

18. Harold Coward, *Sin and Salvation in the World Religions: A Short Introduction* (Oxford: Oneworld, 2003), 117.

example to follow. Although many movements (of Mahayana particularly) acknowledge the concept of grace and (divine) assistance in search of liberation, ultimately liberation is dependent on one's own effort.

"Enlightenment"—or insight—is the favored soteriological term. Following the teachings of Buddha as expressed in the Noble Eightfold Path,[19] as well as emulating his experience, it alone paves the way to release from false attachment, including the error of considering one's self permanent. Mahayana in particular has also developed a growing tradition of spiritual exercises in pursuit of liberative insight.[20]

The most distinctive vision of liberation can be found in the Mahayana Pure Land tradition developed by Shinran (1173–1263), which, as discussed, is deeply theistic and envisions a kind of savior. But that movement is an exception to the Buddhist rule of everyone being one's own savior.

Now that we have introduced the broad visions of salvation and liberation in four other living traditions, it is time to delve into key Christian soteriological topics. In each case, where relevant in light of the self-understanding of other faiths, a sympathetic and critical dialogue will be attempted.

The Divine Favor and Invitation for Eternal Fellowship (Election, Calling)

The Doctrine of Election in History

In patristic theology, until Augustine there was very little specific interest in formulating any theory of election. While the fathers were convinced of divine election, their concerns were different from those of later tradition in which the individual person's salvation (or damnation) became the burning issue. For patristic thinkers, particularly in the Christian East, pagan fatalism loomed large. A related factor is that it took until Augustine's time to have an established doctrine of original sin (in the Christian West). Fathers universally believed in the freedom of the will (without of course denying sinfulness per se).

The controversy between Pelagius and Augustine was a watershed, the former rejecting the Augustinian (and later mainline Christian) idea of the serious weakness of the will because of the Fall. Pelagius maintained that men

19. Walpola Rahula, *What the Buddha Taught*, rev. ed. (New York: Grove, 1974), chap. 5.

20. Kristin Johnston Largen, *What Christians Can Learn from Buddhism: Rethinking Salvation* (Minneapolis: Fortress, 2009), 108–29.

and women are able to choose between good and evil not only concerning this life but also "before God."[21] Although Pelagianism died hard, as early as the Council of Orange (529) it was ruled that the human person is not free apart from God's grace to believe and that God's salvific response does not come as the rewarding of the uttermost effort of humanity.[22] Not unaware of criticism by his opponents,[23] Augustine consolidated his view of the sovereignty of God and unconditionality of divine election in eternity. The "double predestination" view resulted: people are destined for condemnation unless they will be rescued from it by God's sovereign choice.[24]

Much later, in Calvin's theology,[25] particularly among his followers, and in Anglicanism,[26] this idea came to its fullest fruition and, not surprisingly, was vehemently resisted by the Arminian party.[27]

While in Luther's view the human will is unable to take any initiative toward salvation—as evident in his extended fight with the humanist Catholic Erasmus[28]—there is, strictly speaking, no doctrine of double predestination. A further difference between the Reformed and Lutheran traditions is that the latter do not distinguish between the "external" and "effectual" calling[29] but rather consider the Spirit's invitation effective unless one willfully resists. Between Roman Catholics and Protestants, particularly the Reformed, there is, generally speaking, a marked difference in the approach to election. Notwithstanding

21. *Pelagius' Commentary on St. Paul's Epistle to the Romans*, trans. Theodore DeBruyn (Oxford: Oxford University Press, 1998). Written before the controversy with Augustine.

22. Consult Pelikan, *CT* 1:307–31 (the patristic era), and Pelikan, *CT* 3:80–95 (the medieval period).

23. He responded to criticism in *On the Predestination of the Saints* and *On the Gift of Perseverance*.

24. Augustine, *A Treatise on the Soul and Its Origin* 4.16.

25. Calvin, *Institutes* 3.21.5.

26. Jonathan Edwards, *Freedom of the Will* [1754], vol. 1 of *The Works of Jonathan Edwards*, ed. Paul Ramsey (New Haven: Yale University Press, 2009).

27. Jacobus Arminius, "On Predestination," V.I, in vol. 1 of *Works of James Arminius* (available at http://www.ccel.org/ccel/arminius/works1.iii.ii.html). The classic texts with critical notes of Five Points of the Remonstrants (1610) on the Arminian side and the Canons of Dort (1618–1619) on the Calvinist side can be found in Philip Schaff, ed., *The Creeds of Christendom*, 3 vols. (New York: Harper & Row, 1877; 6th ed. reprint, Grand Rapids: Baker, 1990), vol. 3, www.ccel.org.

28. Luther's *Bondage of the Will* (1525) and Erasmus's *Freedom of the Will* (1524) can be found in Gordon Rupp and Philip S. Watson, eds., *Luther and Erasmus: Free Will and Salvation* (Philadelphia: Westminster, 1969); highly useful discussion can be found in the editors' introduction (1–32).

29. Michael Horton, *The Christian Faith: A Systematic Theology for Pilgrims on the Way* (Grand Rapids: Zondervan, 2011), 572–75.

Augustine's heritage, the Roman Catholic Church does not endorse the doctrine of divine predestination or reprobation apart from human response.[30]

What can be named "milder predestinarianism"[31] became the mainstream opinion in the Christian West, according to which election to salvation is affirmed, but not reprobation. Although the Eastern Church is of course not Pelagian, it is totally removed from the Protestant views and debates. They reject the idea of God choosing to send part of humanity to damnation prior to making any choices and they uphold the freedom of the will.

Contemporary Formulations

The Reformed theologian Karl Barth attempted a massive revision of the standard Augustinian-Calvinistic view, which for him appeared both "obscure" and "dark" in its one-sided emphasis on divine determinism as it cast a shadow on the freedom of grace. In a radical departure from tradition, Barth famously shifted the focus from the election of human beings to that of Christ, the Mediator who is both the Electing God and the Elected Man.[32] Christ is the only elected and "the organ and instrument of the whole election of God" from eternity.[33] The traditional "double predestination" is strictly rejected, and a radically revised "double predestination" in terms of the dual role of Christ and his "dual treatment"—rejection (crucifixion) and vindication (resurrection)—is put in its place. Assessments regarding Barth's proposal vary. What concerns critics particularly is that there hardly is any biblical basis for making Christ the "object" of election. Barth's proposal also suffers from the dangers of universalism[34] (a topic to be discussed in eschatology).

Pannenberg has also radically revised the discussion. He places it after soteriology and the church, and it is ominously titled "Election and History."[35] Having critiqued harshly the Augustinian-Calvinistic view of election (§1, on which more below), he discusses "the church as the people of God" (§2) and makes the case that God's election has its focus and aim in building up the

30. *Catholic Catechism* ##600, 1037.

31. So named by Paul King Jewett, *Election and Predestination* (Grand Rapids: Eerdmans, 1985), 7.

32. Barth, *CD* II/2, 103.

33. Barth, *CD* II/2, 116.

34. Oliver D. Crisp, "The Letter and the Spirit of Barth's Doctrine of Election: A Response to Michael O'Neil," *Evangelical Quarterly* 79 (2007): 53–67.

35. Pannenberg, *ST*, vol. 3, chap. 4. Section numbers in the following text refer to this work.

church; Pannenberg widens the sphere of discussion and speaks of even nations and peoples in history.

Revising and Reorienting the Doctrine of Election

A number of reorientations have emerged among contemporary theologians. Rather than abstract speculation into the "mind of God," the discussion would do well to take its lead from the doctrine of revelation, as discussed in chapter 1:

> In His goodness and wisdom God chose to reveal Himself and to make known to us the hidden purpose of His will (see Eph. 1:9) by which through Christ, the Word made flesh, man might in the Holy Spirit have access to the Father and come to share in the divine nature (see Eph. 2:18; 2 Peter 1:4). Through this revelation, therefore, the invisible God (see Col. 1:15; 1 Tim. 1:17) out of the abundance of His love speaks to men as friends (see Ex. 33:11; John 15:14–15) and lives among them (see Bar. 3:37), so that He may invite and take them into fellowship with Himself.[36]

This profound statement assures us that the Father, out of abundant love, having revealed himself in the Son, through the Spirit is actively and passionately seeking fellowship with us. This anchors election in history, and its context is the spiritual community. Theological tradition should have borne this in mind rather than—as happened in the Augustinian-driven theology—locating divine election in eternity, apart from and unrelated to historical happenings and choices of human beings, and focusing it on individuals. In this light, we can see the liabilities and limitations of the traditional doctrine of election originally devised by Augustine:

1. It makes the divine decision timeless, in abstraction from the concrete historicity of the divine acts of election as the Bible bears witness to them.
2. It detaches individuals as the object of election from all relations to society.
3. It restricts the purpose of election to participation in future salvation in disjunction from any historical function of the elect.[37]

36. *Dei Verbum*, #2.
37. Pannenberg, *ST* 3:442.

All these lacunae need correction, as we can learn from the biblical narrative.[38] In the Old Testament, persons such as Abraham and David are elected for the sake of the community and the mission of Yahweh to the nations. Similarly, in the New Testament persons are called to salvation for which they have been foreordained; indeed, one has a hard time finding programmatic statements about "double predestination" when it comes to our eternal destiny. Consider Ephesians 1:4, which is routinely misappropriated to support the traditional view. Having mentioned that God "chose us in him [Christ] before the foundation of the world," the text says that its goal is "that we should be holy and blameless before him" and continues highlighting the salvific gifts in Christ, culminating in the Spirit. The conclusion is that "God wills the salvation of all, offers it to all, and holds those to be without excuse who reject it, his predestination must be based on his foreknowledge of who will and who will not accept the grace offered in Christ."[39] Along with the earliest patristic theology, this view dominates throughout the Eastern Orthodox tradition and is materially similar to that of Arminianism. Furthermore, the biblical theology of election is intertwined with the idea of calling and sending out for God's mission, as can be seen in the case of Abraham (Gen. 12:2–3).

Election is based on God's "unbounded generosity." "The God we love and trust is not One to be satisfied until there is a healing of the nations and an innumerable host of redeemed people around his throne (Rev 7:9; 21:24–26; 22:2–6)." This attitude speaks of hospitality, a "hermeneutic of hopefulness"[40] as opposed to the "fewness doctrine," according to which only a small number of people will be saved.[41]

On the other hand, should the human person refuse the invitation, the Creator honors the (relative) human freedom graciously granted by that same Creator. Eliminating all human choice—on the basis of eternal divine determination done before time and unrelated to historical happenings—seems a strange and perverted way of appreciating the fatherly love of the Creator God. Could we think of the heavenly Father as any "worse" than an earthly father? This personal-relational aspect is lost in the Augustinian-Calvinist scheme. What it rightly emphasizes is the sovereignty and grace of God in salvation. It misses relationality in the way it formulates the idea of God's graciousness and power in terms of the human person's total incapacity and passivity.

38. Jewett, *Election and Predestination*, chap. 2.

39. Jewett, *Election and Predestination*, 68.

40. Clark H. Pinnock, *A Wideness in God's Mercy: The Finality of Jesus Christ in a World of Religions* (Grand Rapids: Zondervan, 1992), 18–20.

41. Pinnock, *Wideness in God's Mercy*, 13–14.

What about other religions? Do they know election? Is there freedom of choice?

Determinism, Fatalism, and Freedom of Will among Religions

On the one hand, "the essential presupposition of most major religions is that humans are born with freedom of choice."[42] On the other hand, most of the religions at the same time embrace the idea of divine election or divine determinism of some sort.

Election and Free Will in Abrahamic Traditions

The most peculiar and formative doctrine of election can be found in Judaism. The idea of "chosen people" defines her identity. It is based on the covenant between Yahweh and his people, going back to Abraham. Deuteronomy 7:6 summarizes election succinctly: "For you are a people holy to the Lord your God; the Lord your God has chosen you to be a people for his own possession, out of all the peoples that are on the face of the earth" (see also 14:2).[43]

Election is solely based on Yahweh's love and purposes. It happens despite the unworthiness of the elected one. The selection of some is for the sake of the people and her mission to other nations rather than for their own benefit.

As with everything else in Jewish tradition, catastrophic events helped consolidate and reshape theological views. With regard to election, the exile was the first such formative event, and the destruction of the temple and ensuing diaspora in 70 CE another. The rabbinic emphasis on Yahweh's election also had to do with the strong resistance to Christian theology's implication that Israel was no longer the chosen people.

What about freedom of the will? Differently from Christian and Islamic versions of robust predeterminism, Jewish tradition does not interpret divine action in a way that would frustrate the exercise of human free will and consequently responsibility. According to Moses Maimonides's oft-cited statement, "Man does what is in his power to do, by his nature, his choice, and his will; and his action is not due to any faculty created for the purpose."

42. Ileana Marcoulesco, "Free Will and Determinism," in *ER* 5:3200.

43. Ellen M. Umansky, "Election," in *ER* 4:2744.

Not only that, but "all species of irrational animals likewise move by their own free will."[44]

In Islam, election does not play the same crucial role as in Judaism. Islamic theology emphasizes the election of several key persons such as Noah, Abraham, and prophets. The greatest stress understandably is placed on the election of the Prophet, Muhammad, and the community established by him (*ummah*). The Qur'an teaches that while other nations might have known God, only Muslims know Allah intimately and are rightly related to God (37:40; 38:40).[45]

A dominant principle of the Qur'anic teaching has to do with human responsibility, the shorthand for which is obedience (submission) to Allah. Indeed, there are hundreds of such Qur'anic texts.[46] That said, as is well known, other important Qur'anic passages seem to deny any notion of human freedom of choice. Consider 35:8: "Indeed God leads astray whomever He will and guides whomever He will" (also 8:17–18). Hence, similarly to Christian theology, fierce continuing debates have been fought in Islamic philosophy and theology.

Already at the end of the first Islamic century, a vigorous protest arose to challenge and refute the prevailing deterministic, often fatalistic, emphasis on divine determinism. One of the most ironic—if not also confusing—terms in Muslim tradition is "Qadarites." From the term "to determine," *qadar*, it was applied astonishingly to both those who subscribed to divine determinism and those who exempted human free choice from divine determination![47] The term, however, eventually came to be applied to the latter group. Generally speaking, the Qadarites wished to affirm human free will, which in turn justified God's punishment for intentional wrongdoings. In other words, freedom of the will entails responsibility. Later the influential Mu'tazilite movement adopted materially the Qadarite view in contrast to the fierce opposition by the dominant Asharite tradition, ratified by the majority Sunni movement. The most famous philosopher, al-Ghazali, an Asharite, helped found "occasionalism," a theory of causation according to which God is the sole acting agent and created beings are not acting agents. This, however, does not rule out all human freedom.

44. Moses Maimonides, *The Guide for the Perplexed*, trans. M. Friedländer (sacred-texts .com [1903]), 3.17; 287.

45. Umansky, "Election," 2748.

46. M. A. Rauf, "The Qur'ān and the Free Will [I]," *Muslim World* 60, no. 3 (1970): 206.

47. William Montgomery Watt, *Islamic Philosophy and Theology: An Extended Survey* (Edinburgh: Edinburgh University Press, 1962), chap. 5.

Modernist Muslim commentators argue that, notwithstanding diversity, the Qur'an endorses the concept of human freedom in choosing one's belief and human responsibility for human actions. God has foreknowledge of human actions, but this divine knowledge does not compel humans to commit sin.[48]

In sum: all Abrahamic faiths are bound to robustly affirm relative yet genuine freedom of the will and ensuing moral and religious responsibility. What about Asiatic traditions?

Determinism, Fatalism, and Free Will in Asiatic Traditions

The following statement helps put in perspective Abrahamic and Asiatic traditions in this regard: "The main traditions of Hinduism and Buddhism do not posit a personal deity with an omnipotent will, and thus the polarity of free will and predestination in relation to the salvation of souls has not been so prominent as in Judaism, Christianity, and Islam. The doctrine of *karman* can constitute a kind of determinism whereby an individual's lot in life is determined by his behavior in past lives, but the doctrine can also imply that a soul is in charge of its future destiny; its modern proponents therefore sometimes consider the doctrine to imply freedom more than fatalism."[49]

From the perspective of the Abrahamic faiths, it is not readily evident how to negotiate freedom and determinism in relation to karma, an ironclad principle. The freedom principle comes to the fore particularly in the ancient concept of *svaraj* (self-ruling), which Mahatma Gandhi took as the basis for his social activism.[50] The Hindu expert Klostermaier affirms, "*Karma* does not cancel free will and genuinely free decision, nor do free will and one's own decisions neutralize *karma*."[51] Be that as it may, a whole spectrum of interpretations is found in diverse Hindu traditions.[52]

Talk about divine election is even more marginal to Buddhists than to Hindus. This is not to deny the possibility of an idea of divine favor or election

48. William Montgomery Watt and Asma Afsaruddin, "Free Will and Predestination: Islamic Concepts," in *ER* 5:3213.

49. Dewey D. Wallace, "Free Will and Predestination: Christian Concepts," in *ER* 5:3204.

50. Mohandas K. Gandhi, *Hind Swaraj or Indian Home Rule*, https://www.mkgandhi.org/hindswaraj/hindswaraj.htm.

51. Klostermaier, *Survey of Hinduism*, 176.

52. For the complexity of the issue in theistic, particularly *bhakti* spiritualities, see Ankur Barua, "The Dialectic of Divine 'Grace' and 'Justice' in St Augustine and Sri-Vaisnavism," *Religions of South Asia* 4, no. 1 (2010): 46.

among some theistically driven Mahayana movements; it is rather a summary statement about Buddhist doctrine at large.[53] Scriptures add to the complexity. Because of causal relations and interdependence of the world, as well as the denial of the existence of "soul," there seems to be very little room for personal choice, even responsibility. On the other hand, because there is no god to depend on, the human person is left totally on one's own in the pursuit of "salvation."[54] Following the Buddhist "middle way," a fitting conclusion says something like this: "The Buddha rejected the philosophical extremes of both determinism and indeterminism and discouraged his followers from embracing any view that might undermine their inspiration to devote themselves to an ethical life in the pursuit of liberation."[55]

Now that we have looked at the divine initiative in salvation, it is natural to move to the human response under the classic rubrics of conversion, repentance, and forgiveness of sins.

(Re-)Turning to God—and to the Neighbor (Conversion, Repentance, and Forgiveness of Sins)

A Theology of Conversion

A common term in the Christian and wider religious thesaurus, "conversion"[56] also elicits a number of debates about its meaning[57] and suitability for the current postmodern[58] and pluralistic context of ours. "Conversion" also has a loaded history, as it has been linked with proselytism, colonialization, and similar suspicious activities.

53. Nicholas F. Gier and Paul Kjellberg, "Buddhism and the Freedom of the Will: Pali and Mahayanist Responses," in *Freedom and Determinism*, ed. Joseph Keim Campbell, Michael O'Rourke, and David Shier (Cambridge, MA: MIT Press, 2004).

54. Asaf Federman, "What Kind of Free Will Did the Buddha Teach?" *Philosophy East & West* 60, no. 1 (2010): 1–19.

55. B. Alan Wallace, "A Buddhist View of Free Will: Beyond Determinism and Indeterminism," *Journal of Consciousness Studies* 18 (2011): 217–33.

56. Bryant M. Darroll and Christopher Lamb, eds., *Religious Conversion: Contemporary Practices and Controversies* (New York: Casell, 1999).

57. Hugh T. Kerr and John M. Mulder, eds., *Conversions: The Christian Experience* (Grand Rapids: Eerdmans, 1983; republished as *Famous Conversions: The Christian Experience*, 1994).

58. Brad J. Kallenberg, "Conversion Converted: A Postmodern Formulation of the Doctrine of Conversion," *Evangelical Quarterly* 67 (1995): 335–64.

The traditional theological *ordo salutis* included "repentance" under conversion as the way to turn away from sin, with accompanying regret and remorse as conditions for turning to Christ in faith. Depending on one's theological tradition, conversion is either followed by regeneration/new birth (Lutheranism) or preceded by it. Similarly to forgiveness, repentance and conversion, as personal acts, are also integrally related to sacraments, particularly to the sacrament of reconciliation (penance) and the Eucharist. In all Abrahamic faiths, conversion also relates to the neighbor.[59]

Biblical Perspectives

The very first public announcement of Jesus in Mark's Gospel has to do with repentance (1:15). Like the main term denoting conversion in the Old Testament, *shuv*, the New Testament *epistrephō* means "to turn (around)." The religious usage of these terms entails turning away from evil and disobedience to serving God. Other important New Testament terms are *metanoeō*, "to repent" (from the literal meaning "thinking-after"), and *metamelomai*, "to regret." The presence together of the first two in Acts 3:19–20 demonstrates the idea of conversion in terms of re-turning and repentance/regret.[60]

Unlike common assumptions, in the Bible, particularly in the Old Testament, conversion is rarely linked with the change of religion; it is rather a call for the people of Israel to (re-)turn to God. This is of course not to undermine the possibility of changing religion in our contemporary pluralistic world, but rather to remind us of the central place of the idea of conversion in the life of the people of God.

What was the main target of conversion and repentance in Jesus's message? Did he address mainly individuals or the whole people of God? While both opinions have honored advocates, it seems that they should not be taken as alternatives and that Jesus's focus was on the individual. This is a marked revision of the Old Testament prophets' focus mainly on nations and their leaders.

Saint Paul's conversion experience has drawn wide interest (as narrated in Acts 9:1–19; 22:3–21; 26:1–23 and referred to by Paul in his own writings).[61]

59. Dawn DeVries, "What Is Conversion?" in *How Shall We Witness? Faithful Evangelism in a Reformed Tradition*, ed. Milton J. Coalter and Virgil Cruz (Louisville: Westminster John Knox, 1995), 28.

60. Richard V. Peace, *Conversion in the New Testament: Paul and the Twelve* (Grand Rapids: Eerdmans, 1999), 346–53.

61. Seyoon Kim, *The Origin of Paul's Gospel* (Grand Rapids: Eerdmans, 1981), 3–31.

While we have to leave to the New Testament experts the continuing debate about whether Paul's was a call (to ministry) more than an initial conversion, theologically it seems best not to keep these two at arm's length from each other.

A Comprehensive Theology of Conversion

Theologically, conversion is "a work of the Holy Spirit, involving the mystery of divine initiative and human response at the same time. It is a restoration of relationship between us and God which involves a reordering of relationships with others."[62] The American Methodist biblical scholar Joel B. Green's account of conversion as "a many-sided affair" illustrates this inclusive meaning: "It is first the story of God's provenience, God's gracious visitation that precedes and opens the way for human responses of changed hearts and lives. This conversion reaches the whole of life and cannot be reduced to one's inner being."[63]

Indeed, one of the emerging themes in contemporary theology of conversion involves its linking with the whole human being, not merely the inner or spiritual. What about the emphasis on "spiritual," onetime conversion in this light?

Conversion in Revivalism

Conversion has been a main theme in revivalism throughout history, all the way to today. Understandably, it has also been criticized as an overly eager method to win converts and for its "onetime-fix" mentality.

Clearly, in the New Testament, conversion is both an event and a process, not merely a onetime experience. When the process nature is taken into consideration, the typical complaints against revivalism—that its message is thin, its follow-up is weak, it tends to triumphalism, and it neglects previous religious experiences of the people—can be defeated. On the other hand, those who see conversion only as a lifelong gradual process could take a lesson from the decisive challenge coming from revivalism toward a conscious

62. Ross Langmead, "Transformed Relationships: Reconciliation as the Central Model for Mission," *Mission Studies* 25, no. 1 (2008): 10.

63. Joel B. Green, *Why Salvation?* (Nashville: Abingdon, 2013), 115.

decision of faith.[64] The Anabaptist ethicist Erin Dufault-Hunter's expression of "conversion to thick faith [that] envelops all aspects of a person's life," illustrates this.[65]

In light of the perceived liabilities of the revivalistic traditions' view of conversion, some leading advocates are working toward redefining conversion: "Older revivalism assumed that conversion was punctiliar, that the focus of a converted life was religious activities, in anticipation of a life 'in heaven' that would come after death, and that this 'conversion' was essentially an interior, personal, and subjective transaction. Revivalists had little appreciation of the place of the sacraments or the intellect in spiritual life. For the revivalists, the church has only one agenda: to obtain conversions; to be successful, congregations should have plenty of growth by conversion."[66] To that litany can be added the use of fear of death as a motive for conversion, as is evident, for example, in John Wesley.[67] As a way of correction, a new paradigm for understanding conversion is emerging in which

- heart and mind will be integrated;
- body and mind will be integrated;
- individual and communal aspects will be noted;
- human will and divine initiative will be put in a dialectical mutual relationship;
- conversion will be seen as both an "arrival" and a "beginning";
- the sacraments will be incorporated into conversion;
- the transmission of Christian faith from one generation to another will not be dismissed; and
- the hope for the world to come and this-worldly focus will be put in a dialectical relationship.[68]

The maturation of the revivalist tradition, as clearly evident in this revised account of conversion, possesses amazing ecumenical potential. It may also

64. Peace, *Conversion*, chaps. 11; 12; 13.

65. Erin Dufault-Hunter, *The Transformative Power of Faith: A Narrative Approach to Conversion* (Lanham, MD: Lexington Books, 2012), x.

66. Gordon T. Smith, *Transforming Conversion: Rethinking the Language and Contours of Christian Initiation* (Grand Rapids: Baker Academic, 2010), ix; for details, see 1–16.

67. Kenneth J. Collins, "John Wesley and the Fear of Death as a Standard of Conversion," in *Conversion in the Wesleyan Tradition*, ed. Kenneth J. Collins and John H. Tyson (Nashville: Abingdon, 2001), 56–68.

68. Smith, *Transforming Conversion*, 17–18.

help the more traditional ecclesiastical families to rediscover in their daily practice the importance of conversion.

What about conversion studied from a human perspective?

A Theological Assessment of Interdisciplinary Study of Conversion

The rise of new religious movements in recent decades has elicited interest among researchers of conversion.[69] The American pragmatist William James's *Varieties of Religious Experience* (1902) famously defined the *experience* of conversion in terms of a transformed self-perception related to religious ideas and realities. For him the content of these ideas was secondary; what mattered was a new kind of attitude and direction for life. A much more thoroughgoing dismissal of the *content* of the experience of conversion came from nineteenth-century atheism, followed by current neo-atheism. The assumption is that not only is there no content behind religious conversion but also that whatever there is, is harmful and even violent. Not infrequently, in sociology (of religion) the convert appears not only as an object of proselytizing activity but even as a victim of it.[70] Conversion may be attributed, for example, to overwhelming emotional states. Part of this tendency is the linkage of religious conversion with social and economic deprivation.

Although the theologian has no need to deny that in some cases conversion can be explained with the help of these models, many—probably most—seemingly healthy, rational, and well-to-do people undergo and sustain a religious conversion experience. Similar critique can be targeted against the neuropsychological and neurocognitive study of conversion that has tended to explain conversion with the help of abnormal experiences such as seizures or epilepsy. Although, for example, the relationship between epilepsy and heightened religious activity and mystical experiences can be statistically established,[71] it would be absurd to make all conversions a merely neuronal act!

All these approaches to the study of conversion among various disciplines tend to be reductionist in that they focus solely on phenomenology or experience or alleged sociological reasons such as deprivation. Second, the main theological lacuna has of course to do with the dismissal of the content of belief.

69. James T. Richardson, "Conversion and New Religious Movements," in *Encyclopedia of Social and Political Movements*, ed. D. Snow et al. (Oxford: Blackwell, 2013).

70. William Sims Bainbridge, "The Sociology of Conversion," in *HRC*, 178–91.

71. Warren S. Brown and Carla Caetano, "Conversion, Cognition, and Neuropsychology," in *HRC*, 147–58.

More conducive to theological intuitions is the emerging study of conversion in "neurotheology" or "spiritual neuroscience," which, on the one hand, takes seriously the neurological basis of all human experiences but, on the other hand, does not necessarily reduce conversion experience to the physical basis. It rather allows the human being to be reshaped over the years.[72]

Conversion in the Religiously and Culturally Pluralistic World

Conversion continues to be an area of interest to anthropologists, who have gathered valuable information in various global and religious contexts.[73] Because of its deeply missionary nature, conversion to Islam has also been widely studied in various global locations.[74]

Not surprisingly, postcolonialist theorists have approached the topic with great suspicion, as "conversion to a world religion, such as Islam or Christianity, is interpreted as a part of the 'colonization of the mind and spirits' of the dominated peoples."[75] Some feminist theorists have asked whether there is a "power play" behind at least some conversions.[76]

Particularly in two geographical and cultural areas, Africa and India, discussions of conversion have received a lot of attention. The main challenge to African Christianity has been the question of how to conceive of conversion in a way that would not mean abandoning one's cultural heritage and identity, as well as power and privilege.[77] In India, the continuing heated discussions around conversion also have everything to do with proselytism and the question of the legitimacy of evangelization.[78]

Contemporary theology has to take very seriously all these challenges concerning the ideological, power-play-driven, and otherwise destructive potential implications of conversion. That said, there is no justification for the

72. Andrew B. Newberg and Bruce Y. Lee, "The Neuroscientific Study of Religious and Spiritual Phenomena: Or Why God Doesn't Use Biostatistics," *Zygon: Journal of Religion and Science* 40 (2005): 469–89.

73. Andrew Buckser and Stephen D. Glazier, eds., *The Anthropology of Religious Conversion* (Lanham, MD: Rowman & Littlefield, 2003).

74. Nehamia Levtzion, ed., *Conversion to Islam* (New York: Holmes & Meier, 1979).

75. Lewis R. Rambo and Charles F. Farhadian, "Conversion," in *ER* 3:1971.

76. Susan Juster, "'In a Different Voice': Male and Female Narratives of Religious Conversion in Post-evolutionary America," *American Quarterly* 41 (March 1989): 34–62.

77. Caroline Ifeka-Moller, "White Power: Social Structural Factor in Conversion to Christianity, Eastern Nigeria, 1921–1966," *Canadian Journal of African Studies* 8, no. 1 (1974): 55–72.

78. Dick Kooiman, *Conversion and Social Equality in India* (Delhi: Manohar, 1989).

blunt judgment that any experience of conversion by default is harmful and counterproductive.

Divine Forgiveness

Biblical Theology of Forgiveness

In recent years forgiveness has caught the attention of behavioral and social scientists, who have undertaken massive research projects.[79] A flood of "self-help" books on forgiveness has also seen daylight.[80] While these contributions will be noted in the discussion, as always, we will begin from the Trinitarian theological framework.

All Abrahamic faiths affirm that the source of forgiveness is God. In Christian theology, this is based on reconciliation (atonement) brought about by the triune God in Christ.[81] Following his resurrection, the seal of reconciliation, the risen Christ authorized and mandated his church: "If you forgive the sins of any, they are forgiven; if you retain the sins of any, they are retained" (John 20:23).

Forgiveness played a crucial role in the ministry of Jesus of Nazareth[82] and of his followers;[83] it is also the only soteriological concept mentioned in the ecumenical creeds. The theme is also prevalent in the Old Testament, including in a number of narratives about human forgiveness (e.g., Joseph and his brothers; Gen. 45–46). The horizontal and vertical dimensions are intertwined, in the midst of all the ambiguities of dramatic human stories.

Notwithstanding the debates about whether (and when) in the preexilic period Israel knew divine forgiveness, certainly during and after the exile it became a treasured belief.[84] Although turning to God (repentance) is required

79. Michael E. McCullough, Kenneth I. Pargament, and Carl E. Thoresen, eds., *Forgiveness: Theory, Research, and Practice* (New York: Guilford, 2002).

80. Frederic Luskin, *Forgive for Good: A Proven Prescription for Health and Happiness* (San Francisco: HarperCollins, 2002).

81. Chap. 5 in John McIntyre, *The Shape of Soteriology: Studies in the Doctrine of the Death of Christ* (Edinburgh: T&T Clark, 1992).

82. Just observe key passages in one gospel: Matt. 6:12, 14–15; 9:2, 5–6; 12:31–32; 18:21–23, 35; 26:28.

83. Luke 24:47; Acts 2:38.

84. Exod. 34:6–7; Num. 14:18–19; Pss. 86:15; 103:8–10; 145:8–9. For details, see Shults and Sandage, *Faces of Forgiveness*, 127–30.

(2 Kings 17:13–14; Jer. 3:11–24; Isa. 22:14), the later prophets also emphasized that what really matters is the right attitude rather than the mechanical following of cultic practices (Amos 5:21–25; Isa. 1:11–17; Hos. 6:6).

The two main words in the New Testament are *aphiēmi* ("let go, cancel, remit, leave") and *aphesis* ("release, pardon, cancellation"); however, they are used unevenly and in contexts not always related to religion. Of the almost 150 occurrences of the former, only one-third refer, strictly speaking, to "forgiveness"; the latter, which appears fewer than twenty times, almost always has the meaning of "forgiveness." Furthermore, as is well known, both terms are virtually limited to the Gospels; Paul hardly knows them. Why so? Paul expresses the idea using other words, particularly "justification," "reconciliation," "redemption," and similar ones. Often the *idea* of forgiveness may be present even if the word is missing (as in the parable of the prodigal son).

Two issues strike the reader of the Gospel stories of forgiveness (whether or not that word appears). First, Jesus's teaching on forgiveness is often striking in its generosity. Particularly important is the table fellowship with "sinners," a technical term that includes those outside the covenant. It seems that repentance is often presented in the Gospels as the response to forgiveness rather than the condition for it. As Joseph Liechty brilliantly observes, "forgive" may be read as "fore-give," that is, "give before."[85] But second, even a cursory reading of the Gospels reveals that both John the Baptist (Mark 1:4) and Jesus also link forgiveness with repentance (1:15); the same mandate is given by the risen Lord to the disciples (Luke 24:46–47), and the early church carries on with this tradition (Acts 2:38; 5:31; 8:22; 26:18). How these two aspects can be negotiated will be taken up below.

Are There Any Conditions for Forgiveness?

Christian tradition does not speak with a unanimous voice about the unconditionality of forgiveness. Historically, from the early centuries repentance came to be linked with the more or less technically defined rite of penitence, linked with the demand for satisfaction as the prerequisite for forgiving. A related, important development was the emerging distinction between sins forgiven at baptism and those committed after baptism. Fortunately, at Vatican II, the

85. Joseph Liechty, "Putting Forgiveness in Its Place," in *Explorations in Reconciliation: New Directions for Theology*, ed. David Tombs and Joseph Liechty (Aldershot, UK: Ashgate, 2006), 62n6, cited in David Tombs, "The Offer of Forgiveness," *Journal of Religious Ethics* 36, no. 4 (2008): 590.

Roman Catholic Church redefined and clarified the theology of penance, including a proper attitude toward the violated neighbor.[86]

Repentance should not be made a prerequisite of forgiveness: "God unilaterally makes forgiveness possible by offering forgiveness 'while we were yet sinners' (Rom. 5:8)."[87] Here is a difference between Jewish and Christian theologies of forgiveness. Although Judaism of course knows divine forgiveness, it normally entails repentance and restitution as the condition, as well as the forgiving of others.[88] With Jesus comes "judgment of *grace*," which not only condemns sin and wrongdoings but also gives the energy and capability to re-turn to God and others in repentance and acknowledgment of one's faults.[89]

That said, the affirmation of unconditionality is not an abandonment of repentance. On the contrary, repentance (and restitution) becomes the necessary *consequence* of the reception of divine forgiveness. Furthermore, Jesus's message made a radical shift in the whole idea of repentance: rather than meant only for some, its audience was everybody, including the "poor" and the marginalized; that is, both the perpetrators and victims were called to repentance. This is because forgiveness always has in view not only reconciliation but also transformation and change.[90] This principle of unconditional forgiveness should also guide our understanding of forgiveness between human persons.

Forgiveness with Neighbors—and Enemies

"As We Also Have Forgiven Our Debtors"

Forgiven people are called to imitate that act of hospitality. In forgiving, humans mediate the gift of forgiveness they have received themselves. "Failure to offer forgiveness indicates a devaluation of God's forgiveness."[91] Withholding

86. *Catholic Catechism* (##1422–24).

87. Jesse Couenhoven, "Forgiveness and Restoration: A Theological Exploration," *Journal of Religion* 90, no. 2 (2010): 165.

88. Louis E. Newman, "The Quality of Mercy: On the Duty to Forgive in the Judaic Tradition," *Journal of Religious Ethics* 15, no. 2 (Fall 1987): 155–72.

89. L. Gregory Jones, *Embodying Forgiveness: A Theological Analysis* (Grand Rapids: Eerdmans, 1995), 136, 145–50.

90. Miroslav Volf, *Exclusion and Embrace: A Theological Exploration of Identity, Otherness, and Reconciliation* (Nashville: Abingdon, 1996), 111–19.

91. Don McLellan, "Justice, Forgiveness, and Reconciliation: Essential Elements in Atonement Theology," *Evangelical Review of Theology* 29 (2005): 13.

forgiveness would mean the exclusion of another and would be nothing other than the exclusion of God.[92]

Miroslav Volf locates forgiving in the context of two opposing movements, namely, embrace and exclusion. Exclusion may happen in many ways, including elimination (as in ethnic cleansing), assimilation (when acceptance is based on the demand to be like us), domination, and abandonment. Embrace, on the contrary, is based on "the mutuality of the self-giving love in the Trinity," "the outstretched arms of Christ on the cross for the 'godless,'" the welcoming by the father of the prodigal son.[93] This "will to embrace" includes both opening to the other and drawing to intimate touching, making space for the otherness of the other.

Forgiveness is not done for our own sake; it is a manifestation of love for the neighbor. The victims decide "no longer to hold the injury they have suffered against their offender."[94] This gift has the potential to set the violator free from the guilt and grip of the wrongful act. However, the act of gift giving is costly. Indeed, forgiving means willingness to pay the price for the neighbor, even the one who has sinned against us.

The assertion that forgiveness is done out of love for the neighbor is not to deny the potential benefits to the forgiver; it is rather to make those benefits secondary. This principle goes contrary to the emphasis in much of contemporary popular self-help literature and behavioral sciences concerning the therapeutic value of forgiveness and its benefits to the forgiver.

If the act of forgiveness has as its ultimate goal the well-being and restoration of the neighbor, it means that it looks not only into the past but also to the future. The orientation to the future is present in God's forgiveness. Its ultimate goal is the eschatological shalom and peace with the coming of God's righteous rule.

Beyond Resentment

A long tradition of philosophical and theological reflection on forgiveness has linked it with resentment. In this view, forgiveness primarily means a process of overcoming resentment, the feeling of anger caused by having been the ob-

92. Miroslav Volf, "Exclusion and Embrace: Theological Reflections in the Wake of 'Ethnic Cleansing,'" *Journal of Ecumenical Studies* 29, no. 2 (1992): 241.

93. Volf, *Exclusion and Embrace*, 29.

94. Justyn Terry, "The Forgiveness of Sins and the Work of Christ: A Case for Substitutionary Atonement," *Anglican Theological Review* 95 (Winter 2013): 13.

ject of wrongdoing.[95] A version of this view is that forgiveness is supposed to free the wronged person from all forms of negative feelings, even disappointment.[96] Often this is linked with demands that even the critical judgment of the offender be suspended.

The resentment theory is contrary to Jesus's teaching that invites us not only to "turn the other cheek" and embrace the offender in forgiveness but also to expose the wrong act for the sake of justice and to allow the wrongdoer to find reconciliation in accepting guilt and receiving forgiveness.[97] Here Christian tradition may follow Aristotle's oft-cited rule (in opposition to Plato's view), according to which a truly moral person is "angry at the right things and with the right people, and, further, as he ought, when he ought, and as long as he ought."[98]

Restoration cannot happen without the wrongdoing being exposed and judged. As Moltmann aptly puts it, forgiveness is about "the new life to which [God] desires to awaken the guilty."[99] To that act may also belong a protest, even an emotional protest.

Forgiveness, Justice, and Memory

The talk about unconditional forgiveness raises questions such as the following: What about justice? Shouldn't an authentic act of forgiveness be able to erase from the offended person's mind all negative feelings? In much of earlier self-help literature, it was taken for granted that an authentic act of forgiveness also helps erase the painful and negative memories of the offender's acts from the victim's mind. Hence, book titles such as *Forgive and Forget.*[100] On the contrary, theology claims that for authentic forgiveness

95. Peter A. French et al., "Forgiveness and Resentment," *Midwest Studies in Philosophy* 7 (1982): 503–16.

96. Uma Narayan, "Forgiveness, Moral Reassessment, and Reconciliation," in *Explorations of Value*, ed. Thomas Magnell (Amsterdam: Rodopi, 1997), 169–78.

97. Nicholas Wolterstorff, "Jesus and Forgiveness," in *Jesus and Philosophy: New Essays*, ed. Paul K. Moser (Cambridge: Cambridge University Press, 2009), 194–214.

98. Aristotle, *Nicomachean Ethics* 1125b32, in *The Complete Works of Aristotle*, ed. Jonathan Barnes, 2 vols. (Princeton: Princeton University Press, 1984).

99. Jürgen Moltmann, *In the End—the Beginning: The Life of Hope*, trans. Margaret Kohl (Minneapolis: Fortress, 2004), 75, cited in Elaine C. Ledgerwood, "The Hope of Forgiveness," *Compass* 47, no. 1 (2013): 14.

100. Lewis B. Smedes, *Forgive and Forget: Healing the Hurts We Don't Deserve* (New York: Harper & Row, 1984).

and healing to happen, it is essential that we remember *rightly*[101] the pain of the wrongdoings against us. This is to establish the truth. Acknowledging and recalling the wrong act is indeed a moral obligation, or else justice and righteousness cannot be established. Furthermore, it is also required for the healing and restoration of the victim. But not remembering is also required for the offender to be restored. Mere forgetting can be nothing more than a way of repressing negative memories yet leaving the victim with the enmity and hatred.

Only right remembering allows the victim to let the offender know the moral wrongdoing and so help that person seek forgiveness and reconciliation. "If your brother sins against you, go and tell him his fault, between you and him alone. If he listens to you, you have gained your brother" (Matt. 18:15). At times, help from other trusted persons and the Christian community is needed (vv. 16–20).[102] But this condemnation of the wrongful act should not be confused with retribution or vengeance. Rather, forgiveness is the refusal to press charges against the violator and instead offering the way of reconciliation even if the victim has the right to press charges.[103]

Commensurately, the reception of forgiveness entails the acceptance of condemnation, and this is why the reception may sometimes be too difficult. The person who says *no* to forgiveness offered is in reality saying that he or she has not done anything wrong. To the art of remembering rightly also belongs the capacity to make a distinction between violator as *violator* and as a human person. Perhaps apart from some extreme cases of violence and abuse (such as the mass murder of Hitler and other mass murderers), the victim should avoid reducing the violator to the violation.[104]

Only in a qualified sense does forgiveness, after all, mean "forgetting." The forgiver has as the ultimate goal the imitation of God, who does not remember our sins anymore (Jer. 31:34; Heb. 8:12; 10:17).[105]

101. Miroslav Volf, *The End of Memory: Remembering Rightly in a Violent World* (Grand Rapids: Eerdmans, 2006), 11–16.

102. See further, James McClendon, *Ethics*, vol. 1 of *Systematic Theology* (Nashville: Abingdon, 1986), 227–28.

103. Miroslav Volf, *Free of Charge: Giving and Forgiving in a Culture Stripped of Grace* (Grand Rapids: Zondervan, 2005), 168–71.

104. Marjorie Hewitt Suchocki, *The Fall to Violence* (New York: Continuum, 1995), 150–53.

105. Volf, *Exclusion and Embrace*, 131–40.

Conversion, Repentance, and Forgiveness among Religions

Repentance, Forgiveness, and Conversion in Jewish Tradition

In Jewish tradition, the basic scriptural word for repentance is *sub*, which develops into the rabbinic term *teshuvah*, "to return." In Torah it "is constantly and closely connected with eschatological ideas of the Judgment and of the Messianic Age."[106] The Christian message of repentance and forgiveness in the ministries of John the Baptist and Jesus builds on these same themes.

Although the idea of forgiving was known by the Israelites since the beginning of their existence, the topic became all the more important as the elected people, as people of God, continued sinning. Particularly in the aftermath of the exile, the importance of repentance became an urgent theme.[107] The availability of God's forgiveness was taken as the confirmation of election and covenant. Even more widely, "the conception could involve the prophetic notion of restoration as well as the conversion of pagans."[108] Although God is the ultimate source of forgiveness, obedience to Torah based on the covenant is emphasized. What about the role of sacrifices? According to a defining Mishnah text (Yoma 8:8–9), the sin offering atones for all unintentional sins, but intentional sins require repentance and returning to God—even though full atonement may come only at death or through the Day of Atonement (provided that the sinner refrains from further intentional sins).[109]

Jacob Neusner concludes that although the "sinner should be, and is punished . . . sin is not indelible. If the sinner repents the sin, atones, and attains reconciliation with God, the sin is wiped off the record, the sinner forgiven, the sinner's successors blameless." Forgiveness entails repentance because without it the rule of justice is violated as repentance "defines the key to the moral life."[110]

Similar to revivalistic movements, mystically oriented Jewish movements such as Hasidism have focused much on repentance and forgiveness as a way to ensure the genuine nature of spiritual life. The Kabbalistic tradition's emphasis on repentance as the way of rectification (*tikkun*) belongs to the same category.[111]

106. C. G. Montefiore, "Rabbinic Conceptions of Repentance," *Jewish Quarterly Review* 16, no. 2 (January 1904): 211.

107. Louis Jacobs, *A Jewish Theology* (London: Darton, Longman & Todd, 1973), chap. 17.

108. David E. Aune, "Repentance," in *ER* 11:7755.

109. Jacob Neusner, "Repentance in Judaism," in *RCP*, 64.

110. Neusner, "Repentance in Judaism," 60, 61–62, respectively.

111. Simon Shokek, *Kabbalah and the Art of Being: The Smithsonian Lectures* (London: Routledge, 2001), 135–40.

Similar to other Abrahamic faiths, Jewish tradition highlights the importance of forgiveness in relation to the neighbor as well. Divine forgiveness cannot be had if an intentional violation against the neighbor has been committed and there is not yet reconciliation.

Islamic Interpretations

Similar to the Old Testament, the earliest Qur'anic passages were not calling people to convert to a new religion. Rather, the Meccans were called to "worship the Lord of this House [Ka'ba]" (Q 106:3).[112] Only later, with rising opposition from worshipers of local deities, was a decisive break announced (106:9) and the confession became "There is no god except God" (37:35).[113]

Because the Qur'an teaches that "there is no compulsion in religion" (2:256), conversion should be a matter of one's choice.[114] This is not to deny—similar to Christian history—occasions of forced conversions, but those have to be considered anomalies rather than the norm.[115] What, however, is strictly forbidden is conversion to another religion, an apostasy potentially resulting in punishment by death.

Conversion to Islam entails confession of two simple but necessary convictions: that Allah is the only god and that Muhammad is the prophet of God (usually recited in Arabic and followed by "the greater ablution" of the whole body). Part of the conversion process is a continuous mind-set of penitence and contrition, although there are no mandatory formal rites or rituals. The internal process of remorse and repentance is accompanied with ritual prayers and *zakat*, "almsgiving" (9:5, 11); submission (*islam*) to God is part of the act (39:54).

Recall that Muhammad declared, "I am the Prophet of repentance."[116] In the Qur'an, and particularly in the later Hadith tradition, repentance plays an important role. Among several terms denoting repentance and remorse, the

112. The Ka'ba is the center of the holy place in Mecca.

113. J. Dudley Woodberry, "Conversion in Islam," in *HRC*, 24.

114. Yohanan Friedmann, *Tolerance and Coercion in Islam: Interfaith Relations in the Muslim Tradition* (Cambridge: Cambridge University Press, 2003).

115. William M. Brinner and Devin J. Stewart, "Conversion," in *The Oxford Encyclopedia of the Islamic World*, ed. John L. Esposito (Oxford: Oxford University Press, 2009); *Oxford Islamic Studies Online*, http://www.oxfordislamicstudies.com/article/opr/t236/e0165.

116. Quoted in Atif Khalil, "Early Sufi Approaches to *Tawba*: From the Qur'ān to Abū Ṭālib al-Makkī" (PhD diss., University of Toronto, 2009), 2.

key scriptural term, akin to Hebrew, is *tawbah* (3:90; 4:17; 40:3; 43:25), meaning not only "to return" but also to do so frequently.[117] The Qur'an speaks of the process of re-turning in terms of "people entering God's religion in throngs" and asking for forgiveness (110:2, 3). While forgiveness is based on God's grace, clearly human initiative is needed: "Indeed God does not alter the state of a people unless they have altered the state of their souls" (13:11).

Continuous repentance is particularly important in Sufi mysticism, which is deeply concerned about repentance and conversion in its desire for deepening spiritual life.[118] The normative medieval theologian al-Ghazali, who also gleans from Sufi mysticism, names repentance as the starting point for followers of the spiritual path, and therefore "it must be put first in the Quarter of Salvation."[119]

What about its conditions? It requires a true change of heart. A prideful and arrogant attitude blocks forgiveness. That said, materially similar to Judeo-Christian tradition, "God's mercy takes precedence over God's wrath."[120] Yet—again like other Abrahamic traditions—Islamic theology has to be able to maintain God's justice in all of that.

As in the other Abrahamic traditions, forgiveness in Islam encompasses both divine and human forgiveness. In keeping with Judeo-Christian teaching, before praying to God one must be reconciled with one's neighbor. It calls for a change of heart toward the violator without excluding the need to expose and judge the wrong act.[121]

Conversion, Repentance, and Forgiveness in Hinduism

Rather than conversion, what counts in Hinduism is a religious experience, spiritual "realization," and conduct.[122] Rather than "deliverance from sin,"

117. Mahmoud Ayoub, "Repentance in the Islamic Tradition," in *RCP*, 96–98; Frederick Mathewson Denny, "The Qur'anic Vocabulary of Repentance: Orientations and Attitudes," *Journal of the American Academy of Religion* 47, no. 4 (1979): 649–64.

118. Khalil, "Early Sufi Approaches," iii.

119. *Al-Ghazzali on Repentance*, trans. M. S. Stern (New Delhi: Sterling Publishers, 1990), 29–30, http://www.ghazali.org/books/gzrepent.pdf.

120. Bahar Davary, "Forgiveness in Islam: Is It an Ultimate Reality?" *Ultimate Reality and Meaning: Interdisciplinary Studies in the Philosophy of Understanding* 27, no. 2 (2004): 135.

121. Davary, "Forgiveness in Islam," 128–29.

122. Sir Sarvepalli Radhakrishnan, *The Hindu View of Life* (London: George Allen & Unwin, 1961 [1927]), 13.

conversion is "progressive enlightenment in which the ignorance and desire that keep us trapped in our human dilemma are expelled."[123] With this view, Hinduism rejects the Abrahamic traditions' call for conversion.

Notwithstanding the hesitancy against conversion, Hinduism knows not only the reconversion of lapsed faithful but also active missionary efforts to convert "pagans." This was certainly the case in the third to fifth centuries during the establishment of Hindu rajas in South India to replace Buddhism. More recently, Hare Krishna and a number of less well-known revival movements in the West have sought new converts.

What about repentance? Notwithstanding a radically different theological context from Abrahamic faiths, both in classical Vedic religion and in theistic (particularly *bhakti*) traditions, repentance is present. The seriousness of sin is certainly present, although, unlike the classical Christian interpretation, there is not an "original sin" but rather a form of contamination and defilement. Related to the key Vedic concept of *rita*, the cosmic and moral order, sin in Hinduism ultimately has to do with violation of this cosmic order, the guarantee of peace, harmony, and blessings. This accrues "debt" that should be paid in order to regain balance.[124]

Somewhat like Christian tradition, some Vedic traditions make a distinction between unintentional and intentional sins: whereas the former can be cleansed with the help of reciting proper Vedic passages, the latter can only be rectified by restitution. The most serious offenses can be "burned off" only in the process of numerous reincarnations, including temporary time spent in various hells. In Hinduism, the reconciliation of the most serious offenses may also entail various kinds of vows, a practice echoing the rationale of merits to be earned in the process of penance (rite of reconciliation) in Roman Catholic tradition.

Although atonement by the deity is not an unknown idea in Vedic religion, the emphasis by and large is still on "self-atonement." The situation is different with *bhakti* spirituality: grace and divine forgiveness are in the forefront as taught in the Bhagavad Gita (18.66): "Setting aside all noble deeds, just surrender completely to the will of God (with firm faith and loving contemplation). I shall liberate you from all sins (or bonds of Karma). Do not grieve." Various opportunities and ways for forgiveness are offered in these traditions, from pilgrimage to a sacred site, to bathing in the sacred river Ganges, to

123. Paul G. Hiebert, "Conversion in Hinduism and Buddhism," in *HRC*, 10.

124. Jeanine Miller, *The Vision of Cosmic Order in the Vedas* (London: Routledge & Kegan Paul, 1985), 142.

being tutored by the guru (who is believed to bear sins as well), and so forth. Particularly important is the recitation of Sanskrit hymns and divine names.[125]

Similar to Abrahamic traditions, there are Hindu teachings about the need to extend forgiveness also to fellow humans. Rig Veda (5.85.7) contains the plea to Varuna: "if we have sinned against the man who loves us, have ever wronged a brother, friend, or comrade, The neighbour ever with us, or a stranger, O Varuṇa, remove from us the trespass."

Buddhist Perspectives

As in Hinduism, Buddhist traditions display an ambiguity concerning conversion.[126] On the one hand, it looks as though beginning from Gautama's enlightenment experience a radical break with the past is the norm; on the other hand, it can also be argued that (apart from some exceptions such as conversion by force)[127] the people who joined the movement hardly underwent any radical crisis experience. One way to reconcile this apparent tension is to argue that only when the religious seeker made the decisive choice to break off from the "world" and become a Theravadin (an ascetic), the break was a crisis. That said, a significant number of disciples who joined Gautama already belonged to religious movements.[128]

As a general rule, it can be said that (with perhaps the exception of Pure Land) forgiveness is not linked with divine pardon for ensuring entrance to eternal blessedness. Gods play little (or virtually no) role in conversion, repentance, and forgiveness. Furthermore, "the early Buddhist doctrine of kamma allows for mitigation, though not eradication, of the consequences of actions under some circumstances";[129] the kind of expiation of sins present in Hindu traditions discussed above is not present, however. What is in the forefront

125. Guy L. Beck, "Fire in the Ātman: Repentance in Hinduism," in *RCP*, 85.

126. Asanga Tilakaratne, "The Buddhist View on Religious Conversion," *Dialogue* (Colombo, Sri Lanka) 32–33 (2005–2006): 58–82.

127. Charles F. Keyes, "Monks, Guns, and Peace," in *Belief and Bloodshed: Religion and Violence across Time and Tradition*, ed. James K. Wellman Jr. (Lanham, MD: Rowman & Littlefield, 2007), 145–63.

128. Torkel Brekke, "Conversion in Buddhism?" in *Religious Conversion in India*, ed. Rowena Robinson and Sathianathan Clarke (New York: Oxford University Press, 2007), 181–91.

129. Jayarava Michael Attwood, "Did King Ajātasattu Confess to the Buddha, and Did the Buddha Forgive Him?" *Journal of Buddhist Ethics* (n.d.): 279, http://www.academia.edu/1327910/Did_King_Aj%C4%81tasattu_Confess_to_the_Buddha_and_did_the_Buddha_Forgive_Him.

in the Buddhist tradition are the "practices of self-examination, feelings of remorse, the renunciation of unwholesome patterns of life, and the possibility of radical moral change."[130]

The major difference exists between Theravada and Mahayana: whereas in the former the renunciation of the world ideally means devotion to full-time religious life with a view to personal salvation, including joining the community (*sangha*), the latter accepts the simple fact that for most of the masses this radical call is too much. Hence, Mahayana with its theistic orientation offers the way of "salvation" somewhat similarly to forms of theistic Hinduism, that is, with devotion to the Ultimate Reality ("divinized" Buddha figure), and encourages delaying one's own stepping into nirvana for the sake of helping others. In keeping with other faith traditions, all Buddhist traditions highlight the importance of forgiving other persons.[131]

The next lengthy section takes up key Christian soteriological themes of justification, sanctification, and deification.

One with God: Justification, Deification, and Sanctification

In the Christian West, justification by faith has become an umbrella concept that covers virtually all aspects of the salvific relationship to God. That usage cannot be established biblically, as the Bible portrays the concept of justification/righteousness as but one of many metaphors of salvation, nor historically (before the Reformation era). It is often forgotten that the way the Western doctrine of justification emerged—as the defining form of soteriology—is related to the late medieval culture of a divinely sanctified hierarchical society, the prominence of guilt, condemnation, and penitential attitude.[132] Contemporary global cultures may not play with those motifs. Be that as it may, in the Eastern Church justification is virtually unknown; in its place stands deification (or divinization, *theōsis*). This is more than just a terminological difference, though.

We will first study critically the Western churches' Reformation disputes in light of historical developments and the Eastern churches' radically different soteriology. The second task inquires into several significant ecumenical achievements on the way toward a reconstructed contemporary theology of

130. Malcolm David Eckel, "A Buddhist Approach to Repentance," in *RCP*, 122.

131. Kinrei Bassis, "Forgiveness," n.p., accessed March 14, 2014, http://www.berkeleybuddhistpriory.org/pages/articles/online_articles/forgiveness.htm.

132. Paul R. Hinlicky, "Theological Anthropology: Toward Integrating *Theosis* and Justification by Faith," *Journal of Ecumenical Studies* 34, no. 1 (Winter 1997): 44–47.

salvation. The last major task is to relate these doctrines to the teachings of four other living faiths.

Justification in Pre-Reformation Traditions

Patristic writers did not express the doctrine of salvation under the concept of justification, even though the term is not totally missing. Consider that the two-volume *Commentary on the Epistle to the Romans* by Origen neither caused debates nor offered substantially new perspectives. One of the reasons is that Pauline theology did not play the *central* role that it did later in medieval and Reformation debates. Only with the rise of Pelagian "works righteousness" did the Western Church have to begin to articulate a doctrine that later became highly technically formulated.

The roots of the Western doctrine of justification can be found in Augustine. The bishop of Hippo considered it the work of the Holy Spirit. Related to this is the emphasis on love rather than "faith alone" as the primary aspect of justification (Rom. 5:5). Building on the Pauline rule of "faith working through love" (Gal. 5:6), Augustine established the highly influential "faith formed by love" principle, which was followed by the Catholic tradition but strongly opposed by Protestants because they feared it would introduce the need for human merit at the expense of faith (though Augustine took both love and faith as divine gifts). The Holy Spirit poured out as love at justification is the key to renewal; love is nothing else but the Spirit himself.[133] Very importantly, unlike the later Protestant Reformation's separation of justification from sanctification, Augustine unambiguously taught that justification means "to make righteous."[134] Technically put, he endorsed both the "forensic" (to declare the sinner righteous) and the "effective" (to make righteous), that is, sanctification, aspects.[135]

The greatest medieval theologian, Aquinas, built on and further developed Augustine's thought. Holding on to the two-aspect account of justification, he went further in that he came to talk about "habitual grace," meaning that the remission of sins elevates the sinner to a "state of justice."[136] In other words, justification brings about something "inherent" to reside in the believer.

133. Augustine, *The Spirit and the Letter* 5.

134. Augustine takes the Latin word *iustificare*, rooted in *facere* (to make), in its literal, obvious meaning.

135. Augustine, *Treatise on Grace and Free Will* 33.

136. Aquinas, *ST* 1-2ae113; see Alister E. McGrath, *Iustitia Dei: A History of the Christian Doctrine of Justification*, 2 vols. (Cambridge: Cambridge University Press, 1986), 1:43–51.

Another key development—which Luther came to resist vehemently—is related to a pre-Reformation former teacher of his, Gabriel Biel, who formulated the famous slogan "God does not deny grace to the one who does everything in his or her power."[137] In other words: do your best and God takes care of the rest.

Before continuing the story in the Christian West, let us survey Eastern soteriology.

Salvation as Theōsis *in the Christian East*

A number of distinctive terms and metaphors of salvation are used in the Christian East, including participation, union, and deification (divinization, *theōsis*).[138] Irenaeus spoke of the "Word of God, our Lord Jesus Christ who because of his limitless love became what we are in order to make us what even he himself is."[139] Athanasius taught that "he, indeed, assumed humanity that we might become God."[140]

The two cardinal biblical texts are 2 Peter 1:4, which speaks of becoming "partakers of the divine nature," and Psalm 82:6 (as quoted by the Johannine Jesus in John 10:34): "I said, you are gods."[141] The Petrine passage accentuates the key idea of release from the corruption and mortality caused by the evil desires of the world. Eastern theology does not focus so much on guilt as on mortality as the main problem of humanity; neither does it juxtapose divine grace (and initiative) with human freedom (and responsibility). It speaks of divine-human synergy.

The fourteenth-century theologian Gregory of Palamas helped conclusively establish the main theological ramifications of the doctrine. The key aspects of his teaching are (1) the creation of the human being "in the image and after the likeness of God," (2) the incarnation of the Logos of God, and (3) the strength of the human being's communion with God in the Holy

137. McGrath, *Iustitia Dei*, 1:81–93.

138. Georgios Mantzaridis, *The Deification of Man: St. Gregory Palamas and the Orthodox Traditions*, trans. Liadain Sherrar (Crestwood, NY: St. Vladimir's Seminary Press, 1984); Panayiotis Nellas, *Deification in Christ: Orthodox Perspectives on the Nature of the Human Person*, trans. Norman Russell (Crestwood, NY: St. Vladimir's Seminary Press, 1987).

139. Irenaeus, *Against Heresies* 5, preface.

140. Athanasius, *On the Incarnation* 8.54.

141. Other texts referred to by Orthodox theologians include Exod. 34:30; Matt. 17:4; John 17:21–23; 2 Cor. 8:9; 1 John 3:2; 4:12.

Spirit.[142] Palamas further taught that the distinction between God's essence and God's "energies" makes it possible to say that deification means participating in divine energies but not in the divine essence as such. Pantheism is thus avoided. God still remains God, and humans remain human, though participating in the divine.

The Protestant Reformation on Justification

Although the Protestant Reformation failed to provide a coherent, single understanding of justification,[143] it is fair to say that mainline Protestantism from the 1530s until the heyday of Protestant orthodoxy (mid-eighteenth century) embraced the following tenets, which obviously represent new developments from earlier tradition: justification as forensic declaration rather than a process of change; consequently, a categorical distinction between justification as an initial "once-and-for-all" change of state and progressive growth in renewal (sanctification); and, subsequently, the vehement rejection of the idea of habitual grace.[144]

That said, the overall picture of a Reformation theology of justification is far more complex and complicated. Most importantly, Martin Luther himself did not by and large endorse what is presented above as the standard view; for him Christ's presence and union are linked not only, or even primarily, with forensic declaration, but also with continuous change of life.[145] His right hand, Philipp Melanchthon, who drafted significant parts of the Lutheran Confessions, helped consolidate the standard view, notwithstanding several changes throughout his career. Furthermore, Calvin's Reformed interpretation introduces an important shift, as for him both justification and sanctification stand under union with God—and surprisingly, sanctification is talked about before justification! The classic opening passage of the third book of the *Institutes*, a preamble to *ordo salutis*, states "that so long as we are without Christ and separated from him, nothing which he suffered and did for the salvation of

142. Mantzaridis, *The Deification of Man*, 15–39.

143. Carl E. Braaten, *Justification: The Article by Which the Church Stands or Falls* (Minneapolis: Fortress, 1990), 10–15.

144. See Michael Horton, "Traditional Reformed View," in *Justification: Five Views*, ed. James K. Beilby and Paul Rhodes Eddy (Downers Grove, IL: IVP Academic, 2011), 85–91.

145. Olli-Pekka Vainio, *Justification and Participation in Christ: The Development of the Lutheran Doctrine of Justification from Luther to the Formula of Concord (1580)* (Leiden: Brill, 2008), 42–53.

the human race is of the least benefit to us. To communicate to us the blessings which he received from the Father, he must become ours and dwell in us."[146] Thereby he links together tightly justification and sanctification in order to refute the charge of "cheap grace" and complaints about a lack of emphasis on good works as the fruit of salvation.[147]

The most significant deviation from the Reformation forensic orientation came from the Radical Reformers.[148] The legitimate concern among the Anabaptists was the lack of emphasis on good works and neighborly love. Like Saint James of the New Testament, Balthasar Hubmaier, echoing a number of others, declared: "Mere faith alone is not sufficient for salvation . . . for a true faith can never exist without deeds of love."[149]

In sum: the Protestant camp stood divided by the time the harsh Roman Catholic rebuttal came in the middle of the sixteenth century, and it has continued this divergence since.

The Roman Catholic Rebuttal of Protestant Doctrine

Concerning the response of the Council of Trent in 1547, one has to remember that as a *reaction*, it hardly attempted any kind of comprehensive formulation of the doctrine. That said, it still is the binding formulation for this church.

Although it takes God's gracious preparation of the will for reception of justification (#6),[150] it cannot happen without human consent (##4, 9). Although faith is necessary for justification, without love it does not suffice (##11, 12); on the basis of Hebrews 11:6 ("without faith it is impossible to please [God]"), the Protestant emphasis on justification as a free gift is rejected (#8). Most controversial to Protestants is the formulation on merit. Although, following Augustine, merit means God's crowning of his own work, Trent teaches that on the basis of inherent righteousness Christians may merit eternal life (#16). What is probably a concession to Luther is the statement on justification as "alien," although Trent does not deny its being inherent righteousness

146. Calvin, *Institutes* 3.1.1.

147. Calvin, *Institutes* 3.16.1.

148. A. J. Beachy, *The Concept of Grace in the Radical Reformers* (Nieuwkoop: De Graaf, 1977).

149. Cited in James McClendon, *Doctrine*, vol. 2 of *Systematic Theology* (Nashville: Abingdon, 1994), 117.

150. "Decree on Justification: Sixth Session" (January 13, 1547), in Schaff, *The Creeds of Christendom*, 2:89–118. Numbers in parentheses refer to this document.

as well. It is "alien" in the sense of coming from outside human efforts and resources (#16). Finally, Trent rejects the Protestant claim of assurance of salvation as well as perseverance (##9 and 16).[151]

Notwithstanding its polemics, Protestants would have done well to heed the call from Catholics to hold on to the two aspects of justification: declaring righteous and making righteous (sanctification). Furthermore, Protestants could have welcomed the definite anti-Pelagian teaching of the inability of human persons to restore fellowship with God. Protestants similarly missed the best intentions of the complex teaching of the council on the role of grace in preparation for and in the process of justification. Finally, the council's highlighting of the role of the freedom of the will could have been interpreted as conditioned by grace rather than as an affirmation of human independence.

Having now surveyed historical developments till the Reformation era, we will tap into a number of current resources and ecumenical developments.

Resources for Reconceptualization of the Doctrine of Justification

The "New Perspective" in Biblical Theology

Significant advances have been made in recent decades to better understand the New Testament teaching on faith and justification, particularly with regard to Pauline materials. Related to this, the Old Testament background of these and related concepts as well as the nature of Judaism as a religion of grace rather than legalistic rules have been rediscovered in the new perspective (on Paul).

What does the biblical term "righteousness/justification" mean?[152] Paul and other early Christians adopted this Hebrew, covenant-based terminology of law/justice/righteousness. The important new thing was to place this terminology in the context of the coming of the Messiah and the awaited kingdom with a view toward its eschatological consummation. Here we come to a major breakthrough in the biblical study of the new perspective. Heralded by E. P. Sanders's 1977 *Paul and Palestinian Judaism*, it was distinctively developed by J. D. G. Dunn and N. T. Wright, among others.

151. Gerald O'Collins, SJ, and Oliver P. Rafferty, SJ, "Roman Catholic View," in Beilby and Eddy, *Justification*, 280–81.

152. John Reumann, "Justification and Justice in the New Testament," *Horizons in Biblical Theology* 21, no. 1 (1999): 26–45.

Rather than taking the Judaism of biblical times as legalism, this new perspective takes it as a religion of grace, with human obedience always understood as a response to that grace. According to Sanders's key term "covenantal nomism," God's dealings with his people are based on covenant, which, on the one hand, is based on grace and provides atonement, and on the other hand, requires obedience. Obedience, hence, is not about works righteousness. The major difference between the Old and New Testaments, hence, is not that one moves from law-based to grace-based religion, but that in the Old Testament the covenant community was defined by external boundary markers, whereas in the New Testament it is governed by faith in Christ. As Dunn aptly notes, the "Judaism of what Sanders christened as 'covenantal nomism' can now be seen to preach good Protestant doctrine: that grace is always prior; that human effort is ever the response to divine initiative; that good works are the fruit and not the root of salvation."[153] The reason, then, for Paul's rejection of his own religion was not legalism but rather its stern rejection of Christ as the crucified Messiah of Israel and the pagans. Paul's concern was also that the "boundary markers" of Judaism, such as circumcision and Sabbath observance, were taken as a means of keeping the nations outside the salvation that belongs to the people of God alone.

Hence, Paul's replacement of the covenant identity markers with faith in Christ, based on grace (Rom. 3:21–31), becomes understandable. He wanted to open the way of salvation to gentiles as well, apart from sticking with Jewish particularities. What has caused fierce debate later—and was misunderstood by Lutheran Reformers—was the equally important witness by Saint James. He labored to correct those who—like their later "antinomist"[154] successors to whom laissez-faire complacency replaced willing obedience as a response to grace—made faith a nominal external confession without any commitment to following Christ. Whereas for Paul "faith" denotes trusting dependence on Christ for salvation, for James it is about (intellectual) affirmation of certain beliefs without life commitment. Similarly, "works" for Paul means pressure for noncovenant persons (gentiles) to adopt Jewish identity markers in order to be included, whereas for James it means authentic fruit of salvation in terms of good deeds and right behavior.[155]

153. James D. G. Dunn, "The Justice of God: A Renewed Perspective on Justification by Faith," *Journal of Theological Studies*, n.s., 43 (1992): 8.

154. A group of Protestant Reformation–period heretics who believed that faith in Christ relieved them from the obedience based on God's grace.

155. Michael F. Bird, "Progressive Reformed View," in Beilby and Eddy, *Justification*, 152–56.

Another set of resources comes from ecumenical conversations and agreements among churches, to which we turn next.

Contemporary Ecumenical Breakthroughs

The establishment in the aftermath of Vatican II (1962–1965) of the influential dialogue between the Vatican and the Lutheran World Federation (LWF) prepared the way for the focused conversation process that finally led to the groundbreaking 1999 *Joint Declaration on the Doctrine of Justification.*[156] Its purpose was to show evidence that despite continuing different orientations, a convergence could be found and earlier condemnations nullified. Although its scope is limited in that it only focuses on the doctrine of justification and matters directly related to it (rather than on many other dividing issues) and, even when discussing them, does not seek to be comprehensive or to hide some remaining differences, its ecumenical significance is unsurpassed. Following the currently widely used convergence methodology, it both states what the agreements are and makes room for each party to delineate (within this consensus) dearly held distinctive views and emphases.

Even though both Catholic and Lutheran emphases and qualifications are not lost in the process, a summary of the main mutual agreement goes something like this: not by works but solely on the basis of God's grace, in union with Christ, through faith sinners are forgiven and made righteous even when the fight with sin and pursuit of renewal are a daily task; renewed persons bring forth good works, and they can be confident that the just and faithful God will see to their final salvation.

Importantly, the World Methodist Council cosigned the joint agreement in 2006 and so expanded the Protestant participation. Most recently (2017) the Reformed churches endorsed it. Other responses to the joint document have been understandably diverse, either affirming or critical. While the *Joint Declaration on the Doctrine of Justification* is the most well-known and far-reaching ecumenical agreement, similar kinds of advances can be found in many other encounters, such as when Catholics and Reformed agreed not only on "justification by grace, through faith" but also on the importance of good works as the fruit of salvation.[157]

156. Available at http://www.vatican.va/roman_curia/pontifical_councils/chrstuni/documents/rc_pc_chrstuni_doc_31101999_cath-luth-joint-declaration_en.html.

157. "Towards a Common Understanding of the Church: Reformed/Roman Catho-

What about Justification and Deification?

One of the most groundbreaking ecumenical advances is a new mutual understanding between the Protestant (Lutheran) doctrine of justification and the Eastern Orthodox doctrine of deification. Under the leadership of the late Professor Tuomo Mannermaa, a number of Luther scholars at the University of Helsinki have not only helped radically revise the Reformer's own theology of justification but also accomplished unprecedented ecumenical achievements. The breakthrough came at the end of the 1970s, thanks to ecumenical contacts with the Orthodox tradition (of Russia). Soon it was also discovered that similarly important convergences could be discerned between the soteriologies of Luther and of Catholics.

The basic theses and claims of the new interpretation can be summarized as follows:[158]

1. Luther's understanding of salvation can be expressed not only in terms of the doctrine of justification, but also as *theōsis.* Thus, while there are differences between the Eastern and Lutheran understandings of soteriology, over questions such as free will and understandings of the effects of the Fall, Luther's own theology should not be set in opposition to the ancient Eastern idea of deification.
2. For Luther, the main idea of justification is "Christ present in faith" (*in ipsa fide Christus adest*). Justification for Luther means a real participation in God through the indwelling of Christ in the heart of the believer through the Spirit.
3. In contrast to the theology of the Lutheran Confessions, Luther himself does not make a distinction between forensic and effective justification, but rather argues that justification includes both. In other words, in line with Catholic theology, justification means both declaring righteous and making righteous.
4. Therefore, justification means not only sanctification but also good

lic International Dialogue; Second Phase (1984–1990)," http://www.vatican.va/roman_curia/pontifical_councils/chrstuni/alliance-reform-docs/rc_pc_chrstuni_doc_19900101_second-phase-dialogue_en.html.

158. As detailed in Veli-Matti Kärkkäinen, *One with God: Salvation as Deification and Justification* (Collegeville, MN: Liturgical Press, 2004); Carl E. Braaten and Robert W. Jenson, eds., *Union with Christ: The New Finnish Interpretation of Luther* (Grand Rapids: Eerdmans, 1998); Tuomo Mannermaa, *Christ Present in Faith: Luther's View of Justification*, ed. Kirsi Stjerna (Minneapolis: Augsburg Fortress, 2005 [1979]).

works, since Christ present in faith makes the Christian a "christ" to the neighbor. In other words, the believer begins to do the works of Christ.

As mentioned, Luther's view of justification can also be called *theōsis*, union, participation in God. Of this participation, Luther says boldly: "It is true that a man helped by grace is more than a man; indeed, the grace of God gives him the form of God and deifies him, so that even the Scriptures call him 'God' and 'God's son.'"[159]

To no one's surprise, responses to the Mannermaa School's reinterpretation of Luther have been varied. Whereas the Continental, particularly German, Luther scholarship has been deeply critical, a number of leading American Lutherans have enthusiastically endorsed it.[160]

A Summary of Current Perspectives on Justification

Without undue repetition of previous discussion, it suffices to remind us of the key insights:

- A key to a proper understanding of justification by faith is to see its biblical basis in the covenant theology of the Old Testament and its continued use in the New Testament but now in the wider context of the coming of Jesus Christ and the anticipation of the eschatological consummation.
- Revisiting the Old Testament background of the terms helps us gain a more proper perspective on Judaism of the biblical times as a religion of grace based on covenant and its call for obedience to Yahweh as stipulated in the divinely given law.
- Justification by faith is an important metaphor and concept of salvation, but neither biblically nor historically can it claim any exclusivity.
- The separation of forensic and effective justification—declaring and making just (holy)—by the time of the Reformation had to be corrected in light of biblical and historical pedigree. Although it is legitimate for Protestant and Anglican theology to continue making a distinction between justification and sanctification, separation is to be avoided at all costs.

159. WA 2:247–48; *LW* 51:58.
160. Braaten and Jensen, *Union with Christ*, among others.

- These said advances make it now possible for Protestants and Roman Catholics to come to a convergence about key aspects of justification, namely, that it is based on grace rather than human merits, and that while based on faith, it results in good works or else one is relying on "cheap grace." Similarly, it makes it possible for Protestants, Roman Catholics, and Eastern Orthodox to mutually appreciate the different approaches to the question of salvation without a need to pass judgment on each other, any more than give up one's dearest heritage.
- That superb ecumenical advances have been gained is reason for congratulation. That serious disagreements and differences still exist, particularly with regard to questions other than justification/deification, calls for continued collaborative work.

Sanctification and Renewal of Life

Beyond Justification: The Pursuit of Spiritual Progress

Although, as discussed, Calvin linked sanctification and justification tightly together through the concept of union—even to the point of placing union first—and expressed grave concerns about the liability of the Protestant doctrine of justification's lapse into complacency, that was not enough for the post-Reformation Pietist movement and other renewal movements. Regeneration rather than (forensic) declaration became the chief aspect in their soteriology. Regeneration was understood as a dynamic event and—unlike external forensic acquittal—an act that brought about inner change. It pointed to new life, holiness, sanctification. Whereas forensic justification is a onetime event, the same to all, holiness is a matter of growth and progress, and a typical Orthodox and Catholic idea.

A radical turn to the pursuit of renewal and change of life in the justified person was taken in the former Anglican John Wesley's theology. Like his Pietist and Puritan forebears, as well as the Anabaptists, Wesley faced the dilemma of wanting to hold on to the forensic Protestant understanding of justification, including the distinction between justification and sanctification, while also, with Pietists, understanding justification as regeneration,[161] and as such, as an inner change. Sanctification marks the "last and highest

161. John Wesley, "The Principles of a Methodist," ed. Albert C. Outler, in *The Works of John Wesley* (Nashville: Abingdon, 1986), 8:369.

state" of this progress.[162] Wesley even used at times the daring word "perfection" to mark the highest level of progress in spiritual life. Although—against misunderstandings—perfection for him did not entail perfect sinlessness, it definitely set Wesley's vision of soteriology outside the Protestant mainstream. It held on tightly to Jesus's admonition to "be perfect, as your heavenly Father is perfect" (Matt. 5:48). In sum, Wesley firmly believed that salvation includes both justification and sanctification and that they cannot be separated.[163]

As suspicious as the desire for perfectionism may sound to mainstream Protestant and Anglican ears, Wesley's vision aligns itself with deep and wide Christian tradition. The pursuit of perfection is evident among the fathers, both in the East and in the West, and subsequently. It is not without significance that Wesley read and helped translate some of the key texts of the Eastern fathers.[164]

Rediscovering Life-Affirming Holiness for Today

The Protestant Reformation's categorical separation between justification and sanctification should be corrected without compromising the underlying legitimate concern about lapsing into "works righteousness" or making the state of progress the basis for salvation. Protestant theology should have listened to the Anabaptist, Orthodox, and Catholic critique of lack of emphasis on change and good works. Most ironically, the Lutheran tradition has come to be known as one that supports "bold sinning."[165]

On the contrary, the biblical tradition approaches the question of salvation from the perspective of the likeness of God's people to God. For this to happen, a change has to take place in the human person. Of course, this may entail a change of status, as if somebody who has committed a crime is being pardoned. This, however, is not the main direction of the biblical data. For a corrective, Protestants should learn from Luther's teaching on Christ present in faith through the Spirit, making the believer a "christ," although perfection

162. Wesley, "Principles of a Methodist," 8:373.

163. William J. Abraham, "Christian Perfection," chap. 34 in *The Oxford Handbook of Methodist Studies*, ed. James E. Kirby and William J. Abraham (Oxford: Oxford University Press, 2014), 587–601.

164. M. Christensen, "Theosis and Sanctification: John Wesley's Reformulation of a Patristic Doctrine," *Wesleyan Theological Journal* 31, no. 2 (Fall 1996): 71–94.

165. Eric W. Gritsch, "Bold Sinning: The Lutheran Ethical Option," *Dialog* 14 (1975): 26–32.

can only be had in the eschaton. They would also benefit from Wesley's insight that sanctification, rather than an optional second moment, so to speak, is "the inevitable consequence of justification."[166] Although the pursuit of holiness and likeness with God should be made a stated theme and daily affair, talk about "perfectionism" has to be qualified. Here one may acknowledge the wisdom of the Lutheran slogan *simul iustus et peccator*, "simultaneously just and sinner"—or *peccator in re et iustus in spe*, "sinner in fact, just in hope."[167]

What would a life-affirming and inviting holiness look like in the third millennium? Although human effort is called forth, ultimately growth—both natural and spiritual—is a matter of the divine Spirit. As in justification, of which divine righteousness is the source, in sanctification God's holiness is the basis. Sanctification and deification reach their goal once we are fully one with God through Christ in the Spirit.

Protestants need to work toward a better balance of two mutually conditioned aspects of sanctification, *mortificatio sui* and *vivificatio in Spiritu*, dying to oneself and worldly propensities, on the one hand, and being made alive in the Spirit, on the other. The former has tended to dominate Western traditions, which have been deeply influenced by the penitential culture of the medieval and Reformation period and its overly negative anthropology. For the Eastern Church and Wesleyan movements, the finding of balance is easier because of a more robust pneumatological orientation and an idea of sin not so much as a transgression to be atoned for as a sickness to be healed.[168]

There is profound truth in the assumption that holiness is "something 'contagious,' that is, humans and things become holy from contact with the holy God."[169] That kind of holiness has nothing to do with such misconceptions of holiness as the withdrawal-from-the-world or related "elitist 'privatizing' of spiritual experience" that lead to "detachment from the community of faith and the service to the world." That kind of escapist holiness is only "attained at the expense of the more pressing task of serving Christ in the world."[170] Liberationists and others have rightly critiqued this perversion. Indeed, as Moltmann insightfully reminds us, sanctification means "rediscovering *the sanctity of life* and *the divine mystery of creation*, and defending them from life's manipulation, the secularization of nature, and the destruction

166. Moltmann, *The Spirit of Life*, 165.

167. See also Moltmann, *The Spirit of Life*, 164.

168. For comments, see Moltmann, *The Spirit of Life*, 164.

169. Simon K. H. Chan, "Sanctification," in *GDT*, 789.

170. David Fergusson, "Reclaiming the Doctrine of Sanctification," *Interpretation* 53, no. 4 (1999): 380.

of the world through human violence."[171] Recall the etymology of the term "holy" in various Western languages: "entire, healthy, unhurt, complete, and 'belonging especially' to someone."[172] Holy life is a "whole" life.

A cure against individualism and elitism is the New Testament observation that it is not an individual "saint"—in exclusion from the community—but rather every Christian, even one in the beginning states (or even temporarily backslidden), who is called holy. "Saints" appears in the plural in the biblical testimonies![173]

The last topic to be discussed in this chapter seeks to link the Christian doctrines of justification/deification and sanctification to distinctive, relevant ideas of other faith traditions.

Justification, Deification, and Holiness among Religions

The current chapter's topics do not easily yield to interfaith comparisons. Justification/deification/holiness is the distinctively Christian vision of salvation and liberation. Of course, this is not to say that no parallels whatsoever exist—the most obvious one (as exceptional as it may be in itself) is the importance of "faith" (trust) and "grace" in Pure Land Buddhism or forms of piety in (deeply) theistic *bhakti* traditions of Hinduism, as discussed above. Instead, what is argued here is that these kinds of "exceptional" (or at least not mainstream) orientations should be put in perspective against the wider "theological" framework of each living faith. Where parallels exist among religions on topics such as conversion, forgiveness, and healing, they have to be acknowledged and carefully compared. Where alleged parallels are only superficial or not representative of the whole faith tradition, they should not be given undue attention. Indicative of that, in a project called "Explorations in Lutheran Perspectives on People of Other Faiths,"[174] the term "justification by faith" (unless used to describe generally Lutheran soteriology) is virtually absent in all comparative exercises.

Although the Jewish scriptural tradition knows the idea of justification by faith, its meaning differs vastly from Christian teaching because Christian

171. Moltmann, *The Spirit of Life*, 171.

172. Moltmann, *The Spirit of Life*, 175.

173. Fergusson, "Reclaiming the Doctrine," 381.

174. Paul Martinson, "Explorations in Lutheran Perspectives on People of Other Faiths: Toward a Christian Theology of Religions," in *Theological Perspectives on Other Faiths: Toward a Christian Theology of Religions*, ed. Hance A. O. Mwakabana, LWF Documentation 41 (Geneva: Lutheran World Federation, 1997).

theology claims that even the salvation of Abraham (Gen. 15:6) is because of the Messiah's having come, Jesus the Christ. Israel's faith categorically rejects all those claims. Instead, the Jewish vision of redemption and deliverance focuses on following Torah. Unlike the Christian vision, its eschatological dimension is marginal, with its focus on this-worldly renewal with the coming of the yet-awaited Messiah of Israel. No need to mention that to Jewish intuitions, the idea of salvation by faith being contingent on the sacrificial death of the innocent Messiah borders on blasphemy.

Salvation in Islam is about submission to Allah and has little to do with the Christian idea of justification by faith; the only role of "faith" in Islam has to do with the knowledge of the Qur'anic (and later, the Prophet's traditional) teachings and confidence in the truth of Islam. Furthermore, a significant difference between Christian and Islamic traditions is that whereas in the former, forgiveness "costs" God (and hence, requires a sacrifice or satisfaction or similar), in Islam God just forgives, without any sacrifice.[175] While "salvation" in Islam is ultimately dependent on Allah, the idea of an "undeserved" gracious gift is foreign to that sister tradition.

The differences between the Christian doctrine of justification by faith and Asiatic traditions are too deep and wide to permit any meaningful comparison. A potential bridge might be found in some aspects of the doctrine of deification. This work, however, is just beginning at the time of this writing, and no report can yet be provided. Although holiness and sanctity are common themes among religions, commonalities with the Christian theology of sanctification based on God's work of salvation are foreign to Asiatic faiths.

Healing, Restoration, and Empowerment

The Omission of Healing in Theology

Healing Ministry in Christian History and Today

A deep irony and profound omission come to the surface when we speak of healing, restoration, and empowerment. The dilemma is simply this: although no major Christian tradition at any historical period has denied the healing and empowering capacity of the Creator God, no major doctrinal/systematic presentation has cared to include the topic of healing in the *ordo salutis*. With the

175. I am indebted to the British Islamicist David Marshall of Duke University.

exception of an important discussion of healings, exorcisms, and charismatic effects in the revisionist *ordo salutis* of Moltmann's *Spirit of Life* (chap. 9), one looks in vain for that category in any noteworthy doctrinal manuals, unless they are written by Pentecostals and charismatics.[176] Yet Jesus of Nazareth was an itinerant healer and exorcist, and his followers were sent out not only to preach and teach but also to heal and deliver from oppressive powers. In the book of Acts, healings and exorcism continued as an integral part of the church's regular activity of prayer, liturgy, sacraments, and missionary outreach. Throughout Christian history healing in various forms has continued,[177] including also the establishment of hospitals and sanitoriums. Yet theologians have failed to include the topic under the vision of Christian salvation.

Some Christian traditions hold a predominantly sacramentally oriented approach to healing in the forefront, particularly in Eastern Orthodoxy, Roman Catholicism, and Anglicanism; in others, the charismatic gifts and hope for instantaneous healing are more typical, as in Pentecostal/charismatic movements. With the expansion of Christianity beginning in the early twentieth century to the Global South, healing practices, approaches, and theological interpretations are intensifying.[178] Focusing on the contemporary scene, the Czech Reformed theologian Pavel Hejzlar has discerned "two paradigms for divine healing." The "healing evangelists" expect an instantaneous recovery to normally take place, and often the charismatically endowed healer is the instrument. The "pastoral healers" equally believe in a rapid restoration of health, but they are open to both the gradual and the instantaneous work of God; the healer's role is less pronounced and may also include a group of Christians over a period of time.[179] In recent years, collaboration between health professionals and Christian ministers has emerged.

The importance of healing and restoration to theology and religion is attested not only by their centrality in the life of the church, but also by the wide interest in the topics in secular interdisciplinary studies in psychology, sociology, and various health sciences, as well as in the media and popular press—let alone in new religious movements.

176. Kimberly Ervin Alexander, *Pentecostal Healing: Models in Theology and Practice* (Dorset, UK: Deo, 2006).

177. Ronald A. N. Kydd, *Healing through the Centuries: Models for Understanding* (Peabody, MA: Hendrickson, 1998).

178. Amanda Porterfield, *Healing in the History of Christianity* (New York: Oxford University Press, 2005), chap. 5.

179. Pavel Hejzlar, *Two Paradigms for Divine Healing: Fred F. Bosworth, Kenneth E. Hagin, Agnes Sanford, and Francis MacNutt in Dialogue* (Leiden: Brill, 2010).

Why the Omission in Theology?

What might be the reasons for such a blunt ignorance of a topic so prevalent in the Bible and the experience of the church throughout her history? Two factors appear to be determinative. First, academic theology's uncritical embrace of the naturalistic epistemology of the contemporary scientific worldview, rooted in the Enlightenment, has blocked the way to something as "supernatural" as healing and exorcism. Second, known under the nomenclature of "cessationism," formative theological movements throughout history have concluded that while healings could happen—and did happen during the first centuries of Christian history—their time and validity ended when the biblical canon was ratified.

Having already critiqued and defeated the naive naturalist epistemological standpoint that refuses to grant the possibility of real divine action, and hence of healings and restoration, we now focus on the cessationist argument. It is deeply embedded in some Christian traditions, particularly traditional Protestantism and current conservative Reformed churches; its roots, however, go back to patristic theology, particularly Augustine (although before the Reformation, cessationism rarely was a formulated, strict doctrinal standpoint).[180] Theological cessationism readily affirms the presence and reality of miracles in the biblical world and until the time of the closing of the Christian canon by the end of the fourth century; after that, the argument goes, miracles ceased. Once the written Word of God (the Bible) came to function as the "norming norm," no spiritual experiences, even the charismatic ones that had previously been taken as divine confirmations, were needed.

There are two forms of theological cessationism, which can be named the "soft" and the "hard-core" views. Whereas the former does not categorically reject the possibility of miraculous events now, they are made nonexistent, practically speaking, not only because they are not needed but also because they seem not to take place anymore. The "hard-core" version categorically denies the existence of all miraculous events after the apostolic era and judges all claims to their existence as counterfeits, as argued in the fundamentalist Reformed theologian B. B. Warfield's classic *The Counterfeit Miracles* (1918).[181] What is highly ironic about cessation-

180. Jon Ruthven, *On the Cessation of the Charismata: The Protestant Polemic on Post-biblical Miracles* (Sheffield: Sheffield Academic, 1993), 24–40.

181. Benjamin Breckinridge Warfield, *The Counterfeit Miracles* (New York: Charles Scribner's Sons, 1918), http://www.monergism.com/thethreshold/sdg/warfield/warfield_counterfeit.html. The most recent highly aggressive fundamentalist-Reformed cessationist

ism is that it boasts no biblical reasons to support it, yet its advocates are fundamentalist scriptural "inerrantists." Clearly, the New Testament data speaks against any idea of a certain historical time bringing to an end charismatic gifts.

The rejection of cessationism, however, should not lead to a return to the idyllic pre-Enlightenment mind-set in order to be more receptive to healings, exorcisms, and other miracles. That theological tactic would make a certain cultural epoch (pre-Enlightenment times) a precondition for experiencing fullness of salvation. It would also cut off bridges with the rest of the modern world. A related theologically suspicious claim is that Christians in certain global locations, particularly in Africa, are by default more open to the miraculous and that this attitude should function as the template for the rest of Christians.[182]

A Contemporary Theology of Healing and Restoration

A Holistic, All-Embracing Salvation

Healings feature prominently in the Bible.[183] The New Testament Gospels narrate numerous healings and miraculous cures, and the Synoptic Gospels add to the picture acts of deliverance and exorcisms.[184] Jesus used various "methods," from touch, to laying on of hands, to healing from a distance, to curious things such as use of saliva (Mark 7:33; 8:23; John 9:6). No doubt there are similarities to shamanic healing techniques, widely known in ancient cultures—and in those of today's Global South. What are we to think of them? On the one hand, the use of then-common techniques is a given; what else would one expect in a culture of the times?

The healing ministry of Jesus is a robust statement about the all-inclusive nature of God's salvation; it includes the physical and emotional as well as the spiritual. Healings and exorcisms were also signs of profound sympathy, cosuffering (Matt. 14:14). Jesus's healing bodily contact with people considered

---

campaign in the USA is the "Strange Fire" movement; see http://www.monergism.com/thethreshold/sdg/warfield/warfield_counterfeit.html.

182. David Tonhou Ngong, *The Holy Spirit and Salvation in African Christian Theology: Imagining a More Hopeful Future for Africa* (New York: Peter Lang, 2010), chap. 2.

183. Michael L. Brown, *Israel's Divine Healer* (Grand Rapids: Zondervan, 1995).

184. Steven L. Davies, *Jesus the Healer: Possession, Trance, and the Origins of Christianity* (New York: Continuum, 1995).

"untouchable," such as the woman with bleeding (Mark 5:24–34), helped defeat the belief that women's bodies are dirty.

Importantly, the Eastern Orthodox bishop George M. Nalunnakkal of India says that not only is "the theme of healing . . . central to the theology, and particularly the soteriology, of almost all churches," but it is so central that "in Orthodox theology, 'healing' is almost a synonym for 'salvation.'"[185] With the spread of Christianity to the Global South, the significance of a holistic view of salvation in Christian theology has been rediscovered.[186]

Atonement, Faith, and Healing: A Need for Clarification and Theological Critique

Christian theology affirms the close link between the atonement and healing based on Old Testament testimonies (Isa. 53:4–5) and their creative use in the New Testament (Matt. 8:17; 1 Pet. 2:24). Modern healing movements established the doctrine of "healing in atonement." Many twentieth-century "healing evangelists" argue vocally that as surely as there is atonement for sin, there is also healing by virtue of the cross.

But how exactly are the two—atonement and healing—linked theologically?[187] It is instructive to see how Matthew (8:17) applies Isaiah 53:4–5 to Jesus's healing ministry: "He took our infirmities and bore our diseases." There is no reference to the cross here. Even less can that formula be supported in the context of 1 Peter's use of Isaiah's passage. Both in the context of the epistle as a whole and in the immediate context, it appears that Jesus's suffering provides encouragement for Christians to follow Jesus in suffering. Whereas in Matthew the link to (physical) healings is clearly presented, in Peter that connection is missing altogether. Thus, the first conclusion is that the link between healing and atonement can be affirmed only at a general level, that is, in light of Christian salvation stemming from the atoning and reconciling work of Christ. But there is nothing "causal" or automatic there.

185. George Mathew Nalunnakkal, "Come Holy Spirit, Heal and Reconcile: Called in Christ to Be Reconciling and Healing Communities," *International Review of Mission* 94, no. 372 (2005): 17–18.

186. Timothy C. Tennent, *Theology in the Context of World Christianity: How the Global Church Is Influencing the Way We Think about and Discuss Theology* (Grand Rapids: Zondervan, 2007), 109–22.

187. W. Kelly Bokovay, "The Relationship of Physical Healing to the Atonement," *Didaskalia* 3, no. 1 (October 1991): 24–39.

Second, like salvation in general, healing "now" is a foretaste of the coming eschatological fulfillment based on the reconciling work of the triune God. Living as we are now between the "already" of the coming kingdom and the "not yet" of its consummation, healings serve as signs affirming for us the final victory.

What about healing and faith? There are healing evangelists and others who have not only made faith the necessary condition for healing to take place but have also devised a "faith formula"—that is, a certain type of faith automatically leads to healing and deliverance. They speak of faith in terms of "claiming" God's promises and assign to "positive confession" almost a magical power. Faith in that case is like a signed check to be redeemed![188] The faith formula leads to preoccupation with one's own faith rather than recognition of divine power and mercy. It also brings about anxiety and pressure to perform. This criticism is not to undermine the importance Jesus placed on faith but rather to put it in proper perspective. While the faith formula must be rejected as a theologically mistaken idea and pastorally disastrous technique,[189] systematic reflection is needed for a proper understanding of the relation between faith and healing.

The Gospels show an integral link between faith and healing. Jesus seemed to attribute some healings to faith (Mark 1:40–44; Matt. 8:2–4; Luke 17:11–19). At times Jesus rebuked people for lack of faith (Matt. 14:31; 17:20). A closer look at the Gospels' data (alone), however, yields a more complex and elusive link between the two. A number of healing incidents make no mention of faith (Mark 3:1–5; Matt. 8:5–13; Luke 4:38–39; John 9:1–7). While in many instances the healed person's faith played a role, there are also incidents in which the faith of other involved persons was commended (Mark 2:1–12; Matt. 9:1–8; Luke 5:17–26). Furthermore, at times faith seemed to precede healing (Mark 2:4; Matt. 8:10; Luke 7:50), and at other times faith emerged as a result of healing (Matt. 11:4; Luke 24:13–35; John 12:37).

Several theological conclusions follow from this discussion. First, there is no "causal" relationship between the work of God and human response (faith). God's works are based on grace and compassion. Second, when speaking of faith in relation to healing, we also have to insist on hope (for God's continuing care amidst sickness and suffering) and love (for those who were

188. For a critique, see Ken Blue, *Authority to Heal* (Downers Grove, IL: InterVarsity Press, 1987), chap. 3.

189. Gordon D. Fee, *The Disease of the Health and Wealth Gospels* (Vancouver, BC: Regent College Publishing, 2006 [1985]).

not healed). We have to remember that "God's power is as near to us in sickness and in death as it is in healing."[190] Third, although there is no direct link between faith and healing, prayer for healing matters. As the American Lutheran Old Testament scholar Frederick J. Gaiser succinctly puts it: "God does not become a God of love and healing because of our prayer. But our prayer opens us to the God of love, who desires our healing."[191]

Fourth, healing can be experienced at personal and communal levels in a variety of ways. Healing can be focused on a "healing evangelist" or "pastoral healer" paradigm; it can be instantaneous or gradual; it may be attributed mainly to prayer and spirituality or to medical expertise; it may be had in a healing meeting or at a sacramental encounter.[192] Fifth, although sickness and healing are personal matters, the role of the faith community is not unimportant. James (5:13–16) recommends that a sick person contact the elders of the church for prayer and anointing with oil (a common Old Testament practice).[193] After all, healing ministry is an integral part of the church's daily life and ministry. Finally, as established above, ultimately healings and deliverances point to the eschatological consummation. Healings are "signs" pointing toward fullness.

What about suffering in relation to healing? It is clear from the biblical teaching that both the pain of suffering and hope for healing coexist until the eschaton. While the acknowledgment of the presence of suffering is not to be made a pretext for not praying for divine healing, theological reflection on suffering, pain, and disability is an important part of a theology of restoration.

To widen the interfaith dimension, let us continue looking at the topics of this chapter in relation to other faiths.

Healing and Sickness among Religions

Health and sickness feature prominently in religions.[194] All scriptural traditions deal with the problem of sickness and the possibility of restoration.

190. Blue, *Authority to Heal*, 49.

191. Frederik J. Gaiser, *Healing in the Bible: Theological Insights for Christian Ministry* (Grand Rapids: Baker Academic, 2010), 55.

192. Charles W. Gusmer, *And You Visited Me: Sacramental Ministry to the Sick and the Dying*, rev. ed. (Collegeville, MN: Liturgical Press, 1990).

193. Keith Warrington, "James 5:14–18: Healing Then and Now," *International Review of Mission* 93, no. 370/371 (July/October 2004): 346–67.

194. David Kinsley, *Health, Healing, and Religion: A Cross-Cultural Perspective* (Upper Saddle River, NJ: Prentice Hall, 1996).

Abrahamic Traditions

The three Abrahamic traditions speak of healing and well-being as a promise of God. Well known are the Old Testament promises of Yahweh as healer. Indeed, in the Israelite faith both calamity and healing come from one and the same Lord (Deut. 32:39). So deeply is healing instilled in Jewish scriptural tradition that a petition from Jeremiah (17:14) is recited in daily Jewish liturgy: "Heal us, O Lord, and we shall be healed."[195]

According to the Qur'anic promise in 41:44, the divine word is "guidance and a healing" for believers but brings about deafness to the disobedient. God is the healer (26:80). The Hadith tradition continues and deepens this idea. According to the Prophet, "God has not sent down a disease without sending down a remedy for it."[196] Not surprisingly, all Islamic traditions also invite the faithful to pray for healing; it is particularly important in the mystical Sufi tradition. Folk healing tradition is long and wide in Islam.[197]

Asiatic Traditions

If there is a common denominator between widely divergent Asiatic faith traditions concerning insights into wellness, it has to do with harmony and balance.[198] The human being's health is part of a larger cosmic network. Although all faith traditions locate sickness and health in a matrix of influences and factors, from religious to secular, in Hinduism the network of effects is unusually wide. It includes not only karma, the spiritual "cause-effect" chain, and other foundational theological themes such as "ignorance," as well as complicated rules and rites regarding ritual pollution and purity, but also caste and class, gender, and other such issues related to the sociocultural hierarchy. The medical and religious are deeply inter-

195. David L. Freeman and Judith Z. Abrams, eds., *Illness and Health in the Jewish Tradition: Writings from the Bible to Today* (Philadelphia: Jewish Publication Society, 1999).

196. *Mishkat al-Masabih*, ed. Al-Baghawi, trans. James Robinson, 4 vols. (Lahore: Sh. Muhammad Ashraft, 1965–1966), 3:945; Fazlur Rahman, *Health and Medicine in the Islamic Tradition* (New York: Kazi Publications, 1998).

197. See, e.g., "Islamic Folk Healing," Islamic Healing Systems, http://islamichealingsystems.wordpress.com/islamicfolkhealing/.

198. Ivette Vargas-O'Bryan, "Keeping It All in Balance: Teaching Asian Religions through Illness and Healing," chap. 4 in *Teaching Religion and Healing*, ed. Linda L. Barnes and Inés Talamantez (New York: Oxford University Press, 2006).

twined.[199] Some diseases are conceived to be the result of the anger of a god. Commensurately with other faith traditions, Hinduism also provides for deliverance from possession and demonic influence.[200]

The question of the place of suffering and sickness in all diverse Buddhist traditions is of course linked with the concept of *dukkha*. Another foundational concept, namely, the interrelatedness of everything in the cosmos, comes into play here: "Suffering is not unique to those who struggle with chronic disability or illness. The point is that even those who are physically healthy and materially wealthy nonetheless experience a chaotic, continually festering dissatisfaction."[201]

If the original Theravada tradition has focused much more energy on "healing" in terms of spiritual healing, the theistically oriented Mahayana traditions imagine healing as both spiritual and physical. Not unlike other theistic traditions, Mahayana can link healing directly to Buddha.[202] Indeed, one of the most interesting developments in this regard is the emergence of the "Medicine Buddha," a hugely important object of worship and prayer in devotional movements throughout East Asia.[203] An authoritative, widely used manual is *The Sutra of Medicine Buddha*. No doubt this theistic version of healing in Buddhism echoes important themes not only in Abrahamic but also in other theistic traditions.

Empowerment, Charismatic Gifting, and Spirit Baptism

Various Interpretations of the Baptism in the Holy Spirit

If possible, doctrinal theology's omission of the category of empowerment is even more striking than its omission of healing. The themes of Spirit bap-

199. Prakash N. Desai, *Health and Medicine in the Hindu Tradition: Continuity and Cohesion* (New York: Crossroad, 1989).

200. B. S. Bharathi, "Spirit Possession and Healing Practices in a South Indian Fishing Community," *Man in India* 73, no. 4 (1968): 343–52.

201. Darla Schumm and Michael Stoltzfus, "Chronic Illness and Disability: Narratives of Suffering and Healing in Buddhism and Christianity," in *Disability and Religious Diversity: Cross-Cultural and Interreligious Perspectives*, ed. Darla Schumm and Michael Stoltzfus (New York: Palgrave Macmillan, 2011), 164.

202. Raoul Birnbaum, *The Healing Buddha* (Boulder, CO: Shambhala, 1989), 3–26.

203. Deepak Chopra, *Journey into Healing: Awakening the Wisdom within You* (London: Ebury, 2010).

tism, charismatic empowerment, and gifting are simply missing altogether in *ordo salutis* presentations (with the exception of Pentecostal/charismatic ones). Why should we be concerned about this category? There are at least three reasons. The first has to do with early Christian tradition. Both in the biblical and early Christian tradition, the charismatic element, at times named Spirit baptism, was integral to the process of Christian initiation. Second, the rise of Pentecostal/charismatic Christianity has again made Spirit baptism prominent. Third, a holistic view of salvation properly includes the dynamic element of gifting, inspiration, and empowerment.

Let us divide the many interpretations of Spirit baptism into four broad categories,[204] the first of which I call the "traditional soteriological view." Its main idea is that Spirit baptism is another name for everything that the Holy Spirit is doing in salvation. The Reformed theologian John Calvin's identification of baptism in the Holy Spirit with the work of regeneration[205] and Roman Catholic theologian Yves Congar's identification of Spirit baptism with water baptism[206] represent this mainstream conception. Barth's view also belongs to this tradition: in distinction from water baptism, the human response, Spirit baptism virtually includes everything the Spirit is doing with regard to salvation.[207] The implication of the traditional soteriological view is that if the term were not used, nothing would be lost, because it is just another way to speak of the Spirit's work in Christian initiation and life.

The most novel interpretation is provided by the Pentecostal movement. Therein Spirit baptism is a necessary and distinct category in the *ordo salutis* and cannot be removed or replaced by something else. Most Pentecostal movements teach that Spirit baptism is distinct from and subsequent to conversion (or new birth).[208] Spirit baptism happens "after" one has become a Christian. Whereas Spirit baptism happens only once in life, it is supposed to be followed by daily fillings with the Spirit. The experience belongs to every Christian, and its main purpose is empowerment for witness and service (Acts 1:8). The most distinctive feature of the Pentecostal interpretation is the expectation that every believer experiences glossolalia (speaking in tongues)

204. See Henry I. Lederle, *Treasures Old and New: Interpretations of "Spirit-Baptism" in the Charismatic Renewal Movement* (Peabody, MA: Hendrickson, 1981), chap. 4

205. Calvin, *Institutes* 3.1.4.

206. Yves Congar, *I Believe in the Holy Spirit*, trans. David Smith (New York: Seabury, 1983; 3 vols. in 1, New York: Herder, 1997), 3:218, 222–24.

207. Barth, *CD* IV/4, 30–31.

208. Frank D. Macchia, *Baptized in the Spirit: A Global Pentecostal Theology* (Grand Rapids: Zondervan, 2006), chap. 2.

as the "initial physical evidence." Whereas this is a normative experience for all, many may also receive the continuing gift of speaking in tongues throughout their Christian life. In other words, there is a distinction between the onetime "evidential" glossolalia patterned after several instances in the book of Acts (2:4–6; 10:46; 19:6) and a regular "prayer language" as mentioned in 1 Corinthians (12:28–30). This last item is not universally affirmed by all Pentecostals, although a majority of world Pentecostals own the belief in some form or other.

The third view, which I name "charismatic-sacramental," represents a radical middle way between the first two views. It forges an integral link between the sacramental water baptism in which the Holy Spirit is given to the baptized and the later experience of Spirit baptism as an occasion for the actualization and surfacing of the Spirit initially received in water baptism through a conscious charismatic experience.[209] Similar to the Pentecostal interpretation, this charismatic-sacramental view expects the release of a charismatic gift, but unlike the Pentecostal, it leaves open what kind of gift that might be. This general template is followed by the majority of theologians in the Roman Catholic charismatic movement and is also influential among some leading Anglican and Lutheran renewal movements.

The final category I name the "nonsacramental-charismatic view." In this outlook, represented by the influential Roman Catholic theologian Francis Sullivan, Spirit baptism is seen as a new imparting of the Spirit without any direct link with the sacrament.[210] Not uncommon in Catholic theology, it seeks to oppose the tendency to limit the conferring of charisms merely to the sacramental context. Nonsacramental Protestants, such as all free churches, may also follow this template in their own theological framework.

Spirit Baptism: A Constructive Ecumenical Proposal

The expression "baptism with the Holy Spirit" does not appear as a noun in the New Testament; only "baptize," the verb, appears. The earliest version in Mark associates baptism with power as the Baptist presents Jesus, the Baptizer with the Spirit, as the "mightier" (or more powerful) one (Mark 1:7). Mark

209. Kilian McDonnell, OSB, and George T. Montague, *Christian Initiation and Baptism in the Holy Spirit: Evidence from the First Eight Centuries* (Collegeville, MN: Liturgical Press, 1991), 84.

210. Francis A. Sullivan, SJ, "Baptism in the Spirit," in *Charisms and Charismatic Renewal* (Ann Arbor, MI: Servant, 1982), 59–75.

assumes the continuation of this ministry by the disciples (and by implication, the church; see Mark 3:14–15, among other passages).

Particularly in the theology of Luke, the Spirit's charismatic work stands in the forefront. In a well-known gospel passage (Luke 7:18–23), Jesus took miraculous deeds as divine confirmation, and already earlier (4:18–19) had introduced his ministry as charismatic. The programmatic passage of Acts 1:8 extends the promise of the Spirit's empowerment to the church, and to Luke we are indebted for the Pentecost event narrative, including the sign of tongues and fire (chap. 2).[211] Similarly, the theology of Paul, as conversant as it is with a wide range of the Spirit's ministry, including the soteriological and ethical, highlights also the Spirit's charismatic dimensions (1 Cor. 12; 14; among others).[212] The same template seems to have been at work during the first centuries of the Christian church, although after the patristic era and with the rise of infant baptism, the charismatic element began to lose prominence.[213]

In light of this New Testament and patristic evidence, the traditional soteriological view is to be deemed reductionist because it simply says too little about empowerment. This is of course not to undermine—and certainly not to debunk—the authenticity of Christian initiation that lacks the charismatic and "experiential" element, but it is to say that a more holistic and integral vision of salvation is needed. The other three Spirit baptism interpretations are clearly superior on this count. They all in their distinctive manner incorporate the charismatic element in a holistic vision of the *ordo salutis.*

The Pentecostal interpretation does this most robustly. Ironically, its separation of Spirit baptism from water baptism is both its strength and its liability. The benefit of the separation lies in the legitimate reminder to us that there are no necessary biblical or theological (any more than pastoral) reasons to limit the charismatic breakthrough, even in its first occurrence, to water baptism. "The Spirit blows where it wills" (John 3:8). On the other hand, so categorically separating it from the wider framework of Christian initiation is also a liability because in the New Testament, particularly in the book of Acts, water baptism and Spirit baptism are clearly related. In that respect, more coherent theologies of Spirit baptism are offered by the sacramental and nonsacramental charismatic views.

211. Roger Stronstad, *The Charismatic Theology of St. Luke* (Peabody, MA: Hendrickson, 1984).

212. Gordon D. Fee, *God's Empowering Presence: The Holy Spirit in the Letters of Paul* (Grand Rapids: Baker Academic, 2009 [1994]).

213. McDonnell and Montague, *Christian Initiation*, 315.

Which of the two views—sacramental-charismatic or nonsacramental-charismatic—is to be preferred? Ecumenically, it is best to be open to both. The nonsacramental is appealing to those Protestant traditions whose theology is not sacramental.[214] Apart from the sacramental apparatus, all three views, in a qualified yet real sense, establish a link between initiation and Spirit baptism; even for Pentecostals, the Holy Spirit indwells believers' hearts at the moment they become Christians, followed by water baptism (if not immediately, then soon thereafter). Another important common denominator among the three interpretations is the desire to be continually filled with the Holy Spirit after the initial breakthrough experience.

What about the external manifestations of Spirit baptism? All three interpretations have to be commended for expecting, as normal, an experiential dimension to Spirit baptism. That consensus should not be lost when differences of opinion about its exact nature are being negotiated. It seems clear that the Pentecostal insistence on one definite and exclusive "initial physical evidence" such as glossolalia cannot be found convincing. While there is some biblical precedent in Acts for the link between speaking in tongues and Spirit baptism, one can hardly make a strong exegetical case for such a rule.[215] Even more impossible is the novel and artificial distinction between the tongues of the day of Pentecost and those mentioned by Paul in 1 Corinthians.

In no way undermining the importance of charismatic experience and accompanying signs, we also have to keep clearly in mind that Spirit baptism is meant for empowerment and gifting, that is, for vocation and ministry. Rather than self-glorification or spiritual enjoyment, Spirit baptism brings about a loving heart and serving hands in the service of the kingdom of God. Following the biblical precedent, particularly the Lukan Jesus's inauguration speech, the empowerment by the Spirit also has social and political implications. Those who are sent out to share testimony to Christ (Acts 1:8) are also mandated to care for the poor, support the marginalized, heal the sick, and free prisoners.

The last main section widens the horizons of the *ordo salutis* to include social, communal, and political dimensions in the search for a holistic vision of salvation.

214. McDonnell and Montague, *Christian Initiation*, 84.

215. See also the Pentecostal exegete Gordon D. Fee, "Baptism in the Holy Spirit: The Issue of Separability and Subsequence," *Pneuma* 7, no. 2 (1985): 87–99.

Widening the Salvific Horizon: Reconciliation, Liberation, and Peacebuilding

The Work of the Spirit in Liberation and Reconciliation of Communities

It has been repeatedly stated that in the holistic and comprehensive vision of salvation sought in this work that salvation, while personal, is never individualistic; it encompasses also communities at various levels. Furthermore, while spiritual at its core, the Christian view of salvation does not separate spirituality and the rest of life; rather, these two belong together. In addition, while the ultimate aim of Christian salvation is eternal communion with God and God's people, it is not escapist, as there is a dynamic continuity-in-discontinuity between the "now" and the "then."

The Spirit of God works in the midst of particular earthly realities, social conflicts, and personal problems.[216] Already in the Old Testament narratives, the Spirit's advocacy and liberative work in the midst of chaos, anarchy, and confusion can be discerned as evident, for example, in the book of Judges, in which cycles of deliverance, chaos, defeat by enemies, and loss of hope follow one after another.[217] The same formative presence of the Spirit is at work in the midst of the early church: "And all who believed were together and had all things in common; and they sold their possessions and goods and distributed them to all, as any had need" (Acts 2:44–45).

An increasing number of theological reports are confirming the rediscovery of the liberative work of the Spirit under way in various global contexts. According to José Comblin, a Belgian-born Catholic theologian, "the experience of God found in the new Christian communities of Latin America can properly be called experience of the Holy Spirit" in its liberative, empowering, and uniting ministry.[218] Working among the Catholic base communities, he discerns various liberative dimensions to the experience of the Spirit, including the experience of action: rather than being acted upon, now the poor take initiative; rather than being passive, Amerindians, black slaves, slum dwellers, the unemployed, and peasants are now being energized by the Spirit. This "earthly" liberation is not exclusive of "spiritual" transformation; the two belong together.

216. Moltmann, *The Spirit of Life*, 110–12.

217. Michael Welker, *God the Spirit: A Problem of Experience in Today's World*, trans. John F. Hoffmeyer (Minneapolis: Fortress, 1994), chap. 3.

218. José Comblin, *The Holy Spirit and Liberation*, trans. Paul Burns (Maryknoll, NY: Orbis, 1989), xi.

"Truth and Reconciliation": Forgiveness and Peacebuilding

In his passionate book *The Principle of Mercy*, Jon Sobrino issues a powerful call for a sociopolitically responsible spirituality that does not shy away from painful issues of reconciliation and forgiveness in a world of violence and oppression. Therein he joins a growing number of theologians and leaders from diverse contexts.[219] Forgiveness also comes to bear on interfaith relations.[220] One important form of political forgiveness is the establishment of processes that aim at reaching reconciliation and forgiveness after conflicts have been resolved. The most well-known is the truth and reconciliation process in South Africa, which, unlike most others, also had a determined Christian orientation in its matrix. It also employed robustly the African form of communalism expressed with the term *ubuntu.*[221]

What are we to think *theologically* of attempts for political forgiveness? L. Philip Barnes has pointed to some potential liabilities such as their often thin theological basis, particularly with regard to the wider atonement and reconciliation narrative of Christian faith, and the tendency of these attempts to operate at a too-general level. He also notes a frequent lack of critical reflection on what "unconditional" forgiveness may or may not mean.[222] On the positive side, we can refer to the seasoned note by Mark R. Amstutz, a leading authority in the field: having studied the process of twenty or so truth commissions of sorts in various global locations, he concludes that the significance of a truth commission is "not that it deemphasizes punishment but that it focuses on the reformation of communal bonds by encouraging moral reflection based on truth telling, confession, forgiveness, and reconciliation."[223]

219. Raymond G. Helmick and Rodney L. Petersen, eds., *Forgiveness and Reconciliation: Religion, Public Policy, and Conflict Transformation* (Philadelphia: Templeton Foundation, 2001).

220. Rodney L. Petersen, "A Theology of Forgiveness: Terminology, Rhetoric, and the Dialectic of Interfaith Relationships," in Helmick and Petersen, *Forgiveness and Reconciliation*, 3–25.

221. Lyn S. Graybill, *Truth and Reconciliation in South Africa: Miracle or Model?* (Boulder, CO: Lynne Rienner, 2002).

222. L. Philip Barnes, "Talking Politics, Talking Forgiveness," *Scottish Journal of Theology* 64 (2011): 72–78.

223. Mark R. Amstutz, *The Healing of Nations: The Promise and Limits of Political Forgiveness* (Lanham, MD: Rowman & Littlefield, 2005), 188.

Reconciliation as the Ultimate Aim of Salvation

In this holistic work of reconciliation, particularly important in our global and pluralistic world are peacebuilding and resolving conflicts.[224] Not for nothing did the recent WCC International Ecumenical Peace Convention make this programmatic statement: "We understand peace and peacemaking as an indispensable part of our common faith. Peace is inextricably related to the love, justice and freedom that God has granted to all human beings through Christ and the work of the Holy Spirit as a gift and vocation. It constitutes a pattern of life that reflects human participation in God's love for the world."[225]

In many contexts such as Australia and North America, an integral, continuing part of reconciliation has to do with relationships between the First Nations and "latecomers."[226] The call for churches to work toward reconciliation is heightened by the sad observation that throughout history "so-called Christian nations have gone to war readily over the centuries, more often than not with the blessing of their chaplains and archbishops."[227]

When God begins the work of reconciliation on earth, the starting point is with the victim.[228] Beginning with the victim means taking the side of the weak and the vulnerable; it seeks to reestablish her or his humanity. A distinctively Christian work of reconciliation also seeks to help the victim turn to God, although that should not be made a precondition for the work of reconciliation concerning current earthly realities. Divine love and forgiveness are unconditional. But there also is the need to help the perpetrator find repentance, remorse, and forgiveness through which his or her humanity can be reestablished. Both the victim and the perpetrator have an urgent need for healing.[229]

The final, brief section of this chapter links reconciliation at all levels and the whole order of salvation with the ultimate eschatological consummation.

224. Robert J. Schreiter, R. Scott Appleby, and Gerard F. Powers, eds., *Peacebuilding: Catholic Theology, Ethics, and Praxis* (Maryknoll, NY: Orbis, 2010).

225. "Glory to God and Peace on Earth: The Message of the International Ecumenical Peace Convocation," May 17–25, 2011, Kingston, Jamaica, available at http://meet-junge-oekumene.de/wp-content/uploads/2015/11/iepcreportonyouthparticipation.pdf.

226. Norman C. Habel, *Reconciliation: Searching for Australia's Soul* (Sydney: HarperCollins, 1999).

227. Langmead, "Transformed Relationships," 12.

228. Robert J. Schreiter, "A Practical Theology of Healing, Forgiveness, and Reconciliation," in Schreiter, Appleby, and Powers, *Peacebuilding*, 371–72, 385–90.

229. Schreiter, "Practical Theology of Healing," 372–76.

Epilogue: The Faithfulness of God and the End of Human Yearning

Traditionally, the last "step" in the order of salvation has been glorification, the ultimate consummation of salvation in God's blessed eternity.[230] The classical biblical support for the doctrine of glorification comes from Romans 8:29–30. Confidence in the final victory is expressed in the Reformed doctrine of "the perseverance of the saints to the end" that not only speaks to spiritual assurance but—as any deeply existential issue—also has to do with the life situation of the faithful. As Moltmann, himself Reformed, puts it, for "Christians living in a minority situation or under persecution," this concern arose: Can the experience of the Holy Spirit in the rebirth to new life and to a living hope ever be lost or not? On all sides of the Reformed movement, from Huguenots to the Dutch and others, it was a deeply felt concern testing the reliability of the faithfulness of God.[231] The Lutheran version of perseverance is ecclesiologically founded. According to the Augsburg Confession, "one holy Christian church will be and remain forever."[232] Notwithstanding differences in nuancing the doctrine of perseverance,[233] the Protestant theologians agreed on the following: "1. God the Father is faithful; he cannot deny himself (II Tim. 2.13). He never lets go of the person he has chosen. 2. God the Son prayed for those who are his 'that your faith might not fail' (Luke 22.32). 3. As advance payment and beginning of eternal life, the Holy Spirit remains with the people who are his to the end (*usque ad finem*). The Holy Spirit 'seals' God's children for the day of redemption."[234]

The Catholic rebuttal of the Reformation doctrine of assurance of salvation and perseverance at the sixteenth-century Council of Trent (*Decree on Justification*, chaps. 9 and 16) mistook it for self-assurance and overly optimistic trust in human steadfastness. Trent was unwilling to acknowledge that the Reformation doctrine of perseverance indeed highlighted the same principle of divine faithfulness that the Catholic doctrine also underlined. Interestingly, in the Arminian-Calvinist exchange about election (as discussed above in this chapter), the Arminian critique of the technically formulated Calvinist doctrine of the perseverance of the saints wanted to shift the focus on to the faithfulness of God rather than on "cold" philosophico-theological reasoning.

230. Bernard Ramm, *Them He Glorified: A Systematic Study of the Doctrine of Glorification* (Grand Rapids: Eerdmans, 1963).

231. Moltmann, *The Spirit of Life*, 156.

232. Augsburg Confession VII, in *BC*, 32.

233. See chap. 11 in Berkhof, *Systematic Theology*.

234. Moltmann, *The Spirit of Life*, 156.

The conclusion, hence, is that as long as the locus of the doctrine of perseverance—whether it be formulated by Protestants or Catholics—is placed in God's faithfulness, it provides confident assurance to the believer. It does not mean that a Christian could not fall away from grace (defined in a semi-automatic way) but that, even in their darkest moments of life, men and women, as well as the whole church of Christ, may confidently rest in the assurance of God's fatherly love and care.

Christian tradition believes that the insatiable human yearning for fulfillment and happiness can be met only by the ultimate encounter with God that "glorification" seeks to conceptualize. In mystical experiences, there is already "an anticipation of the eschatological, immediate and direct seeing of God 'face to face.'"[235] Although it is not a biblical term, the Roman Catholic tradition speaks of the consummation of salvation in terms of the "beatific vision," a dream of ultimate fulfillment of all human yearnings expressed in the Eastern traditions as the completion of deification. Having first concluded that no created good may bring ultimate and final happiness,[236] Saint Thomas teaches that human yearning finds fulfillment in the vision of God, indeed, in the "essence" of God as based on the scriptural promise in 1 John 3:2 ("we shall see him as he is").

As constantly repeated in this project, the hope for personal salvation is to be set within the widest horizons of Christian soteriological vision and the providential world governance of the loving Creator. Barth rightly saw that the idea of world governance speaks of God's faithfulness to his creation.[237] According to the biblical testimonies, it first comes to manifestation in Yahweh's dealings with his people and culminates in the pronouncement of the dawning of the righteous rule of the Father as announced by Jesus, the Son. The same God who in the first place created the heavens and earth is going to show his faithfulness in renewing creation.

In sum: the hope of salvation for humanity is deeply embedded in the wider context of cosmic renewal. God, the Creator, will show himself to be loving and faithful in redeeming the promises of Holy Scriptures for the establishment of the new heaven and new earth. That is the topic for the final chapter of this book with its focus on eschatology; before that, a careful discussion of ecclesiology, the doctrine of the church, is in order.

235. Moltmann, *The Spirit of Life*, 205.

236. Aquinas, *ST* 2a.2.

237. E.g., Barth, *CD* III/3, 40–41.

9 | Church

Introduction: The Christian Church and Ecclesiology in the Matrix of Secularism(s) and Religious Pluralism(s)

As important a role as ecclesiology, the doctrine of the church, plays in contemporary theology, it did not emerge until the time of the Reformation. This is of course not to ignore the many church-related themes discussed already in the patristic and later doctrinal manuals, particularly sacramentology. It is rather to remind us of the polemical setting of the Reformation theology out of which a full-orbed ecclesiology, an understanding of the "true" church, emerged. Currently, similarly to the doctrine of the Trinity and of the Spirit, ecclesiology has risen to the center of attention.

To do ecclesiology for our times, it no longer suffices to center on only the established churches; indeed, the rapid growth and proliferation of the global Christian community require attention to many kinds of ecclesial expressions, including the free churches and Pentecostals/charismatics, the "emerging churches," the liberationist communities, and communities of the Global South. In keeping with our methodology, it is also pertinent to relate to the ways other faith traditions understand the nature, life, and practices of their communities. An essential part of the re-formation of the church is its rapid and robust globalization.

The Christian Church Goes Global—and More Diversified

From its humble beginnings, the Christian church has grown to be the world's largest religious community, with over 2.4 billion adherents, the majority of whom reside in the Global South. Africa is now the biggest "Christian" continent. Consequently, most church members in the near future—and already now—are not adult European–North American Caucasians but people of all ages, both genders, and diverse ethnic backgrounds from across the globe.

As of now, one-half of all Christians are Roman Catholics, another quarter comprises Pentecostals/charismatics, and the rest are Eastern Orthodox, Anglicans, mainline Protestants, and members of free churches. This means that Roman Catholics and Pentecostals/charismatics together constitute three-fourths of the global membership. Particularly, the "Pentecostalization" of the Christian church in terms of Pentecostal/charismatic spirituality and worship patterns infiltrating all churches is yet another implication of the transformation.[1]

A defining feature of current globalization is the massive movement of peoples and people groups around the globe, as migrant churches and diaspora communities shape the life of the church. Currently, of the over 200 million migrants, about one-half are Christians, the majority of them in the United States and Europe. The next largest group is Muslims.[2] Particularly visible are the Pentecostal/charismatic immigrant and diaspora communities, a significant number of whom are of African descent.[3]

Related to these dramatic shifts in the epicenter of global Christianity from north to south are the unprecedented transformations, changes, and hybrid identities of various ecclesial forms.

1. Neil J. Ormerod and Shane Clifton, eds., *Globalization and the Mission of the Church: Ecclesiological Investigations* (New York: T&T Clark, 2009).

2. Pew Research Center, "Faith on the Move—the Religious Affiliation of International Migrants," March 8, 2012, http://www.pewforum.org/2012/03/08/religious-migration-exec/.

3. Frieder Ludwig and J. Kwabena Asamoah-Gyadu, eds., *African Christian Presence in the West: New Immigrant Congregations and Transnational Networks in North America and Europe* (Trenton, NJ: Africa World, 2011).

Continuing Transformations and Changes in Ecclesial Life and Structures in the Global Church

New Forms of Ecclesial Existence

The free church congregational[4] model might well be the major paradigm in the third millennium, alongside the Catholic.[5] It stems from the Radical Reformation and early Anabaptism and currently represents a plethora of free churches and (later) independent churches that have emerged. A tendency toward a free-church mentality can be found even in the Roman Catholic Church with the mushrooming of base communities[6] in Latin America and similar phenomena.

A radical challenge and inspiration to the global church have come from the rapidly growing Pentecostal/charismatic phenomenon, which divides into three subgroups:

1. (Classical) Pentecostal denominations such as the Assemblies of God and Foursquare Gospel, which owe their existence to the famous Azusa Street Revival in 1906.
2. Charismatic movements, Pentecostal-type spiritual movements within the established churches beginning in the 1960s (the largest of which is the Roman Catholic Charismatic Renewal).
3. Neo-charismatic movements, including Vineyard Fellowship in the United States and African Initiated Churches, as well as countless independent churches and groups all over the world; usually even China's rapidly growing house-church movements are included here.[7]

The American ecclesiastical environment is characterized by unprecedented denominational diversity, originally going back to the pilgrimage of

4. In contrast with the "episcopal," in which the bishop is the highest authority, and the "presbyterian," with a presbytery, in "congregational" the whole community is the highest authority.

5. Miroslav Volf, *After Our Likeness: The Church as an Image of the Trinity* (Grand Rapids: Eerdmans, 1998), 12.

6. Leonardo Boff, *Ecclesiogenesis: The Base Communities Reinvent the Church* (Maryknoll, NY: Orbis, 1986).

7. Following Stanley M. Burgess and Eduard M. van der Maas, eds., *New International Dictionary of Charismatic and Pentecostal Movements*, rev. and expanded ed. (Grand Rapids: Zondervan, 2010).

European immigrants from the old continent and now fostered by immigration and diaspora. Although the Catholic Church is today the biggest ecclesiastical player, large numbers of the first generations of new settlers also came from various types of Protestant and Anglican constituencies in which particularly the nonconformists often felt marginalized and were even occasionally oppressed. As a result, what Europeans would name free-church ecclesiality forms the "mainline" American church reality. Among the Protestants, Baptists of various stripes are the largest group.

Alongside the historically unheard-of denominational plurality, the American experiment is also characterized by a deepening and widening multiculturalism.[8] Among the several major American-based ethnic group families, none is growing as fast and proliferating as widely as the Hispanic American churches. The special challenge and asset of Hispanic communities in the United States are their ecumenical background in both Catholicism and Protestantism, lately also in Pentecostal/charismatic spiritualities.[9] Most recently, Asian-descent churches and movements have been gaining significance with the mushrooming of diverse communities.[10] Predominantly evangelical in theological orientation, these churches reflect amazing diversity and plurality. Before the Hispanics and Asians, African American Christianity had already established its significant place in American religiosity. Black churches continue to grow, whether one speaks of Episcopal or evangelical or Pentecostal communities.[11]

The newest and most complex set of ecclesiastical developments is linked with late modern/postmodern cultures, virtual connections, and new "tribalism."

8. Jonathan Chaplin, *Multiculturalism: A Christian Retrieval* (London: Theos, 2011).

9. Justo L. González, *Mañana: Christian Theology from a Hispanic Perspective* (Nashville: Abingdon, 1990), chap. 4.

10. For the difficulty and complexity in defining "Asian American," see Peter Cha, "Ethnic Identity Formation and Participation in Immigrant Churches: Second-Generation Korean American Experiences," in *Korean Americans and Their Religions: Pilgrims and Missionaries from a Different Shore*, ed. Ho-Youn Kwon, Kwang Chung Kim, and R. Stephen Warner (University Park: Pennsylvania State University Press, 2001), 141–56.

11. Jeremiah Wright Jr., "Protestant Ecclesiology," in *The Cambridge Companion to Black Theology*, ed. Dwight N. Hopkins and Edward P. Antonio (Cambridge: Cambridge University Press, 2012), 184–97.

Churches for Postmodern Times: Emerging Churches and "Fresh Expressions"

What does the church look like in the "post-world"?[12] Titles such as *ChurchNext* (2000)[13] and *The Liquid Church* (2002)[14] testify to this ecclesial "post-existence." A few decades ago, ecclesiologists spoke of the baby boomer generation. It was served with the so-called seeker-friendly suburban-based churches that catered to all kinds of needs of individuals and families. Thereafter, "purpose-driven" churches and the like caught our attention. Most recently, these kinds of models, while still having an appeal with their own generation, are giving way to Gen X and other postmodern generations. Among them, a most exciting phenomenon ecclesiologically is known under the rubric of "emerging church" (USA) and "fresh expressions of the church" (UK). Highly active in virtual networks and ways of connecting, their ecclesiologies are fluid.[15] Nor do they always meet in sanctuaries but may instead rent comedy clubs or pubs. Deeply missional in orientation with a focus on practices and everyday Christian service, they do not typically bother to delve into theological debates about ecclesiology, although many of their leaders may have a solid academic training in religion.

Emerging churches (1) identify with the life of Jesus, (2) transform the secular realm, and (3) live highly communal lives. Because of these three activities, they (4) welcome the stranger, (5) serve with generosity, (6) participate as producers, (7) create as created beings, (8) lead as a body, and (9) take part in spiritual activities.[16] The church life and the emerging theological activity among these communities are an interesting mix of old and new. On the one hand, they harken back to some aspects of sacramentality and mysticism, as well as neomonasticism, and on the other hand, they desire to connect with the latest moves and techniques in postmodern culture and ways of communication.

12. Gerard Mannion, *Ecclesiology and Postmodernity: Questions for the Church in Our Time* (Collegeville, MN: Liturgical Press, 2007).

13. Eddie Gibbs, *ChurchNext* (Downers Grove, IL: InterVarsity Press, 2000).

14. Pete Ward, *The Liquid Church* (Peabody, MA: Hendrickson, 2002).

15. Tony Jones, *The Church Is Flat: The Relational Ecclesiology of the Emerging Church Movement* (Minneapolis: JoPa Group, 2011).

16. Eddie Gibbs and Ryan Bolger, *The Emerging Churches: Creating Christian Community in Postmodern Cultures* (Grand Rapids: Baker Academic, 2005), 45. An important recent theological study is Patrick Oden, *The Transformative Church: New Ecclesial Models and the Theology of Jürgen Moltmann* (Minneapolis: Fortress, 2015).

The basic difference between the US-based emerging churches and UK fresh expressions is that whereas the former is usually separatist, forming their own communities, most communities of the latter are birthed by and stay within the Church of England (and other mainline denominations).[17]

Having now briefly outlined and highlighted some radical transformations and changes within the global Christian church, we will scrutinize two more formative features of the third millennium's "global village," namely, secularisms and religious pluralisms.

Religious Pluralism(s) and Secularism(s) as Ecclesiological Challenges

As discussed, secularism has not won the day, but rather, alongside its growth, religions continue gaining more strongholds all over the world. Side by side with the Christian church (2.4 billion), about a quarter of the world population is comprised of Muslims (1.6 billion). The 1 billion Hindus make up about 15 percent, followed by Buddhists at half that number. Jews number fewer than 15 million, and over 400 million people belong to various kinds of "folk religions." Whereas Hinduism and Buddhism are mainly regional (Asian) religions, Christians are by far the most evenly distributed around the globe. Only about 15 percent (1 billion) label themselves religiously unaffiliated (even though the majority of them entertain some kind of religious-type beliefs and practices).[18]

Because of the overwhelming continuing presence and force of religious plurality and forms of religious pluralisms, this challenge can no longer be ignored. It has to be tackled theologically. We face, similarly, the challenges from forms of secularism(s).

Secularism is a complex phenomenon, as will be discussed below. Suffice it to mention here that while it continues to exercise huge influence over American and particularly European societies, it is also diversifying with forms of "post-"secularism and their complex relation to religiosity. In all its forms, secularism is a major contender to all religions.

17. See the Fresh Expressions website: https://www.freshexpressions.org.uk/about/introduction.

18. Pew Research Center, *The Global Religious Landscape: A Report on the Size and Distribution of the World's Major Religious Groups as of 2010*, Pew Forum on Religion & Public Life, December 2012, http://www.pewforum.org/files/2014/01/global-religion-full.pdf.

Brief Orientation to the Chapter

The chapter's first task regards the exposition of visions of community among Jewish, Muslim, Hindu, and Buddhist traditions without any intentional Christian engagement; that will be taken up next. Thereafter, the construction of the distinctively Christian doctrine of the church will begin with the anchoring of the community in the triune God; after that we will delve into the most complex question of "ecclesiality," that is, the conditions of what makes the church, church. To complete that "foundational" ecclesiological discussion, further investigation into so-called communion-theology resources will help clarify the nature of life in Christian community and within the whole church.

Clarifying the nature of the Christian communion through the resources of Trinitarian communion theology also brings to the fore the essentially missional nature of the church. Mission, rather than being a task given to the church, belongs to the very nature of the church. The following two sections envision the missional existence of the church in the world in terms of the liturgical and sacramental and what is called here the "charismatic-diaconal" ministry.

Although the concern for the unity of the one church of Christ characterizes the whole ecclesiological task in this project, the many complex details about ecumenisms will be the focus of the next section. The final, long section again puts Christian community in the matrix of four other faith traditions. At the very end, not to ignore secularism(s), we will take up a similar engagement from the Christian perspective.

Visions of Community among Religions

Orientation

Although it would make only little sense to speak of "ecclesiology," the doctrine of the church, in pan-religious terms, "it is part of the belief-structure of most religions that there should be a particular society which protects and sustains their basic values and beliefs, within which one may pursue the ideal human goal, as defined within the society."[19] That said, there are important differences:[20] First, whereas the Abrahamic traditions are integrally communal, neither of the Asiatic faiths engaged here is; commensurately, the Asiatic

19. Keith Ward, *Religion and Community* (Oxford: Oxford University Press, 1999), 1.
20. Inspiration comes from Ward, *Religion and Community*, 1–4.

faiths' visions of "salvation" focus neither on the whole of humanity nor on the reconciliation of the cosmos, as in Jewish-Christian traditions, but rather on personal "release." Second, whereas for Abrahamic traditions the religious community is rooted in God and divine election, in Asiatic faiths that is not the case. Third, whereas the Asiatic faiths seek to renounce the world in pursuit of final release, the Christian faith particularly seeks to both renounce "the world" and penetrate it for the sake of God's kingdom.

Now, with each of the four religious traditions, three descriptions are attempted: first, the nature of the religious community; second, her liturgical and ritual life; and third, the relation to other religious communities.

Synagogue—the Jewish Community

The Emergence of the Jewish People and Community

Like her Abrahamic sister faiths, Judaism is communally oriented and community centered. But it is the only Abrahamic religion that originally was purely tribal and still continues to be ethnic. While beliefs, particularly uncompromising monotheism (Deut. 6:4), came to be part of Jewishness from early times, the basis of the Jewish identity "is not a creed but a history: a strong sense of a common origin, a shared past and a shared destiny."[21] Indeed, one's Jewishness is not cast away by the lack of faith or even a pronounced atheism—an unthinkable situation for a Muslim or Christian. One either is a Jew, by birth (of a Jewish mother), or one is not.

So far the term "Jewish" has been used in the established contemporary sense. However, totally differently from sister Abrahamic faiths (and Buddhism), the emergence and birth of the religion of Judaism are unique in that it happened in two distinct phases and over a millennium of time. "Israelite" community has Moses's legacy as the defining origin, as recounted in the Tanakh (the Old Testament of Christians). "Judaism" emerged beginning with the renewals led by Ezra following the Babylonian exile in the sixth century; its defining identity is shaped by the rabbinic tradition's Talmud. The emergence of the synagogue as the religious community in that phase is an important event. In the following, however, "Israel" and "Judaism" are used interchangeably.

21. Nicholas De Lange, *An Introduction to Judaism* (Cambridge: Cambridge University Press, 2000), 26.

As discussed, Israel's distinctive identity is based on Yahweh's election of her as a "chosen people," based on covenant and its call for total devotion to Yahweh. Basically, separatism follows from this status, and at the same time from a claim for a specific territory, the Holy Land. Due to separatism, intermarriage has not been encouraged (as common as that has been in various eras), nor are conversions sought, although proselytism is possible under certain conditions.[22] Separatism and ethnic orientation, however, are only one part of the Jewish identity. A strong trend in the Old Testament is a missionary calling to bring other nations of the world to know the name of Yahweh and to be a vehicle of divine blessings (Gen. 12:1–3). Although Israel's missional vocation is not similar to that of Islam and Christianity in terms of making concentrated efforts to reach nonbelievers, it still is embedded in Israel's identity in terms of expecting a universal end-time pilgrimage to Jerusalem to worship God (Isa. 2:1–4; Mic. 4:1–4).

A further defining feature of Jewish identity and her community is the continuing diaspora status beginning from the fall of Jerusalem in the sixth century BCE and continuing until the founding of Israel in 1948. The large majority live in diaspora outside the Holy Land, with the majority of that in the United States.

Liturgy and Religious Cycle

The origin of Jewish religious community, the synagogue,[23] stems from the time of the sixth century BCE crisis of losing the land and the temple, the beginning of (what became) rabbinic Judaism. The first synagogues were like ordinary houses, but the perception of holiness later led to fairly elaborate sacred building structures. Ten men are usually needed to establish a synagogue. Traditionally women have been separated from men into a different space in the synagogue; in modern and contemporary times that varies.[24]

Led by an elected council or official, a synagogue is autonomous, without any authoritative superstructure. Unlike in most Christian churches, but similar to Islam, no professional clergy is needed to lead prayers and worship in the synagogue. That said, in practice the rabbi, the religious leader and teacher

22. David Shatz, "A Jewish Perspective," in *OHRD*, 369–71.

23. The Greek-derived word "synagogue" means "gathering together," that is, community, and thus resembles *ekklēsia*.

24. Joseph Gurmann and Steven Fine, "Synagogue," in *ER* 13:8920–26.

since the founding of (rabbinic) Judaism, presides over the liturgy—but a rabbi's status should not be confused with that of a priest.[25] Rabbis used to be only men; nowadays, in diaspora Judaism, many Reform movements endorse a gender-inclusive view.

Jewish (rabbinic) liturgy is founded around the Shema (Deut. 6:4–9) and the related Eighteen Benedictions (or prayers, the *Amidah*).[26] Another ancient practice is the encouragement to recite one hundred prayers per day, covering all aspects of life and faith. The reading of Torah is an essential part of the worship. Contemporary diaspora, particularly in the United States, has produced a wide variety of liturgical patterns and orientations

Not unlike other religions, there is a religiously ordered pattern for both the Jewish person's life cycle[27] and the life of the community following the sacred calendar.[28] What is unique is the centrality of weekly Sabbath, around which the weekly religious ritual is totally centered (beginning with the common Friday evening pre-Sabbath service).

Perceptions of the Religious Other

The main thrust—and dynamic—in the Jewish relation to others is this: as much as Yahweh's covenant with Israel calls for unreserved commitment, it also implies that the same God could covenant with other nations. In other words, there are both particularity (separatism) and universalism (missionary calling). Just consider Deuteronomy 32:8–9. No wonder Israel's relation to other religions has fluctuated over the centuries between exclusivism and inclusivism. The diversity of approaches has only intensified in contemporary times.[29]

There are important theological reasons behind the wide-openness projected toward the religious other, particularly the "Talmudic position that embracing Judaism is not necessary for a Gentile's entering the world to come" for the simple reason that "God wants to give all people just rewards."[30] This is not to deny the presence of exclusivism, particularly toward Christians, but

25. De Lange, *Introduction to Judaism*, 121–22.

26. Ruth Langer, "Worship and Devotional Life: Jewish Worship," in *ER* 14:9805–9.

27. De Lange, *Introduction to Judaism*, 110–12 and 147–50.

28. De Lange, *Introduction to Judaism*, 141–47.

29. Alan Brill, *Judaism and Other Religions: Models of Understanding* (New York: Palgrave Macmillan, 2010).

30. Shatz, "A Jewish Perspective," 367.

rather to appreciate the fact that despite horrible and inhumane treatment of Jews throughout the centuries and particularly in the twentieth century, there is this robust inclusivist impulse.

Ummah—*the Islamic Community*

The Birth and Meaning of the *Ummah*

Islam as a religion shares with Judaism and Christianity a deep communal orientation anchored in one God.[31] The term for the community, *ummah*, appears in the Qur'an over sixty times, with diverse and varying meanings.[32] The incipient universal vision of early Islam is evident in Qur'an 10:19: "Mankind was but one community; then they differed," obviously implying an original "single *ummah* with a single religion."[33]

There is a marked development in the relation of the *ummah* to the other during the Prophet's lifetime, beginning as inclusive of Muslims, Jews, and Christians, based on belief in one God, toward a narrower view limited basically to the followers of the Prophet. A definite limiting took place after his death, with also a shift toward more sociopolitical and juridical aspects present.

Alongside the early inclusivism, the idea of the superiority of this community was established with appeal to passages such as 3:110: "You are the best community brought forth to men, enjoining decency, and forbidding indecency, and believing in God." At times, however, a more hospitable interpretation could also include other God-fearing communities as exemplary.

The Divisions of the *Ummah*: The Emergence of the Sunnis and Shi'ites

The major division, between the Sunnis and Shi'ites, arose over the issue of the Prophet's successor after his death (632 CE). The Prophet's beloved wife

31. Ward, *Religion and Community*, 33.

32. Abdullah Saeed, "The Nature and Purpose of the Community (Ummah) in the Qur'ān," in *The Community of Believers: Christian and Muslim Perspectives*, ed. Lucinda Mosher and David Marshall (Washington, DC: Georgetown University Press, 2015), 15–28; Frederick Mathewson Denny, "The Meaning of Ummah in the Qur'ān," *History of Religions* 15, no. 1 (1975): 34–70.

33. Brannon Wheeler, "Ummah," in *ER* 14:9446.

Aisha's father, Abu Bakr, was made the first leader (*amir*, "commander") by the majority, but that did not settle the matter, as the minority of the community preferred Ali, Muhammad's daughter Fatima's husband, as leader. Both theological and political issues were involved. Whereas for the majority, the leadership choice after the passing of the Prophet belonged to the *ummah* at large, for the rest it was a divine choice falling on Ali—with the ambiguous claim that he had divine endorsement as well as the Prophet's. The majority wanted to stay in the line of Mecca's dominant tribe, the Prophet's own tribe, Quraysh; whereas a minority received support from Medina. Full separation of the *ummah*, however, did not come about until after the brief leadership of Umar I and the longer office of the caliph Uthman, whose assassination in 656 brought Ali to power for half a decade, a period of virtual civil war. At the end, the community's separation was final, between the majority Sunnis (currently over 80 percent) and a minority of Shi'ites following Ali's legacy. Both sides further continued splitting internally, leading to the kind of complex denominationalism characteristic of most religions.

All Shi'ites share the belief in the divinely ordered status of Ali as the successor to the Prophet (Q 2:124; 21:72–73).[34] By far the largest and most important Shi'ite denomination, the Twelvers, has developed a highly sophisticated genetic line of succession from Ali through his two sons (Hasan and Husayn) all the way to the Twelfth one. The most distinctive claim therein has to do with the last imam (after Hasan ibn Ali al-Askari of the ninth century), titled Muhammad b. Hasan, who allegedly went into "occultation" (that is, concealment) and whose return they await. In this interpretation, all imams possess inerrancy in order to be able to prevent the community from being led astray. That said, there are a number of fiercely debated issues among the three main Shi'ite traditions (the Twelvers, the Ishmaelites, and the Zaydis, the first two sharing much more in common concerning the imamate) about the line of succession and related issues.

What is amazing and confusing to the outsider about the global Muslim community is that, despite how extremely much they share in tradition and doctrine, their mutual relationships are so antagonistic and condemnatory. Both parties share the same Qur'an, the same prophethood, and the five pillars, including prayers, fasting, and other rituals (albeit somewhat differently nuanced and practiced).[35] Yet it seems that any kind of global ecumenical

34. Najam Haider, *Shī'ī Islam* (Cambridge: Cambridge University Press, 2014).

35. Shmuel Bar, "Sunnis and Shiites: Between Rapprochement and Conflict," in *Current Trends in Islamist Ideology*, ed. Hillel Fradkin et al. (Washington, DC: Center on Islam, Democracy, and the Future of the Muslim World, Hudson Institute, 2005), 2:87–96.

reconciliation is not on the horizon[36]—although the Qur'an mandates work for unity. "And hold fast to God's bond, together, and do not scatter" (3:103–5).

Spiritual Life and Worship

Obedience; submission to Allah, including willing service; and honoring *tawhid*, the absolute unity/oneness of God, shape Muslim life in all aspects, including what we call devotion and liturgy.[37] It consists of "five pillars"—confession, ritual prayer, fasting, pilgrimage, and alms—routinely preceded by the important rites of purification, both physical and spiritual.[38]

The ritual prayer is the most visible form of piety. Muslims ought to pray five times a day at designated times, regardless of their location. Prayer is preceded by ablution and employs a prescribed form and content. Prayer is also the main activity in the mosque;[39] nowadays the Friday afternoon gathering there includes a sermon. Holy scripture is highly honored and venerated. Since there is no clergy and no theologically trained priesthood, any male in principle is qualified to lead; he is usually chosen from among those most deeply knowledgeable in the tradition.

Although the Prophet Muhammad was but a human being, particularly in folk Islam and forms of Sufism his status gets elevated to a (semi)divine object of veneration. Sufi mysticism also knows a number of saints similarly highly elevated, particularly Ali (even among the Sunnis).

As in other religions, the annual life cycle follows the religious calendar, starting from the honoring of the date when Muhammad migrated from Mecca to Medina. Friday is not considered a holy day, although it is the day of congregation. Instead, a number of other holy days commemorate significant days in the life of the Prophet and early *ummah*.[40] Globalization has caused much diversity in rituals and rites, but not in doctrine and prayers.

36. Feras Hamza, "Unity and Disunity in the Life of the Muslim Community," in *The Community of Believers*, ed. Lucinda Mosher and David Marshall (Washington, DC: Georgetown University Press, 2015), 74.

37. Vernon James Schubel, "Worship and Devotional Life: Muslim Worship," in *ER* 14:9815–20.

38. Frederick Mathewson Denny, *An Introduction to Islam*, 2nd ed. (New York: Macmillan, 1994), chap. 7.

39. Rusmir Mahmutcehagic, *The Mosque: The Heart of Submission* (New York: Fordham University Press, 2007).

40. George W. Braswell Jr., *Islam: Its Prophet, Peoples, Politics, and Power* (Nashville: Broadman and Holman, 1996), 77–80.

Mission to Nonbelievers and Perception of the Religious Other

Like Christianity's, Islam's outlook is universal. Echoing biblical theology, the Qur'an teaches that "'to God belongs the kingdom (*mulk*) of the heavens and earth' (e.g., 2:107)."[41] The Qur'an instructs us that "had God willed, He would have made them one community" (42:8; see also 42:10). The key verse is well known: "God is our Lord and your Lord. Our deeds concern us and your deeds concern you. There is no argument between us and you. God will bring us together, and to Him is the [final] destination" (42:15).

In this light it is understandable that the earliest Qur'anic passages were not calling people to convert to a new religion; rather, the Meccans were called to "worship the Lord of this House [Ka'ba]" (106:3).[42] Only later, with the rising opposition from the worshipers of local deities, was a decisive break announced (106:9), and the confession became "There is no god except God" (37:35). We know that in Medina the Prophet with his companions lived among the Jews, and we may safely infer that he assumed the new faith was in keeping with theirs as well as with the Christian faith (2:40–41). Recall also that at that time the term *muslim* could also be applied to non-Muslims such as Solomon (27:45) and disciples of Jesus (3:52). Only when the Jews rejected the Prophet was the direction of prayer changed from Jerusalem to Mecca (2:142).

In keeping with this is the special status assigned to Abrahamic sister faiths. Between what Muslims call "the Abode of Peace and the Abode of War," a third region was acknowledged, "the Abode of the People of the Book," that is, Jews and Christians.[43] These two traditions enjoy a unique relation to Islam (2:135–36; 5:12; 5:69), implying that in some real sense the diversity of religions is not only tolerated by Allah but even planned and endorsed, at least when it comes to those who are the "people of the book" (48:29; 5:48; 3:114).

This inclusive tendency notwithstanding, Islam retains a unique place in God's eyes. The inclusion is similar to Catholic inclusivism: while other nations might have known God, only Muslims know Allah intimately and are rightly related to God. That is most probably the meaning of the Qur'anic statements that Muslims, in distinction from others, are "God's sincere servants" (37:40), and "they are of the elect, the excellent" (38:40). Therefore, ultimately even

41. J. Dudley Woodberry, "The Kingdom of God in Islam and the Gospel," in *Anabaptists Meeting Muslims: A Calling for Presence in the Way of Christ*, ed. James R. Krabill, David W. Shenk, and Linford Stutzman (Scottdale, PA: Herald Press, 2005), 49.

42. The Ka'ba is the holiest place in Islam, in Mecca.

43. William Montgomery Watt, *Muslim-Christian Encounters: Perceptions and Misperceptions* (London: Routledge, 1991), 26–27.

Jewish and Christian traditions suffer from corruption and misunderstanding of the final revelation.

At her core, Islam is an active missionary community, based on the Qu'ranic mandate to reach out to nonbelievers (16:125–26). This is often expressed with the Arabic term *da'wah*, literally "call, invocation, or summoning."[44] Combining a universalizing tendency and fervent missionary mandate, Islam's goal of outreach is comprehensive, including ideally social, economic, cultural, and religious spheres. Ideally it would result in the establishment of Sharia law and the gathering of all peoples under one *ummah*.[45]

During various historical eras, *da'wah* has been exercised with the help of military and political means, as Christianity did as well, although the Qur'an prohibits evangelism by force (2:256).[46] Alliance with earthly powers, militarism, and economic interests were all employed to spread Islam with force and brutality. In other words, not only Christianity but also Islam bears the long legacy of colonialism.

Hindu Spiritual Life and Community

In Search of Hindu Identity and Religious Community

Both Judaism and Hinduism emerged over a long period of time. Neither one has a human founder. They are also similar in that while one can be a Jew only by birth (through a Jewish mother), the assumption is that to have been born as an Indian, one is Hindu. Doctrine does not determine belonging in either tradition, although holy scriptures are honored in both.

Differently from Abrahamic faiths, community does not play an essential role in Hinduism, as the religion's main goal is the spiritual release of the individual rather than either reform of the society or communal (let alone cosmic) eschatological renewal. This does not mean in any way to undermine the deeply and widely communal orientation of Indian culture and, as part of that, the celebration of religious rites in communal settings in the family, village, or temple. Rather, it means that the basic orientation of Hinduism lacks an internal and ultimate communal goal. In keeping with this, there is no single

44. William D. Miller, "Da'wah," in *ER* 4:2225–26.

45. Badru D. Kateregga and David W. Shenk, *Islam and Christianity: A Muslim and a Christian in Dialogue* (Ibadan, Nigeria: Daystar, 1985), 79–81.

46. Miller, "Da'wah," 2225.

term to describe the communal side of Hindu spirituality. Perhaps closest in intention comes the term *sampradaya*, which, however, is not universally nor even very widely used.[47]

The plurality of Hinduism allows a plethora of local deities to be worshiped. That said, the existing diversity does not translate into personal choice of the deity, as might be misunderstood in the manner of the hyperindividualism of the Global North. It is, rather, the family and wider community's religion and rites that one follows.

Hindu "Sacraments" and Ways of Spirituality

Without any claim for material similarity between Christian sacraments and Hindu life-cycle-related *samskaras*, through which one becomes a full member of the community and society, the Christian interpreter may duly identify them as "Hindu sacraments." Similarly to rites of passage in most all religions, they cover all life from birth to death, as prescribed in the sacred literature.[48]

Highly important is one called "the second birth," which occurs at eight to twelve years of age. The exact time of this rite of initiation is determined by an astrologer, and it helps make a shift from childhood to the first of the four ashrams, which is studenthood, including religious education.

A central role is also played by the last sacrament, that of death, universally practiced by all Hindus, even secular ones. The funeral, in which the body is burned, includes elaborate rites and rituals. Following the funeral, ancestor rites typically continue over the years to "establish the deceased harmoniously within their appropriate worlds and prevent them from becoming hungry and haunting their living descendants."[49]

As explained in our chapter on soteriology, Hinduism knows three paths to liberation: devotion, knowledge, and work. The most typical at the grassroots level is the way of devotion, and for the large majority, this *bhakti* devotion comes in the form of theistic Vaishnavism. Based on the Bhagavad Gita, this loving, intimate devotion is often focused on Krishna.

47. Gavin D. Flood, *An Introduction to Hinduism* (Cambridge: Cambridge University Press, 1996), 134.

48. Klaus Klostermaier, *A Survey of Hinduism*, 3rd ed. (Albany: State University of New York Press, 2010), chap. 11.

49. Paul B. Courtright, "Worship and Devotional Life: Hindu Devotional Life," in *ER* 14:9821.

In India's worship life, "space and time are permeated with the presence of the supreme."[50] Among artistic manifestations of the supreme, the most profound is *murti*, or image, which can also be called "embodiment," the highest form of manifestation of the divine. In temples, the devout Hindus are surrounded and embraced by this divine presence. In that presence, masses of devotees may experience *darsana*, the special kind of spiritual "seeing" or insight.[51] Indeed, this "auspicious seeing" is mutual as, on the one hand, the deity makes herself or himself to be seen, and, on the other, the god is "seen" by the devotee. Regular *pujas*, acts of worship to the deities, open to all Hindus, take place from day to day to celebrate the divine presence.[52] Closely related to the centrality of divine presence is a special kind of prayer rite, originating in Vedic religion,[53] the mantra "OM," which functions as the representation not only of God (Brahman) but in some sense also of the whole reality. It is typical to have the head of the household utter this word first thing in the morning after purification rituals.

Similarly to other religious traditions, along with rites of passage, a rich and diverse annual festival menu is an essential part of Hindu devotion and worship life. Although the basic structure of festivals may be simple, to outsiders these festivals look extremely complex. They may last several days and exhibit unusually rich local and denominational diversity.

Not unlike in other faiths, there is also the "professional" religious class, the Brahmins, related to the ancient class system of India, formerly a caste society.[54] Whereas ordinary devotees have Puranas, the rich narrative and epic literature, as their holy scripture, only the Brahmins are experts in Vedic literature. Another related structure of Indian society and culture has to do with the four ashrams. Ideally one reaches at the end of life the final stage of the "renouncer," after studenthood, family life, and the period of forest hermit. Only a tiny minority of Hindus belong to the Brahmin class or reach the stage of renouncer. Along with these two classes, there is an innumerable group of gurus of various sorts, many highly respected, others less so. Around the guru, a *sampradaya* is formed, a main community concept for masses of Hindus.

50. Klostermaier, *A Survey of Hinduism*, 263.

51. Klostermaier, *A Survey of Hinduism*, 262–70.

52. For details, see Theodore M. Ludwig, *The Sacred Paths: Understanding the Religions of the World*, 4th ed. (Upper Saddle River, NJ: Pearson, 2006), 109–10; Courtright, "Worship and Devotional Life," 9823.

53. The classic passage is Rig Veda 3.62.10.

54. The four classes are Brahmins, Kshatriyas, Vaishyas, and Shudras. Arvind Sharma, *Classical Hindu Thought: An Introduction* (Oxford: Oxford University Press, 2000), chap. 19.

The Perception of Religious Diversity Both within and in Relation to the Other

Hinduism embraces diversity in a way that no other major living tradition does. This diversity, however, differs from the modernist Western pluralism in many respects. First of all, Hindus, even in their tolerance of other rites and deities, typically take their own beliefs as true. Second, Hindu tolerance has much to do with the idea that since God is bigger than any other concept of ours, various ways of approaching God are complementary in that the infinite God is beyond and transcends any particular path.[55]

What about mission and desire to convert others? It is clear that Hinduism is not a missional religion after Buddhism, Christianity, and Islam. Considering itself the "original" religion, it tends to assimilate others under its own purview, not necessarily inviting them to change.

Understandably, Hinduism faces grave difficulties when encountering Christian and Islamic types of claims for the finality of revelation and uniqueness of God.[56] In keeping with the assimilationist principle, Hindus resist and oppose any efforts at evangelization by other traditions. In that light it appears inhospitable that some movements, such as Arya Samaj, oppose the conversion of Hindus to Islam and Christianity while at the same time strongly advocating reconversion of recent converts to Christianity back to Hinduism.[57]

All in all, notwithstanding the hesitancy about conversion, Hinduism not only knows the reconversion of lapsed faithful but also engages in active missionary efforts to convert "pagans." This was certainly the case in the third to fifth centuries during the establishment of Hindu rajas in South India to replace Buddhism. Itinerant "evangelists" played a critical role in this enterprise. More recently, Hare Krishna and a number of less well-known revival movements in the West have sought new converts.

55. Ward, *Religion and Community*, 82–84, 96–99.

56. Arvind Sharma, "A Hindu Perspective," in *OHRD*, 309–20.

57. Kewal Ahluwalia, "Shudhi Movement: 85th Shardhanand Shudhi Divas—December 23rd," http://www.aryasamaj.com/enews/2012/jan/4.htm.

The Buddhist Sangha *and Spiritual Pursuit*

The Rise of *Sangha* and Rapid Proliferation of Dhamma

Differently from the parent religion of Hinduism, Buddhism has a founder, Siddhartha Gautama. Although the historical details of Gautama's life are very scarce,[58] the religion- and community-forming narrative is based on the enlightenment experience of this former noble prince and renouncer. The teaching of the emerging new religion, similarly to Hinduism, is not centered on faith as much as on commitment to pursuing release from attachment to the world of impermanence and the resulting *dukkha*.

The enlightened Sakyamuni (Gautama) established the *sangha* (or *samgha*) community with five initial disciples. Originally it was an inclusive community, open to both male monks and female nuns. The nuns lived separately from the men but belonged to the community. That inclusive vision, however, came to be limited through the centuries, and it is normal (particularly in Theravada contexts) to have only male monks.

Soon after the founding of *sangha*, Buddha began to send the enlightened monks (*arhats*, "worthy ones") out on missionary trips to preach the Dhamma, the Buddha's teachings. So, unlike Hinduism, but like Christian and Muslim traditions, Buddhism is a missionary religion,[59] and one can find scriptural commissioning for it. Particularly during the founding centuries, the missionary vision was fervent. Similarly to Christianity, the new religion also proliferated through merchants and other travelers.[60]

Following Buddha's *parinirvana* (complete liberation at death), the First Ecumenical Council was summoned, gathering together five hundred *arhats* to whom Buddha's Dhamma was entrusted, comprising Tipitaka, the "Three Baskets" of teachings, the middle one of which (Vinaya Pitaka) contains all instructions and teachings for the life of the *sangha*. Subsequently, the Second Council, one hundred years later, brought to the surface disagreements and strife. A number of other councils followed, along with deep disagreements and splits.

Around the beginning of the common era, the most significant split occurred, giving birth to the Mahayana school.[61] Later, it made a foundational

58. Gajin Nagao, "The Life of the Buddha: An Interpretation," *Eastern Buddhist*, n.s., 20, no. 2 (1987): 1–31.

59. Jonathan S. Walter, "Missions: Buddhist Missions," in *ER* 9:6077–82.

60. Linda Learman, ed., *Buddhist Missionaries in the Era of Globalization* (Honolulu: University of Hawai'i Press, 2005).

61. Whereas Theravada is dominant in Thailand, Myanmar, and Sri Lanka, Mahayana

claim to Buddha's own teaching, though so far such a teaching document has not been discovered.

Mahayana advocates a much more open access to the pursuit of nirvana for all men and women, not only to a few religious. It also adopted a more theistically oriented cosmology and highlighted the importance of notions of grace and mercy, particularly in its later developments having to do with the Pure Land and related movements. Mahayana has also developed a growing tradition of spiritual exercises in pursuit of liberative insight.

The third major strand is commonly called Vajrayana ("Diamond Vehicle") or Tantrism, and it can be found in Tibet. Broadly related to Mahayana, it has also contextualized itself in rich Tibetan folk religiosity and mysticism with a focus on diverse rituals, mantras, and esoteric rites.

Devotion and Liturgy

Differently from Jewish-Christian tradition, but in keeping with Hindu traditions, becoming a Buddhist does not usually entail any initiatory rite (whereas joining the *sangha* takes a long period of discipline and teaching, culminating in "ordination" by a legitimate leader). Instead of an initiatory act, it is (almost) universally taught among Buddhists that taking refuge in Buddha, Dhamma, and *sangha* constitutes becoming a Buddhist. It normally entails adhering to the five precepts of abstaining from killing, stealing, adultery, lying, and drinking. At the same time, one commits oneself to the pursuit of liberation from *dukkha* following the Noble Eightfold Path.

Although in Theravada the releasing enlightenment is typically thought to be attained only by the monks, and even among them, by few, Gautama included in the sphere of the *sangha* also laypersons, regardless of their profession.

Sanghas are supposed to be located near the rest of the society, distinct from it but not so separated as to be isolated. Monks go out every morning to collect gifts and donations, and they also serve the people in the temples and homes in religious rituals.

While in principle there are no mandatory rituals or rites to perform, Buddhist lands are filled with most elaborate devotional and worship acts and

---

is currently present in India, Vietnam, Tibet (mainly in the form of Tantric Buddhism or Vajrayana), China, Taiwan, Korea, and Japan, among other locations. That tradition is also the most familiar form of Buddhism in the Global North.

patterns, liturgy at the center.[62] Furthermore, all denominations, astonishingly even Theravada, are highly "animistic": in everyday religiosity, spirits and spirituality are alive and well.

Furthermore, not unlike most religions, "many Buddhists believe that ritual and devotion are also instrumental in bringing about blessings in life and even inner spiritual transformation."[63] Indeed, notwithstanding wide and deep variety in the Buddhist world, rites related to giving or offering in worship form the basic structure. Giving with the right attitude is the key, and only then meritorious. To the honoring posture toward Buddha belongs the use of candles, water, food, flowers, and so forth.

Yet another defining feature across the varied Buddhist world is meditation, whose aim is to bring about "a state of perfect mental health, equilibrium and tranquility." Unlike in many other contexts, Buddhist meditation is not an exit from ordinary life but, on the contrary, is deeply embedded in it. Its core has to do with mindfulness, an aptitude and skill to be developed throughout one's life.[64]

Because of the nontheistic orientation and nondivine status of Buddha, strictly speaking there is no prayer in original Buddhist devotion; "it is only a way of paying homage to the memory of the Master who showed the way."[65] Similarly, the scriptures—as much as they are honored and venerated in many forms of (particularly Mahayana) liturgy—are not looked upon as divine revelation but rather as guides to human effort. Furthermore, Buddhist devotion, similarly to Islamic religious life, particularly in folk spirituality, has elevated the founder to a (semi)divine status.

Similarly to all other religions, Buddhism embraces daily rituals and worship patterns as well as holy days and festivals, including rites of passage from birth to initiation into (young) adulthood to death.[66] Counterintuitively, all over the Buddhist world, the worship patterns, rituals, and rites seem to be similar to those of theistic faiths, with a strong focus on devotion.

62. Peter Skilling, "Worship and Devotional Life: Buddhist Devotional Life in Southeast Asia," in *ER* 14:9826–34.

63. Ludwig, *Sacred Paths*, 158.

64. Martine Batchelor, "Meditation and Mindfulness," *Contemporary Buddhism* 12, no. 1 (May 2011): 157–64.

65. Walpola Rahula, *What the Buddha Taught*, rev. ed. (New York: Grove, 1974), 81. See also Rita M. Gross, "Meditation and Prayer: A Comparative Inquiry," *Buddhist-Christian Studies* 22 (2002): 77–86.

66. Ludwig, *Sacred Paths*, 159–63.

The Religious Other

Similarly to Hinduism, the proper perspective on investigating the discerning of the religious other among Buddhists embraces both intra- and interfaith dimensions. Yet another shared feature is that it is typical for Buddhist movements to consider other Buddhist movements through the lens of "hierarchical inclusivism." Here is also a resemblance to Catholicism. All of these three traditions consider their own movement as the "fulfillment," while others are at a lower level and yet belong to the same family. An aspect of that tolerance of sectarian diversity is to lift up one's own scriptures as superior to the other sister movements' ones.

Encounter with the non-Buddhist religious other is not new to the tradition; on the contrary, during Buddhism's rise in India, along with emerging Jainism, it had to negotiate its identity not only in relation to Hinduism and other local religions but also (when moving outside India) in relation to Taoism, Confucianism, Shintoism, and others.[67] Although Buddhism's past—or present life—is not without conflicts with the other, occasional campaigns of coercion, and other forms of religious colonialism, by and large Buddhism has sought a peaceful coexistence. The inclusivist paradigm has also applied at times at least to its closest cousin faiths.[68] That said, as can be said of Hinduism, one cannot find many clear examples of what we Westerners call religious pluralism.[69] Only recently have a growing number of Buddhists, many of them scholars from or residing in the Global North, begun more systematic work toward Buddhist comparative theology and interfaith engagement.[70]

Having now briefly and tentatively presented the visions of community as well as the devotional and liturgical life of Judaism, Islam, Buddhism, and Hinduism, we will delve into distinctively Christian ecclesiology. Throughout the discussion, relevant minor comparisons will be attempted until a full-scale comparative theological exercise is conducted in the last section of the chapter.

67. Masao Abe, *Buddhism and Interfaith Dialogue*, ed. Steven Heine (Honolulu: University of Hawai'i Press, 1995); D. W. Chappell, "Buddhist Interreligious Dialogue: To Build a Global Community," in *The Sound of Liberating Truth: Buddhist-Christian Dialogues in Honor of Frederick J. Streng*, ed. S. B. King and P. O. Ingam (Richmond, UK: Curzon, 1999), 3–35.

68. Kristin Beise Kiblinger, *Buddhist Inclusivism: Attitudes toward Religious Others* (Burlington, VT: Ashgate, 2005).

69. David Burton, "A Buddhist Perspective," in *OHRD*, 324–26.

70. E.g., Alexander Berzin, "A Buddhist View of Islam," in *Islam and Inter-Faith Relations*, ed. P. Schmidt-Leukel and L. Ridgeon (London: SCM, 2007), 225–51.

Community after the Trinity

The Trinitarian "Foundation" of the Church

The Church and the Trinity: A Distinctively Christian Vision of the Community

Similarly to her Abrahamic sister faiths, Christian tradition anchors the religious community in God. Herein is a radical difference from the Asiatic faiths; neither the Buddhist *sangha* nor Hindu communities claim any divine origin or purpose. The internal difference within the Abrahamic family has to do with the distinctive Christian confession of faith in the Trinitarian God. Whereas both Jewish and Muslim communities are guardians of strict monotheism, the Christian church's understanding of monotheism is Trinitarian; hence, the church is linked with and shaped by belief in one God as Father, Son, and Spirit.

Among numerous metaphors and symbols of the church in the New Testament,[71] the following three have gained particular importance in Christian parlance, reflecting the Trinity: people of God (1 Pet. 2:9; Rev. 5:9–10), body of Christ (Eph. 1:22–23; 1 Cor. 12:27; Col. 1:18), and temple of the Spirit (Eph. 2:19–22; 1 Pet. 2:5). Ecumenically it is of utmost importance that virtually all Christian churches are currently in agreement about the Trinitarian basis and nature of the church and the anchoring of communion (*koinōnia*) in the shared divine life itself.

Let us delve in more detail into the mystery of the Trinitarian structure and basis of the church and begin from the last, that is, from the work of the Spirit, and then proceed to the Son and Father, although the order is usually the other way around.

Church as Temple of the Spirit

In the Bible, the Spirit not only works in personal life but has also a community-forming role, as is clearly evident on the day of Pentecost, at the founding of the church. This is not to contend that Pentecost in itself is the "birthday" of the church—it is rather Easter, because without the raising of the crucified

71. Paul S. Minear, *The Images of the Church in the New Testament* (London: Lutterworth, 1960); Everett Ferguson, *The Church of Christ: A Biblical Ecclesiology for Today* (Grand Rapids: Eerdmans, 1997).

Messiah, the church would not have emerged—but to highlight the importance of the Spirit, along with the Son, as the "dual foundation" of the Christian community. Everywhere the Son works, the Spirit is there as well, as our discussion of "Spirit Christology" (chap. 5) suggested.

Here the Christian West (Catholics, Anglicans, and Protestants) may take a lesson from the Christian East (Orthodox tradition). Whereas Western ecclesiologies are predominantly built on christological categories, the Eastern doctrine of the church seeks a balance between Christology and pneumatology. Eastern theologians speak about the church as the body of Christ and the fullness of the Holy Spirit.[72]

As the Spirit-ed community, the church is charismatically endowed and empowered to accomplish her mission. The Spirit also guides and shapes the life of the community, themes to be developed in detail below.

Church as Body of Christ

In Pauline theology, body terminology abounds. Whereas in 1 Corinthians and Romans "body" refers to the individual community, in Ephesians and Colossians it refers to the whole church. The body metaphor for individual communities has to do with interrelated virtues and qualities of love, unity, and working for the common good (1 Cor. 12–14). In relation to the whole church, at the fore is a cosmological Christology working out eternal purposes toward the reconciliation of all peoples and all of creation.[73]

Early in Christian tradition, the body metaphor (in reference to the whole church) began to be developed in primarily institutional and hierarchic terms. This development reached its zenith in medieval Catholic ecclesiology and subsequently. Unfortunately, it led to the virtual identification of the church with Christ, a mistake to be corrected (below).

For a proper and balanced ecclesiology, the whole history of Jesus the Christ is determinative, beginning from his earthly life with teachings and miraculous acts and works, as well as the pronouncement of forgiveness and inclusion of even "outsiders," all the way to his suffering, cross, and death, and culminating in his glorious resurrection, ascension, the Pentecost pouring out of the Spirit, and finally his current cosmic rule. With this kind of

72. John D. Zizioulas, *Being as Communion: Studies in Personhood and the Church* (Crestwood, NY: St. Vladimir's Seminary Press, 1985), 22.

73. Hans Küng, *The Church* (Garden City: Doubleday, 1976), 298–313.

wide and comprehensive christological grounding, the church's mission can be framed in a dynamic and multilayered manner.

Church as People of God

Peoplehood is understandably based on divine election. That election, as discussed, means both particularity and opening to the world. Whereas in the theology of the early church the concept of the people of God played a significant role, it receded into the background subsequently, particularly with the entrance of Christendom and Christianity's official status as the civic religion. Fortunately, the peoplehood of the church has been rediscovered, first in the Reformation and then more recently in the Catholic Church's Vatican II theology of the church as the people of God,[74] and beyond it, ecumenically. Conceiving the church as the pilgrim people on the way to her destiny further highlights the eschatological, future-driven nature of God's community.[75]

The people of God is the most comprehensive among the three main metaphors. It not only means everything that the "church" denotes, but also highlights the inclusiveness and equality of all Christians, and importantly, includes Israel, the "first" people of God. The church-Israel relationship will be carefully investigated in the last section.

Having now reflected briefly on the implications of the church of the triune God as the Spirit's temple, Christ's body, and God's people, we deepen this consideration of the Trinitarian basis by clarifying first what the expression in the heading "Community after the Trinity" may mean.

The Church as the Image of the Trinity

Correspondence and Limitations of the Trinitarian Analogy

The most foundational ecclesiological statement in early theology, continued in the Eastern tradition, is that the church is an image of the Trinity. Just as each person is made according to the image of the Trinity, so the church as a whole is image. Happily, this claim has become an ecumenical consensus. The triune God is the eternal communion of Father, Son, and Spirit.

74. *LG*, chap. 2.
75. *LG*, chap. 7.

That said, before searching more intently for potential correspondence between the divine communion (Trinity) and the ecclesial (human) community, an important question has to be raised: Provided that Trinity gives guidance to the formation of human community, how should we imagine the correspondence? In other words, how much can we claim to learn from the "divine society" for the sake of human societies? Both continuities and discontinuities between the divine and ecclesial communion should be acknowledged. The discontinuity is obvious: whereas divine life is uncreated and infinite, the human is not; whereas divine life is perfect, the human is not; and so forth.[76] Furthermore, the Brazilian Catholic liberationist Leonardo Boff reminds us: we shouldn't approach the Trinity from a "utilitarian" perspective, that is, by asking how the Trinity might help inform our conceptions of the nature of the community, because, in the first place, the doctrine is about God.[77] Hence, let us be reverently cautious.

The Nature and Life of the Church in the Trinitarian Analogy

Suggestively, the following connecting points between the triune God as community and the church as community on earth may be discerned:[78]

relationality
presence-for-the-other
equality
nondomination
unity
difference

Relationality. Relationality is based on the communion of Father, Son, and Spirit in mutual relations to each other, traditionally named *perichōrēsis*, mutual interpenetration. Never a "closed" circle, the divine relationality encompasses and invites the church and humanity to participate. Relationality implies that the church is more than an institution; people and their relationships are essential.

76. Volf, *After Our Likeness*, 191–200.

77. Leonardo Boff, *Trinity and Society*, trans. Paul Burns (Maryknoll, NY: Orbis, 1988), 3.

78. Robert A. Muthiah, *The Priesthood of All Believers in the Twenty-First Century: Living Faithfully as the Whole People of God in a Postmodern Context* (Eugene, OR: Pickwick, 2009), 57–68.

Presence-for-the-other. "The relational nature of the Trinity means that each Person of the Trinity is present with and for the others. Being present with another means assuming an inviting posture that hears and receives the other, and involves a movement toward the other."[79] Another way to speak of this kind of turning to others is "self-donation."[80] Church members are not living for themselves but for Christ and other people; they give themselves to others, as it were—without losing their own identity or personhood.

Equality. Similarly to the Father, Son, and Spirit, who in their distinctive personhoods are equal and in concert serve the common cause of the triune God's eternal purposes, in a qualified and broken, yet authentic manner, the church reflects equality. Equality is not pushed away with gender, status, or other human differences. In Christ, all are equal—if different.

Nondomination. Not only characterized by equality but also, as Muthiah puts it, "the trinitarian relations are characterized by nondomination. The relations are consensual and free."[81] Too often, forms of hierarchical church structures, often echoing secular institutions, have caused domination, even abuse. They have to be rejected.

Unity. Even with the starting point in the threeness rather than the oneness of God, contemporary Trinitarian theology is not thereby ignoring the centrality of unity in the Trinity. Yet that unity is relational, as it is the unity of the Father, Son, and Spirit. In that kind of diversified unity, "personal character and social character are only two aspects of the same thing. The concept of person must therefore in itself contain the concept of unitedness or at-oneness."[82]

Difference. The simple reason why unity *alone* can never be affirmed is this: "Unity presupposes differentiation; if no differences exist, we have nothing to unite."[83] With regard to the Trinity, the basic axiom agreed on by all is that "each of the Persons possesses the divine nature in a noninterchangeable way; each presents it in his own way."[84] The currently oft-used expressions of "unity-in-diversity" and "diversity-in-unity" illustrate well the Trinity-driven differentiation in the one God. The Christian church of old saw unity-in-diversity/diversity-in-unity illustrated wonderfully in the many tongues of

79. Muthiah, *Priesthood of All Believers*, 59–60.

80. Miroslav Volf, "'The Trinity Is Our Social Program': The Doctrine of the Trinity and the Shape of Social Engagement," *Modern Theology* 14, no. 3 (1998): 412–17.

81. Muthiah, *Priesthood of All Believers*, 63.

82. Jürgen Moltmann, *The Trinity and the Kingdom of God: The Doctrine of God*, trans. Margaret Kohl (San Francisco: Harper & Row; London: SCM, 1981), 150.

83. Muthiah, *Priesthood of All Believers*, 67.

84. Moltmann, *Trinity and the Kingdom*, 171.

the day of Pentecost (Acts 2). Having now established a limited but significant analogy between the triune God and the church as communion, we take up an important task in the last segment of this section: looking more closely at the place and task of the church in the Trinitarian economy of God, that is, the church as an eschatological anticipation of the coming of God's kingdom in the person of Christ in the power of the Spirit.

The Church as an Eschatological Anticipation of the Kingdom

Church as Anticipation

An essential aspect of the church's nature and status in the Trinitarian economy is its reference to the future, the consummation in the coming of God's kingdom. As Volf argues, the New Testament "authors portray the church, which emerged after Christ's resurrection and the sending of the Spirit, as the anticipation of the eschatological gathering of the entire people of God."[85]

Although thoroughly an earthly community, the church is not only that. The scope of the church's anticipation is wide and comprehensive, as the ultimate goal "as a provisional manifestation and significatory anticipation of the eschatological people of God" is to gather men and women "from every tribe and tongue and people and nation" (Rev. 5:9) before the one God in the new Jerusalem.[86] Even more, there is also the consummation of God's eternal plans regarding the whole cosmos,[87] as will be argued in the next chapter.

The anticipation of God's future links the church integrally with the coming of the kingdom, a relationship in need of theological clarification.

The Church as the Sign of the Coming Reign of God

While related to the kingdom of God, the church in herself is not to be equated with God's rule. God's reign, his kingdom, is much wider than the church, or even human society. The church is a preceding sign pointing to the coming

85. Volf, *After Our Likeness*, 128.

86. Pannenberg, *ST* 3:478.

87. Duly noted also in "The Church as Community of Common Witness to the Kingdom of God," *Reformed World* 57 (2007): 105–207, here 108; this is the report of the third phase of the International Theological Dialogue between the Catholic Church and the World Alliance of Reformed Churches (1998–2005).

righteous rule of God in the eschaton, an anticipation of the coming consummation and gathering of all God's people under one God (Rev. 21:3–4). The distinction between the sign and the "thing" sets the church and her function in relation to God's rule in the proper place: "A sign points beyond itself to the thing signified. It is thus essential to the function of the sign that we should distinguish them,"[88] or else we repeat what happened with Christendom when the church and God's kingdom were virtually equated.

Acknowledging the anticipatory nature of the church's existence helps avoid uncritical alignment with any political or ideological order. As Barth put it succinctly, "Christians will always be Christians first, and only then members of a specific culture or state or class or the like."[89]

Having anchored the church in the triune God, we are prepared to tackle one of the most "foundational" ecclesiological questions, namely, exactly what makes the church, church—the question of "ecclesiality."

The Ecclesiality of the Church: What Makes the Church, Church

What Is at Stake in the Discussion of Ecclesiality?

The Twofold Ecclesiological-Ecumenical Dilemma

The question of the ecclesiality of the church—that is, what makes the church, church[90]—has to do with two unresolved issues. The first of the two relates to the continuing impossibility of mutual recognition of the ecclesiality (the "churchliness") of other Christian communities. In other words, some churches do not consider others as churches but as something "less" or "defective." This wound is particularly deep between the "older" (Roman Catholic and Orthodox) and "younger" churches (free churches and various types of independent churches), but it also relates to Protestant and Anglican communities, which stand somewhere in the middle of this debate. The second impasse has to do with the disconnect between what the church is claimed to be—call it ecclesiality "proper"—and what the church does, that is, the church's "mission" or "ministry."

88. Pannenberg, *ST* 3:32.

89. Barth, *CD* IV/1, 703; see Carys Moseley, *Nations and Nationalism in the Theology of Karl Barth* (New York: Oxford University Press, 2013).

90. See also Volf, *After Our Likeness*, 127.

The Debate about the Conditions of Ecclesiality

The first unresolved problem of ecclesiality ("proper") has to do with the radically different ways of conceiving what makes the church, church. The key debate has to do with the role of sacraments, episcopacy (the office of the bishop), and personal confession of faith. There are three main positions.[91]

First, for Orthodox and Catholic ecclesiology, not only does the church carry out the sacraments, but the sacraments make the church. Only where there is the celebration of the sacrament of the Eucharist (attendance at which requires water baptism) is the Christian church. And for that celebration to be ecclesiologically valid, there needs to be a bishop in proper "apostolic" continuity (somewhat differently defined in those two traditions). In sum: this is the "sacramental" and "episcopal"[92] (lowercase) rule of ecclesiality.

Second, for free churches, decisive is the presence of personal confession of faith of men and women who then gather together as the church. That personal faith is mediated directly, as it were, and does not necessarily require mediation by the sacraments or office. The celebration of the sacraments of water baptism and the Lord's Supper is an important part of the church's life, but they are not considered ecclesiologically constitutive and, where personal faith is missing, might even be taken as something formal and useless.

Third, there is the Protestant mainline definition of the church's "foundation" in terms of the administration of the sacraments (baptism and Eucharist) and the preaching of the gospel. Even if their theology is sacramental in the sense that one comes to faith and is sustained by the sacraments (and Word), neither sacraments nor ministerial patterns are considered ecclesiologically constitutive. As a result, even if they have a bishop (as a large number of Lutherans do),[93] that office is not constitutive for the being of the church and can also be otherwise.

Now, the ecumenical and ecclesiastical implication is this: these three groups are neither willing nor able to mutually recognize each other as authentic churches. This impasse of the mutual recognition is an open wound for ecclesiology and ecumenism. If we were not so used to it, it would appear to be unbearable, excruciating. And it is!

91. A materially similar presentation (limited to Orthodox/Catholics and free churches) can be found in Volf, *After Our Likeness*, 130–35.

92. Hence, in the following, the word "episcopal" (as distinct from the proper name of the Episcopal Church, i.e., Anglican) is used in that technical theological sense.

93. Even some free churches, particularly Pentecostals in the global context, may have bishops, without an episcopal ecclesiology.

The Question of the "Being" and "Doing" of the Church

The second problem, the disconnect between the "being" (ecclesiality proper) and "doing" (mission) of the church, is simply that, a *disconnect*. Mission is then considered a second moment, as it were, auxiliary to the being of the church, or as most often happens in practice, one of the many "tasks" of the church. In other words, missional existence is something separate from ecclesial existence.

Instead, in keeping with an emerging ecumenical consensus, we should define the church as mission. In other words, the church is not only *doing* mission, it *is* mission; mission belongs to her very nature, as will be detailed below.

Having now outlined the twofold ecclesiological-ecumenical impasse, we seek resources to resolve it.

Toward Transcending the Ecclesiality Impasse

There is an ecumenical consensus about the presence of Christ (and therefore, of the Spirit or the triune God) as ecclesiologically constitutive. This rule goes back to the fathers and is solidly based in the New Testament, particularly Matthew 18:20: "For where two or three are gathered in my name, there am I in the midst of them." The early fathers (Ignatius, Irenaeus, and others) agreed. The debated issues have to do with the way Christ's (and the Spirit's) presence can be determined, as it is hardly self-evident.

Here Miroslav Volf takes up the task in an important ecclesiological proposal searching for a minimalist, yet significant, principle of ecclesiality, seeking to develop a theology of the church based on the best and "redeemable" elements of congregationalist–free church traditions, in dialogue with Catholic and Orthodox ecclesiologies. Building on Matthew 18:20, Volf puts forth his tentative description of what makes the church, church: "Where two or three are gathered in Christ's name, not only is Christ present among them, but a Christian church is there as well, perhaps bad church, a church that may well transgress against love and truth, but a church nonetheless." Volf claims that this definition expresses what the above-mentioned church fathers argued, and that it is also in keeping with the rule of ecclesiality propounded by the seventeenth-century English founder of the Baptist movement, John Smyth.[94] Volf further argues

94. Volf, *After Our Likeness*, 135–37 and passim (136; emphasis removed); John Smyth, *Principles and Inferences concerning the Visible Church*, in *The Works of John Smyth, Fellow of*

that while neither sacramental nor episcopal, all free churches also practice and honor baptism and the Lord's Supper.[95]

Now the all-important question arises: Would this proposal yield any ecumenical results?

Toward a Mutual Recognition of the Ecclesiality of the Church: A Constructive Proposal

Locating the Proposal

Taking a lesson from it but also going further, this present text argues that a more solid resource toward a mutual recognition may be found in "mainstream" Protestantism, particularly its Lutheran tradition's rule of ecclesiality, followed by virtually the rest of Protestants. According to the Augsburg Confession (article 7), the church "is the assembly of all believers among whom the gospel is preached in its purity and the holy sacraments are administered according to the gospel. For it is sufficient for the true unity of the Christian church that the gospel be preached in conformity with a pure understanding of it and that the sacraments be administered in accordance with the divine Word." In other words, as long as the gospel and sacraments are there, it "is not necessary for the true unity of the Christian church that ceremonies, instituted by men, should be observed uniformly in all places."[96] Clearly, the theological and ecumenical cash value of CA 7 lies in that as long as the gospel and sacraments are there, most everything else can be named a matter of *adiaphora*, including church structures and ministerial patterns.

Other Protestant churches by and large follow this rule of ecclesiality. Even when adding "discipline," that is, obedience, as a necessary condition[97] and insisting on biblically sanctioned structures and offices,[98] the Reformed tradition firmly agreed with Lutherans. The same can be said of the Baptist movement, although it added, similarly to the Reformed, fixed structures and obedience.[99] Likely even the Radical Reformation, the "left-wing" sector of

---

Christ's College 1594–8, vol. 1, ed. W. T. Whitley (Cambridge: Cambridge University Press, 1915), 252, https://archive.org/stream/cu31924092458995/cu31924092458995_djvu.txt.

95. Volf, *After Our Likeness*, 152–54; Smyth, *Principles and Inferences*, 254.

96. CA 7; *BC*, 32.

97. Calvin, *Institutes* 4.1.9.

98. Calvin, *Institutes* 4.3.1.

99. Smyth, *Principles and Inferences*, 252, 253, respectively.

Protestantism with appeal to more radical renewal of the church, fits in here, although they really insist on some distinctive features such as separation from the world, pacifism, and the like.[100] These "additions" to the Augsburg rule, one may assume, do not have to be seen in any way as blocking the way from the foundational common view of the ecclesiality.

The Ecumenical Promise of the Gospel and Sacraments as Mutually Agreed Ecclesial Rule

Ecumenically, it is of utmost importance that, notwithstanding serious challenges to the acknowledgment of full ecclesiality to Protestant (and Anglican communities), "Catholic theology has never had any positive objection to raise against the two classic Protestant signs: without the preaching of the gospel in accordance with Scripture and the administering of the sacraments as divinely ordained there can be no true Church according to the Catholic view either; both are absolute prerequisites for the Catholic Church too."[101] That Catholic theology requires "more," the presence of legitimate episcopacy at the Eucharist (*LG*, #26), does not have to be taken as a final *no* to the others. What if it could be placed in a bit different context?

I find useful Küng's note that at the core of the Catholic objection to the sufficiency of the CA 7 principle of ecclesiality lies the fear that "these two characteristics of the true Church are not truly distinguishing features" and hence do not fulfill the required task of identifying where the true church really is.[102] If that is the case, there is some hope of bringing the divergent viewpoints closer together if we consider the issue in light of the marks of the church, classically taken as the distinguishing distinctives of or pointers to the true church. It is fair to claim an ecumenical consensus for the stance that the two defining features of the ecclesiality of CA 7 are integrally and irreconcilably linked with the four marks (to be discussed in more detail below): unity, holiness, catholicity, and apostolicity. Indeed, Küng himself, as a Catholic theologian, contends that the marks "do not mean anything if they are not based on the pure Gospel message, valid baptism, and the proper celebration of the Lord's Supper."[103] Isn't there

100. See 1527 Swiss Brethren's Schleitheim collection of Seven Articles in http://www.anabaptists.org/history/the-schleitheim-confession.html.

101. Küng, *The Church*, 346.

102. Küng, *The Church*, 346.

103. Küng, *The Church*, 347.

some kind of real mutuality between the two "marks" of CA 7 and the four "marks" of the creed? Neither one alone is specific and concrete enough to help us discern where the presence of the triune God may lie in an ecclesiologically constitutive manner. When linked together, they help us be more confident.

The legitimate fear among the Catholics and Orthodox concerning the challenge of being able to discern Christ's community-forming presence may also be eased by the observation that as much as Protestant Reformers emphasized the immediacy of believers to Christ (to defeat what they saw as the destructive human-made hierarchy-related and institutional obstacles), in no way could CA 7 be made a matter of a "community of believers" merely coming together as individuals to be the church. That would of course make the claim for ecclesiality random, as one could believe just for oneself. Indeed, that liability should be carefully kept in mind by free churches, as they at times tend to emphasize problematically the mere unmediated access to Christ by all. The community's ecclesiality depends on the preaching and sacraments, which both represent apostolicity as they go back to Jesus and the institution by the apostles.

Furthermore, sticking with the two foundational standards, *pure* gospel and *right* administration of sacraments—as much as it is true and routinely noted that the Protestant Reformation at large failed to provide any specific criteria for their ascertainment—also functions toward the unity in faith and love for all communities committed to them. The Lutheran theologian Pannenberg succinctly argues that, on that basis, "the universal unity of the church across the ages finds manifestation in the worship of the local congregation that exists in virtue of its apostolic basis, having fellowship with past saints and martyrs. For the pure teaching of the apostolic gospel and administration of the sacraments that is faithful to their institution constitute the church's unity across the centuries and at the same time characterize each local congregation of believers as the church of Christ."[104]

This Protestant Reformation–originated ecumenical proposal toward a mutual recognition of the churchly nature of other Christian communities has to be linked tightly with the classical "marks" of the church—and their missional orientation.

104. Pannenberg, *ST* 3:101.

The Four Marks of the Church in Action[105]

What Do the "Marks" of the Church Mark?

Unlike too often in later tradition, the four classical marks of the church (also called "notes" or "signs" in tradition)—unity, holiness, apostolicity, and catholicity—were not used first in any apologetic sense. The marks were most probably added to the creed somewhat haphazardly. Rather than abstract definitions of the church, the marks are first and foremost the object of faith. Whereas in the creeds we believe *in* the triune God as Father, Son, and Spirit, when it comes to the third article, an accurate rendering of the original text states that we believe the church. As a result, they are as much also "statements of hope." Eventually, they also become "statements of action," because they urge us to realize what is believed and hoped for.[106]

It is usual and useful to consider the marks as "gifts" and "tasks." Indeed, the twofold sense is already implied in the above. On the one hand, they are gifts from God. We do not make the church one, holy, apostolic, and catholic; only God can. On the other hand, we see only too clearly that any church in the world, including our own, is far from those markers. Hence, each description is also a matter of hope, which leads to action to more closely attain their realization.

To underline the dynamic and missional orientation of the marks, the naming of them as "adverbs" by the leading American Reformed mission theologian Charles Van Engen points in the right direction. Rather than static adjectives, the adverbial conception is a call for the church to be "the unifying, sanctifying, reconciling, and proclaiming presence of Jesus Christ in the world," thereby "challenging local congregations to a transformed, purpose-driven life of mission in the world, locally and globally."[107]

105. This heading modifies "The Four Attributes in Action," in Charles Van Engen, *God's Missionary People: Rethinking the Purpose of the Local Church* (Grand Rapids: Baker Academic, 1991), 66.

106. Jürgen Moltmann, *The Church in the Power of the Spirit: A Contribution to Messianic Ecclesiology*, trans. Margaret Kohl (London: SCM, 1977), 339–40.

107. Charles Van Engen, "Church," in *Evangelical Dictionary of World Christian Missions*, ed. A. Scott Moreau et al. (Grand Rapids: Baker Academic, 2000), 193.

The Church as One—and Many: Unity in Diversity or the Scandal of Division?

The most striking and dramatic plague of Christianity is not the diversity and plurality of churches (and denominations) but that these churches do not recognize each other. The divisions and lack of love should cause all churches to repent and turn to each other in order to build unity, in obedience to the numerous exhortations and warnings in the New Testament (John 17:20–26; Acts 2:42; Rom. 12:3–8; 1 Cor. 1:10–30; Eph. 4:1–6). Although the unity of the church has been a spiritual and theological conviction from the beginning of history, we should not idealize the early church. As is evident already in the New Testament, divisions and strife emerged as soon as new communities mushroomed. Importantly, early in patristic theology deep concern for restoring unity emerged, as is evident in ecumenical tracts such as the early third-century *On the Unity of the Church* by Cyprian.

That said, for Christians living in postmodern times and pluralist settings, talk about unity might not be good news, as it might be perceived as forced uniformity.[108] That legitimate fear can be set aside; in current ecumenical consciousness unity is never seen as eliminating diversity. True unity is diverse, even pluralistic.[109]

The Church as Catholic—and Local: Oppressing Universality or Flourishing Contextuality?

The term "catholic"—literally in Greek, "directed toward the whole"—at first merely meant the "whole" church in distinction from local communities.[110] There is no indication yet of the later meaning attached to catholicity of "fullness" and "perfection," that is, lacking in nothing, based on Ephesians 1:23. Out of that, in polemical debates, it came to mean "orthodox." This came to its zenith with the establishment of Christianity as the only legitimate state religion in Christendom.

The contemporary understanding has to remember the original New Testament meaning of the term "catholic" (notwithstanding the lack of the

108. Carl E. Braaten and Robert W. Jenson, eds., *In One Body through the Cross: The Princeton Proposal for Christian Unity* (Grand Rapids: Eerdmans, 2003), #2 (p. 12).

109. Roger J. Haight, SJ, *Christian Community in History*, vol. 3, *Ecclesial Existence* (New York: Continuum, 2008), 92.

110. Ignatius, *To the Smyrnaeans* 8.

term therein): it simply means the whole church as that consists of all local churches, which in themselves are full churches insofar as they are in communion with other, similar communities. "While the individual local Church is *an* entire Church, it is not *the* entire Church." So, each local church is truly catholic.[111] Furthermore, although spatial extension, numerical quantity, and temporal continuity are not irrelevant to catholicity, they do not alone—or even primarily—constitute it. It is often noted—rightly—that the term "catholic" comes close to "ecumenical," whose basic meaning, "pertaining to the whole inhabited world," came to mean (the search for) the wholeness, that is, oneness and unity, of the Christian church.

The Church as Holy—and Sinful: Sainthood by Separation or Pursuit of Holiness by Patient Love?

The Christian scandal, simply, is that "the essential holiness of the Church stands in contrast to sin, individual as well as communal."[112] Not surprisingly, various tactics have been tried to ensure the church's holiness. One of them is isolating the "holy members" from the rest. This goes back all the way to the (in)famous Donatist controversy.[113] Whereas the rigorist Donatists started off from the premise of the purity of the church, Augustine's mainline party insisted on the primacy of love and the nature of the church as a "mixed body" on this side of the eschaton. Their point of departure, based on the legacy of Cyprian (and others), was the unity of the body of Christ and the principle of love.[114] Another tactic makes a distinction between a church that is holy in herself and her sinful members; that is, it considers the *church* holy and her membership sinning. The obvious question arises, however: What is a church without Christians? Is it an abstract concept? An "invisible" nonearthly reality?

What, then, would be a theologically and pastorally appropriate way to envision a "holy" church of the creed despite the necessary sinfulness of all

111. Küng, *The Church*, 387–88.

112. *The Nature and Mission of the Church—a Stage on the Way to a Common Statement*, Faith and Order Paper no. 198, World Council of Churches, December 15, 2005, https://www.oikoumene.org/en/resources/documents/commissions/faith-and-order/i-unity-the-church-and-its-mission/the-nature-and-mission-of-the-church-a-stage-on-the-way-to-a-common-statement), #54; see also #51.

113. J. N. D. Kelly, *Early Christian Doctrines*, rev. ed. (New York: Harper & Row, 1978 [1960]), 409–17.

114. J. N. D. Kelly, *Early Christian Doctrines*, 203–7, 409–17.

her members? The starting point is the honest and bold acknowledgment of the sinfulness of the church. Even in her holiness, the church is "sinful and yet holy." This is true as much as the confession of the unity of the church in the midst of rampant divisions—or else we are not speaking of a real, concrete church composed of human beings! This means that the church does not derive her holiness from the members—as free church ecclesiologies too often tend to imply—but from her Lord; nor does the church lose her holiness because of the presence of sin in the lives of men and women.

Yet the idea of separation is at the core of the biblical notion of holiness in both Testaments. Church members should turn away from all that is ungodly and anti-God(ly) and turn to the things of God. But notwithstanding the human act of turning (away and toward), ultimately holiness is the work of the triune God.

The Church as Apostolic—and Charismatic: A Conserving Institution or an Expanding Organism?

Although the adjective "apostolic" never occurs in the Bible, the term "apostle" occurs frequently in the New Testament, most often in Luke and Paul, where its meaning resembles that of "ambassador" (for Christ). The term is not limited to the Twelve, as is often popularly assumed. It can also refer to various persons and groups; Paul himself is of course often its object, and he also mentions "false apostles."

The original meaning of the term simply had to do with the linkage to apostles. Apostolicity, then, essentially involves continuity with the life and faith of the apostles and the apostolic church of the New Testament, not in an artificial technical sense but as a matter of continuity in faith, worship, and mission. To the resemblance with the apostolic church belong the following of Jesus and his teachings as recorded in the Scripture, charismatic endowment, and a holistic mission and service. In that light, the claim to apostolicity by the youngest Christian family, Pentecostalism, gains a new credibility and significance—a movement of most enthusiastic missionary activity as well; no wonder numerous such communities adopted the name "apostolic."[115] This claim is as legitimate as the one based on episcopal succession (Orthodox and

115. Cecil M. Robeck, "A Pentecostal Perspective on Apostolicity" (paper presented to Faith and Order, National Council of Churches, Consultation on American-Born Churches, March 1992).

Roman Catholics) and as that with an appeal to the Bible as the apostolic Word (Reformation churches).

Having now clarified and attempted to contribute to the most "foundational" ecclesiological topic—what makes the church, church—we are in a place to widen and deepen the discussion on the meaning of church as a communion grounded in the triune God.

Church as Communion of Communions

Trinitarian Communion as the Source of Ecclesial Communion

Orientation

Having anchored the Christian community in the life of the triune God and in the missionary ("sending") movement of the coming kingdom for the salvation and reconciliation of the world, as well as tentatively establishing the criteria for where and how the ecclesially constitutive presence of Christ and Spirit may be discerned, we focus here on the life of the church as communion. The investigation begins by expanding on the many dimensions and facets of *koinōnia* springing forth from the triune God. Thereafter, we look at the implications of communion with regard to the local church and then the ways local churches are in communion with other local churches. Following that, the discussion on the one church of Christ as the communion of communions also brings to light the ancient problems of "visibility" and "invisibility," topics to be carefully nuanced for the sake of our pluralistic world.

Writing to the global and ecumenical church, I cannot dismiss a topic that is routinely ignored in systematic ecclesiological presentations, although its importance is evident among the faithful. It has to do with the "communion of saints" that also includes those believers who are deceased, including its particular manifestations in relation to ancestors in the churches of the Global South.

The Rich and Multidimensional Nature of *Koinōnia*

The New Testament term "communion," *koinōnia*, as the Orthodox theologian John Zizioulas's celebrated *Being as Communion* (1985) argues, is foundational to God's being: God is not first "one substance" and only then exists as "trinity"; rather, the Trinity is the primary, most "essential" statement about the one

God who exists in eternal relationship of Father, Son, and Spirit.[116] This term, widely embraced already in early theology, contains a number of interrelated, dynamic meanings that make it ideal to describe the relationship between God and the church as well as among the churches:

fellowship with the triune God (1 Cor. 1:9; 2 Cor. 13:13; 1 John 1:3, 6)
sharing in faith and the gospel (Rom. 15:27; 1 Cor. 9:23; 1 John 1:3, 7)
sharing in the Eucharist (Acts 2:42; 1 Cor. 10:16)
participation in (co)sufferings (Phil. 3:10; Heb. 10:33)
partnering in common ministry (2 Cor. 8:23; Philem. 17)
sharing in and contributing to economic and financial needs (Acts 2:44; Rom. 15:26; 2 Cor. 12:13; 1 Tim. 6:18)[117]

Let us first discuss the importance of *koinōnia* to personal faith and Christian existence.

The Ecclesial Mediation of Personal Faith

If prior to the Enlightenment, before the full emergence of individual personhood in the modern sense, Christian faith (like any other religion or ideology) was often imposed by the community on the individual without giving the individual an opportunity to embrace it, in the post-Enlightenment Global North the opposite liability arose. Particularly among Protestants and free church Christians, hyperindividualism has too often not only taken over communal commitment but even blurred the meaning of faith as a communal event. The task of a balanced communion ecclesiology is to keep in dynamic mutual conditioning both personal embrace of faith and its communal mediation by the Word, sacraments, and significant Christian persons in family and at church. Rightly understood, every believer receives his or her faith from the church, but then that faith must be personally embraced and owned for it to be more than an external religious or cultural feature.[118]

Particularly free church communities need to be constantly reminded that the gathering of Christians together around the gospel and sacraments is

116. Zizioulas, *Being as Communion*, 17.

117. Lorelei F. Fuchs, SA, *Koinonia and the Quest for an Ecumenical Ecclesiology: From Foundations through Dialogue to Symbolic Competence for Communionality* (Grand Rapids: Eerdmans, 2008), appendix 1 (519–25).

118. See also Volf, *After Our Likeness*, 160–81.

more than an arbitrary social get-together. Call it the "objective basis" of the fellowship. The "subjective basis" is called forth by a personal appropriation and embrace of the received gospel message and sacramental celebration. This subjective side, based on personal faith, is more than just a human person's faith as a disposition, as an isolated capacity. If it were only that, the church would not be needed; one could believe in God "directly," as it were. The common content of faith, based on the Bible received from the church, establishes the communal nature of personal faith.[119]

This is not to undermine the importance of the individual's right—and in case of a mature person, responsibility—to think through one's faith critically and carefully. In fact, even when the person, often a young person or a person young in faith, receives the Christian message by the church's authority, personal appropriation and assessment are essential in due course. The relationship between personal embrace and communal mediation is mutually conditioning.

Furthermore, as will be detailed below in the discussion on ecumenism, the common confession of faith has also wider ecumenical ramifications. By sharing in confession with the same content and object, namely, the triune God, we participate in the common confession of all churches and Christians.

Having anchored the ecclesial communion in the life of the triune God and God's "mission" in the world, and having established the coexistence and mutuality of personal and communal/ecclesial faith, we next look at the meaning of *koinōnia* to the local communion and its relation to all other local communions, the communion of communions.

The Communion of Communions

Church as Local Communion

The New Testament does not clarify the relationship between what later tradition calls the "local" church and the "universal" church; it speaks of both, sometimes in the same context. Theologically speaking, it is clear that the basic unit is the particular, concrete, local gathering of people in Jesus's name around the gospel and sacraments, as well as missional ministry in which fellowship or *koinōnia* signifies a common participation (Acts 2:42–47). This local *koinōnia* around the Word, sacraments, and common sharing is the church in the full sense of the term.

119. Pannenberg, *ST* 3:110–14, particularly 110.

But that is not everything. Equally important is to insist that the *communion* of local congregations among themselves is "essential to the integrity of each congregation as a form and manifestation of the one universal church of Christ."[120] Each local church is a communion of many (local) communions; that is the communion of communions.

Local Church, "Universal Church," and Eschatological Consummation

Defining the "essence" of the church as a local communion in communion with all other churches in one body of Christ calls for a careful systematic clarification of three interrelated yet clearly distinct relationships:

What is the relationship between the local church and the "universal" church?
What is the relationship between the local church and the eschatological consummation?
What is the relationship between the visible church and the invisible church?

The local church and the universal church. Early in the Christian West, this relationship was conceived in terms of the local churches being "parts" of the universal church. Hence, a schism was envisioned as a fragmentation of the one body, as it were. Another view, more akin to Eastern sensibilities, was the microcosm/macrocosm scheme. Both views are not so much wrong as inadequate and somewhat unhelpful. Minding the full ecclesiality of each local gathering, we are not helped by thinking of the local church merely as a part of the universal church. Rather, as stated, each local church is a full church. At the same time, this local church, as a "full" church, is necessarily part of the one universal body of Christ. Hence, to speak of the local and universal is to speak dialectically of "two distinct perspectives on the church which always mutually interact and influence each other."[121]

The local church and the eschatological consummation. With the church placed in the context of the coming kingdom, the question has to do with

120. Pannenberg, *ST* 3:103.

121. Roger J. Haight, SJ, *Christian Community in History*, vol. 1, *Historical Ecclesiology* (New York: Continuum, 2004), 41–42; similarly *Nature and Mission of the Church*, #65.

the relation of the local church to "the totality of the eschatological people of God" gathered under one God in the eschaton.[122] Following uncritically the free church template would suggest that the eschatological totality is but the composition or sum of all local churches. But that raises the question of how a local church could be a full church. It couldn't in that logic. Hence, it looks as if the Orthodox idea of identifying the local church with the universal church would help negotiate the dilemma: if the whole Christ is fully present in all eucharistic gatherings, then in each local communion the whole church is present (and of course in the eschatological gathering as well). The problem here is what Volf rightly calls "overrealized eschatology" and the accompanying problem of equating the church with Christ.[123] What, then, about the Roman Catholic view in which, so to speak, the local church receives its ecclesiality from the universal church or, to put it another way, "the local church participates in the reality of the larger church; the larger church is actualized in the local church"?[124] The problem with this has to do with the neglect of the still-eschatological and thus anticipatory nature of the universal church prior to consummation.

Only by minding the eschatologically oriented and therefore provisional nature of the church communion do we arrive at a proper understanding of the relation of the local church to the eschatological communion. While not an identification, there is an overlapping relationship between the local church and the universal church "insofar as the universal church includes all local churches, and every local church is a part of the universal church understood in this way."[125]

The visible church and the invisible church. Although the New Testament speaks of the church most often in concrete local terms, as a visible fellowship in a particular location, also implied is the idea that came to be known in tradition as the invisible church.[126] Quite early, particularly in the Christian East, the emphasis began to shift to the invisible church, the "true" church, the company of the elect. Although the Western counterpart stuck more firmly with the importance of the visible, Augustine also brought about a classic understanding of what the invisible church may mean: over against many who had been baptized, only a minority were truly Christians, and those only God

122. Following Volf, *After Our Likeness*, 139–45.

123. Volf, *After Our Likeness*, 99–101.

124. Volf, *After Our Likeness*, 140.

125. Volf, *After Our Likeness*, 140–41, here 140.

126. Donald G. Bloesch, *The Church: Sacraments, Worship, Ministry, Mission* (Downers Grove, IL: InterVarsity Press, 2002), 70–75.

knew.[127] This distinction reemerged many a time in history, for example, in Pietism with its concern for personal possession of faith as opposed to mere formal membership.

The solution goes something like this: first, there simply is not a completely invisible community without visible people and acts. Second, that said, the distinction between these two aspects should be cautiously affirmed—or else why would believing be required? But rather than the two separate aspects of the church being alternatives, they are mutually conditioned and integrated: "The real Church is the Church we believe, and yet is visible; it is at once visible and invisible."[128]

Linked with the question of the invisible church is the relation of the communion of saints still on earth to that communion binding it together with the deceased.

The Wider Context of the "Communion of Saints" in Relation to the Deceased and Ancestors

Communion of the Faithful, Both "Below" and "Above"

According to the New Testament testimonies, communion between believers in God stretches beyond the boundary of physical death (Heb. 12:1). Communion links our lives to the lives of those who have gone before and sets before us the hopeful future to which we aspire. In early Christian theology and in Eastern Orthodox and Roman Catholic traditions throughout church history, this extension of the communion of saints beyond the faithful living in the same age has also led to certain prayer and ritual practices not embraced by Protestant communities.

Ecumenically we are in a place to acknowledge together the importance of this God-given communion (as God is the God of the living and the dead) without necessarily embracing a unified theology of the saints departed or of shared rituals.[129] Churches also have much to learn from each other in terms of how to best incorporate that aspect of the communion of saints in their life and liturgies.

127. Augustine, *On Baptism, against the Donatists* 4.3.5.

128. Küng, *The Church*, 62.

129. WCC, "A Cloud of Witnesses: Message to the Churches from a Symposium in Bose," November 2, 2008, https://www.oikoumene.org/en/resources/documents/wcc-programmes/unity-mission-evangelism-and-spirituality/visible-unity/a-cloud-of-witnesses-message-to-the-churches-from-a-symposium-in-bose.

An ecumenical project by the WCC has worked toward a common "ecumenical martyrology,"[130] a continuing pressing need for the global church. As is well known, there have never been as many martyrs as in the last century.[131]

Should We Have a Communion with the Ancestors?

An important theological question has to do with the attitude toward the ancestors, common in various religio-cultural contexts in the Global South, the epicenter of Christianity now.[132] Especially important is the link between generations in contexts where honoring ancestral relations is an essential part of the culture, particularly in various African and Asian cultural locations[133] where the ancestor theme has also been linked with Christ and the Trinity (chaps. 2 and 5 above). The Nigerian Jesuit priest A. E. Orobator speaks of "warm communion with the ancestors" as a way to underline the intimacy of the connection.[134] Whereas Protestants to a large extent have rejected this communion, the Roman Catholic Church has tried to critically "baptize" these cultural elements into the Christian liturgy. Promisingly, more recently, Protestant churches have begun to engage the topic, including even evangelicals.[135]

Theologically, the defining question is the avoidance of idol worship, which is strictly prohibited in the Bible and is thus applicable to both Jewish and Christian faiths (Exod. 20:3–5). To safeguard that, it is best to follow the theologically useful distinction between "worship" of God and "veneration" or paying homage to or honoring ancestors.

130. Guido Dotti, "The Bose Monastery's Ecumenical Martyrology" (lecture, Bose, Italy, July 9, 2013), www.strasbourginstitute.org/wp-content/uploads/2013/08/Bose-Monastery.docx.

131. Lawrence S. Cunningham, "Saints and Martyrs: Some Contemporary Considerations," *Theological Studies* 60 (1999): 529–37.

132. Russell Lynn Staples, "Christianity and the Cult of the Ancestors: Belief and Ritual among the Bantu-Speaking Peoples of Southern Africa; An Interdisciplinary Study Utilizing Anthropological and Theological Analyses" (PhD diss., Princeton Theological Seminary, 1981).

133. Helen Hardacre, "Ancestor Worship," in *ER* 1:320–25; Choon-Sup Bae, *Ancestor Worship: The Challenges It Poses to the Christianity Mission and Ministry* (Saarbrücken, Germany: VDM Verlag, 2008).

134. Heading in Agonkhianmeghe E. Orobator, *Theology Brewed in an African Pot* (Maryknoll, NY: Orbis, 2008), 115.

135. Sammuel Anye Ndingwan, "Ancestor Veneration among the Mankon of the Cameroon Republic" (PhD diss., Fuller Theological Seminary, School of World Mission, 1981); Bong Rin Ro, ed., *Christian Alternatives to Ancestor Practices* (Taichung, Taiwan: Asia Theological Association, 1985).

Now, what constitutes making "another god," that is, an idol, of any object? No object in itself is an idol. Humans make idols by their worship. Worship in this sense has to be understood as a qualitatively unique way of honoring and giving allegiance to the object. Should that happen, idolatry follows, which is totally forbidden for all Abrahamic faiths. As long as the religio-cultural understanding does not consider the ancestors in terms of idols—divine-like beings—to be worshiped but rather as images or symbols that recall the dead ancestors, honoring that memory would constitute something closer to a Christian memorial service than illegitimate idol worship. Particularly in folk religiosity, whether in African or Asian folk religions or Christianity's folk versions, this border is easily transgressed, and therefore, should ancestral honoring be practiced, most careful continuous catechesis is required.

The next task will be to delve into many details of the claim for the missionary nature of the Christian communion, tentatively established so far. That discussion will then lead into various aspects of the missional existence in sacramental life, liturgy, and the manifold ministries of the church.

The Church as Mission

Mission in the New Context(s)

The Many Meanings—and Challenges—of "Mission(s)"

Few other terms in the theological thesaurus have undergone as much change and still embrace as many meanings as "mission." Whereas until the Reformation it denoted simply the "sending" (*missio*) of the Son by the Father, thereafter its meaning became related to the work for the conversion by Catholics (spearheaded by the Jesuits) of non-Catholics (mainly Protestants rather than non-Christians), until in modern times it adopted a meaning virtually synonymous to "foreign" mission. Only in recent decades has its basic meaning in theology and missiology become comprehensive and inclusive, referring to the basic nature of the church as a "sent" community, as Vatican II put it: "The pilgrim Church is missionary by her very nature."[136]

Before getting into many implications of the missional existence of the church, the two main obstacles have to be tackled, that is, the rise of Christendom and colonialism.

136. *Ad Gentes: Decree on the Mission Activity of the Church* (Vatican II), #2.

Christendom and Colonialism as Deviations from Missionary Existence

What was the Christianity of Christendom like? What were its problems?[137] Many resulted from the radical shift of the church "from a marginal position to a dominant institution in society," a religio-political force rather than a gospel-driven pilgrim-people endowed with a mission to all, particularly for the marginalized.[138] Although it is not of course literally true that "the Christendom model of church may be characterized as *church without mission*"[139]—just recall the numerous missionaries and mission agencies particularly of the various Catholic orders throughout the medieval and later church—it is regrettable that the idea of the church as mission was virtually lost with the establishment of the church as the custodian of the religion of the empire. At the same time, we can be confident that God had not left his church even during the peak of her earthly power and its abuses, so prevalent in church history.

Not unlike Christendom, colonialism seeks power and earthly influence. At its heart is the will to subjugate and take advantage of the other. Just think of the massive occupation of land and resources in the majority world by the Western powers beginning from the seventeenth century. Colonialism includes but is not limited to racial discrimination, economic poverty, and political marginalization. The more subtle manifestations of colonialism encompass ideological, cultural, epistemological, and other means of violence and oppression. In its extreme form—slavery—as happened with blacks and the first nations of America, it means making human beings a commodity. Sadly, colonialism is not limited to Western powers; the history of Asia also bears its legacy (Japan's subjugation of Korea or the power of the Ottoman Empire).

Although it is crystal clear that the Christian church at large was involved with the colonial expansion of modern times and bears guilt for it, that should not lead to uncritical and unnuanced debunking of modern missions. In light of the newest missions history, there is no doubt that missionaries

137. Judith Herrin, *The Formation of Christendom* (London: Fontana, 1989); Stuart Murray, *Post-Christendom: Church and Mission in a Strange New World* (Carlisle, UK: Paternoster, 2004), chap. 4.

138. Michael W. Goheen, *As the Father Has Sent Me, I Am Sending You: J. E. Lesslie Newbigin's Missionary Ecclesiology* (Zoetermeer: Uitgeverij Boekencentrum, 2000), 2–3.

139. Wilbert Shenk, *Write the Vision: The Church Renewed*, Christian Mission and Modern Culture (Valley Forge, PA: Trinity, 1995), 35.

also helped not only to establish and cultivate local languages ("mission as translation")[140] but also to empower local economies and cultures by declining to further colonialists' agendas.[141] That same missionary translation also empowered indigenous resistance to colonialism. While the colonial system represented a worldwide economic and military order, mission represented vindication for the vernacular.

The Missional Nature of the Church

As emphasized in this project, there is a consensus across the ecumenical spectrum concerning the essentially missionary nature of the church.[142] The theological conviction birthed among WCC churches of mission as *missio Dei*, God's mission, encapsulates this vision and is now widely embraced. This idea of course lies behind the anchoring of the church and her mission in the sending of the triune God.

While *missio Dei* has been universally embraced by all traditions, a healthy debate has been going on for decades about its focus and emphasis. The debate relates to the place and role of the "agenda" provided by the world in relation to God's mission. Simply put: Should the missional existence of the church be guided primarily by the agenda provided by the world with its socioeconomic, racial, gender, environmental, and other issues, or should it primarily flow from the mandate of proclamation, worship, witnessing, and serving the needs of the people?

Eventually, a loosely defined and still-under-continuous-debate middle stance has emerged in ecumenical theology that seeks to radically balance both perspectives, with the caveat that for a distinctively *Christian* ecclesiological existence the primacy be given to a scripturally driven agenda focused on the triune God's mission to the world. As will be detailed, this vision is conceived in a most holistic and world-embracing manner.

140. Lamin Sanneh, *Translating the Message: The Missionary Impact on Culture* (Maryknoll, NY: Orbis, 1989).

141. Brian Stanley, "Conversion to Christianity: The Colonization of the Mind?" *International Review of Mission* 92, no. 366 (July 2003): 315–31.

142. For key influences and shapers, see WCC, *TTL*; Lesslie Newbigin, *The Gospel in a Pluralist Society* (Grand Rapids: Eerdmans; Geneva: WCC, 1989); Darrell Guder, ed., *Missional Church: A Vision for the Sending of the Church in North America* (Grand Rapids: Eerdmans, 1998); The Gospel and Our Culture, http://www.gospel-culture.org.uk/index.htm.

Multidimensional Mission in the Service of the Coming of God's Kingdom

The Interrelated "Layers" of the Mission of the Church

The church's existence as a missional communion derives from and is integrally linked with the life of the triune God, the sending God, in whose sending the church may graciously participate for the sake of the coming of God's kingdom. The kind of missional existence and life appropriate for the missional community consists of a number of dimensions and facets:

mission as evangelism and common witness
mission as healing and restoration
mission as social justice and equality
mission as integrity and flourishing of nature
mission as reconciliation and peacebuilding
mission as dialogue and interfaith engagement

In what follows, we will discuss the theological basis and significance of each of these six layers, gleaning also (but not unduly) from themes already investigated throughout the book.

Mission as Evangelism and Common Witness

Currently we are testifying to a widespread resurgence of evangelism, not only in younger churches but also in older churches, especially in the Catholic Church.[143] Although a widely attested biblical term (*euangelion* and related words), "evangelism" (or "evangelization") in normal church usage was not rediscovered until the nineteenth century. In contemporary ecumenical understanding, "it is at the heart of Christian mission to foster the multiplication of local congregations in every human community [as the] planting of the seed of the Gospel will bring forward a people gathered around the Word and sacraments and called to announce God's revealed purpose."[144] It is agreed that since the gospel is meant for every human person, everyone has the right to hear it. Evangelization should be done in a holistic manner and following the example of Jesus.

143. Ralph Martin and Peter Williamson, eds., *John Paul II and the New Evangelization* (San Francisco: Ignatius, 1995).

144. WCC, *Mission and Evangelism: An Ecumenical Affirmation* (Geneva: WCC, 1982),

While engaging in evangelization, a number of pertinent, interrelated theological issues routinely arise, including proselytism and common witness. In other words: What are the role and justification of conversion and repentance—or does evangelism with that goal represent a perverted power play? What, if anything, is the difference between evangelistic persuasion with the aim of initiating a response and proselytism? Under what conditions could Christians from various churches collaborate in giving a common witness? Since the first topic—conversion—is discussed above (chap. 8), only the twin themes of proselytism and common witness will now be taken up.

Proselytism has emerged as one of the most hotly debated topics between older, more established historic churches and younger churches with enthusiastic evangelizing activities. Routinely, free churches and other "newcomers" are labeled as proselytizers, and only recently have they been invited to mutual conversations about the topic. These conversations are yielding promising results. Consider the common statement by Catholics and the WCC titled "Towards Common Witness: A Call to Adopt Responsible Relationships in Mission and to Renounce Proselytism" (TCW) issued in 1997 with an invitation to a wide participation of Christian communities.

Although "proselyte" originally meant a convert to Judaism and later, by derivation, a convert to any other religion, "'proselytism' is now used to mean the encouragement of Christians who belong to a church to change their denominational allegiance, through ways and means that 'contradict the spirit of Christian love, violate the freedom of the human person and diminish trust in the Christian witness of the church,'" and it is "the corruption of witness."[145] Some of the features of proselytism in contrast to authentic evangelism include "unfair criticism or caricaturing of the doctrines, beliefs, and practices of another church without attempting to understand or enter into dialogue on those issues, presenting one's church or confession as 'the *true* church' and its teachings as 'the *right* faith' and the only way to salvation . . . offering humanitarian aid or educational opportunities as an inducement to join another church," and similar unethical acts.[146] While all churches should condemn and reject these kinds of proselytizing activities and attitudes,[147] it is equally important not to confuse authentic evangelism and common witness with proselytism.

145. TCW, II.

146. TCW, II.

147. See the important Pentecostal contribution by Cecil M. Robeck, "Mission and the Issue of Proselytism," *International Bulletin of Missionary Research* 20, no. 1 (1996): 2–8.

Authentic Christian witness, including common witness, "is constructive: it enriches, challenges, strengthens and builds up solid Christian relationships and fellowship" instead of the proselytizing "counterwitness," which "brings about tensions, scandal and division, and is thus a destabilizing factor for the witness of the church of Christ in the world." Furthermore, as long as the person decides to move from one Christian community to another out of the person's own volition and freedom, charges of proselytism should not be leveled.[148] A related ecumenical consensus is that "all Christians have the right to bear witness to the Gospel before all people, including other Christians."[149]

An important goal for all Christian churches is to work toward new initiatives in engaging common witness, "standing together and sharing together in witness to our common faith"—be it proclamation, worship, service, or evangelism in concert.[150]

Mission as Healing and Restoration

Unlike proclamation and evangelism, healing—whether physical or mental—has not been the hallmark of Christian mission for a long time, nor does healing occupy any place in standard theological discussions. This is markedly different from the early church and the long history of the church's life—let alone from the importance attached to healing, deliverance, and restoration among Pentecostals/charismatics and churches of the Global South across the ecumenical spectrum. Since this topic was discussed in detail above (chap. 8), there is no need to repeat it here. Let it suffice to emphasize that any missionary activity and presence worth its salt cannot afford to dismiss it.

Mission as Social Justice and Equality

The church's sociopolitical mandate has been taken up in the discussions of revelation, Trinity, Christology, and pneumatology, and will be revisited in the next chapter on eschatology. Hence, it suffices to just link tightly with the missional existence of the church.

148. TCW, II.
149. *EPCW*, ##94–95, here 94.
150. *EPCW*, #118.

Mission as Integrity and Flourishing of Nature

The theological basis of healing, flourishing, and integrity of creation is a key concern in contemporary theology and has been developed in the doctrine of creation (chap. 3) and pneumatology; it will be revisited in the next chapter on eschatology. An appeal suffices here: to the comprehensive missionary existence of the church belongs essentially concern for God's creation.

Mission as Reconciliation and Peacebuilding

Not only has this text treated the work of reconciliation and peacebuilding as an integral part of the Christian doctrine of Trinity ("divine hospitality") and salvation (*ordo salutis*), it has also adopted reconciliation as the widest and most inclusive concept denoting the various dimensions and aspects of salvation, God's gift of shalom (chap. 8). Here we can sum it up in the words of the WCC document *Together towards Life*: "God did not send the Son for the salvation of humanity alone or give us a partial salvation. Rather, the gospel is the good news for every part of creation and every aspect of our life and society. It is therefore vital to recognize God's mission in a cosmic sense and to affirm all life, the whole *oikoumenē*, as being interconnected in God's web of life."[151]

Mission as Dialogue and Interfaith Engagement

The last dimension of the church's missionary activity, interfaith engagement, will be investigated in some detail in the very last section of this chapter. If anything, this belongs to the core of the most comprehensive vision of reconciliation.

151. *TTL*, #4.

Missional Existence as the Sacramental and Liturgical Celebration

Liturgy and Worship at the Heart of the Church's Missional Existence

The Spiritual Source of Mission

Moving from the previous section, "The Church as Mission," to the current one with a focus on liturgy, worship, and sacraments is to leave behind neither mission nor missional existence. On the contrary, the missional communion gathered around the gospel and sacraments constantly feeds, renews, and reinvigorates the church's spiritual life and missional fervency in regular prayer, reading of Scripture, and sacramental and liturgical participation. Nowhere else is this deep and wide connection between liturgy, sacramental life, and missionary orientation as evident as in the life of the first church in the Acts of the Apostles (2:42–47), according to which the liturgical-sacramental life, filled with prayer and Bible study, helped launch this world-transforming mission with proclamation, healings, and deliverance to the ends of the earth.

In keeping with the triune nature of the church as the image of the triune God, it is appropriate to conceive of the church's worship and liturgy in Trinitarian terms as well. Just think of the great liturgical hymn in Revelation 5, in which "the Lamb receives the very same kind of worship as the Almighty YHWH does in chapter 4."[152]

One of the topics central to contemporary theology in general and the use of language in liturgy and everywhere in church life—language's inclusive nature—will not be taken up in this chapter because it was discussed above (chap. 2). Let it suffice to summarize that discussion's main conclusion: On the one hand, the traditional naming of God as Father, Son, and Spirit should be retained because there are no credible theological reasons not to. On the other hand, to insure inclusivity from women's perspective, complementary ways of naming God need to be creatively employed with a view to contextual appropriateness as well.

Should a poll be taken among ordinary churchgoers on the question, "Should we consider liturgy 'spiritual' or 'bodily' in nature?" it is safe to assume that the responses would be on the spiritual side. To the question, "Is liturgy a 'religious' or a 'political' event?" the answers most probably would fall on the

152. Brad Harper and Paul Louis Metzger, *Exploring Ecclesiology: An Evangelical and Ecumenical Introduction* (Grand Rapids: Brazos, 2009), 86.

side of "religious." What if these obvious responses were not so much wrong as only partially true? Indeed, liturgy and worship is a spiritual act, but it is done very much "as body language," as the American-based Nigerian Catholic Elochukwu W. Uzukwu's book title has it.[153] And as religious an act as liturgy is, it also has political connotations and expresses the core values of the missional community. Let us take up these two issues in succession.

"Worship as Body Language"

After the long dominance of body-soul dualism in Western culture, embodiment has had a hard time in Christian theology. As discussed above, only recently have theologians come to a more nuanced and also (self-)critical understanding of the holistic, embodied nature of the human person (chap. 4). Consider a recent book title by two Christian neuropsychologists, *The Physical Nature of Christian Life*.[154] Importantly, some theologians from the Global South, particularly from African contexts, are reminding us of the significant place given to the body in the traditional cultures in the contexts of nonanalytic, holistic views of humanity.

Indeed, while spiritual, worship is an act that expresses movement toward God, and it engages the whole human being. In this light, it is ironic that in the church, shaped by the Greco-Roman classical cultures, bodily gestures, movement, and enthusiasm were eschewed, and somewhat rigid "immobility" in liturgy came to be the norm. Just think of dance: for a long time, it was not considered proper in worship because of its sensuous and bodily aspects. Not surprisingly, still a routine object of ridicule in the African Instituted Churches, in African American churches, and among Pentecostal/charismatic communities everywhere has been their enthusiastic worship style with movements, shouts, and emotional expressions. Interestingly enough, those kinds of enthusiastic expressions are well regarded in other societal gatherings, from sports to politics to art.

One benefit of highlighting the embodied nature of liturgical life is to save it from a narrow "spiritual" reductionism and thus make space for a holistic participation of men and women; note that "liturgy" comes from the Greek

153. Elochukwu Uzukwu, *Worship as Body Language: Introduction to Christian Worship, an African Orientation* (Collegeville, MN: Liturgical Press, 1997).

154. Warren S. Brown and Brad D. Strawn, *The Physical Nature of Christian Life: Neuroscience, Psychology, and the Church* (Cambridge: Cambridge University Press, 2012).

word meaning work (of the people). This is not meant to undermine the importance of the liturgy also as ritual, an ordered and planned event. It is rather meant to help—for the sake of the global church with many colors, sounds, movements, and tastes—open up diverse and dynamic ways of expressing the liturgy. Even the most enthusiastic worship styles such as Pentecostal/charismatic ones get ritualized.[155]

A robust linking of embodiment, dynamic enthusiasm, and ritual has the promise of yielding an experience of the "heavenly liturgy" that is grounded in earthly realities of Christian life and is spiritually enriching. A creative example of that is a feminist theologian's effort "to develop a theology of the Eucharist that holds together the materiality of bodies and ordinary things as they are lifted up and shared in liturgical practice" in the holy meal.[156] This orientation helps link "spiritual" liturgy deeply and solidly with this-worldly, earthly experiences. That is the reminder of the public role of liturgies.

"Cultural Liturgies"

In his provocative and innovative "Cultural Liturgies" project, the American Reformed philosopher J. K. A. Smith advances the claim that whatever else the human being is, she or he is *homo liturgicus*, a worshiping animal. Or, to put it another way, following Augustine: "We are what we love." We are not only rational, thinking beings, or even believing beings, although we are also that; for Smith, we are basically imaginative and desiring (loving) creatures who express their desires and love in "liturgies." Mere focus on ideas and beliefs may yield a picture of the human person in quite abstract and disembodied terms. Smith sees us "persons as embodied agents of desire and love." "Rather than being pushed by beliefs alone, we are pulled by a *telos* that we desire."[157]

By looking at our cultural liturgies, whether in the shopping mall or at school or on the football field or as a citizen of the nation, others can determine what we vision as the good life, which can replace love of God, the highest value, with lesser loves. Rather than worshiping idols, Christians are

155. Daniel E. Albrecht, *Rites in the Spirit: A Ritual Approach to Pentecostal/Charismatic Spirituality* (Sheffield: Sheffield Academic, 1999).

156. Andrea Bieler and Luise Schottroff, *The Eucharist: Bodies, Bread, and Resurrection* (Minneapolis: Fortress, 2007), 3.

157. James K. A. Smith, *Desiring the Kingdom: Worship, Worldview, and Cultural Formation*, Cultural Liturgies 1 (Grand Rapids: Baker Academic, 2009), 46–47, 54, respectively.

meant to practice true worship that is guided by the love of God. True worship also corrects misguided cultural liturgical directions as it "functions as a counter-formation to the mis-formation of secular liturgies into which we are 'thrown' from an early age."[158]

Embodiment and "doing" also belong to preaching and proclamation correctly understood.

Proclamation as a "Dramatic Event"

"Why is it . . . that Christian doctrine so often appears strikingly dull," K. Vanhoozer wonders in the beginning of his programmatic work *The Drama of Doctrine*, if "at the heart of Christianity lies a series of vividly striking events that together make up the gospel of Jesus Christ," an "intrinsically dramatic" event?[159] Joining some other contemporary theologians,[160] Vanhoozer is seeking to (re)discover the "dramatic" nature of Scripture and—they are related—of preaching and doctrine.

Vanhoozer's "theo-drama" is both "divine speech and action." From the beginning of the Bible, God "does" many things with speech. Hence, theology needs to rediscover the nature of the word of God "as something God both says and does."[161] Or, as he wittily puts it: "The gospel is something *said* about something *done*. . . . *Speaking is one of God's mighty acts*."[162] Preaching that misses this is liable to the same fallacy that merely propositional theology is: "*dedramatizing* Scripture."[163]

Along with liturgical life and worship, the missional existence of the Christian communion is sustained and cultivated by sacramental participation and celebration.

158. James K. A. Smith, *Desiring the Kingdom*, 88.

159. Kevin J. Vanhoozer, *The Drama of Doctrine: A Canonical-Linguistic Approach to Christian Theology* (Louisville: Westminster John Knox, 2005), xi; see also his recent, less scholarly, more pastorally oriented *Faith Speaking Understanding: Performing the Drama of Doctrine* (Louisville: Westminster John Knox, 2014). See also Michael Horton, *A Better Way: Rediscovering the Drama of God-Centered Worship* (Grand Rapids: Baker, 2002), chap. 2.

160. Horton, *A Better Way*; see also William A. Dyrness, *Poetic Theology: God and the Poetics of Everyday Life* (Grand Rapids: Eerdmans, 2011).

161. Vanhoozer, *Drama of Doctrine*, 45, emphasis removed.

162. Vanhoozer, *Drama of Doctrine*, 46.

163. Vanhoozer, *Drama of Doctrine*, 87. For useful reflections on preaching, see also Bloesch, *The Church*, chap. 9.

The Sacramental Life of the Missional Communion in a Theological Outlook

Although "sacramental" or sacrament-type phenomena and gestures—call them "doors to the sacred"—can be found in the wider history of religions, theologically defined ecclesial acts, sacraments, at the center of ecclesial existence, are a uniquely Christian thing. While in Orthodox theology, beginning from the seventeenth century, the number of sacraments (usually named "mysteries") is usually seven, throughout history there has been no defined number. The Roman Catholic Church acknowledges seven sacraments: baptism, confirmation, Eucharist, penance, anointing the sick, ordination, and matrimony.[164] For Protestants, the number is two (although the Lutheran confessions also know "confession" as the third). Furthermore, although sacraments carry a fixed meaning (notwithstanding their number), in principle we could list a number of other acts that, if not sacraments, certainly carry a strong sacramental ring, such as healings, acts of mercy, or the proclamation of the word.[165]

With the exception of the (original) Quakers, even free churches, following Protestantism, practice sacraments—some Pentecostals and members of other churches also practice foot washing.[166] Often, instead of "sacrament," these communities speak of "ordinances."[167] Reacting vehemently against gross misuses of sacraments in the Catholic Church, Radical Reformers and their Baptist forebears went to the other extreme, away from the *ex opere operato* type of (semi)magical effectuality, as they saw it, to emphasize obedience: baptism and the Lord's Supper were to be celebrated because they had been "ordained" by the Lord in the Bible. Rather than divine acts bringing about what they symbolized, ordinances were primarily a means of human response to God's command.[168]

Notwithstanding differences on the meaning and scope of the sacraments, all (Western) Christian traditions build on Augustine's teaching on the sacraments as signs.[169] He makes the needed thematic distinction between

164. *LG*, #11.

165. Pannenberg, *ST* 3:355–56; for a fascinating theological reflection on "marriage as reminder of a broader sacramental understanding," see 358–64.

166. Harold D. Hunter, "Ordinances," in *The New International Dictionary of Pentecostal and Charismatic Movements*, ed. Stanley M. Burgess and Eduard M. van der Maas, rev. and expanded ed. (Grand Rapids: Zondervan, 2002), 948–49.

167. Stanley J. Grenz, *Theology for the Community of God* (Grand Rapids: Eerdmans, 1994), 512–18.

168. Grenz, *Theology for the Community*, 514–15.

169. J. N. D. Kelly, *Early Christian Doctrines*, 422–24.

the "sign" and the thing signified.[170] While not equated, they are closely and intimately related. This distinction has to be affirmed in a way that allows for the thing signified to already be present in a true anticipatory manner in the sign.[171]

The process of signification is always combined with God's command and promise, the Word. Speaking of baptism, Augustine put it succinctly: "Take away the word, and the water is neither more nor less than water. The word is added to the element, and there results the Sacrament, as if itself also a kind of visible word."[172] Hence, it is not the ritual itself, it is a receiving and believing embrace that counts. With this tight linking of the sacrament with the Word of promise, we can say that "Christ's own presence at the Supper fulfills the promise contained in the words of institution."[173] With the Word and promise in mind—but only so doing—what Saint Thomas defined as the core of the sacraments can be justly maintained, namely, that "they effect what they signify."[174] So much can be—and should be—said even if the Protestant tradition at large eschews the (semi)automatic and technical *ex opere operato*.

Baptism

Baptism and Christian Initiation

Baptism has been part of Christian initiation from the beginning. Orthodox, Catholic, Anglican, and Lutheran traditions uniformly understand it sacramentally; that is, linked with faith and the Word of God, it brings about what it promises, new birth. In the Reformed family, there are well-known internal differences. For the Zwinglian covenant theology, baptism indicates belonging to the people of God (somewhat similarly to the Old Testament rite of circumcision). The Calvinist majority oscillates between Lutheran and Zwinglian understandings in the sense that while it does not consider the rite regenerative in the sense that the sacramental traditions do, it does consider it a "seal" of the covenant with God. As such, it is done with a view to forthcoming faith.[175]

170. Augustine, *On Christian Doctrine* 1 and 2.

171. Pannenberg, *ST* 3:352–53, here 353.

172. Augustine, *Lectures or Tractates on the Gospel according to St. John* 80.3.

173. Pannenberg, *ST* 3:352.

174. Aquinas, *ST* 3.62.1.

175. Russell Haitch, *From Exorcism to Ecstasy: Eight Views of Baptism* (Louisville: Westminster John Knox, 2007), chap. 5.

Baptists, Anabaptists, and most all other free churches understand water baptism as an "ordinance," in other words, as an act ordained by Christ. Rather than a sacrament, it is a public response of a believer. Rather than infant baptism as in Catholic, Orthodox, Anglican, and Lutheran churches, free churches practice believers' ("adult") baptism by immersion.[176]

The Diversity of New Testament Perspectives: A Brief Assessment

Although baptism is not without pagan and Jewish antecedents, the New Testament establishes a distinctively Christian view of baptism with close links not only to the preparatory work of John the Baptist but also, more importantly, to Jesus's own baptism (recorded in all four Gospels). That said, as is well known, there hardly is a single baptismal theology in the New Testament. The Acts of the Apostles provides the most baptismal data and examples of the first Christian baptisms (chaps. 2; 8; 9; 10; 11; 16; 18–19; 22). The initiation included hearing the gospel, repentance, faith, forgiveness of sin, and the reception of the Holy Spirit (at times with charismatic manifestations). Baptism follows conversion immediately. All the baptized were in the age of responsibility. No information is given as to what kind of person performed baptism. Immersion was the normal baptismal mode. Baptism was done in the name of Jesus (although the church adopted soon the Trinitarian formula present in Matthew and elsewhere). Baptism is received from the community; one cannot baptize oneself.[177] It is not repeated. Baptism is a gate to church membership.[178]

In the Pauline and other New Testament epistles, the theology of baptism is depicted with the help of a number of images and metaphors, without any attempt at harmonizing. These include participation in the death and resurrection of Christ (Rom. 6:3–5; Col. 2:12), "a washing away of sin (I Cor. 6:11); a new birth (John 3:5); an enlightenment by Christ (Eph. 5:14); a re-clothing in Christ (Gal. 3:27); a renewal by the Spirit (Titus 3:5)," and so forth.[179] Baptism has both a human and a divine aspect, a gift of divine grace and an expression of human commitment.

When it comes to the spiritual effects of baptism, there are three types of orientations. Important passages link regeneration with baptism (John 3:5; 1 Pet.

176. Haitch, *From Exorcism to Ecstasy*, chap. 2.

177. *BEM*-B, #12.

178. Everett Ferguson, *Baptism in the Early Church: History, Theology, and Liturgy in the First Five Centuries* (Grand Rapids: Eerdmans, 2009), parts 1 and 2.

179. *BEM*-B, #2.

3:21; 1 Cor. 12:13). Others seem to imply that what is decisive are repentance and faith, to be followed by baptism (Mark 16:16; Acts 2:38; 8:12, 13, 36; 10:45–48; etc.). And finally, there are sayings in which repentance and faith without sacraments are linked with regeneration and new birth (Luke 24:47; Acts 4:4; 5:14; 11:21; etc.). Two broad conclusions seem warranted: First, in a number of passages baptism is seen as effecting or "causing" salvation. That said, second, baptism happens in the context of hearing the gospel, repentance, and faith. That speaks of the importance of human response to God's doing. This dynamic divine-human aspect of baptism should be kept in mind when weighing out how to define the way a person becomes a Christian in relation to baptism.

The Emergence and Establishment of Baptismal Theologies in Postbiblical Early Christianity

The (early) second-century Didache offers the first known description of baptismal practice (chap. 7): it was done in the triune name in "living" (or running) water (where available), and the candidates were expected to have fasted. Before baptism, preparatory teaching was obviously given. Eucharistic participation followed (chap. 9), as well as instructions for ethics and Christian life. In the theology of the leading second-century teachers, such as Irenaeus, faith, forgiveness, cleansing of sins, and reception of the Spirit are closely linked. Following earlier traditions, a three-year catechumenate for the sake of thorough instruction in faith before baptism became a norm. New components that seem to be established patterns in the West by that time include anointing with oil and exorcism.[180]

Augustine's influence towers over the theology of baptism in the Latin Church. While following the tradition prescribed above, he introduced innovative teachings that emerged out of his painful encounters with the Donatists and Pelagians. Against the former, he leveled the charge of rejecting Christian baptism and developed a thick theology of the sacrament in terms of its "indelible character"; its efficacy is immune to the quality of the administrator or the recipient. Augustine also comes to strongly endorse infant baptism, which of course fits this framework. The fight with the Pelagians further helped consolidate the doctrine of original sin (see chap. 4) that required infant baptism.[181]

180. Ferguson, *Baptism in the Early Church*, part 3, covers the second century, and part 4 the third, with meticulous documentation.

181. Ferguson, *Baptism in the Early Church*, chaps. 51; 52.

The Rise of Infant Baptism

Infant baptism is a new development in relation to the New Testament and the earliest patristic theology. It emerged slowly and sporadically in various Christian locations, and its legitimacy had to be demonstrated (Origen) and was sometimes rejected outright (Tertullian). This momentous shift began slowly from the end of the second century, and not earlier than the end of the fourth and beginning of the fifth, infant baptism had established itself as the main form of baptism.[182]

The first documented evidence for infant baptism at the end of the second century comes from Tertullian's strict opposition to it. He strongly recommended delaying baptism in order to ensure proper instruction in faith. Like the early fathers, he regarded children as innocent, as the later Western Augustinian doctrine of original sin was not yet in place. Ironically, instrumental in the slow rise of infant baptism were debates about baptism by heretics/schismatics and "clinical" or deathbed baptisms. Disputes about infant baptism's legitimacy continued for a long time. The first authoritative ecclesiastical pronouncement in favor of infant baptism—along with adult baptism—doesn't come until the mid-third century (at a council presided over by Cyprian). The main theological justification is that the divine gift belongs to all, young and old.[183]

In the first five centuries, apart from the emergency baptism, with healthy children "there is no evidence that their parents presented them for baptism. The instruction to parents to baptize their children begins in the late fourth century . . . and the routine baptism of babies belongs to the fifth century and after." Only with Augustine at the turn of the fifth century did infant baptism become the norm, although believers' baptism did not thereby disappear at once.[184] Notwithstanding the rise of infant baptism, believers' baptism as the dominant form of Christian baptism survived at least until the fourth century and continued as an alternative, legitimate form at least until the fifth (or even sixth) century.

182. In addition to Ferguson, *Baptism in the Early Church*, reliable are David F. Wright, *What Has Infant Baptism Done to Baptism? An Enquiry at the End of Christendom* (Carlisle, UK: Paternoster, 2005); David F. Wright, *Infant Baptism in Historical Perspective: Collected Studies* (Carlisle, UK: Paternoster, 2007); Hendrick F. Stander and Johannes P. Louw, *Baptism in the Early Church*, rev. ed. (Pretoria: Didaskalia Publishers; Leeds, UK: Reformation Today Trust, 1994 [1988]), chap. 1.

183. Ferguson, *Baptism in the Early Church*, chaps. 23 and 39.

184. Ferguson, *Baptism in the Early Church*, 627–28, here 627.

Faith and Baptism

In keeping with the New Testament teaching in which faith normally precedes baptism and the act of baptism is a personal choice, all churches agree that baptism and faith belong together irreversibly.[185] "Not the sacrament, but the faith of the sacrament, justifies," declared Luther.[186] Faith commitment should follow the baptized throughout life. Christian initiation is just that—*initiation*—rather than completion of the Christian life. It is particularly important for parents and mentors of baptized infants to be reminded that "personal commitment is necessary for responsible membership in the body of Christ,"[187] or else the goal and fruit of the sacrament may very well be lost. Indeed, baptism places a lifelong claim on the whole life of the Christian as a responsible member of the community.[188]

That said, the relationship between baptism and human response is dynamic and mutual: the irreducible link with faith should be connected with the equally important link in the New Testament between seeing baptism as "both God's gift and our human response to that gift."[189] In contrast to *wrongly* conceived, extreme ideas of the sacrament as a semimechanical *ex opere operato* or a merely human act, the divine-human/human-divine nature of baptism helps steer a radical middle road. Ultimately, neither baptism nor faith "have their bases in themselves, but alike in the saving act of God in Christ," in the eschatological act of salvation. In short: "baptism comes from faith, and faith leads to baptism."[190]

The emphasis on the close link between personal faith and baptism brings to light the problems and liabilities related to infant baptism. These were already recognized early on in Christian theology, as the discussion above indicates.

Believers' Baptism as the Theological Norm

The basic ecumenical argument is that believers' baptism should be adopted as the theological norm and standard when assessing various baptismal practices. The term "believers' baptism" refers not to the age of the candidate (although

185. *BEM*-B, #8.
186. WA 6:532.29; *LW* 36:66.
187. *BEM*-B, #8.
188. *BEM*-B, #10.
189. *BEM*-B, #9, #8, respectively.
190. Küng, *The Church*, 271.

it is related to it) but rather to the baptismal act in which a candidate with personal faith requests to be baptized in accordance with the New Testament and early Christianity. This is affirmed by *Baptism, Eucharist, and Ministry*.[191] Adopting believers' baptism as the theological standard does not have to lead to discrediting infant baptism, but rather helps those churches that continue this practice to constantly evaluate its theological value and hopefully reconsider the adoption of both believers' and infant baptism models as legitimate. Rather than continuing the often frustrating and fruitful dispute about infant versus believers' baptism, theologically trained persons should embrace the scholarly consensus and begin to work toward a common understanding.

The adoption of believers' baptism as the theological norm raises the question of how to negotiate the presence of faith in the context of infant baptism. In support of infant baptism in the absence of faith, ingenious tactics have been devised, but none of them sounds theologically—and *logically*—very convincing. Augustine's justification of vicarious faith of the infant (that is, parents or other believing adults believe for the child) with the reasoning that, similarly to original sin, which comes from outside the child (from parents), the family members and the church bring faith on behalf of the yet-to-mature infant[192] and Luther's idea of "infant faith" are not only without biblical support but also artificial and hardly convincing.

Indeed, the general effort to find a "substitute" faith for that of the infant baptized is not convincing. The reasons are many, not the least of which is lack of biblical support. Faith in the New Testament, as much as it is a divine gift communicated through the Holy Spirit, is also normally viewed as a personal choice that leads to commitment. In the New Testament, no one is baptized without the person's request or consent. This is not to deny the importance of either the Christian family or the church in cultivating the child's spiritual life, nor is there any reason to expect an infant to display cognitive and volitional features of faith similar to those of a mature person. Those concessions, however, have very little to do with baptismal practice. In contemporary culture, a further question arises as to whether baptizing infants may at least implicitly fail to honor each human person's integrity and inviolability.

Other typical arguments set forth in support of infant baptism are hardly convincing, including an appeal to the unconditionality of God's mercy. Were

191. *BEM*-B, #11; see also Jean Giblet, "Baptism—the Sacrament of Incorporation into the Church according to St. Paul," in *Baptism in the New Testament: A Symposium*, trans. David Askew (Baltimore: Helicon, 1964), 161–88.

192. Augustine, *Against the Two Letters of the Pelagians* 1.40.

the unconditionality really the theological basis for infant baptism, it would necessarily lead to the conclusion that *all* infants, whether those of Christians or of non-Christians, should be baptized indiscriminately, which is a procedure all churches condemn. Indeed, nowhere in the New Testament is the connection between unconditional grace and baptism established; rather, where unconditionality comes to the fore is in Jesus's blessing of children—but that is unrelated to baptism (notwithstanding its uncritical use in its support).

Nor is the reference to Israelite circumcision finding its Christian counterpart in baptism successful. The origins of baptism in the New Testament point in completely different directions, including that John's baptism has no relation to circumcision but rather is linked with repentance—for the circumcised people! Not to mention that circumcision is part of Jewish religion, which is based on birthright, whereas Christian baptism is a public commitment of both Jews and gentiles willing to commit their lives for Christ and the church.

Finally, Augustine's appeal to infant faith because of the alleged "deadly" original sin falls short of theological basis. First of all, the Augustinian doctrine of original sin is not universally endorsed by the church, and even if it were, nowhere in the New Testament is the sinfulness of humanity linked with baptism. As Pannenberg, a Lutheran theologian, categorically puts it: "The idea of exclusion of unbaptized children from eternal salvation on the basis of the doctrine of original sin is not in keeping with the total witness of the NT."[193] If original sin was the reason for baptizing infants, surely the early church would have adopted that practice immediately.

Ecumenical Suggestions for a Renewed Baptismal Theology and Practice

All churches should make concentrated efforts to learn to recognize the baptismal practices of other churches. Sacramental churches ought to give up the misguided insistence on infant baptism as the "default position," too often coupled with harsh rejection of believers' baptism. That would help churches strive toward considering both infant and believers' baptism as parallel and legitimate practices. Herein lies also a practical challenge—and an asset—to both baptismal traditions: whereas believer baptizers should seek to highlight more robustly that already before baptism all children are put under the care

193. Pannenberg, *ST* 3:264.

and grace of God, infant baptizers should make every effort to stay away from indiscriminate baptisms and continuously encourage parents and guardians to work toward helping the growing young person to find personal faith. Here much can be learned from the experiences of those churches that are practicing both forms of baptism.[194] The long-term ecumenical goal should be, on the one hand, a full mutual acknowledgment of both forms of baptism and, on the other hand, gradual transition toward believers' baptism as the normal form of the beginning of Christian initiation.

The timing of baptism should be left to the parents. Consequently, those churches whose bylaws require the bringing of infants for baptism (such as the Lutheran church) should change this ruling. It is somewhat ironic that in many secularized contexts of the Global North, particularly on the old continent, an increasing number of parents already do not baptize their children (even without any theological reason for or against).

Furthermore, minding the criteriological role of believers' baptism also means that all churches should consider carefully rediscovering the original mode of immersion, as that "can vividly express the reality that in baptism the Christian participates in the death, burial and resurrection of Christ."[195] That practice is of course used widely in Eastern Christianity and as a norm by most churches practicing believers' baptism.

In the absence of and in place of infant baptism, a rite of blessing for infants and young children, ideally in the worship service setting, could be adopted as a standard practice, as is already the case for most believers' baptism communities. That would match the New Testament example of Jesus's blessing of children. Naming—"christening"—of the child could be related to the event, if so desired, but it is not necessary. If naming is done, then through teaching and preaching, it should be made clear to the community witnessing the baptism that the act is much more than a mere cultural event.

Finally, what about confirmation, an important rite linked to baptism (whether viewed as a sacrament, as in Catholic and Orthodox churches, or merely a "sacramental" act, as in Protestantism)? Ironically, there is hardly any New Testament evidence for what confirmation means today. Unless one keeps baptism and confirmation together, as the Eastern Church has always done, the delegating of the reception of the Spirit to a future rite is not justifiable. This is not to deny the important practical and pastoral function confirmation

194. *One Baptism: Towards Mutual Recognition; A Study Text*, Faith and Order Paper no. 210 (2011), #97.

195. *BEM*-B, #18.

has served over the centuries among Western churches, as it has provided an occasion for both catechesis for the baptized and public confession of faith. The focus here is its theological basis—which is questionable. Instead of confirmation classes, churches should make a focused effort for Christian teaching of the youth, and the content of that teaching can glean much from hundreds of years of confirmation classes.

Eucharist

Theological and Spiritual Dimensions of the Eucharist

Apart from long-standing and ongoing differences in the interpretation of the meaning of the Eucharist, whose celebration has stood at the center of Christian worship from the beginning (Acts 2:44–46), ecumenically we have come to a place where it is possible to discern a significant consensus about the basic dimensions and aspects of the meal. The Lord's Supper is a profound embodiment of divine hospitality.[196] As with any other work of God, the Eucharist is Trinitarian in its nature and form: "the sacrament of the gift which God makes to us in Christ through the power of the Holy Spirit."[197] In the sacred meal, none other than the Lord and Savior hosts and presides.

Based on this *theological*-Trinitarian grounding of the sacred meal, *Baptism, Eucharist, and Ministry* expresses the significance and manifold meanings of this divine act of hospitality in a most comprehensive manner:

- Thanksgiving to the Father (as the term *eucharisteo* literally means)
- *Anamnesis*, the memorial of Christ's passion and resurrection as the resurrected Christ himself has instituted (1 Cor. 11:23–25)
- Invocation of the Spirit
- Communion of the faithful
- Meal of the kingdom, pointing to the return of Christ (1 Cor. 11:26; Matt. 26:29)

Furthermore, related to a number of these dimensions is proclamation, which has been integrally linked with the celebration of the Supper from the beginning; just observe the accounts of the early church in Acts 2–4 and beyond, as

196. *BEM*-E, #1.
197. *BEM*-E, #2.

well as Pauline teachings about the Eucharist (1 Cor. 11:26). Proclamation is of course most closely linked with the *anamnesis* and memorial.

Anamnesis means "representation and anticipation." It re-presents to the gathered community the significance and meaning of Christ's suffering and victory over death and thus anticipates the final consummation. The challenge for Roman Catholic sacramentology is to negotiate *anamnesis* in relation to the sacrifice of the Mass. Trent's view of the Eucharist as a re-presentation of Christ's sacrifice is not acceptable either theologically or ecumenically, if for no other reason than it potentially obscures the completed nature of the work of the cross (Heb. 10:14).

Remembrance is a clear biblical command. We can be confident that when Christians recall Christ's suffering and glorious resurrection and the words of institution are pronounced and embraced in faith, the Holy Spirit effects Christ's presence among the gathered people. It is a "literal re-membering of Christ's body, a knitting together of the body of Christ by the participation of many in His sacrifice."[198]

The Spirit's role is to bring Christ's memory and presence to the church. This is in keeping with the integral link between Easter and Pentecost. The readoption of the *epiclesis*, the prayer for the descent of the Spirit, has helped Western Christianity to rediscover the pneumatological dimension of the Lord's Supper.

Similarly to water baptism, which issues a claim on the whole life of the baptized person, the Eucharist also binds the celebrant to the values of the Lord of the Supper, particularly reconciliation with God and others. "All kinds of injustice, racism, separation and lack of freedom are radically challenged when we share in the body and blood of Christ."[199]

Christ's Presence in the Eucharist

All churches agree that Christ is present in the celebration of the Eucharist because of the New Testament statements about "this is my body" and "my blood." What is debated is the mode of his presence. Whereas Orthodox theology has refused to define in any conceptual manner the nature of the presence, the Roman Catholic tradition formulated it in terms of "transubstantiation,"

198. William T. Cavanaugh, *Torture and Eucharist: Theology, Politics, and the Body of Christ* (Oxford: Blackwell, 1998), 229.

199. *BEM*-E, #20.

that is, the elements become Christ's body and blood by virtue of the words of institution. The Lutheran version is "consubstantiation" (Christ "under," "in," and "above" the elements), the idea that Christ is truly present but without the elements changing their essence. Among the Reformed churches, the Zwinglian version focuses on commemoration of Christ's work, whereas the Calvinist view oscillates between the Lutheran and Zwinglian understandings, affirming commemoration but insisting on Christ's presence through the Holy Spirit.[200]

It is clear now that Luther's rejection of the Catholic doctrine of transubstantiation was in no way an attempt to undermine the full and robust presence of Christ in the Eucharist. Rome also ignored Luther's concessions that he was not so much opposing the doctrine of transubstantiation per se as emphasizing its voluntary, thus nonbinding, status.[201] Even Trent's authoritative formulations of 1551 are deeply controversial and nondiscerning concerning the Reformers' sacramental theologies.[202]

Ecumenically we can say this much without artificially ignoring differences: in keeping with classical sacramental theology, the eucharistic celebration shows the intimate relationship between the "sign" (bread and wine) and the "thing" (Christ's presence)—unlike typically when the sign indicates the clear distinction between it and the thing (as in a signpost that points to the destination away from it). At the Eucharist, "sign and thing are together, as when the sign indicates the presence of the things signified."[203] Terms such as "transsignification," invoked by both Catholic and Protestant theologians, might be useful here: it means a change in the "meaning" of an act, such as when a sheet of paper is "changed" into a letter, but not in any kind of literal or technical manner.

We can only hope that Rome would be willing to consider transubstantiation a *theologoumenon*, a traditional way of affirming the real presence but not binding on other traditions that materially affirm the real presence in their own respective ways. Other Christians should be able to affirm the real presence of Christ in the Eucharist without requiring a certain kind of semitechnical apparatus. The technical Lutheran term "consubstantiation" says materially the same and claims no exclusivity.

Similarly, the intra-Protestant disputes should be put under critical scrutiny. The seeming impasse between the Zwinglian incapacity to intuit how

200. For details and sources, see Gordon T. Smith, ed., *The Lord's Supper: Five Views* (Downers Grove, IL: InterVarsity Press, 2008).

201. Smalcald Articles, *BC*, I.6.5, 311.

202. See Pannenberg, *ST* 3:297–98.

203. Pannenberg, *ST* 3:299–300.

the ascended heavenly Christ could have his body present at the table and the ingenious Lutheran solution of the "omnipresence" (ubiquity) of Christ's body due to *communicatio idiomatum* can now be resolved with the help of the idea of the whole of Christ being present in the celebration, rather than the "body." Already pointing in that direction was Calvin's middle position that, in critique of Luther (and Catholics), contested the "real presence" in the elements and, in critique of Zwingli, still insisted on a "real *spiritual* presence" through the Holy Spirit.[204] As long as Christ's presence is conceived personally, the abstract and forced options among the Protestant Reformers can be healed and overcome. To that also points Calvin's "representational" understanding, according to which—in contrast to Zwingli's anti-Catholic "memorial" or symbolic understanding—the elements "point beyond themselves to bring to heart and mind the reality of salvation."[205]

As emphasized throughout the project, everything that the church is and does is related to mission. So even the most sacred sacrament, the Eucharist, bears a connection to the church's missional existence. That theme will be the focus of the next section.

"The Eucharist and Human Liberation"

Unlike in almost all contemporary celebrations of the Eucharist, the socioeconomic aspect was part of the New Testament church's sacramental life. This is why Paul's exhortation and rebuke come as prelude to what we now know as the words of institution (1 Cor. 11:20–22): he chastises Christians for not waiting on others. Similarly remarkable is the link between economic sharing and spiritual *koinōnia*, including the Word, prayers, and Eucharist in Luke (Acts 2:42–46; 4:32–37). This is what the feminist scholars A. Bieler and L. Schottroff call "Eucharistic life—a way of living with regard to food, body politics, economic exchange, and memory practices that flows out of liturgical practice." It is sacramental life deeply embedded in socioeconomic and justice issues at the local and global levels.[206]

The Sri Lankan Catholic Tissa Balasuriya's *The Eucharist and Human Liberation* rightly notes the irony of the colonial times when once a week those

204. Calvin, *Institutes* 4.17.31.

205. Leanne Van Dyk, "The Reformed View," in Gordon T. Smith, *The Lord's Supper*, 70.

206. Bieler and Schottroff, *The Eucharist*, 4. See also Monika Hellwig, *The Eucharist and the Hunger of the World* (New York: Paulist, 1976); Joseph A. Grassi, *Broken Bread and Broken Bodies: The Lord's Supper and World Hunger* (Maryknoll, NY: Orbis, 1985).

who colonized and those colonized were brought into the same place to share in the common bread and wine "while the rape of these colonial countries was going on."[207]

Eucharist and the Unity of Christian Communion

Throughout history, the Pauline "unworthiness" ban on partaking of the Lord's Supper (1 Cor. 11:27) has been conceived in terms of moral lapses. Although there is no reason to deny the importance of minding one's moral and spiritual condition when approaching the Lord's Table, contemporary exegesis is unanimous that what Paul had in his mind when urging his hearers to discern "the body" (v. 29) had to do primarily with church unity. The celebrants are warned seriously not to split or divide the one church body. Hence, the advice about self-examination (v. 28) is less about scrutiny of one's own conscience as an individual person and more about paying attention to one's behavior and attitudes with regard to unity.

That interpretation also brings to surface weighty ecumenical issues—keeping unity among all who wish to come to the table. Not without reason, then, a call has been issued to open the Eucharist to all Christians as long as they desire fellowship with the Lord and his people.[208]

Having now reflected on the church's missional existence gathered around the gospel and sacraments in liturgy and worship, we highlight in the following section the missional nature of the church by looking specifically at her ministry.

Missional Existence as the Charismatic-Diaconal Ministry

The People of God as the Missional Minister

To the question of who serves as the minister in the missionary church, the foundational answer is: every church member, the people of God. Even when tasks vary and some persons are dedicated to a lifelong and full-time ministry,

207. Tissa Balasuriya, *The Eucharist and Human Liberation* (Maryknoll, NY: Orbis, 1977), 4–5, here 5. See also the Latin American Catholic liberationist Juan Luis Segundo's *The Sacraments Today*, trans. John Drury (Maryknoll, NY: Orbis, 1974).

208. Pannenberg, *ST* 3:329.

everything is part of the common calling and vocation of the whole church. All are called and endowed (1 Pet. 2:9). This is an ecumenical consensus, including Catholic theology.

The "priesthood" of all believers became a leading theological theme in Luther's theology.[209] Differently from Catholic theology—including even Vatican II's *Lumen Gentium* (#10)—Luther's theology of ministry refused to grant any special status to ministers; they are merely set apart by the community for the community.[210] Other Reformers, including Anabaptists, enthusiastically followed this lead.

Notwithstanding different charisms and callings, there are no classes or hierarchies that compromise the equal status of all men and women regardless of sex, ethnicity, social status, or other human markers (Gal. 3:28). According to the New Testament, the "*whole* people, filled with the Spirit of Christ, becomes a priesthood set apart; all Christians are priests."[211]

What about the administration of sacraments? It is clear without any debate that in the New Testament there are no restrictions: all baptized men and women have the right to baptize and serve the Lord's Supper. That most churches have in the course of history reserved the right to the ordained clergy may be justifiable for the reason of order,[212] but even then the New Testament teaching and practice should be kept in mind as the leading principle.

Diaconal-Charismatic Ministry of the "Polycentric Community"

It is curious that the New Testament does not use any particular term equivalent to our term "ministry." Two terms are used that come close to "ministry." The first is "charism." For Paul (Rom. 12; 1 Cor. 12; 14; Eph. 4) and others (1 Pet. 4), a normal part of the church's worship and ministry is the exercise by the body of believers of various types of charisms, spiritual gifts. The second one is *diakonia*, "service." It refers to the work of serving food and waiting at table, despised by all free Greek citizens. In Jesus's teaching and example, it focuses on living for and serving others, even to the point of self-sacrifice.[213]

209. Luther, *To the Christian Nobility of the German Nation* (1520), WA 6:407–10; *LW* 44:125–31.

210. Luther, *The Babylonian Captivity* (1520), *LW* 36:113; WA 6:564.6–14.

211. Küng, *The Church*, 473–76, here 475.

212. So, e.g., CA 14.

213. Norbert Mette and James Aitken Gardiner, *Diakonia: Church for Others*, Concilium (Edinburgh: T&T Clark, 1988).

With the focus on lowly and unselfish service, we may speak of the "diaconal structure" of the church and link it tightly with the charismatic structure of the church.[214] Miroslav Volf says the same when he sets forth the participatory principle of ministry: "The church lives through the participation of its members, that is, the laity and the office holders, and is constituted through them by the Holy Spirit."[215] This leads to a "polycentric community" model of the communion with the participation, gifting, and responsibility of all instead of the traditional "bipolar" model in which those in office do the church work and the laity observes.

Consequently, ministries and offices of the church "only come into being by virtue of the common commissioning of the community itself." Those people are not separated or isolated from the community but rather render service among the people and on their behalf.[216] Lutheran ecclesiology rightly anchored the need for ordained ministers in the need to take care of the public ministry and order. Importantly, it presupposes a "general call" by the church.[217]

Following the New Testament testimonies and intuitions, any commission, charge, or ministry can "be full-time or part time. They can be carried out by men and women, by the married and the unmarried, by the theologically trained and people without any theological training. They can be exercised by individuals and groups. None of these circumstances and aptitudes amount to a law."[218]

Yet another noteworthy contribution of the Protestant Reformation to the theology and practice of ministry is its emphasis on preaching and proclamation, as particularly in the medieval church the cultic function of the priest had taken over. Vatican II moved definitely in the same direction with a remarkable emphasis on proclamation.[219]

The Charismatic Structure of the Church

The Church Is Charismatic

In the New Testament, each and every Christian and each and every church is charismatic, not only some. The term "charism" (from the Greek *charis*,

214. Küng, *The Church*, 502.
215. Volf, *After Our Likeness*, 222.
216. Moltmann, *Church in the Power*, 302–3, here 302.
217. CA 14, in *BC*, 36.
218. Moltmann, *Church in the Power*, 308.
219. Presbyterorum Ordinis, ##2 and 4.

"grace") is used loosely and nontechnically in the New Testament with reference to various types of charismatic endowments, giftings, and capabilities. They range from more extraordinary (miraculous works, words of wisdom, prophetic words) to fairly "mundane" (teaching, exhortation, giving generously), and there is no fixed number of them.[220]

Charisms are not only for the individual believers, although they of course are that. They are first and foremost gifts for the whole church, in keeping with the focus on the whole church as the minister of the charismatic gifting and endowment of all.

Christian communities that have followed more closely the ministry patterns present in the Pastoral Epistles have tended to prefer order over spontaneity, structures over improvisation, and the body of Christ metaphor over that of the temple of the Spirit. Those communities in the footsteps of the Pauline teaching for the Corinthian and Thessalonian congregations have sought a continuing, fresh experience of the charisms and spiritual manifestations. Without pitting these New Testament traditions against each other, it is vital for the church of the third millennium to rediscover the charismatic structure of the church and its integral link with the diaconic structures of ministry.

The Charismatic Workings of the Spirit in the Church

Three important principles can be drawn from the New Testament teachings and testimonies, particularly in Pauline literature.[221] First and foremost, the charisms are distributed and delivered by the sovereign Spirit of God, "who apportions to each one individually as he wills" (1 Cor. 12:11). At the same time, we are urged to "earnestly desire the higher gifts" (v. 31).

Second, charisms are not only exceptional and sensational phenomena—although there are also those, including glossolalia, powerful works, exorcisms, and healings (1 Cor. 12 and 14; Acts 10:46; Mark 16:17)—but also everyday ministry energies and giftings, from giving and exhortation to helping and leading, from teaching and discernment of spirits to acts of mercy and administration (Rom. 12:7–8; 1 Cor. 12:8, 10; 1 Pet. 4:10–11). The main goal of both types of charisms is the common good of the church (1 Cor. 12:7).

Charisms are diverse and plural. There is no definite or exhaustive list of gifts anywhere in the New Testament, but rather we find various types of

220. Max Turner, "Spiritual Gifts Then and Now," *Vox Evangelica* 15 (1985): 7–63.

221. Following closely Volf, *After Our Likeness*, 228–33; Küng, *The Church*, 236–50.

descriptions, open-ended in nature (Rom. 12:6–8; 1 Cor. 12:28–31; Eph. 4:11–13; 1 Pet. 4:10–11).

Third, there is a universal distribution of charisms, as every Christian is charismatic (Rom. 12:3; 1 Cor. 12:7; Eph. 4:7; 1 Pet. 4:10). No members are without any charisms, although there might be some—perhaps many—who are yet to discern and acknowledge them. Hence, the principle of "common responsibility" for the life of the church.

Minding the common calling of the whole people of God and the charismatic endowment of every church member determines the kinds of governance and community structures appropriate for missional existence.

The Missional Organization of the Community Structures

Ministry patterns, leadership models, administrative procedures, and other aspects of the structures of the community should be in the service of mission. As C. Van Gelder aptly puts it, "the church organizes what it does."[222] As practical and hands-on as the question of structures is, ultimately it is a deeply *theological* and *ecclesiological* question. Rather than fixed patterns, Scripture clearly underdetermines instructions concerning structures and what we call polity.[223]

It is important to acknowledge the improvised and fluid emergence of church structures in the New Testament and early Christianity.[224] Just consider the long-term and still-continuing scholarly debates about the diverse list of "offices" and ministers in 1 Corinthians 12:28–29 alone.

Even in the latter New Testament period, routinely named "early Catholicism," the organizational structures are still flexible. Along with the simple need in the church (as evinced in the selection of the first deacons in Acts 6), the unity of and need to care for the fledgling communities seemed to have been the major catalyst behind the appointment of leaders. In that sense, Lutheran ecclesiology's refusal to endorse any particular kind of ministry pattern or church structure is in keeping with the New Testament witness.

That said, historically it is undisputed that as early as the second century the office of the bishop—and a fairly straightforward three-tiered ministry,

222. Craig Van Gelder, *The Essence of the Church* (Grand Rapids: Baker, 2000), 37.

223. See Barry Ensign-George, "Denomination as Ecclesiological Category: Sketching an Assessment," in *Denomination: Assessing an Ecclesiological Category*, ed. Paul M. Collins and Barry Ensign-George (London: Bloomsbury, 2011), 11–12.

224. Adam Hood, "Governance," in *Routledge Companion to the Christian Church*, ed. Gerard Mannion and Lewis S. Mudge (New York: Routledge, 2012), 536–49.

with priests and deacons as assistants—emerged. The central tasks given to the bishop included presiding over the liturgy, particularly the Eucharist, teaching, and governing, and that assignment has continued throughout history.[225] That said, we do not yet have a firm knowledge of the extent that our contemporary conception of the bishop corresponds to the early episcopacy.

Ordained Ministers in the Service of the Community

The Missional Reassessment of the Nature and Role of the Ordained Ministry

Although the term "priest" in the New Testament is not applied to any specific persons (except for Christ) but rather to all Christians, as early as the time of Tertullian, priests as ordained persons are mentioned along with bishops, presbyters, and deacons.

With much justification Luther was troubled about the way the theology and practice of the priesthood had developed in his former church. He refused to include ordination as a sacrament not only because in his understanding there was no promise of grace attached to it in the New Testament,[226] but also—polemically—because he found the contemporary view of ordination into a sacrificial priesthood repulsive to evangelical faith. It is clear in light of the New Testament teaching that Luther's rejection of a sacrificial priesthood was correct. At the same time, Luther did not of course reject ordination per se.

Ordination as the Divine-Human Commissioning and Gifting

Placing the ordained ministry within the missional communion rather than over it or separate from it honors the principle of mutuality between all church members. The ordained and lay members work together and need each other. Hence, ordination is a "public reception of a charisma given by God and focused on the local church as a whole . . . [and] an act of the entire local church led by the Spirit of God."[227]

In summary, we can list the following interrelated aspects and effects of ordination:

225. Haight, *Christian Community in History*, 1:153–54.
226. Luther, *The Babylonian Captivity of the Church*, WA 6:560.20–23; *LW* 36:106.
227. Volf, *After Our Likeness*, 249, emphasis removed; so also *BEM*-M, #42.

- Reception of the gift of the Spirit (1 Tim. 4:14; 2 Tim. 1:6–7)
- Public commissioning (Acts 13:3)
- Acknowledgment of God's gifting and calling in the ordained person's life
- Commissioning of the person by the local church
- Mutual commitment between the community and the ordained
- Public declaration to the world outside the church, as the minister will minister in and to the world[228]

Although the New Testament endorses no definite ministry patterns, no more than it endorses particular forms of governance, it is clear about what it takes and means to be the holder of a church office: rather than above the people of God in their own category, ministers are but cobelievers, and rather than dignitaries to be served, they are servants willing to minister to others.[229] All appeals to superiority over others are totally foreign to the biblical teaching (see Mark 9:33–35; 10:42–45; and par.).[230]

An Inclusive Theology and Practice of Ordination

Although there have existed deeply negative attitudes toward women in Christian history, which are alive and well even in contemporary churches, only a few women theologians have gone as far as urging women to withdraw (at least for the time being) from the male-dominated churches.[231] Instead, a growing number of women are looking for a more inclusive, affirmative way of conceiving the Christian community and her ministry.[232]

Orthodox and Catholic churches—alongside a number of the most conservative Protestant churches—do not allow female ordination, whereas Anglican and most mainline Protestant churches do. Related blocks to women include the support for patriarchal top-down structures dominated

228. I am indebted to Volf, "Systematic Theology III: Ecclesiology and Eschatology" (unpublished lecture notes, Fuller Theological Seminary, Pasadena, CA, Summer 1988).

229. See also Küng, *The Church*, 465.

230. See further *BEM*-M, ##15, 16.

231. Rosemary Radford Ruether, *Women-Church: Theology and Practice of Feminist Liturgical Communities* (San Francisco: Harper & Row, 1985).

232. Letty M. Russell, *Church in the Round: Feminist Interpretation of the Church* (Louisville: Westminster John Knox, 1993); Kwok Pui-lan, "Women and the Church," in *Introducing Asian Feminist Theology* (Cleveland: Pilgrim, 2000), 98–112.

by males, a strongly biased androcentric writing of church history, and so forth.

The late American Reformed feminist L. Russell's celebrated *Church in the Round* utilizes the symbolism of the table to create new images of the church by employing the common cultural image of hospitality. The table represents inclusivity. An inclusive understanding of ministry takes it for granted that both the reception and the recognition of God's gifting for ministry apply to women and men alike. In patriarchal styles of leadership, authority is exercised by standing above in the place of power. Feminist styles of leadership draw their model from a partnership paradigm that is oriented toward community formation. The inclusive and hospitable vision of the communion would help us imagine an inclusive theology of ordination.

Let us divide typical arguments against women's ordination into three broad categories: (1) biblical-exegetical (focused on well-known New Testament passages seemingly barring women from ministry: 1 Cor. 11:3–16; 14:34–35; 1 Tim. 2:11–15); (2) traditional-historical (related to the beliefs about the lack of access of women to ministry during history); and (3) anthropological/gender-related assumptions (based on conceptions of women's nature and role in Christian theological understanding).[233] Since all these and related arguments in favor of exclusive male ordination have been so thoroughly investigated and rebutted in contemporary theological scholarship, the shortest possible response suffices.

Concerning the alleged biblical prohibitions, exegetes and theologians have presented the following types of counterarguments and rebuttals that—if not absolutely convincing one by one—seriously undermine their credibility as a whole and, indeed, have convinced the supporters of the inclusive view:[234]

- The equality in Christ of both men and women is a central affirmation (Gal. 3:28).
- The gifts of the Spirit have been promised for both men and women (Joel 2:28–29; Acts 2:17–18).
- The hermeneutics of passages used to prohibit female ordination in the New Testament (particularly in 1 Cor. 11 and 14, as well as 1 Tim. 2) have

233. E.g., Sacred Congregation for the Doctrine of the Faith, *Inter Insigniores: Declaration on the Question of Admission of Women to the Ministerial Priesthood* (1996); the typology used is from Una Stroda, "The Ordination of Women: The Experience of the Evangelical Lutheran Church of Latvia" (master's thesis, Catholic Theological Union, Chicago, 2008).

234. Any major critical commentary can be consulted for details of exegesis and hermeneutics, including arguments pro and con.

been successfully defeated with reference to lack of authenticity, cultural conditioning of texts, the occasional nature of prohibitions, translation alternatives, and so forth.

- The presence of female leaders in the New Testament such as Lydia (Acts 16:40), the four daughters of Philip (Acts 21:9), Priscilla (Acts 18:18; Rom. 16:3), Euodia and Syntyche (Phil. 4:2–3), among others, is established.
- Furthermore, the appeal to the precedent of twelve male apostles lost its scholarly credibility long ago; this is even acknowledged by some Catholic critics of their own church.
- We have to agree with the feminist theologians that the gender of Jesus is not a problem; the way Jesus's maleness is used in tradition to establish hierarchy, exclusivity, and power structures is the problem.

The minimal conclusion by those who continue supporting exclusion of women should be that since arguments in favor of their position are non-conclusive at their best, the matter should at least be left inconclusive, that is, open for continuing discussion. At the same time, the question of ordination and ministry should be placed in the wider context of the equality, inclusivity, and hospitality of the Christian communion vision: "Where Christ is present, human barriers are being broken."[235]

Although the unity of the church has been a recurring theme in the discussion so far, it is so essential as to deserve a section of its own.

Missional Existence as the Pursuit of the Diversified and Plural Unity of the Church

The Task and Landscape in the Search for the Unity of the Church

A Trinitarian Vision of Diversified Unity

Any credible and energetic work on the continuing healing of divisions and working for the unity of the church has to acknowledge honestly that "for the first time . . . the scandal of divided Christendom has reached such a head that it has become intolerable for the faith consciousness of countless modern Christians."[236] Faced with this painful reality and urgent mandate,

235. *BEM*-M, #18.
236. Pannenberg, *ST* 3:411.

the Christian church—each local communion in communion with other communions—shaped after the triune communion and drawn graciously into the sending of the Son by the Father in the power of the Spirit for the salvation of the world, anticipates the final gathering of all God's people in the new Jerusalem under one God. This eschatological gathering will consist of a ransomed people "from every tribe and tongue and people and nation" (Rev. 5:9).

This means that the ultimate vision for the unity of God's people will be unity characterized by diversity and plurality—without divisions, tensions, and strife pertinent to even the best attempts for oneness on this side of the eschaton. Hence, the somewhat counterintuitive expression in the section title: "The Diversified and Plural Unity of the Church."

Unity in Mission—Mission in Unity

Before proceeding, we should remember the deep and integral connection of unity with mission, as evinced so clearly in the modern ecumenical movement, birthed by the enthusiasm of the 1910 Edinburgh Missionary Conference. Its initial vision for the unity of Christ's church was fueled by the "practical" missionary need to collaborate and remove obstacles, including questions of ethics and reconciliation. As a result, various kinds of ecumenical processes and ways of collaboration have emerged, from the Life and Work movement, to the Faith and Order movement, and beyond. Since the beginning, the lofty goal of the ecumenical movement has been to "proclaim the oneness of the Church of Jesus Christ and to call the churches to the goal of visible unity in one faith and one Eucharistic fellowship, expressed in worship and in common life in Christ, in order that the world may believe."[237]

In the 1948 founding of the World Council of Churches,[238] this vision was commonly accepted as the shared goal. Standing in the widening river of these (and related) streams, the current ecumenical movement strives to work toward a fuller unity.

237. Faith and Order Commission of the World Council of Churches, "Faith and Order By-Laws, 3.1," in *Faith and Order at the Crossroads: Kuala Lumpur 2004; The Plenary Commission Meeting*, ed. Thomas F. Best, Faith and Order Paper no. 196 (Geneva: WCC, 2005), 450.

238. For history, functions, and resources, see https://www.oikoumene.org/en.

On Different Perceptions of the Unity among Church Traditions

The somewhat technical-sounding expression "models of unity" means "statements of the nature and form of the full visible unity of the church, which is the final goal of the ecumenical movement."[239] As mentioned, visible unity is the stated goal of the ecumenical movement. That said, no one (at the moment at least) knows or has the authority to formulate in any authoritative manner what that might imply. That is why there are various—take them either as competing or complementary—notions of what that unity may imply. All ecumenists agree that visible unity means more than a mere generic acknowledgment of "spiritual unity," as important as that in itself is (the idea that all believers throughout the ages belong to the same body of Christ).

All ecumenists also agree—against common misconceptions and "rumors"—on what visible unity does not entail: no credible vision of visible unity in the modern ecumenical movement has ever meant canceling out denominational markers; nor does it mean an effort to eradicate distinctive features between different traditions; and, needless to say, visible unity has nothing to do with the caricature of a "world church" taking over other churches.

The effort to discern the Eastern Orthodox Church's "model of unity" is highly challenging due to the scarcity of official pronouncements and doctrinal statements. What is clear is that schism is taken as a grave problem, on the one hand, and, on the other hand, that the church itself is confident in standing in the unbroken line of the apostolic tradition and church. Without recognition of the apostolic succession and, related, the sacramental priesthood, the Orthodox are hardly able or willing to proceed in full mutual recognition.[240]

No other church has defined as carefully and publicly its model of unity than the Roman Catholic Church. Recall that "the restoration of unity among all Christians" was "one of the principal concerns" of Vatican II.[241] Along with the Orthodox, Catholics affirm only one church of Christ on the earth. Importantly, *Lumen Gentium* replaced the older idea of the "perfect society" with the church as a "pilgrim people" on the way, not yet arrived.[242] Rather than equating the church of Christ with the Catholic Church, it teaches that

239. Thomas F. Best, "Unity, Models of," in *Dictionary of the Ecumenical Movement*, ed. Nicolas Lossky et al., 2nd ed. (Geneva: WCC, 2002), 1173.

240. C. G. Patelos, ed., *The Orthodox Church in the Ecumenical Movement* (Geneva: WCC, 1978).

241. *UR*, #1.

242. *LG*, chap. 7.

Christ's church "subsists in the Catholic Church,"[243] leaving open the possibility of the same for other Christian communities. Although the council affirmed that the church "is necessary for salvation,"[244] it also famously set forth the most comprehensive and inclusive vision of the levels with which other Christians and even followers of other faith traditions may be linked to the Catholic Church. Of other Christians with whom the Catholic Church shares so much in common, from its Scriptures to the triune God to the sacraments, it says, "in many ways she is linked with those who, being baptized, are honored with the name of Christian."[245] What remains a grave challenge to other communities is that even though the Vatican I mentality of the "return of separated brethren" was qualified by Vatican II, it still is part of the Catholic ecumenical view.[246]

For the Anglican Communion, as explicated in the Thirty-Nine Articles of 1563 and 1571, the unity of the church is based on the preaching of the Word of God and the sacraments (##19, 34). However, the later Chicago-Lambeth Quadrilateral from 1870 went further in its specifications regarding unity and outlined four aspects that shift the ecclesiological identity definitely toward the Roman Catholic and Orthodox view (and away from the Protestant one): Scripture, the Apostles' Creed, the two sacraments, and the episcopate.[247]

As explained, for the mainstream Protestants, under the tutelage of Lutheran tradition, to have union, possession of the gospel and the sacraments suffices. The youngest Christian churches, the free churches, have entertained many kinds of suspicions, even doubts, concerning the idea of ecumenism. The guiding principle for them has been the idea of "spiritual union," according to which the God-given unity already exists among "true" churches, or at least among "true" individual believers. The free churches have not located unity in creeds or even the Bible, although for most of them these two have been very important, but rather in the believing hearts of individuals.[248]

243. *LG*, #8.

244. *LG*, #14.

245. *LG*, #15.

246. *UR*, #4.

247. "Resolution 11," in *Book of Common Prayer and Administration of the Sacraments and Other Rites and Ceremonies of the Church: Together with the Psalter or Psalms of David according to the Use of the Episcopal Church* (New York: Church Hymnal Corp., 1979), 877–78.

248. E.g., William L. Pitts, "The Relation of Baptists to Other Churches," in *The People of God: Essays on the Believers' Church*, ed. Paul Basden and David S. Dockery (Nashville: Broadman, 1991), 235–50.

Toward Mutual Recognition of Churches

Ecumenical recognition "focuses on the possibility of recognizing the other [church] as a true church."[249] Or else no hope of visible unity can be had. Working toward full mutual recognition includes recognition of each other's baptism, ministry, liturgy, and so forth. Note that, at the moment, "full mutual recognition thus far only occurs among certain Protestant denominations but not outside of Protestantism."[250] As said, in its striving for mutual recognition, the modern ecumenical movement's goal is not to delete ecclesial identities but rather to help differences flourish in the shared diverse unity.

While making every effort toward a full recognition on the way to visible unity, the churches could also rejoice over and appreciate reaching less than full measure. The term "partial communion" has been invented to aid in that respect. It "means mutual recognition despite substantial or significant differences or disagreements."[251] That kind of goal may better help a church enter into a relationship of communion with another church that may seriously differ from it. This notion of communion admits many degrees.

In keeping with the modest call of partial communion, ecumenism could envision flexible, creative, and diverse processes and structures in the service of seeking unity. That kind of imagination, rather than rigid structures, better fits the mosaic of the Christian church at both local and global levels. That would allow for new kinds of ecumenical players, such as the Global Christian Forum,[252] to be engaged as a full partner. It would also allow for free churches, emerging communities, Christian coalitions, and similar groups to have a stronger voice.

Encouragement also may come from the simple theological acknowledgment that by definition all denominational identities and claims for the ecclesiality of any particular church are provisional on this side of the eschatological consummation. The church as a whole is an anticipation of the final gathering of all people and churches under one God.[253]

249. Minna Hietamäki, "Recognition and Ecumenical Recognition—Distinguishing the Idea of Recognition in Modem Ecumenism," *Neue Zeitschrift für systematische Theologie und Religionsphilosophie* 56 (2014): 458.

250. See Timothy T. M. Lim, "Ecclesial Recognition: An Interdisciplinary Proposal" (PhD diss., Regent University, School of Divinity, 2014), 4.

251. Haight, *Christian Community in History*, 3:277.

252. http://www.globalchristianforum.org/.

253. Christian Duquoc, *Provisional Churches: An Essay in Ecumenical Ecclesiology* (London: SCM, 1986).

Recall that in the listing of the tasks of the missional community in the previous section, the last one was named "mission as dialogue and interfaith engagement." To that complex quest we turn last in this chapter.

Missional Existence as Hospitable Dialogue: The Church among Religions and Secularism(s)

The Theological Mandate of Engaging Other Faith Traditions

There are certainly many "practical" reasons for the church to engage the religious other, from establishing a pedagogical contact and preparing to witness to Christ in the matrix of religious convictions, to helping Christians live in a civil way with the other, and so alleviating conflicts. These reasons alone would suffice; on top of those, there are also weighty theological reasons, that is, reasons related to the way systematic theology is to be conducted.

One of the reasons for the interfaith mandate stems from the Abrahamic faiths' monotheistic nature. The English philosopher of religion R. Trigg tells us why: "Christianity and Islam both believe that they have a universal message. If there is one God, one would expect that He would be regarded as the God of all people, and not just some." As a result, "Monotheism can have no truck with relativism, or alternative gods. Beliefs may construct gods, but those who believe in one God cannot allow for other parallel deities, even in the sense that other people have their gods while monotheists look to their one deity."[254]

The second theological reason for robust engagement with the religious other lies in the common origin and destiny of humanity, an offshoot from monotheism. This was clearly set forth in the beginning of Vatican II's statement on other religions (*Nostra Aetate*, #1): "One is the community of all peoples, one their origin, for God made the whole human race to live over the face of the earth. One also is their final goal, God."

On the basis of these two foundational convictions, the mandate for hospitable relating to the other establishes itself. It seeks to cultivate inclusivism, welcoming testimonies, insights, and interpretations from different traditions and contexts, and so foster mutual dialogue. A hospitable posture honors the otherness of others as human beings created by the same God and reconciled

254. Roger Trigg, *Religious Diversity: Philosophical and Political Dimensions* (Cambridge: Cambridge University Press, 2014), 114–15.

by the same Lord. Hospitality also makes space for an honest, genuine, authentic sharing of one's convictions.

The introduction to this book explained the meaning of comparative theology (alongside the related fields of comparative religion and Christian theology of religions). The God-centered pursuit of truth, acknowledging the deep belonging together of all men and women, leading to hospitable dialogue and mutual engagement, facilitates the scholarly work of comparative theology. Comparative theological work does not brush aside or undermine deep dynamic tension concerning religions and their claims for truth; in the spirit of hospitality they are brought to the dialogue table.

The many meanings of religious pluralism(s) have already been tackled in some detail above (chap. 2). Rather than repeating them, as a way of orientation, a theological critique is called for.

Healing the Broken Promises of Pluralism(s)

The leading Roman Catholic comparative theologian of England, Gavin D'Costa, rightly considers pluralisms at their core to be representations of modernity's "hidden gods." Ultimately, these pluralisms fail to deliver the promises of the Enlightenment: "openness, tolerance, and equality." Why so? Because, "in granting a type of equality to all religions, [the Enlightenment] ended up denying public truth to any and all of them."[255] As argued above, that would be an impasse to a monotheist.

The remedy to pluralisms, however, is not exclusivism but rather an attitude that takes delight in the potential of an encounter with the other without denying either party's distinctive features. The aim is to make room for a "critical, reverent, and open engagement with otherness, without any predictable outcome."[256] That kind of engagement does not water down real differences in the way of modernism. Too easily, pluralisms tend to deny the self-definitions of particular religions.

Plurality and diversity of religions are not the problem. Indeed, "for a religious person, to *accept* disagreement is to see it as within the providence of God"—even disagreement due to diversity of religious beliefs and convictions. Religions are not here without God's permission and allowance. The continu-

255. Gavin D'Costa, *The Meeting of Religions and the Trinity* (Maryknoll, NY: Orbis, 2000), 1–2.

256. D'Costa, *Meeting of Religions*, 9.

ing challenge, particularly for the staunch monotheist, is how to reconcile the existence of one's own deeply felt (God-given?) beliefs with different, often opposite, kinds of convictions.[257]

A Trinitarian Theology of Interfaith Hospitality of Witness and Dialogue

The Trinitarian Shape of Interfaith Engagement

Trinity is a proper framework for interfaith dialogue and hospitality because in the triune God there are both unity and plurality, communion and diversity. The Trinity as communion allows room for both genuine diversity (otherwise we could not talk about the Trinity) and unity (otherwise we could not talk about one God).

Borrowing from the biblical scholar Walter Brueggemann, we can make the term "other" a verb to remind us of the importance of seeing the religious other not as a counterobject but rather as a partner in "othering," which is "the risky, demanding, dynamic process of relating to one that is not us."[258] What matters is the capacity to listen to the distinctive testimony of the other, to patiently wait upon the other, and to make a safe space for him or her.

Naming it "The Holy Spirit's Invitation to Relational Engagement,"[259] D'Costa urges us to appreciate other religions important for the Christian church in that they help the church penetrate more deeply into the divine mystery and so also enrich their own spirituality and insight. While testifying to salvation in Christ, Trinitarian openness toward other religions fosters the acknowledgment of the gifts of God in them by virtue of the presence of the Spirit—as well as the critical discernment of these gifts by the power of the same Spirit.[260]

At the same time, the Trinity not only determines the Christian view of God, it also shapes our understanding of Christ. Only when Christ is confessed as truly divine and truly human, following the ancient symbols (creeds) of faith confessed by all Christian churches, can the Christian doctrine of the Trinity be maintained. Many problems in theologies of religions derive from a less than satisfactory conception of the Trinity, including the typical pluralistic pitfalls of

257. Ward, *Religion and Community*, 25.

258. Walter Brueggemann, *The Covenanted Self: Explorations in Law and Covenant* (Minneapolis: Augsburg Fortress, 1999), 1.

259. Section title in D'Costa, *Meeting of Religions*, 109.

260. D'Costa, *Meeting of Religions*, 115.

turning to "theo-centrism" in an effort to replace Jesus as *the* Way, or turning to the "Spirit" to get around the centrality of Jesus and the Father, as if the Spirit's ministry were independent from that of the other Trinitarian members.

Witness, Dialogue, and Tolerance

A true dialogue does not mean giving up one's truth claims but rather entails patient and painstaking investigation of real differences and similarities. The purpose of the dialogue is not necessarily to soften the differences among religions but rather to clarify similarities and differences as well as issues of potential convergence and impasse. The contemporary secular mind-set often mistakenly confuses tolerance with lack of commitment to any belief or opinion. That is to misunderstand the meaning of the term "tolerance." Deriving from the Latin term meaning "to bear a burden," tolerance is needed when real differences are allowed.[261]

The secular mind-set seeks to block the way to an authentic witness and proclamation in its fear of the power play and embraces only "neutral" dialogue. For a missionary faith, however, mission and dialogue, proclamation and interfaith engagement belong together and are not alternatives, and include common service, healing, and reconciliation.[262]

Having now clarified Christian theological guidelines for interfaith engagement and constructed some directives for continuing comparative theological work, we move from methodology toward actual material interfaith engagement with Jewish, Muslim, Hindu, and Buddhist traditions from a Christian perspective, with the focus on community and its mission.

The Church and the Synagogue

The Pain and Promise of Christian-Jewish Relations

What makes the encounter between Jews and Christians ironic and unique is that only after the Jewish people had rejected Jesus, the Messiah, did he be-

261. Consult Harold A. Netland, *Encountering Religious Pluralism: The Challenge to Christian Faith and Mission* (Downers Grove, IL: InterVarsity Press, 2001), chap. 4.

262. Pontifical Council for Inter-Religious Dialogue, "Dialogue and Proclamation," May 19, 1991, http://www.vatican.va/roman_curia/pontifical_councils/interelg/documents/rc_pc_interelg_doc_19051991_dialogue-and-proclamatio_en.html.

come the "Savior of the nations."[263] Along with these and related theological reasons, what has damaged the relations between the two Abrahamic communities is the "supersessionist ideolog[y] of Christian identity," which rejects that Israel continues to be the people of God,[264] and its corollary, Christian anti-Semitism.

It is against this sad and regrettable background—including also Jewish omission until modern times of a thoughtful engagement of Christianity and the proliferation of caricatures and prejudices—that promising signs of a fruitful mutual dialogue appear on the horizon.[265]

Jews and Christians as the People of God

It was established above that the concept of the "people of God" includes both Jews and Christians. Consequently, the idea of the church as the "new" people replacing Israel as the "old" people is to be rejected.

As orientation to this complex discussion, it may be useful to outline briefly (but hopefully not in an oversimplified manner) the main options among Christian theologians with regard to this issue:[266]

- In the *supersessionist* (or traditional) view, the church as the "new people" replaces Israel and takes her place in the divine economy.
- *Dispensationalists* make a categorical distinction between God's dealings with church and Israel, and they expect a literal fulfillment of Old Testament prophecies, including the rebuilding of the temple and its cult in the eschaton before the final consummation.[267] Because this view is novel and therefore marginal in Christian theology, it will not be further engaged.
- For the *revisionists*, there is ultimate redemption for both Israel and the church, and while for the latter it is through Christ, for the former it is

263. Pannenberg, *ST* 2:312.

264. John G. Kelly, "The Cross, the Church, and the Jewish People," in *Atonement Today*, ed. John Goldingay (London: SPCK, 1995), 168.

265. Edward Kessler and Neil Wenborn, eds., *A Dictionary of Jewish-Christian Relations* (Cambridge: Cambridge University Press, 2005); Edward Kessler, *An Introduction to Jewish-Christian Relations* (Cambridge: Cambridge University Press, 2010).

266. Following, with minor modifications, Donald G. Bloesch, *The Last Things: Resurrection, Judgment, Glory* (Downers Grove, IL: InterVarsity Press, 2004), 43–46 and chap. 10.

267. Robert G. Clouse, "Fundamentalist Eschatology," in *OHE*, 263–77.

not; indeed, the nonacceptance of Jesus as the Messiah for Israel is made a matter of obedience to God in this scheme.

- In *reunionism*, God's covenant with Israel will never be annulled but will be fulfilled through Christ, Israel's and all peoples' Messiah; ultimately both peoples of God, that of the Old Testament and that of the New Testament, will be reunited and saved.

In support of the reunionist vision—and thus rejecting supersessionism—it seems clear in the biblical testimonies, first, that God's covenant with Israel is irrevocable (Amos 9:14–15; Rom. 11:1, 29). Although for Paul the church embodied the true Israel (Rom. 2:29; 9:6; Phil. 3:3), this did not mean God put Israel aside (Gal. 3:17) after the supersessionist scheme. Second, in the divine plan of salvation, Israel plays a unique role as the "light" to the nations (Isa. 42:6; 49:6; Acts 13:47). That commission is not made void by Israel's disobedience. Third, in Jesus Christ, Israel's Messiah and the Savior of the whole world, the line of enmity between the chosen people and gentiles has been eradicated forever (Eph. 2:12–22), hence making possible the coming eschatological reunion.

Taking for granted the inviolability of God's covenant in Romans 9–11, Paul holds that Israel is the "trunk" of God's tree, and that the church, as the newcomer, can be compared to branches. In God's plan the branches could be united with the trunk (9:25)! This is a diametrically opposite angle from later Christian theology. At the same time, Paul is of course deeply troubled with Israel's unwillingness to embrace Christ as the Messiah, although he finds some consolation in the Old Testament remnant theology. He is confident that Israel's current "hardening" is but temporary and, ironically, is used by God to further God's plans for the salvation of the whole world (11:11). As a result, God's purposes will be fulfilled: "a hardening has come upon part of Israel, until the full number of the Gentiles come in, and so all Israel will be saved" (11:25–26). There is thus a united eschatological goal for both Israel and the church, and they are set in mutual, yet distinct, roles in relation to each other. All this means that the church should take a careful and self-critical look at herself as the people of God.[268]

While holding to the continuation of God's covenant with Israel, the Christian church and theology also should exercise critical judgment in not identifying that status with the current secular state of Israel. Israel's political sins and wrongdoings, like those of her Arabic neighbors, should be sub-

268. Pannenberg, *ST* 3:476–77, here 476.

jected to the same kinds of ethical and theological judgments as are other nations' deeds.

The Unique Nature of the Christian Mission to the Jews

Unlike Judaism, Christianity—like Islam—is an active missionary faith. We have to critique the revisionist view, which, while agreeing with much that has been said above, would oppose any notion of Jewish evangelization. Neither Paul nor the rest of the New Testament was advocating a "special path" for Israel in terms of the Jews not needing Jesus the Messiah. The one people of God will all be saved in and through Christ. Not only did Paul preach to both gentiles and Jews (Acts 9:15), but bringing the gospel of Christ to Israel took priority for him over other works of mission (Rom. 1:16).

At the same time, the unique and special nature of Jewish evangelization and mission have to be noted. The gospel of Christ, even when rejected by Jews, is not calling the people of God into something "new" in the way gentiles are being called. After all, Jesus Christ is Israel's Messiah before he is the Savior of the world. Mission to the Jews should also include a contrite and repentant spirit and acknowledgment of guilt for the sins in which Christians have participated throughout history. At the same time, Christians should acknowledge their indebtedness to Israel for the message of salvation and the Messiah.

These two broad theological principles help us better appreciate this continuing dynamic tension facing Christian theology, put well by a Jewish theologian: how "to be faithful to the New Testament command to witness for Christ to all peoples and to convert all nations, while, at the same time, affirming the ongoing validity of the covenant between God and Israel via Abraham and Moses."[269] At the center of this tension lies the obvious but important fact that "historically Christianity has been theologically exclusive and humanistically universal, while Judaism has been theologically universal and humanistically exclusive." Christian theological exclusivism, however, does not entail a view to disqualifying others from salvation but—as the sympathetic Jewish observer further rightly notes—is funded by the conviction that Christ's salvific work is meant for the benefit of all.[270]

269. Michael S. Kogan, *Opening the Covenant: A Jewish Theology of Christianity* (Oxford: Oxford University Press, 2008), xii.

270. Kogan, *Opening the Covenant*, xii–xiii.

Church and Ummah

Muslim-Christian Relations in a Theological Perspective: A Brief Assessment

Not only does Judaism stand in a unique position in relation to the Christian church, so does Islam, albeit differently. That said, it is too rarely appreciated how different the Christianity first encountered by the Prophet and the early Muslim *ummah* was from the contemporary global Christian church now. In the seventh century, notwithstanding internal differences, there was one undivided church (at least formally). Importantly, the segments of the church that early Islam engaged were either marginal or heretical in the eyes of the mainstream Christianity, namely, advocates of Nestorianism and monophysitism (of various sorts). Most ironically, many of the objections of Muslims against the orthodox Christian doctrine of the Trinity and Christology either stem from or are strongly flavored by these Christian divergences.[271]

On the one hand, the Christian-Muslim encounters throughout history have been characterized by misperceptions, misrepresentations, and even hostility. On the other hand, more often than not there has been more tolerance than would be expected from, say, cultures of the Middle Ages.[272] There was also a shift in Christian perception: whereas for Christian apologists from the seventh century, such as John of Damascus, to the late medieval period, Islam was represented more like a heresy, from the late medieval period onward it was taken as a false religion, apostasy. In the contemporary situation, a number of promising signs indicate that concentrated efforts are under way to continue constructive mutual engagement, heal memories, and improve understanding of the two faiths.[273]

Recall the wise words from Vatican II's *Nostra Aetate*: "The Church regards with esteem also the Moslems. They adore the one God, living and subsisting in Himself; merciful and all-powerful, the Creator of heaven and earth, who has spoken to men; they take pains to submit wholeheartedly to even His inscrutable decrees, just as Abraham, with whom the faith of Islam takes pleasure in linking itself, submitted to God. Though they do not acknowledge

271. Watt, *Muslim-Christian Encounters*, chap. 1.

272. Clinton Bennett, *Understanding Christian-Muslim Relations: Past and Present* (London: Continuum, 2008); Watt, *Muslim-Christian Encounters*.

273. "A Common Word between Us and You," A Common Word, https://www.acommonword.com/the-acw-document/; for "The Building Bridges Seminar," see Berkley Center for Religion, Peace, and World Affairs, https://berkleycenter.georgetown.edu/projects/the-building-bridges-seminar.

Jesus as God, they revere Him as a prophet. They also honor Mary, His virgin Mother; at times they even call on her with devotion."[274] A common basis in monotheism, scriptural heritage, doctrine of creation, theological anthropology, eschatology, and the person of Jesus has been detailed above, and it alone mandates a continuous, sustained dialogue. Commonalities and differences also come to the surface in the missional orientation of both traditions.

Mission, Colonialism, and Political Power: Shared Concerns

Similarly to Judaism, Islam sees "the appropriate way to human fulfillment in obedience to a divinely revealed law," named in that tradition the Sharia, which differs from Judaism in that it is "given to be followed by all humanity, and not just by one special community."[275] How does Christian mission relate to that claim? Instead of a divinely given law to govern all of life as in a theocracy, Christian mission aims at providing a holistic way of life based on love of God and neighbor, leaving open issues of government (most inclusively understood). From a Christian perspective, it is highly ironic that the Islamic pursuit of global Sharia has from the beginning been closely allied with a specific ethnicity and language (Arabic) and, in modern and contemporary times, often allied with nationalism, particularly in the regions of the world colonized by European powers.[276] How would a universal reach to all humanity be reconciled with that? "If Islam is indeed meant to be a global community, then it is self-defeating for Islam to oppose 'the West,' when Westerners should be Muslims, too, and when many are."[277]

As mentioned above, both Islam and Christianity carry a legacy of colonialism as part of their mission history. Unbeknownst to many is the fact that "while from the first there were considerable numbers of Christians under Muslim rule, yet until the appearance of European colonialism there were virtually no Muslims under Christian rule except for limited periods."[278] Everywhere Christians lived under Muslim rule, the Sharia law totally forbade Christian sharing of the gospel with Muslims. Indeed, according to Sharia law, the penalty for apostasy—the Islamic perception of converting to Christianity—is death.[279]

274. *Nostra Aetate: Declaration on the Relation of the Church to Non-Christian Religions* (Vatican II), #3.

275. Ward, *Religion and Community*, 31.

276. See Bernard Lewis, *Islam and the West* (Oxford: Oxford University Press, 1993).

277. Ward, *Religion and Community*, 32–33, here 33.

278. Watt, *Muslim-Christian Encounters*, 74.

279. See Watt, *Muslim-Christian Encounters*, 70.

The Church and Hindus

Differences of Orientation

Because of the difference of orientations between Hindu and Christian traditions—the former's individualistic pursuit of release and the latter's deeply communal faith—dialogue with Hindus focused on ecclesiology yields fewer results and areas of shared concerns than dialogue between the church and the synagogue or the *ummah*.

In many ways Hindu spiritual life and devotion are oriented differently than Judeo-Christian traditions—for example, prayer for the Hindu, rather than petition and pleading, as in the Judeo-Christian tradition, is more about chanting the sacred mantra, linked with the search for *darsana* in the divine presence. There is also what can be called "ritual enhancement," that is, a devotional practice that "aims at sustaining or improving the circumstances of the worshiper," whether that means practical life situations like sickness or business or family concerns, or the spiritual aims of liberation and release.[280] This is of course also a common feature of Abrahamic traditions.

What is a foundational difference has to do with another common theme in Hindu devotional life, namely, "negotiation or exchange, in which devotional performances become occasions for giving human resources of food, gifts, and devotion to supernatural entities and powers in exchange for human well-being, which is understood to flow from those persons and powers as a consequence of the rite."[281] Although this kind of exchange mentality is not unknown in Christian spirituality, theologically it is a foreign concept.

Religious Diversity: Connections and Disconnections

Hinduism exhibits internal diversity unlike any other living faith tradition, and its relation to the religious other is also more open than in Abrahamic faiths. Its tendency to assimilate others under itself, believing itself to be the "original" and perhaps best revelation, makes it in some real sense a counterpart to Roman Catholicism. At the same time, the Hindu attitude toward Christian faith is more complicated than that. Consider the well-known spokespersons of Hinduism in the West, Swami Vivekananda, India's delegate to the World

280. Courtright, "Worship and Devotional Life," 9820.
281. Courtright, "Worship and Devotional Life," 9820.

Parliament of Religions meeting in Chicago in 1893, and Sarvepalli Radhakrishnan, the former president of India. Known for tolerance and religious coexistence, they are also critics of Christianity.[282]

Indeed, there is no standard, universal Hindu response to the religious other.[283] In light of this complexity, it is important to recall that the roots of Hindu-Christian engagement and coexistence go far back in history. It is probable that there was a Christian presence in India as early as the first century. Syrian Christianity is believed to have reestablished itself beginning in the fourth century.[284] Although Western colonialism helped poison mutual relations between Hindus and Christians in a number of ways, it is significant that, beginning from the end of the nineteenth century, a new wave of interpretations of Christ related to the so-called Indian renaissance or neo-Hindu reform emerged, testing affinities between the two traditions.

These and related experiences in the past both speak to the complexity of relations between the two traditions and open up some possibilities for continuing mutual exploration of common themes and concerns. It is promising to hear from a Hindu scholar that "the dialogue initiative has come to stay in India."[285]

The Church and Buddhists

The Slow Emergence of Buddhist and Christian Engagement

In contrast to Christianity's interaction with Judaism and Islam, Christian and Buddhist theologies do not have a history of dialogue and mutual engagement; indeed, until the nineteenth century, very little exchange took place, notwithstanding some meaningful encounters between Nestorian Christians and Buddhists in India and China from the sixth to the eighth century.

282. Lowell D. Streiker, "The Hindu Attitude toward Other Religions," *Journal of Religious Thought* 23, no. 1 (1966/1967): 75–90.

283. P. S. Daniel, *Hindu Response to Religious Pluralism* (Delhi: Kant Publications, 2000), 233–36.

284. Anantanand Rambachan, "Hindu-Christian Dialogue," chap. 20 in *The Wiley-Blackwell Companion to Inter-Religious Dialogue*, ed. Catherine Cornille (Chichester, UK: Wiley & Sons, 2013), 325–45.

285. Anand Amaladass, "Viewpoints: Dialogue in India," *Journal of Hindu-Christian Dialogue* 1, no. 7 (June 1988): 7–8.

The best-chronicled friendship-based and intimate knowledge of Buddhism among Christians comes from the sixteenth-century Jesuit Francis Xavier.[286]

Similarly to all other faith traditions, Buddhism in the contemporary world faces massive challenges, many of which have to do with relations to Christianity and the linked colonialist burden. The effects of modernization are aptly named by D. L. McMahan as "detraditionalization" and "demythologization." Well known also in post-Enlightenment Christianity, they seek to highlight the importance of reason and critique over traditional beliefs and authorities.[287] Part of this process is the coming of Buddhism into the Global North in new contextualized forms, from Zen Buddhism to Buddhist theosophical societies, among others.

Discerning Differences and Potential Common Concerns

For the sake of continuing dialogue, let us register some foundational differences:

- Although the *sangha* is an important part of Buddhist pursuit of spiritual liberation, as in Hinduism, spiritual liberation is ultimately a matter of each individual's effort. Hence, Buddhism is not, ecclesiologically, a religion of "communion."
- Although not atheistic in the Western sense, a deity is marginal to Buddhists. One's salvation depends on one's own effort.
- Although Buddhism does not lack a social ethic or noble examples of working toward peace, reconciliation, and improvement of the society and world, as a religious-ethical system it is not optimistic about the future consummation. Ultimately, as with Hinduism, it is a religion of renouncement.

Despite these radical differences of orientation, what is common to both traditions is their missionary nature.[288] That said, its missional nature is

286. See Hans Küng, "A Christian Response [to Heinz Bechert: Buddhist Perspectives]," in *Christianity and the World Religions: Paths of Dialogue with Islam, Hinduism, and Buddhism*, by Hans Küng, with Josef van Ess, Heinrich von Stietencron, and Heinz Bechert, trans. Peter Heinegg (New York: Doubleday, 1986), 307–8.

287. David L. McMahan, *The Making of Buddhist Modernism* (New York: Oxford University Press, 2008), chap. 2.

288. Lisbet Mikaelsson, "Missional Religion—with Special Emphasis on Buddhism, Christianity and Islam," *Swedish Missiological Themes* 92 (2004): 523–38.

nothing like that of the Christian tradition, whose mission is anchored in the sending God. The *sangha*'s mission is to spread the knowledge of the liberating insight of the Buddha for the sake of men and women pursuing a similar path and for the well-being and benefit of all.

Concerning women's status in religion and the religious community, the Christian church may be in a position to inspire and instruct the Buddhist community. Despite the inclusive vision of Buddha discussed above, almost as a rule throughout the Buddhist world, females are either completely banned from the highest religious calling—full monastic life—or relegated to lower monastic levels. Religious authority is kept firmly in men's hands.[289]

Having engaged the four religious communities and their spiritual life from a Christian perspective, we now intend to do the same with secularisms.

The Christian Church and Ecclesiology in the "Secular City"

Forms and Ways of Secularism

With the founding of the United States of America in 1789, a new kind of officially formulated relation between religion and society emerged as the Constitution endorsed freedom of religion and prohibited privileging any particular faith. The same was reaffirmed with the founding of India and Israel in 1947. One may also think of the Russian Federation. Whereas particularly in the United States the desire not to affiliate the state with religion was motivated mostly by the need for tolerance and freedom of choice, in France, Spain, and Italy it was a protest-secularism against the dominant religion, Catholicism. These events testify to a growing desire to ensure freedom of religion, including the choice not to follow any faith tradition.[290]

Even though secularism enjoys overwhelming influence in the Global North, religions are not being marginalized; rather, the opposite is true. Linked with that is the rise of fundamentalist and ethnic projects to endorse the "religion of the land," whether by Islamic, Hindu, and some right-wing American constituencies.

Unknown to many, secularization is not limited to the Global North, although its epicenter definitely is in Europe and North America. The meaning

289. Suat Yan Lai, "Engendering Buddhism: Female Ordination and Women's 'Voices' in Thailand" (PhD diss., Claremont Graduate University, 2011).

290. Roger Trigg, *Equality, Freedom, and Religion* (Oxford: Oxford University Press, 2012).

and manifestations of secularism, however, are quite different in various contexts of the Global South. Unlike in the West, religion in Africa is not separate from the rest of life. This is not to say that secularism is unknown in Africa, but rather that its appearance and meaning differ vastly from that of European and North American contexts. As one may expect, secularism in the vast continent of Asia comes in various forms. India is a case in point. There are those who argue for its absence in that subcontinent while others discern secularism there.[291]

The latest "turn" in secularism discourse owes to the leading German philosopher Jürgen Habermas and the concept of the postsecular that he has helped launch.[292] Taking notice of the obvious "multifaceted transformation" in the landscape of religions in the Global North and beyond, as a result of which "religious symbols and language games are being transposed into other, not genuinely religious domains," including literature, performing arts, and advertising, among others, he observes the ways "the semantic and symbolic potentials of religions are becoming a universal social resource which shapes public and cultural life in a whole variety of ways."[293]

What would the Christian church's response look like? Understandably, a number of strategies have been tried, to which we turn in the last section of this chapter.

Churches Respond to (Post)secularism(s)

Classical liberals sought to encounter the emerging secular age with the strategy of accommodation or "correlation" in which Christian doctrines were reinterpreted in ways that were believed to be appealing to those who rejected religion. This led to a reductionist pick-and-choose collection of beliefs, carving out the miraculous and transcendent. This same "demythologization" program in various forms continues even to the third millennium, but in a more radical form. Consider book titles representing "postreligion" such as D. Bass's *Christianity after Religion* (2012) and Phil Zuckerman's *Faith No More: Why People Reject Religion* (2012).

291. Israel Selvanayagam, "Indian Secularism: Prospect and Problem," *Implicit Religion* 15, no. 3 (2012): 357–61.

292. Jürgen Habermas, *Between Naturalism and Religion*, trans. Ciaran Cronin (Cambridge, UK: Polity, 2008).

293. As paraphrased by Michael Reder and Josef Schmidt, SJ, "Habermas and Religion," in *An Awareness of What Is Missing: Faith and Reason in a Post-secular Age*, by Jürgen Habermas et al., trans. Ciaran Cronin (Cambridge: Polity, 2010 [2007]), 1–2.

Not all churches, not even a majority of them, are excited by these versions of accommodation (some may say, capitulation of faith). Briefly put: those strategies would not only mean compromising the identity of the church and her missional calling, but they would also mean basically constructing a new "secular religion" not based on any known tradition. On the other extreme of the spectrum (on the American scene) stands the "Constantinian" project of the Religious Right, which seeks to reestablish a "Christian nation" in alignment with political powers.[294] There is no need to elaborate on problems related to it. Another, very different extreme strategy is recommended by the British Radical Orthodoxy movement, which rejects any project of correlation and apologetic. It not only opposes but also denies secularism. Rather than correlation, a robustly and distinctively *Christian* theological vision is put in place—without a dialogue.[295] The project's liabilities are obvious as well.

Rightly the American ethicist Stanley Hauerwas critiques "secular liberalism" for having caused the church to capitulate under its claim that only if religion is privatized may true democracy and (religious) freedom occur.[296] In this respect, somewhat similarly, L. Newbigin critiqued tirelessly the Western church for retreating into a harmless position of caring for individuals' "souls" rather than arguing for the truth of the Christian message.[297]

The missional calling outlined in this text leads to a robust, hospitable encounter with (post)secularism(s) through the church's missional existence as a worshiping-liturgical and diaconal-charismatic communion, presenting a credible Christian gospel for religionless secularists, the nones, and followers of other religious paths.[298]

294. For a critique, see Stanley Hauerwas and William H. Willimon, *Resident Aliens: A Provocative Christian Assessment of Culture and Ministry for People Who Know That Something Is Wrong* (Nashville: Abingdon, 1989), 17–24.

295. See James K. A. Smith, *Introducing Radical Orthodoxy: Mapping a Post-secular Theology* (Grand Rapids: Baker Academic, 2004).

296. Stanley Hauerwas, *Dispatches from the Front: Theological Engagements with the Secular* (Durham, NC: Duke University Press, 1995).

297. See Veli-Matti Kärkkäinen and Michael Karim, "Community and Witness in Transition: Newbigin's Missional Ecclesiology between Modernity and Postmodernity," in *The Gospel and Pluralism Today: Reassessing Lesslie Newbigin in the 21st Century*, ed. Scott W. Sunquist and Amos Yong (Downers Grove, IL: InterVarsity Press, 2015), 71–100, and the original literature cited therein.

298. Robert Gascoigne, *The Church and Secularity: Two Stories of Liberal Society* (Washington, DC: Georgetown University Press, 2009); Andrew Sempell, "God, Society and Secularism," *St. Mark's Review* 221 (September 2012): 56–65.

10 | Eschatology

Introduction: On the Possibility and Conditions of a Christian Eschatology

The (Omni)Presence of Eschatology

All living religions have a vision of the future and "end." Eschatology, however, is not limited to the religious sphere. Just think of the growing concern, at times anxiety, in secular culture and scientific study over the impending "end"—either of our planet or of human life. In light of the omnipresence of the expectation of the end around us, eschatology's eclipse in Christian theology calls for a commentary.

The Eclipse of Eschatology in Christian Tradition

For the earliest followers of Christ, the intense expectation of the imminent return of their Lord was just that—*intense*; the (early) patristic church continued this focus.[1] Even such intellectually oriented writers as the apologists of the second century employed urgent eschatological warnings and visions in their defense of the faith before the unbelieving world. Although the eschatological hope waned some after the establishment of Christendom, in no way

1. Brian E. Daley, *The Hope of the Early Church: A Handbook of Patristic Eschatology*, rev. ed. (Peabody, MA: Hendrickson, 2003 [1991]).

did it die out. Indeed, more often than not, particularly in the Middle Ages and all the way to the Reformation era, eschatological-apocalyptic imagination fueled spirituality.

A dramatic shift happened when eschatological hope lost its meaning among the intelligentsia, about the time of modernity. Kant's focus on religion's effect on morality undoubtedly helped the nineteenth-century liberal Protestants and others to reduce faith to the subjective and moral dimensions. And even the "rediscovery" of eschatology at the turn of the twentieth century in liberal New Testament scholarship (Johannes Weiss, Albert Schweitzer, and others) hardly signaled a robust interest in the *theological* significance of the end times. Not only did these scholars not believe the content of the New Testament claims regarding eschatology, but they were more keen on apocalypticism and, most ironically, its naive but totally mistaken application by Jesus and the disciples!

Simultaneously, though for different reasons, dismissal—or even an aggressive disavowal—of eschatological hope was funded by other leading philosophical and cultural figures. As is well known, L. Feuerbach took the human desire for life after death as a form of egotism.[2] Sigmund Freud's rejection of (religious) imagination of the afterlife merely as a (neurotic, or at least immature) form of an illusion attracted many followers. Indeed, the Freudian interpretation sticks well with the contemporary naturalist worldview. Many philosophers have continued their persistent critique, targeting any belief in an afterlife and personal survival after death.[3]

No wonder that in much of post-Enlightenment theology any traditional talk about the "end" lacked content and became marginalized. The work begun by A. Schweitzer and other liberals was picked up in the latter part of the twentieth century by the (in)famous American Jesus Seminar. The late Marcus J. Borg advocated a totally noneschatological interpretation of Jesus and took the kingdom of God as merely a this-worldly entity.[4]

Some leading systematic theologians similarly dismissed or radically revised eschatology. There is almost no mention of eschatological themes in the late Harvard theologian Gordon Kaufman's *In Face of Mystery: A Constructive Theology*. *The Cambridge Companion to Postmodern Theology* contains no entry on eschatology—the index does not even list the term! Some

2. Ludwig Feuerbach, *The Essence of Christianity*, trans. George Eliot (New York: Harper & Brothers, 1957), 170–84 particularly.

3. Anthony Flew, "The Logic of Mortality," in *DIRW*, 171–87.

4. Marcus J. Borg, *Jesus, a New Vision: Spirit, Culture, and the Life of Discipleship* (San Francisco: Harper & Row, 1987).

leading feminist pioneers have charged the (Christian) hope for afterlife as "a patriarchal concept arising predominantly from the male psyche," while others argue that it necessarily neglects the destiny of the nonhuman creation and the cosmos.[5]

Some Attempts at Rediscovery and Reconceiving of Eschatology

It is not that all twentieth-century theological movements are willing to ignore eschatology. There is also the desire to reconceive it. One of the most sophisticated revisions comes from the soil of American process theology's deeply panentheistic and in many ways immanentist conception of God: therein God provides the "lure" for the future events but is not the one who guarantees an eschatological solution.[6] There is neither an *ex nihilo* beginning (as God emerges with the cosmos) nor a final eschaton. Furthermore, rather than resurrection hope for humanity, there is an idea of "objective immortality," that is, some kind of nonpersonal recollection of us in divine memory (to be explained below).

Another marked reorientation of eschatology is the feminist theologian Kathryn Tanner's "eschatology without a future" proposal (to be engaged below). This relates to the obvious fact that the natural sciences' bleak picture of all life, and the cosmos itself, seems to be heading eventually toward annihilation, the vision of which conflicts with Christian hope.[7]

The Rise of Contemporary Constructive Christian Eschatologies

Some leading contemporary theologians have helped rediscover eschatology and even put it at the center of theological conversations. K. Barth's classic rediscovery of eschatology is routinely mentioned as the clarion call: he claimed that without eschatology, no theology is worth its salt.[8] The publication of German Reformed theologian J. Moltmann's *Theology of Hope* in the mid-1960s

5. Valerie A. Karras, "Eschatology," in *Cambridge Companion to Feminist Theology*, ed. Susan Frank Parsons (Cambridge: Cambridge University Press, 2002), 243–44, here 244.

6. John B. Cobb Jr., *Christ in a Pluralistic Age* (Philadelphia: Westminster, 1975), chaps. 15 and 16.

7. Kathryn E. Tanner, "Eschatology without a Future," in *EWEG*, 222.

8. Karl Barth, *The Epistle to the Romans*, trans. Edwyn C. Hoskyns, 6th ed. (London: Oxford University Press, 1968 [1933]), 314.

launched a new movement called "theology of hope."[9] For him, eschatology is the "first" chapter of Christian theology. Another German, the Lutheran W. Pannenberg, talks about the "causal priority of the future"[10] and makes the surprising and counterintuitive claim of "the present as an effect of the future, in contrast to the conventional assumption that past and present are the cause of the future."[11] Because of that, for Pannenberg the concept of anticipation of the future became a leading theme.

Several Americans have joined the turn to the future, including the two Lutherans Ted Peters, with his concept of "retroactive ontology" materially repeating Pannenberg's futuristic causality,[12] and Robert W. Jenson, to whom God's true "triune identity" can be known in the course of history's unfolding toward consummation, in which process God shows his faithfulness.[13] Yet another American, the Anabaptist Thomas N. Finger, not only makes room for eschatology in his doctrinal presentation but even gives it the primary place by making it the leading theme.[14]

The British Anglican New Testament scholar N. T. Wright has importantly reflected on the biblical basis of future hope. He has been recently joined by another senior New Testament expert, A. Thiselton.[15] Some leading science-religion experts, particularly the British physicist-priest John Polkinghorne and the American physicist-theologian Robert J. Russell, in collaboration with systematicians such as the German Michael Welker, have done groundbreaking work in helping rediscover the centrality of eschatology after the advent of modern science. And so forth. This is to say that with all the push toward ignoring eschatology in some theological quarters, in others it is alive and well.

Not only in theology but also among the Christian communities, particularly when looked at from a global perspective, eschatology has returned. Whereas in the Global North on the old continent, eschatology rarely plays

9. Veli-Matti Kärkkäinen, "Hope, Theology of," in *GDT*, 404–5.

10. So named by Robert J. Russell, *Time in Eternity: Pannenberg, Physics, and Eschatology in Creative Mutual Interaction* (Notre Dame: University of Notre Dame Press, 2012), 117–19.

11. Wolfhart Pannenberg, *Theology and the Kingdom of God*, trans. Richard John Neuhaus (Philadelphia: Westminster, 1969), 54.

12. Ted Peters, *Anticipating Omega: Science, Faith, and Our Ultimate Future* (Göttingen: Vandenhoeck & Ruprecht, 2006).

13. Robert W. Jenson, *The Triune Identity: God according to the Gospel* (Philadelphia: Fortress, 1982).

14. Thomas N. Finger, *Christian Theology: An Eschatological Approach* (Scottdale, PA: Herald Press, 1985).

15. Anthony C. Thiselton, *Life after Death: A New Approach to the Last Things* (Grand Rapids: Eerdmans, 2012).

a visible role in churches' spirituality and liturgy, large sections of American Christianity still cultivate a vital hope for the return of Christ, not only among the fundamentalists but also beyond. Furthermore, among majority-world Christianity (Africa, Asia, Latin America), where churches are mushrooming and flourishing, eschatological proclamation still is very much a part of the daily tapestry of spirituality.

On the Nature and Conditions of a Comprehensive Eschatology

The "end" that eschatology speaks of is a notoriously polyvalent term; "end" can mean both completion (that is, coming or bringing to an end) and fulfillment (as in the Greek term *telos*). Both meanings are present in the Christian eschatological expectation. When put in the wider context of religions, "in its broadest sense the term 'eschatology' includes all concepts of life beyond death and everything connected with it such as heaven and hell, paradise and immortality, resurrection and transmigration of the soul, rebirth and reincarnation, and last judgment and doomsday."[16] Although the equivalent of the term "eschatology," the Latin *de novissimis* ("the last things"), was used much earlier, only at the time of Protestant orthodoxy did the term establish itself.

What makes Christian eschatology distinctive among religions is that it encompasses all of creation, not only humans, nor merely Earth—but the whole vast cosmos. This widest horizon, however, has not been at the center of Christian eschatology. Indeed, what happened early in Christian theology was that personal eschatology became the focus of the Christian hope. And the concept of the kingdom of God was soon marginalized. Even worse, when employed, its meaning was reduced mainly to hope for the personal resurrection of the body. Communal and cosmic horizons were marginalized.

Only in twentieth-century theology have the centrality and comprehensive nature of eschatology been rediscovered, including not only the personal but also the communal. But even here, a key weakness can still be discerned: the lack of a cosmic orientation. Gradually, the implications of what we know of the vastness of the cosmos—in terms of size, "age," and expansion—have begun to emerge as integral themes.

The development of a viable Christian eschatology has to encompass the following spheres:

16. Hans Schwarz, *Eschatology* (Grand Rapids: Eerdmans, 2000), 26.

- personal and communal hope
- human and cosmic destiny
- present and future hope

Personal and communal hope. A crucial theological problem has to do with negotiating personal and communal hopes not only as parallel with each other but also as mutually linked. Only such an eschatology that can successfully envision "the perfecting of individual life after death . . . with the consummation of humanity and world in the kingdom of God" will suffice.[17] In the Old Testament and Jewish tradition, the communal hope lay in the forefront and the individual hope emerged only later, gradually. Even when the hope for individuals developed, it was not divorced from but rather integrated into the hope for all humanity. The Christian church adopted this view and faced the task of even expanding it with the inclusion of gentiles into the hope for a common destiny. In comparison, the pagan hope of the immortality of the soul (as in Plato) has no reference to the whole of humanity, only to the individual. Nor is the contemporary secular hope for the completion of human dreams in an ideal society, as expressed particularly in Marxism, satisfactory, as it only deals with those currently living; those who have passed away will totally miss it.

Human and cosmic destiny. Christian hope should not be "separated from the destiny of the universe,"[18] as the eschatological consummation includes the whole of God's creation, including history and nature. This holistic and "earthly" eschatological vision is masterfully expressed by the American Anabaptist theologian Thomas A. Finger: "Since the new creation arrives through God's Spirit, and since it reshapes the physical world, every theological locus is informed by the Spirit's transformation of matter-energy."[19]

Present and future hope. The present and future are linked tightly with each other through the presence of the Spirit by whom "the eschatological future is present already in the hearts of believers" and anticipates the consummation.[20] This is a corrective to merely this-worldly "eschatologies" mentioned above. It is also a defeat of those fundamentalist and other otherworldly eschatological visions that end up being escapist and dismissive of work toward

17. Pannenberg, *ST* 3:546.

18. Paul Tillich, *Systematic Theology*, vol. 3 (Chicago: University of Chicago Press, 1963), 418.

19. Thomas N. Finger, *A Contemporary Anabaptist Theology: Biblical, Historical, Constructive* (Downers Grove, IL: InterVarsity Press, 2004), 563.

20. Pannenberg, *ST* 3:552.

improving the current world. This dynamic between "already" and "not yet" will be carefully discussed below through the dynamic of "continuity" and "discontinuity."

Plan of the Chapter

The immediately following two sections present the visions of the "end" of the cosmos and human life as conjectured among natural sciences and as envisioned in four living faiths. With regard to the sciences, clarifications of what is at stake theologically will be carefully considered. Jewish, Muslim, Buddhist, and Hindu eschatologies will be briefly outlined without a critical analysis or comparison. Thereafter, in the rest of the chapter, the implications of the eschatologies of science and the religions will be compared with Christian theology.

As a theological prelude to the rest of the presentation of a Christian eschatology, similarly to all other doctrines, a Trinitarian approach will first be outlined, a distinctively Trinitarian theology of hope. Thereafter, two long sections will seek to develop and defend a comprehensive Christian vision of the transition from this world to new creation, paying special attention to how to conceive this transition in relation to the time-space continuum, which obviously has to be radically transformed; to the transposition from the state of decay and death to one of life in the resurrected body; and to the role of judgment and purification as necessary conditions for living in the holiness of God. A particularly complex problem of the identity-continuity between now and "then" in relation to the hope for physical resurrection will also be inspected.

The subsequent section will take up issues only marginally (if at all) discussed in systematic eschatologies: first, the value of nature and the environment, as well as justice and equality, in relation to hope for life eternal. It seeks to defeat the persistent critique of liberationists of various sorts and environmentally sensitive theologians to whom the Christian vision of the end represents egoism and leads to dismissal of this earthly life. This will be followed by a consideration of the presence of evil and suffering in a world created good.

In the next to last section of the chapter, we will reflect on the difficult and complex questions related to access to eternal salvation and the possibility of eternal condemnation in light of Christian tradition and contemporary theological and religious plurality. The last section of the chapter takes up the remaining standard issues regarding final consummation, from the signs of Jesus's return, to its nature and significance, to the possibility of the earthly millennial rule of Christ, to the nature of heaven and new creation.

The "End" of the Cosmos and Life in Natural Sciences' Conjectures

Scientific Predictions about the "Future" of the Universe

Conjectures of the sciences about the future are based on our current best knowledge about the cosmos's origins, evolvement, and workings. Since a detailed discussion of scientific cosmology's views of origins was conducted in chapter 3, it is not repeated here.

Yet, what are the implications of current scientific knowledge for the future of the universe—and for life on this earth or life elsewhere? It is convenient to divide that question into three interrelated time frames: the near future (the end of life conditions on the earth), the distant future (the end of the earth, sun, and our solar system), and the far-distant future (the "end" of the whole cosmos).[21] Let us work our way from the far-distant end to questions related to the future of humanity on this earth.

The Far-Distant, Distant, and Near-Future Predictions concerning the Cosmos and Life Conditions

The most distant future of the cosmos, according to current scientific predictions, looks something like the following:

- In 5 billion years, the sun will become a red giant, engulfing the orbits of Earth and Mars.
- In 40–50 billion years, star formation in our galaxy will have ended.
- In 10^{12} years, all massive stars will have become neutron stars or black holes.
- If the universe is closed, then in 10^{12} years, the universe will have reached its maximum size and then will recollapse back to a singularity like the original hot big bang.
- In 10^{31} years, protons and neutrons will decay into positrons, electrons, neutrinos, and photons.
- In 10^{34} years, all carbon-based life-forms will inevitably become extinct.[22]

21. With minor adaptations from Kate Grayson Boisvert, *Religion and the Physical Sciences* (Westport, CT: Greenwood, 2008), 229–34.

22. R. Russell, *Time in Eternity*, 60–61.

The end result is that, ultimately, after an amazingly long period of time, all will come to nil. But what if there are other forms of "life" or platforms other than carbon-based ones for life to continue? Not surprisingly, a number of proposals have been put forth, but since all of that is mere speculation at the time, the topic merits only a mention in this primer.[23]

What about the distant future prospects beyond the conditions of life on this earth and in this solar system? Well known and well documented is the possibility of Earth being hit by a comet or asteroid.[24] A familiar example from history is the dinosaur extinction due to a comet's hitting Earth about 65 million years ago. Be that as it may, in 5 billion years Earth will be uninhabitable and eventually lifeless. The sun will come to the end of its available hydrogen fuel and will begin to swell up and eventually run out of its energy, as it were.

All the above-mentioned conditions are totally out of human control, as opposed to the relatively significant human factor concerning the near future of this earth and its life conditions. The impending catastrophes facing the future, threatening all life on Earth, are well known and well documented, including pollution, global warming, and nuclear threat (chap. 3). In sum: "if current trends continue, we will not."[25]

Given these scientific predictions, the all-important question now emerges: What is at stake theologically?

What Is at Stake for Theology?

Briefly and nontechnically put, the theological challenge is this: How can we even begin to reconcile Christian eschatology's expectation of the imminent return of Christ and the bringing about of the "new heavens and new earth" in light of the extremely, almost infinitely long horizons of the sciences? Wisely, Pannenberg acknowledges that "to this question there are no easy solutions," and therefore, at least for the time being, theologians perhaps should just accept the tension and conflict.[26] The mutual tension between the two disciplines is

23. David Wilkinson, *Christian Eschatology and the Physical Universe* (London: T&T Clark, 2010), 7–10.

24. Chap. 2 in Paul C. Davies, *The Last Three Minutes: Conjectures about the Ultimate Fate of the Universe* (New York: Basic Books, 1994).

25. Daniel Maguire, *The Moral Core of Judaism and Christianity: Reclaiming the Revolution* (Philadelphia: Fortress, 1993), 13.

26. Wolfhart Pannenberg, "Theological Questions to Scientists," in *Beginning with the*

intensified by the fact that Christian eschatology envisions not only bodily resurrection but also a radical transformation of life conditions in new creation.[27]

Of course, a tempting tactic for theology would be simply to ignore the scientific challenge. Having already investigated that and other approaches to science (chap. 3), we remember that the model of critical mutual interaction was adopted. This approach was already anticipated at Vatican II when the council stated that the church "will attain its full perfection only in the glory of heaven, when there will come the time of the restoration of all things [when] the entire world, which is intimately related to man and attains to its end through him, will be perfectly reestablished in Christ."[28] Happily, a growing number of theologians are doing constructive, critical work in this area, including the late W. Pannenberg, J. Moltmann, R. Russell, D. Wilkinson, J. Polkinghorne, T. Peters, and D. Edwards, among others.

Both sides have to bear in mind that "the idea of a hope after death and an end that fulfills history as a whole is as intrinsic to the Christian tradition as it is foreign to the project of science."[29] Indeed, not only for most scientists but also for the wider public, this theological conviction sounds incredible. While carefully listening to scientists and learning about the continuous flow of new information and insights, theologians should continue challenging scientists. Theology's challenge to scientists is that "an unaided scientific account of the world does not succeed in making complete sense of cosmic history"[30] and science has no means of reaching beyond the observed world and empirically verified observations.

Before constructing a contemporary Christian eschatology, an investigation into four living faith traditions' eschatological intuitions comes next.

Eschatological Visions and Symbols among Religions

Although the Christian theologian has to be careful when speaking of "eschatology" as a pan-religious theme, it is true that all world religions express

---

End: God, Science, and Wolfhart Pannenberg, ed. Carol Rausch Albright and Joel Haugen (Chicago: Open Court, 1997), 48.

27. R. Russell, *Time in Eternity*, 67–70.

28. *LG*, #48.

29. Philip C. Clayton, "Eschatology as Metaphysics under the Guise of Hope," in *World without End: Essays in Honor of Marjorie Suchocki*, ed. Joseph Bracken (Grand Rapids: Eerdmans, 2005), 134.

30. John Polkinghorne, "Eschatology: Some Questions and Some Insights from Science," in *EWEG*, 38.

a concern over mortality and a vision of life after death. That said, insofar as eschatology is "the study of the final end of things, the ultimate resolution of the entire creation," then it applies much more easily to Abrahamic and other theistic views that teach an absolute beginning and coming to a definite end of life and the cosmos as opposed to the great Asiatic faiths, which envision a continuous emergence and destruction of the cosmos in endless cycles, so to speak.

This investigation surveys but does not yet engage religions' eschatologies; that will happen throughout the rest of the chapter.

Jewish Eschatology

The Gradual Emergence of Eschatological Consciousness

No Old Testament books are devoted to death or afterlife; indeed, the theme is marginal. The Old Testament worldview is very much this-worldly (although it is deeply *theo*logical, God-driven). When eschatological themes appear occasionally, they pertain less to the individual and much more to national hope and to Yahweh's intervention in the world. This-worldly blessings from Yahweh are at the center of the Israelite religion. Yahweh's role as judge is also envisioned in relation to earthly affairs, particularly with the establishment of justice and righteousness.[31]

In stark contrast to neighboring lands, particularly Egypt, Israelite culture was definitely not death driven.[32] The Old Testament describes the condition of the dead as some sort of shadowy existence (Isa. 38:18). An eschatological consciousness only arose in the Old Testament gradually. The hope for an afterlife in terms of resurrection evolved slowly toward the end of the Old Testament, although intimations and anticipations appear here and there (Job 19:25–26; Pss. 49:15; 73:24; Isa. 26:19). Daniel 12:2 is widely taken as the summit of that development: "And many of those who sleep in the dust of the earth shall awake, some to everlasting life, and some to shame and everlasting contempt."

Only during the postexilic period did intimations of life beyond emerge slowly.[33] The outlook changes radically in the theology of rabbinic Judaism.

31. Walter Brueggemann, *Theology of the Old Testament: Testimony, Dispute, Advocacy* (Minneapolis: Augsburg Fortress, 1997), 233–50.

32. Schwarz, *Eschatology*, 32–35.

33. George W. E. Nickelsburg, *Resurrection, Immortality, and Eternal Life in Intertestamental Judaism* (Cambridge, MA: Harvard University Press, 1972).

The Talmud and related writings delve deeply and widely into eschatological and apocalyptic speculations. Eschatology becomes a defining feature, and against that background it can be said "that no significant movement in the course of Jewish history had lacked an eschatology."[34] Whence the rise of an eschatological orientation? The standard scholarly response is that it had to do with the question of suffering and theodicy: Why is the believer in Yahweh suffering?[35]

With the rise of the eschatological impulse (beginning in the second century BCE), the hope for the afterlife also becomes more defined, as death is no longer looked upon as the end. In rabbinic thought, eschatological topics can be classified in three mutually related categories: the world-to-come, the resurrection of the body, and the Messiah. Although the communal orientation still is dominant, under these categories one can see also hope for the individual. This kind of "eschatology is manifested in the expectation of a future eon radically discontinuous with the present." Yet this means no escapism, because in this eschatological vision "the circumstances of history will be transformed but not transcended."[36]

In very broad strokes, Jews came to believe that, at the end of days, the dead will be resurrected and come before God to account for their lives on earth; the righteous will be rewarded and the evil punished; Jews, free from the yoke of the exile, will return to their homeland, rebuild it, and become masters of their own destiny; they will rebuild the temple and reinstitute the temple cult; the nations of the world will flock to study Torah with the Jewish people; peace and justice will rule; and all people will come to know and worship the God of Israel. This entire scenario will be brought to pass through the initiative of the Messiah.[37]

Like younger sister faiths, postbiblical Judaism also knows apocalypticism, which is escapist.[38] Some of these movements were also related to Christian ones.[39] A defining feature of apocalypticism has to do with a changing understanding of history. Not only Israel's enemies (as in the Old Testament) but all powers, including cosmic and heavenly powers, would be destroyed.[40]

34. Neil Gillman, *The Death of Death: Resurrection and Immortality in Jewish Thought* (Woodstock, VT: Jewish Lights, 1997), 12.

35. David Novak, "Jewish Eschatology," in *OHE*, 115.

36. Bill T. Arnold, "Old Testament Eschatology and the Rise of Apocalypticism," in *OHE*, 24–25, here 24.

37. Gillman, *The Death of Death*, 22.

38. John J. Collins, "Apocalyptic Eschatology in the Ancient World," in *OHE*, 40–55.

39. James D. Tabor, "Ancient Jewish and Early Christian Millennialism," in *OHM*, 252–53.

40. Schwarz, *Eschatology*, 51–55, here 53.

Salvation and Condemnation—Heaven and Hell

As in other traditions, eschatological hermeneutics in Judaism often takes its departure from the earthly scene, such as the description of David's encounter with the angel of death in the garden in the hereafter. On the other hand, both Scripture and rabbinical tradition make the realities of the hereafter so incomparable with the current world that we can hardly say anything about those realities.[41] Indeed, with all its this-worldly orientation, classic Jewish theology has developed quite sophisticated accounts of heaven.

Who then will inherit salvation? As discussed (chap. 8), following (or not following) the Torah is the key to salvation or condemnation. Rabbinic theology mentions a number of types of people who might end up in hell, including those who deny resurrection or Torah's heavenly origin, or the heretic, or the one who abuses the divine name, and so forth.[42] This much almost all Jewish traditions agree upon—keeping Torah and doing good deeds. Debated issues include for example the balance between good and bad deeds, on which no final agreement exists.[43]

Yet an important long-standing, unresolved issue of debate relates to the destiny of gentiles. Not surprisingly, no canonical opinion was reached among the different rabbinical schools. This much can be said: while the Christian type of "no salvation outside the church" principle was often held as the normal opinion, there is also undoubtedly a strong prophetic tradition in the Old Testament that envisions some kind of "universal scope of salvation." Rather than leading to ultimate destruction and annihilation, Yahweh's judgment will have shalom as the final word (Amos 9:11–15; Isa. 2:2–4). But even then, no unanimity exists about whether "nations" (as opposed to the "people" of Yahweh) are included in this salvation, which also encompasses nature and the whole world.

Broadly speaking, until modernity, the core rabbinic belief in two destinies stood intact. In contrast, the majority of modern and contemporary Jews have left it behind or at least qualified it significantly. This is possible because the Torah, as is well known, explains quite little about the nature of judgment and blessedness beyond this world. As it is in Christian theology, particularly difficult for contemporary Jewish theologians is the affirmation of hell.

41. Novak, "Jewish Eschatology," 118.

42. Daniel Cohn-Sherbok, "Death and Immortality in the Jewish Tradition," in *DIRW*, 26.

43. Novak, "Jewish Eschatology," 117.

The Resurrection of the Body

Although the doctrinal solidification took centuries, the resurrection of the dead is a central belief in classical Judaism. Indeed, condemned are those who deny the centrality of this belief. Briefly stated, resurrection and the authority of Torah "are the two dogmas the rabbis required, minimally, that no Jew deny and, maximally, that every Jew affirm."[44] That said, there were of course dissenting voices within Jewish orthodoxy: while the Pharisees fully endorsed the doctrine, the Sadducees did not.[45]

For rabbinic theology, it was not enough to merely affirm immortality: a *bodily* resurrection was to be affirmed. A robust affirmation of embodiment comports well with Jewish anthropology with its holistic orientation (chap. 4). Somewhat similarly to the New Testament, in their attempts to imagine the nature of the bodily resurrection, the Jewish sources use various metaphors, from awakening from sleep, to nature metaphors of morning dew and plants sprouting, to being clothed, and so forth.

Afterlife, Resurrection, and Immortality in Contemporary Jewish Theology

By and large, modern/contemporary Jewish theologies have not paid much attention to end times. While there might be many reasons, certainly the experience of Auschwitz stands among them. On the other end of the spectrum are radical millenarian and apocalyptic expressions similar to those of other Abrahamic faiths.[46]

Contemporary Jewish eschatologies, similarly to Christianity, follow the ordinary lines of distinction on the continuum from most traditional/conservative to reconstructionist views, and are ultimately reactions to modernity. Significant in this regard was the Reform movements' reworking of key doctrines beginning in the early nineteenth century. Resurrection as a doctrine came to be replaced by the idea of immortality. Along with resurrection went the classic doctrines of hell and heaven.[47]

Understandably, opposition arose among the conservatives. However, even conservative Judaism of the early twentieth century did not necessar-

44. Novak, "Jewish Eschatology," 123.

45. Gillman, *The Death of Death*, 115–22.

46. Yaakov Ariel, "Radical Millennial Movements in Contemporary Judaism in Israel," in *OHM*, 1–15.

47. Gillman, *The Death of Death*, 196–204.

ily demand a return to resurrection; rather, it insisted on a sort of spiritual immortality. In other words, by the mid-twentieth century, immortality had been adopted as the mainstream Jewish opinion.[48] With the Reconstructionist movement headed by Mordecai Kaplan, a radically new paradigm was offered. His religious naturalism sought to reformulate radically old eschatological beliefs to stick with modern science.[49] On the other end of the spectrum remained Orthodox Judaism, which firmly continued to uphold the doctrine of the resurrection of the body.[50]

At the same time, some other leading contemporary Jewish thinkers have been persuaded of the necessity for belief in the bodily resurrection, as difficult as that may be for the modern mind. Those include Arthur A. Cohen, whose short essay "Resurrection of the Dead" seeks to rehabilitate the doctrine as an indispensable tenet of faith for contemporary Judaism. Another formative scholar, Neil Gillman, finds two powerful reasons for refusing to let the critical mind *alone* dictate one's ultimate vision. On the one hand, with every other Jew, he is fully convinced of the omnipotence of God, even over death. Along with this theological argument, on the other hand, the anthropological argument seems convincing: the biblical view of the human as a "psychophysical unity" makes him believe that without the body his own self is not complete.[51]

What about the eschatological vision of the youngest Abrahamic tradition? To the consideration of Islamic theology of the end we turn next.

Islamic Eschatology

The Significance of Eschatology in Islam

Eschatology plays an extraordinary role in Islam. Recall that the Prophet's first and continuing message was about coming judgment and the need for submission to Allah to avoid the hell of judgment. Both the Qur'an and particularly Hadith texts go to great lengths in discussing the afterlife.[52] Eschatological beliefs are also prominent fare in many Muslim creedal statements.[53]

48. Gillman, *The Death of Death*, 205–8.
49. Gillman, *The Death of Death*, 208–11.
50. Gillman, *The Death of Death*, 212–13.
51. Gillman, *The Death of Death*, 243–74.
52. William C. Chittick, "Muslim Eschatology," in *OHE*, 132–50.
53. See Ahmad Ibn Hanbal's "Hanbalī Traditionalist Creed," trans. W. Montgomery

Generally speaking, contemporary Muslims tend to take the traditional teaching on eschatology much more seriously than do most Jews and Christians. The "eschatological narrative" lays claim on everything in the Muslim's faith and life. Similarly to Judaism and Christianity, a rich tradition of apocalypticism can be found in Islam,[54] including radical millenarian and jihadist movements.[55]

On Discerning the Signs of the "Hour"

As in Christian tradition, in Islam the (final) hour is unknown to all but God (Q 31:34).[56] As the Prophet stated: "Knowledge thereof lies only with God—and what do you know, perhaps the Hour is near" (33:63). Differently from Hadith and apocalyptic traditions, the Qur'an is reticent to talk about signs. That said, eschatological undergirding lies beneath a number of suras such as "The Hour" (22), "The Smoke" (45), and "The Darkened Sun" (82).

Understandably, Muslims have not stopped looking for signs. Books, blogs, and talks on "signs of the hour" abound.[57] The search for the signs is fueled by the presence in the Hadith of detailed lists of signs. "Geological, moral, social, and cosmic signs . . . [as well as] the erosion of the earth, the spread of immorality, the loss of trust among the people, and the administration of unjust rulers [are perceived] as some signs of the Hour." In distinction from these "minor" signs, the Hadith lists as "major" ones the "emergence of the Antichrist, the descent of Jesus, and the rising of the sun in the west," which all point to the imminence of the end. Quite similarly to the descriptions in the book of Revelation, trumpets, archangels, and cataclysmic changes on earth, including earthquakes, play a role in the final consummation (81:1–14; 99:1–4; 39:67–69); there will also be intense suffering by the unfaithful. The rise of the mysterious nations of Gog and Magog also plays a role in the eschatological scheme of Islam.[58]

Watt, in *Islamic Theological Themes: A Primary Source Reader*, ed. John Renard (Oakland: University of California Press, 2014), 104–9.

54. David Cook, "Early Islamic and Classical Sunni and Shi'ite Apocalyptic Movements," in *OHM*, 267–83.

55. Jeffrey T. Kenney, "Millennialism and Radical Islamist Movements," in *OHM*, 688–716.

56. Zeri Saritoprak, *Islam's Jesus* (Gainesville: University Press of Florida, 2014), 38–40.

57. Mehmood Alam, "Signs of Hour," July 23, 2014, Darussalam, http://darussalamblog.com/signs-of-hour/.

58. Saritoprak, *Islam's Jesus*, 58–59.

Mahdi, Jesus, and the Antichrist: The Major End-Time Figures

Muslim eschatology widely embraces the figure of the Mahdi, who reflects messianic characteristics.[59] The task of the Mahdi is to defeat the antichrist and bring justice and peace to the world and lead people to truth. An ordinary human being rather than a divine figure, the Mahdi is endowed supernaturally to accomplish his task. While affirmed by all major denominations, particularly important is the role of the Mahdi among the Shi'ites. Yet he is unknown in the Qur'an and also in the two main Hadith traditions, that of Bukhari and that of Muslim.

Debate persists about a number of issues related to the Mahdi, not least as to whether there is one Mahdi or more than one, as well as the related question of pseudo- (or anti-) Mahdi. Not surprisingly, various Mahdist movements throughout history have tended to identify a specific person. Whatever else the Mahdi tradition may mean to Islamic eschatology, it is linked closely with the yearning for justice and righteousness in a world of evil.

The relationship between the Mahdi and Jesus is close yet somewhat undefined. While the Qur'an itself does not directly mention Jesus's "descent" to earth, it is widely attested in the Hadith.[60] According to the standard Islamic interpretation, Jesus of Nazareth was not killed on the cross but was instead "taken up" by Allah to heaven to wait for the return. Then he will fight alongside the Mahdi against the antichrist and defeat him.[61] Jesus will slaughter pigs, tear down crosses, and destroy churches and synagogues; most probably he will also kill Christians unwilling to embrace Islamic faith.

The picture of the antichrist in Islam is not radically different from that in Christianity. Obviously an archenemy of Jesus, the antichrist can be seen as the personification of evil (similarly to Satan and Iblis). Although the term itself (*al-Dajjal*) does not appear in the Qur'an, there is wide agreement in Islamic tradition that allusions and indirect references are found therein, including the saying attributed to Jesus: "Nay, but verily man is [wont to be] rebellious" (96:6).[62]

Understandably, the Hadith traditions greatly expand and elaborate on the description and influence of the antichrist: "The antichrist is short, hen-

59. Riffat Hassan, "Messianism and Islam," *Journal of Ecumenical Studies* 22 (Spring 1985): 261–91.

60. Saritoprak, *Islam's Jesus*, chap. 4.

61. Q 4:156–58; 3:55; see chap. 5 above.

62. Bernard McGinn, *Antichrist: Two Thousand Years of the Human Fascination with Evil* (New York: Columbia University Press, 2000), 111.

toed, woolly-haired, one-eyed, an eye-sightless, and neither protruding nor deep-seated. If you are confused about him, know that your Lord is not one-eyed."[63] The antichrist will fight against the believers until the Mahdi and Jesus come and help defeat his power.

Death and Resurrection

For the Muslim, life on this earth is but preparation for eternity, at the core of which is obedience to and desire to please Allah. Hence, death should be properly kept in mind (Q 23:15; 3:185). There is given a "fixed" time, a stated life span (6:2).

Although the Qur'an provides precious few details about what happens between death and resurrection, later traditions have produced fairly detailed accounts.[64] Similarly to Christian tradition, whereas the body decays, the "soul" (or "spirit") continues to exist (see 39:42). According to a major Muslim tradition, the deceased person meets two angels—named Munkar and Nakir—who test the faith of the person and help determine the final destiny. In all Muslim accounts of the afterlife, there is thus an intermediate state that, according to some Muslim theologians, approaches the Roman Catholic idea of purgatory.[65] Muslims also believe in the resurrection of the body, as well as (eternal) retribution (sura 75; 36:77–79; and so forth).

The main theological debate about the resurrection is whether it entails a total annihilation of the person before re-creation or a reconstitution and renewal. The lack of unanimity is understandable in light of two kinds of directions in scripture itself. Just compare 28:88, "Everything will perish except His Countenance," which clearly assumes the annihilationist view, with 10:4, "To Him is the return of all of you. . . . Truly He originates creation, then recreates it," which teaches the other option.

63. *Abu Dawud*, bk. 37 ("Battles"), #4306.

64. Jane Idleman Smith and Yvonne Yazbeck Haddad, *The Islamic Understanding of Death and Resurrection* (Albany: State University of New York Press, 1981; Oxford: Oxford University Press, 2002), 32–33.

65. Asma Afsaruddin, "Death, Resurrection, and Human Destiny in Islamic Tradition," in *Death, Resurrection, and Human Destiny: Christian and Muslim Perspectives*, ed. David Marshall and Lucinda Mosher (Washington, DC: Georgetown University Press, 2014), 46.

Heaven and Hell—Salvation and Judgment

Consider that a typical list of the basic beliefs of Islam includes "belief in one God, His messengers, His books, His angels, and the day of judgement."[66] The final accounting happens when in the hereafter men and women "return" to their God (32:7–11). Almost every chapter of the Qur'an speaks of or refers to the theme of judgment.[67] Similarly to the New Testament, even the evil spirits (*jinn*) will be judged.

The general picture of the day of judgment is very similar to that given in the Bible. Great earthquakes will rock the earth, setting mountains in motion (sura 99). The sky will split open and heaven will be "stripped off," rolled up like a parchment scroll. The sun will cease to shine; the stars will be scattered and fall upon the earth. The oceans will boil over. Graves will be opened, the earth bringing forth its burdens (sura 82). All will bow, willingly or not, before God. After resurrection, each human person is given a "book" that indicates the final destiny (18:49), either heaven or hell.

A debated issue among the Muslim schools is the lot of the (gravely) sinning believer, and no agreement has been reached. A related debate asks: How do the person's good and bad deeds account for the final judgment received? Common to all opinions is the centrality of obedience to Allah or lack thereof; furthermore, it is widely agreed that only grave sins bring about judgment (4:31).

What about non-Muslims? It seems that the Qur'an teaches a fairly inclusive view of salvation: "Surely those who believe, and those of Jewry, and the Christians, and the Sabaeans, whoever believes in God and the Last Day, and performs righteous deeds—their wage is with their Lord, and no fear shall befall them, neither shall they grieve" (2:62). The implications of this passage are of course widely debated among historical and contemporary Muslim scholars. Echoing the biblical view for those who have never heard the gospel, the Qur'an teaches that "we do not punish unless We send a messenger" (17:15).

What is not debated is that there are two destinies as taught in the scripture (9:100–102; 7:37–51; and so forth). Hell is a place of great pain and torture.

66. Muhammad [A. S.] Abdel Haleem, "Qur'an and Hadith," in *The Cambridge Companion to Classical Islamic Theology*, ed. Tim Winter (Cambridge: Cambridge University Press, 2008), 25.

67. Allen Fromherz, "Judgment, Final," in *The Oxford Encyclopedia of the Islamic World*, ed. John L. Esposito (Oxford: Oxford University Press, 2009), http://www.oxfordislamicstudies.com/article/opr/t236/e1107.

What about heaven? Often depicted in the Qur'an with garden images (sura 37), paradise is a place of great enjoyment, peace, and reunion. The Qur'an offers sensual descriptions, including the pleasures of exquisitely delicious food and drink, as well as sexual relations with divine maidens (often interpreted metaphorically). Particularly splendid and elaborate accounts of paradise ("Garden") can be found in the Hadith. Similarly to the Bible, there are also various levels of rewards for the blessed ones.

"End-Time" Visions and Symbols in Hindu Traditions

In Search of a Distinctive Hindu Vision of the "End"

Unlike Abrahamic traditions with a linear and historical view of history, "Hinduism has no last day or end time, nor any completion of history, resurrection of the dead, and universal last judgment."[68] The focus lies rather on "the deliverance of the individual from the unreal realm of the empirical and temporal to the timeless realm of the spirit."[69] Even the role of the deities is ambiguous, as a number of them undergo death and even rebirth in another form.[70]

"Cosmic eschatology" is usually described in terms of *kalpas*. Each *kalpa* encompasses the life span from origination to dissolution.[71] At the end of a *kalpa*, a great dissolution occurs, "which coincides with the end of the life of Brahma. The world will be reabsorbed into Brahma by involution and remain in that state until the hatching of a new cosmic age."[72] And so on, ad infinitum.

Are there any millennial elements in various Hindu traditions? Only with the rise of anticolonialist movements in the nineteenth century did millennial groups emerge. At the same time, various types of self-made gurus appeared, and their activities included millennial features.[73]

68. David M. Knipe, "Hindu Eschatology," in *OHE*, 171.

69. Mariasusai Dhavamony, "Death and Immortality in Hinduism," in *DIRW*, 100–101, here 100.

70. Wendy Doniger, *On Hinduism* (Oxford: Oxford University Press, 2014), online ed., 97–103.

71. Chap. 13 in Arvind Sharma, *Classical Hindu Thought: An Introduction* (Oxford: Oxford University Press, 2000).

72. Dhavamony, "Death and Immortality," 100–101, here 101.

73. Hugh B. Urban, "Millenarian Elements in the Hindu Religious Traditions," in *OHM*, 369–81.

Death, Rebirth, and Karmic Samsara

The last two books (ninth and tenth) of the oldest Vedic scripture, Rig Veda, speak extensively of death.[74] The Funeral Hymn (10.14), dedicated to Yama, the god of death—the first one to die and show the rest of mortals the way to go—speaks of death in terms of meeting Yama and the "Fathers" (the honored ancestors). Yama is assisted by two messenger dogs, the guardians of death's pathway. Yama and the Fathers prepare a wonderful place for the deceased (10.14.8–11). The last part of the Vedas, the Upanishads, further develop the view of death and afterlife.

The most innovative and theologically significant Upanishadic development has to do with the evolvement of the doctrines of karma and transmigration of the soul (rebirth). The soul continues its afterlife journey from one state to another conditioned by the deeds of one's lifetime. Until one is ready to be absorbed into "Reality" (*satya*), the migration continues. Known as karmic samsara, continuous rebirths are believed by all Hindu movements, both theistic and otherwise. It is essential to note that samsara is a "universal" law concerning "the conditioned and ever changing universe as contrasted to an unconditioned, eternal, and transcendent state (*moksa* or *nirvāna*)." The liberated one is no longer under karma.[75]

Karma evolves from moral and immoral actions from the past lives to their consequences and one's actions in subsequent lives. While personal, both good and bad karma may also be transferred to another person. At death, "the various component parts of . . . [the deceased person's] body unite with [his] corresponding counterparts in nature, while the sum total of his karma remains attached to his self (*atman*). The force of this karma decides the nature of his next birth where he reaps the fruit of what he merits."[76]

That teaching helps put death in a different perspective: as aversive as it may appear to human desire to cling to life, death is not the ultimate reality and has only relative significance. Death is an "earthly" matter and hence belongs to the "appearance" part of reality. "The knowing (Self) is not born, it dies not; it sprang from nothing, nothing sprang from it. The Ancient is unborn, eternal, everlasting; he is not killed, though the body is killed."[77] That said, however, reverence for the dead and the obligation of the relatives to the deceased are

74. Knipe, "Hindu Eschatology."

75. Brian K. Smith, "Samsāra," in *ER* 12:8098.

76. Dhavamony, "Death and Immortality," 94.

77. Katha Upanishad 1.2.18; so also Gita, see 2.12.

an integral part of Hindu cultures, and sophisticated funeral rites have evolved to help start the journey in the afterlife.

Bhagavad Gita affirms the basic Upanishadic teachings: the inevitability of death, its transitory nature because of transmigration, and two destinies (at least as long as one has not yet achieved the ultimate goal). As is well known, the Gita pays special attention to one's last thoughts, that is, whether one is totally devoted to one's deity or to some earthly goal.[78]

Avidya and *Moksa*: "Ignorance" and "Salvation"

Similarly to the doctrine of resurrection, rebirth raises the question of the constitution of human nature and the corollary question of what continues beyond physical death. Although the Vedanta Hindu philosophical schools do not typically lean toward the Hellenistic type of body-soul dualism (or if they do, they frame it differently), there is a dualism of "true" (real) and "not-self." As long as one does not grasp the single most important insight that "Self [*atman*] is indeed Brahman [the eternal Self],"[79] one is distanced from the real self.[80] Only with the removal of "ignorance" (*avidya*) can the effects of karma be overcome and final release (*moksa*) be attained (see chap. 4).

Only vaguely intuited in the Vedic literature, a fairly clearly defined picture of heaven and hell does not appear until the great epics, particularly the *Mahabharata*.[81] Because of rebirth, their meaning is obviously different from those of Abrahamic traditions. Neither one is the ultimate destiny.

Buddhist Visions of End and "Release"

Although Buddhism, similarly to Hinduism, does not know any final closure, already during the time of Gautama himself a diversity of views of the "end" of human life had emerged, although Buddha himself showed great reticence toward such speculations. Somewhat similarly to Hindu tradition, Buddhism speaks of the "history" of the cosmos in terms of exceedingly long ages, called

78. Bhagavad Gita 8.

79. Brihadaranyaka Upanishad 4.4.5.

80. R. Balasubramanian, "The Advaita View of Death and Immortality," in *DIRW*, 110–17.

81. Alf Hiltebeitel, "The 'Mahābhārata,' and Hindu Eschatology," *History of Religions* 12, no. 2 (1972): 95–135.

"great eons," and divides them into four periods, beginning with the destruction of the cosmos and extending to various durations of renovation when the universe again reemerges.[82]

To be liberated from the illusion of being permanent and hence clinging to anything conditioned, the "salvific" insight into the true nature of reality, leading to *nibbana* (or nirvana) as "ultimate release," is needed as a way of release from samsara, the cycle of rebirths. Lest one conceive of the karmic samsara cycle of rebirths along the lines of Hinduism—and common sense—that is, that the deceased self will be reborn, Buddhism only imagines some kind of "a flux of becoming in which successive lives are linked together by causal transmission of influence rather than by substantial identity."[83]

What, if anything, then can be said of the nature of *nibbana*? Recall that this is the only nonconditioned aspect of reality and therefore free from change and decay.[84] The main logical challenge to such a vision is well known among both Buddhists and its critics: If everything is nonpermanent, how can nirvana then be the "final" goal? I am not aware of satisfactory solutions.[85]

The end result of reaching *nibbana* in the Theravada tradition is the *arahant*, the enlightened one who has reached final release. In the Mahayana tradition, this original concept of *arahant* was revised into Boddhisattva, the Enlightened One who for the sake of others postpones the stepping into *nibbana*.

Having now outlined in some detail the visions of the "end" and "consummation" in four living faith traditions, we will begin to develop a distinctively Christian eschatology. In the course of that process, the other faith traditions as well as the insights of the sciences will be critically evaluated.

A Trinitarian Christian Theology of Hope

Similarly to all other works of God, there is a Trinitarian structure to eschatological consummation.

82. Jan Nattier, "Buddhist Eschatology," in *OHE*, 152–53.

83. Bhikkhu Ňānamoli and Bhikku Bodhi, introduction to *The Middle Length Discourses of the Buddha*, in *Majjhima Nikāya*, trans. Bhikkhu Ňānamoli and Bhikku Bodhi (Kandy, Sri Lanka: Buddhist Publication Society, 1995), 45.

84. "Nibbana Sutta: Total Unbinding (1)" (*Udana* 8.1), trans. T. Bhikkhu, *Access to Insight (BCBS Edition)*, September 3, 2012, http://www.accesstoinsight.org/tipitaka/kn/ud/ud.8.01.than.html.

85. See also Keith Ward, *Images of Eternity: Concepts of God in Five Religious Traditions* (London: Darton, Longman & Todd, 1987), 61–62.

God of Hope

Whereas before modernity, belief in God served as the source of hope and confidence, in the post-Enlightenment world, self-confidence and trust in human resources were put in its place. That led to naive optimism about progress and further funded secularization and distance from God. By the latter part of the twentieth century, though, that confidence had encountered dramatic defeats in terms of world wars and international conflicts, impending natural catastrophes and nuclear threat, as well as other related dangers. No wonder that alongside theologians, philosophers and even psychologists and psychiatrists have joined the investigation of the influence, necessity, and nature of hope.[86] Joint projects such as *Interdisciplinary Perspectives on Hope* (2005) have recently appeared.[87]

What are the theological implications of the loss of hope? According to the astute analysis of the German Lutheran theologian H. Schwarz, Christian eschatology helps the confused world discern two vital truths: First, "it shows that the modern idea of progress alienated itself from its Christian foundation . . . [as it] deprived history of its God-promised goal." Thereby, "we promoted ourselves from God-alienated and God-endowed actors *in history* to deified agents *of history*." As a remedy to this dilemma, Christian eschatology, second, "provides a hope and a promise that we are unable to attain through our own efforts."[88]

The Promised Hope

As an alternative and challenge to either pessimism stemming from the loss of hope or optimism derived from naive confidence in human progress, Christian faith proposes a solid, historically based but also history-transcending hope based on the faithfulness of God, who raised from the dead the crucified Son in the power of the Spirit. Rather than based on a human utopia, Christian hope intuits history as meaningful based on God's providence. The redemption of the future is possible because "the laws and forces of the past are no longer 'compul-

86. James R. Averill, George Catlin, and Kyum Koo Chon, *Rules of Hope* (New York: Springer, 1990).

87. Jaklin A. Eliott, ed., *Interdisciplinary Perspectives on Hope* (Hauppauge, NY: Nova Science, 2005).

88. Schwarz, *Eschatology*, 17–21, here 20.

sive' . . . [as] God's messianic future wins power over the present."[89] This historically anchored perspective of hope distinguishes Christian theology from Asiatic faiths in which, as discussed, historical events are merely an "appearance."

Historically engaged, Christian eschatology takes time seriously, an idea deeply rooted in the Old Testament narrative in which the people of God are conceived as a nomadic people on the way to the promised land. In contrast, in Asiatic religions, time is cyclical. The future is not "new"; it is a repeat. In the biblical worldview, hope is expressed in terms of promise.[90] Divine promises often contradict human expectation. The promise of Christ's resurrection, the "anchor" of concrete hope, illustrates this best. In the biblical drama, the greatest threat is death—and the greatest promise is deliverance from under the power of death.

The Resurrection of the Son as the Basis of Hope

According to Saint Paul, Christ's resurrection forms the basis for the Christian hope (1 Cor. 15:14–15). Indeed, the apostle goes so far as to claim that had Christ not been raised, Christian faith is futile and there is no hope for eternal life (vv. 17–19). In order for Christ's resurrection to guarantee eschatological consummation, it has to be historical and factual, a topic widely discussed in Christology above (chap. 5). Without Christ's resurrection, we are left with only the possibility of falsification of Christian hope: "Such a falsification would come in two forms, one looking backward and one looking forward. Looking backward, we could imagine evidence put forward to claim that Jesus hung on the cross, died, and remained dead. . . . Looking forward, we could imagine a future without a consummation, without the new creation promised by the Easter resurrection. . . . The resurrection of Christ, according to Christian faith . . . was the advent of the world's transformation. Without the consummation of this transformatory promise, the Christian faith is in vain."[91] Theologically, it can be said that resurrection is both an event that happens in history and an event that goes beyond (but not against) history; it is a "*new kind of historical happening.*"[92]

89. Jürgen Moltmann, *The Coming of God: Christian Eschatology*, trans. Margaret Kohl (Minneapolis: Fortress, 1996), 45.

90. Chap. 2 of Jürgen Moltmann, *Theology of Hope: On the Ground and the Implications of a Christian Eschatology* (London: SCM, 1967 [1964]).

91. Ted Peters, "Introduction: What Is to Come," in *RTSA*, viii.

92. Thomas F. Torrance, *Space, Time, and Incarnation* (Edinburgh: T&T Clark, 1968), 88.

What about the challenge from sciences? The theologian Michael Welker reminds us of the obvious, that "there is perhaps no topic that seems less suited for the dialogue between theology and the so-called exact sciences than the topic of the resurrection."[93] The reason of course lies with the current secular naturalist worldview that reigns among the scientific communities in the Global North, with its aversion to all notions of life after death and the category of the "supernatural." Along with naturalism, the main challenge from the sciences concerning the resurrection is that it seems to violate the regularity of natural occurrences, the role of laws of nature.

Having critiqued and put naturalism in a proper theological perspective and having constructed an account of divine action without the threat of intervention with the so-called NIODA-template (chap. 3), we here merely highlight the theological cash value for eschatology. A proper way to speak of resurrection in this context is as pointing to "a transformation of the present nature *beyond* what emergence refers to,"[94] that is, beyond what natural processes and their evolution in themselves may deliver. Rather than going against nature, the resurrection of Christ—who, himself, in biblical testimonies is the very agent of creation (Col. 1:15–17)—transcends and lifts up the natural.[95] It points to the eschatological consummation when, according to the biblical promises, creation "will be set free from its bondage to decay" (Rom. 8:21), so much so that, as a result, even death will be defeated (1 Cor. 15:55).

The Perfecting Work of the Spirit

While a christological event, the resurrection is of course also a Trinitarian and pneumatological event, as Christ was raised to new life by the Father through the Holy Spirit (Rom. 1:4).[96] As a result, the indwelling Spirit in believers constantly reminds them of the certainty of their own resurrection by the same Spirit who raised Christ (Rom. 8:11).[97] This Spirit is also the life-giving "cos-

93. Michael Welker, "Resurrection and Eternal Life: The Canonic Memory of the Resurrected Christ, His Reality, and His Glory," in *EWEG*, 279.

94. Robert J. Russell, *Cosmology: From Alpha to Omega; The Creative Mutual Interaction of Theology and Science* (Minneapolis: Fortress, 2008), 37.

95. R. Russell, *Cosmology*, 309–10.

96. See Günther Thomas, "Resurrection to New Life: Pneumatological Implications of the Eschatological Transition," in *RTSA*, 255–76.

97. Pannenberg, *ST* 3:622.

mic" Spirit. That observation relates to a key argument in the current project: Christian hope of the eschatological consummation, as much as it means to humanity, also includes the whole of God's creation.

Christ's resurrection through the life-giving Spirit is already a foretaste of the "transformation of matter-energy" in new creation.[98] The pneumatologically loaded eschatological openness of creation points to a final consummation in which matter and physicality—no more than time—are not so much "deleted" as they are transformed, made transcendent, so to speak.[99]

Now we are ready to inquire into the ways the Trinitarian theology of hope may facilitate and fund the Christian vision of the new creation.

The Transition from Time to Eternity and New Creation

Introduction: The "Already–Not Yet" Dynamic

Although one of the new movements of the twentieth century, known as the "theology of hope" headed by Moltmann and others, definitely helped theology turn toward the future as the main focus,[100] a number of contemporary forms of eschatology have turned their back on the future orientation and occupy themselves merely with a this-earthly "hope." Examples were given in the introduction to this chapter and include, for instance, the American Jesus Seminar with its idea of Jesus as a this-worldly ethical teacher or provocateur. Another, a representative turn to the historical present, is K. Tanner's suggestion of an "eschatology without a future" in which "eternal life is ours now as in the future . . . [and] is therefore not directly associated with the world's future."[101] The main problem with merely present-driven proposals is that all Abrahamic faiths—differently from Asiatic traditions—are historical in nature and thus futurist; they are based on divine promises to be fulfilled. The future orientation of Christian hope, however, does not mean escapism, a flight from this world, but rather, as the science-religion expert Polkinghorne puts it, "new creation is to be related to the present creation in a way that involves both continuity and discontinuity."[102]

98. R. Russell, *Cosmology*, 37.

99. R. Russell, *Cosmology*, 37–38.

100. See Kärkkäinen, "Hope, Theology of."

101. Tanner, "Eschatology without a Future," 230.

102. John Polkinghorne, "Introduction to Part 1: Eschatology and the Sciences," in *EWEG*, 17.

Because it is future oriented, Christian eschatology is anticipatory in nature. Anticipation brings to the fore the important dynamic between "already" and "not yet." Rather than juxtaposing a future appearance of eschatological consummation ("futurist eschatology") and an already-happened eschaton ("realized eschatology"), anticipation points to "inaugurated eschatology," that is, while already having arrived, God's kingdom has not yet appeared in fullness.

The establishment of the future orientation of Christian eschatology yields several important tasks for theology. Under the comprehensive umbrella term "new creation" (which could also be named the kingdom of God or simply eschatological consummation), the following topics will be clarified here in order to make sensible the Christian talk about transitioning from "here" to "beyond." First, the notions of time and space, essential coordinates of our current existence, need to be theologically investigated in terms of relationship to the transition to new creation. Only then, second, may we hope to be equipped to clarify in more detail the template of "continuity *versus* (or in) discontinuity." Finally, as a precondition for the "change" required for "this perishable nature . . . [to] put on the imperishable, and this mortal nature . . . [to] put on immortality" (1 Cor. 15:53), judgment and reconciliation have to take place.

Time-Space and Eternity

The Reality of the Future: In Defense of a "Flowing Time" Conception

A key theological issue of negotiation for properly conceiving the transition from creation to new creation has to do with time and space. Having investigated carefully the topic in the doctrine of creation and having offered a constructive proposal (chap. 3), we will focus on the most pertinent issue with regard to the science-eschatology dialogue. It has to do with the radical difference between two notions of time, conveniently named "flowing time" (A-time) and "block time" (B-time). What is at stake for theology? Indeed, very much: only the vision in which the future brings about something new (flowing time) may secure the judgment, reconciliation, and healing of our lives and memories in new creation.

Other problems result from the adoption of the block-time view. One of the most serious involves the question of authentic human freedom if the future does not mean potentialities. Furthermore, without insistence on the openness of the future, divine freedom is also at stake. Finally, in terms of interfaith engagement, it seems that for Abrahamic faith traditions, a block-time model would be a major theological obstacle, whereas the Asiatic faiths' cyclical worldview of eternal emergence and return points in a different direction from the Abrahamic faiths' emphasis on history and historical time.

Alongside theological considerations, there are scientific and logical reasons for supporting the flowing-time conception, notwithstanding the majority opinion among scientists favoring the block-time template. These include the second law of thermodynamics, entropy, which seems to require unidirectionality and irreversibility of time; the expansion in size and increase in complexity of the universe; and the apparent cause-effect dynamic (as far as we know, the cause precedes the effects). Similarly, the majority (Copenhagen) interpretation of quantum physics with its indeterminacy principle makes much less sense (if any) if the future is not truly future and potentially open for processes to evolve in an indeterminate way. Without being able to further engage this highly complex and technical (philosophical-scientific) discussion, suffice it to state that the theologian's claim for the reality of the future (based on flowing time) is a reasonable and justified proposal even in relation to the sciences.

Eternity as the Ultimate Fulfillment of God's New Creation

Rather than "outside" time, we should vision God as transcending space-time. Although the almighty Creator "God cannot be limited in space-time," this understanding allows God to be "in time," so to speak. Indeed, both divine omnipresence (that God is present everywhere at all times) and incarnation imply some kind of temporality in divine life. Furthermore, the openness of the future seems to require some relation to temporality.[103] R. Russell's conception of eternity as the "boundless temporality of the trinitarian God" summarizes this brilliantly.[104] In other words, eternity is neither timelessness nor lack of movement. Rather, "we find God on both sides of the fence, both as eternal and as temporal."[105]

103. Keith Ward, "God as a Principle of Cosmological Explanation," in *QCLN*, 250.

104. R. Russell, *Time in Eternity*, 5.

105. Ted Peters, "The Trinity in and beyond Time," in *Quantum Cosmology and the Laws of Nature: Scientific Perspectives on Divine Action*, ed. Robert J. Russell, Nancey Murphy, and C. J. Isham (Vatican City and Berkeley, CA: Vatican Observatory and Center for Theological and the Natural Sciences, 1993), 263–64, here 264.

This kind of conception of time gives us the needed resources to imagine the final eschatological redemption that makes possible final reconciliation and peace with the "entry of eternity into time."[106] As will be explained below, God's eternity not only brings fulfillment but also judges all that does not hold up to the standard of eternity.[107]

What about space(-time) in relation to eschatological fulfillment?

The Transition from Time to Eternity: The Dynamic of Continuity and Discontinuity

Would the transition from time to eternity imply total destruction of the world? Or is there a way to think of the transformation in other terms? Biblical symbols, visions, and teachings assume a dynamic tension and interrelationship between continuity and discontinuity. The very term "new creation" implies this twofold dynamic: that it is "new" reflects discontinuity, and that it is "creation" bespeaks continuity. A striking juxtaposition and mutual conditioning can also be found in sayings according to which "flesh and blood" may not enter God's eternity, and yet it is *physical* resurrection that stands at the forefront of that hope![108] Polkinghorne puts it well: "the new creation does not arise from a radically novel creative act *ex nihilo*, but as a redemptive act *ex vetere*, out of old."[109]

It has taken a long time for Christian theology to reach a dynamic balance in this understanding. On the basis of 2 Peter 3:10 and related passages (Rev. 20:11; 21:1), in Lutheran orthodoxy the view of the annihilation of the world established itself: following final judgment, the world will be burned to ashes, so to speak. This is the classic annihilation view. An opposite position is that of transformation, which finds support in Romans 8:19–25 and was taught by Calvinist theology. It highlighted God's faithfulness as Creator to creation. The Reformed theologian Moltmann's conclusion reflects well this standpoint: "The eschatological transformation of the universe embraces both the identity of creation and its newness, that is to say both continuity and discontinuity.

106. Pannenberg, *ST* 3:603.

107. R. Russell, *Time in Eternity*, 5–6, here 5.

108. See also John Polkinghorne and Michael Welker, "Introduction: Science and Theology on the End of the World and the Ends of God," in *EWEG*, 2.

109. John Polkinghorne, *The God of Hope and the End of the World* (New Haven: Yale University Press, 2002), 116; John Polkinghorne, *The Faith of a Physicist: Reflections of a Bottom-Up Thinker; The Gifford Lectures for 1993–4* (Princeton: Princeton University Press, 1994), 167.

All the information of this world remains in eternity, but is transformed."[110] This corresponds to the vision in Revelation (21:1): "Then I saw a new heaven and a new earth."

Annihilation and transformation should not be juxtaposed, however, but rather put in a dynamic mutual conditioning. There is much in the "old creation" to be annihilated, particularly decay and effects of sin and fall. That said, differently from the annihilation position, the final cleansing and sanctification are not unrelated to the "first creation"; in all of God's works, there is continuity, even in discontinuity. Among other things, the bodily resurrection view demands that there is some real correspondence between current conditions making possible embodied life and new creation. This template has implications for the location of the new creation, the eschatological kingdom of God.[111]

A proper negotiation of the dynamic tension between annihilation and transformation has tremendous effects on a number of lifestyle and attitudinal issues. Whereas the implications for ecology will be touched on below, let us mention here the value of work and human effort to improve the conditions of earthly life. If *human* work (inclusively understood) is related to the divine purpose of creation that points to new creation, then work gains its ultimate meaning from God's future; work is not only a matter of the present world.[112] On the contrary, the annihilationist vision does not leave much hope for this world.

Transformed "Space" and "Time" in New Creation

What does it mean to envision time-space in the new creation (in some sense) analogously to the current world? What does the biblical idea that "there is no more time (*chronos*)"[113] mean (Rev. 10:6)? In light of the continuity-discontinuity template, temporality as the condition for creaturely life cannot be taken as sinful or against God's purposes to be destroyed. Rather, God is patient, "who acts through temporally unfolding processes in the old cre-

110. Jürgen Moltmann, "Cosmos and Theosis: Eschatological Perspectives on the Future of the Universe," in *The Far-Future Universe: Eschatology from a Cosmic Perspective*, ed. George F. R. Ellis (Philadelphia: Templeton Foundation, 2002), 257.

111. See Miroslav Volf, *Work in the Spirit: Toward a Theology of Work* (Eugene, OR: Wipf & Stock, 2001), 95.

112. Volf, *Work in the Spirit*, 91–92,

113. Translated routinely in contemporary English versions as "[no more] delay."

ation."[114] Hence, temporality in itself cannot be something to be deleted, because that would mean nothing less than the destruction of creation! Rather, the idea of the "end of time" has to be understood in terms of the eternity bringing about the "fulfillment of time," a "new" time that lacks the potentiality for sin and entropy and, unlike earthly time, does not denote creaturely limitations characteristic of current space-time. This can be called "finitude beyond transience."[115]

This, in turn, has to assume a new kind of time-space environment in the new creation. It is built on the assumption that if "in this universe, space, time and matter are all mutually interlinked in the single package deal of general relativity . . . [then it] seems reasonable to suppose that this linkage is a general feature of the Creator's will. If so, the new creation will also have its 'space' and 'time' and 'matter'"[116] in a new form of existence bearing some real resemblance with the old but also radically transforming it to make possible life in physical resurrection never tasting death. The current life without this divine transformation is not fit for God's eternity (1 Cor. 15:50).

Judgment, Purification, and Reconciliation

For the new creation to be "new," there needs to be "redemptive purging and healing of our lives." Sins and omissions need to be confessed and forgiven, good deeds and virtues to be celebrated and honored. As established, eternity "is not only a time of endless rejoicing in all that is true and good and beautiful, it is also a time of leaving off and destroying of all that is wrong and false and ugly in this creation."[117] Divine judgment is in keeping with the holiness and purity of God, the Creator.

Judgment is a frequent biblical theme. The agent of judgment in the New Testament is the Father (Matt. 6:4; Rom. 3:6; 1 Cor. 5:13). Jesus's role as judge is more complicated: it is said, on one hand, that Jesus judges no one (John 3:17), but on the other hand, that he serves as judge (John 5:22). However, at his coming Christ brings grace (1 Pet. 1:13), and even now he acts as our Advocate (1 John 2:1).[118]

114. Polkinghorne, *God of Hope*, 120.

115. David E. Aune, *Revelation 6–16*, Word Biblical Commentary (Dallas: Word, 1986), 567.

116. Polkinghorne, *God of Hope*, 117.

117. R. Russell, *Time in Eternity*, 6.

118. Pannenberg, *ST* 3:613–14, here 614, on the basis of Joseph Ratzinger, *Eschatology: Death and Eternal Life* (Washington, DC: Catholic University of America Press, 2007), 205–6.

The New Testament speaks of the standard of judgment in many complementary ways; it calls it God's will (cf. Matt. 6:10), the word of Jesus (John 12:48), or more widely, the message of Jesus (see particularly Luke 12:8–9). Indeed, "the message of Jesus is the norm by which God judges even in the case of those who never meet Jesus personally," not of course in relation to the response to the gospel (which is impossible in that case), but in keeping with the direction in which Jesus's message points.[119] Theologically this can be expressed in the following way: "Eternity is judgment . . . [because it] brings the truth about earthly life to light." That, however, does not mean the annihilation or destruction of creatures, because God, the Judge, is also Creator, who holds fast to his creatures.[120]

Indeed, already in this life judgment has begun, and those who submit their lives under purifying and reconciling judgment may hope to be preserved at the last judgment.[121] Even if the faithful may suffer loss as their lifework "burns up" like wood or stubble, their lives will be saved (1 Cor. 3:12–15).[122] This cleansing effect of judgment is the necessary precondition for the bodily resurrection to happen in the new creation as the "perishable puts on the imperishable, and the mortal puts on immortality" (1 Cor. 15:54).[123]

Who or what will be judged? According to the New Testament teaching, it is works (1 Cor. 3:12–15), whether as affirmation of their value in God's sight or as condemnation. Although fair and thoroughgoing, judgment is not an act of divine wrath or vengeance. The judge is not only the Creator but also the Savior.[124] This judge is fair and his judgment is in proportion to our opportunities and resources (Luke 12:48). Ultimately, we can be confident that "the final judgment is not a judgment of our merits, but of our response to God's grace which he has extended to us in Jesus Christ."[125]

Christ's resurrection is the basis of not only personal hope but also that of the cosmos.

119. Pannenberg, *ST* 3:614–15 (615).

120. Moltmann (*The Coming of God*, 236) rightly notes that ultimately the question of judgment is "the question about God" and whether he wishes to hold on to his creatures.

121. For judgment as a means of purification, see Isa. 1:25; Mal. 3:2–3.

122. Pannenberg, *ST* 3:610–12.

123. Pannenberg, *ST* 3:619–20.

124. Schwarz, *Eschatology*, 392.

125. Schwarz, *Eschatology*, 391.

Resurrection as the Destiny of the Cosmos and Humanity

The Cosmic Significance of Jesus's Resurrection

An indication of the significance of "reclaiming the resurrection in its cosmological setting"[126] is the fact that patristic theology at large (however differently cosmology was understood at the time) widely affirmed the link between Christ's resurrection and the future of the world.[127] Highly significant is the fact that in several early theologies "the resurrection was based on a strong understanding of God as Creator, and this led to a strong sense of God's purposes for this material creation and its goodness."[128] Early Christian theology rightly rejected Gnosticism, which could not embrace an eschatological vision related to bodily and earthly realities because it "shared the conviction that the present, embodied condition of human consciousness is not a natural or ideal state, but is itself the sign of a fallen world."[129]

The emphasis on physicality and embodiment reminds us of the necessary mortality and decay not only of humans and other creatures but also of the cosmos at large. As Thomas Torrance puts it, we can speak of the "mutual involution of mortality and immortality, death and life, the crucifixion and the resurrection of Christ."[130]

Recall that above we defined eternity as the "boundless temporality of the Trinitarian God," the source of the earthly and the transformed new creation's "time." The eschatological dimension of the resurrection reminds us of the integral link between creation and new creation; the redemption of space and time also bespeaks the healing and renewal of nature. In sum: Christ's resurrection, as "miraculous" as it is, is an event that belongs to this world, time, and space in order to secure the redemption not only of human life on this earth, but also of all created life, as well as space and time.

126. Title for chap. 5 in Wilkinson, *Christian Eschatology*, 89.

127. Brian E. Daley, "A Hope for Worms: Early Christian Hope," in *RTSA*, 136–64.

128. Wilkinson, *Christian Eschatology*, 103.

129. Brian E. Daley, "Eschatology in the Early Church Fathers," in *OHE*, 94.

130. Torrance, *Space, Time, and Resurrection*, 48.

The Meaning and Theology of Death

The Question of Death

It says something about our modern culture in the Global North that a best seller since the 1970s has been the anthropologist and philosopher Ernst Becker's book *The Denial of Death*. Its main thesis is that humanity fears death and hence seeks to either ignore or overcome it. Death seems to make null and void all hopes of any lasting value. Not surprisingly, modern society has pushed death out of its purview and does everything in its power to deny its reality. That said, a new academic field named thanatology has emerged.[131] Furthermore, debates about what constitutes death have been with us for some time.[132]

What makes death unique to humanity is that, differently from all other creatures, we alone have an awareness of the coming to an end of life. Animals (similarly to human infants) do not have that capacity, as far as we know. Even if higher animals may experience an instinctual awareness of impending death in danger, only humans can make it a theme and reflect on it. In that light, it is not a surprise that hope for life after death is deeply embedded in human evolution. The custom of burials going back at least to the (Middle) Paleolithic age (300,000 to 50,000 years ago) is an indication of that hope.

Toward a Contemporary Theology of Death

Early in Christian theology, building on Paul's teaching, death came to be seen as an enemy and punishment for sin. It was linked tightly to original sin and the Fall in Christian tradition. Only in modern theology, also related to the rise of evolutionary theory, has this belief been replaced by the "naturalness" of death because of finitude and necessary decay of all created life.

The traditional position of course claimed biblical support. There is no denying that for Paul "it is not possible to exclude so-called natural death as not being cointended" in passages such as Romans 5:12 and 1 Corinthians 15:44–48.[133]

131. For basic issues and methods, see David K. Meagher and David E. Balk, eds., *Handbook of Thanatology: The Essential Body of Knowledge for the Study of Death, Dying, and Bereavement*, 2nd ed. (New York: Routledge, 2013).

132. David J. Bleich, "Establishing Criteria of Death," in *Ethical Issues in Death and Dying*, ed. Tom L. Beauchamp and Robert M. Veatch, 2nd ed. (Upper Saddle River, NJ: Prentice Hall, 1996), 28–32.

133. Pannenberg, *TA*, 129.

Yet contemporary theology claims that we hardly find solid basis in the biblical narrative for the idea of the immortality of humanity before the Fall. In modern theology, a correct terminological distinction was made between "natural" death that is not related to sin but to finite nature and the death of "judgment" that manifests intensification of the personal feeling toward death in light of the possibility of being cut off from the life of God.

The idea of death as "natural"—while true—has to be handled with care and qualified theologically. The Catholic catechism puts this seemingly paradoxical statement in perspective: "Even though man's nature is mortal God had destined him not to die" (#1008).[134] Second, as mentioned, death, while inevitable, is seen as an "enemy" (1 Cor. 15:26). In the Old Testament, death means separation from God (Ps. 88:5).

Christian theology should "understand death as a necessary companion of life, and its actual presupposition,"[135] yet as something to be defeated because it is the "last enemy" (1 Cor. 15:26). Although all created life necessarily comes to an end, Christian faith envisions a world in which death, as the last enemy, will be destroyed, and in which God, as the giver of life, grants eternal life as a gift. Death then is "natural" only in the sense that no creature can avoid it in our kind of world.

The overcoming of mortality as a divine gift from the Creator (rather than as an innate capacity) can be only imagined in view of the "new creation." Only in new creation are resources infinite—a necessary precondition for the continuation of life forever—in contrast to this world, in which only death guarantees the availability of limited resources.

What about "after" physical death? With some overgeneralization we might say that among theologians there are two ways to intuit the relationship of each individual person's death and the resurrection of all at the eschaton. On the one hand, there is the idea according to which physical death marks a total cessation and there is no continuity in the "intermediate state." On the other hand, the traditional dualistic anthropology feeds the idea that while the body decays totally, the soul more or less independently continues its existence until the two finally become united again; this latter view is shared with Jewish and Islamic traditions.

In contrast to these two, a radical middle position can be argued. On the one hand, we have to underline the radical coming to an end of human life at physical death; it is final in this sense. On the other hand, to combat the

134. I am indebted to Schwarz, *Eschatology*, 259.
135. Schwarz, *Eschatology*, 253.

obvious implication that therefore the newly resurrected body means once again creation *ex nihilo* (because of the lack of any form of continuity), hope for a personal resurrection in the new creation means that death is not the final end. A good way to put this dynamic is to speak of "death as finality and transition."[136] Even if one may no longer find compelling the traditional idea of the soul's survival without the body, there are satisfactory ways of speaking of "continuity" in God's memory or similarly. Moltmann puts it succinctly: "God's relationship to people is a dimension of their existence which they do not lose even in death."[137]

However exactly the theology of death is conceived, Christian tradition agrees that the belief in the resurrection of the body is hope for defeating death in the new creation.

Resurrection as Human Destiny

The Theological Dilemma of Personal Identity between This Life and the Life to Come

As established, the resurrection of Jesus Christ on the first Easter morning provided the "first fruit," an anticipation, of the coming new creation in which the power of entropy, ultimate decay and death, is overcome. The whole of the cosmos anticipates the new creation in which all of creation will participate (Rom. 8:19–27). Humanity's hope participates in this cosmic hope.

It is one thing to affirm the theological significance of the bodily resurrection in the Christian eschatological vision; it is another thing to intuit how it may happen. In other words, how could we envision the transition from premortem embodied existence (via physical death as well as general resurrection and judgment) to postmortem "physical" resurrection existence in the new creation—particularly when the person we speak of has to be the same person! The main challenge is this: based on one's conception of human nature, one has to choose from among various options in philosophical and theological traditions concerning the idea of the transition.[138] Currently we know that not only with regard to the afterlife, but even in this life, the conti-

136. Schwarz, *Eschatology*, 296.

137. Moltmann, *The Coming of God*, 76.

138. See Lynne Rudder Baker, "Persons and the Metaphysics of Resurrection," in *Personal Identity and Resurrection: How Do We Survive Our Death?*, ed. Georg Gasser (Surrey, UK: Ashgate, 2010), 168–75.

nuity of personal identity cannot be a matter of material continuity since atoms are in constant flux through wear and tear.[139]

The problem of continuity between this life and the hoped-for bodily resurrection was already clearly acknowledged in early theology. What can be conveniently called the "anthropology of composition" became a fairly standard view in patristic theology: once the body decays at death, on the last day God reassembles it from the last constitutive material particles available and rejoins it with the soul that did not die. The fathers were aware of obvious problems such as death by cannibalism or in the sea when there was no trace of the deceased person's material body available, and they sought creative solutions.[140]

Another standard early tactic was to establish the identity on the basis of the identity of the soul, separated at death but immortal. The pagan Hellenistic idea of immortality, however, was significantly reshaped and strictly limited to one individual to avoid the (Platonic) doctrine of reincarnation.

Philosophical Attempts

Moving from theology to philosophy, we may note two standard tactics that attempt to ensure the continuation of personal identity, namely, the "memory criterion" that, beyond mere memory, encompasses complex mental functioning, and the "bodily criterion," that is, this person can be considered to be identical with that person if and only if they have the same body throughout the person's life. Although neither one alone, or both together, hardly suffices because the demand that there be continuous brain activity in order to ensure the psychical structure supporting mental properties cannot be met in resurrection, a related classic version thereof points in the right direction—the "consciousness continuity," or to be more precise, "self-consciousness continuity." The key to identity continuity is the ability to have a first-person perspective, that is, self-reflective capacity. That of course has to be assumed in order to have judgment, forgiveness, and responsibility and for it to be meaningful in the new creation. But even that alone hardly suffices.

In summative response to these proposals, we can say this much: it is obvious that minimally both physical (corporeal) and psychological (mental) criteria are required for identity continuation, particularly if topped with

139. Derek Parfit, *Reasons and Persons* (Oxford: Oxford University Press, 1986), part 3.

140. E.g., Athenagoras, *On the Resurrection of Flesh* 4–8.

the capacity for self-consciousness. To these, "character formation" has to be added. More than mere moral-ethical integrity, this component has to do with practices and virtues. When placed in the wider context of communities that shape us and essential relationships, we have advanced considerably the pursuit of identity continuity in this life.[141]

Without downplaying these insights, something more is needed when considering postmortem continuity. Not surprisingly, a number of competing sophisticated options have been proposed in contemporary philosophy and philosophical theology, the discussion of which, however, would require philosophical learning way beyond a theological primer. Let us instead seek for some key biblical-theological resources.

Personal Identity in New Creation: Divine Faithfulness and Continuity-in-Discontinuity

The starting point for all inquiries into the possibility of the resurrection of the body has to be Paul's note of the "change" (1 Cor. 15:51). Change is neither total replacement nor replication. Another critical theological insight is the theology of the human being as the image of God, which signals our relatedness to and contingency on God. The moment the divine life-giving Spirit is taken away, all creaturely life comes to an end (Ps. 104:29–30).

The personal identity that defines me as a person cannot be "transferred" from this earthly life to the afterlife with my own innate powers; divine faithfulness and creative power are needed. But *what* will transition from here to there: Is it the "whole package" of what has made me the kind of person I am? The judgment of my life, and its reconciliation, will be based on my capacity to recognize myself as the actor of the deeds attributed to me, on the quality of my character both at the personal and at the communal level.

What about the body in this regard? Nancey Murphy rightly argues that as essential as it is for identity formation and persistence, it is "that which provides the substrate for all of the personal attributes . . . ; that which allows one to be recognized by others; that which bears one's memories." In this life, all these activities are based on and tightly linked with embodiment. But because the human being is a "person" rather than a "material object," "there is no reason *in principle* why a body that is numerically distinct but similar in all

141. Nancey Murphy, "The Resurrection Body and Personal Identity: Possibilities and Limits of Eschatological Knowledge," in *RTSA*, 212–13.

relevant aspects could not support the same personal characteristics."[142] In any case, my physical composition changes several times during my lifetime (albeit gradually rather than instantly, as in resurrection). Temporal interval (however that may be understood) does not in principle frustrate the continuity of identity. Indeed, for "new creation" to be *new*, as discussed already, the "matter" (body, physicality) must be different from the earthly body (notwithstanding the continuity to the point that it still makes sense to speak of "body" rather than merely "spirit").

Useful is Polkinghorne's way of speaking of the "how" of the continuity of identity in the transition from here to there in terms of "the almost infinitely complex, information-bearing pattern in which the matter of the body is organized at any one time." While there is no need necessarily to endorse the traditional conception of soul, it is also the case that "this surely is the meaning of the soul."[143] In that regard, Aquinas's hylomorphic account of human nature (discussed in chap. 4) intuited something similar, notwithstanding his vastly different intellectual context. Utilizing the concept of information, it can be stated that what the older soul theory rightly intuited was that "the faithful God will remember the pattern that is me and reembody it in the eschatological act of resurrection." Polkinghorne continues: "In making this assertion, I want to affirm the intrinsically embodied character of human being, without supposing that the flesh and blood of this world represents the only possible form that embodiment might take."[144]

Recall as well, on the basis of the discussion of the time-eternity relationship, that "what takes place in time can never be lost so far as God's eternity is concerned. To God all things that were are always present, and as what has been they are present in the totality of their existence." The conclusion is that "the identity of creatures needs no continuity of their being on the time line but is insured by the fact that their existence is not lost in God's eternal present."[145]

Having discussed the thorny problem of the continuity of identity in the transition from earthly life via death to resurrection life in the new creation, we move to clarify theologically the related issue of the "intermediate state."

142. Murphy, "The Resurrection Body," 214–15.

143. John Polkinghorne, "Anthropology in an Evolutionary Context," in *God and Human Dignity*, ed. R. K. Soulen and L. Woodhead (Grand Rapids: Eerdmans, 2006), 98.

144. Polkinghorne, "Anthropology in an Evolutionary Context," 99–100.

145. Pannenberg, *ST* 3:606.

The "Intermediate State" and the Linking Together of Personal and Communal Destinies

The "gap" theory, advocated by nonreductive physicalists, among others, holds that between my personal death and the final resurrection there is nothing—and it is problematic from the point of view of systematic theology. As established, the idea of physical death as literally bringing to an end all of the human person has to be qualified with the equally important thesis that "God is the future of the finite from which it again receives its existence as a whole."[146] A related theological concern is that all talk about the completion of one's personal destiny in the eschaton has to be linked tightly with the common destiny of other human beings (and of course, the whole of creation). Four principles point to an appropriate solution.

First, following the continuity-in-discontinuity schema, it can be said that the earthly "body" (that is, the whole human person) has to undergo a radical change, without losing the person's identity. Second, the information-bearing pattern (or similar idea) is kept in God's "memory," preserving all that makes human identity—despite the "gap" between the deceased person's entrance into eternity and the general resurrection of all at the transitioning to new creation.

Third, because God in his eternity is on both sides of death whereas we are time-bound, "all individuals go into eternity at the moment of death," and "yet it is only at the end of the age that all those who sleep in Christ receive in common by the Spirit of God the being-for-self of the totality of their existence that is preserved in God, and thus live with all others before God."[147] Fourth, because we are "constituted by relation to God,"[148] even death is not able to separate us from God and God's love (Rom. 8:38–39). If there is any meaning to an intermediate state, it is "God holding us fast until the resurrection."[149]

This constructive theological work is all the more important because the Bible does not give a coherent picture of what happens after physical death. Passages such as Philippians 1:20–24 seem to merely imply some type of continuation of personal life. Other passages can be read as supporting immediate entrance into blessedness at death (2 Cor. 5:8; Phil. 1:23; 1 Thess. 5:10). The bib-

146. Pannenberg, *ST* 3:607; see also Miroslav Volf, "Enter into Joy! Sin, Death, and the Life of the World to Come," in *EWEG*, 268.

147. Pannenberg, *ST* 3:606–7.

148. Elizabeth Johnson, *Friends of God and Prophets: A Feminist Theological Reading of the Communion of Saints* (New York: Continuum, 1998), 194.

149. Stanley J. Grenz, *Theology for the Community of God* (Grand Rapids: Eerdmans, 1994), 597.

lical data also include a number of references to what became the "soul-sleep" view in tradition (Dan. 12:2; Luke 8:52; 1 Cor. 15:51; 2 Pet. 3:4). Whereas "sleep" entails inactivity, some passages seem to imply conscious activity (particularly the parable in Luke 16:22–23).[150] It seems that the focus of all these diverse biblical testimonies and metaphors is, first, to assure us that as final and inevitable as death is, it is not the last word; God is. Similarly, they clearly seem to be saying that, second, in no way is the "intermediate" state usurping the bliss of one's eternal destiny. At its best, the "gap" between personal death and general resurrection is transient, awaiting final consummation.

As long as our contemporary reflection on the nature and mode of the intermediate state is in keeping with these general biblical pointers, there is leeway for diverse interpretations. In the traditional body-soul view, we must acknowledge the liability of the problematic idea of the soul continuing its life apart from the body to the extent that in resurrection—so to speak—the body and soul to be united are not the same as those of the deceased person (the soul having accumulated experiences). That said, why couldn't we think of this period as time for the beginning of healing, transformation, and change—without in any way taking away from the all-important role of resurrection? Polkinghorne puts it well: "We may expect that God's love will be at work, through the respectful but powerful operation of divine grace, purifying and transforming the souls awaiting resurrection in ways that respect their integrity."[151] Ecumenically speaking, that insight would make it easier for non–Roman Catholics to understand the possibility of the doctrine of purgatory. Could that intuition also correspond to the traditional idea of paradise (or Abraham's bosom) as the "waiting room" for the blessed?

Speculatively, one may also consider that, if we are kept by God during the intermediate state, then the biblically based intuition of some kind of connection between the living and the dead becomes meaningful. Setting aside some unhelpful—and perhaps heretical—beliefs and customs stemming from the medieval period and even before, theologically it is not only permissible but also appropriate to reserve a place, for example, for prayer for the dead. Similarly, there is no reason to exclude their prayer for us.

Having outlined and defended in some detail the distinctively Christian vision of resurrection as a hope for the cosmos and humanity, we engage next a comparative exercise with competing and alternative views of life after death (or lack thereof).

150. Grenz, *Theology for the Community*, 593–94.

151. Polkinghorne, *God of Hope*, 111.

Competing Views of the Afterlife

Immortality, Karma, and Rebirth: A Christian Engagement of the Hindu Vision

Much older than the belief in bodily resurrection is the belief in immortality and reincarnation (rebirth) among ancient and living faith traditions. With all their differences, the Greek and Hindu versions of immortality share some common "ground beliefs" that differ significantly from those of the Abrahamic faiths. First, rather than the soul possessing inherent powers out of itself, in the Abrahamic view life eternal is a gift from God. Second, rather than the soul being the person itself, let alone the "true" person, the resurrection doctrine considers the whole human being as the human person. Third, rather than the soul having its endless journey and history through incarnations, the person, after once-for-all earthly life, looks forward to eternal life in communion with the Creator.[152] Finally, for Abrahamic faiths, each human life and human personality (individuality) is unique and nonrepeatable.

With the Abrahamic faiths' doctrine of bodily resurrection, Asiatic faiths' teaching on reincarnation/transmigration shares the problem of identity constitution, though in the latter that is of course differently framed, that is, "how to preserve the identity of the soul in the mutability of the forms which the soul assumes." The problem of identity continuation from one human life to another is a huge challenge. But it becomes hugely more challenging when we think of a sequence of lives from human to animal and back to human. Is the "soul" still the carrier of the identity?[153]

A common and persistent misunderstanding among Christian observers of Hinduism is that rebirth signifies a "second chance." That is a fatal mistake. Belief in rebirth has nothing to do with yet another potential opportunity to fix one's life. Rebirth is rather the result of the karmic law of cause and effect. Even gods cannot break the power of karma. As a result, Hinduism (and Buddhism) at large rather seeks a way to defeat the possibility of having to be born again. Rather than a positive offer, rebirth is more like a curse.

The Christian notion of grace differs significantly from the ironclad power of karma. In it God acts "contingently and historically," continuously interrupting "the chain of act and destiny," which means the repelling of karma. That is of course what forgiveness does: while not doing away with

152. Pannenberg, *ST* 3:571–73.

153. Moltmann, *The Coming of God*, 112–13.

punishment—because it does not deny the "sowing and reaping" principle taught in the Bible (Gal. 6:7; Jer. 31:29)—it opens up the possibility of being saved without being destroyed or consumed by the consequences. That is truly a second chance in life.

A standard question to both Hindu and Buddhist eschatologies has to do with the assignment of this-worldly fortunes or ills to previous lives. It seems morally highly questionable to refer the sufferings of the poor, sick, handicapped, and other unfortunate people to their past deeds. Nor does it seem morally fair to count the fortunes of the rich, famous, and healthy as their own accomplishments. Rather, in our kind of world evil and good seem to be mixed together.[154]

Provided (for the sake of the argument) that the karmic cause-and-effect logic were to work, a problem arises with regard to memory. How many persons recall their former lives in order to see the logic and learn from them? Hindu philosophy has so far failed to offer a reasonable explanation. It is merely assumed that something is allegedly recalled from past lives and it is believed to guide in some way or another one's life choices. But even if those memories do not appear, the person is claimed to have lived his or her life in the "shadow" of past lives' experiences and memories.

An even more difficult question has to do with the capacities of the "soul" of nonhuman entities in the samsaric cycle. Rebirth (or transmigration) of course assumes some kind of "animating principle, however defined, from one more or less physical, terrestrial body to another."[155] Now, believing that karma may lead the human being not only upward but also downward in the evolutionary tree results in a highly problematic assumption: all souls must know and understand, make choices; in other words, they must have self-consciousness and high-level intellectual skills. While that is not a problem with most humans—unless they die as infants or are mentally impaired—with subhuman entities it is a problem, beginning from even the highest animals. For example: How could the "soul" of the insect or dog have these capacities in its way "upward" in the cycle of rebirths? Again, no satisfactory reasonable account is available.

To the outsider, belief in reincarnation seems highly individualistic. Obviously, it neglects the effects on each person's behavior and attitudes of environmental, social, cultural, sociopolitical, and economic factors, to name

154. Keith Ward, *Religion and Human Nature* (Oxford: Clarendon, 1998), 60–62.

155. Robert P. Goldman, "Karma, Guilt, and Buried Memories: Public Fantasy and Private Reality in Traditional India," *Journal of the American Oriental Society* 105, no. 3 (1985): 414.

a few. However, we know that much of what we are is the result of effects from the milieu in which we evolve and live. Of course, the counterargument could be that we are put in this place of suffering because of our previous deeds, but even then, the effects of the community and human relatedness are not properly addressed. A corollary problem is that if another person—or even a divine being—seeks to alleviate my suffering, then it must lead to the postponement of my final release. Is that charitable act then really charitable, or rather an unintentional way of adding to my suffering?[156]

Hindu and Buddhist visions of afterlife also seem to defeat any permanent meaning of embodiment, and this is a major difference from Abrahamic faith traditions' focus on the resurrection of the body. Final release is understood in terms of liberation *from* all bodily life, not a renewal.

"No-Self" and Eschatological Hope: A Christian Engagement of the Buddhist Vision

As mentioned, by far the biggest problem for Abrahamic traditions is the denial of individuality ("self"). The Christian commentator is of course deeply troubled by any kind of possibility of a "rebirth" of something that does not exist. Indeed, in the absence of self, it is impossible—at least for the Western mind—to imagine "who" is the one who clings to life due to desire, suffers from the effects of karma, and particularly comes to the enlightening realization. This also has to do with what seems to me a deep and wide difference of orientation between Semitic faiths and Theravada Buddhism: the notion of individuality and the individual's relation to others. Related to this is the question, how do we affirm the dignity of human personhood if there is nothing "permanent"? Finally, how should we conceive the principle of kamma in the absence of the "self" whose destiny it should determine?

Although there are no major Christian movements that, strictly speaking, endorse the Asiatic faiths' idea of reincarnation (and rebirth), several contemporary theologians have creatively gleaned from these resources in their desire to challenge the traditional Christian eschatological hope. Well-known radical proposals come from the philosopher J. Hick and feminist theologian R. R. Ruether. To the list could also be added a more complicated version of the American process theology's eschatology. Let us consider them briefly.

156. Ward, *Religion and Human Nature*, 66–67.

Transcendence of Individuality and Dissolution into "the Matrix of the Whole"

Ruether bluntly denies the notion of "personal immortality."[157] One of her more obscure reasons has to do with her conviction that immortality is usually sought by males who "are primarily concerned about their own self-perpetuation," while for women that is not important due to their heavy inclination toward relationality.[158] Furthermore, Ruether opines, hope for immortality fosters dualism of the body and the spirit, of this world versus the world to come, making the former without value.[159] Even worse, female sexuality and giving birth are conceived as representing this lower domain of bodily (and even sinful) existence as opposed to the "spiritual body" in eternal life.[160] The final dissolution of each being into the "ongoing creative Matrix of the whole" is impermanence and lack of life after death writ large.[161] Apart from its novelty and highly speculative nature, the obvious critical question to Ruether is, by what logic can it be maintained that hope for an afterlife per se is a particularly male characteristic and that women do not care for it?

Although American process theology at large does not speak with one voice on the question of the afterlife,[162] mainstream process thought stands "against any subjective immortality, holding that as objectively experienced by God our lives are wholly preserved and cherished forever."[163] The elusive and somewhat undefined notion of "objective immortality" of course radically deviates from any mainstream Christian vision. Even the concept of "subjective immortality" advocated by a few process thinkers in no way matches the biblical-Christian idea of personal physical resurrection.[164]

157. See Rosemary Radford Ruether, "Eschatology in Christian Feminist Theologies," in *OHE*, 335.

158. Rosemary Radford Ruether, *Sexism and God-Talk: Toward a Feminist Theology* (Boston: Beacon, 1983), 235–37, here 235.

159. Ruether, *Sexism and God-Talk*, 239–40.

160. Ruether, *Sexism and God-Talk*, 245–49.

161. Rosemary Radford Ruether, *Gaia and God: An Ecofeminist Theology of Earth Healing* (San Francisco: HarperCollins, 1992), 248–53, here 253.

162. Alfred North Whitehead, "Immortality," *Harvard Divinity School Bulletin* 7 (1941–1942): 5–21; Joseph A. Bracken, SJ, ed., *World without End: Christian Eschatology from a Process Perspective* (Grand Rapids: Eerdmans, 2005).

163. Lewis S. Ford, *The Lure of God: A Biblical Background for Process Theism* (Philadelphia: Fortress, 1978), 114.

164. Marjorie Hewitt Suchocki, *The End of Evil: Process Eschatology in Historical Context* (Albany: State University of New York Press, 1988), chap. 5.

Undoubtedly, the most sophisticated challenge to the Christian view comes from Hick. In his earlier work on theodicy, *Evil and the God of Love*, he advocated the possibility of progress and development in the afterlife for the simple reason that one life hardly is long enough for the attainment of the goal of perfection set by God.[165] In his later eschatological monograph, *Death and Eternal Life* (1976), Hick rejected both the traditional Abrahamic faiths' belief in resurrection (including two destinies) and Asiatic faiths' doctrine of repeated reincarnations on earth. Instead, he chose "a third possibility . . . , namely that of a series of lives, each bounded by something analogous to birth and death, lived in other worlds in spaces other than that in which we now are,"[166] ultimately leading to the transcending of individuality in corporeality in which persons will "no longer be separate in . . . [the] sense of having boundaries closed to one another . . . [but rather will] be wholly open to another." In that final sense, even embodiment will be transcended and "the individuals' series of lives culminates in a last life beyond which there is no further embodiment but instead entry into the common Vision of God, or nirvana, or the eternal consciousness of the atman in its relation to Ultimate Reality."[167] Although Hick's hybrid construct of the afterlife is highly ingenious, its main challenge from the Christian perspective is its radical deviation from both biblical and traditional contours. Furthermore, his kind of invention is representative of no known religious tradition.

Regarding religious (and perhaps also other) eschatological visions, a lingering question involves whether they are ultimately so otherworldly that concerns for the well-being of this world—with regard to both the flourishing of nature and the pursuit of justice and equality among men and women—are marginalized. To these pertinent issues we turn next.

165. John Hick, *Evil and the God of Love*, 2nd reissued ed. (New York: Palgrave Macmillan, 2010), 337–41.

166. John Hick, *Death and Eternal Life: With a New Preface by the Author* (Louisville: Westminster John Knox, 1994 [1976]), 456; for details, see 414–22 (titled "Many Lives in Many Worlds").

167. Hick, *Death and Eternal Life*, 459–64, here 461, 463–64.

Would Eschatological Hope Stifle Work toward Improvement of This World?

Liberation and Hope

Eschatological Hope under Suspicion among Liberation Theologians

There is word out that eschatology may be the most suspicious doctrinal locus for liberationists and eco-theologians of various stripes. How helpful is it for the well-being and flourishing of nature to await the final judgment and establishment of a new heaven and new earth? No wonder liberationists do not typically discuss eschatology at any length.

Generally speaking, not only assigning eschatology a marginal role but also treating it with deep suspicion is typical of much of liberationism. Particularly apprehensive about eschatology has been feminist theology (with the exception of important scholars such as E. Johnson). As discussed in the previous section, R. Ruether and some other leading feminists have totally rejected the idea of personal survival in the resurrected body.

If eschatology is included in the theological menu, most liberationists seek to revise quite radically its canons and orientations. Again, feminist theologians have been among the pioneers, as they "have refocused eschatology from the distant future ('unrealised eschatology') to the here-and-now ('realised eschatology'). Simultaneously, these feminist thinkers have shifted the thematic centre from humanity, as the apex of creation, to creation itself, with humanity removed from centre stage to a supporting position as an interwoven, interdependent component of that creation. In short, realised eschatology has become the ethical culmination of ecofeminism."[168]

In response to these rebuttals and rejections of the Christian eschatological hope for the coming of God's kingdom and hope for personal resurrection life in new creation, a liberationist-sensitive eschatological vision will be needed.

Eschatological Hope as the Catalyst for Liberation and Reconciliation

To defeat the criticism about the stifling effect of the eschatological hope on liberation, contemporary theology argues that ultimately reconciliation of peo-

168. Karras, "Eschatology," 243.

ples and societies requires the reconciliation of the basic relationship between the individual and society. Although efforts toward that should be pursued persistently, it may only happen finally at the eschaton with the coming of God's righteous rule.

Christian vision is superior to secular and (merely) political dreams, including atheist Marxism-Leninism. First of all, the Marxist dream of a just society never materialized, based as it was only on human resources. And more importantly: even if it were to happen by earthly means, it would only relate to that particular generation—never to countless generations that have passed away.[169]

Knowing that the ultimate reconciliation of peoples and groups can only happen in new creation does not lead the church into passivity, let alone apathy. The church is joining the work for liberation and justice exactly because it knows that thereby it participates in the work of the Trinitarian God.[170]

The missionary church participates in the liberative work for its own sake; that is, helping people in need is a Christian "thing." At the same time, "being aware that all of its efforts are at best patchwork, bandages on the wounds of a hurting world, the church also witnesses with its action to a world that will be without anguish and suffering."[171] In sum: rather than fostering passivity and apathy, Christian hope for the future, God's future, inspires commitment to liberation.

A Theological Acknowledgment and Assessment of Eco-Feminist Critique

According to the leading American eco-feminist R. R. Ruether, "ecofeminism seeks to dismantle the basic paradigm of male over female, mind over body, heaven over earth, transcendent over immanent, the male God outside of and ruling over the created world—and to imagine an alternative to it."[172] She and others have relentlessly critiqued Christian (and by implication, any such theistic) eschatology for wrongful tendencies like these in its dismissal of the destiny and well-being of nature and, by implication, for the disastrous effects on the current lifestyle of Christians. Other eco-feminists, including Catherine Keller, have joined the critics of the escapist view of nature in Christian

169. Pannenberg, *ST* 3:585–86, here 585.

170. Leonardo Boff, *Liberating Grace*, trans. John Drury (Maryknoll, NY: Orbis, 1979), 152. I am indebted to Schwarz, *Eschatology*, 156.

171. Schwarz, *Eschatology*, 371.

172. Ruether, "Eschatology in Christian Feminist Theologies," 337.

eschatology.[173] Keller believes that traditional eschatology necessarily leads to escapism that justifies the unashamed utilitarian rape of nature, as hope is relegated merely to the future divine intervention, including desire for immortality. Even worse, the traditional eschatological myth includes the total destruction of this world and its replacement with a totally new world.[174] As a solution, Keller recommends an immanentist, this-worldly solution to the impending eco-crisis. The burden and hopes are placed on humanity's capacity to deliver the promise.

While contemporary theology definitively agrees with the feminist critique of certain ways Christian eschatology has been abused to frustrate work for the protection of nature and the integrity of creation's life, it also has to critique this uncritical and unnuanced rejection of mainline Christian hope. Not only is it one-sided, but it is also dismissive not only of a number of nature-embracing theologies of Christian tradition but also of a large number of contemporary constructive theological proposals from the "left" and the "right" that combine robust eschatological hope and intense work for the environment and "green" values.[175] Furthermore, it is highly suspicious to claim that building a this-worldly, human-made hope for the future of creation would *necessarily* deliver a nature-affirming lifestyle (as Keller's passionate and often-obscure prose seems to suggest).

As a counterargument, we should remember the most obvious viewpoint: in all scientific accounts, not only the earth and her life but also the whole cosmos will come to an end; and in terms of near-future prospects, even if human-made threats such as pollution, waste, and nuclear disaster could be avoided, sooner or later "super"-human asteroid collisions or something similar may totally wipe us out. In that light, how appealing and realistic is a merely this-worldly vision, including the hope for eternal life for individuals?[176] In sum: "it is hardly possible to motivate people to care for the earth unless they are convinced that there is indeed some future for themselves on

173. Catherine Keller, "Eschatology, Ecology, and a Green Ecumenacy," *Ecotheology: Journal of Religion, Nature & the Environment* 5 (January 1997): 84–99.

174. Catherine Keller, *Apocalypse Now and Then: A Feminist Guide to the End of the World* (Boston: Beacon, 1996).

175. In addition to Moltmann's important works engaged in this text, see, e.g., C. Birch, W. Eaking, and J. B. McDaniel, eds., *Liberating Life: Contemporary Approaches to Ecological Theology* (Maryknoll, NY: Orbis, 1990); Leonardo Boff, *Ecology and Liberation: A New Paradigm* (Maryknoll, NY: Orbis, 1995).

176. Theodore David McCall, *The Greenie's Guide to the End of the World* (Adelaide: ATF Theology, 2011), 46–50.

earth." Indeed, it is the case that despair before the impending eco-crisis most likely elicits resignation and apathy.[177]

As established, in its widest horizon, a Christian eschatological vision includes not only human and cosmic hope but also hope for nature, the environment. This kind of hope-filled expectation may provide a superior incentive for working toward preservation of the earth in anticipation of the "new heaven and new earth."

Overcoming Evil: The Question of Theodicy

Toward an "Eschatological" Theodicy

Having discussed suffering and pain in nature in the doctrine of creation and the flourishing of human life against the horizon of created life as vulnerable and decaying in theological anthropology, we continue the same themes particularly with regard to eschatology and with the focus on what in classical philosophy and theology is called theodicy. Theodicy refers to attempts to defend the goodness and love of God, the Creator and Provider, in the world full of suffering, pain, and decay.

Theodicy is a highly complex issue, and the basic theological question about it is the negotiation among three kinds of claims: (1) God is perfectly good, (2) God is omnipotent, and (3) evil exists. Negotiating among these three claims can result in vastly different solutions; that is the classic dilemma of theodicy. Unless one is willing to pay the price for compromising any of the three—almost universally assumed to be givens in classical theistic (at least Abrahamic) traditions—a dynamic tension between them must be tolerated.

In Christian understanding, the theodicy question can only be fully discussed in the context of the End, although it also deals with creation and anthropology. Pannenberg describes the eschatological hope succinctly: "Hence it is only the union of creation and redemption against the background of eschatology that makes possible a tenable answer to the question of theodicy, the question of the righteousness of God in his work." Until

177. Ernst M. Conradie, "What Is the Place of the Earth in God's Economy? Doing Justice to Creation, Salvation and Consummation," in *Christian Faith and the Earth: Current Paths and Emerging Horizons in Ecotheology*, ed. Ernst M. Conradie et al. (London: Bloomsbury, 2014), 75.

then, "the world looks only at its uncompleted and unredeemed present," and the presence of evil remains but "an insoluble riddle and offense."[178] So far so good, but some critics hasten to argue that perhaps the whole effort of constructing a theodicy is mistaken. Let us consider that claim before proceeding.

Beyond Theodicy: No Resolution but Resistance?

Not surprisingly, some theologians, both Jewish and Christian, have rejected the whole project of theodicy—or they have attempted a theistic "protest theodicy."[179] These theologians want to shift the focus of theodicy from philosophical-theological reflection to practical ways of tackling suffering and evil. A case in point is Moltmann's *Theology of Hope*. Rather than a philosophical-theological theodicy, he wishes to help defeat suffering and its causes. The only theodicy left is joining the questioning of the dying Christ, "My God, my God, why hast thou forsaken me?"[180]

Several liberationists have found in Job a paragon not only of suffering but also of protest and rejection of theodicy explanations.[181] Consider the senior American black theologian James Cone. He seeks to go beyond the abstract turn to practical theodicy in his locating the experience of evil in "the struggle of an oppressed community for justice."[182]

In response, it can be argued that even though suffering is an existential problem, it is not only that. It is a deep *theological* question as well. The turn to praxis should be welcomed—but not as an alternative to continuing sophisticated and careful "theoretical" thinking. Deepening of analysis and reasoning can go hand in hand with a more robust tackling of issues and cultivation of a patient and hopeful attitude.

178. Pannenberg, *ST* 2:164.

179. Terrence W. Tilley, *The Evils of Theodicy* (Washington, DC: Georgetown University Press, 1991).

180. Jürgen Moltmann, *The Crucified God: The Cross of Christ as the Foundation and Criticism of Christian Theology*, trans. Margaret Kohl (Minneapolis: Fortress, 1993), 4.

181. Gustavo Gutiérrez, *On Job: God-Talk and the Suffering of the Innocent*, trans. Matthew J. O'Connell (Maryknoll, NY: Orbis, 1995), 32–37.

182. James H. Cone, *God of the Oppressed*, rev. ed. (Maryknoll, NY: Orbis, 1997; originally New York: Seabury, 1975), 168.

Overcoming Evil as the Ultimate Eschatological Hope

We should follow Augustine in that "metaphysical evil," namely, the finitude and "natural" limitations of the created reality in itself, is not sinful, as the philosopher Leibniz mistakenly assumed;[183] indeed, creation is good even as something finite, including the material world. Similarly correct is Augustine's denial of evil's ontological existence. Evil is a later intrusion into God's world.

Although neither the exercise of human will nor human corruption can be made solely responsible for evil and suffering—not even in human life (as illustrated in rampant innocent suffering), let alone in the life of nature—a carefully nuanced free will defense (FWD), such as that of the American analytic philosopher Alvin Plantinga (based on the Augustinian tradition), is useful. It is designed to rebut the atheistic charge that it is impossible for God and evil to coexist in any possible world. Simply put, the critics say, a good, omnipotent, omniscient God would want to prevent evil and be able to do so. To counter this objection to theism, Plantinga's defense aims to show that the existence of evil and the existence of God are logically compatible.[184] Plantinga is quite successful in establishing the minimum thesis that it is not impossible to think that God allows evil for a good and honorable purpose, in this case, for bringing about truly (relatively speaking) independent conscious beings endowed with freedom of choice. Free choice of course entails its misuse.

Where Plantinga errs is that (following Augustine) he seeks to absolve God of responsibility, assuming that free, independent creatures rather than the Creator are to be held ultimately responsible. In the final analysis God is to be held responsible for allowing evil's presence in God's world. Otherwise dualism (that is, ultimately there will be two "powers" or "realities" at the End instead of one, God) follows and will not be resolved even eschatologically. Having decided to create this kind of world and independent creatures, God assumed (at least the indirect) responsibility for suffering and the misuse of freedom. The kind of evolutionary world we know entails growth and decay, pain and joy. It is a world filled with death and decay, suffering and pain, as well as violence and cruelty. Happily, we know from the biblical testimonies that God, the Creator, did not shirk responsibility for evil and suffering. Rather, according to the biblical testimony, God, in the suffering of his Son, embraced evil and made sin his own.[185]

183. See Suchocki, *The End of Evil*, chap. 1.

184. Alvin Plantinga, "God, Evil and the Metaphysics of Freedom," in *PE*, 83–109; Alvin Plantinga, *God, Freedom, and Evil* (London: Allen & Unwin, 1975), part Ia.

185. Pannenberg, *ST* 2:165–66.

Making God responsible for sin, however, should not lead theology to the conclusion of Schleiermacher, according to which God was "ultimately ordaining sin and suffering" and hence bears the ultimate responsibility.[186] Nor should we say that God wills sin—any more than, say, a medical doctor wishes a car accident in order to have a surgery. On the contrary, in a world like ours, car accidents—negative and bad events in themselves—happen, and surgery is a way to "redeem" many.

At the same time, we also have to handle with great care the Irenaean-Hickian insistence on the pedagogical and sanctifying role of suffering. Although no one contests the occasional redemptive value of suffering and pain, the limitations of that argument are severe and well known. First of all, it seems that much less (and much less random) suffering and pain would deliver the same results. Furthermore, this reasoning hardly helps explain natural catastrophes and much violence and pain.

Ultimately, the eschatological coming of the kingdom of God also brings about the needed monistic resolution: Abrahamic faiths can only have one ultimate reality, although prior to that, depending on one's theology, it seems like two powers are in place.[187]

Christian theodicy also raises questions about how this vision of the overcoming of evil may relate to hopes in other faith traditions. To that topic we turn next.

Evil and Suffering among Religions: The Challenge to Abrahamic Traditions

All religions are bound to offer some explanations for the presence of suffering and evil in relation to Ultimate Reality. That said, each religious tradition has its own specific kinds of evils to account for.[188] Particularly pertinent is the challenge of theodicy among the three Abrahamic traditions. Hence, Jewish and Islamic resources will be scrutinized here.[189]

186. As paraphrased by Hick, *Evil and the God of Love*, 228.

187. For details, see Hick, *Evil and the God of Love*, chap. 2.

188. John Westerdale Bowker, *Problems of Suffering in Religions of the World* (Cambridge: Cambridge University Press, 1970).

189. For theodicies in the Indian context, see Wendy Doniger, *The Origins of Evil in Hindu Mythology* (Berkeley: University of California Press, 1976); Arthur L. Herman, *The Problem of Evil and Indian Thought* (Delhi: Motilal Banarsidass, 1993).

Jewish Theodicies—and Antitheodicies

As discussed, the rise of Jewish eschatology is widely attributed to the theodicy question, as the conviction arose that final resolution of innocent suffering could only be had in the life to come. The urgency of the theodicy question to Judaism is unsurpassable for several reasons.[190] First, unlike in the Asiatic religions, locating God's deeds in the historical arena naturally raises the question of God's responsibility for evil. Second, its theology of election, based on the covenant, elicits the painful question of why this people has suffered so much. Third, the sheer amount and absurdity of suffering, not only at Auschwitz but also throughout Israel's existence, make the issue a burning one.

Although the Deuteronomic tradition more or less unequivocally sees evil as the result of disobedience, in some later Old Testament traditions in the Writings and the Prophets, final retribution and vindication are relegated to the eschatological future and "new covenant." The testimony of Job also offers a decisive rebuttal to the Deuteronomic direct cause-and-effect link between suffering and human behavior.[191]

In the Scripture, there is also another kind of marked shift: whereas in the preexilic writings God is seen as the sovereign source of both good and evil, after the catastrophe a more dualistic understanding begins to emerge in which God's power and human disobedience each play their roles. At the same time, confidence in the capacity of God to bring good out of evil—as is evident in the life testimonies of Joseph and Job—is maintained.

In later Jewish literature, one finds opinions according to which evil must have come through some other intermediary, most prominently human freedom to sin (as also attested in Lev. 26:14–20 and Deut. 11:13–17). This is the theory of divine retribution, which does not deny but presupposes divine mercy, but not without punishment (in order to maintain God's holy nature). Similarly to the Christian tradition, divine retribution is often linked with messianic redemption and eschatological fulfillment.[192]

At some point, the divine-retribution template turns out to be unsatisfactory to those who suffer too much and too long, without seeing any sign

190. Jacob Neusner, "Theodicy in Classical Judaism," in *Encyclopaedia of Judaism*, ed. Jacob Neusner, Alan J. Avery-Peck, and William Scott Green (New York: Continuum; Leiden: Brill, 2006).

191. M. Peterson, "Religious Diversity, Evil, and a Variety of Theodicies," in *OHRD*, 156–57.

192. Byron L. Sherwin, "Theodicy," in *Contemporary Jewish Religious Thought: Original Essays on Critical Concepts, Movements, and Beliefs*, ed. Arthur A. Cohen and Paul Mendes-Flohr (New York: Free Press, 1987), 960–63.

of retribution (see Jer. 12:1–2; Job 9:24). Not surprisingly, by the time of the Holocaust, retribution theology came under radical shaking and revision—to the point that many Jewish theologians saw it as completely useless for the post-Holocaust world. The reason is that ultimately "in a monotheistic faith evil as well as good must ultimately be referred back to God."[193]

Concerning contemporary Jewish responses, even when theodicy is not rejected in the first place—for the simple reason that for many "to speak the name of Auschwitz in the same sentence as the word 'theodicy' seems unconscionable"[194]—they all respond to the Holocaust. It suffices to merely mention that these post-Shoah-era theodicies range from protest atheism, to nontheistic responses, to Deism, to reaffirmation of traditional Jewish theism;[195] a detailed scrutiny of them would go well beyond the contours of this primer.

Happily, some Christian theologians have recently begun to engage the theodicy question in a more intentional manner from the perspective of the Jewish experience.[196] Since they share the same scriptural heritage, more mutual work between the two Abrahamic traditions could be attempted in tackling suffering and theodicy.

Suffering and Evil in Light of Allah's Sovereignty and Justice

At the center of Islamic tradition is God's unqualified power rather than divine vindication, as it is in Judeo-Christian theodicies. As a result, the urgency of theodicy in Islam is far less intense than in Judaism.[197] That said, there is also a long tradition of reflection on suffering and evil. Just think of the narrative of Job—"Ayyub" (one of the prophets!)—scattered over several places (Q 4:163; 6:84; 21:83; 38:41–44). Although Ayyub stands out as the paragon of patience in the midst of calamities, the focus overall is less on theodicy and more on the instructions God gives Ayyub for him to settle the problems.[198]

193. Sherwin, "Theodicy," 966.

194. See Richard L. Rubenstein, *After Auschwitz: Radical Theology and Contemporary Judaism* (Upper Saddle River, NJ: Prentice Hall, 1966), 153.

195. Steven T. Katz, ed., *The Impact of the Holocaust on Jewish Theology* (New York: New York University Press, 2005).

196. Robert E. Willis, "Christian Theology after Auschwitz," *Journal of Ecumenical Studies* 12, no. 4 (1975): 493–519.

197. Eric L. Ormsby, *Theodicy in Islamic Thought: The Dispute over al-Ghazali's "Best of All Possible Worlds"* (Princeton: Princeton University Press, 1984).

198. Gohar Mukhtar, "A Comparative and Critical Analysis of the Story of Job as Found

In light of the divine sovereignty, almost an antitheodicy results. This is not to deny the equally strong insistence in the Qur'an of the compassion of Allah, but rather to indicate the main focus of discussion in this arena. Nor is it to ignore the fact that, somewhat similarly to Judaism (although less vocally expressed), at times suffering may be taken as punishment for sin. That said, in light of divine omnipotence, the idea of suffering as the test of character and faithfulness is more prominent a theme in the Qur'an. Furthermore, similarly to Judaism and Christianity, Islam also invokes the final eschatological resolution.

The two remaining sections of the chapter engage two central topics in Christian eschatology, namely, the question of religious ends and visions of "new creation."

Who Will Be Saved? A Christian Theology of Religious Ends

The Traditional Theology of Two Destinies and Its Rebuttals

Hell in Christian Tradition

All Abrahamic traditions and Asiatic faiths engaged in this book endorse the doctrine of hell as an unparalleled eschatological suffering and penalty. The mainline Jewish belief is that those who do not obey Yahweh, along with heretics and the like, should prepare for eternal judgment. The destiny of gentiles is disputed. Similarly to modern Christian tradition, among Jews there are diametrically opposed beliefs about the reality of hell—for and against. Islam has unusually rich traditions about hell.[199] Against common misconceptions, even the two Asiatic faiths affirm hell and consider it necessary, if not for other reasons, then because karma/kamma alone makes it so; however, it is not the most ultimate destiny.[200]

---

in the Bible and the Quran," *Gohar Mukhtar's Weblog*, July 22, 2011, http://goharmukhtar.wordpress.com/2011/07/22/a-comparative-and-critical-analysis-of-the-story-of-job-as-found-in-the-bible-and-the-quran/.

199. Einar Thomassen, "Islamic Hell," *Numen: International Review for the History of Religions* 56, nos. 2–3 (2009): 401–16.

200. Jens Braarvig, "The Buddhist Hell: An Early Instance of the Idea?" *Numen: International Review for the History of Religions* 56, nos. 2–3 (2009): 254–81; Knut A. Jacobsen, "Three Functions of Hell in the Hindu Traditions," *Numen: International Review for the History of Religions* 56, nos. 2–3 (2009): 385–400.

Both advocates and opponents freely grant a strong biblical support for what became the Christian doctrine of hell (Isa. 66:15–16; Jer. 7:30–34; Joel 3:1–2; Matt. 13:42, 49–50; 22:13; and Synoptic parallels; 2 Thess. 1:9; Jude 7; Rev. 14:10–14).[201] That said, despite its wide, almost universal attestation, there is no single Christian understanding of hell.[202] What might be called the "traditional" understanding includes the following arguments: hell is for punishment for sins in earthly life and refusal to receive forgiveness from God; it is a final judgment from which there is no escape once executed; at least part of humanity will end up there; and it invokes the "eternal existence thesis: hell is a place of conscious existence."[203] An important alternative model denies the eternity of hell (in terms of unending existence). That version fits both universalism, according to which after one has suffered for a period of time in hell, all will be saved, and annihilationism, which teaches the ultimate destruction (coming to an end) of those who are not believers. Yet another revision of the traditional interpretation—which can be called the "punishment model"—considers hell rather the outcome of one's own choices. In other words, hell means the honoring of the human person's choice to live separately from God.[204]

While the two destinies were almost universally embraced in early theology, hell was not in any way the focus of early Christians' hope for the future. Rather, they "portrayed an optimistic certainty concerning salvation and focused much more on heaven as a desirable state to reach." Early creeds make no mention of hell. Only after the establishment of Christianity as a state religion with unprecedented mass conversions and a rapid increase of nominalism did the need to highlight the reality of perdition give the topic increasing significance. By the Middle Ages, occupation with hell had become an intensive affair.[205]

With the widely spread opposition to hell in modern theology,[206] it is curious that after a century-long neglect of the topic in literature, beginning from the 1960s a steady flow of studies has appeared.[207] Both rebuttals and

201. The Greek transliteration *gehenna* comes from the Hebrew *ge hinnom*, a valley south of Jerusalem where garbage was brought and children were sacrificed to Molech in fire (2 Kings 16:3; 2 Chron. 28:3; 33:6). Details are readily available in standard biblical encyclopedias.

202. William Crockett, ed., *Four Views on Hell* (Grand Rapids: Zondervan, 1997).

203. Jonathan L. Kvanvig, "Hell," in *OHE*, 414.

204. Kvanvig, "Hell," 416–21.

205. Schwarz, *Eschatology*, 399–404, here 399–400.

206. Albert Mohler, "Modern Theology: The Disappearance of Hell," in *Hell under Fire: Modern Scholarship Reinvents Eternal Punishment*, ed. Christopher W. Morgan and Robert A. Peterson (Grand Rapids: Zondervan, 2004), 15–42.

207. Joel Buenting, ed., *The Problem of Hell: A Philosophical Anthology* (Surrey, UK: Ashgate, 2009).

revisionist attempts have emerged as a result. Gleaning from the mainstream contemporary theological contributions, the following kinds of broad principles can be discerned:[208] First, physical punishment and suffering are not an integral or necessary part of the doctrine. Metaphors such as "gnashing of teeth" and similar in the Bible are just that, *metaphors*. Second, punishment does not have to be the leading motif (although it is certainly an aspect in biblical testimonies): the logic of hell may be supported by other forms of justice (such as restorative), the integrity of the divine nature, the irrevocability of human freedom, and so forth. Third, the position that hell will be "densely populated" should not be the default position; rather, our desire and prayer should be that as few as possible would be found there. Fourth, making hell an absolutely unending form of damnation to all that may end up there does not necessarily follow. And finally, although normally one's eternal destiny is sealed at the moment of death, one could also imagine some kind of possibility of purification and preparation before final consummation.

The other major alternatives are annihilation/conditional immortality and universalism.

Annihilation and Conditional Immortality

Particularly among evangelicals in the UK and North America, a view of religious ends called annihilationism has in recent decades garnered interest.[209] It argues that the "impenitent wicked will cease to exist after (or soon after) the last judgment." It is usually coupled with conditional immortality, according to which believers may live forever as the gift of God (because no human person is immortal on one's own account).[210]

Annihilationists believe that their view is in keeping with human persons' freedom. The biblical support for annihilationism comes from the numerous allusions in the Bible, both Old and New Testaments, to the effect that the "wicked" face destruction at the end (Ps. 37:9–10; Mal. 4:1; Matt. 3:10–12; Phil. 3:19; 2 Thess. 1:9; 2 Pet. 3:7; Rev. 20:14–15). Opponents are of course quick

208. Jerry L. Walls, *Hell: The Logic of Damnation* (Notre Dame: University of Notre Dame Press, 1992), 10–11.

209. Edward W. Fudge, *The Fire That Consumes: A Biblical and Historical Study of Final Punishment* (Houston: Providential, 1982); Clark H. Pinnock, "The Conditional View," in *Four Views on Hell*, ed. William Crockett (Grand Rapids: Zondervan, 1997), 135–66.

210. Clark H. Pinnock, "Annihilationism," in *OHE*, 462.

to resort to other biblical texts that seem to support the idea of the ultimate finality of hell (Matt. 25:46; Rev. 14:9–11; 20:10; among others).

Much is at stake with conditionalism and the interpretation of the term "eternal" (*aionios*). Although there used to be a strong case for understanding *aionios* to mean less than "eternal," in recent years the tide has turned. The general scholarly consensus does not support the idea that "eternal," though a very long time, means only "temporary."[211] Furthermore, it is often noted that the idea of just passing out of existence is not greatly comforting to many, and it also raises the question: Can we so easily escape the consequences of choosing alienation from God rather than reconciliation and fellowship with God?[212]

The Logic of Hell and Its Objections

Typical objections to hell are concisely listed by the universalist John Hick:

> For a conscious creature to undergo physical and mental torture through unending time . . . is horrible and disturbing beyond words; and the thought of such torment being deliberately inflicted by divine decree is totally incompatible with the idea of God as infinite love; the absolute contrast of heaven and hell, entered immediately after death, does not correspond to the innumerable gradations of human good and evil; justice could never demand for finite human sins the infinite penalty of eternal pain; such unending torment could never serve any positive or reformative purpose precisely because it never ends; and it renders any coherent Christian theodicy impossible by giving the evils of sin and suffering an eternal lodgment within God's creation.[213]

Advocates of hell are not of course convinced by the force of these arguments—if not for other reasons, then for its prevalence in the biblical teaching. Importantly, the British New Testament scholar C. F. D. Moule bluntly acknowledges the presence of two destinies in the New Testament, even if he himself supports the universalistic interpretation.[214]

211. Richard Bauckham, "Universalism: An Historical Survey," *Themelios* 4 (1978): 52.

212. Grenz, *Theology for the Community*, 640–41.

213. Hick, *Death and Eternal Life*, 200–201.

214. See C. F. D. Moule, *The Meaning of Hope: A Biblical Exposition with Concordance* (Philadelphia: Fortress, 1953), 46 particularly.

But even they who advocate the possibility of hell have to face the obvious biblical dynamic: one can easily find passages that warn us of the possibility of eternal damnation (Matt. 18:8–9; 25:41; Mark 9:43–48; Luke 16:26) and passages that carry a "universalist" orientation (Rom. 5:18; 11:32; 1 Cor. 15:22, 28; 1 Tim. 2:4). Perhaps the theologically most responsible way to approach this is to maintain both types of passages, rather than pitting them against each other. Yet, it seems to mainstream theology that in the New Testament "we notice that the tenor is not one of universal homecoming but of a twofold outcome of human history, namely acceptance and rejection." The New Testament seems to make the human response a condition. Hence, the "universalistic message would contradict the New Testament's insistence that our response to the gospel determines our final destiny."[215]

Recently, it has been claimed that rather than eternal damnation of the human person, hell is something this-worldly, a "hellish" suffering and torment men and women undergo,[216] or the "hell" of forsakenness and judgment of Christ on the cross.[217] What to think of the revision? Although there is no reason to prohibit metaphorical usage of hell, its problem lies in making hell mean *merely* that.

Assuming two destinies poses severe philosophical and theological challenges, the most serious of which is perhaps the seeming conflict between hell and divine love and goodness. To negotiate that dilemma, very important is the argument of the Eastern fathers that "God did not create hell: it was created by humans for themselves. The source of eschatological torment is the will of those humans who are unable to partake in God's love, to feel God's love as a source of joy and blessedness."[218] At the same time, "God does everything he can to save all persons, short of destroying their freedom."[219] The Orthodox bishop Kallistos Ware rightly reminds us of the importance of holding tightly to the tension between God's love and human freedom.[220]

215. Schwarz, *Eschatology*, 346.

216. Nicolas Berdyaev, *Truth and Revelation*, trans. R. M. French (New York: Collier, 1962), 138.

217. Moltmann, *The Coming of God*, 251.

218. Hieromonk Hilarion Alfeyev, "Eschatology," in *The Cambridge Companion to Orthodox Christian Theology*, ed. Mary B. Cunningham and Elizabeth Theokritoff (Cambridge: Cambridge University Press, 2008), 113–14.

219. Walls, *Hell*, 87–88.

220. Bishop Kallistos Ware, "Dare We Hope for the Salvation of All? Origen, St. Gregory of Nyssa and St. Isaac the Syrian," in *The Inner Kingdom, The Collected Works,* vol. 1 (Crestwood, NY: St. Vladimir's Seminary Press, 2001), 194.

A useful insight comes from the Catholic liberationist L. Boff's claim that the "human person has absolute value: he can say *no* to God. He can decide alone for his future which centers around himself and his navel."[221] Along similar lines, Polkinghorne adds that although "God's offer of mercy and forgiveness is not withdrawn at death," because God's love lasts forever, it is also the case that "no one will be carried into the kingdom of heaven against their will by an empowering act of divine power."[222]

The Appeal and Problems of Universalisms

The Evolvement of Universalism in Christian Tradition

Universalism—a.k.a. universal salvation or the restoration of all things (*apokatastasis panton*)[223]—is undoubtedly the most vividly and widely disputed concept in Christian eschatology. It did not arise until the third century and is routinely attributed to Origen. His main argument is twofold: that at the end, all things will be restored to their original state and all things will be subjected under the lordship of Christ; his most often-cited biblical passage in support is 1 Corinthians 15:22–28. At the end, even hell will be destroyed.[224]

Although other noted early theologians proposed ideas that either taught universalism or echoed that orientation (such as Gregory of Nyssa),[225] universalism encountered strong opposition—notwithstanding early theology's great interest in and hope for postmortem salvation.[226] Augustine's strict doctrine of predestination led him to firmly assure two destinies and reject universalism.[227] The view was officially condemned at the Second Council of

221. Leonardo Boff, *Was kommt nachher? Das Leben nach dem Tode*, translated from Portuguese to German by Horst Goldstein (Salzburg: Otto Müller Verlag, 1982), 75, my translation.

222. Polkinghorne, *God of Hope*, 136.

223. The noun itself occurs only once in the New Testament: Acts 3:21.

224. Origen, *First Principles* 1 and 3 (in *ANF*, vol. 4).

225. Constantine N. Tsirpanlis, "The Concept of Universal Salvation in Saint Gregory of Nyssa," *Studia Patristica* 17, no. 3 (1982): 1131–44.

226. The biblical passages invoked included 1 Cor. 15:29; 1 Pet. 3:19–20; 4:6; Jeffrey A. Trumbower, *Rescue for the Dead: The Posthumous Salvation of Non-Christians in Early Christianity* (Oxford: Oxford University Press, 2001).

227. Augustine, *City of God* 21.

Constantinople (552). Most creeds and confessions all the way through Reformation times ruled against universalism and in favor of two destinies.[228]

Theology had to wait until the time of the Enlightenment and modernity to have another generation of fully developed universalisms. Schleiermacher's extended theology of universalism, based on the theology of election, was an important trailblazer. Notwithstanding the acceptance of two types of divine elections, both positive and negative, he refused to see that as an occasion for *eternal* damnation.[229]

Famously, Barth ended up embracing a form of universalism deeply anchored in Christocentrism. Behind Barth's universalism is his radically reworked Reformed doctrine of election, in which Jesus Christ rather than the human person (or even humanity at large) is in focus (see chap. 8). The traditional "double predestination" is strictly rejected and a radically revised doctrine of predestination in terms of the dual role of Christ and his "dual treatment"—rejection (crucifixion) and vindication (resurrection)—is put in its place. The logical conclusion from Christ's rejection on the cross and his resurrection on the day of Easter is that no one else will be rejected.[230]

Among contemporary systematic theologians, Moltmann's tightly argued and carefully nuanced universalism is most widely debated. His main arguments include these: that divine grace is more powerful than human sinfulness; that divine judgment "serves the universal establishment of the divine righteousness and justice"; that God's loving and compassionate desire to save is able to overcome the sinner's resistance; that at stake is "confidence in God: what God wants to do he can do, and will do," that is, salvation rather than condemnation—otherwise ultimately human destiny is left in the hands of the human;[231] and finally, "if *the double outcome of judgment* is proclaimed, the question is then: why did God create human beings if he is going to damn most of them in the end, and will only redeem the least part of them?"[232]

Although mostly a phenomenon of the post-Enlightenment Global North, nowadays universalism can also be found among some theologians

228. Gerald R. McDermott, "Will All Be Saved?" *Themelios* 38, no. 2 (2013): 232–43, http://tgc-documents.s3.amazonaws.com/themelios/Themelios38.2.pdf#pag.

229. Friedrich Schleiermacher, *The Christian Faith,* ed. H. R. Mackintosh and J. S. Stewart (Edinburgh: T&T Clark, 1999), 548–51, 720–22.

230. Barth, *CD* II/2, 163.

231. Moltmann, *The Coming of God,* 243–46, here 243, 244.

232. Moltmann, *The Coming of God,* 239–40.

in the Global South, including theologians from Africa[233] and Asia.[234] Furthermore, against common intuition, universalisms have also emerged lately among some American and British evangelicals, despite evangelicalism's significant opposition to that kind of theology.[235] Theologically and philosophically, the most sophisticated representative is Thomas Talbott, whose main motive for universalism has to do with the prominence of divine love, which he sees as utterly incompatible with the idea of eternal judgment.[236]

Another wave of pluralisms is in one way or another related to the robust rise of religious pluralisms. Gleaning from the Enlightenment ideals of the common essence of religions that leads to the idea of a "rough parity" of all faiths, any demand for subscribing to a particular kind of tradition as a precondition for salvation is compromised or outright rejected. John Hick's pluralistic universalism is well known. Whereas in his earlier work *Evil and the God of Love* (1966) the rejection of hell was funded by the incompatibility of theodicy and hell (for reasons we do not have to go into here),[237] after his decisive turn to pluralism, a universalistic orientation entered the context of interfaith issues. On top of rejecting any claims for the unique role of Christ as the door to salvation and similar pluralistic orientations, talk about hell and judgment lost its traditional legacy. The final and highly novel universalistic vision came to full fruition in Hick's monumental *Death and Eternal Life*. It bases "universal salvation"[238] on the idea that "since man has been created by God for God, and is basically oriented towards him, there is no final opposition between God's saving will and our human nature acting in freedom."[239]

233. Andrew Olu Igenoza, "Universalism and New Testament Christianity," *Evangelical Review of Theology* 12 (1998): 261–75.

234. Daniel J. Adams, "Universal Salvation? A Study in Myanmar Christian Theology," *Asia Journal of Theology* 22 (2008): 219–36.

235. Gregory McDonald [Robin A. Parry], *The Evangelical Universalist*, 2nd ed. (Eugene, OR: Cascade, 2012); Rob Bell, *Love Wins: A Book about Heaven, Hell, and the Fate of Every Person Who Ever Lived* (New York: HarperOne, 2012).

236. Thomas Talbott, *The Inescapable Love of God* (Eugene, OR: Cascade, 2014 [1999]).

237. Hick, *Evil and the God of Love*, 341–45.

238. Title of chap. 13 in Hick, *Death and Eternal Life*, 242.

239. Hick, *Death and Eternal Life*, 254.

Against Universalisms and in Support of "Optimism of Salvation"

Universalisms come in many forms and versions, as the previous discussion has indicated.[240] In addition to negative objections to hell and eternal punishment, universalisms also enjoy support from the following kinds of viewpoints: the power of divine love to accomplish its salvific purposes, even when the human person resists (cf. 2 Tim. 2:13), and the nonreality of evil, which means that only God, the goodness, lasts, whereas everything evil does not. Furthermore, general human feelings of resistance to the whole idea of eternal punishment and compassion for all humans are often invoked.

On the other hand, reasons against universalisms include these: the argument from free will cannot imagine that God, the giver of freedom, will overrule it if the human person wishes to choose otherwise; "the point of no return" argument opines that although God is patiently waiting for repentance, physical death constitutes a final boundary mark; the argument from justice simply means that if everybody ends up in the same eternal destiny, all demands of justice and fairness may be in danger of compromise; the pastoral and missiological argument opposes universalism for the obvious reason that it has the potential of making Christian outreach and discipline meaningless.

Mainstream theology claims that universalism as a stated, dogmatic position is not a coherent Christian resolution for many reasons: First of all, it "contradicts the vision of the historical process as a path to the final transfiguration and change into a better state." Furthermore, an unreserved universalism also ignores the importance of human freedom to choose to live with God. Finally, universalism raises grave questions about "the moral sense of the entire drama of human history, if good and evil are ultimately irrelevant before divine mercy and justice."[241] That said, we have to be very cautious about wanting to say any final word on this complicated issue.

All Christians, notwithstanding their denominational affiliation, could gladly acknowledge the radical widening in the offer of salvation in New Testament passages such as Matthew 8:11–12, in which Jesus says: "I tell you, many will come from east and west and sit at table with Abraham, Isaac, and Jacob in the kingdom of heaven, while the sons of the kingdom will be thrown into the outer darkness; there men will weep and gnash their teeth." The passage seems to be saying that those who take for granted their entrance into God's

240. Michael Murray, "Three Versions of Universalism," *Faith and Philosophy* 16 (1999): 55–68.

241. Alfeyev, "Eschatology," 116.

kingdom—be it Israelites or Christians—may face condemnation, whereas pagans (non-Jews) or non-Christians may be included.[242]

In light of these considerations, it is useful to follow the distinction between "strong" and "hopeful" universalism: whereas the former assumes "universal salvation," the latter concedes to hope that as few as possible find themselves in eternal punishment.[243] The late Canadian Baptist Clark Pinnock coined the term "optimism of salvation." It is based on one's understanding of God as "unbounded generosity." Says Pinnock: "The God we love and trust is not One to be satisfied until there is a healing of the nations and an innumerable host of redeemed people around his throne (Rev. 7:9; 21:24–26; 22:2–6)." This attitude speaks of hospitality, a "hermeneutic of hopefulness,"[244] as opposed to the "fewness doctrine," according to which it is certain that only a small number of people will be saved.[245] On the basis of biblical teaching and Christian tradition, not much more can be conclusively claimed. Ware puts it well: "Our belief in human freedom means that we have no right to categorically affirm, 'All *must* be saved.' But our faith in God's love makes us dare to *hope* that all will be saved. . . . Hell exists as a possibility because free will exists."[246]

There is also a further reason to link heaven ("salvation") and hell closely together, one that has to do with the ancient biblical and creedal doctrine of Christ's descent into hell.

The Soteriological Implications of Christ's Descent into Hell

Although the biblical basis is scanty, Christ's descent into hell became a vibrant topic in patristic theology[247] and Christian spirituality. Except for the two references in 1 Peter (3:18–20; 4:6), which in themselves have stirred a lot of exegetical debate, the New Testament leaves us with fairly little.[248] In that

242. Pannenberg, *ST* 3:616; he draws a parallel between this passage and 1 Pet. 3:19–20 in this regard.

243. Robin A. Parry and Christopher H. Partridge, eds., *Universal Salvation? The Current Debate* (Grand Rapids: Eerdmans, 2003), xx–xxii.

244. Clark H. Pinnock, *A Wideness in God's Mercy: The Finality of Jesus Christ in a World of Religions* (Grand Rapids: Zondervan, 1992), 18–20, 99.

245. Pinnock, *Wideness in God's Mercy*, 13–14.

246. Ware, "Dare We Hope?," 215.

247. Hieromonk Hilarion Alfeyev, *Christ the Conqueror of Hell: The Descent into Hades from an Orthodox Perspective* (New York: St. Vladimir's Seminary Press, 2009).

248. Important allusions in Paul include Eph. 4:9 and 1 Cor. 15:54–57.

light, it is surprising that the descent of Christ into hell is part of the Apostles' Creed.[249]

Both in Catholic and in Orthodox traditions, the descent into hell was originally related mainly to the deliverance of the Old Testament righteous ones, but it soon became "an expression of the universal significance of Christ's death for salvation," encompassing all deceased before the coming of Christ.[250] It is hard to contest the fact that "the natural reading of 1 Peter . . . is that Jesus' preaching is to the disobedient, and that preaching is meant to lead to penitence."[251] The late Reformed theologian D. Bloesch coined the term "divine perseverance," which expresses this hope in contemporary theology. The view "holds that God in his love does not abandon any of his people to perdition but pursues them into the darkness of sheol or hell, thereby keeping open the opportunity for salvation. . . . God's grace penetrates the barrier of death, thus kindling the hope of conversions beyond the pale of death."[252] Bloesch is not advocating universalism (or the "harrowing of hell" to the point of making it empty), but he acknowledges that various kinds of hopeful expectations can be based on this template.

Theologically, Christ's proclamation and releasing work can be seen as dramatic expressions of the victory over death and the underworld after the Pauline statement: "Death is swallowed up in victory" (1 Cor. 15:54). With the inclusion of this statement in the creed, the church meant "not only to indicate that Christ has triumphed over all possible dimensions, even over that dimension where death usually reigns, but also to express something of the divine compassion."[253]

The Consummation: "New Heavens and New Earth"

The Ambivalence and Dynamic of the Imminent Return of Christ

Having discussed widely a number of topics related to eschatology, we will provide a summative statement about the consummation as understood in mainstream Christian tradition that includes the "signs" of Christ's return

249. See Pelikan, *CT* 1:151.

250. Pannenberg, *ST* 3:616.

251. Ward, *Religion and Human Nature*, 273.

252. Donald G. Bloesch, *The Last Things: Resurrection, Judgment, Glory* (Downers Grove, IL: InterVarsity Press, 2004), 40.

253. Hans Schwarz, *Christology* (Grand Rapids: Eerdmans, 1998), 294.

and its nature (as well as "delay"), the possible "interim" in the process of the establishment of the "new heavens and new earth" (known under the umbrella concept of the millennium), as well as intimations of the nature and "newness" of the symbol of heaven. Finally, as with other topics, a comparison with other faith traditions' intimations of the end and fulfillment will be attempted.

The Problem of the Interim

On the one hand, Jesus's proclamation was thoroughly eschatological, but on the other hand, Jesus did not provide any kind of prophetic timetable for future events.[254] This entails a radical departure from apocalypticism, which is prone to setting dates.[255] A robust dynamic between the "already" (arrival of the kingdom in Jesus's words and deeds) and the "not yet" (the final consummation) is reflected well in the classic title of the late American New Testament scholar G. E. Ladd, *The Presence of the Future.*

What about the problem in the Gospel traditions regarding an interim? Is it the case that the original Gospel writers and Paul were simply and sadly mistaken in expecting the coming of God's kingdom during their lifetime? The data in the Synoptic Gospels is far more complex. Notwithstanding their internal differences, all sought to combat the apocalyptic enthusiasm that set dates, which would first have led to disenchantment and then to final disappointment with the overly long delay in meeting the intense expectation. All three Synoptics seem to balance statements that can be interpreted to propose an immediate eschatological consummation within their lifetime (Mark 9:1; 13:10) with those that postpone its coming to the future (if not necessarily to the distant future, at least to a later period of time).[256] Highly illustrative is the intentional dynamic contained within one and the same saying preserved in all three: "Truly, I say to you, this generation will not pass away before all these things take place. Heaven and earth will pass away, but my words will not pass away. But of that day or that hour no one knows, not even the angels in heaven, nor the Son, but only the Father" (Mark 13:30–32; par. Matt. 24:34–36; Luke 21:32–33). Clearly, the first part is speaking of the imminent end, whereas the latter leaves it open, perhaps even to the distant future.

254. Benedict T. Viviano, "Eschatology and the Quest for the Historical Jesus," in *OHE*, 73–90.

255. Collins, "Apocalyptic Eschatology in the Ancient World," 40–51.

256. Anthony A. Hoekema, *The Bible and the Future* (Grand Rapids: Eerdmans, 1979), chap. 10.

Whereas Mark, as the earliest account, is closest to the enthusiasm of imminent expectation, he also importantly makes the interim period the time of mission to the world (16:9–20). For Matthew it is important to highlight the continuity in Jesus's ministry with the old covenant and the fulfillment in him of the divine promises. Matthew is also the only one to speak explicitly of the church (16:18), including its structures and how to cope with practical problems (18:15–17), thus implying a significant interim. Finally, it was given to Luke to move "beyond the notion of a strict interim period by introducing a salvation-historical understanding of history" and place Jesus in the wider context of the history of the whole world (1:5–6; also 2:1–4). Most striking in this respect is the Lukan Jesus saying that "when you hear of wars and tumults, do not be terrified; for this must first take place, but the end will not be at once" (21:9). As is well known, in the Gospel of John, a "realized eschatology" seems to take the upper hand, although not exclusively, as C. H. Dodd and others have claimed.[257]

Similarly, Paul intuits the Christian's and church's life between two ages, this age and the age to come. Hence, mission and labor in the service of Christ's gospel were the call to Christians. In this way the apostle "saved Christian eschatology from two blind alleys: unhistorical spiritualism and overanxious disappointment."[258]

Signs of the Return of Christ

Despite the repeated reservation of Jesus, the signs of the end have been quite popular among Christians (Matt. 12:38–39; 24:36; Luke 11:16; John 4:48; Acts 1:7). The same is true of Islam—if not more true (as discussed above).

That said, a cautious and discerning scrutiny of signs is not discouraged in the New Testament. Among the expected signs, the New Testament mentions a heightened excitement over the occult, coupled with self-appointed prophets eager to lead astray the faithful (Matt. 24:24; 2 Thess. 2:3, 9–11; among others).[259] The gathering back to their homeland of the Jews and their restoration is an abiding mark of the coming end in both Testaments (Isa. 11:11; Luke 21:24; Acts 15:14–17; Rom. 9–11). Dramatic cosmic changes and portents in nature and the heavens (Isa. 13:13; Joel 2:30; 3:14–16; Matt. 24:29; Luke 21:26; Acts

257. This paragraph is based on Schwarz, *Eschatology*, 83–90, here 86.

258. Schwarz, *Eschatology*, 91–96, here 95.

259. Bloesch, *The Last Things*, 74.

2:20), including seismic events and famines (Luke 21:10–11; Rev. 6:12), as well as intensified wars and conflicts (Mark 13:7; Matt. 24:6; Luke 21:9), signal the parousia of the Lord. To the end-time signs belongs also the proclamation of the gospel unto the whole world (Matt. 24:14).[260] A sure sign of the impending end is the appearance of the antichrist, indeed antichrists—christ counterfeits.

Indeed, a prominent figure in the Christian (and Islamic) imagination of the end times is the antichrist, a human opponent of Christ. In light of the prominence of Jesus in Muslim eschatology, it is not surprising that the picture of the antichrist in Islam is not radically different from that of Christianity. In the biblical testimonies (2 Thess. 2:3–12), he is depicted as "a universal ruler whose reign of unprecedented evil . . . Christ will defeat at his parousia." We glean from the Jewish apocalyptic prophecy concerning the Syrian ruler Antiochus Epiphanes, who defiled the temple (Dan. 11:29–45), that he is not only a religious but also a political figure, seeking to establish a "counterfeit theocracy."[261]

Jewish apocalypticism also provided cues for corollary adversaries with its depiction of the enticing false prophet (Deut. 13:1–5), which lies behind the Christian Apocalypse's (book of Revelation) account of two monsters, the sea beast and land beast (Rev. 13:1–18), the former a blasphemous ruler and the latter a false prophet (16:13; 19:20). Similarly to the false prophet of old, these antagonists in the New Testament perform miracles and seek to entice people away from worship of the true God to idols. Chapter 17 of Revelation adds yet another evil figure, the harlot of Babylon, likely representing economic enticement.[262]

Fascination with the figure of antichrist has been intense throughout history. Although the appearance of such an evil figure has been assigned to the future, there has also been constant attention to identifying his appearance in contemporary life. For the Reformers, it was the pope; for twentieth-century Christians, Hitler or Stalin or the European Union.[263] Although modern and contemporary academic theology has virtually dismissed the topic as something mythical without any content, the expectation of the antichrist persists vividly in popular apocalypticism, particularly in Christian and Islamic forms.

In light of the long history of failed attempts by Christians to identify the antichrist, we should be very cautious. Theologically, we have to say that, on

260. Bloesch, *The Last Things*, 74–75.

261. Richard Bauckham and Trevor A. Hart, *Hope against Hope: Christian Eschatology at the Turn of the Millennium* (Grand Rapids: Eerdmans, 1999), 111–12, here 111.

262. See Bauckham and Hart, *Hope against Hope*, 112–13.

263. For a massive study, see McGinn, *Antichrist*. Useful also is G. C. Jenks, *The Origin and Development of the Antichrist Myth* (London: de Gruyter, 1991).

the one hand, the God-opposing "mystery of lawlessness is already at work" (2 Thess. 2:7) in any given historical time, and that, on the other hand, the final culmination of the growth of evil will happen on the eve of the final consummation.

Parousia: The Presence and Appearance of Christ

According to Jewish expectations, the Messiah is yet to appear. In Islamic eschatology, the one to return is the Mahdi—accompanied by Jesus. For Christian theology, Christ's return clearly is the central image of hope in Christian eschatology.

The term "parousia," as is well known, has the dual meaning of both "appearance" (as in "coming") and "presence."[264] His "return" is not a return as in going back or coming again, but rather a cosmic "re-turn," as in making a turn to usher in God's promised new creation. Rather than a "private" meeting with a tiny flock of the faithful, Christ's return will be an establishment of God's righteous rule and renewal of cosmic dimensions.

An essential part of the parousia is Christ's assumption of universal rule and execution of righteous judgment over the whole cosmos and all people (Matt. 25:31–46; Acts 10:42; 2 Thess. 1:9–10; Heb. 9:28; 1 Pet. 4:5). This is no whimsical vengeance and illegal usurping of power by a tyrant, but rather the "revelation" or "appearance" of the faithful Creator, Sustainer, Reconciler, and Consummator.

The biblical vision of Christ's return and cosmic renewal, as dramatically new as that is vis-à-vis expectations based on the normal course of history, differs significantly from apocalypticism. Thus, a careful assessment and critique of contemporary forms of apocalypticism is a necessary theological task.

Contemporary Neo-Apocalypticism and Its Liabilities

Tapping into the long and rich tradition of apocalypticism with its deeply dualistic view of the world and expectation of the imminent catastrophic end of history, contemporary neo-apocalypticism is gaining strongholds not only

264. N. T. Wright, *Surprised by Hope: Rethinking Heaven, the Resurrection, and the Mission of the Church* (New York: HarperOne, 2008), chap. 8.

in conservative and fundamentalist Christian but also in Jewish[265] and Islamic movements.[266] Although it is easy to dismiss these kinds of movements as harmless or excessive, their importance to the faithful should not be underestimated. From the ranks of Christian fundamentalist neo-apocalypticism come best-selling titles such as *The Late, Great Planet Earth* (1970) by Hal Lindsey and the Left Behind series by Tim LaHaye (and Jerry B. Jenkins).

The neo-apocalyptic vision of the world is deeply dualistic, dividing the world into evil and good, them and us, enemies and friends. A common hallmark of the fundamentalist movements in all Abrahamic traditions is the expectation of the terror of Armageddon.[267] Often the advocates of neo-apocalypticism also consider themselves agents of God's righteous judgment, in extreme cases even leading to violence.[268]

The theological and ethical liabilities of neo-apocalypticism are obvious given its deep dualism and built-in potential violence. It reads Scripture ideologically in its attempt to justify its own cause and show the falsehood of the other. The neo-apocalyptic eschatological timetable is deterministic and may lead to fatalism. Furthermore, work for the peace of the world, cleaning and caring for the environment, erasing poverty and injustice, and similar good efforts for the improvement of the world are pushed away as efforts that impede the coming of the Day.

Although the dangers and liabilities of neo-apocalypticism should be theologically exposed, academic theology and established churches should also take a self-critical look and ask why apocalypticism garners such an appeal. Furthermore, the observer of neo-apocalypticism has to be reminded that not all evangelical Christians, not even a majority, support the extreme features described above. Even among fundamentalists, that is most probably the case.

Although closely related to fundamentalist and neo-apocalyptic eschatological sensibilities, millennial hopes are in no way limited to those movements.

265. Gershom Gorenberg, *The End of Days: Fundamentalism and the Struggle for the Temple Mount* (New York: Oxford University Press, 2000).

266. David Cook, *Studies in Muslim Apocalyptic* (New York: Syracuse University Press, 2005).

267. For a broad overview, see Michael A. Sells, "Armageddon in Christian, Sunni, and Shia Traditions," in *The Oxford Handbook of Religion and Violence*, ed. Michael Jerryson, Mark Juergensmeyer, and Margo Kitts (Oxford: Oxford University Press, 2012), 467–95. See also Victoria Clark, *Allies for Armageddon: The Rise of Christian Zionism* (New Haven: Yale University Press, 2007).

268. Daniel L. Migliore, *Faith Seeking Understanding: An Introduction to Christian Theology*, 2nd ed. (Grand Rapids: Eerdmans, 2004), 334–35.

The Critical and Inspiring Role of the Millennium as the Penultimate Earthly Hope

Disputes about Millennial Hopes

Although there is only one explicit statement in the New Testament regarding what became the hope for the millennium in Christian theology[269]—Revelation 20:1–15—a number of other biblical references in both Testaments have been linked to it.[270] The idea also appears in the Jewish apocalyptic tradition (2 Bar. 40:1–3). While in early theology some opted for an allegorical interpretation, the majority went with a more-or-less literal expectation of a thousand-year rule.[271] Named in hindsight premillennialism, this doctrine teaches that following Christ's return to earth, the millennium will be set up for a thousand-year period, after which the new heaven and new earth will be established. That was the default option in earliest theology.[272]

Beginning from Augustine, the enthusiasm for an earthly rule of Christ began to wane, undoubtedly because of the new status of the Christian religion. Instead, the church became the locus and embodiment of God's kingdom.[273] Usually named amillennialism, this view soon established itself as the normative one. It believes that there is no other "reign" of Christ but that which already happens in the church. Significantly, the Council of Ephesus condemned outright the millennial hope (a gesture followed by later confessions among the Protestant churches, both Lutheran and Reformed).[274]

Earthly millennial hopes did not, however, die out. Various types of mystical and spiritualist movements took up the importance of the millennial hope. Similarly, premillennialism did not disappear, notwithstanding a steady and strong resistance from the establishment. Beginning from various types of revival movements during the Protestant Reformation, such as the Ana-

269. Comprehensive resources are *OHM*; Stephen Hunt, ed., *Christian Millennialism: From the Early Church to Waco* (Bloomington: Indiana University Press, 2001).

270. 1 Cor. 15:23–25; Dan. 7:18, 27; and numerous passages in the book of Revelation, among others. In the Old Testament, typical passages invoked include Isa. 2 and 11; Jer. 31–33; Ezek. 36–37; and Mic. 4.

271. Timothy P. Weber, "Millennialism," in *OHE*, 369–71.

272. See, e.g., Tertullian, *The Five Books against Marcion* 3.24.

273. Augustine, *City of God* 20.9.

274. Moltmann, *The Coming of God*, 153–56.

baptists, many other free churches, including Pentecostal/charismatic groups, adopted it as a favorite expectation.[275]

The third form of millennialism, which emerged later in history, is named postmillennialism, according to which Christ's reign is progressing in history with the presence and proclamation of the church and will culminate in a "Christianized" world. Postmillennialists "locate the Second Coming after a long period of gradual and incremental 'gospel success' in which the vast majority of humanity is converted to Christ and human society is radically reformed."[276] Their understanding of the golden era of Christ's rule on earth is consequently less literal than that of the premillennialists. This belief of course fits well the optimism related to missions movements as expressed particularly in the modern missionary movements.

Whereas in twentieth-century academic theology the millennium became marginalized and virtually forgotten—except for conservative Protestant traditions—a striking exception to the omission is Moltmann.[277] Linking the millennium with the "future" of history, Moltmann places the millennium hope between personal and cosmic expectations.[278] Devising his idiosyncratic terminology, he makes a distinction between "apocalyptic eschatology" that focuses on history's "end" and "millenarian eschatology" that thinks of history's goal. The latter is divided into either "historical millennialism," which envisions the present (in various forms) as the "golden era," or "eschatological millennialism," which "hopes for the kingdom of Christ as the future which will be an alternative to the present, and links this future with the end of 'this world' and the new creation of all things." Forms of mistaken historical millennialism include the political, in which a nation becomes the focus of all hope, and ecclesiastical, with a focus on a religious power. Furthermore, the Enlightenment era in itself appeared to many as "millennial" in its promise of unending development and progress.[279]

All these forms of historic millennialism diagnosed by Moltmann are based on "messianic violence," and they legitimate earthly power in the service of reaching the desired dream. Their opposite, what Moltmann names "eschatological millennialism," "is a necessary picture of hope in resistance, in suffering, and in the exiles of this world." It is open to God's new creation and the coming to an end of these illegitimate human edifices. It is a millennialism

275. Weber, "Millennialism," 367.

276. Weber, "Millennialism," 368.

277. Moltmann, *The Coming of God*, 147.

278. Moltmann, *The Coming of God*, 131–34.

279. Moltmann, *The Coming of God*, 159–92.

that "must be firmly incorporated into eschatology" or else "it leads to the catastrophes of history" and to disillusionment.[280]

What Would the Millennium Mean for Us Today: "The Realizing Millennium"

Never should we take the millennium as the center of Christian hope; it is but temporary. Were Christians too occupied with millennial hopes—which are this-world and this-globe centered—they would commit a sin of reductionism. There is much to commend in the argument that the main reason for the millennium in the narrative of Revelation is the vindication of the martyrs. Those who have laid down their lives because of the testimony of Christ appear to be victorious, whereas the haughty earthly rulers are not. But that is not the only reason.

Rightly understood, the millennial hope's true significance has to do with its "earthly" orientation. It represents the this-worldly part of the eschatological hope. With its earthly orientation, millennium hope may also contribute to liberative and redemptive work.[281]

One way of speaking of the millennial hope in a manner that seeks to keep in a dynamic tension the human-initiative *and* God-centered activity as well as this-globe-centered *and* cosmic expectations is to use the nomenclature "realizing or unfolding millennium."[282] This language seeks to combine "elements of apocalyptic, realized eschatology, and millenarian eschatology." Therein, "the kingdom of God bursts into history and advances in history as an invading force of righteousness."[283] This kind of template has the promise of holding together (and at the same time defeating the one-sidedness of) the optimism of postmillennialism in its reliance on the role of the church in advancing the kingdom and the pessimism of premillennialism in its apocalyptic expectation of divine intervention at the expense of human initiative.[284]

As emphasized, millennial hopes are penultimate hopes—to use Hick's language, they belong to par-eschatology. The consummation in its fullness in Christian theology has to do with the establishment of a new heavens and new earth.

280. Moltmann, *The Coming of God*, 192.

281. Mardon Lee Morgan, "Eschatology for the Oppressed: Millenarianism and Liberation in the Eschatology of Jürgen Moltmann," *Perspectives in Religious Studies* 4 (2012): 379–93.

282. Bloesch, *The Last Things*, 110.

283. Bloesch, *The Last Things*, 32.

284. See chap. 7 in Stanley J. Grenz, *The Millennial Maze* (Downers Grove, IL: InterVarsity Press, 1994).

A Theological Rediscovery of "Heaven"

The Eclipse and "Immanentization" of Heavenly Hopes in Modern Theology

As widely and deeply as the imagination and spirituality of heaven occupied the minds of patristic and medieval theologians,[285] so theological reflection on heaven is ominously missing in contemporary academic theology. The omission is so frequent in almost all biblical and systematic theologies that—embarrassingly!—the world's largest and most prestigious theological encyclopedia, *Theologische Realenzyklopädie*, in thirty-six volumes, has no entry on "heaven"!

A delightful exception to contemporary theology's lack of discussion about heaven is Moltmann. His *Coming of God* devotes a whole section to the topic of heaven, under the weighty heading "Cosmic Temple: The Heavenly Jerusalem."[286] That said, Moltmann's discussion of cosmic eschatology under the wider rubric of "New Heaven—New Earth"[287] is so strongly focused on the hope for the "new earth" that at times one is left wondering how much newness he dares to hope for. Readers are constantly warned not to be too otherworldly minded. While this warning is timely, one also wonders what exactly is the meaning and nature of heaven!

A highly important and thoughtful challenge to the traditional notion of future-driven hope for heaven comes from the Scottish New Testament scholar N. T. Wright. Although not denying the future hope per se, he also reinterprets the Gospels' teachings in a quite radical manner. Wright, a fairly traditional scholar, takes the "Small Apocalypse" of Mark 13 (and parallels in other Synoptics) almost exclusively as a description of the return of Israel's Yahweh to his people having been announced and embodied in Jesus's own person. These sayings are thus not prophetic in the sense of a future orientation.[288] "Heaven, in the Bible, is not a future destiny but the other, hidden, dimension of our ordinary life—God's dimension, if you like."[289] That said,

285. Jerry L. Walls, *Heaven: The Logic of Eternal Joy* (Oxford: Oxford University Press, 2002).

286. Moltmann, *The Coming of God*, 308–19.

287. Moltmann, *The Coming of God*, part 4.

288. N. T. Wright, *Jesus and the Victory of God*, vol. 2 of *Christian Origins and the Question of God* (Minneapolis: Fortress, 1996), 339–68, 612–53.

289. Citations in N. T. Wright, *Surprised by Hope*, 19; similar argumentation in J. Richard Middleton, *New Heaven and New Earth: Reclaiming Biblical Eschatology* (Grand Rapids: Baker, 2014).

he still acknowledges the future orientation elsewhere in the New Testament, although still quite minimally.[290] The critical question to Wright is obvious: Why cannot "heaven" be both a future dimension and a hidden dimension of our ordinary life? Where is the newness of eschatological hope?

The main critical theological challenge to the merely this-worldly vision is whether it is able to support a truly cosmic and comprehensive vision of God's making "all things new." How would a fixing of our globe's life conditions be a lasting solution to the problems of entropy and decay? In other words, how *cosmic* (in light of our current scientific knowledge) is a vision of a "new earth" if "cosmic" (by and large) is understood as our globe?

So, what would be a more balanced view? While we have to clearly acknowledge the many pitfalls of overly spiritual, overly otherworldly, overly human projection–driven dreams of the future, we also must hold on to the continuity-in-discontinuity template. Whereas contemporary theology has one-sidedly opted for the idea of continuity and traditional theology has taken the opposite side, a robust account of the radically new future with the consummation of God's kingdom seeks a radical middle. Consider the astute assertion of the Christian philosopher J. L. Walls: "Theism raises the ceiling on our hopes for happiness for the simple reason that God provides resources for joy that immeasurably outstrip whatever the natural order can offer."[291] With these desiderata in mind, let us piously inquire into the nature of heaven.

Heaven as Communion and Consummation

As is routinely mentioned, the biblical narrative provides a meager account of the nature of heaven—and when it engages the theme, the chosen genre is imaginative and poetic. Pictures, images, and metaphors rather than definitions, statements, and analyses are provided. It is also noteworthy that none of the classical creeds rule on the nature of heaven and eternal life; they are merely assumed.[292]

290. N. T. Wright, *The New Testament and the People of God,* vol. 1 of *Christian Origins and the Question of God* (London: SPCK; Minneapolis: Fortress, 1992), 459–61 particularly.

291. Jerry L. Walls, "Heaven," in *OHE*, 399.

292. Alongside Walls, *Heaven*, standard scholarly resources are Colleen McDannell and Bernhard Lang, *Heaven: A History* (New York: Vintage Books, 1990), and Jeffrey Burton Russell, *A History of Heaven* (Princeton: Princeton University Press, 1997); highly accessible is Alister E. McGrath, *A Brief History of Heaven* (Oxford: Blackwell, 2003).

The biblical symbols and metaphors of heaven could be conveniently classified under three linguistic forms: space language, person language, and time language.[293] Space-language-driven metaphors abound, including the "city" and "garden," gleaning from the rich traditions of Jerusalem, the holy city, and the paradise of Genesis 3. The garden stands as a symbol "of innocence and harmony, a place of peace, rest, and fertility."[294] The city speaks of the security and community of people, as well as settlement (for a nomadic, wandering people). The new Jerusalem of Revelation is a walled city, denoting protection, but also a city with permanently open gates, implying constant access. Examples of person language are expressions such as "being with Christ" (Phil. 1:22–23), "seeing God face-to-face" (Matt. 5:8; 1 Cor. 13:12), and related metaphors such as glorification (John 17:4–5, 22–26). Time language relates to expressions such as "eternal life" and corollary terms.

An essential aspect of heaven is the consummation of union with God as expressed in Aquinas's pursuit of the beatific vision; this "seeing" of God alone satisfies the endless human thirst for union.[295] Augustine put it memorably: "He shall be the end of our desires who shall be seen without end, loved without cloy, praised without weariness."[296] Even though one has "arrived" in eternity, progress and evolvement do not have to stop, as there might be an endless journey of new explorations.[297]

Because of bodily resurrection, life in heaven is embodied life. In this regard, N. T. Wright's observation is to the point, namely, that Revelation's vision "is not about people leaving 'earth' and going to 'heaven,' but rather about the life of 'heaven,' more specifically the New Jerusalem, coming down from heaven to earth—exactly in line with the Lord's Prayer."[298]

The "new heaven" must be imagined as cosmos-wide: the mere fixing of life conditions in one part of the cosmos would only be a temporary solution. Human knowledge at the moment has very few resources at its disposal for imagining such a cosmic renewal (somewhat similarly to the question of the ultimate origins of the cosmos in the first place).

293. Tibor Horvath, SJ, *Eternity and Eternal Life: Speculative Theology and Science in Discourse* (Waterloo, ON: Wilfrid Laurier University Press, 1993), 124–32.

294. McGrath, *Brief History of Heaven*, chap. 2 (p. 41).

295. As explained by Walls, "Heaven," 402.

296. Augustine, *City of God* 22.30; I am indebted to Walls, *Heaven*, 37.

297. Polkinghorne, *God of Hope*, 132–33.

298. N. T. Wright, *For All the Saints: Remembering the Christian Departed* (Harrisburg, PA: Morehouse, 2003), 59, cited in Walls, "Heaven," 2–3.

A fitting way to end this chapter is yet another short visit to other faith traditions' imaginations about the ultimate end and destiny.

Visions of Consummation among Religions: A Brief Statement

The Jewish tradition has not spent much ink trying to describe the final consummation because of its this-worldly orientation. Similarly to Christian tradition, a virtual omission of heaven occurs in post-Enlightenment nontraditional Jewish movements. Even in the rabbinic writings, reservation in speaking about the future is the norm. Somewhat similarly to the Christian vision, various stages on the way to the final messianic consummation can be seen in Judaism; the Christian counterparts are the intermediate state and the millennium. Although the cosmic eschatological vision is not totally foreign to Judaism, neither is it at the heart of that tradition.

Islam's vision of heaven is the most transcendent, rich with elaborate descriptions of the final consummation, which take their departure from the beauties and enjoyment of this world but also develop them into highly sophisticated accounts of otherworldly bliss. In that sense, the danger of escapism looms large in many forms of Muslim spirituality, not least in Sufi traditions.

A radical difference concerning consummation can be found between Asiatic and Abrahamic faiths. The Asiatic traditions reject final resolution in their cyclical and ever-repeating cosmologies (even if the individual person's cycle may come to an end in nirvana). A major difference also has to do with the decidedly theo-centric vision of Abrahamic faiths in their expectations of consummation. Even in theistic Hinduism as well as Buddhism's Mahayana traditions, which freely acknowledge deities, their role is ambiguous or at least marginal. Particularly for Buddhism, any talk about "eschatology" in reference to a doctrine of "last things" or "consummation" with any meaning of closure is highly problematic in principle. For the sake of interfaith hospitality, these dramatic differences have to be highlighted and respected.

EPILOGUE: Christian Doctrine as the Trinitarian Unfolding of the Divine Economy

The popular version of Moltmann's massive eschatology, *The Coming of God*, is wittily titled *In the End—the Beginning*. Apart from its aptness for materially describing the core of the Christian doctrine of eschatology, the title also communicates that reflection on Christian doctrine at large is a task without end. It is a continuous work.

Briefly stated, Christian doctrine is but an observation of the Trinitarian unfolding of the divine economy. The Father, having revealed himself to us in the Son through the power of the Spirit, acts jointly with them to create the world and human beings in his image. The Son, sent by his Father in tandem with the Spirit, lives, dies on the cross, and rises to new life for us and our salvation, to be seated on the Father's right hand as coruler. The life-giving Spirit, who sustains all life in this cosmos, is also the One who, with the Father, raises the Son from the dead, brings about faith in Christ, and empowers the Christian walk in obedience to Christ's teaching. The triune God's salvific gifts are donated by the Spirit to us as persons and members of the Christian community. The church/temple of the Spirit, body of Christ, people of God, images the triune God by being a sent community and an agent of reconciliation toward the unity of all people in God. The eschatological consummation, the joint work of Father, Son, and Spirit, brings to realization the eternal promises of God for men and women, as well as this whole cosmos created by the same God.

This is the Christian vision, based on the biblical revelation, and it has to be put in dialogue with other faith traditions' visions as well as the rest of human knowledge as discovered in the sciences. If the triune God is the Creator, Provider, and Consummator of all things, then nothing in the world—including religions as ways of pursuing God's truth—escapes the theologian's notice. Hence, constant dialogue with living faiths (Jewish, Muslim, Buddhist, and Hindu) as well as secular knowledge are hallmarks of this new way of doing Christian theology.

Christian theology can be confident about the truthfulness of its teaching, but in the aftermath of the Enlightenment, it is not possible to reach modernity's dream of "indubitable certainty." A modest goal is "proper confidence," to cite L. Newbigin's essay title. While intellectually rigorous in its pursuit, certainty in theology—as in other disciplines in the humanities—readily acknowledges its relatedness to a wide and comprehensive network of basic beliefs that sustains our thinking. Ultimately, it awaits the eschatological confirmation of the final divine manifestation. It is deeply value-driven and has to do with the deepest and most ultimate questions of death and life. In that sense, it is living by faith, rather than seeing. On the other hand, as an academic discipline, theology's claims, including claims concerning revelation, also have to be subjected to proper critical scrutiny and debate. To theology, as well as philosophy and similar fields, disagreements and different viewpoints belong as an essential part of the inquiry. That is simply because theological "views are extremely wide-ranging beliefs about the nature of things in general; they aim at unrestricted generality and comprehensiveness."[1]

While faith and reason should not be juxtaposed, ultimately theological convictions and beliefs are just that: *convictions* and beliefs. They are person related. The American philosopher William James's classic essay "The Will to Believe" sets forth some characteristics of a commitment to believe when one is faced with a lack of conclusive evidence. The three basic conditions James outlines are that, first, the decision to believe does not leave any choices ("belief is forced") because of its urgency; second, that it makes a vital difference in life; and third, that it presents itself as a plausible or realistic option.[2] It is easy to see the application of James's reasoning to the discussion of certainty with regard to revelation and faith. Although there is no conclusive evidence available—and in this sense, to quote Kierkegaard, the believer lives in "objective

1. Keith Ward, *Religion and Revelation: A Theology of Revelation in the World's Religions* (Oxford: Clarendon, 1994), 12.

2. William James, "The Will to Believe," in *"The Will to Believe" and Other Essays in Popular Philosophy* [1897], *and Human Immortality* [1898] (Mineola, NY: Dover, 1956), 1–31 (see esp. 1–4 for a brief presentation and discussion of these conditions). I am indebted to Ward (*Religion and Revelation*, 26–27) for turning my attention to this essay for the consideration of this topic.

uncertainty"—the call of the gospel comes to one's life as a total call for surrender. Even when the intellectual and rational homework is done, that alone will persuade no one to surrender, particularly when the Christian gospel also calls for moral obedience, similarly to Jewish and Islamic traditions.

In his discussion James refers to French philosopher Blaise Pascal's famous wager metaphor, which introduces the concept of risk as well—but risk worth taking. Advises the French philosopher: "Let us weigh the gain and the loss in wagering that God is. Let us estimate these two chances. If you gain, you gain all; if you lose, you lose nothing. Wager, then, without hesitation that He is."[3] The recommendation to take up this wager is another fitting way of repeating the message of this epilogue: "In the End—the Beginning."

3. Blaise Pascal, "Of the Necessity of the Wager," in *Pensées*, trans. W. F. Trotter (1944 [1690]), section 3, citation in #233.

Bibliography

Abdalla, Mohamad. "Ibn Khaldūn on the Fate of Islamic Science after the 11th Century." In *ISHCP* 3:29–38.

Abd-Allah, Umar F. "Do Christians and Muslims Worship the Same God?" *Christian Century* 121, no. 17 (August 24, 2004).

Abdulaziz, Daftari. "Mulla Sadra and the Mind-Body Problem: A Critical Assessment of Sadra's Approach to the Dichotomy of Soul and Spirit." PhD diss., Durham University, 2010. http://etheses.dur.ac.uk/506/.

Abe, Gabriel Oyedele. "Redemption, Reconciliation, Propitiation: Salvation Terms in an African Milieu." *Journal of Theology for Southern Africa* 95 (1996): 3–12.

Abe, Masao. *Buddhism and Interfaith Dialogue*. Edited by Steven Heine. Honolulu: University of Hawai'i Press, 1995.

———. "Kenotic God and Dynamic Sunyata." In *Divine Emptiness and Historical Fullness: A Buddhist-Jewish-Christian Conversation with Masao Abe*, edited by Christopher Ives, 25–90. Valley Forge, PA: Trinity, 1995.

Abelson, Joshua. *The Immanence of God in Rabbinical Literature*. London: Macmillan, 1912.

Abhedananda, Swami. *Vedanta Philosophy*. Calcutta: Ramakrishna Vedanta Math, 1959.

Abraham, William J. "Christian Perfection." Chapter 34 in *The Oxford Handbook of Methodist Studies*, edited by James E. Kirby and William J. Abraham, 587–601. Oxford: Oxford University Press, 2014.

Abrahams, Israel, Jacob Haberman, and Charles Manekin. "Belief." In *EJ* 3:290–94.

Adams, Daniel J. "Universal Salvation? A Study in Myanmar Christian Theology." *Asia Journal of Theology* 22 (2008): 219–36.

Ad Gentes: Decree on the Mission Activity of the Church (Vatican II). http://www.vatican.va/archive/hist_councils/ii_vatican_council/documents/vat-ii_decree_19651207_ad-gentes_en.html.

Adiswarananda, Swami. "Hinduism." Part 2. Ramakrishna-Vivekananda Center of New York, 1996. http://www.ramakrishna.org/activities/message/message15.htm.

Afsaruddin, Asma. "Death, Resurrection, and Human Destiny in Islamic Tradition." In *Death, Resurrection, and Human Destiny: Christian and Muslim Perspectives*, edited by David Marshall and Lucinda Mosher, 43–60. Washington, DC: Georgetown University Press, 2014.

Ahluwalia, Kewal. "Shudhi Movement: 85th Shardhanand Shudhi Divas—December 23rd." http://www.aryasamaj.com/enews/2012/jan/4.htm.

Ahn, Byung Mu. "Jesus and the People (Minjung)." In *Asian Faces of Jesus*, edited by R. S. Sugirtharajah, 163–72. Maryknoll, NY: Orbis, 1993.

———. "Minjung: Suffering in Korea." In *The Lord of Life: Theological Explorations of the Theme "Jesus Christ—the Life of the World,"* edited by William H. Lazareth. Geneva: WCC, 1983.

Alam, Mehmood. "Signs of Hour." July 23, 2014. Darussalam. http://darussalamblog.com/signs-of-hour/.

Albrecht, Daniel E. *Rites in the Spirit: A Ritual Approach to Pentecostal/Charismatic Spirituality*. Sheffield: Sheffield Academic, 1999.

Alexander, Kimberly Ervin. *Pentecostal Healing: Models in Theology and Practice*. Dorset, UK: Deo, 2006.

Alfeyev, Hieromonk Hilarion. *Christ the Conqueror of Hell: The Descent into Hades from an Orthodox Perspective*. New York: St. Vladimir's Seminary Press, 2009.

———. "Eschatology." In *The Cambridge Companion to Orthodox Christian Theology*, edited by Mary B. Cunningham and Elizabeth Theokritoff, 107–20. Cambridge: Cambridge University Press, 2008.

Alston, William P. *Perceiving God: The Epistemology of Religious Experience*. Ithaca, NY: Cornell University Press, 1991.

Altekar, A. S. *The Position of Women in Hindu Traditions: From Prehistoric Times to the Present Day*. 2nd ed. Delhi: Motilal Banarsidass, 2005.

Amaladass, Anand. "Viewpoints: Dialogue in India." *Journal of Hindu-Christian Dialogue* 1, no. 7 (June 1988): 7–8.

Amaladoss, Michael, SJ. "Other Scriptures and the Christian." *Indian Theological Studies* 22, no. 1 (March 1985): 62–78.

Amstutz, Mark R. *The Healing of Nations: The Promise and Limits of Political Forgiveness*. Lanham, MD: Rowman & Littlefield, 2005.

Anatolios, Khaled. *Athanasius*. Early Church Fathers. London: Routledge, 2004.

Anguttara Nikaya. In *The Book of the Gradual Sayings (Anguttara Nikaya) or More-Numbered-Suttas*. Edited and translated by F. L. Woodward. Oxford: Pali Text Society, 1992.

Anselm of Canterbury. *Proslogium*. Chapter 2 in *Anselm of Canterbury: The Major Works*, edited by G. R. Evans and Brian Davies. Oxford: Oxford University Press, 1998.

Aquinas, Thomas. *Summa contra Gentiles*. Edited by Joseph Kenny, OP. Translated by Anton C. Pegis et al. New York: Hanover House, 1955–1957. http://www.dhspriory.org/thomas/ContraGentiles.htm.

Ariel, Yaakov. "Radical Millennial Movements in Contemporary Judaism in Israel." In *OHM*, 1–15.

Aristotle. *The Complete Works of Aristotle*. Edited by Jonathan Barnes. 2 vols. Princeton: Princeton University Press, 1984.

———. *On the Soul*. Translated by J. A. Smith. Internet Classics Archive. http://classics.mit.edu//Aristotle/soul.html.

Arminius, Jacobus. "On Predestination." In *Works of James Arminius*, vol. 1. http://www.ccel.org/ccel/arminius/works1.iii.ii.html.

Arnold, Bill T. "Old Testament Eschatology and the Rise of Apocalypticism." In *OHE*, 23–39.

Arnold, Clinton E. *Ephesians: Power and Magic—the Concept of Power in Ephesians in Light of Its Historical Setting*. Cambridge: Cambridge University Press, 1989.

———. *Powers of Darkness: Principalities and Powers in Paul's Letters*. Downers Grove, IL: InterVarsity Press, 1992.

Asvaghosa. *Açvaghosha's Discourse on the Awakening of Faith in the Mahâyâna*. Translated by Teitaro Suzuki. 1900. Available at http://sacred-texts.com/bud/taf/index.htm.

Attwood, Jayarava Michael. "Did King Ajātasattu Confess to the Buddha, and Did the Buddha Forgive Him?" *Journal of Buddhist Ethics* (n.d.): 279–307. http://www.academia.edu/1327910/Did_King_Aj%C4%81tasattu_Confess_to_the_Buddha_and_did_the_Buddha_Forgive_Him.

Augustine. *The Literal Meaning of Genesis*. Translated and annotated by John Hammond Taylor, SJ. 2 vols. Ancient Christian Writers 41–42. Edited by Johannes Quasten, Walter J. Burghardt, and Thomas Comerford Lawler. New York: Paulist, 1982.

———. *On the Free Choice of Will*. Translated by Thomas Williams. Indianapolis: Hackett, 1993.

Aune, David E. "Repentance." In *ER* 11:7755–60.

———. *Revelation 6–16*. Word Biblical Commentary. Dallas: Word, 1986.

Averill, James R., George Catlin, and Kyum Koo Chon. *Rules of Hope*. New York: Springer, 1990.

Avicenna's Psychology [*De Anima*; *The Treatise on the Soul*]. Translated and edited by Fazlur Rahman. Oxford: Oxford University Press, 1952.

Aviezer, Nathan. "The Anthropic Principle: What Is It and Why Is It Meaningful to the Believing Jew?" *Jewish Action* (Spring 1999): n.p. http://www.ou.org/publications/ja/5759spring/anthropic.pdf.

Ayoub, [Mahmud] Mahmoud [Mustafa]. "Creation or Evolution? The Reception of Darwinism in Modern Arab Thought." In *SRPW*, chap. 11.

———. "Repentance in the Islamic Tradition." In *RCP*, 96–121.

———. "Towards an Islamic Christology, II: The Death of Jesus, Reality or Delusion (a Study in the Death of Jesus in Tafsīr Literature)." *Muslim World* 70, no. 2 (1980): 91–121.

Bae, Choon-Sup. *Ancestor Worship: The Challenges It Poses to the Christianity Mission and Ministry*. Saarbrücken, Germany: VDM Verlag, 2008.

Bainbridge, William Sims. "The Sociology of Conversion." In *HRC*, 178–91.

Baker, Lynne Rudder. "Persons and the Metaphysics of Resurrection." In *Personal Identity and Resurrection: How Do We Survive Our Death?*, edited by Georg Gasser, 161–76. Surrey, UK: Ashgate, 2010.

Baker, Mark D., and Joel B. Green. *Recovering the Scandal of the Cross: Atonement in New Testament and Contemporary Contexts*. Downers Grove, IL: InterVarsity Press, 2000.

Baker-Fletcher, Garth Kasimu. *Xodus: An African American Male Journey*. Minneapolis: Fortress, 1996.

Baker-Fletcher, Karen. *Dancing with God: The Trinity from a Womanist Perspective*. St. Louis: Chalice, 2006.

Baker-Fletcher, Karen, and Garth Kasimu Baker-Fletcher. *My Sister, My Brother: Womanist and Xodus God-Talk*. Maryknoll, NY: Orbis, 1997; Eugene, OR: Wipf & Stock, 2002.

Balasubramanian, R. "The Advaita View of Death and Immortality." In *DIRW*, 109–27.

Balasuriya, Tissa. *The Eucharist and Human Liberation*. Maryknoll, NY: Orbis, 1977.

Bales, Kevin. *Disposable People: New Slavery in the Global Economy*. 2nd ed. Berkeley: University of California Press, 2004.

Bammel, Ernst. "Christian Origins in Jewish Tradition." *New Testament Studies* 13, no. 4 (1967): 317–35.

Bar, Shmuel. "Sunnis and Shiites: Between Rapprochement and Conflict." In *Current Trends in Islamist Ideology*, edited by Hillel Fradkin et al., 2:87–96. Washington, DC: Center on Islam, Democracy, and the Future of the Muslim World, Hudson Institute, 2005.

Barbour, Ian G. *Religion in the Age of Science*. New York: Harper & Row, 1990.

Barker, Gregory A., and Stephen E. Gregg. "Muslim Perceptions of Jesus: Key Issues." In *JBC*.

Barnes, L. Philip. "Talking Politics, Talking Forgiveness." *Scottish Journal of Theology* 64 (2011): 64–79.

Barnes, Michel René. "The Beginning and End of Early Christian Pneumatology." *Augustinian Studies* 39, no. 2 (2008): 169–86.

Barrow, John D. *New Theories of Everything*. Oxford: Oxford University Press, 2007.

Barrow, John D., and Frank J. Tipler. *The Anthropic Cosmological Principle*. Oxford: Oxford University Press, 1986.

Barth, Karl. *The Epistle to the Romans*. Translated by Edwyn C. Hoskyns. 6th ed. London: Oxford University Press, 1968 [1933].

Bartlett, Anthony W. *Cross Purposes: The Violent Grammar of Christian Atonement*. Harrisburg, PA: Trinity, 2000.

Barua, Ankur. "The Dialectic of Divine 'Grace' and 'Justice' in St. Augustine and Sri-Vaisnavism." *Religions of South Asia* 4, no. 1 (2010): 45–65.

Bassis, Kinrei. "Forgiveness." n.p. Accessed March 14, 2014. http://www.berkeleybuddhistpriory.org/pages/articles/online_articles/forgiveness.htm.

Batchelor, Martine. "Meditation and Mindfulness." *Contemporary Buddhism* 12, no. 1 (May 2011): 157–64.

Batchelor, Martine, and Kerry Brown, eds. *Buddhism and Ecology*. London: Cassell, 1992.

Bathrellos, Demetrios. "The Sinlessness of Jesus: A Theological Exploration in the Light of Trinitarian Theology." Chapter 9 in *Trinitarian Soundings in Systematic Theology*, edited by P. L. Metzger, 113–26. New York: T&T Clark, 2005.

Bauckham, Richard. *The Theology of Jürgen Moltmann*. Edinburgh: T&T Clark, 1995.

———. "Universalism: An Historical Survey." *Themelios* 4 (1978): 47–54.

Bauckham, Richard, and Trevor A. Hart. *Hope against Hope: Christian Eschatology at the Turn of the Millennium*. Grand Rapids: Eerdmans, 1999.

Bauman, Zygmunt. *Globalization: The Human Consequences*. New York: Columbia University Press, 1998.

Beachy, A. J. *The Concept of Grace in the Radical Reformers*. Nieuwkoop: De Graaf, 1977.

Bebawi, George H. "Atonement and Mercy: Islam between Athanasius and Anselm." In *Atonement Today*, edited by John Goldingay. London: SPCK, 1995.

Beck, Guy L. "Fire in the Ātman: Repentance in Hinduism." In *RCP*, 76–95.

Beck, Ulrich. *Risk Society: Towards a New Modernity*. Translated by Mark Ritter. London: Sage, 1992.

Bediako, Kwame. *Jesus in African Culture: A Ghanaian Perspective*. Accra: Asampa, 1990.

Bell, Rob. *Love Wins: A Book about Heaven, Hell, and the Fate of Every Person Who Ever Lived*. New York: HarperOne, 2012.

Bennett, Clinton. *Understanding Christian-Muslim Relations: Past and Present*. London: Continuum, 2008.

Berdyaev, Nicolas. *Truth and Revelation*. Translated by R. M. French. New York: Collier, 1962.

Bergen, Jeremy M. "The Holy Spirit in the World." *Vision: A Journal for Church and Theology* 13, no. 1 (Spring 2012): 84–92.

Berger, Peter L. *A Rumor of Angels: Modern Society and the Rediscovery of the Supernatural*. Garden City, NY: Doubleday, 1969; Harmondsworth, UK: Penguin, 1970.

Bering, Jesse M. "The Folk Psychology of Souls." *Behavioral and Brain Sciences* 29 (2006): 453–98.

Berkhof, Hendrikus. *Christ and Powers*. Translated by John H. Yoder. Scottdale, PA: Herald Press, 1962.

Berkhof, Louis. *Systematic Theology*. Grand Rapids: Eerdmans, 1996.

Berzin, Alexander. "A Buddhist View of Islam." In *Islam and Inter-Faith Relations*, edited by P. Schmidt-Leukel and L. Ridgeon, 225–51. London: SCM, 2007.

Bharat, Sandy. "Hindu Perspectives on Jesus." In *The Blackwell Companion to Jesus*, edited by Delbert Burkett. Oxford: Wiley-Blackwell, 2011.

Bharathi, B. S. "Spirit Possession and Healing Practices in a South Indian Fishing Community." *Man in India* 73, no. 4 (1968): 343–52.

Bickerton, Derek. "Did Syntax Trigger the Human Revolution?" In *Rethinking the Human Revolution: New Behavioural and Biological Perspectives on the Origin and Dispersal of Modern Humans*, edited by Paul Mellars, Katie Boyle, Ofer Bar-Yosef, and Chris Stringer, 99–105. Cambridge: Short Run Press, 2007.

Bieler, Andrea, and Luise Schottroff. *The Eucharist: Bodies, Bread, and Resurrection*. Minneapolis: Fortress, 2007.

Birch, C., W. Eaking, and J. B. McDaniel, eds. *Liberating Life: Contemporary Approaches to Ecological Theology*. Maryknoll, NY: Orbis, 1990.

Bird, Michael F. "Progressive Reformed View." In *Justification: Five Views*, edited by James K. Beilby and Paul Rhodes Eddy, 131–57. Downers Grove, IL: IVP Academic, 2011.

Birnbaum, Raoul. *The Healing Buddha*. Boulder, CO: Shambhala, 1989.

Bleich, David J. "Establishing Criteria of Death." In *Ethical Issues in Death and Dying*, edited by Tom L. Beauchamp and Robert M. Veatch, 28–32. 2nd ed. Upper Saddle River, NJ: Prentice Hall, 1996.

Bloch, Maurice. *Prey into Hunter: The Politics of Religious Experience*. Cambridge: Cambridge University Press, 1992.

Blocher, Henri A. "The Sacrifice of Jesus Christ: The Current Theological Situation." *European Journal of Theology* 8, no. 1 (1999): 23–36.

Bloesch, Donald G. *The Church: Sacraments, Worship, Ministry, Mission*. Downers Grove, IL: InterVarsity Press, 2002.

———. *Jesus Christ: Savior and Lord*. Downers Grove, IL: InterVarsity Press, 1997.

———. *The Last Things: Resurrection, Judgment, Glory*. Downers Grove, IL: InterVarsity Press, 2004.

Bloom, Alfred. "Jesus in the Pure Land." Chapter 3 in *JWF*.

Blue, Ken. *Authority to Heal*. Downers Grove, IL: InterVarsity Press, 1987.

Boersma, Hans. *Violence, Hospitality, and the Cross: Reappropriating the Atonement Tradition*. Grand Rapids: Baker Academic, 2006.

Boff, Leonardo. *Ecclesiogenesis: The Base Communities Reinvent the Church*. Maryknoll, NY: Orbis, 1986.

———. *Ecology and Liberation: A New Paradigm*. Maryknoll, NY: Orbis, 1995.

———. *Jesus Christ Liberator: A Critical Christology for Our Time*. Translated by Patrick Hughes. Maryknoll, NY: Orbis, 1978.

———. *Liberating Grace*. Translated by John Drury. Maryknoll, NY: Orbis, 1979.

———. *Trinity and Society*. Translated by Paul Burns. Maryknoll, NY: Orbis, 1988.

———. *Was kommt nachher? Das Leben nach dem Tode*. Translated from Portuguese to German by Horst Goldstein. Salzburg: Otto Müller Verlag, 1982.

Boisvert, Kate Grayson. *Religion and the Physical Sciences*. Westport, CT: Greenwood, 2008.

Bokovay, W. Kelly. "The Relationship of Physical Healing to the Atonement." *Didaskalia* 3, no. 1 (October 1991): 24–39.

Bolt, Peter G. "Jesus, the Daimons and the Dead." Chapter 5 in *The Unseen World: Christian Reflections on Angels, Demons, and the Heavenly Realm*, edited by Anthony N. S. Lane. Carlisle, UK: Paternoster, 1996.

Bonhoeffer, Dietrich. *Christology*. Translated by John Bowden. London: Collins, 1966.

———. *Christ the Center*. Translated by John Bowden. New York: Harper & Row, 1960.

Book of Common Prayer and Administration of the Sacraments and Other Rites and Ceremonies of the Church: Together with the Psalter or Psalms of David according to the Use of the Episcopal Church. New York: Church Hymnal Corp., 1979.

Boonyakiat, Satanun. "A Christian Theology of Suffering in the Context of Theravada Buddhism in Thailand." PhD diss., Fuller Theological Seminary, School of Theology, 2009.

Borg, Marcus J. *Jesus, a New Vision: Spirit, Culture, and the Life of Discipleship*. San Francisco: Harper & Row, 1987.

Boslooper, Thomas. *The Virgin Birth*. London: SCM, 1962.

Bowker, John Westerdale. *Problems of Suffering in Religions of the World*. Cambridge: Cambridge University Press, 1970.

Boyd, Gregory A. *God at War: The Bible and Spiritual Conflict*. Downers Grove, IL: InterVarsity Press, 1997.

———. *Satan and the Problem of Evil: Constructing a Trinitarian Warfare Theodicy*. Downers Grove, IL: InterVarsity Press, 2001.

Boyd, Robin H. S. *An Introduction to Indian Christian Theology*. Madras: Christian Literature Society, 1969.

Braarvig, Jens. "The Buddhist Hell: An Early Instance of the Idea?" *Numen: International Review for the History of Religions* 56, nos. 2–3 (2009): 254–81.

Braaten, Carl E. *Justification: The Article by Which the Church Stands or Falls*. Minneapolis: Fortress, 1990.

Braaten, Carl E., and Robert W. Jenson, eds. *In One Body through the Cross: The Princeton Proposal for Christian Unity*. Grand Rapids: Eerdmans, 2003.

———. *Union with Christ: The New Finnish Interpretation of Luther*. Grand Rapids: Eerdmans, 1998.

Bracken, Joseph A., SJ, ed. *World without End: Christian Eschatology from a Process Perspective*. Grand Rapids: Eerdmans, 2005.

Braswell, George W., Jr. *Islam: Its Prophet, Peoples, Politics, and Power*. Nashville: Broadman and Holman, 1996.

Brekke, Torkel. "Conversion in Buddhism?" In *Religious Conversion in India*, edited by Rowena Robinson and Sathianathan Clarke, 181–91. New York: Oxford University Press, 2007.

Brill, Alan. *Judaism and Other Religions: Models of Understanding*. New York: Palgrave Macmillan, 2010.

Brinner, William M., and Devin J. Stewart. "Conversion." In *The Oxford Encyclopedia of the Islamic World*, edited by John L. Esposito. Oxford: Oxford University Press, 2009; *Oxford Islamic Studies Online*, http://www.oxfordislamicstudies.com/article/opr/t236/e0165.

Brock, Rita Nakashima. *Journeys by Heart: A Christology of Erotic Power*. New York: Crossroad, 1988.

Brockington, John. *Hinduism and Christianity*. New York: St. Martin's, 1992.

Brothers, Leslie A. *Friday's Footprints: How Society Shapes the Human Mind*. New York: Oxford University Press, 1997.

Brown, Colin. *Jesus in European Protestant Thought (1778–1860)*. Durham, NC: Labyrinth, 1985.

Brown, Dee. *Bury My Heart at Wounded Knee*. New York: Holt, Rinehart & Winston, 1971.

Brown, Joanne Carlson, and Rebecca Parker. "For God So Loved the World." In *Christianity, Patriarchy, and Abuse: A Feminist Critique*, edited by J. Carlson Brown and C. R. Bohn, 1–30. New York: Pilgrim, 1989.

Brown, Michael L. *Israel's Divine Healer*. Grand Rapids: Zondervan, 1995.

Brown, Raymond E. *An Introduction to the New Testament*. New York: Doubleday, 1997.

———. *The Virginal Conception and Bodily Resurrection of Jesus*. New York: Paulist, 1992.

Brown, Warren S. "Cognitive Contributions to Soul." In *WHS*, 99–125.

Brown, Warren S., and Carla Caetano. "Conversion, Cognition, and Neuropsychology." In *HRC*, 147–58.

Brown, Warren S., and Brad D. Strawn. *The Physical Nature of Christian Life: Neuroscience, Psychology, and the Church*. Cambridge: Cambridge University Press, 2012.

Browning, George. "Sabbath Reflections 5: Capitalism and Inequity versus a Gospel Mandate." Anglican Communion Environmental Network, 2012. http://acen.anglicancommunion.org/media/61249/Sabbath-Study-5.pdf.

Brueggemann, Walter. *The Covenanted Self: Explorations in Law and Covenant*. Minneapolis: Augsburg Fortress, 1999.

———. *The Land: Place as Gift, Promise, and Challenge in Biblical Faith*. Overtures to Biblical Theology 1. Philadelphia: Fortress, 1977.

———. "The Liturgy of Abundance, the Myth of Scarcity." *Christian Century*, March 24–31, 1999. https://www.religion-online.org/article/the-liturgy-of-abundance-the-myth-of-scarcity/.

———. *Theology of the Old Testament: Testimony, Dispute, Advocacy*. Minneapolis: Augsburg Fortress, 1997.

Buckser, Andrew, and Stephen D. Glazier, eds. *The Anthropology of Religious Conversion*. Lanham, MD: Rowman & Littlefield, 2003.

Buenting, Joel, ed. *The Problem of Hell: A Philosophical Anthology*. Surrey, UK: Ashgate, 2009.

Bulgakov, Sergius. *The Comforter*. Translated by Boris Jakim. Grand Rapids: Eerdmans, 2004.

Bultmann, Rudolf. "New Testament and Mythology." In *Kerygma and Myth: A Theological Debate*, edited by Hans Werner Bartsch, 1–44. New York: Harper & Row, 1961.

Burgess, Stanley M. *The Holy Spirit: Ancient Christian Traditions*. Peabody, MA: Hendrickson, 1984.

———. *The Holy Spirit: Eastern Christian Traditions*. Peabody, MA: Hendrickson, 1989.

———. *The Holy Spirit: Medieval Roman Catholic and Reformation Traditions*. Peabody, MA: Hendrickson, 1997.

Burgess, Stanley M., and Eduard M. van der Maas, eds. *New International Dictionary of Charismatic and Pentecostal Movements*. Revised and expanded ed. Grand Rapids: Zondervan, 2010.

Burton, David. "A Buddhist Perspective." In *OHRD*, 321–36.

Cabezón, José Ignacio. "Buddhism and Science: On the Nature of the Dialogue." In *Buddhism and Science: Breaking New Ground*, edited by B. Alan Wallace, 35–68. New York: Columbia University Press, 2003.

———. "Buddhist Views of Jesus." Chapter 1 in *JWF*.

Cahill, Lisa Sowle. *Sex, Gender, and Christian Ethics*. Cambridge: Cambridge University Press, 1996.

Caird, G. B. *Principalities and Powers: A Study in Pauline Theology*. Oxford: Clarendon, 1956.

Calvin, John. *Commentary on Psalms 93–119*. In *Commentary on the Psalms*, translated by James Anderson. Vol. 4. Grand Rapids: Christian Classics Ethereal Library, n.d. https://www.ccel.org/ccel/calvin/calcom11.html.

———. *Commentary on the Epistle of Paul the Apostle to the Romans*. Available at https://www.ccel.org/ccel/calvin/calcom11.html.

Campbell, Douglas A. "Reconciliation in Paul: The Gospel of Negation and Transcendence in Galatians 3:28." In *The Theology of Reconciliation*, edited by Colin E. Gunton, 39–65. London: T&T Clark, 2003.

Campese, Gioacchino, CS. "The Irruption of Migrants: Theology of Migration in the 21st Century." *Theological Studies* 73 (2012): 3–32.

Candasiri, Sister Ajahn. "Jesus: A Theravadan Perspective." Chapter 2 in *JWF*.

Cantor, Geoffrey, and Marc Swetlitz, eds. *Jewish Tradition and the Challenge of Darwinism*. Chicago: University of Chicago Press, 2006.

Carman, John B. *Majesty and Meekness: A Comparative Study of Contrast and Harmony in the Concept of God*. Grand Rapids: Eerdmans, 1994.

Carter, J. Kameron. *Race: A Theological Account*. Oxford: Oxford University Press, 2008.

Cartmill, Matt, and Fred H. Smith. *The Human Lineage*. Hoboken, NJ: Wiley-Blackwell, 1989.

Cavanaugh, William T. *Torture and Eucharist: Theology, Politics, and the Body of Christ*. Oxford: Blackwell, 1998.

Cha, Peter. "Ethnic Identity Formation and Participation in Immigrant Churches: Second-Generation Korean American Experiences." In *Korean Americans and Their Religions: Pilgrims and Missionaries from a Different Shore*, edited by Ho-Youn Kwon, Kwang Chung Kim, and R. Stephen Warner, 141–56. University Park: Pennsylvania State University Press, 2001.

Chan, Simon K. H. "Sanctification." In *GDT*, 789–91.

Chaplin, Jonathan. *Multiculturalism: A Christian Retrieval*. London: Theos, 2011.

Chappell, D. W. "Buddhist Interreligious Dialogue: To Build a Global Community." In *The Sound of Liberating Truth: Buddhist-Christian Dialogues in Honor of Frederick J. Streng*, edited by S. B. King and P. O. Ingam, 3–35. Richmond, UK: Curzon, 1999.

Chapple, Christopher. "Asceticism and the Environment: Jainism, Buddhism, and Yoga." *Cross Currents* 57, no. 4 (2008): 514–25.

Charter of the United Nations (June 26, 1945). Preamble. http://www.un.org/en/sections/un-charter/introductory-note/index.html.

Chatterjee, Susmita. "Acharya Jagadish Chandra Bose: Looking beyond the Idiom." Chapter 8 in *Science, Spirituality, and the Modernization of India*, edited by Makarand Paranjape, 3–14. Anthem South Asian Studies. London: Anthem, 2008.

Chishti, Saadia Khawar Khan. "*Fiṭra*: An Islamic Model for Humans and the Environment." In *I&E*, 67–82.

Chittick, William C. "Muslim Eschatology." In *OHE*, 132–50.

Chopra, Deepak. *Journey into Healing: Awakening the Wisdom within You*. London: Ebury, 2010.

Christensen, M. "Theosis and Sanctification: John Wesley's Reformulation of a Patristic Doctrine." *Wesleyan Theological Journal* 31, no. 2 (Fall 1996): 71–94.

"The Church as Community of Common Witness to the Kingdom of God." *Reformed World* 57 (2007): 105–207. Report of the third phase of the International Theological Dialogue between the Catholic Church and the World Alliance of Reformed Churches (1998–2005).

Clark, Victoria. *Allies for Armageddon: The Rise of Christian Zionism.* New Haven: Yale University Press, 2007.

Clarke, Sathianathan, Deenabandhu Manchala, and Philip Vinod Peacock, eds. *Dalit Theology in the Twenty First Century: Discordant Voices, Discerning Pathways.* New Delhi: Oxford University Press, 2010.

Clayton, Philip C. "The Case for Christian Panentheism." *Dialog* 37, no. 3 (Summer 1988): 201–8.

———. "Eschatology as Metaphysics under the Guise of Hope." In *World without End: Essays in Honor of Marjorie Suchocki*, edited by Joseph Bracken, 128–49. Grand Rapids: Eerdmans, 2005.

———. "The Impossible Possibility: Divine Causes in the World of Nature." In *God, Life, and the Cosmos: Christian and Islamic Perspectives*, edited by Ted Peters, Muzaffar Iqbal, and Syed Nomanul Haq, 249–80. Surrey, UK: Ashgate, 2002.

———. *Mind and Emergence: From Quantum to Consciousness.* Oxford: Oxford University Press, 2004.

———. "Neuroscience, the Person, and God: An Emergentist Account." In *NP*, 181–214.

———. "The Spirit in Evolution and in Nature." Chapter 13 in *IRDSW*, 187–96.

Cleary, J. C. "Trikaya and Trinity: The Mediation of the Absolute." *Buddhist-Christian Studies* 6 (1986): 63–78.

Clifford, Anne M. "Creation." In *Systematic Theology: Roman Catholic Perspectives*, edited by Francis Schüssler Fiorenza and John P. Galvin, 1:193–248. Minneapolis: Fortress, 1991.

Clooney, Francis X., SJ. *Comparative Theology: Deep Learning across Religious Borders.* West Sussex, UK: Wiley-Blackwell, 2010.

———. "Trinity and Hinduism." In *Cambridge Companion to the Trinity*, edited by Peter C. Phan, 309–24. Cambridge: Cambridge University Press, 2011.

Clouse, Robert G. "Fundamentalist Eschatology." In *OHE*, 263–77.

Coakley, Sarah. "Introduction: Religion and the Body." In *RB*, 1–12.

———. "What Does Chalcedon Solve and What Does It Not? Some Reflections on the Status and Meaning of the Chalcedonian 'Definition.'" In *The Incarnation: An Interdisciplinary Symposium on the Incarnation of the Son of God*, edited by Stephen T. Davis et al., 143–63. Oxford: Oxford University Press, 2004.

Cobb, John B., Jr. *Christ in a Pluralistic Age.* Philadelphia: Westminster, 1975.

Cobb, John B., Jr., and David Ray Griffin. *Process Theology: An Introductory Exposition.* Philadelphia: Westminster, 1976.

Cohen, Hermann. *Religion of Reason out of the Sources of Judaism.* Translation and introduction by Simon Kaplan. 2nd rev. ed. New York: Frederick Ungar, 1972 [1919].

Cohn-Sherbok, Daniel. "Death and Immortality in the Jewish Tradition." In *DIRW*, 24–36.

Cohon, Samuel S. *Essays in Jewish Theology.* Cincinnati: Hebrew Union College Press, 1987.

———. *Jewish Theology: A Historical and Systematic Interpretation of Judaism and Its Foundations*. Assen: van Gorcum, 1971.

Collins, John J. "Apocalyptic Eschatology in the Ancient World." In *OHE*, 40–55.

Collins, Kenneth J. "John Wesley and the Fear of Death as a Standard of Conversion." In *Conversion in the Wesleyan Tradition*, edited by Kenneth J. Collins and John H. Tyson, 56–68. Nashville: Abingdon, 2001.

Collins, Robin. "Evolution and Original Sin." In *Perspectives on Evolving Creation*, edited by K. B. Miller, 469–501. Grand Rapids: Eerdmans, 2003.

Comblin, José. *The Holy Spirit and Liberation*. Translated by Paul Burns. Maryknoll, NY: Orbis, 1989.

"A Common Word between Us and You." A Common Word. https://www.acommonword.com/the-acw-document/.

Cone, James H. *A Black Theology of Liberation*. 2nd ed. Twentieth anniversary ed. Maryknoll, NY: Orbis, 1986.

———. *God of the Oppressed*. Rev. ed. Maryknoll, NY: Orbis, 1997; original New York: Seabury, 1975.

Congar, Yves. *I Believe in the Holy Spirit*. Translated by David Smith. New York: Seabury, 1983. 3 vols. in 1, New York: Herder, 1997.

Conradie, Ernst M. "What Is the Place of the Earth in God's Economy? Doing Justice to Creation, Salvation and Consummation." In *Christian Faith and the Earth: Current Paths and Emerging Horizons in Ecotheology*, edited by Ernst M. Conradie, Sigurd Bergmann, Celia Deane-Drummond, and Denis Edwards, 65–96. London: Bloomsbury, 2014.

Cook, David. "Early Islamic and Classical Sunni and Shi'ite Apocalyptic Movements." In *OHM*, 267–83.

———. *Studies in Muslim Apocalyptic*. New York: Syracuse University Press, 2005.

Cook, Michael J. "Jewish Perspectives on Jesus." In *The Blackwell Companion to Jesus*, edited by Delbert Burkett. Oxford: Wiley-Blackwell, 2011.

Cooper, John W. *Body, Soul, and Life Everlasting: Biblical Anthropology and the Monism-Dualism Debate*. 2nd ed. Grand Rapids: Eerdmans, 2000.

———. *Panentheism: The Other God of the Philosophers—from Plato to the Present*. Grand Rapids: Baker Academic, 2006.

Copan, Paul, and William Lane Craig. *Creation out of Nothing: A Biblical, Philosophical, and Scientific Exploration*. Grand Rapids: Baker Academic, 2004.

Cornell, Vincent. "Listening to God through the Qur'an." In *Scriptures in Dialogue: Christians and Muslims Studying the Bible and the Qur'an Together*, edited by Michael Ipgrave, 36–62. London: Church House, 2004.

Couenhoven, Jesse. "Forgiveness and Restoration: A Theological Exploration." *Journal of Religion* 90, no. 2 (2010): 148–70.

Council of Trent, Fourth Session. "Decree concerning the Canonical Scriptures." In *The Canons and Decrees of the Sacred and Oecumenical Council of Trent*, translated by J. Waterworth. London: Dolman, 1848. http://history.hanover.edu/texts/trent/ct04.html.

Courtright, Paul B. "Worship and Devotional Life: Hindu Devotional Life." In *ER* 14:9820–26.

Coward, Harold. Introduction to *Experiencing Scripture in World Religions*, edited by H. Coward, 1–14. Maryknoll, NY: Orbis, 2000.

———. *Sacred Word and Sacred Text: Scripture in World Religions*. Maryknoll, NY: Orbis, 1988.

———. *Sin and Salvation in the World Religions: A Short Introduction*. Oxford: Oneworld, 2003.

Cragg, Kenneth. *The Call of the Minaret*. Rev. ed. Maryknoll, NY: Orbis, 1985 [1956].

———. "God and Salvation (an Islamic Study)." *Studia Missionalia* 29 (1980): 154–66.

———. *Jesus and the Muslim: An Exploration*. London: George Allen & Unwin, 1985; Oxford: Oneworld, 1999.

———. *The Privilege of Man: A Theme in Judaism, Islam, and Christianity*. London: Athlone Press, 1968.

Craig, William Lane. "The Middle Knowledge View." In *Divine Foreknowledge, Four Views*, edited by James K. Beilby and Paul R. Eddy, 119–43. Downers Grove, IL: InterVarsity Press, 2001.

———. *The Only Wise God*. Eugene, OR: Wipf & Stock, 1999.

———. *Time and Eternity: Exploring God's Relationship to Time*. Wheaton, IL: Crossway, 2001.

Crisp, Oliver D. *Divinity and Humanity: The Incarnation Reconsidered*. Cambridge: Cambridge University Press, 2007.

———. "The Letter and the Spirit of Barth's Doctrine of Election: A Response to Michael O'Neil." *Evangelical Quarterly* 79 (2007): 53–67.

Crockett, William, ed. *Four Views on Hell*. Grand Rapids: Zondervan, 1997.

Culpepper, Robert H. *Interpreting the Atonement*. Grand Rapids: Eerdmans, 1966.

Cunningham, David S. "The Trinity." In *The Cambridge Companion to Postmodern Theology*, edited by Kevin J. Vanhoozer, 186–202. Cambridge: Cambridge University Press, 2003.

Cunningham, Lawrence S. "Saints and Martyrs: Some Contemporary Considerations." *Theological Studies* 60 (1999): 529–37.

Daley, Brian E. "Eschatology in the Early Church Fathers." In *OHE*, 91–109.

———. "A Hope for Worms: Early Christian Hope." In *RTSA*, 136–64.

———. *The Hope of the Early Church: A Handbook of Patristic Eschatology*. Rev. ed. Peabody, MA: Hendrickson, 2003 [1991].

Damasio, Antonio R. *Descartes' Error: Emotion, Reason, and the Human Brain*. New York: Grosset/Putnam, 1994.

Danan, Julie Hilton. "The Divine Voice in Scripture: *Ruah ha-Kodesh* in Rabbinic Literature." PhD diss., University of Texas at Austin, 2009. http://repositories.lib.utexas.edu/bitstream/handle/2152/17297/dananj31973.pdf?sequence=2.

Daniel, P. S. *Hindu Response to Religious Pluralism*. Delhi: Kant Publications, 2000.

"Dark Matter." Berkeley Cosmology Group. http://astro.berkeley.edu/~mwhite/darkmatter/dm.html.

Darroll, Bryant M., and Christopher Lamb, eds. *Religious Conversion: Contemporary Practices and Controversies*. New York: Casell, 1999.

Darwin, Charles. *Origin of Species*. With additions and corrections from the sixth and last English edition. New York: D. Appleton, 1896. In volume 49 of *Great Books of the Western World*, edited by Robert Maynard Hutchins. Chicago: Encyclopaedia Britannica, 1952.

Davary, Bahar. "Forgiveness in Islam: Is It an Ultimate Reality?" *Ultimate Reality and Meaning: Interdisciplinary Studies in the Philosophy of Understanding* 27, no. 2 (2004): 127–41.

Davies, Paul C. *The Last Three Minutes: Conjectures about the Ultimate Fate of the Universe*. New York: Basic Books, 1994.

Davies, Steven L. *Jesus the Healer: Possession, Trance, and the Origins of Christianity*. New York: Continuum, 1995.

Davis, John R. *Poles Apart: Contextualizing the Gospel in Asia*. Bangalore, India: Theological Book Trust, 1998.

Dawkins, Richard. *The Selfish Gene*. Oxford: Oxford University Press, 1989 [1976].

D'Costa, Gavin. "The Holy Spirit and the World Religions." *Louvain Studies* 34, no. 4 (2010): 279–311.

———. *The Meeting of Religions and the Trinity*. Maryknoll, NY: Orbis, 2000.

Deacon, Terrence. "The Symbolic Threshold." In *The Symbolic Species: The Co-Evolution of Language and the Brain*, 79–92. New York: Norton, 1997.

De Lange, Nicholas. *An Introduction to Judaism*. Cambridge: Cambridge University Press, 2000.

Denny, Frederick Mathewson. *An Introduction to Islam*. 2nd ed. New York: Macmillan, 1994.

———. "The Meaning of Ummah in the Qur'ān." *History of Religions* 15, no. 1 (1975): 34–70.

———. "The Qur'anic Vocabulary of Repentance: Orientations and Attitudes." *Journal of the American Academy of Religion* 47, no. 4 (1979): 649–64.

Desai, Prakash N. *Health and Medicine in the Hindu Tradition: Continuity and Cohesion*. New York: Crossroad, 1989.

Descartes, René. *Meditations on the First Philosophy* [1641]. In *The Method, Meditations, and Philosophy of Descartes*, translated by John Veitch, introduced by Frank Sewall. Washington, DC: M. Walter Dunne, 1901. http://oll.libertyfund.org/titles/1698.

DeVries, Dawn. "What Is Conversion?" In *How Shall We Witness? Faithful Evangelism in a Reformed Tradition*, edited by Milton J. Coalter and Virgil Cruz, 27–46. Louisville: Westminster John Knox, 1995.

Dhavamony, Mariasusai. "Death and Immortality in Hinduism." In *DIRW*, 93–108.

Dionysius the Areopagite. *Works*. Translated by John Parker. 1899. http://www.tertullian.org/fathers/index.htm#Dionysius_the_Areopagite.

Dobkowski, Michael. "'A Time for War and Time for Peace': Teaching Religion and Violence in the Jewish Tradition." Chapter 2 in *TRV*.

Dogmatic Constitution on the Catholic Faith. Vatican I (1780). Session 3, chap. 3. http://www.papalencyclicals.net/Councils/ecum20.htm.

Doniger, Wendy. "The Body in Hindu Texts." In *RB*, 167–84.

———. *On Hinduism*. Oxford: Oxford University Press, 2014. Online ed.

———. *The Origins of Evil in Hindu Mythology*. Berkeley: University of California Press, 1976.

Dotti, Guido. "The Bose Monastery's Ecumenical Martyrology." Lecture, Bose, Italy, July 9, 2013. www.strasbourginstitute.org/wp-content/uploads/2013/08/Bose-Monastery.docx.

Douglas, Kelly Brown. *The Black Christ*. Maryknoll, NY: Orbis, 1994.

Driver, G. R. *Understanding the Atonement for the Mission of the Church*. Scottdale, PA: Herald Press, 1986.

Dufault-Hunter, Erin. *The Transformative Power of Faith: A Narrative Approach to Conversion*. Lanham, MD: Lexington Books, 2012.

Dulles, Avery. *Models of Revelation*. Maryknoll, NY: Orbis, 1992 [1983].

Dunn, James D. G. *Christology in the Making: A New Testament Inquiry into the Origins of the Doctrine of the Incarnation*. 2nd ed. London: SCM, 1989 [1980].

———. "The Justice of God: A Renewed Perspective on Justification by Faith." *Journal of Theological Studies*, n.s., 43 (1992): 1–22.

Dünzl, Franz. *A Brief History of the Doctrine of the Trinity in the Early Church*. Translated by John Bowden. London: T&T Clark, 2007.

Duquoc, Christian. *Provisional Churches: An Essay in Ecumenical Ecclesiology*. London: SCM, 1986.

Dwivedi, O. P. "Dharmic Ecology." In *Hinduism and Ecology: The Intersection of Earth, Sky, and Water.* Edited by Christopher Key Chapple and Mary Evelyn Tucker, 3–22. Religions of the World and Ecology. Cambridge, MA: Harvard University Press, 2000.

Dyrness, William A. *Poetic Theology: God and the Poetics of Everyday Life*. Grand Rapids: Eerdmans, 2011.

Dyson, Freeman J. *Disturbing the Universe*. New York: Harper & Row, 1979.

Eckel, Malcolm David. "Buddhism." In *Eastern Religions: Hinduism, Buddhism, Taoism, Confucianism, Shinto*, edited by Michael D. Coogan. Oxford: Oxford University Press, 2005.

———. "A Buddhist Approach to Repentance." In *RCP*, 122–42.

Eddy, Paul Rhodes, and James K. Beilby. "Introduction: Introducing Spiritual Warfare; A Survey of Key Issues and Debates." In *Understanding Spiritual Warfare: Four Views*, edited by James K. Beilby and Paul Rhodes Eddy, 1–45. Downers Grove, IL: InterVarsity Press, 2012.

Edwards, Denis. *Ecology at the Heart of Faith: The Change of Heart That Leads to a New Way of Living on Earth*. Maryknoll, NY: Orbis, 2007.

———. "Original Sin and Saving Grace in Evolutionary Context." In *EMB*, 377–92.

Edwards, Jonathan. *Freedom of the Will* [1754]. Vol. 1 of *The Works of Jonathan Edwards*, edited by Paul Ramsey. New Haven: Yale University Press, 2009.

Efron, Noah J. *Judaism and Science: A Historical Introduction*. Westport, CT: Greenwood, 2007.

Eliott, Jaklin A., ed. *Interdisciplinary Perspectives on Hope*. Hauppauge, NY: Nova Science, 2005.

Enns, Peter. *The Evolution of Adam: What the Bible Does and Doesn't Say about Human Origins*. Grand Rapids: Brazos, 2012.

Ensign-George, Barry. "Denomination as Ecclesiological Category: Sketching an Assessment." In *Denomination: Assessing an Ecclesiological Category*, edited by Paul M. Collins and Barry Ensign-George, 1–21. London: Bloomsbury, 2011.

Enuma Elish. In *The Babylonian Genesis: The Story of Creation*, by Alexander Heidel, 18–60. Chicago: University of Chicago Press, 1951.

Erickson, Millard J. *Christian Theology*. 3 vols. in 1. Grand Rapids: Baker, 1984.

Evans, James H., Jr. *We Have Been Believers: An African-American Systematic Theology*. Minneapolis: Fortress, 1992.

Faith and Order Commission of the World Council of Churches. "Faith and Order By-Laws, 3.1." In *Faith and Order at the Crossroads: Kuala Lumpur 2004; The Plenary Commission Meeting*, edited by Thomas F. Best. Faith and Order Paper no. 196. Geneva: WCC, 2005.

Federman, Asaf. "What Kind of Free Will Did the Buddha Teach?" *Philosophy East & West* 60, no. 1 (2010): 1–19.

Fee, Gordon D. "Baptism in the Holy Spirit: The Issue of Separability and Subsequence." *Pneuma* 7, no. 2 (1985): 87–99.

———. *The Disease of the Health and Wealth Gospels*. Vancouver, BC: Regent College Publishing, 2006 [1985].

———. *God's Empowering Presence: The Holy Spirit in the Letters of Paul*. Grand Rapids: Baker Academic, 2009 [1994].

Ferguson, Everett. *Baptism in the Early Church: History, Theology, and Liturgy in the First Five Centuries*. Grand Rapids: Eerdmans, 2009.

———. *The Church of Christ: A Biblical Ecclesiology for Today*. Grand Rapids: Eerdmans, 1997.

Fergusson, David. "Reclaiming the Doctrine of Sanctification." *Interpretation* 53, no. 4 (1999): 380–90.

Feuerbach, Ludwig. *The Essence of Christianity*. Translated by George Eliot. New York: Harper & Brothers, 1957.

Finger, Thomas N. *Christian Theology: An Eschatological Approach*. Scottdale, PA: Herald Press, 1985.

———. *A Contemporary Anabaptist Theology: Biblical, Historical, Constructive*. Downers Grove, IL: InterVarsity Press, 2004.

Finlan, Stephen. *Options on Atonement in Christian Thought*. Collegeville, MN: Glazier, 2007.

———. *Problems with Atonement: The Origins of, and Controversy about, the Atonement Doctrine*. Collegeville, MN: Liturgical Press, 2005.

Fischer, John Martin. "Putting Molinism in Its Place." In *Molinism: The Contemporary Debate*, edited by Kenneth Perszyk, 208–26. New York: Oxford University Press, 2011.

Flew, Anthony. "The Logic of Mortality." In *DIRW*, 171–87.

Flood, Gavin D. *An Introduction to Hinduism*. Cambridge: Cambridge University Press, 1996.

———."Jesus in Hinduism: Closing Reflection." In *JBC*.

Florovsky, Georges. "And Ascended into Heaven." *St. Vladimir's Seminary Quarterly* 2, no. 3 (1954): 23–28.

Foltz, Richard C. "Islamic Environmentalism: A Matter of Interpretation." In *I&E*, 249–79.

Ford, Lewis S. *The Lure of God: A Biblical Background for Process Theism*. Philadelphia: Fortress, 1978.

Fox, Matthew. *The Coming of the Cosmic Christ: The Healing of Mother Earth and the Birth of a Global Renaissance*. San Francisco: Harper & Row, 1988.

Freeman, David L., and Judith Z. Abrams, eds. *Illness and Health in the Jewish Tradition: Writings from the Bible to Today*. Philadelphia: Jewish Publication Society, 1999.

French, Peter A., et al. "Forgiveness and Resentment." *Midwest Studies in Philosophy* 7 (1982): 503–16.

Friedmann, Yohanan. *Tolerance and Coercion in Islam: Interfaith Relations in the Muslim Tradition*. Cambridge: Cambridge University Press, 2003.

Fromherz, Allen. "Judgment, Final." In *The Oxford Encyclopedia of the Islamic World*, edited by John L. Esposito. Oxford: Oxford University Press, 2009. http://www.oxfordislamicstudies.com/article/opr/t236/e1107.

Fuchs, Lorelei F., SA. *Koinonia and the Quest for an Ecumenical Ecclesiology: From Foundations through Dialogue to Symbolic Competence for Communionality*. Grand Rapids: Eerdmans, 2008.

Fudge, Edward W. *The Fire That Consumes: A Biblical and Historical Study of Final Punishment*. Houston: Providential, 1982.

Gaiser, Frederik J. *Healing in the Bible: Theological Insights for Christian Ministry*. Grand Rapids: Baker Academic, 2010.

Gandhi, Mohandas K. *The Message of Jesus Christ*. Bombay: Bharatiya Vidya Bhavan, 1963 [1940].

———. *Non-Violent Resistance (Satyagraha)*. New York: Schocken, 1951.

Gascoigne, Robert. *The Church and Secularity: Two Stories of Liberal Society*. Washington, DC: Georgetown University Press, 2009.

Gaudium et Spes: Pastoral Constitution on the Church in the Modern World (Vatican II). Available at www.vatican.va.

Gertel, Elliot B. "The Holy Spirit in the Zohar." *CCAR Journal: A Reform Jewish Quarterly* 56, no. 4 (2009): 80–102.

Ghazali [Ghazzali], [Abu Hamid Muhammad] al-. *Al-Ghazzali on Repentance*. Translated by M. S. Stern. New Delhi: Sterling Publishers, 1990. http://www.ghazali.org/books/gz-repent.pdf.

———. *The Incoherence of the Philosophers*. Provo, UT: Brigham Young University Press, 1997.

Gibbs, Eddie. *ChurchNext*. Downers Grove, IL: InterVarsity Press, 2000.

Gibbs, Eddie, and Ryan Bolger. *The Emerging Churches: Creating Christian Community in Postmodern Cultures*. Grand Rapids: Baker Academic, 2005.

Giblet, Jean. "Baptism—the Sacrament of Incorporation into the Church according to St. Paul." In *Baptism in the New Testament: A Symposium*, translated by David Askew, 161–88. Baltimore: Helicon, 1964.

Gier, Nicholas F., and Paul Kjellberg. "Buddhism and the Freedom of the Will: Pali and Mahayanist Responses." In *Freedom and Determinism*, edited by Joseph Keim Campbell, Michael O'Rourke, and David Shier. Cambridge, MA: MIT Press, 2004.

Gillman, Neil. "Creation in the Bible and in the Liturgy." In *J&E*, 133–54.

———. *The Death of Death: Resurrection and Immortality in Jewish Thought*. Woodstock, VT: Jewish Lights, 1997.

Girard, René. *The Girard Reader*. Edited by James G. Williams. New York: Crossroad, 1996.

———. *Things Hidden Since the Foundation of the World*. Translated by Stephen Bann and Michael Metteer. Stanford, CA: Stanford University Press, 1987.

"Glory to God and Peace on Earth: The Message of the International Ecumenical Peace Convocation." May 17–25, 2011, Kingston, Jamaica. http://meet-junge-oekumene.de/wp-content/uploads/2015/11/iepcreportonyouthparticipation.pdf.

Gnanakan, Chris. "The Manthiravadi: A South Indian Wounded Warrior-Healer." Chapter 7 in *A&D*, 140–57.

Goetz, Stewart, and Charles Taliaferro. *Naturalism*. Grand Rapids: Eerdmans, 2008.

Goheen, Michael W. *As the Father Has Sent Me, I Am Sending You: J. E. Lesslie Newbigin's Missionary Ecclesiology*. Zoetermeer: Uitgeverij Boekencentrum, 2000.

Goldingay, John. *Israel's Gospel*. Vol. 1 of *Old Testament Theology*. Downers Grove, IL: InterVarsity Press, 2003.

Goldman, Robert P. "Karma, Guilt, and Buried Memories: Public Fantasy and Private Reality in Traditional India." *Journal of the American Oriental Society* 105, no. 3 (1985): 413–25.

Golshani, Mehdi. "Does Science Offer Evidence of a Transcendent Reality and Purpose?" In *ISHCP* 2:95–108.

———. "Islam and the Sciences of Nature: Some Fundamental Questions." In *ISHCP* 1:67–79.

González, Justo L. *A History of Christian Thought*. Vol. 1, *From the Beginning to the Council of Chalcedon*. Nashville: Abingdon, 1970.

———. *Mañana: Christian Theology from a Hispanic Perspective*. Nashville: Abingdon, 1990.

Goosen, Gideon. *Spacetime and Theology in Dialogue*. Milwaukee: Marquette University Press, 2008.

Gordon, Haim, and Leonard Grob. *Education for Peace: Testimonies from World Religions*. Maryknoll, NY: Orbis, 1987.

Gorenberg, Gershom. *The End of Days: Fundamentalism and the Struggle for the Temple Mount*. New York: Oxford University Press, 2000.

Gorringe, Timothy. *God's Just Vengeance: Crime, Violence, and the Rhetoric of Salvation*. Cambridge Studies in Ideology and Religion 9. Cambridge: Cambridge University Press, 1966.

Gosling, David L. "Darwin and the Hindu Tradition: 'Does What Goes Around Come Around?'" *Zygon: Journal of Religion and Science* 46, no. 2 (June 2011): 345–69.

Grant, Jacquelyn. "Womanist Theology: Black Women's Experience as a Source for Doing Theology, with Special Reference to Christology." In *Constructive Christian Theology in the Worldwide Church*, edited by William R. Barr, 337–54. Grand Rapids: Eerdmans, 1997.

Grassi, Joseph A. *Broken Bread and Broken Bodies: The Lord's Supper and World Hunger*. Maryknoll, NY: Orbis, 1985.

Graybill, Lyn S. *Truth and Reconciliation in South Africa: Miracle or Model?* Boulder, CO: Lynne Rienner, 2002.

Green, Joel B. "'Bodies—That Is, Human Lives': A Re-examination of Human Nature in the Bible." In *WHS*, 149–73.

———. *Body, Soul, and Human Life: The Nature of Humanity in the Bible*. Studies in Theological Interpretation. Grand Rapids: Baker Academic, 2008.

———. *Why Salvation?* Nashville: Abingdon, 2013.

Greene, Brian. *The Elegant Universe: Superstrings, Hidden Dimensions, and the Quest for the Ultimate Theory*. 2nd ed. New York: Vintage Books, 2000.

Gregersen, Niels Henrik. "Special Divine Action and the Quilt of Laws: Why the Distinction between Special and General Divine Action Cannot Be Maintained." In *SPDA*, 179–99.

Grenz, Stanley J. *The Millennial Maze*. Downers Grove, IL: InterVarsity Press, 1994.

———. *The Named God and the Question of Being: A Trinitarian Theo-Ontology*. Louisville: Westminster John Knox, 2005.

———. *Rediscovering the Triune God: The Trinity in Contemporary Theology*. Minneapolis: Fortress, 2004.

———. *The Social God and Relational Self: A Trinitarian Theology of the* Imago Dei. Louisville: Westminster John Knox, 2001.

———. *Theology for the Community of God*. Grand Rapids: Eerdmans, 1994.

Grenz, Stanley J., and John R. Franke. *Beyond Foundationalism: Shaping Theology in a Postmodern Context*. Louisville: Westminster John Knox, 2001.

Griffin, David Ray. *God, Power, and Evil: A Process Theodicy*. Philadelphia: Westminster, 1976.

Gritsch, Eric W. "Bold Sinning: The Lutheran Ethical Option." *Dialog* 14 (1975): 26–32.

Gross, Rita M. "Meditating on Jesus." In *Buddhists Talk about Jesus, Christians Talk about the Buddha*, edited by Rita M. Gross and Terry C. Muck. New York: Continuum, 2000.

———. "Meditation and Prayer: A Comparative Inquiry." *Buddhist-Christian Studies* 22 (2002): 77–86.

Guder, Darrell, ed. *Missional Church: A Vision for the Sending of the Church in North America*. Grand Rapids: Eerdmans, 1998.

Guessoum, Nidhal. *Islam's Quantum Question: Reconciling Muslim Tradition and Modern Science*. London: I. B. Tauris, 2011.

Gunton, Colin E. *Act and Being: Towards a Theology of the Divine Attributes*. Grand Rapids: Eerdmans, 2003.

———. *Enlightenment and Alienation*. Grand Rapids: Eerdmans; Basingstoke: Marshall, Morgan & Scott, 1985.

———. *The Triune Creator: A Historical and Systematic Study*. Edinburgh Studies in Constructive Theology. Grand Rapids: Eerdmans, 1998.

Gurmann, Joseph, and Steven Fine. "Synagogue." In *ER* 13:8920–26.

Guruge, Ananda W. P. "The Buddha's Encounters with Mara the Tempter: Their Representation in Literature and Art." *Access to Insight (BCBS Edition)*, November 30, 2013. http://www.accesstoinsight.org/lib/authors/guruge/wheel419.html.

Gushee, David P. *The Sacredness of Human Life: Why an Ancient Biblical Vision Is Key to the World's Future*. Grand Rapids: Eerdmans, 2013.

Gusmer, Charles W. *And You Visited Me: Sacramental Ministry to the Sick and the Dying*. Rev. ed. Collegeville, MN: Liturgical Press, 1990.

Gutierrez, Cathy, ed. *Handbook of Spiritualism and Channeling*. Leiden: Brill, 2015.

Gutiérrez, Gustavo. *On Job: God-Talk and the Suffering of the Innocent*. Translated by Matthew J. O'Connell. Maryknoll, NY: Orbis, 1995.

———. *The Power of the Poor in History: Selected Writings*. Maryknoll, NY: Orbis, 1983.

———. *A Theology of Liberation: History, Politics, and Salvation*. Translated and edited by Sister Caridad Inda and John Eagleson. Maryknoll, NY: Orbis, 1986 [1973]; rev. ed. with a new introduction, 1988.

Habel, Norman C. *Reconciliation: Searching for Australia's Soul*. Sydney: HarperCollins, 1999.

Habermas, Jürgen. *Between Naturalism and Religion*. Translated by Ciaran Cronin. Cambridge, UK: Polity, 2008.

Habito, Ruben L. F. "Environment or Earth Sangha: Buddhist Perspectives on Our Global Ecological Well-Being." *Contemporary Buddhism* 8, no. 2 (2007): 131–47.

Haider, Najam. *Shīʿī Islam*. Cambridge: Cambridge University Press, 2014.

Haight, Roger J., SJ. *Christian Community in History*. Vol. 1, *Historical Ecclesiology*. Vol. 2, *Comparative Ecclesiology*. Vol. 3, *Ecclesial Existence*. New York: Continuum, 2004, 2005, 2008.

Haitch, Russell. *From Exorcism to Ecstasy: Eight Views of Baptism*. Louisville: Westminster John Knox, 2007.

Haleem, Muhammad [A. S.] Abdel. "Qur'an and Hadith." In *The Cambridge Companion to Classical Islamic Theology*, edited by Tim Winter, 19–32. Cambridge: Cambridge University Press, 2008.

Hamza, Feras. "Unity and Disunity in the Life of the Muslim Community." In *The Community of Believers*, edited by Lucinda Mosher and David Marshall, 65–80. Washington, DC: Georgetown University Press, 2015.

Hardacre, Helen. "Ancestor Worship." In *ER* 1:320–25.

Harper, Brad, and Paul Louis Metzger. *Exploring Ecclesiology: An Evangelical and Ecumenical Introduction*. Grand Rapids: Brazos, 2009.

Harris, Sam. *The End of Faith: Religion, Terror, and the Future of Reason*. New York: Norton, 2004.

———. *Free Will*. New York: Free Press, 2012.

Hasker, William. *Providence, Evil, and the Openness of God*. New York: Routledge, 2004.

Hassan, Riffat. "Messianism and Islam." *Journal of Ecumenical Studies* 22 (Spring 1985): 261–91.

Hauerwas, Stanley. *Dispatches from the Front: Theological Engagements with the Secular*. Durham, NC: Duke University Press, 1995.

Hauerwas, Stanley, and William H. Willimon. *Resident Aliens: A Provocative Christian Assessment of Culture and Ministry for People Who Know That Something Is Wrong*. Nashville: Abingdon, 1989.

Haught, John F. *Is Nature Enough? Meaning and Truth in the Age of Science.* Cambridge: Cambridge University Press, 2006.

Hawking, Stephen. *A Brief History of Time.* Updated and expanded tenth anniversary ed. New York: Bantam Books, 1998 [1988].

Hefner, Philip. "Biocultural Evolution: A Clue to the Meaning of Nature." In *EMB*, 329–56.

Heidel, Alexander. *The Babylonian Genesis: The Story of Creation.* Chicago: University of Chicago Press, 1942.

Heim, S. Mark. *The Depth of the Riches: A Trinitarian Theology of Religious Ends.* Grand Rapids: Eerdmans, 2001.

———. *Saved from Sacrifice: A Theology of the Cross.* Grand Rapids: Eerdmans, 2006.

Hejzlar, Pavel. *Two Paradigms for Divine Healing: Fred F. Bosworth, Kenneth E. Hagin, Agnes Sanford, and Francis MacNutt in Dialogue.* Leiden: Brill, 2010.

Hellwig, Monika. *The Eucharist and the Hunger of the World.* New York: Paulist, 1976.

Helmick, Raymond G., and Rodney L. Petersen, eds. *Forgiveness and Reconciliation: Religion, Public Policy, and Conflict Transformation.* Philadelphia: Templeton Foundation, 2001.

Hengel, Martin. *Crucifixion in the Ancient World and the Folly of the Message of the Cross.* Philadelphia: Fortress, 1977.

Henriksen, Jan-Olav. *Desire, Gift, and Recognition: Christology and Postmodern Philosophy.* Grand Rapids: Eerdmans, 2009.

Herman, Arthur L. *The Problem of Evil and Indian Thought.* Delhi: Motilal Banarsidass, 1993.

Herrin, Judith. *The Formation of Christendom.* London: Fontana, 1989.

Heschel, Susannah. "Jewish Views of Jesus." Chapter 17 in *JWF*.

Hick, John. *Death and Eternal Life: With a New Preface by the Author.* Louisville: Westminster John Knox, 1994 [1976].

———. *Evil and the God of Love.* 2nd reissued ed. New York: Palgrave Macmillan, 2010.

———. *God and the Universe of Faiths: Essays in the Philosophy of Religion.* 2nd ed. London: Macmillan, 1977.

———. *The Metaphor of God Incarnate: Christology in a Pluralistic Age.* London: SCM, 1993.

———, ed. *The Myth of God Incarnate.* London: SCM, 1977.

Hiebert, Paul G. "Conversion in Hinduism and Buddhism." In *HRC*, 9–21.

———"Discerning the Work of God." In *Charismatic Experiences in History*, edited by Cecil M. Robeck, 147–63. Peabody, MA: Hendrickson, 1985.

———. "The Flaw of the Excluded Middle." *Missiology: An International Review* 10, no. 1 (1982): 35–47. http://hiebertglobalcenter.org/blog/wp-content/uploads/2013/09/29.-1999.-The-Flaw-of-the-Excluded-Middle.pdf.

Hietamäki, Minna. "Recognition and Ecumenical Recognition—Distinguishing the Idea of Recognition in Modem Ecumenism." *Neue Zeitschrift für systematische Theologie und Religionsphilosophie* 56 (2014): 454–72.

Hiltebeitel, Alf. "The 'Mahābhārata,' and Hindu Eschatology." *History of Religions* 12, no. 2 (1972): 95–135.

Hinlicky, Paul R. "Theological Anthropology: Toward Integrating *Theosis* and Justification by Faith." *Journal of Ecumenical Studies* 34, no. 1 (Winter 1997): 38–73.

Historic Creeds and Confessions. Edited by Rick Brannan. Available on Christian Classics Ethereal Library website: http://www.ccel.org/ccel/brannan/hstcrcon.html.

Hodge, Charles. *Systematic Theology*. Vol. 3. Grand Rapids: Eerdmans, 1973 [1872].

Hoefer, Herbert. "Gospel Proclamation of the Ascended Lord." *Missiology* 33, no. 4 (2005): 43–49.

Hoekema, Anthony A. *The Bible and the Future*. Grand Rapids: Eerdmans, 1979.

Hood, Adam. "Governance." In *Routledge Companion to the Christian Church*, ed. Gerard Mannion and Lewis S. Mudge (New York: Routledge, 2012), 536–49.

Hopkins, Julie M. *Towards a Feminist Christology: Jesus of Nazareth, European Women, and the Christological Crisis*. Grand Rapids: Eerdmans, 2005.

Horton, Michael. *A Better Way: Rediscovering the Drama of God-Centered Worship*. Grand Rapids: Baker, 2002.

———. *The Christian Faith: A Systematic Theology for Pilgrims on the Way*. Grand Rapids: Zondervan, 2011.

———. "Traditional Reformed View." In *Justification: Five Views*, edited by James K. Beilby and Paul Rhodes Eddy, 85–91. Downers Grove, IL: IVP Academic, 2011.

Horvath, Tibor, SJ. *Eternity and Eternal Life: Speculative Theology and Science in Discourse*. Waterloo, ON: Wilfrid Laurier University Press, 1993.

"Human Trafficking Basics." U.S. Committee for Refugees and Immigrants. Accessed February 26, 2018. http://refugees.org/explore-the-issues/our-work-with-survivors-of-human-trafficking/human-trafficking-basics/.

Hunt, Stephen, ed. *Christian Millennialism: From the Early Church to Waco*. Bloomington: Indiana University Press, 2001.

Hunter, Harold D. "Ordinances." In *The New International Dictionary of Pentecostal and Charismatic Movements*, edited by Stanley M. Burgess and Eduard M. van der Maas. Revised and expanded ed. Grand Rapids: Zondervan, 2002.

Ibn Hanbal, Ahmad. "Hanbalī Traditionalist Creed." Translated by William Montgomery Watt. In *Islamic Theological Themes: A Primary Source Reader*, edited by John Renard, 104–9. Oakland: University of California Press, 2014.

Ibn Taymiyyah Expounds on Islam: Selected Writings of Shaykh al-Islam Taqi ad-Din Ibn Taymiyyah on Islamic Faith, Life, and Society. Compiled and translated by Muhammad 'Abdul-Haqq Ansari. Virginia: Institute of Islamic and Arabic Sciences in America, 2007. http://ahlehadith.files.wordpress.com/2010/07/expounds-on-islam.pdf.

Ickert, Scott. "Luther and Animals: Subject of Adam's Fall?" Chapter 8 in *AOA*.

Idinopulos, Thomas A., and Roy Bowen Ward. "Is Christology Inherently Anti-Semitic? A Critical Review of Rosemary Ruether's *Faith and Fratricide*." *Journal of the American Academy of Religions* 45, no. 2 (1977): 193–214.

Ifeka-Moller, Caroline. "White Power: Social Structural Factor in Conversion to Christianity, Eastern Nigeria, 1921–1966." *Canadian Journal of African Studies* 8, no. 1 (1974): 55–72.

Igenoza, Andrew Olu. "Universalism and New Testament Christianity." *Evangelical Review of Theology* 12 (1998): 261–75.

Iqbal, Muhammad. *The Reconstruction of Religious Thought in Islam*. Lahore, Pakistan: Ashraf Press, 1960.

Iqbal, Muzaffar. *Islam and Science*. Aldershot, UK: Ashgate, 2002.

Isasi-Díaz, Ada María. *En la Lucha* [In the struggle]: *A Hispanic Women's Liberation Theology*. Minneapolis: Fortress, 1993.

———. *Mujerista Theology: A Theology for the Twenty-First Century*. Maryknoll, NY: Orbis, 1996.

Jacobs, Louis. *A Jewish Theology*. London: Darton, Longman & Todd, 1973.

Jacobs, Mark X. "Jewish Environmentalism: Past Accomplishments and Future Challenges." In *J&E*, 449–80.

Jacobsen, Knut A. "Three Functions of Hell in the Hindu Traditions." *Numen: International Review for the History of Religions* 56, nos. 2–3 (2009): 385–400.

James, William. "Report on Mrs. Piper's Hodgson-Control." *Proceedings of the English Society for Psychical Research* 23 (1909).

———. "The Will to Believe." In *"The Will to Believe" and Other Essays in Popular Philosophy* [1897], *and Human Immortality* [1898], 1–31. Mineola, NY: Dover, 1956.

Jeffery, Arthur. *The Foreign Vocabulary of the Qur'ān*. Leiden: Brill, 2007.

Jenks, G. C. *The Origin and Development of the Antichrist Myth*. London: de Gruyter, 1991.

Jenson, Robert W. *Systematic Theology*. 2 vols. New York: Oxford University Press, 1997, 1999.

———. *The Triune Identity: God according to the Gospel*. Philadelphia: Fortress, 1982.

Jewett, Paul King. *Election and Predestination*. Grand Rapids: Eerdmans, 1985.

Jewett, Paul King, with Marguerite Shuster. *Who We Are: Our Dignity as Human; A Neo-Evangelical Theology*. Grand Rapids: Eerdmans, 1996.

"Jinn." In *The Oxford Dictionary of Islam*, edited by John L. Esposito. *Oxford Islamic Studies Online*. http://www.oxfordislamicstudies.com/article/opr/t125/e1204.

Joh, Wonhee Anne. *Heart of the Cross: A Postcolonial Christology*. Louisville: Westminster John Knox, 2006.

John Paul II. *Laborem Exercens*, "On Human Work" (1981). http://w2.vatican.va/content/john-paul-ii/en/encyclicals/documents/hf_jp-ii_enc_14091981_laborem-exercens.html.

Johnson, Elizabeth. *Friends of God and Prophets: A Feminist Theological Reading of the Communion of Saints*. New York: Continuum, 1998.

———. *Quest for the Living God: Mapping Frontiers in the Theology of God*. New York: Continuum, 2007.

———. *She Who Is: The Mystery of God in Feminist Theological Discourse*. New York: Crossroad, 1993.

———. *Women, Earth, and Creator Spirit*. Mahwah, NJ: Paulist, 1993.

Jones, Ken. *The New Social Face of Buddhism: A Call to Action*. Somerville, MA: Wisdom, 2003.

Jones, L. Gregory. *Embodying Forgiveness: A Theological Analysis*. Grand Rapids: Eerdmans, 1995.

Jones, Serene. *Feminist Theory and Christian Theology: Cartographies of Grace*. Minneapolis: Fortress, 2000.

Jones, Tony. *The Church Is Flat: The Relational Ecclesiology of the Emerging Church Movement*. Minneapolis: JoPa Group, 2011.

Joseph, P. V. *Indian Interpretation of the Holy Spirit*. Delhi: ISPCK, 2007.

Juergensmeyer, Mark. *Terror in the Mind of God: The Global Rise of Religious Violence*. 3rd rev. ed. Berkeley: University of California Press, 2003.

Juster, Susan. "'In a Different Voice': Male and Female Narratives of Religious Conversion in Post-evolutionary America." *American Quarterly* 41 (March 1989): 34–62.

Kallenberg, Brad J. "Conversion Converted: A Postmodern Formulation of the Doctrine of Conversion." *Evangelical Quarterly* 67 (1995): 335–64. http://www.biblicalstudies.org.uk/pdf/eq/1995-4_335bk.pdf.

Kant, Immanuel. *The Critique of Practical Reason*. Translated by Thomas Kingsmill Abbott. University Park: Pennsylvania State University Press, 2010. http://www2.hn.psu.edu/faculty/jmanis/kant/Critique-Practical-Reason.pdf.

———. *The Critique of Pure Reason* [1781]. Translated by J. M. D. Meiklejohn. A Penn State Electronic Classic Series. 2010. http://www2.hn.psu.edu/faculty/jmanis/kant/Critique-Pure-Reason6x9.pdf.

Kapolyo, Joe M. *The Human Condition: Christian Perspectives through African Eyes*. Downers Grove, IL: InterVarsity Press, 2005.

Kärkkäinen, Veli-Matti. *Christian Understandings of the Trinity: The Historical Trajectory*. Minneapolis: Fortress, 2017.

———. *Christology: A Global Introduction*. 2nd rev. ed. Grand Rapids: Baker Academic, 2016.

———. *Creation and Humanity*. A Constructive Christian Theology for the Pluralistic World, vol. 3. Grand Rapids: Eerdmans, 2016.

———. *The Doctrine of God: A Global Introduction*. 2nd rev. ed. Grand Rapids: Baker Academic, 2017.

———, ed. *Holy Spirit and Salvation: The Sources of Christian Theology*. Louisville: Westminster John Knox, 2010.

———. "Hope, Theology of." In *GDT*, 404–5.

———. "'How to Speak of the Spirit among Religions': Trinitarian 'Rules' for a Pneumatological Theology of Religions." *International Bulletin of Missionary Research* 30, no. 3 (July 2006): 121–27.

———. *An Introduction to the Theology of Religions: Biblical, Historical, and Contemporary Perspectives*. Downers Grove, IL: InterVarsity Press, 2003.

———. *One with God: Salvation as Deification and Justification*. Collegeville, MN: Liturgical Press, 2004.

———. "*Ordo Salutis*." In *GDT*, 622–23.

———. *The Trinity and Religious Pluralism: The Doctrine of the Trinity in Christian Theology of Religions*. Aldershot, UK: Ashgate, 2004.

———. *Trinity and Revelation*. A Constructive Christian Theology for the Pluralistic World, vol. 2. Grand Rapids: Eerdmans, 2014.

Kärkkäinen, Veli-Matti, and Michael Karim. "Community and Witness in Transition:

Newbigin's Missional Ecclesiology between Modernity and Postmodernity." In *The Gospel and Pluralism Today: Reassessing Lesslie Newbigin in the 21st Century*, edited by Scott W. Sunquist and Amos Yong, 71–100. Downers Grove, IL: InterVarsity Press, 2015.

Karras, Valerie A. "Eschatology." In *Cambridge Companion to Feminist Theology*, edited by Susan Frank Parsons, 243–60. Cambridge: Cambridge University Press, 2002.

Kasper, Walter. *Jesus the Christ*. Translated by V. Green. London: Burns & Oates; New York: Paulist, 1976.

Kateregga, Badru D., and David W. Shenk. *Islam and Christianity: A Muslim and a Christian in Dialogue*. Ibadan, Nigeria: Daystar, 1985.

Katz, Steven T., ed. *The Impact of the Holocaust on Jewish Theology*. New York: New York University Press, 2005.

Kavunkal, Jacob. "The Mystery of God in and through Hinduism." In *Christian Theology in Asia*, edited by Sebastian C. H. Kim. Cambridge: Cambridge University Press, 2008.

Keller, Catherine. *Apocalypse Now and Then: A Feminist Guide to the End of the World*. Boston: Beacon, 1996.

———. "Eschatology, Ecology, and a Green Ecumenacy." *Ecotheology: Journal of Religion, Nature & the Environment* 5 (January 1997): 84–99.

Kellner, Menachem M. *Dogma in Medieval Judaism from Maimonides to Abravanel*. Oxford: Oxford University Press, for the Littmann Library of Jewish Civilization, 1986.

Kelly, J. N. D. *Early Christian Doctrines*. Rev. ed. New York: Harper & Row, 1978 [1960].

Kelly, John G. "The Cross, the Church, and the Jewish People." In *Atonement Today*, edited by John Goldingay, 166–84. London: SPCK, 1995.

Kelsey, David H. *Eccentric Existence: A Theological Anthropology*. 2 vols. Louisville: Westminster John Knox, 2009.

Kenney, Jeffrey T. "Millennialism and Radical Islamist Movements." In *OHM*, 688–716.

Kepnes, Steven. "'Turn Us to You and We Shall Return': Original Sin, Atonement, and Redemption in Jewish Terms." In *Christianity in Jewish Terms*, edited by Tikva Frymer-Kensky et al., 293–319. Boulder, CO: Westview, 2000.

Kerr, Hugh T., and John M. Mulder, eds. *Conversions: The Christian Experience*. Grand Rapids: Eerdmans, 1983; republished as *Famous Conversions: The Christian Experience*. 1994.

Kesich, Veselin. "Resurrection, Ascension and the Giving of the Spirit." *Greek Orthodox Theological Review* 25, no. 3 (Fall 1980): 249–60.

Kessler, Edward. *An Introduction to Jewish-Christian Relations*. Cambridge: Cambridge University Press, 2010.

Kessler, Edward, and Neil Wenborn, eds. *A Dictionary of Jewish-Christian Relations*. Cambridge: Cambridge University Press, 2005.

Keyes, Charles F. "Monks, Guns, and Peace." In *Belief and Bloodshed: Religion and Violence across Time and Tradition*, edited by James K. Wellman Jr., 145–63. Lanham, MD: Rowman & Littlefield, 2007.

Khalidi, Tarif, ed. and trans. *The Muslim Jesus: Sayings and Stories in Islamic Literature*. Cambridge, MA: Harvard University Press, 2001.

Khalil, Atif. "Early Sufi Approaches to *Tawba*: From the Qur'ān to Abū Ṭālib al-Makkī." PhD diss., University of Toronto, 2009.

Khatami, Mahmoud. "On the Transcendental Element of Life: A Recapitulation of Human Spirituality in Islamic Philosophical Psychology." *Journal of Shi'a Islamic Studies* 2, no. 2 (2009): 121–40.

Kiblinger, Kristin Beise. *Buddhist Inclusivism: Attitudes toward Religious Others*. Burlington, VT: Ashgate, 2005.

Kierkegaard, Søren. *Sickness unto Death: A Christian Psychological Exposition for Upbuilding and Awakening*. Edited and translated by Edna H. Hong and Howard V. Hong. Princeton: Princeton University Press, 1983.

Kim, Kirsteen. "The Holy Spirit in Mission in India: Indian Contribution to Contemporary Mission Pneumatology." Presentation at Overseas Christian Missionary Society, April 6, 2004. http://www.ocms.ac.uk/docs/TUESDAY%20LECTURES_Kirsteen.pdf.

———. "The Potential of Pneumatology for Mission in Contemporary Europe." *International Review of Mission* 95, nos. 378–79 (2006).

Kim, Seyoon. *The Origin of Paul's Gospel*. Grand Rapids: Eerdmans, 1981.

Kinsley, David. *Health, Healing, and Religion: A Cross-Cultural Perspective*. Upper Saddle River, NJ: Prentice Hall, 1996.

Klausner, Joseph. *Jesus of Nazareth: His Life, Times, and Teaching*. Translated by Herbert Danby. New York: Macmillan, 1925.

Klein, C. *Anti-Judaism in Christian Theology*. Translated by Edward Quinn. Philadelphia: Fortress, 1978.

Kloetzli, W. Randolph. *Buddhist Cosmology: Science and Theology in the Images of Motion and Light*. Delhi: Motilal Banarsidass, 1989.

Klostermaier, Klaus. *A Survey of Hinduism*. 3rd ed. Albany: State University of New York Press, 2010.

Knipe, David M. "Hindu Eschatology." In *OHE*, 170–90.

Knitter, Paul F. *Jesus and the Other Names: Christian Mission and Global Responsibility*. Maryknoll, NY: Orbis, 1996.

———. *No Other Name? A Critical Survey of Christian Attitudes toward the World Religions*. Maryknoll, NY: Orbis, 1985.

———. *One Earth, Many Religions: Multifaith Dialogue and Global Responsibility*. Maryknoll, NY: Orbis, 1995.

Kogan, Michael S. *Opening the Covenant: A Jewish Theology of Christianity*. Oxford: Oxford University Press, 2008.

Kooiman, Dick. *Conversion and Social Equality in India*. Delhi: Manohar, 1989.

Kotsko, Adam. *The Politics of Redemption: The Social Logic of Salvation*. London: T&T Clark, 2010.

Kritzeck, James. "Holy Spirit in Islam." In *Perspectives on Charismatic Renewal*, edited by Edward D. O'Connor, 101–11. Notre Dame: University of Notre Dame Press, 1975.

Kühnemann, Frank. "When Plants Say 'Ouch.'" Deutsche Welle, February 5, 2002. http://www.dw.de/when-plants-say-ouch/a-510552.

Kulandran, Sabapathy. *Grace in Christianity and Hinduism*. Cambridge: James Clarke, 2000 [1964].

Kumar, B. J. Christie. "An Indian Appreciation of the Doctrine of the Holy Spirit: A Search into the Religious Heritage of the Indian Christian." *Indian Journal of Theology* 30 (1981): 29–35.

Küng, Hans. *Christianity and World Religions: Path to Dialogue*. New York: Doubleday, 1986.

———. "A Christian Response [to Heinz Bechert: Buddhist Perspectives]." In *Christianity and the World Religions: Paths to Dialogue with Islam, Hinduism, and Buddhism*, by Hans Küng, with Josef van Ess, Heinrich von Stietencron, and Heinz Bechert, translated by Peter Heinegg, 306–28. New York: Doubleday, 1986.

———. *The Church*. Garden City, NY: Doubleday, 1976.

———. "God's Self-Renunciation and Buddhist Self-Emptiness: A Christian Response to Masao Abe." In *Divine Emptiness and Historical Fullness: A Buddhist-Jewish-Christian Conversation with Masao* Abe, edited by Christopher Ives, 207–23. Valley Forge, PA: Trinity, 1995.

Küppers, Bernd-Olaf. *Information and the Origin of Life*. Cambridge, MA: MIT Press, 1990.

Kvanvig, Jonathan L. "Hell." In *OHE*, 413–26.

Kydd, Ronald A. N. *Healing through the Centuries: Models for Understanding*. Peabody, MA: Hendrickson, 1998.

LaCugna, Catherine Mowry. "The Baptismal Formula, Feminist Objections, and Trinitarian Theology." *Journal of Ecumenical Studies* 26, no. 2 (Spring 1989).

———. *God for Us: The Trinity and Christian Life*. San Francisco: HarperSanFrancisco, 1991.

La Due, William J. *Jesus among the Theologians: Contemporary Interpretations of Christ*. Harrisburg, PA: Trinity, 2001.

Lai, Suat Yan. "Engendering Buddhism: Female Ordination and Women's 'Voices' in Thailand." PhD diss., Claremont Graduate University, 2011.

Lakoff, George. *Don't Think of the Elephant!* White River Junction, VT: Chelsea Green, 2004.

Lamm, Norman. "Ecology in Jewish Law and Theology." In *Faith and Doubt: Studies in Traditional Jewish Thought*. New York: Ktav, 1972.

Langer, Ruth. "Worship and Devotional Life: Jewish Worship." In *ER* 14:9805–9.

Langmead, Ross. "Transformed Relationships: Reconciliation as the Central Model for Mission." *Mission Studies* 25, no. 1 (2008): 5–20.

Lapide, Franz. *Jewish Monotheism and Christian Trinitarian Doctrine: A Dialogue by Pinchas Lapide and Jürgen Moltmann*. Translated by Leonard Swidler. Philadelphia: Fortress, 1981.

Lapide, Pinchas. *Israelis, Jews, and Jesus*. Translated by Peter Heinegg. Garden City, NY: Doubleday, 1979.

———. *The Resurrection of Jesus: A Jewish Perspective*. Minneapolis: Augsburg, 1983.

Largen, Kristin Johnston. *What Christians Can Learn from Buddhism: Rethinking Salvation*. Minneapolis: Fortress, 2009.

The Laws of Manu. Translated by George Bühler. *SBE* 25. http://www.sacred-texts.com/hin/manu.htm.

Learman, Linda, ed. *Buddhist Missionaries in the Era of Globalization*. Honolulu: University of Hawai'i Press, 2005.

Lederle, Henry I. *Treasures Old and New: Interpretations of "Spirit-Baptism" in the Charismatic Renewal Movement*. Peabody, MA: Hendrickson, 1981.

Ledgerwood, Elaine C. "The Hope of Forgiveness." *Compass* 47, no. 1 (2013): 14–20.

Lee, Jung Young. "Ancestor Worship: From a Theological Perspective." In *Ancestor Worship and Christianity in Korea*, edited by Jung Young Lee, 83–91. Lewiston, NY: Edwin Mellen, 1988.

———. *The Trinity in Asian Perspective*. Nashville: Abingdon, 1996.

———. "The Yin-Yang Way of Thinking." In *Asian Christian Theology: Emerging Themes*, edited by Douglas J. Elwood, 81–88. Philadelphia: Westminster, 1980.

Lee, Sang Hyun. *From a Liminal Place: An Asian American Theology*. Minneapolis: Fortress, 2010.

Lefebure, Leo D. *The Buddha and the Christ: Explorations in Buddhist and Christian Dialogue*. Maryknoll, NY: Orbis, 1993.

———. *Revelation, the Religions, and Violence*. Maryknoll, NY: Orbis, 2000.

Leirvik, Oddbjørn. *Images of Jesus Christ in Islam*. 2nd ed. London: Continuum, 2010.

Leslie, Donald Daniel, David Flusser, Alvin J. Reines, Gershom Scholem, and Michael J. Graetz. "Redemption." In *EJ*, 17:151–55.

Levison, John R., and P. Pope-Levison. "Christology: 4. The New Contextual Christologies: Liberation and Inculturation." In *GDT*.

Levtzion, Nehamia, ed. *Conversion to Islam*. New York: Holmes & Meier, 1979.

Lewin, Roger. *The Origin of Modern Humans*. New York: Scientific American Library, 1993.

Lewis, Bernard. *Islam and the West*. Oxford: Oxford University Press, 1993.

Libet, B., C. Gleason, E. Wright, and D. Pearl. "Time of Conscious Intention to Act in Relation to Onset of Cerebral Activity (Readiness-Potential)." *Brain* 106, no. 3 (1983): 623–42.

Liechty, Joseph. "Putting Forgiveness in Its Place." In *Explorations in Reconciliation: New Directions for Theology*, edited by David Tombs and Joseph Liechty, 59–68. Aldershot, UK: Ashgate, 2006.

Lienhard, Joseph T. "On 'Discernments of Spirits' in the Early Church." *Theological Studies* 4 (1980): 505–29.

Lim, Timothy T. M. "Ecclesial Recognition: An Interdisciplinary Proposal." PhD diss., Regent University, School of Divinity, 2014.

Lindbeck, George A. *The Nature of Doctrine: Religion and Theology in a Postliberal Age*. Philadelphia: Westminster, 1984.

Lints, Richard. "Soteriology." In *Mapping Modern Theology: A Thematic and Historical Introduction*, edited by Kelly M. Kapic and Bruce L. McCormack, 259–91. Grand Rapids: Baker Academic, 2012.

Lipner, Julius J. *Hindus: Their Religious Beliefs and Practices*. London: Routledge, 1994.
Löfstedt, Torsten. "The Creation and Fall of Adam: A Comparison of the Qur'anic and Biblical Accounts." *Swedish Missiological Themes* 93, no. 4 (2005): 453–77.
Lønning, Peter, ed. *Creation—an Ecumenical Challenge: Reflections Issuing from a Study by the Institute for Ecumenical Research, Strasbourg, France*. Macon, GA: Mercer University Press, 1989.
Lopez, Donald S. *Buddhism and Science: A Guide for the Perplexed*. Chicago: University of Chicago Press, 2008.
Lossky, Nicholas, et al., eds. *Dictionary of the Ecumenical Movement*. 2nd ed. Geneva: WCC, 2002.
Ludwig, Frieder, and J. Kwabena Asamoah-Gyadu, eds. *African Christian Presence in the West: New Immigrant Congregations and Transnational Networks in North America and Europe*. Trenton, NJ: Africa World, 2011.
Ludwig, Theodore M. *The Sacred Paths: Understanding the Religions of the World*. 4th ed. Upper Saddle River, NJ: Pearson, 2006.
Luskin, Frederic. *Forgive for Good: A Proven Prescription for Health and Happiness*. San Francisco: HarperCollins, 2002.
Luther, Martin. *The Large Catechism*. Translated by F. Bente and W. H. T. Dau. St. Louis: Concordia, 1921.
Lutheran World Federation and the Catholic Church. *Joint Declaration on the Doctrine of Justification*. October 31, 1999. http://www.vatican.va/roman_curia/pontifical_councils/chrstuni/documents/rc_pc_chrstuni_doc_31101999_cath-luth-joint-declaration_en.html.
Lyden, John C. "Atonement in Judaism and Christianity: Towards a Rapprochement." *Journal of Ecumenical Studies* 29, no. 1 (Winter 1992): 47–54.
Macchia, Frank D. *Baptized in the Spirit: A Global Pentecostal Theology*. Grand Rapids: Zondervan, 2006.
———. "God Says What the Text Says: Another Look at Karl Barth's View of Scripture." Unpublished manuscript, n.d.
Macdonald, Duncan B. *Development of Muslim Theology, Jurisprudence, and Constitutional Theory*. New York: Charles Scribner, 1903. Available at www.sacred-texts.com.
———. "The Development of the Idea of Spirit in Islam: I" and "The Development of the Idea of Spirit in Islam: II." *Moslem World* 22, no. 1 (1932): 25–42; and no. 2 (1932): 153–68.
Maguire, Daniel. *The Moral Core of Judaism and Christianity: Reclaiming the Revolution*. Philadelphia: Fortress, 1993.
Mahmutcehagic, Rusmir. *The Mosque: The Heart of Submission*. New York: Fordham University Press, 2007.
Maimonides, Moses. *The Eight Chapters of Maimonides on Ethics (Shemonah Perakim)*. Translated and edited by Joseph I. Gorfinkle. New York: Columbia University Press, 1912. http://archive.org/stream/eightchaptersofmoomaim#page/n9/mode/2up.
———. *The Guide for the Perplexed*. Translated by M. Friedländer. Sacred-texts.com [1903]. http://www.sacred-texts.com/jud/gfp/index.htm#contents.

Majjhima Nikaya Sutta. In *The Middle Length Discourses of the Buddha*. A new translation of *Majjhima Nikāya*. Translated by Bhikkhu Ñānamoli and Bhikku Bodhi. Kandy, Sri Lanka: Buddhist Publication Society, 1995.

Malek, Sobhi. "Islam Encountering Spiritual Power." In *Called and Empowered: Global Mission in Pentecostal Perspective*, edited by Murray W. Dempster, Byron D. Klaus, and Douglas Petersen, 180–97. Peabody, MA: Hendrickson, 1991.

Mann, William E. "Augustine on Original Sin and Evil." In *Cambridge Companion to Augustine*, edited by Eleonore Stump and Norman Kretzmann, 40–48. Cambridge: Cambridge University Press, 2001.

Mannermaa, Tuomo. *Christ Present in Faith: Luther's View of Justification*. Edited by Kirsi Stjerna. Minneapolis: Augsburg Fortress, 2005 [1979].

Mannion, Gerard. *Ecclesiology and Postmodernity: Questions for the Church in Our Time*. Collegeville, MN: Liturgical Press, 2007.

Mantzaridis, Georgios. *The Deification of Man: St. Gregory Palamas and the Orthodox Traditions*. Translated by Liadain Sherrar. Crestwood, NY: St. Vladimir's Seminary Press, 1984.

Marcoulesco, Ileana. "Free Will and Determinism." In *ER* 5:3199–3202.

Markham, Ian S. *Against Atheism: Why Dawkins, Hitchens, and Harris Are Fundamentally Wrong*. Oxford: Wiley-Blackwell, 2010.

Marks, Jonathan. *What It Means to Be 98% Chimpanzee: Apes, People, and Their Genes*. Berkeley: University of California Press, 2002.

Marshall, Christopher. *Beyond Retribution: A New Testament Vision of Justice, Crime, and Punishment*. Grand Rapids: Eerdmans, 2001.

Martin, F. "Discernment of Spirits, Gift of." In *The New International Dictionary of Pentecostal and Charismatic Movements*, edited by Stanley M. Burgess and Eduard M. van der Maas, rev. and expanded ed., 582–84. Grand Rapids: Zondervan, 2002.

Martin, Ralph, and Peter Williamson, eds. *John Paul II and the New Evangelization*. San Francisco: Ignatius, 1995.

Martin, Raymond, and John Barresi. *The Rise and Fall of Soul and Self: An Intellectual History of Personal Identity*. New York: Columbia University Press, 2006.

Martinson, Paul. "Explorations in Lutheran Perspectives on People of Other Faiths: Toward a Christian Theology of Religions." In *Theological Perspectives on Other Faiths: Toward a Christian Theology of Religions*, edited by Hance A. O. Mwakabana. LWF Documentation 41. Geneva: Lutheran World Federation, 1997.

Marty, Martin E. *When Faiths Collide*. Malden, MA: Blackwell, 2005.

Marx, Karl. *Critique of Hegel's Philosophy of Right*. Edited, with introduction and notes, by Joseph O'Malley. Cambridge: Cambridge University Press, 1970.

May, Peter. "The Trinity and Saccidananda." *Indian Journal of Theology* 7, no. 3 (1958): 92–98.

McCall, Theodore David. *The Greenie's Guide to the End of the World*. Adelaide: ATF Theology, 2011.

McClendon, James. *Systematic Theology*. Vol. 1, *Ethics*. Vol. 2, *Doctrine*. Nashville: Abingdon, 1986, 1994.

McCready, Douglas. *He Came Down from Heaven: The Preexistence of Christ and the Christian Faith*. Downers Grove, IL: InterVarsity Press, 2005.

McCullough, Michael E., Kenneth I. Pargament, and Carl E. Thoresen, eds. *Forgiveness: Theory, Research, and Practice*. New York: Guilford, 2002.

McDaniel, Jay Byrd. "Where Is the Holy Spirit Anyway? Response to a Skeptic Environmentalist." *Ecumenical Review* 42, no. 2 (1990): 162–74.

McDannell, Colleen, and Bernhard Lang. *Heaven: A History*. New York: Vintage Books, 1990.

McDermott, Gerald R. "Will All Be Saved?" *Themelios* 38, no. 2 (2013): 232–43. http://tgc-documents.s3.amazonaws.com/themelios/Themelios38.2.pdf#page.

McDonald, Gregory [Robin A. Parry]. *The Evangelical Universalist*. 2nd ed. Eugene, OR: Cascade, 2012.

McDonnell, Kilian, OSB, and George T. Montague. *Christian Initiation and Baptism in the Holy Spirit: Evidence from the First Eight Centuries*. Collegeville, MN: Liturgical Press, 1991.

McFague, Sallie. *The Body of God: An Ecological Theology*. Minneapolis: Fortress, 1993.

———. *Metaphorical Theology: Models of God in Religious Language*. Philadelphia: Fortress, 1982.

———. *Models of God: Theology for an Ecological, Nuclear Age*. Minneapolis: Fortress, 1987.

McGinn, Bernard. *Antichrist: Two Thousand Years of the Human Fascination with Evil*. New York: Columbia University Press, 2000.

McGrath, Alister E. *A Brief History of Heaven*. Oxford: Blackwell, 2003.

———. Conclusion to *Four Views on Salvation in a Pluralistic World*, edited by Dennis L. Okholm and Timothy R. Phillips, 200–209. Grand Rapids: Zondervan, 1996.

———. *Dawkins' God: Genes, Memes, and the Meaning of Life*. Oxford: Blackwell, 2005.

———. *A Fine-Tuned Universe: The Quest for God in Science and Theology*. Gifford Lectures, 2009. Louisville: Westminster John Knox, 2009.

———. *Iustitia Dei: A History of the Christian Doctrine of Justification*. Vol. 1, *From the Beginnings to 1500*. Vol. 2, *From 1500 to the Present Day*. Cambridge: Cambridge University Press, 1986.

———. *The Open Secret: A New Vision for Natural Theology*. Oxford: Blackwell, 2008.

———. *The Order of Things: Explorations in Scientific Theology*. Oxford: Wiley-Blackwell, 2006.

———. *A Scientific Theology*. Vol. 1, *Nature*. Grand Rapids: Eerdmans, 2001.

McIntyre, John. *The Shape of Soteriology: Studies in the Doctrine of the Death of Christ*. Edinburgh: T&T Clark, 1992.

McLellan, Don. "Justice, Forgiveness, and Reconciliation: Essential Elements in Atonement Theology." *Evangelical Review of Theology* 29 (2005): 4–15.

McMahan, David L. *The Making of Buddhist Modernism*. New York: Oxford University Press, 2008.

McMullin, Ernan. "Creation *Ex Nihilo*: Early History." In *CGA*, 11–23.

———. "How Should Cosmology Relate to Theology?" In *The Sciences and Theology in the Twentieth Century*, edited by A. R. Peacocke, 17–57. Notre Dame: University of Notre Dame Press, 1981.

McNamara, Patrick. *Where God and Science Meet: How Brain and Evolutionary Studies Alter Our Understanding of Religion*. Vol. 1, *Evolution, Genes, and the Religious Experience*. Vol. 2, *The Neurology of Religious Experience*. Vol. 3, *The Psychology of Religious Experience*. Westport, CT: Praeger, 2006.

McNamara, Patrick, and Wesley Wildman, eds. *Science and the World's Religions*. Vol. 1, *Origins and Destinies*. Vol. 2, *Persons and Groups*. Vol. 3, *Religions and Controversies*. Santa Barbara, CA: Praeger, 2012.

Meagher, David K., and David E. Balk, eds. *Handbook of Thanatology: The Essential Body of Knowledge for the Study of Death, Dying, and Bereavement*. 2nd ed. New York: Routledge, 2013.

Meeks, M. Douglas. "The Economy of Grace: Human Dignity in Market System." In *God and Human Dignity*, edited by R. K. Soulen and L. Woodhead, 196–214. Grand Rapids: Eerdmans, 2006.

———. *God the Economist: The Doctrine of God and Political Economy*. Minneapolis: Fortress, 1989.

Mesa, José M. de. "Making Salvation Concrete and Jesus Real: Trends in Asian Christology." January 1, 1999. Available by permission of *SEDOS* on the Network for Strategic Missions: http://www.strategicnetwork.org/index.php?loc=kb&view=v&id=07429&mode=v&pagenum=1&lang=.

Mette, Norbert, and James Aitken Gardiner. *Diakonia: Church for Others*. Concilium. Edinburgh: T&T Clark, 1988.

Middleton, J. Richard. *New Heaven and New Earth: Reclaiming Biblical Eschatology*. Grand Rapids: Baker, 2014.

Migliore, Daniel L. *Faith Seeking Understanding: An Introduction to Christian Theology*. 2nd ed. Grand Rapids: Eerdmans, 2004.

Mikaelsson, Lisbet. "Missional Religion—with Special Emphasis on Buddhism, Christianity and Islam." *Swedish Missiological Themes* 92 (2004): 523–38.

Miller, Jeanine. *The Vision of Cosmic Order in the Vedas*. London: Routledge & Kegan Paul, 1985.

Miller, William D. "Da'wah." In *ER* 4:2225–26.

Milner, Richard, and Ian Tattersall. "Faces of the Human Past: Science and Art Combine to Create a New Portrait Gallery of Our Hominid Heritage." *Natural History*, February 2007, n.p. http://www.naturalhistorymag.com/htmlsite/master.html?http://www.naturalhistorymag.com/htmlsite/0207/0207_feature.html.

Minear, Paul S. *The Images of the Church in the New Testament*. London: Lutterworth, 1960.

Mishkat al-Masabih. Edited by Al-Baghawi. Translated by James Robinson. 4 vols. Lahore: Sh. Muhammad Ashraft, 1965–1966.

Misner, C. W., K. S. Thorne, and J. A. Wheeler. *Gravitation*. New York: Freeman, 1973.

Miyahira, Nozomu. *Towards a Theology of the Concord of God: A Japanese Perspective on the Trinity*. Carlisle, UK: Paternoster, 2000.

Moberly, R. C. *Atonement and Personality*. London: John Murray, 1924 [1901].

Moffett, Samuel Hugh. *A History of Christianity in Asia*. Vol. 1, *Beginnings to 1500*. San Francisco: HarperSanFrancisco, 1992.

Mohamed, Yasien. *Fitrah: The Islamic Concept of Human Nature.* London: Ta-Ha, 1996.

Mohler, Albert. "Modern Theology: The Disappearance of Hell." In *Hell under Fire: Modern Scholarship Reinvents Eternal Punishment*, edited by Christopher W. Morgan and Robert A. Peterson, 15–42. Grand Rapids: Zondervan, 2004.

Moltmann, Jürgen. *The Church in the Power of the Spirit: A Contribution to Messianic Ecclesiology.* Translated by Margaret Kohl. London: SCM, 1977.

———. *The Coming of God: Christian Eschatology.* Translated by Margaret Kohl. Minneapolis: Fortress, 1996.

———. "Cosmos and Theosis: Eschatological Perspectives on the Future of the Universe." In *The Far-Future Universe: Eschatology from a Cosmic Perspective*, edited by George F. R. Ellis, 249–65. Philadelphia: Templeton Foundation, 2002.

———. *The Crucified God: The Cross of Christ as the Foundation and Criticism of Christian Theology.* Translated by Margaret Kohl. Minneapolis: Fortress, 1993.

———. *Experiences in Theology: Ways and Forms of Christian Theology.* Translated by Margaret Kohl. Minneapolis: Fortress, 2000.

———. *God in Creation: A New Theology of Creation and the Spirit of God.* Translated by Margaret Kohl. Minneapolis: Fortress, 1993.

———. *In the End—the Beginning: The Life of Hope.* Translated by Margaret Kohl. Minneapolis: Fortress, 2004.

———. *The Spirit of Life: A Universal Affirmation.* Translated by Margaret Kohl. Minneapolis: Fortress, 2001.

———. *Theology of Hope: On the Ground and the Implications of a Christian Eschatology.* London: SCM, 1967 [1964].

———. *The Trinity and the Kingdom of God: The Doctrine of God.* Translated by Margaret Kohl. San Francisco: Harper & Row; London: SCM, 1981.

———. *The Way of Jesus Christ: Christology in Messianic Dimensions.* Translated by Margaret Kohl. Minneapolis: Fortress, 1993 [1989].

Montefiore, C. G. "Rabbinic Conceptions of Repentance." *Jewish Quarterly Review* 16, no. 2 (January 1904): 209–57.

Morgan, Mardon Lee. "Eschatology for the Oppressed: Millenarianism and Liberation in the Eschatology of Jürgen Moltmann." *Perspectives in Religious Studies* 4 (2012): 379–93.

Morris, Henry M. *Beginning of the World.* Denver: Accent Books, 1977.

Morris, Simon Conway. *The Crucible of Creation: The Burgess Shale and the Rise of Animals.* New York: Oxford University Press, 1998.

Moseley, Carys. *Nations and Nationalism in the Theology of Karl Barth.* New York: Oxford University Press, 2013.

Moule, C. F. D. *The Meaning of Hope: A Biblical Exposition with Concordance.* Philadelphia: Fortress, 1953.

Mukhtar, Gohar. "A Comparative and Critical Analysis of the Story of Job as Found in the Bible and the Quran." *Gohar Mukhtar's Weblog.* July 22, 2011. http://goharmukhtar.wordpress.com/2011/07/22/a-comparative-and-critical-analysis-of-the-story-of-job-as-found-in-the-bible-and-the-quran/.

Muller, Richard A. *Christ and the Decree: Christology and Predestination in Reformed Theology from Calvin to Perkins*. Durham, NC: Labyrinth, 1986.

———. "Scripture." In *Oxford Encyclopedia of the Reformation*, edited by Hans J. Hillerbrand, 4:37. Oxford: Oxford University Press, 1996.

Murphy, Nancey. *Beyond Liberalism and Fundamentalism: How Modern and Postmodern Philosophy Set the Theological Agenda*. Valley Forge, PA: Trinity, 1996.

———. *Bodies and Souls, or Spirited Bodies?* Cambridge: Cambridge University Press, 2006.

———. "Reductionism: How Did We Fall into It and Can We Emerge from It?" In *Evolution and Emergence: Systems, Organisms, Persons*, edited by Nancey Murphy and William R. Stoeger, 19–39. Oxford: Oxford University Press, 2007.

———. "The Resurrection Body and Personal Identity: Possibilities and Limits of Eschatological Knowledge." In *RTSA*, 202–18.

———. "Science and the Problem of Evil: Suffering as a By-Product of a Finely Tuned Cosmos." In *PC*, 131–51.

Murphy, Nancey, and Warren S. Brown. *Did My Neurons Make Me Do It? Philosophical and Neurobiological Perspectives on Moral Responsibility and Free Will*. Oxford: Oxford University Press, 2007.

Murray, Michael. "Three Versions of Universalism." *Faith and Philosophy* 16 (1999): 55–68.

Murray, Stuart. *Post-Christendom: Church and Mission in a Strange New World*. Carlisle, UK: Paternoster, 2004.

Musk, Bill A. "Angels and Demons in Folk Islam." Chapter 10 in *A&D*.

Muthiah, Robert A. *The Priesthood of All Believers in the Twenty-First Century: Living Faithfully as the Whole People of God in a Postmodern Context*. Eugene, OR: Pickwick, 2009.

Myers, Ched. *The Biblical Vision of Sabbath Economics*. Massachusetts: Bartimaeus Cooperative Ministries, 2007.

Nagao, Gajin. "The Life of the Buddha: An Interpretation." *Eastern Buddhist*, n.s., 20, no. 2 (1987): 1–31.

Nalunnakkal, George Mathew. "Come Holy Spirit, Heal and Reconcile: Called in Christ to Be Reconciling and Healing Communities." *International Review of Mission* 94, no. 372 (2005): 7–19.

Ñānamoli, Bhikkhu, and Bhikku Bodhi. Introduction to *The Middle Length Discourses of the Buddha*. In *Majjhima Nikāya*, translated by Bhikkhu Ñānamoli and Bhikku Bodhi, 19–60. Kandy, Sri Lanka: Buddhist Publication Society, 1995.

Nanda, Meera. "Vedic Science and Hindu Nationalism: Arguments against a Premature Synthesis of Religion and Science." Chapter 2 in *SRPW*.

Narayan, Uma. "Forgiveness, Moral Reassessment, and Reconciliation." In *Explorations of Value*, edited by Thomas Magnell, 169–78. Amsterdam: Rodopi, 1997.

NASA/WMAP [Wilkinson Microwave Anisotropy Probe] Science Team. "Cosmology: The Study of the Universe." Last modified June 3, 2011. http://map.gsfc.nasa.gov/universe/WMAP_Universe.pdf.

Nasr, Seyyed Hossein. "Islam and Science." In *OHRS*, 71–86.

———. *Man and Nature: The Spiritual Crisis in Modern Man*. Rev. ed. Chicago: Kazi Publishers, 1997 [1967].

———. *The Need for a Sacred Science*. SUNY Series in Religious Studies. Albany: State University of New York Press, 1993.

Nattier, Jan. "Buddhist Eschatology." In *OHE*, 151–69.

The Nature and Mission of the Church—a Stage on the Way to a Common Statement. Faith and Order Paper no. 198. World Council of Churches. December 15, 2005. https://www.oikoumene.org/en/resources/documents/commissions/faith-and-order/i-unity-the-church-and-its-mission/the-nature-and-mission-of-the-church-a-stage-on-the-way-to-a-common-statement.

Ndingwan, Sammuel Anye. "Ancestor Veneration among the Mankon of the Cameroon Republic." PhD diss., Fuller Theological Seminary, School of World Mission, 1981.

Nellas, Panayiotis. *Deification in Christ: Orthodox Perspectives on the Nature of the Human Person*. Translated by Norman Russell. Crestwood, NY: St. Vladimir's Seminary Press, 1987.

Nelson, Derek R. *What's Wrong with Sin: Sin in Individual and Social Perspective from Schleiermacher to Theologies of Liberation*. London: T&T Clark, 2009.

Nelson-Pallmeyer, Jack. *Is Religion Killing Us? Violence in the Bible and the Quran*. Harrisburg, PA: Trinity, 2003.

Nestorius. *The Bazaar of Heracleides*. Translated from Syriac and edited by G. R. Driver and Leonard Hodgson. London: Oxford University Press, 1925. www.ccel.org.

Netland, Harold A. *Encountering Religious Pluralism: The Challenge to Christian Faith and Mission*. Downers Grove, IL: InterVarsity Press, 2001.

Neufeldt, R. "Hindu Views of Christ." In *Hindu-Christian Dialogue: Perspectives and Encounters*, edited by Harold Coward, 162–75. Maryknoll, NY: Orbis, 1990.

Neumaier, Eva K. "The Dilemma of Authoritative Utterance in Buddhism." In *Experiencing Scripture in World Religions*, edited by H. Coward, 138–67. Maryknoll, NY: Orbis, 2000.

Neusner, Jacob. "Repentance in Judaism." In *RCP*, 60–75.

———. "Theodicy in Classical Judaism." In *Encyclopaedia of Judaism*, edited by Jacob Neusner, Alan J. Avery-Peck, and William Scott Green. New York: Continuum; Leiden: Brill, 2006.

Newberg, Andrew B., and Bruce Y. Lee. "The Neuroscientific Study of Religious and Spiritual Phenomena: Or Why God Doesn't Use Biostatistics." *Zygon: Journal of Religion and Science* 40 (2005): 469–89.

Newbigin, Lesslie. *The Gospel in a Pluralist Society*. Grand Rapids: Eerdmans; Geneva: WCC, 1989.

———. *The Light Has Come: An Exposition of the Fourth Gospel*. Edinburgh: Handsel, 1982.

Newby, Gordon D. "Angels" and "Jinn." In *The Oxford Encyclopedia of the Modern Islamic World*, edited by John L. Esposito. *Oxford Islamic Studies Online*. http://www.oxfordislamicstudies.com/article/opr/t236MIW/e0061.

Newlands, George, and Allen Smith. *Hospitable God: The Transformative Dream*. Surrey, UK: Ashgate, 2010.

Newman, Louis E. "The Quality of Mercy: On the Duty to Forgive in the Judaic Tradition." *Journal of Religious Ethics* 15, no. 2 (Fall 1987): 155–72.

Ngong, David Tonhou. *The Holy Spirit and Salvation in African Christian Theology: Imagining a More Hopeful Future for Africa.* New York: Peter Lang, 2010.

"Nibbana Sutta: Total Unbinding (1)" (*Udana* 8.1). Translated by T. Bhikkhu. *Access to Insight (BCBS Edition)*, September 3, 2012. http://www.accesstoinsight.org/tipitaka/kn/ud/ud.8.01.than.html.

Nicholas of Cusa. *De Pace Fidei and Cribratio Alkorani: Translation and Analysis.* Edited and translated by Jasper Hopkins. 2nd ed. Minneapolis: Arthur J. Banning Press, 1994. http://jasper-hopkins.info/DePace12-2000.pdf.

Nickelsburg, George W. E. *Resurrection, Immortality, and Eternal Life in Intertestamental Judaism.* Cambridge, MA: Harvard University Press, 1972.

Niebuhr, Reinhold. "Sin." In *A Handbook of Christian Theology*, edited by Marvin Halverson and Arthur A. Cohen, 349. New York: World, 1958.

Nietzsche, Friedrich Wilhelm. *Gay Science (The Joyful Wisdom).* Translated by Thomas Common. Lawrence, KS: Digireads, 2009 [1882/1887].

Noll, Stephen F. "Thinking about Angels." In *The Unseen World: Christian Reflections on Angels, Demons, and the Heavenly Realm*, edited by Anthony N. S. Lane, 1–27. Carlisle, UK: Paternoster, 1996.

Nostra Aetate: Declaration on the Relation of the Church to Non-Christian Religions (Vatican II). Available at www.vatican.va.

Novak, David. "Jewish Eschatology." In *OHE*, 113–31.

Nyamiti, Charles. "African Christologies Today." In *Faces of Jesus in Africa*, edited by R. J. Schreiter. Maryknoll, NY: Orbis, 1991.

———. *African Tradition and Christian God.* Eldoret, Kenya: Gaba, 1972.

———. *Christ as Our Ancestor: Christology from an African Perspective.* Gwero, Zimbabwe: Mambo, 1984.

———. "The Trinity from an African Ancestral Perspective." *African Christian Studies* 12, no. 4 (1996): 38–74.

O'Collins, Gerald, SJ. *Christology: A Biblical, Historical, and Systematic Study of Jesus.* New York: Oxford University Press, 1995.

———. "The Incarnation: The Critical Issues." In *The Incarnation: An Interdisciplinary Symposium on the Incarnation of the Son of God*, edited by Stephen T. Davis et al. Oxford: Oxford University Press, 2004.

———. *The Tripersonal God: Understanding and Interpreting the Trinity.* Mahwah, NJ: Paulist, 1999.

O'Collins, Gerald, SJ, and Oliver P. Rafferty, SJ. "Roman Catholic View." In *Justification: Five Views*, edited by James K. Beilby and Paul Rhodes Eddy, 265–66. Downers Grove, IL: IVP Academic, 2011.

O'Connor, David. *God and Inscrutable Evil: In Defense of Theism and Atheism.* Lanham, MD: Rowman & Littlefield, 1998.

Oden, Patrick. *The Transformative Church: New Ecclesial Models and the Theology of Jürgen Moltmann.* Minneapolis: Fortress, 2015.

Olcott, Henry S. *The Buddhist Catechism*. 2nd ed. London and Benares, India: Theosophical Publishing Society, 1903. Available at www.sacredtexts.com.

Oliver, Simon. "Trinity, Motion and Creation *Ex Nihilo*." In *CGA*, 133–51.

O'Murchu, Diamuid. *In the Beginning Was the Spirit: Science, Religion, and Indigenous Spirituality*. Maryknoll, NY: Orbis, 2012.

Onaiyekan, John. "Christological Trends in Contemporary African Theology." In *Constructive Christian Theology in the Worldwide Church*, edited by William R. Barr, 355–68. Grand Rapids: Eerdmans, 1997.

One Baptism: Towards Mutual Recognition; A Study Text. Faith and Order Paper no. 210. Geneva: WCC, 2011.

Opler, Morris E. "Spirit Possession in a Rural Area of Northern India." In *Reader in Comparative Religion: An Anthropological Approach*, edited by William A. Lessa and Evon Z. Vogt, 553–66. Evanston, IL, and White Plains, NY: Row, Peterson, 1958.

Origen. *On First Principles*. In *ANF*, vol. 4.

Ormerod, Neil J., and Shane Clifton, eds. *Globalization and the Mission of the Church: Ecclesiological Investigations*. New York: T&T Clark, 2009.

Ormsby, Eric L. *Theodicy in Islamic Thought: The Dispute over al-Ghazali's "Best of All Possible Worlds."* Princeton: Princeton University Press, 1984.

Orobator, Agonkhianmeghe E. *Theology Brewed in an African Pot*. Maryknoll, NY: Orbis, 2008.

O'Shaughnessy, Thomas J. *The Development of the Meaning of Spirit in the Koran*. Rome: Pont. Institutum Orientalium Studiorum, 1953.

Ott, Heinrich. "The Convergence: Sunyata as a Dynamic Event." In *Divine Emptiness and Historical Fullness: A Buddhist-Jewish-Christian Conversation with Asao Mabe*, edited by Christopher Ives, 127–35. Valley Forge, PA: Trinity, 1995.

Özdemir, İbrahim. "Towards an Understanding of Environmental Ethics from a Qu'ranic Perspective." In *I&E*, 3–37.

Panikkar, Raimundo. "The Jordan, the Tiber, and the Ganges: Three Kairological Moments of Christic Self-Consciousness." In *The Myth of Christian Uniqueness: Toward a Pluralistic Theology of Religions*, edited by John Hick and Paul F. Knitter, 89–116. Maryknoll, NY: Orbis, 1987.

———. *The Trinity and the Religious Experience of Man*. Maryknoll, NY: Orbis; London: Darton, Longman & Todd, 1973. Also titled *The Trinity and the World Religions*.

———. *The Unknown Christ of Hinduism: Towards an Ecumenical Christophany*. London: Darton, Longman & Todd, 1964. Rev. ed. Maryknoll, NY: Orbis, 1981.

Pannenberg, Wolfhart. *Anthropology in Theological Perspective*. Translated by Matthew J. O'Connell. Philadelphia: Westminster, 1985.

———. "Contributions from Systematic Theology." In *OHRS*, 359–71.

———. "The Doctrine of the Spirit and the Task of a Theology of Nature." *Theology* 75 (January 1972): 8–21.

———. "God's Love and the Kenosis of the Son: A Response to Masao Abe." In *Divine Emptiness and Historical Fullness: A Buddhist-Jewish-Christian Conversation with Masao Abe*, edited by Christopher Ives, 246–47. Valley Forge, PA: Trinity, 1995.

———. *An Introduction to Systematic Theology*. Grand Rapids: Eerdmans, 1991.

———. *Metaphysics and the Idea of God*. Translated by Philip Clayton. Grand Rapids: Eerdmans, 1990.

———, ed. *Revelation as History: A Proposal for a More Open, Less Authoritarian View of an Important Theological Concept*. Translated by David Granskou. London: Collier-Macmillan, 1968 [1961].

———. *Systematic Theology*. Translated by Geoffrey W. Bromiley. 3 vols. Grand Rapids: Eerdmans, 1991, 1994, 1998.

———. "Theological Questions to Scientists." In *Beginning with the End: God, Science, and Wolfhart Pannenberg*, edited by Carol Rausch Albright and Joel Haugen, 37–50. Chicago: Open Court, 1997.

———. *Theology and the Kingdom of God*. Translated by Richard John Neuhaus. Philadelphia: Westminster, 1969.

Parekh, Bhikhu. *Colonialism, Tradition, and Reform: An Analysis of Gandhi's Political Discourse*. New Delhi and London: Sage, 1989.

Parfit, Derek. *Reasons and Persons*. Oxford: Oxford University Press, 1986.

Park, Andrew Sung. *The Wounded Heart of God: The Asian Concept of Han and the Christian Doctrine of Sin*. Nashville: Abingdon, 1993.

Parry, Robin A., and Christopher H. Partridge, eds. *Universal Salvation? The Current Debate*. Grand Rapids: Eerdmans, 2003.

Parsania, Hamid. "Unseen and Visible." In *ISHCP* 1:155–69.

Pascal, Blaise. "Of the Necessity of the Wager." In *Pensées*, translated by W. F. Trotter, section 3. 1944 [1690]. ccel.org.

Patelos, C. G., ed. *The Orthodox Church in the Ecumenical Movement*. Geneva: WCC, 1978.

Pathrapankal, Joseph. "Editorial." *Journal of Dharma* 33, no. 3 (1998): 299–302.

Paul, Diana Y. *Women in Buddhism: Images of the Feminine in the Mahāynāna Tradition*. 2nd ed. Berkeley: University of California Press, 1985.

Payutto, P. A. [Venerable Phra Dammapitaka]. *Dependent Origination: The Buddhist Law of Conditionality*. Translated by Bruce Evans. Bangkok: Buddhadhamma Foundation, 1995. http://www.dhammatalks.net/Books3/Payutto_Bhikkhu_Dependent_Origination.htm.

Peace, Richard V. *Conversion in the New Testament: Paul and the Twelve*. Grand Rapids: Eerdmans, 1999.

Peacocke, Arthur. "Chance and Law in Irreversible Thermodynamics, Theoretical Biology, and Theology." In *Chaos and Complexity: Scientific Perspectives on Divine Action*, edited by Robert John Russell, Nancey Murphy, and Arthur R. Peacocke, 123–43. Vatican City and Berkeley, CA: Vatican Observatory and Center for Theological and the Natural Sciences, 1995.

———. "Introduction: '*In* Whom We Live and Move and Have Our Being'?" In *IWWLM*, xviii–xxii.

———. "The Sound of Sheer Silence: How Does God Communicate with Humanity?" In *NP*, 215–47.

Pelagius' Commentary on St. Paul's Epistle to the Romans. Translated by Theodore De Bruyn. Oxford: Oxford University Press, 1998.

Pelikan, Jaroslav. *The Christian Tradition: A History of the Development of Doctrine*. Vol. 1, *The Emergence of the Catholic Tradition (100–600)*. Vol. 2, *The Spirit of Eastern Christendom (600–1700)*. Vol. 3, *The Growth of Medieval Theology (600–1300)*. Vol. 4, *Reformation of Church and Dogma (1300–1700)*. Chicago: University of Chicago Press, 1971, 1974, 1978, 1984.

Perszyk, Kenneth, ed. *Molinism: The Contemporary Debate*. New York: Oxford University Press, 2011.

Peters, Ted. *Anticipating Omega: Science, Faith, and Our Ultimate Future*. Göttingen: Vandenhoeck & Ruprecht, 2006.

———. *God—the World's Future: Systematic Theology for a Postmodern Era*. Minneapolis: Fortress, 1992.

———. "Introduction: What Is to Come." In *RTSA*, viii–xvii.

———. "The Trinity in and beyond Time." In *Quantum Cosmology and the Laws of Nature: Scientific Perspectives on Divine Action*, edited by Robert J. Russell, Nancey Murphy, and C. J. Isham, 263–89. Vatican City and Berkeley, CA: Vatican Observatory and Center for Theological and the Natural Sciences, 1993.

Petersen, Rodney L. "A Theology of Forgiveness: Terminology, Rhetoric, and the Dialectic of Interfaith Relationships." In *Forgiveness and Reconciliation: Religion, Public Policy, and Conflict Transformation*, edited by R. G. Helmick and R. L. Petersen, 3–25. Philadelphia: Templeton Foundation, 2001.

Peterson, Gregory R. "Whither Panentheism?" *Zygon: Journal of Religion and Science* 36, no. 3 (2001): 395–405.

Peterson, M. "Religious Diversity, Evil, and a Variety of Theodicies." In *OHRD*, 154–68.

Pew Research Center. "Faith on the Move—the Religious Affiliation of International Migrants." March 8, 2012. http://www.pewforum.org/2012/03/08/religious-migration-exec/.

———. *The Global Religious Landscape: A Report on the Size and Distribution of the World's Major Religious Groups as of 2010*. Pew Forum on Religion & Public Life, December 2012. http://www.pewforum.org/files/2014/01/global-religion-full.pdf.

———. "Summary of Key Findings." *Pew Forum on Religion & Public Life / U.S. Religious Landscape Survey*, 2008, 3–20.

Phan, Peter C. *Christianity with an Asian Face: Asian American Theology in the Making*. Maryknoll, NY: Orbis, 2003.

Pieris, Aloysius, SJ. *An Asian Theology of Liberation*. Maryknoll, NY: Orbis, 1988.

Pinnock, Clark H. "Annihilationism." In *OHE*, 462–75.

———. "The Conditional View." In *Four Views on Hell*, edited by William Crockett, 135–66. Grand Rapids: Zondervan, 1997.

———. *Flame of Love: A Theology of the Holy Spirit*. Downers Grove, IL: InterVarsity Press, 1996.

———. *Most Moved Mover: A Theology of God's Openness*. Grand Rapids: Baker Academic, 2001.

———. *A Wideness in God's Mercy: The Finality of Jesus Christ in a World of Religions*. Grand Rapids: Zondervan, 1992.

Pitts, William L. "The Relation of Baptists to Other Churches." In *The People of God: Es-*

says on the Believers' Church, edited by Paul Basden and David S. Dockery, 235–50. Nashville: Broadman, 1991.

Pius XII. "The Proofs for the Existence of God in the Light of Modern Natural Science." Address to the Pontifical Academy of Sciences, November 22, 1951.

Placher, William C. *A History of Christian Theology*. Philadelphia: Westminster, 1983.

Plantinga, Alvin. "God, Evil and the Metaphysics of Freedom." In *PE*, 83–109.

———. *God, Freedom, and Evil*. London: Allen & Unwin, 1975.

Plantinga, Cornelius. *Not the Way It's Supposed to Be: A Breviary of Sin*. Grand Rapids: Eerdmans, 1995.

Polkinghorne, John. "The Anthropic Principle and the Science and Religion Debate." *Faraday Paper* 4 (2007): 1–4.

———. "Anthropology in an Evolutionary Context." In *God and Human Dignity*, edited by R. K. Soulen and L. Woodhead, 89–103. Grand Rapids: Eerdmans, 2006.

———. "Eschatology: Some Questions and Some Insights from Science." In *EWEG*, 29–41.

———. *Faith, Science, and Understanding*. New Haven: Yale University Press, 2000.

———. *The God of Hope and the End of the World*. New Haven: Yale University Press, 2002.

———. "Introduction to Part 1: Eschatology and the Sciences." In *EWEG*, 17–18.

———. *The Quantum World*. Princeton Science Library. Princeton: Princeton University Press, 1985.

———. *Science and Christian Belief / The Faith of a Physicist*. Princeton: Princeton University Press, 1994.

———. "Theological Notions of Creation and Divine Causality." In *Science and Theology: Questions at the Interface*, edited by M. Rae, H. Regan, and J. Stenhouse. Grand Rapids: Eerdmans, 1994.

———. *Theology in the Context of Science*. New Haven: Yale University Press, 2009.

Polkinghorne, John, and Nicholas Beale. *Questions of Truth: Fifty-One Responses to Questions about God, Science, and Belief*. Louisville: Westminster John Knox, 2009.

Polkinghorne, John, and Michael Welker. "Introduction: Science and Theology on the End of the World and the Ends of God." In *EWEG*, 1–13.

Pontifical Council for Inter-Religious Dialogue. "Dialogue and Proclamation." May 19, 1991. http://www.vatican.va/roman_curia/pontifical_councils/interelg/documents/rc_pc_interelg_doc_19051991_dialogue-and-proclamatio_en.html.

Porterfield, Amanda. *Healing in the History of Christianity*. New York: Oxford University Press, 2005.

Postmodern Bible. New Haven: Yale University Press, 1995.

"Practising Hospitality in an Era of New Forms of Migration." World Council of Churches, February 22, 2005. http://www.oikoumene.org/en/resources/documents/wcc-commissions/international-affairs/human-rights-and-impunity/practising-hospitality-in-an-era-of-new-forms-of-migration.html.

Prenter, Regin. *Spiritus Creator: Luther's Concept of the Holy Spirit*. Philadelphia: Muhlenberg, 1953.

Pui-lan, Kwok. *Postcolonial Imagination and Feminist Theology*. Louisville: Westminster John Knox, 2005.

———. "Women and the Church." In *Introducing Asian Feminist Theology*, 98–112. Cleveland: Pilgrim, 2000.

Purcell, Brendan. *From Big Bang to Big Mystery: Human Origins in the Light of Creation and Evolution*. Hyde Park, NY: New City Press, 2012.

Queen, Christopher S., and Sally B. King, eds. *Engaged Buddhism: Buddhist Liberation Movements in Asia*. Albany: State University of New York Press, 1996.

Radhakrishnan, Sir Sarvepalli. *The Hindu View of Life*. London: George Allen & Unwin, 1961 [1927].

———. "The Nature of Hinduism." In *The Ways of Religion*, edited by Roger Eastman, 10–22. New York: Harper & Row, 1975.

Rahman, Fazlur. *Health and Medicine in the Islamic Tradition*. New York: Kazi Publications, 1998.

Rahner, Karl. "Current Problems in Christology." In *Theological Investigations* 1, translated by Cornelius Ernst, 149–200. London: Darton, Longman & Todd, 1965.

———. *The Trinity*. Translated by Joseph Donceel. London: Burns & Oates, 1970.

Rahula, Walpola. *What the Buddha Taught*. Rev. ed. New York: Grove, 1974.

Ramakrishna, Sri. *The Gospel of Sri Ramakrishna: Translated into English with an Introduction by Swami Nikhilananda*. New York: Ramakrishna-Vivekananda Center, 1984 [1942]; reproduced in *JBC*.

Rambachan, Anantanand. "Hindu-Christian Dialogue." Chapter 20 in *The Wiley-Blackwell Companion to Inter-Religious Dialogue*, edited by Catherine Cornille, 325–45. Chichester, UK: Wiley & Sons, 2013.

Rambo, Lewis R., and Charles F. Farhadian. "Conversion." In *ER* 3:1969–74.

Ramm, Bernard. *Them He Glorified: A Systematic Study of the Doctrine of Glorification*. Grand Rapids: Eerdmans, 1963.

Ram-Prasad, Chakravarthi. "Hindu Views of Jesus." Chapter 9 in *JWF*.

Rashdall, Hastings. *The Idea of Atonement in Christian Theology*. New York: Macmillan, 1919.

Ratzinger, [Cardinal] Joseph. *Eschatology: Death and Eternal Life*. Washington, DC: Catholic University of America Press, 2007.

Rauf, M. A. "The Qur'ān and the Free Will [I]" and "The Qur'ān and the Free Will [II]." *Muslim World* 60, nos. 3 and 4 (1970): 205–17 and 289–99.

Ray, Reginald A. "Buddhism: Sacred Text Written and Realized." In *The Holy Book in Comparative Perspective*, edited by Frederick M. Denny and Rodney L. Taylor, 148–80. Columbia: University of South Carolina Press, 1985.

Reder, Michael, and Josef Schmidt, SJ. "Habermas and Religion." In *An Awareness of What Is Missing: Faith and Reason in a Post-secular Age*, by Jürgen Habermas et al., translated by Ciaran Cronin, 1–14. Cambridge: Polity, 2010 [2007].

Reumann, John. "Justification and Justice in the New Testament." *Horizons in Biblical Theology* 21, no. 1 (1999): 26–45.

Rezazadeh, Reza. "Thomas Aquinas and Mulla Sadrá on the Soul-Body Problem: A Comparative Investigation." *Journal of Shi'a Islamic Studies* 4, no. 4 (Autumn 2011): 415–28.

Ricard, Matthieu, and Trinh Xuan Thuan. *The Quantum and the Lotus: A Journey to the*

Frontiers Where Science and Buddhism Meet. Translated by Ian Monk. New York: Three Rivers, 2001.

Richardson, James T. "Conversion and New Religious Movements." In *Encyclopedia of Social and Political Movements*, edited by D. Snow, D. della Porta, B. Klandermans, and D. McAdam. Oxford: Blackwell, 2013.

Riddell, Peter G. "How Allah Communicates: Islamic Angels, Devils and the 2004 Tsunami." Chapter 8 in *A&D*.

Rivera, Mayra. *The Touch of Transcendence: A Postcolonial Theology of God*. Louisville: Westminster John Knox, 2007.

Ro, Bong Rin, ed. *Christian Alternatives to Ancestor Practices*. Taichung, Taiwan: Asia Theological Association, 1985.

Robeck, Cecil M. "Mission and the Issue of Proselytism." *International Bulletin of Missionary Research* 20, no. 1 (1996): 2–8.

———. "A Pentecostal Perspective on Apostolicity." Paper presented to Faith and Order, National Council of Churches, Consultation on American-Born Churches, March 1992.

Robinson, John A. T. *The Human Face of God*. London: SCM, 1972.

Robinson, Neil. *Christ in Islam and Christianity*. New York: State University of New York Press, 1991.

Robson, James. "Aspects of the Qur'anic Doctrine of Salvation." In *Man and His Salvation: Studies in Memory of S. G. F. Brandon*, edited by Eric F. Sharpe and John R. Hinnels, 205–19. Manchester: Manchester University Press, 1973.

Rogers, Eugene F., Jr. *After the Spirit: A Constructive Pneumatology from Resources Outside the Modern West*. Grand Rapids: Eerdmans, 2005.

Roy, Raja Ram Mohun. *The English Works of Raja Ram Mohun Roy*. Vol. 3, *The Precepts of Jesus—a Guide to Peace and Happiness; Extracted from the Books of the New Testament Ascribed to the Four Evangelists with Translations into Sungscit and Bengalee*. Calcutta: Baptist Mission Press, 1820. Part I, 172–75, reproduced in *JBC*, 162–64.

Rubenstein, Richard L. *After Auschwitz: Radical Theology and Contemporary Judaism*. Upper Saddle River, NJ: Prentice Hall, 1966.

Ruether, Rosemary Radford. "Eschatology in Christian Feminist Theologies." In *OHE*, 328–42.

———. *Faith and Fratricide: The Theological Roots of Anti-Semitism*. New York: Seabury, 1974.

———. *Gaia and God: An Ecofeminist Theology of Earth Healing*. San Francisco: HarperCollins, 1992.

———. *Introducing Redemption in Christian Feminism*. Introductions in Feminist Theology 1. Sheffield: Sheffield Academic, 1998.

———. *Sexism and God-Talk: Toward a Feminist Theology*. Boston: Beacon, 1983.

———. *To Change the World: Christology and Cultural Criticism*. New York: Crossroad, 1981.

———. *Women-Church: Theology and Practice of Feminist Liturgical Communities*. San Francisco: Harper & Row, 1985.

Rupp, Gordon, and Philip S. Watson, eds. *Luther and Erasmus: Free Will and Salvation*. Philadelphia: Westminster, 1969.

Russell, Jeffrey Burton. *The Devil: Perceptions of Evil from Antiquity to Primitive Christianity*. Ithaca, NY: Cornell University Press, 1977.

———. *A History of Heaven*. Princeton: Princeton University Press, 1997.

———. *Lucifer: The Devil in the Middle Ages*. Ithaca, NY: Cornell University Press, 1984.

———. *Mephistopheles: The Devil in the Modern World*. Ithaca, NY: Cornell University Press, 1986.

———. *Satan: The Early Christian Tradition*. Ithaca, NY: Cornell University Press, 1981.

Russell, Letty M. *Church in the Round: Feminist Interpretation of the Church*. Louisville: Westminster John Knox, 1993.

———. *Just Hospitality: God's Welcome in the World of Difference*. Edited by J. Shannon Clarkson and Kate M. Ott. Louisville: Westminster John Knox, 2009.

Russell, Robert J. "Challenges and Progress in 'Theology and Science': An Overview of the VO/CTNS Series." In *SPDA*, 3–56.

———. *Cosmology: From Alpha to Omega; The Creative Mutual Interaction of Theology and Science*. Minneapolis: Fortress, 2008.

———. *Time in Eternity: Pannenberg, Physics, and Eschatology in Creative Mutual Interaction*. Notre Dame: University of Notre Dame Press, 2012.

Ruthven, Jon. *On the Cessation of the Charismata: The Protestant Polemic on Postbiblical Miracles*. Sheffield: Sheffield Academic, 1993.

Saarinen, Risto. *God and the Gift: An Ecumenical Theology of Giving*. Unitas Books. Collegeville, MN: Liturgical Press, 2005.

Sachedina, Abdulaziz Abdulhussein. *The Islamic Roots of Democratic Pluralism*. New York: Oxford University Press, 2001.

Sacred Congregation for the Doctrine of the Faith. *Inter Insigniores: Declaration on the Question of Admission of Women to the Ministerial Priesthood*. 1996. http://www.vatican.va/roman_curia/congregations/cfaith/documents/rc_con_cfaith_doc_19761015_inter-insigniores_en.html.

Sadakata, Akira. *Buddhist Cosmology: Philosophy and Origins*. Translated by Gaynor Sekimori. Tokyo: Kōsei, 1997.

Saeed, Abdullah. "The Nature and Purpose of the Community (Ummah) in the Qur'ān." In *The Community of Believers: Christian and Muslim Perspectives*, edited by Lucinda Mosher and David Marshall, 15–28. Washington, DC: Georgetown University Press, 2015.

Saiving, Valerie. "The Human Situation: A Feminine View." In *Womanspirit Rising: A Feminist Reader in Religion*, edited by Carol P. Christ and Judith Plaskow, 25–42. San Francisco: Harper & Row, 1979.

Samartha, Stanley J. *Between Two Cultures: Ecumenical Ministry in a Pluralist World*. Geneva: WCC, 1996.

———. *Courage for Dialogue: Ecumenical Issues in Inter-Religious Relationships*. Geneva: WCC, 1981; Maryknoll, NY: Orbis, 1982.

———. "The Cross and the Rainbow: Christ in a Multireligious Culture." In *Asian Faces of Jesus*, edited by R. S. Sugirtharajah, 104–23. Maryknoll, NY: Orbis, 1995.

———. "The Holy Spirit and People of Other Faiths." *Ecumenical Review* 42, nos. 3–4 (July 1990): 250–63.

———. "Unbound Christ: Towards Christology in India Today." In *Asian Christian Theology: Emerging Themes*, edited by Douglas J. Elwood, 145–60. Philadelphia: Westminster, 1980.

Samuel, Reda. "The Incarnation in Arabic Christian Theology from the Beginnings to the Mid-Eleventh Centuries." PhD tutorial, Fuller Theological Seminary, School of Intercultural Studies, Spring 2010.

Sanneh, Lamin. *Translating the Message: The Missionary Impact on Culture*. Maryknoll, NY: Orbis, 1989.

Saritoprak, Zeri. *Islam's Jesus*. Gainesville: University Press of Florida, 2014.

Schaff, Philip, ed. *The Creeds of Christendom*. 3 vols. New York: Harper & Row, 1877. 6th ed. 1931. Reprint, Grand Rapids: Baker, 1990. www.ccel.org.

Schleiermacher, Friedrich. *The Christian Faith*. Edited by H. R. Mackintosh and J. S. Stewart. Edinburgh: T&T Clark, 1999.

Schlossberg, Herbert, Vinay Samuel, and Ronald J. Sider, eds. *Christianity and Economics in the Post–Cold War Era: The Oxford Declaration and Beyond*. Grand Rapids: Eerdmans, 1994.

Schmidt-Leukel, Perry. "Buddha and Christ as Mediators of the Transcendent: A Christian Perspective." In *Buddhism and Christianity in Dialogue*, Gerald Weisfeld Lectures, 2004, edited by Perry Schmidt-Leukel, 151–75. London: SCM, 2005.

Schofer, Jonathan. "The Image of God: A Study of an Ancient Sensibility." *Journal of the Society for Textual Reasoning* 4, no. 3 (May 2006). http://jtr.shanti.virginia.edu/volume-4-number-3/the-image-of-god-a-study-of-an-ancient-sensibility/.

Schrag, Calvin O. "Transversal Rationality." In *The Question of Hermeneutics: Essays in Honor of Joseph J. Kockelmans*, edited by T. J. Stapleton. Dordrecht: Kluwer, 1994.

Schreiter, Robert J. "A Practical Theology of Healing, Forgiveness, and Reconciliation." In *Peacebuilding: Catholic Theology, Ethics, and Praxis*, edited by Robert J. Schreiter, R. Scott Appleby, and Gerard F. Powers, 366–97. Maryknoll, NY: Orbis, 2010.

Schreiter, Robert J., R. Scott Appleby, and Gerard F. Powers, eds. *Peacebuilding: Catholic Theology, Ethics, and Praxis*. Maryknoll, NY: Orbis, 2010.

Schubel, Vernon James. "Worship and Devotional Life: Muslim Worship." In *ER* 14:9815–20.

Schumm, Darla, and Michael Stoltzfus. "Chronic Illness and Disability: Narratives of Suffering and Healing in Buddhism and Christianity." In *Disability and Religious Diversity: Cross-Cultural and Interreligious Perspectives*, edited by Darla Schumm and Michael Stoltzfus, 159–75. New York: Palgrave Macmillan, 2011.

Schwager, Raymund. *Jesus in the Drama of Salvation*. New York: Crossroad, 1999.

Schwarz, Hans. *Christology*. Grand Rapids: Eerdmans, 1998.

———. *Creation*. Grand Rapids: Eerdmans, 2002.

———. *Eschatology*. Grand Rapids: Eerdmans, 2000.

———. *The God Who Is: The Christian God in a Pluralistic World*. Eugene, OR: Cascade, 2011.

Schweizer, Eduard. "On Distinguishing between Spirits." *Ecumenical Review* 41 (July 1989): 406–15.

———. "Pneuma." In *Theological Dictionary of the New Testament*, edited by Gerhard

Friedrich, translated and edited by Geoffrey W. Bromiley, 6:396. 10 vols. Grand Rapids: Eerdmans, 1964–1976.

Schwöbel, Christoph. "Reconciliation: From Biblical Observations to Dogmatic Reconstruction." In *The Theology of Reconciliation*, edited by Colin E. Gunton, 26–32. London: T&T Clark, 2003.

Scotland, Nigel. "The Charismatic Devil: Demonology in Charismatic Christianity." Chapter 4 in *A&D*.

Segundo, Juan Luis. *The Sacraments Today*. Translated by John Drury. Maryknoll, NY: Orbis, 1974.

Sells, Michael A. "Armageddon in Christian, Sunni, and Shia Traditions." In *The Oxford Handbook of Religion and Violence*, edited by Michael Jerryson, Mark Juergensmeyer, and Margo Kitts, 467–95. Oxford: Oxford University Press, 2012.

Selvanayagam, Israel. "Indian Secularism: Prospect and Problem." *Implicit Religion* 15, no. 3 (2012): 357–61.

Sempell, Andrew. "God, Society and Secularism." *St. Mark's Review* 221 (September 2012): 56–65.

Sharma, Arvind. *Classical Hindu Thought: An Introduction*. Oxford: Oxford University Press, 2000.

———. "A Hindu Perspective." In *OHRD*, 309–20.

Shatz, David. "A Jewish Perspective." In *OHRD*, 365–80.

Shenk, Wilbert. *Write the Vision: The Church Renewed*. Christian Mission and Modern Culture. Valley Forge: Trinity, 1995.

Sherwin, Byron L. "Theodicy." In *Contemporary Jewish Religious Thought: Original Essays on Critical Concepts, Movements, and Beliefs*, edited by Arthur A. Cohen and Paul Mendes-Flohr, 959–70. New York: Free Press, 1987.

Shokek, Simon. *Kabbalah and the Art of Being: The Smithsonian Lectures*. London: Routledge, 2001.

Shults, F. LeRon. *Reforming the Doctrine of God*. Grand Rapids: Eerdmans, 2005.

Shults, F. LeRon, and Steven J. Sandage. *Faces of Forgiveness: Searching for Wholeness and Salvation*. Grand Rapids: Baker Academic, 2003.

Siddiqui, Mona. "Being Human in Islam." In *Humanity: Texts and Context; Christian and Muslim Perspectives*, edited by Michael Ipgrave and David Marshall, 15–21. Washington, DC: Georgetown University Press, 2011.

Skilling, Peter. "Worship and Devotional Life: Buddhist Devotional Life in Southeast Asia." In *ER* 14:9826–34.

Smedes, Lewis B. *Forgive and Forget: Healing the Hurts We Don't Deserve*. New York: Harper & Row, 1984.

Smith, Brian K. "*Samsāra*." In *ER* 12:8097–99.

Smith, Gordon T., ed. *The Lord's Supper: Five Views*. Downers Grove, IL: InterVarsity Press, 2008.

———. *Transforming Conversion: Rethinking the Language and Contours of Christian Initiation*. Grand Rapids: Baker Academic, 2010.

Smith, James K. A. *Desiring the Kingdom: Worship, Worldview, and Cultural Formation*. Cultural Liturgies 1. Grand Rapids: Baker Academic, 2009.

———. *Introducing Radical Orthodoxy: Mapping a Post-secular Theology*. Grand Rapids: Baker Academic, 2004.

Smith, Jane Idleman, and Yvonne Yazbeck Haddad. *The Islamic Understanding of Death and Resurrection.* Albany: State University of New York Press, 1981; Oxford: Oxford University Press, 2002.

Smyth, John. *Principles and Inferences concerning the Visible Church.* In *The Works of John Smyth, Fellow of Christ's College, 1594–8*, vol. 1, edited by W. T. Whitley. Cambridge: Cambridge University Press, 1915. https://archive.org/stream/cu31924092458995/cu31924092458995_djvu.txt.

Sölle, Dorothee. *Christ Our Representative.* Philadelphia: Fortress, 1967.

Song, Choan-Seng. *Jesus, the Crucified People.* New York: Crossroad, 1990.

Soskice, Janet M. "*Creatio Ex Nihilo*: Its Jewish and Christian Foundations." Chapter 2 in *CGA*, 24–39.

"Soul." In *A Dictionary of the Bible*, edited by James Hastings. Edinburgh: T&T Clark, 1902.

Spence, Sean A. *The Actor's Brain: Exploring the Cognitive Neuroscience of Free Will.* Oxford: Oxford University Press, 2009.

Spitzer, Robert J., SJ. *New Proofs for the Existence of God: Contributions of Contemporary Physics and Philosophy*. Grand Rapids: Eerdmans, 2010.

Stamoolis, James J. "Scripture and Tradition in the Orthodox Church." *Evangelical Review of Theology* 19, no. 2 (April 1995): 131–43.

Stander, Hendrick F., and Johannes P. Louw. *Baptism in the Early Church*. Rev. ed. Pretoria: Didaskalia Publishers; Leeds, UK: Reformation Today Trust, 1994 [1988].

Stanley, Brian. "Conversion to Christianity: The Colonization of the Mind?" *International Review of Mission* 92, no. 366 (July 2003): 315–31.

Staples, Russell Lynn. "Christianity and the Cult of the Ancestors: Belief and Ritual among the Bantu-Speaking Peoples of Southern Africa; An Interdisciplinary Study Utilizing Anthropological and Theological Analyses." PhD diss., Princeton Theological Seminary, 1981.

Stephens, Walter. "Demons: An Overview." In *ER* 4:2275–82.

Stoeger, William R., SJ. "Entropy, Emergence, and the Physical Roots of Natural Evil." In *PC*, 93–108.

Strauss, David F. *The Life of Jesus Critically Examined.* Translated from the fourth German ed. by George Eliot. 2nd ed. in 1 vol. London: Schwann Sonnenschein; New York: Macmillan, 1892.

Streiker, Lowell D. "The Hindu Attitude toward Other Religions." *Journal of Religious Thought* 23, no. 1 (1966/1967): 75–90.

Stroda, Una. "The Ordination of Women: The Experience of the Evangelical Lutheran Church of Latvia." Master's thesis, Catholic Theological Union, Chicago, 2008.

Stronstad, Roger. *The Charismatic Theology of St. Luke*. Peabody, MA: Hendrickson, 1984.

Suchocki, Marjorie Hewitt. *The End of Evil: Process Eschatology in Historical Context.* Albany: State University of New York Press, 1988.

———. *The Fall to Violence.* New York: Continuum, 1995.

Sugirtharajah, R. S., ed. *Asian Faces of Jesus.* Maryknoll, NY: Orbis, 1993.

Sullivan, Francis A., SJ. "Baptism in the Spirit." In *Charisms and Charismatic Renewal*, 59–75. Ann Arbor, MI: Servant, 1982.

Summers-Minette, Amy. "Not Just Halos and Horns: Angels and Demons in Western Pop Culture." Chapter 13 in *A&D*.

Swinburne, Richard. *The Christian God*. Oxford: Clarendon; New York: Oxford University Press, 1994.

———. *Revelation: From Analogy to Metaphor*. Oxford: Clarendon, 1992.

Tabor, James D. "Ancient Jewish and Early Christian Millennialism." In *OHM*, 252–53.

Talbott, Thomas. *The Inescapable Love of God*. Eugene, OR: Cascade, 2014 [1999].

Tanner, Kathryn E. "Eschatology without a Future." In *EWEG*, 222–37.

———. *God and Creation in Christian Theology: Tyranny or Empowerment?* Minneapolis: Fortress, 1988.

Tattersall, Ian. *The World from Beginnings to 4000 BCE*. New York: Oxford University Press, 2008.

Tattersall, Ian, and Jeffrey H. Schwartz. *Extinct Humans*. New York: Westview, 2000.

Taylor, Charles. *A Secular Age*. Cambridge, MA: Belknap Press of Harvard University Press, 2007.

Taylor, Mark Lewis. *The Executed God: The Way of the Cross in Lockdown America*. Minneapolis: Fortress, 2001.

Tennent, Timothy C. *Theology in the Context of World Christianity: How the Global Church Is Influencing the Way We Think about and Discuss Theology*. Grand Rapids: Zondervan, 2007.

Terrell, JoAnne Marie. *Power in the Blood? The Cross in the African American Experience*. Maryknoll, NY: Orbis, 1998.

Terry, Justyn. "The Forgiveness of Sins and the Work of Christ: A Case for Substitutionary Atonement." *Anglican Theological Review* 95 (Winter 2013): 9–24.

Tertullian. *Against Praxeas*. In *ANF*, vol. 3.

Thiselton, Anthony C. *Life after Death: A New Approach to the Last Things*. Grand Rapids: Eerdmans, 2012.

Thomas, Günther. "Resurrection to New Life: Pneumatological Implications of the Eschatological Transition." In *RTSA*, 255–76.

Thomas, M. M. "The Holy Spirit and the Spirituality for Political Struggles." *Ecumenical Review* 42, nos. 3–4 (1990): 216–24.

Thomassen, Einar. "Islamic Hell." *Numen: International Review for the History of Religions* 56, nos. 2–3 (2009): 401–16.

Thorsen, Donald. *Explorations in Christian Theology*. Grand Rapids: Baker Academic, 2010.

Tilakaratne, Asanga. "The Buddhist View on Religious Conversion." *Dialogue* (Colombo, Sri Lanka) 32–33 (2005–2006): 58–82.

Tilley, Terrence W. *The Evils of Theodicy*. Washington, DC: Georgetown University Press, 1991.

Tillich, Paul. *Systematic Theology*. Vol. 3. Chicago: University of Chicago Press, 1963.

Timoner, Rachel. *Breath of Life: God as Spirit in Judaism*. Brewster, MA: Paraclete, 2011.

"Tipitaka: The Pali Canon." Edited by John T. Bullitt. *Access to Insight*, May 29, 2010. http://www.accesstoinsight.org/tipitaka/index.html.

Tirosh-Samuelson, Hava. "Introduction: Judaism and the Natural World." In *J&E*, xxxiii–lxii.

Tombs, David. "The Offer of Forgiveness." *Journal of Religious Ethics* 36, no. 4 (2008): 587–93.

Torrance, Thomas F. "The Problem of Natural Theology in the Thought of Karl Barth." *Religious Studies* 6 (1970): 121–35.

———. *Space, Time, and Incarnation*. Edinburgh: T&T Clark, 1968.

"Towards a Common Understanding of the Church: Reformed/Roman Catholic International Dialogue; Second Phase (1984–1990)." http://www.vatican.va/roman_curia/pontifical_councils/chrstuni/alliance-reform-docs/rc_pc_chrstuni_doc_19900101_second-phase-dialogue_en.html.

Trigg, Roger. *Equality, Freedom, and Religion*. Oxford: Oxford University Press, 2012.

———. *Religious Diversity: Philosophical and Political Dimensions*. Cambridge: Cambridge University Press, 2014.

Troeltsch, Ernst. "On the Historical and Dogmatic Methods in Theology [1898]." Translated by Jack Forstman, in *Gesammelte Schriften*, 2:728–53. Tübingen: J. C. B. Mohr, 1913.

Troll, C. W., H. Reifeld, and C. T. R. Hewer, eds. *We Have Justice in Common: Christian and Muslim Voices from Asia and Africa*. Berlin: Konrad-Adenauer-Stiftung, 2010.

Trumbower, Jeffrey A. *Rescue for the Dead: The Posthumous Salvation of Non-Christians in Early Christianity*. Oxford: Oxford University Press, 2001.

Tsirpanlis, Constantine N. "The Concept of Universal Salvation in Saint Gregory of Nyssa." *Studia Patristica* 17, no. 3 (1982): 1131–44.

Turner, Max. "Spiritual Gifts Then and Now." *Vox Evangelica* 15 (1985): 7–63.

Twelftree, Graham H. *Jesus the Exorcist: A Contribution to the Study of the Historical Jesus*. Tübingen: Mohr-Siebeck, 1993.

Ubruhe, J. O. "Traditional Sacrifice: A Key to the Heart of the Christian Message." *Journal of Theology for Southern Africa* 95 (1996): 13–22.

Umansky, Ellen M. "Election." In *ER* 4:2744–49.

Urban, Hugh B. "Millenarian Elements in the Hindu Religious Traditions." In *OHM*, 369–81.

Uzukwu, Elochukwu. *Worship as Body Language: Introduction to Christian Worship, an African Orientation*. Collegeville, MN: Liturgical Press, 1997.

Vähäkangas, Mika. "Trinitarian Processions as Ancestral Relationships in Charles Nyamiti's Theology: A European Lutheran Critique." *Revue Africaine de Théologie* 21 (1997): 61–75. Reprinted in *Svensk Missionstidskrift* 86 (1998): 251–63.

Vainio, Olli-Pekka. *Justification and Participation in Christ: The Development of the Lutheran Doctrine of Justification from Luther to the Formula of Concord (1580)*. Leiden: Brill, 2008.

Van Dyk, Leanne. "The Reformed View." In *The Lord's Supper: Five Views*, edited by Gordon T. Smith, 67–82. Downers Grove, IL: InterVarsity Press, 2007.

Van Engen, Charles. "Church." In *Evangelical Dictionary of World Christian Missions*, edited by A. Scott Moreau et al., 193. Grand Rapids: Baker Academic, 2000.

———. *God's Missionary People: Rethinking the Purpose of the Local Church*. Grand Rapids: Baker Academic, 1991.

Van Gelder, Craig. *The Essence of the Church*. Grand Rapids: Baker, 2000.

Vanhoozer, Kevin J. *The Drama of Doctrine: A Canonical-Linguistic Approach to Christian Theology*. Louisville: Westminster John Knox, 2005.

———. *Faith Speaking Understanding: Performing the Drama of Doctrine*. Louisville: Westminster John Knox, 2014.

Van Huyssteen, J. Wentzel. *Alone in the World? Human Uniqueness in Science and Theology.* Grand Rapids: Eerdmans, 2006.

Vargas-O'Bryan, Ivette. "Keeping It All in Balance: Teaching Asian Religions through Illness and Healing." Chapter 4 in *Teaching Religion and Healing*, edited by Linda L. Barnes and Inés Talamantez. New York: Oxford University Press, 2006.

Victoria, Brian Daizen. "Teaching Buddhism and Violence." In *TRV*, 74–93.

———. *Zen War Stories*. London: Routledge, 2003.

Vischer, Lukas, ed. *Spirit of God, Spirit of Christ: Ecumenical Reflections on the Filioque Controversy*. London: SPCK; Geneva: WCC, 1981.

Vivekananda, Swami. *The Complete Works of Vivekananda*. 10th ed. Calcutta: Advaita Ashrama, 1999. Vol. 8, 159–60, reproduced in *JBC*, 177–79.

Viviano, Benedict T. "Eschatology and the Quest for the Historical Jesus." In *OHE*, 73–90.

Volf, Miroslav. *After Our Likeness: The Church as an Image of the Trinity*. Grand Rapids: Eerdmans, 1998.

———. *Allah: A Christian Response.* New York: HarperCollins, 2011.

———. *The End of Memory: Remembering Rightly in a Violent World*. Grand Rapids: Eerdmans, 2006.

———. "Enter into Joy! Sin, Death, and the Life of the World to Come." In *EWEG*, 256–78.

———. *Exclusion and Embrace: A Theological Exploration of Identity, Otherness, and Reconciliation*. Nashville: Abingdon, 1996.

———. "Exclusion and Embrace: Theological Reflections in the Wake of 'Ethnic Cleansing.'" *Journal of Ecumenical Studies* 29, no. 2 (1992): 230–48.

———. *Free of Charge: Giving and Forgiving in a Culture Stripped of Grace*. Grand Rapids: Zondervan, 2005.

———. "Systematic Theology III: Ecclesiology and Eschatology." Unpublished lecture notes, Fuller Theological Seminary, Pasadena, CA, Summer 1988.

———. "'The Trinity Is Our Social Program': The Doctrine of the Trinity and the Shape of Social Engagement." *Modern Theology* 14, no. 3 (1998): 403–23.

———. *Work in the Spirit: Toward a Theology of Work*. Eugene, OR: Wipf & Stock, 2001.

Vondey, Wolfgang. "The Holy Spirit and the Physical Universe: The Impact of Scientific Paradigm Shifts on Contemporary Pneumatology." *Theological Studies* 70 (2009): 3–36.

Vries, Hent de. *Religion and Violence: Philosophical Perspectives from Kant to Derrida*. Baltimore: Johns Hopkins University Press, 2002.

Vroom, Hendrik. *No Other Gods: Christian Belief in Dialogue with Buddhism, Hinduism, and Islam*. Grand Rapids: Eerdmans, 1996.

Wagner, C. Peter [and Rebecca Greenwood]. "The Strategic-Level Deliverance Model." In *Understanding Spiritual Warfare: Four Views*, edited by James K. Beilby and Paul Rhodes Eddy, 173–98. Downers Grove, IL: InterVarsity Press, 2012.

Wallace, B. Alan. "A Buddhist View of Free Will: Beyond Determinism and Indeterminism." *Journal of Consciousness Studies* 18 (2011): 217–33.

Wallace, Dewey D. "Free Will and Predestination: Christian Concepts." In *ER* 5:3202–6.

Wallace, Mark I. *Fragments of the Spirit: Nature, Violence, and the Renewal of Creation*. New York: Continuum, 1996.

———. "The Green Face of God: Recovering the Spirit in an Ecocidal Era." In *Advents of the Spirit: An Introduction to the Current Study of Pneumatology*, edited by Bradford E. Hinze and D. Lyle Dabney, 444–64. Milwaukee: Marquette University Press, 2001.

Walls, Jerry L. "Heaven." In *OHE*, 399–412.

———. *Heaven: The Logic of Eternal Joy*. Oxford: Oxford University Press, 2002.

———. *Hell: The Logic of Damnation*. Notre Dame: University of Notre Dame Press, 1992.

Walter, Jonathan S. "Missions: Buddhist Missions." In *ER* 9:6077–82.

Ward, Keith. "God as a Principle of Cosmological Explanation." In *QCLN*, 247–62.

———. *Images of Eternity: Concepts of God in Five Religious Traditions*. London: Darton, Longman & Todd, 1987. Reissued as *Concepts of God: Images of the Divine in Five Religious Traditions*. Oxford: Oneworld, 1998.

———. *Is Religion Dangerous?* Grand Rapids: Eerdmans, 2006.

———. *More Than Matter: Is Matter All We Really Are?* Grand Rapids: Eerdmans, 2011.

———. "Personhood, Spirit, and the Supernatural." In *All That Is: A Naturalistic Faith for the Twenty-First Century*, by Arthur Peacocke, edited by Philip Clayton, 152–62. Minneapolis: Fortress, 2007.

———. *Religion and Community*. Oxford: Oxford University Press, 1999.

———. *Religion and Creation*. Oxford: Clarendon, 1996.

———. *Religion and Human Nature*. Oxford: Clarendon, 1998.

———. *Religion and Revelation: A Theology of Revelation in the World's Religions*. Oxford: Clarendon, 1994.

Ward, Pete. *The Liquid Church*. Peabody, MA: Hendrickson, 2002.

Ware, [Timothy] Bishop Kallistos. "Dare We Hope for the Salvation of All? Origen, St. Gregory of Nyssa and St. Isaac the Syrian." In *The Inner Kingdom, The Collected Works, 1*:193–215. Crestwood, NY: St. Vladimir's Seminary Press, 2001.

———. "God Immanent Yet Transcendent: The Divine Energies according to Saint Gregory Palamas." In *IWWLM*, 157–68.

———. "The Holy Trinity: Model for Personhood-in-Relation." In *The Trinity and the Entangled World: Relationality in Physical Science and Theology*, edited by John Polkinghorne, 107–29. Grand Rapids: Eerdmans, 2010.

Warfield, Benjamin Breckinridge. *The Counterfeit Miracles*. New York: Charles Scribner's Sons, 1918. http://www.monergism.com/thethreshold/sdg/warfield/warfield_counterfeit.html.

———. *Revelation and Inspiration*. New York: Oxford University Press, 1927.

Warrington, Keith. "James 5:14–18: Healing Then and Now." *International Review of Mission* 93, no. 370/371 (July/October 2004): 346–67.

Warrior, Robert Allan. "Canaanites, Cowboys and Indians: Deliverance, Conquest and Liberation Theology Today." *Christianity and Crisis* 49, no. 12 (September 11, 1989): 261–65.

Waskow, Arthur. "Is the Earth a Jewish Issue?" *Tikkun* 7, no. 5 (1992): 35–37.

Watt, William Montgomery. "His Name Is Ahmad." *Muslim World* 43, no. 2 (1953): 110–17.

———. *Islamic Philosophy and Theology: An Extended Survey*. Edinburgh: Edinburgh University Press, 1962.

———. *Muslim-Christian Encounters: Perceptions and Misperceptions*. London: Routledge, 1991.

Watt, William Montgomery, and Asma Afsaruddin. "Free Will and Predestination: Islamic Concepts." In *ER* 5:3209–13.

Weaver, J. Denny. *The Nonviolent Atonement*. Grand Rapids: Eerdmans, 2001.

Webb, Robert L. *John the Baptizer and Prophet: A Socio-Historical Study*. Sheffield: Sheffield Academic, 1991.

Weber, Timothy P. "Millennialism." In *OHE*, 365–83.

Webster, John. "The Holiness and Love of God." *Scottish Journal of Theology* 57, no. 3 (2004): 249–68.

Welker, Michael. *God the Spirit: A Problem of Experience in Today's World*. Translated by John F. Hoffmeyer. Minneapolis: Fortress, 1994.

———. "Resurrection and Eternal Life: The Canonic Memory of the Resurrected Christ, His Reality, and His Glory." In *EWEG*, 279–90.

Wesley, John. "The Principles of a Methodist." Edited by Albert C. Outler. In *The Works of John Wesley*, vol. 8. Nashville: Abingdon, 1986.

Wessels, Anton. *Images of Jesus: How Jesus Is Perceived and Portrayed in Non-European Cultures*. Grand Rapids: Eerdmans, 1990.

"What Is the Inflation Theory?" NASA/WMAP [Wilkinson Microwave Anisotropy Probe] Science Team. April 16, 2010. http://map.gsfc.nasa.gov/universe/WMAP_Universe.pdf.

Wheeler, Brannon. "Ummah." In *ER* 14:9446–48.

White, Lynn, Jr. "The Historical Roots of Our Ecological Crisis." *Science*, n.s., 155, no. 3767 (March 10, 1967): 1203–7. http://www.drexel.edu/~/media/Files/greatworks/pdf_fall09/HistoricalRoots_of_EcologicalCrisis.ashx.

Whitehead, Alfred North. "Immortality." *Harvard Divinity School Bulletin* 7 (1941–1942): 5–21.

———. *Process and Reality: An Essay in Cosmology*. Edited by David R. Griffin and Donald W. Sherburn. Corrected ed. New York: Free Press, 1978 [1929].

Wiley, Tatha. *Original Sin: Origins, Developments, Contemporary Meanings*. New York: Paulist, 2002.

Wilkinson, David. *Christian Eschatology and the Physical Universe*. London: T&T Clark, 2010.

Williams, Delores S. *Sisters in the Wilderness: The Challenge of Womanist God-Talk*. Maryknoll, NY: Orbis, 1993.

Williams, George Huntson. "Christology and Church-State Relations in the Fourth Century." *Church History* 20, nos. 3 and 4 (1951): 3–33 and 3–26.

Willis, Robert E. "Christian Theology after Auschwitz." *Journal of Ecumenical Studies* 12, no. 4 (1975): 493–519.

Wink, Walter. *Engaging the Powers: Discernment and Resistance in a World of Domination.* Minneapolis: Fortress, 1992.

———. *Naming the Powers: The Language of Power in the New Testament.* Philadelphia: Fortress, 1984.

———. *The Powers That Be: Theology for a New Millennium.* New York: Doubleday, 1998.

———. *Unmasking the Powers: The Invisible Forces That Determine Human Existence.* Philadelphia: Fortress, 1986.

Witzel, Michael. "Vedas and Upanisads." In *The Blackwell Companion to Hinduism*, edited by Gavin Flood, 68–98. Oxford: Blackwell, 2003.

Wolterstorff, Nicholas. "Jesus and Forgiveness." In *Jesus and Philosophy: New Essays*, edited by Paul K. Moser, 215–31. Cambridge: Cambridge University Press, 2009.

Woodberry, J. Dudley. "Conversion in Islam." In *HRC*, 22–41.

———. "The Kingdom of God in Islam and the Gospel." In *Anabaptists Meeting Muslims: A Calling for Presence in the Way of Christ*, edited by James R. Krabill, David W. Shenk, and Linford Stutzman, 48–58. Scottdale, PA: Herald Press, 2005.

World Council of Churches [WCC]. *Churches' Compassionate Response to HIV and AIDS.* September 6, 2006. http://www.oikoumene.org/en/resources/documents/wcc-commissions/international-affairs/human-rights-and-impunity/churches-compassionate-response-to-hiv-and-aids.

———. "A Cloud of Witnesses: Message to the Churches from a Symposium in Bose." November 2, 2008. https://www.oikoumene.org/en/resources/documents/wcc-programmes/unity-mission-evangelism-and-spirituality/visible-unity/a-cloud-of-witnesses-message-to-the-churches-from-a-symposium-in-bose.

———. *Mission and Evangelism: An Ecumenical Affirmation.* Geneva: WCC, 1982. In *The Ecumenical Movement: An Anthology of Key Texts and Voices*, edited by Michael Kinnamon and Brian E. Cope, #25, 372–83. Geneva: WCC; Grand Rapids: Eerdmans, 1997.

"World Report on Violence and Health." Edited by Etienne G. Krug, Linda L. Dahlberg, James A. Mercy, Anthony B. Zwi, and Rafael Lozano, World Health Organization. Geneva, 2002. http://whqlibdoc.who.int/publications/2002/9241545615_eng.pdf.

Wright, David F. "The Atonement in Reformation Theology." *European Journal of Theology* 8, no. 1 (1999): 37–48.

———. *Infant Baptism in Historical Perspective: Collected Studies.* Carlisle, UK: Paternoster, 2007.

———. *What Has Infant Baptism Done to Baptism? An Enquiry at the End of Christendom.* Carlisle, UK: Paternoster, 2005.

Wright, George E. *God Who Acts: Biblical Theology as Recital.* Studies in Biblical Theology 8. London: SCM, 1952.

Wright, Jeremiah, Jr. "Protestant Ecclesiology." In *The Cambridge Companion to Black*

Theology, edited by Dwight N. Hopkins and Edward P. Antonio, 184–97. Cambridge: Cambridge University Press, 2012.

Wright, N. T. *The Climax of the Covenant: Christ and the Law in Pauline Theology*. Minneapolis: Fortress, 1993.

———. *For All the Saints: Remembering the Christian Departed*. Harrisburg, PA: Morehouse, 2003.

———. "Jesus and the Identity of God." *Ex Auditu* 14 (1998): 42–56.

———. *Jesus and the Victory of God*. Vol. 2 of *Christian Origins and the Question of God*. Minneapolis: Fortress, 1996.

———. "Mind, Spirit, Soul and Body: All for One and One for All; Reflections on Paul's Anthropology in His Complex Contexts." Paper presented at Society of Christian Philosophers Eastern Meeting, March 18, 2011. http://www.ntwrightpage.com/Wright_SCP_MindSpiritSoulBody.htm.

———. *The New Testament and the People of God*. Vol. 1 of *Christian Origins and the Question of God*. London: SPCK; Minneapolis: Fortress, 1992.

———. "Redemption from the New Perspective?" In *The Redemption: An Interdisciplinary Symposium on Christ as Redeemer*, edited by Stephen T. Davis, Daniel Kendall, SJ, and Gerald O'Collins, SJ. Oxford: Oxford University Press, 2004.

———. *The Resurrection of the Son of God*. Minneapolis: Fortress, 2003.

———. *Surprised by Hope: Rethinking Heaven, the Resurrection, and the Mission of the Church*. New York: HarperOne, 2008.

Yamamoto, Dorothy. "Aquinas and Animals: Patrolling the Boundary?" Chapter 7 in *AOA*.

Yoder, John Howard. *The Politics of Jesus*. Grand Rapids: Eerdmans, 1972.

Yogananda, Paramahansa. *Man's Eternal Quest*. Los Angeles: Self-Realization Fellowship, 1975.

Yong, Amos. *Beyond the Impasse: Towards a Pneumatological Theology of Religions*. Grand Rapids: Baker Academic, 2013.

———. *The Cosmic Breath: Spirit and Nature in the Christianity-Buddhism-Science Trialogue*. Leiden: Brill, 2012.

———. "Discernment; Discerning the Spirits." In *GDT*, 232–35.

———. "The Holy Spirit and the World Religions: On the Christian Discernment of Spirit(s) 'after' Buddhism." *Buddhist-Christian Studies* 24 (2004): 191–207.

———. *In the Days of Caesar: Pentecostalism and Political Theology*. Grand Rapids: Eerdmans, 2010.

———. "On Binding, and Loosing, the Spirits: Navigating and Engaging a Spirit-Filled World." In *IRDSW*, 1–12.

———. *Pneumatology and the Christian-Buddhist Dialogue: Does the Spirit Blow through the Middle Way?* Leiden: Brill Academic, 2012.

———. *The Spirit of Creation: Modern Science and Divine Action in the Pentecostal-Charismatic Imagination*. Grand Rapids: Eerdmans, 2011.

———. *The Spirit Poured Out on All Flesh: Pentecostalism and the Possibility of Global Theology*. Grand Rapids: Baker Academic, 2005.

———. *Theology and Down Syndrome: Reimagining Disability in Late Modernity*. Waco, TX: Baylor University Press, 2007.

Zaehner, R. C. *Mysticism, Sacred and Profane: An Inquiry into Some Varieties of Praeternatural Experience*. Oxford: Clarendon, 1957.

Zizioulas, John D. *Being as Communion: Studies in Personhood and the Church*. Crestwood, NY: St. Vladimir's Seminary Press, 1985.

Zwemer, Samuel M. *The Moslem Doctrine of God: An Essay on the Character and Attributes of Allah according to the Koran and Orthodox Tradition*. New York: American Tract Society, 1905.

Index of Authors

Index of Subjects

Index of Scripture: Christian and Other Traditions